AMERICA TRANSFORMED

A History of the United States since 1900

Gary Gerstle
University of Maryland

Emily S. Rosenberg
Macalester College

Norman L. Rosenberg
Macalester College

Harcourt Brace College Publishers

Fort Worth Philadelphia San Diego New York Orlando Austin San Antonio
Toronto Montreal London Sydney Tokyo

Publisher:	Earl McPeek
Acquisitions Editor:	David C. Tatom
Product Manager:	Steve Drummond
Developmental Editor:	Margaret McAndrew Beasley
Project Editor:	Charles J. Dierker
Art Director:	Biatriz Chapa
Production Manager:	Diane Gray
Art & Design Coordinator:	Florence Fujimoto

Cover Image: *City Activities with Subway*, Thomas Hart Benton, 1889–1975, The New School for Social Research, New York City, SuperStock/VAGA; © T. H. Benton and R. P. Benton Testamentary Trusts/Licensed by VAGA, New York, NY

ISBN: 0-15-508046-6

Library of Congress Catalog Card Number: 98-87934

Address for Editorial Correspondence:
Harcourt Brace College Publishers,
301 Commerce Street, Suite 3700,
Fort Worth, TX 76102

Address for Orders:
Harcourt Brace & Company,
6277 Sea Harbor Drive,
Orlando, FL 32887-6777
1-800-782-4479

Web site address:
http://www.hbcollege.com

Harcourt Brace College Publishers may provide complimentary instructional aids and supplements or supplement packages to those adopters qualified under our adoption policy. Please contact your sales representative for more information. If as an adopter or potential user you receive supplements you do not need, please return them to your sales representative or send them to:

Attention: Returns Department, Troy Warehouse, 465 South Lincoln Drive, Troy, MO 63379

Printed in the United States of America

8 9 0 1 2 3 4 5 6 7 066 10 9 8 7 6 5 4 3 2 1

About the Authors

Gary Gerstle, University of Maryland

Gary Gerstle is the author of the first section of the text (Chapters 1–6). A specialist in labor, immigration, and political history, he has published *Working-Class Americanism: The Politics of Labor in a Textile City, 1914–1960* (1989), *The Rise and Fall of the New Deal Order, 1930–1980* (1989), and articles in the *American Historical Review, Journal of American History, American Quarterly*, and many other journals. He is a consulting editor, along with James M. McPherson, of *American Political Leaders: From Colonial Times to the Present* (1991) and *American Social Leaders: From Colonial Times to the Present* (1993). He has been awarded many honors, including a National Endowment for the Humanities Fellowship for University Teachers, an Institute for Advanced Study Membership, and a John Simon Guggenheim Memorial Fellowship.

Emily S. Rosenberg, Macalester College

Emily S. Rosenberg is the author, along with Norman L. Rosenberg, of the last section of the text (Chapters 7–12). She specializes in United States foreign relations in the 20th century and is the author of the widely used book *Spreading the American Dream: American Economic and Cultural Expansion, 1890–1945* (1982). Her other publications include (with Norman L. Rosenberg) *In Our Times: America Since 1945*, Fifth Edition (1995) and numerous articles on subjects such as international finance, gender issues, and foreign relations. She has served on the board of the Organization of American Historians, on the board of editors of the *Journal of American History*, and as president of the Society for Historians of American Foreign Relations.

Norman L. Rosenberg, Macalester College

Norman L. Rosenberg is coauthor, along with Emily S. Rosenberg, of the final section of the text (Chapters 7–12). He specializes in legal history with a particular interest in legal culture and First Amendment issues. His books include *Protecting the "Best Men": An Interpretive History of the Law of Libel* (1990) and (with Emily S. Rosenberg) *In Our Times: America Since 1945*, Fifth Edition (1995). He has published articles in the *Rutgers Law Review, Constitutional Commentary, Law & History Review*, and many other legal journals.

Preface

The Story of America's Transformation

To ponder the last hundred years of American history is to reckon with a nation undergoing rapid, and often bewildering change. During that time America transformed itself from a nation of farms into a nation of cities and suburbs, from a vigorous but isolated country into a great world power, from a society built on racial and gender inequities into one striving for greater social equality. In 1900 many Americans still rode in horse-drawn buggies and had never seen a building taller than four stories. They could not have imagined an explosive more powerful than dynamite or a vehicle that could fly. They knew enough about indoor toilets and telephones to hope that their own homes might one day be so-outfitted, but only the most visionary among them could have conceived of a time when Americans would be able to watch their president or a favorite actor on a "TV" in their home. And the idea of storing vast quantities of information—such as an entire U.S. census—on tiny silicon chips and of being able to retrieve any part of it instantaneously would have struck everyone as preposterous.

In *America Transformed,* we tell the story of the remarkable changes that affected the lives of both prominent and ordinary Americans. This story is full of triumphs: of scientific, technological, and managerial breakthroughs that cured disease, placed innumerable consumer goods within reach of the average wage-earner, and created levels of abundance and economic comfort never before experienced by any society; of military victories against foes who threatened American and world civilization; and of reform movements that succeeded—often against great odds—in extending the promise of liberty and equality to all citizens.

The story of transformation is marked, too, by failure, tragedy, and unintended consequences. Economic depressions have followed periods of economic boom, generating widespread suffering. Exercising its growing power in the world, America has sometimes failed to design foreign policies that served its interests or those of the world. Eliminating racial prejudice and poverty in America has proven to be a tough task. Generating economic abundance has damaged the physical environment while unlocking the power of the atom has created weapons of unimaginably destructive power. We have not shied away from discussing these developments, for comprehending them is crucial to an understanding of where America has been and what future transformations may await it.

The Authors' Approach

The first half of this book focuses on the transformation of America from a commercial-agrarian society into an urban-industrial one. This is a traditional topic, but one that remains the best way to frame American history from 1890 to 1950. This transformation entailed the decline of the farming sector, the rise of corporations and labor unions, the proliferation of cities, and the creation—within these urban spaces—of new kinds of civic organizations. In this era, the Democratic Party secured an urban base and developed a political philosophy, liberalism, that would become the 20th century's most consequential creed. This was also the time in which America became a world power and a shaper of world order. To each of these topics, we have devoted a great deal of attention.

We also recognize, however, that industrial transformation affected American society in ways that went well beyond economics, politics, and war. The rise of an industrial society convulsed traditional notions of sexuality, gender roles, racial hierarchy, and leisure. Thus, we have emphasized the emergence of a "New Woman" and the rise of feminism; the struggle for racial equality as it has affected and involved African Americans, Indians, Hispanics, Asians, and immigrants from southern and eastern Europe; and the rise of mass culture as it has manifested itself in movies, music, dress, sports, and comics. Throughout this book we have attempted to relate changes in society and culture to economic and political developments. As a result, we believe that we have overcome the problem of ghettoization that troubles many 20th-century texts. In this volume, the concerns and experiences of women and minorities are integral, rather than peripheral, to the story of economic and political change. The result is a fuller portrait of transformation than is common in histories of this kind.

As one moves beyond 1950, the notion of industrial transformation is less and less useful to comprehending developments in American society and politics. America's more than 40-year struggle against the Soviet Union and the Cold War's influence on the economy, domestic politics, and foreign policy is necessarily a major theme, and we have given it the attention that it deserves. But, at some point during the Cold War, America embarked on a second economic transformation every bit as fundamental as the urban-industrial one. Some scholars have referred to this change as the rise of the "post-industrial society," by which they mean a society no longer so dependent on manufacturing and cities for its economic livelihood. The information and service sectors displaced the industrial sector as the prime generators of jobs and wealth, and sprawling suburban and exurban expanses replaced tightly bounded cities as the prime geographic regions of work and residence.

The computer chip is the technological key to this transformation, assuming the role played by the internal combustion engine 75 years earlier, triggering higher rates of economic growth and convulsive social and political changes. In some respects, this new transformation is reminiscent of the old one: The gap between rich and poor is large, new ideals (conservative rather than radical) are galvanizing politics, immigration levels are high, notions of gender and sexuality are being contested, communication is being revolutionized, and new forms of popular culture are proliferating. But the kind of information-based society being created is also different. "Identity politics" has crosscut the class politics of old, while political campaigns oriented to the mass media have eroded the once prominent role of political parties and machines. We are still in the midst of this transformation, which makes it difficult for historians to be certain about all of its elements, but we have described its major features and effects.

Chapter Organization

Covering the whole of the American 20th century in only 12 chapters represents something of a departure from other texts. In so doing, we have been motivated by two concerns. First, all of the 20th century is now history, not current events. This requires American historians to begin treating the 20th century as we do the 19th and 18th centuries: examining events in a longer and broader historical context for the sake of gaining deeper perspective. As America moves further into the 21st century, we believe that college history instructors will opt increasingly for single-semester classes on "Twentieth-Century America." This text will well serve such a trend.

Second, we have listened to and acknowledged an expressed desire for shorter texts. Teachers recognize the importance of using single books to convey the "big picture" but may also wish to include other materials—secondary works, primary documents, movies, and other sources—in their curricula. Such professors will find our book particularly useful. If instructors wish to cover the 20th century in two courses rather than in one, it would be easy to assign a chapter from this book every other week, leaving the alternate weeks open for the inclusion of supplementary material. We have designed a book, in other words, that offers instructors a great deal of flexibility.

Acknowledgments

We have benefited from the advice, skills, and support of many people. Our students have always been our toughest critics, and their input, both direct and indirect, has been invaluable to the shaping of this book. We would like to thank the many colleagues and fellow history teachers who have given us feedback on earlier drafts of these chapters, and to acknowledge a special debt to John Murrin, James McPherson, and Paul Johnson, who worked closely with us on a related project. The editorial, production, and marketing staff at Harcourt Brace has been superb, and we wish to thank, in particular, David Tatom, senior acquisitions editor; Margaret McAndrew Beasley, developmental editor; Charles Dierker, senior project editor; Diane Gray, production manager; Biatriz Chapa, art director; Steve Drummond, marketing strategist; and Lili Weiner, freelance photo researcher. They have boosted us over many humps and have helped to make the job of writing *America Transformed* a rewarding one.

Contents in Brief

Prologue: The Crisis of the 1890s   1

CHAPTER 1   An Industrial Society, 1890–1920   10

CHAPTER 2   Progressivism   50

CHAPTER 3   Becoming a World Power, 1898–1917   95

CHAPTER 4   War and Society, 1914–1920   127

CHAPTER 5   The 1920s   167

CHAPTER 6   The Great Depression and the New Deal, 1929–1939   208

CHAPTER 7   America during the Second World War   254

CHAPTER 8   The Age of Containment, 1946–1954   301

CHAPTER 9   Affluence and Its Discontents, 1954–1963   347

CHAPTER 10   America during Its Longest War, 1963–1974   391

CHAPTER 11   America in Transition: Economics, Culture, and Social Change in the Late 20th Century   433

CHAPTER 12   Winds of Change: Politics and Foreign Policy from Ford to Clinton   476

APPENDIX   A–1

Contents in Detail

Preface vii

PROLOGUE: The Crisis of the 1890s   1

Economic Crisis   1

Racial and Gender Turmoil   4

The Election of 1896   7

CHAPTER 1 An Industrial Society, 1890–1920   10

Sources of Economic Growth   11
   Technology   11
   Corporate Growth   12
   Mass Production and Distribution   13
   Corporate Consolidation   15
   Revolution in Management   16
   Scientific Management on the Factory Floor   16

"Robber Barons" No More   19

Obsession with Physical and Racial Fitness   21
   Social Darwinism   22

Immigration   23
   Causes of Immigration   24
   Patterns of Immigration   25
   Immigrant Labor   26
   Living Conditions   28

Building Ethnic Communities   28
   A Network of Institutions   28
   The Emergence of an Ethnic Middle Class   29
   Political Machines and Organized Crime   31

African American Labor and Community   33

Workers and Unions   35
   Samuel Gompers and the AFL   35
   "Big Bill" Haywood and the IWW   37

The Joys of the City   39

The New Sexuality and the New Woman 40
The Rise of Feminism 42

Conclusion 44
Chronology 45
Suggested Readings 45

CHAPTER 2 Progressivism 50
Progressivism and the Protestant Spirit 50

Muckrakers, Magazines, and the Turn toward "Realism" 51
Increased Newspaper and Magazine Circulation 52
The Turn toward "Realism" 53

Settlement Houses and Women's Activism 54
Hull House 54
The Cultural Conservatism of Progressive Reformers 56
A Nation of Clubwomen 57

Socialism and Progressivism 58
The Many Faces of Socialism 58
Socialists and Progressives 60

Municipal Reform 61
The City Commission Plan 61
The City Manager Plan 62
The Costs of Reform 62

Political Reform in the States 62
Restoring Sovereignty to "The People" 63
Creating a Virtuous Electorate 63
The Australian Ballot 64
Personal Registration Laws 64
Disfranchisement 64
Disillusionment with the Electorate 65
Woman Suffrage 66

Economic and Social Reform in the States 68
Robert La Follette and Wisconsin Progressivism 68
Progressive Reform in New York 70

A Renewed Campaign for Civil Rights 71
The Failure of Accommodationism 71
From the Niagara Movement to the NAACP 71

National Reform 74
The Roosevelt Presidency 74

Regulating the Trusts 75
Toward a "Square Deal" 75
Expanding Government Power: The Economy 76
Expanding Government Power: The Environment 77
Progressivism: A Movement for the People? 79
The Republicans: A Divided Party 80

The Taft Interregnum 80
Taft's Battles with Congress 81
The Ballinger-Pinchot Controversy 81

Roosevelt's Return 82
The Bull Moose Campaign 82

The Rise of Woodrow Wilson 83
The Unexpected Progressive 84

The Election of 1912 84

The Wilson Presidency 86
Tariff Reform and a Progressive Income Tax 86
The Federal Reserve Act 87
From the New Freedom to the New Nationalism 88

Conclusion 90
Chronology 91
Suggested Readings 91

CHAPTER 3 Becoming a World Power, 1898–1917 95
The United States Looks Abroad 95
Protestant Missionaries 96
Businessmen 96
Imperialists 97

The Spanish-American War 99
"A Splendid Little War" 100

The United States Becomes a World Power 105
The Debate over the Treaty of Paris 106
The American-Filipino War 107
Controlling Cuba and Puerto Rico 108
China and the "Open Door" 110

Theodore Roosevelt, Geopolitician 112
The Roosevelt Corollary 113
The Panama Canal 114
Keeping the Peace in East Asia 116

William Howard Taft, Dollar Diplomat 119

Woodrow Wilson, Struggling Idealist 121

Conclusion 123
Chronology 124
Suggested Readings 125

CHAPTER 4 War and Society 1914–1920 127
Europe's Descent into War 128

American Neutrality 130
Submarine Warfare 131
The Peace Movement 133
Wilson's Vision: "Peace without Victory" 134
German Escalation 135

American Intervention 136

Mobilizing for "Total" War 139
Organizing Industry 139
Organizing Civilian Labor 141
Organizing Military Labor 143
Paying the Bills 145
Arousing Patriotic Ardor 146
Wartime Repression 148

The Failure of the International Peace 151
The Paris Peace Conference and the Treaty of Versailles 152
The League of Nations 153
Wilson versus Lodge: The Fight over Ratification 154
The Treaty's Final Defeat 156

The Postwar Period: A Society in Convulsion 158
Labor-Capital Conflict 158
Radicals and the Red Scare 160
Racial Conflict and the Rise of Black Nationalism 161

Conclusion 163
Chronology 164
Suggested Readings 165

CHAPTER 5 The 1920s 167
Prosperity 167
A Consumer Society 169
A People's Capitalism 170
The Rise of Advertising and Mass Marketing 171

Changing Attitudes toward Marriage and Sexuality   173
Celebrating a Business Civilization   173
Industrial Workers   174

The Politics of Business   176
Harding and the Politics of Personal Gain   176
Coolidge and the Politics of Laissez-Faire   177
Hoover and the Politics of "Associationalism"   179
The Politics of Business Abroad   180

Farmers, Small-Town Protestants, and Moral Traditionalists   183
Agricultural Depression   183
Cultural Dislocation   184
Prohibition   185
The Ku Klux Klan   187
Immigration Restriction   188
Fundamentalism   190
The Scopes Trial   191

Ethnic and Racial Communities   192
European Americans   192
African Americans   195
The Harlem Renaissance   197
Mexican Americans   198

The "Lost Generation" and Disillusioned Intellectuals   201
Democracy on the Defensive   202

Conclusion   203
Chronology   204
Suggested Readings   205

CHAPTER 6 The Great Depression and the
            New Deal, 1929–1939   208
Causes of the Great Depression   209
Stock Market Speculation   209
Mistakes by the Federal Reserve Board   209
An Ill-Advised Tariff   210
A Maldistribution of Wealth   210

Hoover: The Fall of a Self-Made Man   210
Hoover's Program   211
The Bonus Army   212

The Democratic Roosevelt   213
An Early Life of Privilege   213
Roosevelt Liberalism   214

The First New Deal, 1933–1935 215
Saving the Banks 217
Saving the People 217
Repairing the Economy: Agriculture 218
Repairing the Economy: Industry 221
Rebuilding the Nation 221
The TVA Alternative 222
The New Deal and Western Development 222

Political Mobilization, Political Unrest, 1934–1935 224
Populist Critics of the New Deal 224
Labor's Rebirth 226
Anger at the Polls 228
The Rise of Radical Third Parties 228

The Second New Deal, 1935–1937 229
Philosophical Underpinnings 230
Legislation of the Second New Deal 230
Victory in 1936: The New Democratic Coalition 232
Rhetoric versus Reality 233
New Deal Men, New Deal Women 234
Labor Ascendant 238

America's Minorities and the New Deal 239
Eastern and Southern European Ethnics 240
African Americans 240
Mexican Americans 242
Native Americans 243

The New Deal Abroad 245

Stalemate, 1937–1940 247
The Court-Packing Fiasco 247
The Recession of 1937–1938 248

Conclusion 249
Chronology 250
Suggested Readings 250

CHAPTER 7 America during the Second World War 254
The Road to War: Aggression and Response 254
The Rise of Aggressor States 255
Isolationist Sentiment and American Neutrality 255
Growing Interventionist Sentiment 256
Japan's Invasion of China 256
The Outbreak of War in Europe 257

America's Response to War in Europe   259
An "Arsenal of Democracy"   260
The Attack at Pearl Harbor   262

Fighting the War in Europe   263
Campaigns in North Africa and Italy   264
Operation OVERLORD   265

The Pacific Theater   270
Seizing the Initiative in the Pacific   270
China Policy   271
Pacific Strategy   271
Atomic Power and Japanese Surrender   274

The War at Home: The Economy   277
Government's Role in the Economy   277
Business and Finance   278
The Workforce   279
Labor Unions   281
Assessing Economic Change   282

The War at Home: Social Issues   282
Wartime Propaganda   283
Gender Equality   284
Racial Equality   286
Racial Tensions   288

Shaping the Peace   291
The United Nations and International Economic Organizations   292
Spheres of Interest and Postwar Political Settlements   293

Conclusion   296
Chronology   296
Suggested Readings   297

CHAPTER 8 The Age of Containment, 1946–1954   301
Creating a National Security State, 1945–1949   301
Onset of the Cold War   301
Containment Abroad: The Truman Doctrine   303
Truman's Loyalty Program   304
The National Security Act, the Marshall Plan, and the Berlin Crisis   306
The Election of 1948   307

The Era of the Korean War, 1949–1952   309
NATO, China, and the Bomb   309
NSC-68   311

The Korean War   312
Korea and Containment   315

Containment at Home   316
Anticommunism and the Labor Movement   317
HUAC and the Loyalty Program   318
Targeting Difference   320
The Rosenberg Case and "the Great Fear"   320
McCarthyism   322

Domestic Policy: Truman's Fair Deal   323
The Employment Act of 1946 and the Promise of Economic Growth   324
Truman's Fair Deal   327
Civil Rights   329

Social Change and Containment   331
Jackie Robinson and the Baseball "Color Line"   331
The Postwar Suburbs   332
The Suburban Family and Gender Issues   335
Women's Changing Roles   337

From Truman to Eisenhower   338
The Election of 1952   339
Eisenhower Takes Command   340

Conclusion   342
Chronology   342
Suggested Readings   343

CHAPTER 9 Affluence and Its Discontents, 1954–1963   347
Foreign Policy, 1954–1960   347
The New Look and Summitry   347
Covert Action and Economic Leverage   349

America and the Third World   350
Latin America   350
Nasserism and the Suez Crisis of 1956   351
Vietnam   352

Affluence—A "People of Plenty"   353
Highways and Waterways   356
Labor-Management Accord   357
Political Pluralism   359
A Religious People   360

Discontents of Affluence   361
Conformity in an Affluent Society   361

Youth Culture   362
The Mass Culture Debate   364
The Limits of the Mass Culture Debate   365

The Fight against Discrimination, 1954–1960   366
Brown v. *Board*   366
The Montgomery Bus Boycott and Martin Luther King Jr.   368
The Politics of Civil Rights   369
American Indian Policy   370
Growth of Spanish-Speaking Populations   372
Urban Issues   373

Debates over Government's Role in the Economy   374
Eisenhower and the New Conservatives   375
Advocates of a More Active Government   375

The Kennedy Years: Foreign Policy   377
The Election of 1960   378
Kennedy's Foreign Policy Goals   379
Cuba and Berlin   380
Southeast Asia and "Flexible Response"   382

The Kennedy Years: Domestic Policy   383
Policymaking under Kennedy   383
The Civil Rights Crusade, 1960–1963   384
Women's Issues   385
The Assassination of John F. Kennedy   386

Conclusion   387
Chronology   387
Suggested Readings   388

CHAPTER 10 America during Its Longest War, 1963–1974   391
The Great Society   391
Completing Kennedy's Initiatives   392
The Election of 1964   393
Lyndon Johnson's Great Society   394
Evaluating the Great Society   395

Escalation in Vietnam   397
The Tonkin Gulf Resolution   397
The War Widens   399
The Media and the War   403

The War at Home   403
The Rise of the New Left   404
The Counterculture   405

From Civil Rights to Black Power   407
1968: The Violence Overseas   410
1968: The Violence at Home   411
The Election of 1968   412

The Nixon Years, 1969–1974   413
The Economy   414
Social Policy   415
Controversies over Rights   417

Foreign Policy under Nixon and Kissinger   419
Détente   420
Vietnamization   420
The Aftermath of War   422
The Nixon Doctrine   423

The Wars of Watergate   423
The Election of 1972   424
Nixon Pursued   425
Nixon's Final Days   426

Conclusion   428
Chronology   429
Suggested Readings   429

C H A P T E R   1 1   America in Transition: Economics, Culture, and
                Social Change in the Late 20th Century   433
A Changing People   433
An Aging Population   433
Rise of the Sunbelt   434
New Immigration   436
Urbanization and Suburbanization   438

Economic Transformations   440
New Technologies   440
Big Business   441
Postindustrial Restructuring   443

The Environment   446
Environmental Activism and Government Policy   446
Energy   449

Media and Culture   450
The Video Revolution   450
Hollywood and the "MTV Aesthetic"   453
The New Mass Culture Debate   454
The Debate over Multicultural Education   456

Social Activism   457
  A New Women's Movement   458
  Sexual Politics   460

Race, Ethnicity, and Social Activism   461
  Debates within African American Culture   462
  American Indians   463
  Spanish-Speaking Americans   465
  Asian Americans   467
  Dilemmas of Antidiscrimination Efforts   468

The New Right   469
  Neoconservatives   470
  The New Religious Right   470
  Conservative Politics   471

Conclusion   472
Chronology   473
Suggested Readings   473

CHAPTER 12 Winds of Change: Politics and Foreign Policy from
                Ford to Clinton   476

The Ford Presidency   476
  Domestic Issues under Ford   477
  Foreign Policy under Ford   477
  The Election of 1976   478

The Carter Presidency: Domestic Issues   480
  Welfare and Energy   480
  Economic Policy   481

The Carter Presidency: Foreign Policy   482
  Negotiations in Panama and the Middle East   482
  Human Rights Policy   483
  The Hostage Crisis in Iran   483
  The Election of 1980   484

Reagan's "New Morning in America"   486
  Reagan's First Term: Economic Issues   487
  Implementing a Conservative Agenda   488
  The Election of 1984   490

Renewing the Cold War   491
  The Defense Buildup   491
  Military Actions in Lebanon, Grenada, Nicaragua, and Libya   492
  Other Initiatives   494

The Iran-*Contra* Affair   494
Beginning of the End of the Cold War   495

From Reagan to Bush   496
Domestic Policy during Reagan's Second Term   497
The Election of 1988   498

Foreign Policy under Bush   500
The End of the Cold War   500
The Persian Gulf War   504

Toward the 21st Century   506
The Election of 1992   506
Clinton's Domestic Policies   508
Clinton's Foreign Policy   510
Election of 1996 and Aftermath   512

Conclusion   515
Chronology   515
Suggested Readings   516

APPENDIX   A–1

CREDITS   A–29

INDEX   A–31

Prologue: The Crisis of the 1890s

I n *The Wonderful Wizard of Oz* (1900), which may be read as a political parable, the novelist L. Frank Baum uses a tornado to symbolize the turbulent nature of the 1890s. The twister deposits Dorothy and her dog Toto in the land of Oz, a fascinating but troubled world very different than the shabby Kansas farm from which they were hurled. Each of the major characters that Dorothy meets on the way to the Emerald City, the capital of Oz, represents a key movement or figure in 1890s America. The Scarecrow speaks for the western farmer, who is unable to understand the complex economic issues of the day; the Tin Woodsman represents the industrial worker, who has lost both his job and his heart as a result of economic depression; and the Cowardly Lion resembles William Jennings Bryan, a youthful Democratic Party orator who can roar out his political message, but who lacks the courage to wage an all-out fight for the radical Populist Party that he supposedly represents. Farmers, workers, and Bryan were not the only significant figures in the 1890s, but their experiences and actions remain the essential starting point for understanding America at the dawn of its 20th-century transformation.

Economic Crisis

During the 1890s, the United States itself seemed to be caught in a whirlwind of economic and social change. Corporations and cities were displacing family farms and small towns as the most dynamic sectors of American life. The economic energy and wealth being generated in factories and cities were dizzying, and celebrants of the new industrial age saw the United States soon becoming the world's most powerful and affluent nation. But many others caught up in this transformation failed to perceive this promise, for they saw their very livelihoods at risk: These people included the small business operators competing with burgeoning corporations; industrial workers threatened by mechanization; and farmers who found that their land, even when productive, might not generate enough income to support their families and way of life.

Farmers in the South and on the Great Plains, the real-life counterparts of Auntie Em and Uncle Henry in *The Wonderful Wizard of Oz*, were hit particularly hard. As a result of a glut of farm products in the domestic and world markets and a deflationary price spiral that gripped the nation's economy, the value of agricultural commodities, already in decline, continued to plummet during the 1890s. Most

The Wizard of Oz • This illustration, from the original edition of *The Wonderful Wizard of Oz,* suggests the symbolic dimensions of L. Frank Baum's famous novel. Baum's illustrator, William Denslow, used a color scheme that producers later adopted in the 1939 motion picture: The sequences set in Kansas are dominated by the use of gray, while those in Oz feature the lavish display of colors, especially yellow, blue, and (for the Emerald City) green.

farmers were deeply in debt, and the low prices that they received for their crops made it impossible for them to meet their financial obligations. Many blamed their misfortune on the banks that held farm loans and on the grain elevators and railroads that saddled them with seemingly exorbitant charges for storing and transporting crops. Some farm families left their wheat to rot in the fields; others burned their corn for fuel while still others abandoned their land altogether. For those who believed in the Jeffersonian vision, in which the strength and virtue of America lay in family farms and in the small towns that they helped to sustain, the nation seemed in grave peril.

In order to construct a more equitable economic system, farmers in the South and on the northern plains took collective action. They first formed the Farmers Alliance, a bold effort to bypass corporate institutions by creating a network of farmer-run cooperatives to sell implements and market crops. When the Alliance failed, insurgents organized the People's, or Populist, Party. Its 1892 platform expanded upon the insurgent thrust of the Alliance. It called for a government takeover of railroads and communication facilities as a means of eliminating corporate control over pricing; "free and unlimited" coinage of silver at a ratio of 16:1 with gold, a program to inflate the nation's currency and, in the process, break the hold of eastern bankers on the country's financial system; and the direct election of U.S. Senators, a measure designed to strip corporate-dominated state legislatures of the power to determine the makeup of the Senate. Rarely had an American political party mounted such a radical assault on prevailing centers of economic power. The Populists nominated Gen. James B. Weaver of Iowa, a Civil War veteran, as their presidential candidate.

The economic problems that were fueling populism convulsed the industrial sector as well. In July 1892, a bitter strike by unionized iron workers at Andrew Carnegie's Homestead Works near Pittsburgh turned violent and took 16 lives. The governor of Pennsylvania called out the state militia to enforce management's decision to bring in nonunion workers. The union carried on its strike until November but could not avert defeat. Meanwhile, President Benjamin Harrison sent federal troops to Coeur d'Alene, Idaho, where they broke up a miners strike by escorting nonunion replacement workers into the mines and incarcerating hundreds of striking workers in a makeshift prison.

Amidst this turmoil, most voters opted for the familiar in 1892. General Weaver received less than 10 percent of the popular vote, and only 15 Populists gained election to Congress. The Populist Party fared best in Kansas, where it won control of the legislature, and in Nevada and Colorado, mining states in which the party's free silver pledge, rather than its broader political platform, attracted voters. Meanwhile, former President Grover Cleveland, a conservative Democrat, defeated Harrison, the Republican who had ousted him from the White House four years earlier. Cleveland soon confronted worsening economic and political conditions. A precipitous plunge in stock prices during March triggered the "Panic of 1893." Hundreds of banks and more than 15,000 other businesses closed their doors. Eventually, the solvency of the federal treasury seemed at risk as people exchanged paper money for gold. Amidst great secrecy, Cleveland and banker J. P. Morgan negotiated a complex arrangement by which Morgan helped to finance a plan (for a sizable profit of his own) that saved the U.S. Treasury from default. Business leaders credited the Cleveland-Morgan negotiations with saving the nation's entire financial system.

But the Cleveland-Morgan deal did nothing to create jobs or otherwise help the millions of people hard-hit by the continuing depression. Many men, especially younger ones, began "tramping" across the country in search of work. Led by Jacob Coxey, an Ohio businessman with an interest in political reform, a few headed for Washington D.C., in hopes of persuading Congress to hire the unemployed workers for public projects such as road construction. The Cleveland administration quickly dispersed Coxey's ragged "industrial army" from the Capitol grounds but soon confronted a full-scale industrial revolt when the Pullman Palace Car Company, the nation's leading manufacturer of railroad passenger cars, cut the wages of its employees but refused to lower the rents on its company-owned houses in which many Pullman workers lived. The American Railway Union (ARU), a national labor organization headed by Eugene Debs, refused to move any train that included a car manufactured by Pullman. This action disrupted the nation's rail system. In response to an appeal from the railroad industry, Cleveland obtained a sweeping court injunction that, in effect, outlawed the strike and threatened the ARU's leadership with imprisonment. On July 4, 1894, Cleveland dispatched federal troops to Chicago in order to enforce the injunction. The troops arrested Debs and other ARU leaders and ended the strike.

A heated debate over these military actions ensued. The Supreme Court, in reviewing the use of an injunction to halt the Pullman strike, emphasized the need to shore up the social order and uphold the rule of law. "The strong arm of the national government," the Court ruled, "may be put forth to brush away all obstructions to the freedom of interstate commerce or the transportation of the mails." Cleveland hailed the Court's decision for establishing, "in an absolutely authoritative manner and for all time, the power of the national government to protect itself in the exercise of its functions." But the pro-Populist and pro-labor Topeka *Advocate* saw the issue differently: The continued use of troops to break strikes suggested that "military despotism" was coming to the United States.

Racial and Gender Turmoil

The economic crisis, with its associated political unrest, was accompanied by social strains rooted in the increasingly multicultural and multiethnic character of American society. In the East, for example, many native-born Americans believed that their country's labor troubles were being caused by the "new immigrants"—Catholics and Jews from eastern and southern Europe who allegedly belonged to "inferior races" that could never be assimilated into American society. They urged the government to bar these immigrants from entering the country.

In the South, economic distress had given rise not only to populism but to racial violence, as many white southerners made African Americans the target of their rage. Between 1885 and 1900 more than 2,000 African American men were lynched by racist mobs. In response, white southern "moderates" began to construct a new system of "Jim Crow" laws that mandated a rigid system of racial separation. In 1896, the issue of Jim Crow laws reached the Supreme Court. The case of *Plessy* v. *Ferguson* involved the constitutionality of a Louisiana statute that required separate but equal accommodations for "whites" and "coloreds" on intrastate railways. Rejecting the separationist principle on which the measure was based, Justice John Marshall Harlan insisted that, "in the eye of the law, there is in this country no superior, dominant ruling class of citizens. There is no caste here." But his fellow justices disagreed. Writing for the majority that upheld the constitutionality of Jim Crow laws, Justice Henry Billings Brown argued that the Louisiana measure was a reasonable use of the state's police power, in line with "established usages, customs, and traditions." Separate facilities, the Court ruled, did not mark one race to be the inferior of the other, unless "the colored race chooses to put that construction upon it."

Plessy and subsequent Supreme Court decisions sanctioned new laws and separate public facilities that were rarely, if ever, equal. Soon, South Carolina was permitted, under the separate-but-equal principle, to spend about one-eighth as much money on the education of students of African descent as it spent on instruction for those of European ancestry. At the same time, a variety of other Jim Crow measures, including poll-taxes and literacy requirements, effectively denied African Americans the right to vote in southern states. While the Supreme Court was legitimating Jim Crow laws, Congress was refusing to respond to a campaign, spearheaded by the African American journalist Ida B. Wells, aimed at halting the upsurge in lynchings.

In these circumstances, the African American leader Booker T. Washington preached the necessity, if not the virtue, of keeping black and white institutions separate. Washington was a former slave who had founded the Tuskegee Institute in Alabama to train blacks for industrial and agricultural occupations. In 1895, in a

Booker T. Washington • A leading, though controversial, figure in the African American community at century's turn, Booker T. Washington preached a message of black self-help and of accommodation to Jim Crow. Here he is seated at left among teachers of the Tuskegee Institute (Alabama) that he directed.

speech to white leaders at the Atlanta Exposition, he announced his conditional acceptance of Jim Crow as long as whites pledged to help blacks develop their own schools, farms, and businesses. "In all things that are purely social we can be as separate as the fingers," Washington declared, "yet one as the hand in all things essential to mutual progress." He urged African Americans to focus on the task of building their own economic and social institutions, confident that progress there would hasten the day when whites would accept blacks as equals. At a time of great suffering, he gave many blacks hope. But he also angered activists who insisted that no circumstances could justify an accommodation, no matter how temporary, to a system of racial exclusion.

In the West, the 1890s saw the final stage of the long campaign to extinguish the political and cultural independence of the American Indian tribes. The military power of the tribes had been broken; their claims to vast tracts of land rebuffed. Most had been placed on reservations where they suffered from poverty and disease. In 1890, a Lakota group trying to revive its nation and culture faced the U.S. Army at Wounded Knee, in Dakota Territory; 25 soldiers and at least 250 Lakota died. Meanwhile, eastern reformers were trying to assimilate Indians into mainstream American life. Their primary tool was the Dawes Act (1887), which had authorized the breakup of reservations into individual, 160-acre farms, each to be owned by a single Indian family. The goal was to teach Indians to emulate white farmers, in the hope that it would encourage them to abandon their tribal cultures and adopt new economic and social habits. But the act did not promote assimilation; white land developers snatched up most of the 160-acre parcels while Indians remained generally faithful to their own cultures. By 1900, American Indians owned less than half of the land that they had possessed in 1887, while their poverty and isolation had increased.

In the Far West and Southwest, legal sanctions were directed at persons of East Asian and Mexican ancestry. The Chinese Exclusion Act of 1882 had barred the immigration of Chinese laborers for 10 years; when the law was renewed in 1892, it included a new procedure for the swift deportation of Chinese laborers who could not produce documentation for their status as legal aliens. Meanwhile, Mexican Americans from California to Texas, whose families had lived in the Southwest long before the United States had acquired it, were fighting, generally without much success, to keep their land from falling into the hands of Anglo-American newcomers. By the 1890s, the Southwest had undergone "Americanization," and Anglos were numerically and economically dominant, with many Mexican Americans becoming seasonal wage workers in agriculture, railroading, mining, and timber processing. In this region, too, segregationist laws and extra-legal violence often enforced ethnic separation.

In addition to rising racial tension, the 1890s were marked by growing controversy over the proper place of women in the nation's economic, political, and cultural life. The industrial economy was drawing more and more women out of the home and into the paid workforce, undermining the doctrine of "separate spheres" that had long dominated American culture. Groups of women were beginning to question why the female sphere was defined as rigidly separate from and subordinate to the male sphere. They wanted the choice of becoming professionals rather than homemakers. They wanted to vote, a right that was denied them under federal law, and, as late as 1893, by all but two states (Wyoming and Colorado). They wanted to become full participants in the heated political battles of the day. Some women also began seeking a greater degree of personal and sexual freedom, both as single and married individuals. Their demands frequently provoked male anger and fear.

The economic dislocations, racial tensions, and incipient turmoil in gender relations contributed to what many historians call the "crisis of the 1890s." Suffering economic hardship and confusion about how to forge a nation out of people deeply divided by class, race, and culture, many Americans came to believe that the United States stood at a dangerous crossroads. In 1886 Josiah Strong, a congregational minister and one of the most widely read writers of the day, had written, "There are certain great focal points of history . . . from which have radiated the molding influences of the future . . . and such are the closing years of the nineteenth century, second in importance only to the birth of Christ."

The Election of 1896

The sense that the end of the 19th century marked a critical watershed in the nation's history spilled into politics, making the election of 1896 one of the most contentious in U.S. history. Recognizing the appeal of the free silver issue, insurgent Democrats such as Nebraska's William Jennings Bryan challenged the "gold-bug" supporters of Grover Cleveland for control of the party. Bryan's "Cross of Gold Speech" in support of a platform plank calling for the free and unlimited coinage of silver galvanized the delegates to the Democratic national convention. Comparing the situation that the nation faced in 1896 to that which it had confronted at its birth in 1776, Bryan sounded a call to arms:

> We are fighting in defense of our homes, our families, our posterity. We have petitioned, and our petitions have been scorned; we have entreated, and our entreaties have been disregarded; we have begged, and they have mocked when our calamity came. We beg no longer; we entreat no more; we petition no more. We defy them!

The convention endorsed a free silver plank and selected Bryan, then only 34 years old, as its presidential nominee.

The free silver issue, with its special appeal to debt-ridden farmers and mining interests, dominated Bryan's campaign. The "Great Commoner" traveled to every part of the country, even to the East and other places where his core message seemed unlikely to sway the many voters who feared a free silver program would spark inflation. Bryan did offer a broader reform vision, with a potentially wider appeal, but he always returned to the silver issue.

Bryan's campaign presented the Populist Party with a fateful choice: Should it "fuse" with the Democrats or run its own presidential candidate? The Populist platform of 1896, though still committed to free silver, was even more radical than that of 1892. It called for public-works programs as a means of counteracting economic hard times, for instance, and condemned Jim Crow voting laws as "unrepublican and undemocratic." After a bitter debate, the fusionist faction prevailed: The

Populists nominated Bryan as their own standard-bearer, though they selected the Georgia Populist Tom Watson for vice president rather than accept Bryan's Democratic Party running mate, Arthur Sewall, a pro-silver banker with close ties to railroad interests. In the early 1890s, Watson and other white Populist leaders in the South had courageously tried to build their party by making common cause with black tenant farmers and laborers.

To ensure a Republican victory, Marcus Hanna, a wealthy entrepreneur and skilled political organizer, crafted a stark message for William McKinley, the GOP's presidential candidate in 1896: If Bryan and the Populist radicals for whom he was fronting were to lead the nation down the path of free silver, its financial system and social stability would be destroyed. In contrast, a Republican victory would not only guarantee a sound currency system but usher in a new era of widespread economic prosperity. No longer distracted by crackpot ideas, the nation could bask in the radiant glow of a gold-backed financial structure. Hanna made sure that trainloads of people, who had been pre-selected by his political lieutenants and offered special railway rates, came to McKinley's front porch in Canton, Ohio, to hear this message and to pledge their support for the presidential candidate who was promising to save, and then transform, the nation.

William McKinley, Republican Presidential Candidate • William McKinley defeated the Democrat and Populist William Jennings Bryan in the crucial election of 1896. Here he is seated on his front porch in Canton, Ohio, where he received trainloads of people who had come to declare their support for him and the Republican platform.

The 1896 election represented a victory for McKinley's vision of the nation's future. Although Bryan garnered more votes than any previous Democratic presidential candidate, McKinley still prevailed by about 600,000 popular and 95 electoral votes, and the Republicans retained control of Congress. Although the Populist Party ran well in some local and statewide races, particularly in the West, it fared much worse than Bryan. As Tom Watson wrote after the election, "while the fusionists have succeeded in getting some local pie . . . National Populism is almost a dead letter. . . . The sentiment is still there . . . but confidence is gone, and the party organization is almost gone." The defeat of populism further strengthened those who were seeking to disenfranchise black voters and extend Jim Crow in the South. Even Watson, disillusioned by defeat, abandoned the effort to forge interracial political bonds, began to issue racist and anti-Semitic tracts, and ended his political career as a rabid segregationist.

The first national election of the 20th century would take place in a very different economic climate. By early 1897, the depression of the '90s was beginning to end. New discoveries of gold in South Africa and in Alaska increased the world's supply of the precious metal and gave currency systems based on the gold standard, including that of the United States, greater liquidity. After several decades of falling prices, deflation finally began to ease, although the nation's financial system would remain the subject of proposals aimed at overhauling its operations and stabilizing its structure. The return of better economic conditions eliminated the free silver issue from national politics, and many of the Populist Party's other proposals—such as the direct election of U.S. Senators and a national income tax—were adopted by Republicans and Democrats. The fusion controversy of 1896 continued to divide the People's Party, and it ran two different presidential candidates in 1900.

Despite its sympathy for the Populist and labor movements of the 1890s, *The Wonderful Wizard of Oz* ultimately welcomes the new trends. The Scarecrow, the Tin Woodsman, and the Cowardly Lion are all appealing figures who endear themselves to the book's readers. But, neither they nor Dorothy, it turns out, require the kind of fundamental changes that they initially thought they needed. They merely require some fine-tuning to promote their self-confidence: a makeover for Dorothy, some oil and polish for the Tin Woodsman, a good combing and brushing for the Cowardly Lion, and some fresh stuffing for the Scarecrow. All they really need to save themselves, the Wizard of Oz convinces them, is an appreciation of the significant resources already at their command. In this way, *The Wonderful Wizard of Oz* assured Americans, as did McKinley, that the future would be bright and prosperous.

1

An Industrial Society, 1890–1920

With the collapse of the Populist Party in 1896 and the end of the depression in 1897, the American economy embarked on a remarkable stretch of growth. By 1910 America was unquestionably the world's greatest industrial power; in that year, the total output of America's factories exceeded that of its nearest rival, Germany, by a factor of 2 to 1.

Corporations were changing the face of America. Their railroad and telegraph lines crisscrossed the country. Their factories employed millions. Their production and management techniques became the envy of the industrialized world. A new kind of building—the skyscraper—came to symbolize America's corporate power. These modern towers were made possible by the use of steel rather than stone framework and by the invention of electrically powered elevators. Impelled upward by rising real estate values, they were intended to evoke the same sense of grandeur as Europe's medieval cathedrals. But these monuments celebrated man, not God; material wealth, not spiritual riches; science, not faith; corporations, not the commonweal. Reaching into the sky, dwarfing Europe's cathedrals, they were convincing embodiments of America's worldly might.

This chapter explores how the newly powerful corporations transformed America: how they unleashed untold productive power; how the jobs they generated attracted millions of European immigrants, southern blacks, and young single women to northern cities; and how they triggered an urban cultural revolution that made amusement parks, dance halls, vaudeville theater, and movies integral features of American life.

The power of the corporations dwarfed that of individual wage earners, deepening inequality. But wage earners sought to limit the power of corporations through labor unions and strikes, or by organizing institutions of collective self-help within their own ethnic or racial communities. And significant numbers found opportunities and liberties they had not known before: Immigrant entrepreneurs invented ways to make money through legal and illegal enterprise; young, single, working-class women pioneered a sexual revolution; and radicals dared to imagine building a new society where no one—not workers, women, or minorities—suffered from poverty, inequality, and powerlessness. The power of the new corporations, in other words, did not go unchallenged; nor, however, did a more egalitarian society prove easy to attain.

Sources of Economic Growth

A series of technological innovations in the late 19th century ignited the nation's economic engine. But technological breakthroughs alone do not fully explain the nation's spectacular economic boom. New corporate structures and new management techniques—in combination with the new technology—created the conditions that powered economic growth.

Technology

Two of the most important new technologies were the harnessing of electric power and the invention of the gasoline-powered internal combustion engine. Scientists had long been fascinated by electricity, but only in the late 19th century, through the work of Thomas Edison, George Westinghouse, and Nikola Tesla, did they produce the incandescent bulb that made electric lighting practical in homes and offices, and the alternating current (AC) that made electric transmission possible over long distances. From 1890 to 1920 the proportion of American industry powered by electricity rose from virtually nil to almost one-third. Older industries switched from expensive and cumbersome steam power to more efficient and cleaner electrical power. The demand for electric generators and related equipment brought into being new sectors of metalworking and machine-tool industries. Between 1900 and 1920 virtually every major city built electric-powered transit systems to replace horse-drawn trolleys and carriages. By 1912, some 40,000 miles of electric railway and trolley track had been laid. In New York City electricity made possible the construction of the first subways. Electric lighting—on city streets, in department store windows, in brilliantly lit amusement parks like New York's Coney Island—gave cities a new allure. The public also fell in love with the movies, which depended on electricity for the projection of images onto a screen. Electric power, in short, stimulated capital investment and accelerated economic growth.

The first gasoline engine was patented in the United States in 1878, and the first "horseless carriages" began appearing on European and American roads in the 1890s. But few thought of them as serious rivals to trains and horses; rather, they were seen as playthings for the wealthy, who liked to race them along country roads. In 1900 Henry Ford was just an eccentric 37-year-old mechanic who built race cars in Michigan in order to raise the capital he needed to build a different kind of car. By 1909 he had positioned himself at the head of a new transportation revolution. That year, Ford unveiled his Model T: an unadorned, even homely car, but reliable enough to travel hundreds of miles without servicing and cheap enough to be affordable to most working Americans. Ford had dreamed of creating an automobile civilization with his Model T, and his dream soon became a reality. In the ensuing 20 years, Americans bought Model T vehicles (and Model T imitations, built by Ford's competitors) by the millions. The stimulus this insatiable demand gave to the economy can scarcely be exaggerated. Millions of cars required millions of pounds of steel alloys, glass, rubber, petroleum, and other material. Millions of jobs in coal and iron-ore mining, oil refining and rubber manufacturing, steelmaking and machine tooling, road construction and service stations came to depend on automobile manufacturing.

Leading Industries

Cotton Goods	Sugar Refining	Marble and Stone Products
Copper Refining	Paper	Woolen Goods
Lumber Products	Shipbuilding	Diversified
Meatpacking	Automobiles	Rubber Products
Brass and Copper Products	Butter	Petroleum Refining
Leather Goods	Clothing	Lead Smelting
Iron and Steel	Products for Railroads	
Flour Mill Products	Tobacco Products	

Distribution of Factory Output, 1919
in thousands

Over $3,000,000
$1,000,000 to $2,999,000
$500,000 to $999,000
$100,000 to $499,000
Less than $99,000

Cities
o Value of product over $1 billion
• Value of product over $200 million

Industrial America, 1919

Corporate Growth

Successful inventions such as the automobile required more than the mechanical ingenuity and social vision of inventors like Henry Ford. Corporations with sophisticated organizational and technical know-how were also required to mass-produce and mass-distribute the newly invented products. Corporations had played an important role in the nation's economic life since the 1840s, but in the late 19th and early 20th centuries they underwent significant changes—in size, in the scope of their activities, and in their management.

The most obvious change was in their size. Employment in Chicago's International Harvester factory, where agricultural implements were built, nearly quadrupled

Change in Distribution of the American Workforce, 1870–1920

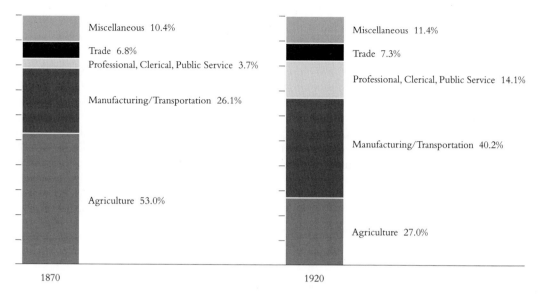

1870   1920

Source: Data from Alba Edwards, *Comparative Occupational Statistics for the United States 1870–1940,* U.S. Bureau of the Census, *Sixteenth Census of the United States, 1940, Population* (Washington, D.C., 1943).

from 4,000 in 1900 to 15,000 in 1916. Delaware's DuPont Corporation, a munitions and chemical manufacturer, employed 1,500 workers in 1902 and 31,000 workers in 1920. Founded with a few hundred employees in 1903, the Ford Motor Company employed 33,000 at its Detroit Highland Park plant by 1916 and 42,000 by 1924. That same year, the 68,000 workers employed at Ford's River Rouge plant (just outside Detroit) made it the largest factory in the world.

This growth in scale was in part a response to the enormous size of the domestic market. By 1900 railroads provided the country with an efficient transportation system that allowed corporations to ship goods virtually anywhere in the United States. A national network of telegraph lines laid out alongside railroad tracks made it possible for buyers and sellers separated by thousands of miles to stay in constant communication. And the population, which was expanding rapidly through both natural increase and immigration, demonstrated an ever-growing appetite for goods and services.

Mass Production and Distribution

The size of this domestic market encouraged manufacturers to perfect mass-production techniques that increased the speed of production and lowered unit costs. Mass production often meant replacing skilled workers with machines. It invariably required the coordination of machines with one another to permit high-speed, uninterrupted production at every stage of the manufacturing process. Mass-production techniques had become widespread in basic steel manufacturing and sugar refining by the 1890s, and spread to the machine-tool industry and automobile manufacturing in the first two decades of the 20th century.

For such production techniques to be profitable, large quantities of output had to be sold. And although the domestic market offered a vast potential for sales, manufacturers often found that distribution systems were inadequate. This was the case with the North Carolina manufacturer of smoking tobacco, James Buchanan Duke, who almost single-handedly transformed the cigarette into one of the best-selling commodities in American history. In 1885, at a time when relatively few Americans smoked, Duke invested in several Bonsack cigarette machines, each of which manufactured 120,000 cigarettes a day. Then, to create a market for the millions of cigarettes he was producing, Duke advertised his product aggressively throughout the country. He also established regional sales offices so that his sales representatives could keep in touch with local jobbers and retailers. Both in his use of national advertising and in his use of regional salesmen, Duke was an innovator. As the sales of cigarettes skyrocketed, more and more corporations sought to emulate Duke's techniques. Over the course of the next 20 years, the characteristics of American "big business" came to be defined by the corporations that were able to integrate mass production and mass distribution, as Duke had done in the 1880s.

A Pioneer in Marketing and Distribution • By 1903, Sears, Roebuck and Co. was already using its famed catalog to sell merchandise not only throughout the United States but around the world as well.

Corporate Consolidation

Corporate expansion also reflected a desire to avoid market instability. The rapid industrial growth of the late 19th century had proved deeply unsettling, not just to farmers and workers caught in predicaments beyond their control, but also to industrialists, who had trouble regulating growth and restraining competition. As promising economic opportunities arose, more and more industrialists sought to take advantage of them. But overexpansion and increasingly furious competition often turned rosy prospects into less-than-rosy results. In the economic cycle, buoyant booms were quickly followed by bankrupting busts. Soon, larger corporations began looking for ways to insulate themselves from the harrowing course of the business cycle.

In tackling this problem, as in so many others, the railroads led the way. Rather than engaging in ruinous rate wars—in which freight rates were reduced to unprofitable levels in an effort to capture the business of competitors—railroads began cooperating with one another. They shared information on costs and profits, established standardized rates, and allocated discrete portions of the freight business among themselves. These cooperative arrangements were variously called "pools," "cartels," or "trusts." The 1890 Sherman Antitrust Act declared such cartel-like practices illegal, but the law's enforcement proved to be short-lived. Still, the railroads' efforts rarely succeeded for long because they depended heavily on voluntary compliance. During difficult economic times, the temptation to lower freight rates and exceed one's market share could become too strong to resist.

Efforts by corporations to restrain competition and inject order into the economic environment continued unabated, however. Mergers now emerged as the favored instrument of control. By the 1890s powerful and sophisticated investment bankers, such as J. P. Morgan, possessed both the capital and the financial skills to engineer the complicated stock transfers and ownership renegotiations that mergers required. James Duke again led the way in 1890 when he and four competitors merged to form the American Tobacco Company. Over the next eight years the quantity of cigarettes produced by companies controlled by Duke quadrupled, from 1 billion to almost 4 billion per year. Moreover, American Tobacco used its powerful position in cigarette manufacture to achieve dominance in pipe tobacco, chewing tobacco, and snuff manufacture as well.

The merger movement intensified as the depression of the 1890s lifted. In the years from 1898 to 1904, many of the corporations that would dominate American business throughout most of the 20th century acquired their modern form: Armour and Swift in meatpacking, Standard Oil in petroleum, General Electric and Westinghouse in electrical manufacture, American Telephone and Telegraph in communications, International Harvester in the manufacture of agricultural implements, and DuPont in munitions and chemical processing. The largest merger occurred in steel in 1901, when Andrew Carnegie and J. P. Morgan together fashioned the U.S. Steel Corporation from 200 separate iron and steel companies. U.S. Steel, with its 112 blast furnaces and 170,000 steelworkers, controlled 60 percent of the country's steelmaking capacity. Moreover, its ownership of 78 iron-ore boats and 1,000 miles of railroad gave it substantial control over the procurement of raw materials and the distribution of finished steel products.

Revolution in Management

The dramatic growth in the number and size of corporations revolutionized corporate management. The ranks of managers mushroomed, as elaborate corporate hierarchies defined both the status and the duties of individual managers. Increasingly, senior managers took over from owners the responsibility for long-term planning. Day-to-day operations were then placed in the hands of numerous middle managers who oversaw particular departments (purchasing, research, production, labor) in corporate headquarters, or who supervised regional sales offices, or directed particular factories. Middle managers also managed the people—accountants, clerks, foremen, engineers, salesmen—in these departments, offices, or factories. The rapid expansion within corporate managerial ranks created a new middle class, intensely loyal to their employers but at odds both with blue-collar workers and with the older middle class of shopkeepers, small businessmen, and independent craftsmen.

As management grew in importance, companies tried to make it more scientific. Firms introduced rigorous cost-accounting methods into departments (such as purchasing) charged with controlling the inflow of materials and the outflow of goods. Many corporations began requiring college or university training in science, engineering, or accounting for entry into middle management. Corporations that had built their success on a profitable invention or discovery sought to maintain their competitive edge by creating research departments and hiring professional scientists—those with Ph.Ds from American or European universities—to come up with new technological and scientific breakthroughs. These departments were modeled on the industrial research laboratory set up by the inventor-entrepreneur Thomas Edison in Menlo Park, New Jersey, in 1876. To the extent that corporations hoped to reshape American life, they would do so in alliance with science.

Scientific Management on the Factory Floor

The most controversial and, in some respects, the most ambitious effort to introduce scientific practices into management occurred in production. Managers understood that the premium mass production placed on speed and efficiency could be magnified through improvements in factory organization as well as through technological innovation. So, in league with engineers, they sought optimal arrangements of machines and deployments of workers that would achieve the highest speed in production with the fewest human or mechanical interruptions. Some of these managers, such as Frederick Winslow Taylor, the chief engineer at Philadelphia's Midvale Steel Company in the 1880s, styled themselves as the architects of scientific management. They methodically examined every human task and mechanical movement involved in each production process. In "time-and-motion studies," they recorded every distinct movement a worker made in performing his or her job, how long it took, and how often it was performed. They hoped thereby to identify and eliminate wasted human energy not evident through more casual observation. Eliminating waste might mean reorganizing an entire floor of machinery so as to reduce "down time" between production steps; it might mean instructing workers to perform their tasks differently; or it might mean replacing uncooperative skilled workers with machines tended by unskilled, low-wage laborers. Regardless of the method chosen, the goal was the same: to make human labor emulate the smooth and apparently effortless operation of an automatic, perfectly calibrated piece of machinery.

Taylor shared his vision widely in the early 20th century, first through speeches to fellow engineers and managers, and then through his writings. By the time he published *The Principles of Scientific Management* (1911), his ideas had already captivated countless numbers of corporate managers and engineers, many of whom sought to introduce "Taylorism" into their own production systems.

But the introduction of scientific management practices rarely proceeded as easily as Taylor's speeches and writings seemed to suggest. Time-and-motion studies were costly, and Taylor's formulas for increasing efficiency and reducing waste were often far less scientific than he claimed. Taylor also overestimated the willingness of workers to play the mechanical role he assigned them. Many workers detested the "time-and-motions" inspector who arrived at their workstation with a stopwatch in one hand and a clipboard in the other. And the skilled workers and general foremen, whom Taylor sought to eliminate, used every available means of resistance. For these reasons, those managers and engineers who persisted in their efforts to apply scientific management invariably modified Taylor's principles.

Henry Ford led the way. His engineers initially adopted Taylorism wholeheartedly, with apparent success. By 1910 they had broken down automobile manufacturing into a series of simple, sequential tasks. Each worker performed only one task—adding a carburetor to an engine, inserting a windshield, mounting tires onto wheels. Some of these tasks were manual; others required the use of complex but easily operated machines. Then, in 1913 Ford's engineers introduced the first moving assembly line, a continuously moving conveyor belt that carried cars-in-production through each workstation. This innovation eliminated precious time previously wasted in transporting car parts (or partially built cars) by crane or truck from one work area to another. It also sharply limited the time available to workers to perform their assigned tasks. The speed of the line could be stopped, or altered, only by the foreman, not by the workers.

The continuous assembly line allowed the potential of the factory's many other organizational and mechanical innovations to be fully realized. By 1913 the Ford Motor Company's new Highland Park plant was the most tightly integrated and continuously moving production system in manufacturing. The pace of production exceeded all expectations. Between 1910 and 1914 production time on Ford Model Ts dropped by 90 percent, from an average of more than 12 hours per car to 1½ hours. A thousand Model Ts began rolling off the assembly line each day. This striking increase in the rate of production enabled Ford to slash the price of a Model T from $950 in 1909 to only $295 in 1923, a reduction of 70 percent. The number of Model Ts purchased by Americans increased sixteenfold between 1912 and 1921, from 79,000 to 1,250,000. The assembly line quickly became the most admired—and most feared—symbol of American mass production, not only in the United

The World's First Automobile Assembly Line • Introduced by Henry Ford at his plant in High-land Park, Michigan, this 1913 innovation cut production time on Ford Model Ts by an astounding 90 percent, allowing Ford to reduce the price of his cars by more than half while doubling his workers' hourly wages.

States but wherever industrialization had taken hold. Ford's Highland Park factory had apparently turned Taylor's vision into reality.

Problems immediately beset the system, however. Ford's workers hated the assembly line. Repeating a single motion all day long induced mental stupor, and managerial efforts to speed up the line produced physical exhaustion—both of which increased the incidence of error and injury. Some workers tried to organize a union to gain a voice in production matters. But most Ford workers expressed their dissatisfaction simply by quitting. By 1913 employee turnover at Highland Park had reached the astounding rate of 370 percent a year. At that rate, Ford had to hire 51,800 workers every year just to keep his factory fully staffed at 14,000.

A problem of that magnitude demanded a dramatic solution. Ford provided it in 1914 by raising the wage he paid his assembly-line workers to $5 a day, double the average manufacturing wage then prevalent in American industry. The result: Workers, especially young and single men, flocked to Detroit. Highland Park's high productivity rate permitted Ford to absorb the wage increase without cutting substantially into profits.

Taylor himself had believed that improved efficiency would lead to dramatic wage gains. With his decision to raise wages, Ford was being true to Taylor's principles. But Ford went even further in his innovations. He set up a sociology department,

Model T Prices and Sales, 1909–1923

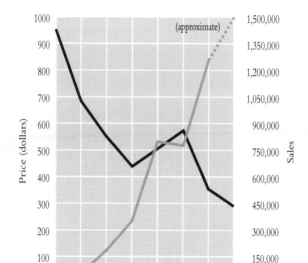

Source: From Alfred D. Chandler Jr., ed., *Giant Enterprise: Ford, General Motors, and the Automotive Industry* (New York: Harcourt, Brace and World, 1964), pp. 32–33.

forerunner of the personnel department, to collect job, family, and other information about his employees. He sent social workers into workers' homes to inquire into (and "improve") their personal lives. For the foreign-born, he instituted Americanization classes. He offered his employees housing subsidies, medical care, and other benefits. In short, Ford recognized that workers were more complex than Taylor had allowed, and that high wages alone would not transform them into the perfectly functioning parts of the mass-production system that Taylor had envisioned.

Ford's success impelled others to move in his direction. But it would take time for modern management to come of age. Not until the 1920s did a substantial number of corporations establish personnel departments, institute welfare and recreational programs for employees, and hire psychologists to improve human relations in the workplace. Until then, Ford remained a pioneer.

"Robber Barons" No More

Beyond being clever, sophisticated, and conducive to industrial harmony, innovations in corporate management were part of a broader effort among elite industrialists to shed their "robber baron" image and appear more responsible and virtuous.

The swashbuckling entrepreneurs of the 19th century—men like Cornelius Vanderbilt, Jay Gould, and Leland Stanford—had wielded their economic power brashly and ruthlessly, while lavishing money on European-style palaces, private yachts, personal art collections, and extravagant entertainments. But the depression of the 1890s—along with the populist political movement and labor protests such as the Homestead and Pullman strikes—shook the confidence of the members of this elite. The anarchist Alexander Berkman's 1892 attempt to assassinate Henry Clay Frick, Andrew Carnegie's right-hand man, by marching into his office and shooting him at point-blank range (Frick survived), terrified industrialists. Although such physical assaults were rare, anger over ill-gotten and ill-spent wealth was widespread. In the 1890s, after Mrs. Bradley Martin spent $370,000 (roughly $3.5 million in 1990s dollars) on an evening of entertainment for her friends in New York's "high society," she and her husband were forced to flee to England to escape the ensuing storm of indignation.

Seeking a more favorable image, some industrialists began to restrain their displays of wealth and use their private fortunes to advance the public welfare. As early as 1889 Andrew Carnegie had advocated a "gospel of wealth." The wealthy, he believed, should consider all income in excess of their needs as a "trust fund" for their communities. In 1901, the year in which he formed U.S. Steel, Carnegie withdrew from industry and devoted himself entirely to philanthropic pursuits, especially in art and education. By the time he died in 1919, he had given away or entrusted to several Carnegie foundations 90 percent of his fortune. Among the projects he funded were New York's Carnegie Hall, Pittsburgh's Carnegie Institute (now Carnegie-Mellon University), and 2,500 public libraries throughout the country.

Other industrialists, including John D. Rockefeller, soon followed Carnegie's lead. Rockefeller, a devout Baptist with an ascetic bent, had never flaunted his wealth (unlike the Vanderbilts and others), but his ruthless business methods in assembling the Standard Oil Company and in crushing his competition made him one of the most reviled of the robber barons. In the wake of journalist Ida Tarbell's stinging 1904 exposé of Standard Oil's business practices, and of the federal government's subsequent prosecution of Standard Oil for monopolistic practices in 1906, Rockefeller transformed himself into a public-spirited philanthropist. Through the Rockefeller Foundation, which was officially incorporated in 1913, he had dispersed an estimated $500,000,000 by 1919. His most significant gifts included money to establish the University of Chicago and the Rockefeller Institute for Medical Research (later renamed Rockefeller University). His charitable efforts did not escape criticism, however; many Americans interpreted them as an attempt to establish control over American universities, scientific research, and public policy. Still, Rockefeller's largesse helped build for the Rockefeller family a reputation for public-spiritedness and good works, a reputation that grew even stronger in the 1920s and 1930s. Many other business leaders, such as Julius Rosenwald of Sears, Roebuck and Daniel and Simon Guggenheim of the American Smelting and Refining Company, also dedicated themselves to philanthropy during this time.

Obsession with Physical and Racial Fitness

The fractious events of the 1890s also induced many wealthy Americans to engage in what Theodore Roosevelt dubbed "the strenuous life." In an 1899 essay with that title, Roosevelt, just back from Cuba, where he had fought in the Spanish-American War (see Chapter 3), urged Americans, especially educated men, to extinguish "the soft spirit of the cloistered life" and "boldly face the life of strife." Roosevelt exhorted Americans to live vigorously, to test their physical strength and endurance in competitive athletics, and to experience nature through hiking, hunting, and mountain climbing. He articulated a way of life that influenced countless Americans from a variety of classes and cultures.

The 1890s were indeed a time of heightened enthusiasm for competitive sports, physical fitness, and outdoor recreation. Millions of Americans began riding bicycles and eating more healthful foods. A passion for athletic competition gripped American universities. The rougher and more strenuous the game, the better. The power and violence of football helped make it the sport of choice at the nation's elite campuses, and for 20 years Ivy League schools were the nation's football powerhouses. In athletic competition, as in nature, one could discover and recapture one's manhood, one's virility. The words "sissy" and "pussyfoot" entered common usage in the 1890s as insults hurled at men whose masculinity was found wanting.

Ironically, this quest for masculinity had a liberating effect on women, who had been barred from strenuous outdoor activity of any sort by Victorian moral codes. In the vigorous new climate of the 1890s, young women began to engage in sports and other activities long considered too manly for "the fragile sex." They put away their corsets and long dresses and began wearing simple skirts, shirtwaists, and other clothing that gave them more comfort and freedom of movement. By the standards of the 1920s, these gentle changes would seem mild. But in the 1890s, they were radical indeed.

In the country at large the new enthusiasm for athletics and the outdoor life reflected a widespread dissatisfaction with the growing regimentation of industrial society. But among wealthy Americans, the quest for physical superiority reflected a deeper and more ambiguous anxiety: These Americans worried about their *racial* fitness. Most of them were native-born Americans whose families had lived in the United States for several generations and whose ancestors had come from the British Isles, the Netherlands, or some other region of northwestern Europe. Those few who were recent immigrants, such as the Scot Andrew Carnegie, nevertheless shared the cultural background and values of the native-born.

Many members of this economic elite liked to attribute their success and good fortune to their "racial superiority." They saw themselves as "natural" leaders, members of a noble Anglo-Saxon race endowed with uncommon intelligence, imagination, and discipline. But events of the 1890s had challenged the legitimacy of the elite's wealth and authority, and the ensuing depression mocked their ability to exert economic leadership. The immigrant masses laboring in factories, despite their poverty and alleged racial inferiority, seemed to possess a vitality that the "superior" Anglo-Saxons lacked. Immigrant families were overflowing with children. The city neighborhoods where they lived exhibited a social and cultural energy (especially apparent in their popular entertainments—vaudeville, amusement parks, nick-elodeons, and dance halls) that was missing in the sedate environs of the wealthy.

Some rich Americans, such as Henry Adams, Henry Cabot Lodge, and other members of Boston's declining political elite, reacted to the immigrants' vigor and industry by calling for a halt to further immigration. But that would not do for the ebullient Roosevelt, who argued instead for a return to fitness, superiority, and numerical predominance of the Anglo-Saxon race. He called on American men to live the strenuous life and on women to devote themselves to reproduction. The only way to avoid "race suicide," he declared, was for every Anglo-Saxon mother to have at least four children.

Such racialist thought was not limited to wealthy elites. Many other Americans, from a variety of classes and regions, also thought that all people demonstrated the characteristics of their race. Racial stereotypes were used to describe not only blacks, Asians, and Hispanics, but Italians ("violent"), Jews ("nervous"), and Slavs and Poles ("slow"). Such aspersions flowed as easily from the pens of compassion-ate reformers, such as Jacob Riis, who wanted to help the immigrants, as from the pens of bitter reactionaries, such as Madison Grant, who argued in *The Passing of the Great Race* (1916) that America should rid itself of inferior races.

Social Darwinism

Racialist thinking even received "scientific" sanction from distinguished biologists and anthropologists, who believed that racially inherited traits explained variations in the economic, social, and cultural lives of ethnic and racial groups. For a large number of the nation's intellectuals who styled themselves "Social Darwinists," human society developed according to the "survival of the fittest" principle articulated by the English naturalist Charles Darwin to describe plant and animal evolution. Human history could be understood in terms of an ongoing struggle among races, with the strongest and the fittest invariably triumphing. The wealth and power of the Anglo-Saxon race was ample testimony, in this view, to its superior fitness.

Social Darwinism was rooted in two developments of the late 19th century, one intellectual and one socioeconomic. Intellectually, it reflected a widely shared belief that human society operated according to principles every bit as scientific as those governing the natural world. The 19th century had been an age of stunning scientific breakthroughs. The ability of biologists, chemists, and physicists to penetrate the mysteries of the natural world generated great confidence in science, in people's ability to know and control their physical environment. That confidence, in turn, prompted intellectuals to apply the scientific method to the human world. The social sciences—economics, political science, anthropology, sociology, psychology—took shape in the late 19th century, each trying to discover the scientific laws governing individual and group behavior. Awed by the accomplishments of natural scientists, social scientists were prone to exaggerate the degree to which social life mimicked natural life; hence the appeal of Social Darwinism, a philosophy that allegedly showed how closely the history of human beings resembled the history of animal evolution.

Social Darwinism was also rooted in a socioeconomic development: the unprecedented interpenetration of the world's economies and peoples. Cheap and rapid ocean travel had bound together continents as never before. International trade, immigration, and imperial conquest made Americans more conscious of the variety of peoples inhabiting the earth. Although awareness of diversity sometimes encourages tolerance and cooperation, in the economically depressed years of the late 19th century, it encouraged intolerance and suspicion, fertile soil for the cultivation of Social Darwinism.

Immigration

Perhaps the most dramatic evidence of the nation's growing involvement in the international economy was the high rate of immigration. The United States had always been a nation of immigrants, but never had so many come in so short a time. Between 1880 and 1920, some 23 million immigrants came to a country that numbered only 76 million in 1900. From 1900 to 1914 an average of 1 million immigrants arrived each year. In many cities of the Northeast and Midwest, immigrants and their children comprised a majority of the population. In 1920s Boston, New York City, Chicago, and Milwaukee they accounted for more than 70 percent of the total population; in Buffalo, Detroit, and Minneapolis, more than 60 percent; and in Philadelphia, Pittsburgh, and Seattle more than 50 percent. Everywhere in the country, except in the South, the working class was overwhelmingly ethnic.

European immigration accounted for approximately three-fourths of the total. Some states received significant numbers of non-European immigrants—Chinese, Japanese, and Filipinos in California; Mexicans in California and the Southwest; and French Canadians in New England—whose presence profoundly affected regional economies, politics, and culture. But their numbers, relative to the number

Sources of Immigration

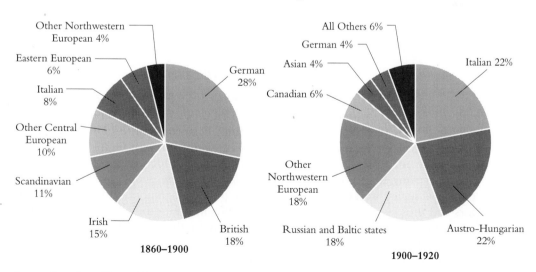

Other Northwestern European 4%
Eastern European 6%
Italian 8%
Other Central European 10%
Scandinavian 11%
Irish 15%
British 18%
German 28%

1860–1900

All Others 6%
German 4%
Asian 4%
Canadian 6%
Other Northwestern European 18%
Russian and Baltic states 18%
Austro-Hungarian 22%
Italian 22%

1900–1920

Source: Data from *Historical Statistics of the United States, Colonial Times to 1970* (White Plains, N.Y.: Kraus International, 1989), pp. 105–109.

of European immigrants, were small. The U.S. government refused to admit Chinese immigrants after 1882 and Japanese male immigrants after 1907 (see Chapter 3). Although immigrants from Latin America were free to enter the United States throughout this period, few did until 1910, when the social disorder caused by the Mexican Revolution propelled a stream of refugees to southwestern parts of the United States. Half a million French Canadians had migrated to New England and the upper Midwest between 1867 and 1901. The rate then slowed as the pace of industrialization in their Quebec homeland quickened.

Most of the European immigrants who arrived between 1880 and 1914 came from eastern and southern Europe. Among them were 3 to 4 million Italians, 2 million Russian and Polish Jews, 2 million Hungarians, an estimated 4 million Slavs (including Poles, Bohemians, Slovaks, Russians, Ukrainians, Bulgarians, Serbians, Croatians, Slovenians, Montenegrins, and Macedonians), and 1 million from Lithuania, Greece, and Portugal. Hundreds of thousands came as well from Turkey, Armenia, Lebanon, Syria, and other Near Eastern lands abutting the European continent.

These post-1880 arrivals were called "new immigrants" to underscore the cultural gap separating them from the "old immigrants," who had come from northwestern Europe—Great Britain, Scandinavia, and Germany. "Old immigrants" were regarded by Americans (and often regarded themselves) as racially fit, culturally sophisticated, and politically mature. The "new immigrants," by contrast, were often regarded by Americans as racially inferior, culturally impoverished, and incapable of assimilating American values and traditions. This negative view of the "new immigrants" reflected in part a fear of their alien languages, religions, and economic backgrounds. Few spoke English. Most adhered to Catholicism, Greek Orthodoxy, or Judaism rather than Protestantism. And most, with the exception of the Jews, were peasants, unaccustomed to urban industrial life. But they were not as different from the "old immigrants" as the label implied. For example, many of the earlier-arriving Catholic peasants from Ireland and Germany had had no more familiarity with American values and traditions than did the Italians and Slavs who arrived later.

Causes of Immigration

In fact, the "old" and "new" European immigrants were more similar than different. Both came to America for the same reasons: either to flee religious or political persecution or to escape economic hardship. It is true that the United States attracted a small but steady stream of political refugees throughout the 19th century: labor militants from England; nationalists from Ireland; socialists and anarchists from Germany, Russia, Finland, and Italy. Many of these people possessed unusual talents as skilled workers, labor organizers, political agitators, and newspaper editors and thus exercised considerable influence in their ethnic communities. However, only the anti-Semitic policies of Russia in the late 19th and early 20th centuries triggered a mass emigration (in this case Jewish) of political refugees.

Most mass immigration was propelled instead by economic hardship. Europe's rural population was growing at a faster rate than the land could support. European factories absorbed some, but not all, of the rural surplus. And industrialization and urbanization were affecting the European countryside in ways that disrupted rural ways of life. As railroads penetrated the countryside, village artisans found themselves unable to compete with the cheap manufactured goods that arrived from city factories. These handicraftsmen were among the first to emigrate. Meanwhile, rising demand for food in the cities accelerated the growth of commercial agriculture in the hinterland. Some peasant families lost their land. Others turned to producing crops for the market, only to discover that they could not compete with larger, more efficient producers. In addition, by the last third of the 19th century, peasants faced competition from North American farmers. Prices for agricultural commodities plummeted everywhere. The economic squeeze that spread distress among American farmers in the 1880s and 1890s caused even more hardship among Europe's peasantry. These were the circumstances that triggered mass emigration.

Patterns of Immigration

An individual's or family's decision to emigrate often depended on having a contact—a family member, relative, or fellow villager—already established in an American city. In 1910 four-fifths of the immigrants who had come from Austria and Hungary reported to congressional investigators that they had had friends or relatives waiting for them in America. These were people who provided immigrants with a destination, with inspiration (they were examples of success in America), with advice about jobs, and with financial aid. Sometimes whole villages in southern Italy or western Russia—or at least all the young men—seemed to disappear, only to reappear in a certain section of Chicago, Pittsburgh, or New York. Villages without contacts in the United States were relatively unaffected by the emigration mania.

A majority of immigrants viewed their trip to the United States as a temporary sojourn. They came not in search of permanent settlement but in search of the high wages that would enable them to improve their economic standing in their homeland. For them, America was a land of economic opportunity, not a land to call home. This attitude explains why men vastly outnumbered women and children in the migration stream. From 1899 to 1910, three-fourths of the immigrants from southern and eastern Europe were adult men. Some had left wives and children behind; more were single. Most wanted merely to make enough money to buy a farm in their native land. And, true to their dream, many did return home. For every 100 Italian immigrants who arrived in the United States between 1907 and 1911, for example, 73 returned to Italy. An estimated 60 to 80 percent of all Slavic immigrants eventually returned to the land of their birth.

The rate of return was negligible among certain other groups, however. Jews had little desire to return to the religious persecution they had fled. Most came as families, intending to make America their permanent home. Only 5 percent of them returned home. The rate of return was also low among the Irish, who saw few opportunities in their long-suffering (though much-loved) Emerald Isle. But in the early 20th century, such groups were exceptional. Most immigrants looked forward to returning to Europe. Not until the First World War shut down transatlantic travel did most immigrants begin to regard their presence in the United States as permanent.

Immigration tended to move in rhythm with the U.S. business cycle. It rose in boom years and fell off during depressions. It remained at a high level during the first 14 years of the new century when the U.S. economy was experiencing a period of sustained growth, broken only by the brief Panic of 1907–1908.

Immigrant Labor

In the first decade of the 20th century, immigrant men and their male children constituted 70 percent of the workforce in 15 of the 19 leading U.S. industries. Their concentration was highest in industries where work was the most backbreaking. Immigrants built the nation's railroads and tunnels; mined its coal, iron ore, and other minerals; stoked its hot and sometimes deadly steel furnaces; and slaughtered and packed its meat in Chicago's putrid packinghouses. In 1909 first- and second-generation immigrants—especially Greeks, Italians, Japanese, and Mexicans—comprised more than 96 percent of the labor force that built and maintained the nation's railroads. Of the 750,000 Slovaks who arrived in America before 1913, at least 600,000 headed for the coal mines and steel mills of western Pennsylvania. The steel mills of Pittsburgh, Buffalo, Cleveland, and Chicago attracted disproportionately large numbers of Poles and other Slavs as well.

Immigrants also performed "lighter" but no less arduous work. Jews and Italians predominated in the garment manufacturing shops of New York City, Chicago, Philadelphia, Baltimore, and Boston. In 1900 French Canadian immigrants and their children held one of every two jobs in New England's cotton textile industry. By 1920 the prosperity of California's rapidly growing agricultural industry—what

Immigrants and the Clothing Industry • Jewish and Italian immigrants predominated in New York City's huge garment industry, with men holding the supervisory and skilled jobs and women the semiskilled positions. Unionists and their supporters often labeled garment factories "sweatshops" because of the low pay, long hours, and poorly ventilated and cramped workplaces.

the writer Carey McWilliams later called "factories in the field"—depended primarily on Mexican and Filipino labor. In these industries, immigrant women and children, who worked for lower wages than men, formed a large part of the labor force. Few states restricted child labor. More than 25 percent of boys and 10 percent of girls aged 10 to 15 were "gainfully employed."

Immigrants were as essential as fossil fuels to the smooth operation of the American economic machine. Sometimes, however, the "machine" consumed workers as well as coal and oil. Those who worked in heavy industry, mining, or railroading were especially vulnerable to accident and injury. In 1901, for instance, 1 in every 400 railroad workers died on the job and 1 in every 26 suffered injury. Between the years 1906 and 1911, almost one-quarter of the recent immigrants employed at the U.S. Steel Corporation's South Works (Pittsburgh) were injured or killed on the job. Lax attention to safety rendered even light industry hazardous and sometimes fatal. In 1911 a fire broke out on an upper floor of the Triangle Shirtwaist Company, a New York City garment factory. The building had no fire escapes. The owners of the factory, moreover, had locked the entrances to each floor as a way of keeping their employees at work. A total of 146 workers, mostly young Jewish and Italian women, perished in the fire or from desperate nine-story leaps to the pavement below.

Chronic fatigue and inadequate nourishment increased the risk of accident and injury. Workweeks averaged 60 hours—10 hours every day except Sunday. Workers who were granted Saturday afternoons off—thus reducing their workweek to a "mere" 55 hours—considered themselves fortunate. Steelworkers were not so lucky. They labored from 72 to 89 hours a week, and were required to work one 24-hour shift every two weeks.

Most workers had to labor long hours simply to eke out a meager living. In 1900 the annual earnings of American manufacturing workers averaged only $400 to $500 a year, although there were substantial variations from region to region and skill to skill. Income in the South averaged only $300 a year; the average in the North was $460, although skilled workers could earn as much as $1,500 or $2,000 a year. Workers who held higher-paying jobs earned far more than those doing comparable work in Europe. In theory, such well-paid work offered immigrants their greatest opportunities. But most of these jobs were held by Yankees and by the Germans, Irish, Welsh, and other Europeans who had come as part of the "old immigration." Through their unions, workers of northern European extraction also controlled access to new jobs that opened up and usually managed to fill them with a son, relative, or fellow countryman. Consequently, relatively few of the "new immigrants" rose into the prosperous ranks of skilled labor. In any case, employers were replacing many skilled workers with machines operated by cheaply paid operatives.

From the 1870s to 1910 real wages paid to factory workers and common laborers did rise, but not steadily. Wages fell sharply during depressions. And the hope for sharp increases during periods of recovery collapsed under the weight of renewed mass immigration, which brought hundreds of thousands of new job seekers into the labor market. One out of every five industrial workers was unemployed, even during the boom years of the early 20th century.

Most working families required two or three wage earners to survive. If a mother could not go out to work because there were small children at home, she might rent rooms to some of the many single men who had recently immigrated. But economic security was hard to attain. In his book, *Poverty,* published in 1904, the social investigator Robert Hunter conservatively estimated that 20 percent of the industrial population of the North lived in poverty.

Living Conditions

Strained economic circumstances confined many working-class families to cramped and dilapidated living quarters. Many of them lived in two- or three-room apartments, with several sleeping in each room. To make ends meet, one immigrant New York City family of eight living in a two-room apartment took in six boarders. Some boarders considered themselves lucky to have their own bed. That luxury was denied the 14 Slovaks who shared eight beds in a small Pittsburgh apartment and the New York City printer who slept on a door he unhinged every night and balanced across two chairs. The lack of windows in city tenements allowed little light or air into these apartments, and few had their own toilets or running water. Crowding was endemic. The population density of New York City's Lower East Side—the principal area of settlement for Jewish immigrants there—reached 700 per acre in 1900, a density greater than that of the poorest sections of Bombay, India. Overcrowding and poor sanitation resulted in high rates of deadly infectious diseases, especially diphtheria, typhoid fever, and pneumonia.

By 1900 this crisis in urban living had begun to yield to the insistence of urban reformers that cities adopt housing codes and improve sanitation. Between 1880 and 1900, housing inspectors condemned the worst of the tenements and ordered landlords to make certain minimal improvements. City governments built reservoirs, pipes, and sewers to carry clean water to the tenements and to carry away human waste. Newly paved roads lessened the dirt, mud, and stagnant pools of water and thus further curtailed the spread of disease. As a result, urban mortality rates fell in the 1880s and 1890s. Nevertheless, improvements came far more slowly to the urban poor than they did to the middle and upper classes. Cities like Pittsburgh built extensive systems of paved roads in wealthy districts but not in working-class areas. And the water supply and water pressure were far better in prosperous than in poor neighborhoods. At the outbreak of the First World War, many working-class families still did not have running water in their homes.

Building Ethnic Communities

The immigrants may have been poor, but they were not helpless. Migration itself had required a good deal of resourcefulness, self-help, and mutual aid—assets that survived in the new surroundings of American cities.

A Network of Institutions

Each ethnic group quickly established a network of institutions that gave it a sense of community and multiplied the sources of communal assistance. Some people simply reproduced those institutions that had been important to them in the "Old

Country." The devout established churches and synagogues. Lithuanian, Jewish, and Italian radicals reestablished Old World socialist and anarchist organizations. Irish nationalists set up clandestine chapters of the Clan Na Gael to keep alive the struggle to free Ireland from the English. Germans felt at home in their traditional *Turnevereins* (athletic clubs) and musical societies.

Immigrants developed new institutions as well. In the larger cities, foreign-language newspapers disseminated news, advice, and culture. Each ethnic group created fraternal societies to bring together immigrants who had known each other in the Old Country, or who shared the same craft, or who had come from the same town or region. Most of these societies provided members with a death benefit (ranging from a few hundred to a thousand dollars) that guaranteed the deceased a decent burial and the family a bit of cash. Some fraternal societies made small loans as well. Among those ethnic groups that prized home ownership, especially the Slavic groups, the fraternal societies also provided mortgage money. And all of them served as centers of sociability—places to have a drink, play cards, or simply relax with fellow countrymen. The joy, solace, and solidarity they generated helped countless immigrants to adjust to American life.

The Emergence of an Ethnic Middle Class

Within each ethnic group, a sizable minority directed their talents and ambitions to economic gain. Some of these entrepreneurs first addressed their communities' needs for basic goods and services. Immigrants preferred to buy from fellow countrymen with whom they shared a language, a history, and presumably a bond of trust. Enterprising individuals responded by opening dry goods stores, food shops, butcher shops, and saloons in their ethnic neighborhoods. Those who could not afford to rent a store hawked their fruit, clothing, or dry goods from portable stands, wagons, or sacks carried on their back. The work was endless, the competition tough. Men often enlisted the entire family—wife, older children, younger children—in their undertakings. Few family members were ever paid for their labor, no matter how long or hard they worked. Although many of these small businesses failed, enough survived to give some immigrants and their children a toehold in the middle class.

Other immigrants turned to industry. Despite the growth of large-scale manufacturing enterprises, the scale of operation in some industries remained small and thus accessible to individuals with little capital. This was particularly true of the garment industry, truck farming, and construction. A clothing manufacturer needed only a few sewing machines to become competitive. Many Jewish immigrants, having been tailors in Russia and Poland, opened such facilities. If a rented space proved beyond their means, they set up shop in their own apartment. Competition among these small manufacturers was fierce, and work environments were condemned by critics as "sweatshops": inadequate lighting, heat, and ventilation; 12-hour workdays and 70-hour workweeks during peak seasons, with every hour spent bent over a sewing machine; poor pay and no employment security, especially for the women and children who made up a large part of this labor force. Even at this level of exploitation, many small manufacturers failed and fell back into the pool of

Immigrant Street Life • Immigrant districts were overcrowded but vibrant. Here crowds of immigrant women shoppers and street merchants carry on their business.

"sweated" labor themselves. But over time, a good many of them managed to firm up their position as manufacturers and to evolve into stable, responsible employers. Their success contributed to the emergence of a Jewish middle class.

The story was much the same in urban construction, where Italians who had established themselves as labor contractors, or *padroni,* went into business for themselves to take advantage of the rapid expansion of American cities. Though few became general contractors on major downtown projects, many of them did well building family residences or serving as subcontractors on larger buildings.

One immigrant who did make the leap from small to big business was Amadeo P. Giannini, who used his savings from a San Francisco fruit and vegetable stand to launch a career in banking. Determined to make bank loans available and affordable to people of ordinary means, Giannini generated a huge business in small loans. Expanding on this strong base, he eventually made his bank—the Bank of America—into the country's largest financial institution.

In southern California, Japanese immigrants chose agriculture as their route to the middle class. Working as agricultural laborers in the 1890s, they began to acquire their own land in the early years of the 20th century. Their small-scale holdings did not amount to much compared to the vast corporate farms of the Imperial and San Joaquin Valleys. Altogether, they owned only 1 percent of California's total farm acreage. But their specialization in fresh vegetables and fruits (particularly strawberries), combined with their labor-intensive agricultural methods (with family members supplying the labor), was yielding $67 million in annual revenues by 1919. That was one-tenth of the total revenue generated by California agriculture that year. Japanese farmers sold their produce to Japanese fruit and vegetable wholesalers in Los Angeles, who had chosen a mercantile route to middle-class status.

Each ethnic group created its own history of economic success and social mobility. From the emerging middle classes came many leaders who would provide their ethnic groups with identity, legitimacy, and power and would lead the way toward Americanization and assimilation. Their children tended to do better in school than the children of working-class ethnics, and academic success served as a ticket to upward social mobility in a society that depended more and more on university-trained engineers, managers, lawyers, doctors, and other professionals.

Political Machines and Organized Crime

The underside of this success story could be seen in the rise of government corruption and organized crime. Many ethnic entrepreneurs operated on the margins of economic failure and bankruptcy—and some of them looked beyond their usual support networks and accepted the help of those who promised to ensure their economic survival. Sometimes the help came from honest unions and upright government officials, but sometimes it did not. Unions were generally weak, and some government officials, themselves lacking experience and economic security, were susceptible to bribery. Economic necessity became a breeding ground for government corruption and greed. A contractor eager to win a city contract—to build a trolley system, a sewer line, or a new city hall, for example—would find it necessary to "pay off" government officials who could throw the contract his way. By 1900 such graft had become essential to the day-to-day operation of government in most large cities. The graft, in turn, made local officeholding a rich source of economic gain. Politicians began building political machines to guarantee their success in municipal elections. The machine bosses used a variety of legal and illegal means to bring victory on election day. They won the loyalty of urban voters—especially immigrants—by providing poor neighborhoods with paved roads and sewer systems. They helped newly arrived immigrants to get jobs (often on city payrolls) and occasionally provided food, fuel, or clothing to families in dire need. Many of their clients were grateful for these services in an age when government itself provided little public assistance.

The bosses who ran the political machines—including "King Richard" Croker in New York, James Michael Curley in Boston, Tom Pendergast in Kansas City, Martin Behrman in New Orleans, and Abe Ruef in San Francisco—served their own needs first. They saw to it that construction contracts went to those who offered the most graft, not to those who were likely to do the best job. They protected gamblers, pimps, and other purveyors of urban vice who contributed large amounts to their machine coffers. They often required city employees to contribute to their campaign chests, to solicit political contributions, and to get out the vote on election day. And they engaged in widespread election fraud: rounding up truckloads of newly arrived immigrants and paying them to vote a certain way; having their supporters vote two or three times; and stuffing ballot boxes with the votes of phantom citizens who had died, moved away, or never been born.

Big city machines, then, were both a positive and negative force in urban life. Reformers despised them for disregarding election laws and encouraging vice. Immigrants valued them for providing social welfare services and for creating opportunities for upward mobility.

The history of President John F. Kennedy's family offers a compelling example of the economic and political opportunities opened up by machine politics. Both of Kennedy's grandfathers, John Francis ("Honey Fitz") Fitzgerald and Patrick Joseph Kennedy, were the children of penniless Irish immigrants who arrived in Boston in the 1840s. Fitzgerald was the more talented of the two, excelling at academics and athletics at Boston Latin School and Boston College and then, in 1885, winning a coveted place in Harvard's Medical School. But Fitzgerald left Harvard that same year, choosing a career in politics instead. Between 1891 and 1905 he served as a Boston city councillor, Massachusetts state congressman and senator, U.S. congressman, and mayor of Boston. For much of this period, he derived considerable income and power from his position as the North End ward boss, where he supervised the trading of jobs for votes and favors for cash in his section of Boston's Democratic and Irish-dominated political machine.

Patrick Kennedy, a tavern owner and liquor merchant in East Boston, never enjoyed Fitzgerald's popularity or electoral success, but he became an equally important figure behind the scenes in Boston city politics. In addition to running the Democratic Party's affairs in Ward Two, he served on the Strategy Board, a secret council of Boston's machine politicians that met regularly to devise policies, settle disputes, and divide up the week's graft. Both Fitzgerald and Kennedy derived a substantial income from their political work and used it to lift their families into middle-class prosperity. Kennedy's son (and the future president's father), Joseph P. Kennedy, had even greater ambitions: He would go on to make a fortune as a Wall Street speculator and liquor distributor and to groom his sons for Harvard and the highest political offices in the land. But his rapid economic and social ascent had been made possible by his father's and father-in-law's earlier success in the local and lucrative world of Boston machine politics.

Underworld figures, too, influenced urban life. In the early years of the 20th century, gangsterism was a scourge of Italian neighborhoods, where Sicilian immigrants had established outposts of the notorious Mafia, and in Irish, Jewish, Chinese, and other ethnic communities as well. Favorite targets of underworld extortionists were small-scale manufacturers and contractors, from whom they extracted large sums of money for protection. They enforced their demands with physical force, beating up or killing those who failed to abide by the "rules." Greedy for money, power, and fame, and willing to use any means necessary, these criminals considered themselves authentic entrepreneurs cut from the American mold. By the 1920s petty extortion had escalated in urban areas, and underworld crime had become big business. Al Capone, the ruthless Chicago mobster who made a fortune from gambling, prostitution, and bootleg liquor during Prohibition, once claimed: "Prohibition is a business. All I do is to supply a public demand. I do it in the best and least harmful way I can." New York City's Arnold Rothstein, whose financial sophistication won him a gambling empire and the power to fix the 1919 World Series, nurtured his reputation as "the J. P. Morgan of the underworld." Mobsters like Rothstein and Capone were charismatic figures, both in their ethnic communities and in the nation at large. Few immigrants, however, followed their criminal path to economic success.

African American Labor and Community

Unlike immigrants, African Americans remained a predominately rural and southern people in the early 20th century. Most blacks were sharecroppers and tenant
farmers. The markets for cotton and other southern crops had stabilized in the
early 20th century, ending the dizzying downward spiral in agricultural prices that
had spread distress throughout rural America in the 1880s and 1890s. But black
farmers remained vulnerable to exploitation. Landowners, most of whom were
white, often forced sharecroppers to accept artificially low prices for their crops. At
the same time, these landowners charged high prices for seed, tools, and groceries
at the local stores that they controlled. Many sharecroppers had no alternative but
to submit to this extortion. Few rural areas generated enough business to support
more than one store, or to create a competitive climate that might force prices
down. Those sharecroppers who traveled elsewhere to sell their crops or purchase
their necessities risked retaliation—either physical assaults by white vigilantes or
eviction from their land. Thus, most remained beholden to their landowners,
mired in poverty and debt.

For a majority of African Americans, the First World War would represent the
first opportunity to escape this economic servitude (see Chapter 4). But during the
1880s and 1890s, some African Americans sought a better life by migrating to

A Sharecropping Family, 1919 • In the early 20th century, a majority of African Americans lived in
the rural South, in circumstances similar to those depicted in this photo of a North Carolina family.

industrial areas of the South and the North. In the South, they worked in iron and coal mines, in furniture and cigarette manufacture, as railroad track layers and longshoremen, and as laborers in the steel mills of Birmingham, Alabama. By the early 20th century, their presence was growing in the urban North as well, where they worked on the fringes of industry as janitors, elevator operators, teamsters, longshoremen, and servants of various kinds. Altogether, about 200,000 blacks left the South for the North and West between 1890 and 1910.

In southern industries, blacks were subjected to hardships and indignities that even the newest immigrants were not expected to endure. Railroad contractors in the South, for example, treated their black track layers (such as the lengendary John Henry) like prisoners. Armed guards marched them to work in the morning and back at night. Track layers were paid only once a month and forced to purchase food at the company commissary, where the high prices claimed most of what they earned. Their belongings were locked up to discourage them from running away. Other employers of black laborers in the South usually did not discipline their workers so severely, but they did isolate them, in steel mills and coal mines, in the dirtiest and most grueling jobs. The Jim Crow laws passed by every southern state legislature in the 1890s legalized this rigid separation of the black and white races (see the Prologue).

Although northern states did not pass Jim Crow laws, the nation's worsening racial climate adversely affected southern blacks who had come north. Industrialists generally refused to hire black migrants for manufacturing jobs, preferring the labor of European immigrants. Only when those immigrants went on strike did employers turn to African Americans. Black workers first gained a foothold in the Chicago meatpacking industry in 1904, when 28,000 ethnic packinghouse workers walked off their jobs. Employers hoped that the use of black strikebreakers would inflame racial tensions between white and black workers and thus undermine labor unity and strength.

African Americans who had long resided in northern urban areas also experienced intensifying discrimination in the late 19th and early 20th centuries. In 1870 about a third of the black men in many northern cities had been skilled tradesmen: blacksmiths, painters, shoemakers, and carpenters. Serving both black and white clients, these men enjoyed steady work and good pay. But by 1910 only 10 percent of black men made a living in this way. In many cities, the number of barber shops and food catering businesses owned by blacks also went into sharp decline, as did black representation in the ranks of restaurant and hotel waiters. These barbers, food caterers, and waiters had formed a black middle class whose livelihood depended on the patronage of white clients. By the early 20th century, this middle class had been dissipated, the victim of growing racism. Whites were no longer willing to engage the services of blacks, preferring to have their hair cut, beards shaved, food prepared and served by European immigrants. The residential segregation of northern blacks also rose in these years, as whites excluded them from more and more urban neighborhoods.

Thus, blacks in the North at the turn of the 20th century had to cope with a marked deterioration in their working and living conditions. But they did not lack for resourcefulness. Urban blacks laced their communities with the same array of institutions—churches, fraternal insurance societies, political organizations—that solidified ethnic neighborhoods. A new black middle class arose, comprised of ministers, professionals, and businesspeople who serviced the needs of their racial group. Black-owned realties, funeral homes, doctors' offices, newspapers, groceries, restaurants, and bars opened for business on the commercial thoroughfares of African American neighborhoods. Many businessmen had been inspired by the words of black educator Booker T. Washington, and specifically by his argument that blacks should devote themselves to self-help and self-sufficiency. Nevertheless, community-building remained a tougher task among African Americans than among immigrants. Black communities were often smaller and poorer than their white ethnic counterparts; economic opportunities were fewer, and the chance of gaining power or wealth through municipal politics almost nonexistent. Yet, some black entrepreneurs succeeded despite these odds. Madame C. J. Walker, for example, built a lucrative business from the hair and skin lotions she devised and sold to black customers throughout the country. In many cities, African American real estate agents achieved significant wealth and power. Still, most black businesspeople could not overcome the obstacles posed by racial prejudice. It was much more difficult for them than for European immigrants to find customers outside their own communities. Thus, the African American middle class remained smaller and more precarious than did its counterpart in ethnic communities, less able to lead the way toward affluence and assimilation.

Workers and Unions

Middle-class success eluded most immigrants and blacks in the years prior to the First World War. Even among Jews, whose rate of social mobility was rapid, most immigrants were working class, not middle class; garment workers, not garment entrepreneurs. For most workers, the path toward a better life lay in the improvement of working conditions, not in escape from the working class. Henry Ford's offering of the $5-a-day wage in 1914, double the average manufacturing wage, raised the hopes of many. Young immigrant men, in particular, flocked to Detroit to work for Ford. But in the early decades of the century few other manufacturers were prepared to follow Ford's daring lead, and most factory workers remained in a fragile economic state.

Samuel Gompers and the AFL

For those workers, the only hope for economic improvement lay in organizing unions powerful enough to wrest wage concessions from reluctant employers. This was not an easy task. The furious, often violent labor protests of the Gilded Age had been put down. The unity of the burgeoning labor movement—as evidenced by the dramatic growth of the Knights of Labor in the 1880s—had been broken. Federal and state governments, time and again, had shown themselves ready to use military force to break strikes. The courts, following the lead of the U.S. Supreme Court, repeatedly found unions in violation of the Sherman Antitrust Act, even though that act had been intended to control corporations, not unions. Judges in most states usually granted employer requests for injunctions—court orders that barred striking workers from picketing their place of employment (and thus from obstructing employer efforts to hire replacement workers). And prior to 1916 no federal laws protected the right of workers to organize or required employers to bargain with the unions to which their workers belonged.

This hostile legal environment retarded the growth of unions from the 1890s through the 1930s. It also made the major labor organization of those years, the American Federation of Labor (AFL), more timid and conservative than it had been prior to the depression of the 1890s. In the aftermath of that depression, the AFL poured most of its energy into organizing craft, or skilled, workers such as carpenters, typographers, plumbers, painters, and machinists. Because of their skills, these workers commanded more respect from employers than did the unskilled. Employers negotiated contracts, or trade agreements, with craft unions that stipulated the wages workers were to be paid, the hours they were to work, and the rules under which new workers would be accepted into the trade. These agreements were accorded the same legal protection that American law bestowed on other commercial contracts.

As the AFL focused on these "bread-and-butter" issues, it withdrew from the political activism that had once occupied its attention. It no longer agitated for governmental regulation of the economy and the workplace. The AFL had concluded that labor's powerful opponents in the legislatures and the courts would find ways to undermine whatever governmental gains organized labor managed to achieve. That conclusion was reinforced by a 1905 ruling, *Lochner* v. *New York,* in which the U.S. Supreme Court declared unconstitutional a seemingly innocent New York state law limiting bakery employees to a 10-hour day.

The AFL's "business" unionism was given its most forceful expression by its president, Samuel Gompers. A onetime Marxist and cigarmaker who had helped found the AFL in 1886, Gompers was reelected to the AFL presidency every year from 1896 until his death in 1924. During that time, he was the most famous trade unionist in the United States. The AFL showed considerable vitality under his leadership, especially in the early years when its membership quadrupled from less than half a million in 1897 to more than 2 million in 1904. Aware of the AFL's growing significance and conservatism, the National Civic Federation, a newly formed council of corporate executives, agreed to meet periodically with the organization's leaders to discuss the nation's industrial and labor policies.

Nevertheless, the AFL's success was limited. Its 2 million members represented only a small portion of the total industrial workforce. Its concentration among craft workers, moreover, distanced it from the majority of workers, who had no identifiable skill that could qualify them for admission to a craft union. Such workers could only be organized into an industrial union (as opposed to a craft union) that offered membership to *all* workers in a particular industry, irrespective of skill. Gompers understood the importance of industrial unions and allowed several of them to participate in the AFL. The most significant in the early 20th century were the United Mine Workers (UMW), the United Textile Workers, and the International Ladies Garment Workers Union (ILGWU). Within the AFL, these unions received support from socialist members, who were trying to make the organization more responsive to the needs of the unskilled and semiskilled. But members of the conservative craft unions, who wanted to keep the industrial unions subordinate, resisted the socialists' efforts. Craftsmen's feelings of superiority over the unskilled were intensified by their ethnic background. Most were from "old immigrant" stock—particularly English, Scottish, German, and Irish—and they shared the common prejudice against immigrants from southern and eastern Europe.

The prejudice demonstrated by AFL members toward black workers was even worse. In the early 20th century, nine AFL unions explicitly excluded African Americans from membership, while several others accomplished the same goal by declaring blacks ineligible for union initiation rituals. National unions that did not officially discriminate often permitted their union locals to segregate African American workers in Jim Crow locals or to bar them from membership altogether. The shrinking numbers of black tradesmen between 1870 and 1910 was partially attributable to the AFL's racist policies.

Nevertheless, white and black workers sometimes managed to set aside their suspicions of each other and cooperate. The UMW allowed black workers to join and to rise to positions of leadership. In New Orleans, black and white dockworkers constructed a remarkable experiment in biracial unionism that flourished from the 1890s through the early 1920s. Their unity gave them leverage in negotiations with their employers and allowed them to exercise a great deal of control over the conditions of work. The cooperation on the docks flowed over into the saloons and clubs of New Orleans, as black and white musicians explored each other's traditions and devised new musical forms, such as ragtime and jazz, that would eventually revolutionize American musical culture. But these moments of cooperation, South and North, were rare. Racism increasingly pulled blacks and whites apart.

Although blacks made up too small a percentage of the working class to build alternative labor organizations that would counteract the influence of the AFL, the "new immigrants" from eastern and southern Europe were too numerous to be ignored. Their participation in the UMW enabled that union to grow from only 14,000 in 1897 to more than 300,000 in 1914. In 1909 a strike of 20,000 women workers against the owners of New York City's garment factories inspired tens of thousands of workers, male and female, to join the ILGWU.

"Big Bill" Haywood and the IWW

When the AFL failed to help them organize, immigrants turned to other unions. The most important was the Industrial Workers of the World (IWW), founded by western miners in 1905 and led by the charismatic William "Big Bill" Haywood. The IWW was everything the AFL was not. It rejected the principle of craft organization, hoping instead to organize all workers into "one big union." It scorned the notion that only a conservative union could survive in American society, declaring its commitment to revolution instead. The IWW refused to sign collective bargaining agreements with employers, arguing that such agreements only trapped workers in capitalist property relations. Capitalism could not be tamed; it had to be overthrown—not through the ballot box but through struggles between workers and their employers at the point of production.

The IWW was too radical and reckless ever to attract a mass membership. Although hundreds of thousands of workers passed through its ranks or participated in its strikes, its regular membership rarely exceeded 20,000. Nevertheless, few

William "Big Bill" Haywood • Born in Utah in 1869, William Haywood worked as a miner with occasional stints as a cowboy and homesteader. He joined the Western Federation of Miners in 1896 and founded the Industrial Workers of the World in 1905, embarking on a career as one of America's most feared labor radicals.

organizations inspired as much awe and fear. The IWW organized the poorest and most isolated workers—lumbermen, miners, and trackmen in the West, textile workers and longshoremen in the East. Emboldened by IWW leaders, these workers waged strikes against employers who were not accustomed to having their authority challenged. Violence lurked beneath the surface of these strikes and occasionally erupted in bloody skirmishes between strikers and police, National Guardsmen, or the private security forces hired by employers. Some blamed the IWW for the violence, seeing it as a direct outgrowth of the IWW's loose, irresponsible calls for a "class war." But others understood that the IWW was not solely responsible. Even in the absence of the IWW, employers had shown themselves quite willing to resort to violence to enforce their will on employees. In 1913, for example, at Ludlow, Colorado, the Colorado Fuel and Iron Company, a subsidiary of Rockefeller's Standard Oil Company, brought in a private security force and then the local militia (which it controlled) to break up a UMW strike. When the company evicted strikers and their families from their homes, the union set up 13 tent colonies to obstruct the entrances to the mines. The standoff came to a bloody conclusion in April 1914 when company police, firing randomly into one colony of tents, killed 66 men, women, and children.

The "Ludlow massacre" outraged and shamed the nation. At public congressional hearings, John D. Rockefeller Jr. was humiliated by Senator Frank Walsh's disclosure of the industrialist's complicity in the events leading up to the violence. The massacre revealed yet again what the IWW strikes had repeatedly demonstrated: that many American workers felt abused by their low wages and poor working conditions; that neither the government nor employers offered workers a mechanism that would allow their grievances to be openly discussed and peacefully settled; and that workers, as a result, felt compelled to protest through joining unions and waging strikes, even if it meant risking their lives. The fame and notoriety of the IWW rested on its ability to force Americans to recognize how ugly and disfiguring the conflict between labor and capital was. On the eve of the First World War, almost 40 years after the anger and destruction unleashed by the Great Railroad Strike of 1877, industrial conflict still plagued the nation.

The Joys of the City

Industrial workers might not have been getting their fair share of the nation's prosperity, but they were crowding the dance halls, vaudeville theaters, amusement parks, and ballparks offered by the new world of commercial entertainment. Above all, they were flocking to the movies. Urban audiences made the motion picture industry the most important media innovation since the 15th-century invention of the printing press.

Coney Island • Amusement parks were new in the early 20th century, and the greatest of all was New York City's Coney Island. Here, park visitors "shoot the chutes" at Dreamland, an early version of the water rides that became one of the parks' most enduringly popular attractions.

Movies were well suited to poor city dwellers with little money, little free time, and little English. Initially, they cost only a nickel. The "nickelodeons" where they were shown were usually converted storefronts in working-class neighborhoods. Movies did not require much leisure time, for at first they lasted only 15 minutes on average. Those with more time on their hands could stay for a cycle of two or three films (or for several cycles). And moviegoers needed no knowledge of English to understand what was happening on the "silent screen." By 1905 immigrants were flocking to the nickelodeons. The number of nickelodeons in New York City rose from a mere handful in 1900 to more than 400 in 1908, and an estimated 200,000 New Yorkers watched movies on one of these 400 screens every day. By 1910, at least 20,000 nickelodeons dotted northern cities.

Every aspect of these early "moving pictures" was primitive by today's standards. But they were thrilling just the same. The figures appearing on the screen were realistic, yet "larger than life." Moviegoers could transport themselves to parts of the world they otherwise would never see, encounter people they would otherwise never meet, and watch boxing matches they could otherwise not afford to attend. The darkened theater provided a setting in which secret desires, especially sexual ones, could be explored. As one newspaper innocently commented in 1899: "For the first time in the history of the world it is possible to see what a kiss looks like."

No easy generalizations are possible about the content of these early films, more than half of which came from France, Germany, and Italy. Among those produced in the United States, slapstick comedies were common, as were adventure stories and romances. Producers did not yet shy away, as they soon would, from the lustier or seedier sides of American life. The Hollywood formula of happy endings had yet to be worked out. In fact, the industry, centered in New York City and Fort Lee, New Jersey, had yet to locate itself in cheery southern California. In 1914 the movies' first sex symbol, Theda Bara, debuted in a movie that showed her tempting an upstanding American ambassador into infidelity and then into ruin. She would be the first of the big screen's many "vamps," so-called because the characters they portrayed, like vampires, thrived on the blood (and death) of men.

The New Sexuality and the New Woman

The introduction of movies was closely bound up with a sexual revolution in American life. For most of the 19th century, the idea of "separate spheres" had dominated relations between the sexes, especially among middle-class Americans. The male sphere was one of work, politics (only men could vote), and sexual passion. The female sphere, by contrast, was one of domesticity, moral education (instructing the young), and sexual reproduction. Men and women were not supposed to intrude into each other's spheres. It was "unnatural" for women to hold jobs, or to enter the corrupting world of politics, or to engage in pleasurable sex. It was equally "unnatural" for men to devote themselves to child-rearing, or to "idle" themselves with domestic chores, or to live a life bereft of sexual passion. Not only did this doctrine of separate spheres—sometimes called Victorianism because it arose during the reign of Queen Victoria in Great Britain—discriminate against women, it also meant that men and women spent substantial portions of their daily lives apart from each other. The ceremonial occasions, meals, and leisure activities that brought them together tended to be closely regulated. The lives of the young, in particular, were closely watched, guided, and supervised by parents, teachers, and ministers.

Although Victorianism never worked as well in practice as it did in theory, throughout the 1880s and 1890s it had a profound influence on gender identity and sexual practice. Then a revolt set in. That revolt came from many sources: from middle-class men who were tiring of a life devoted to regimented work with no time for play; from middle-class women who, after achieving first-rate educations at elite women's colleges, were told they could not participate in the nation's economic, governmental, or professional enterprises; from immigrants, blacks, and other groups who had never been fully socialized into the Victorian world; and from the ready availability of leisure activities far removed from parental supervision.

Among the most influential rebels in the new century were the young, single, working-class women who were entering the work force in large numbers. The economy's voracious appetite for labor was drawing women out of the home and into factories and offices. Men who would have preferred to keep their wives and daughters at home were forced, given their own low wages, to allow them to go to work. Women's employment doubled between 1880 and 1900, and increased by 50

Theda Bara as Cleopatra, 1917 • Theda Bara was the first movie actress to gain fame for her roles as a "vamp"—a woman whose irresistible sexual charm led men to ruin. Because little effort was made to censor movies prior to the 1920s, directors were able to explore sexual themes and film their female stars in erotic, and partially nude, poses.

percent from 1900 to 1920. Meanwhile, the nature of female employment was undergoing a radical change. Domestic service—women who worked in family households as servants—had been the most common occupation for women during the 19th century. (In 1870, one out of every two working women was a domestic servant.) Female servants generally worked alone, or with one or two other servants. They were expected to live according to the Victorian values of the family they served. They worked long hours cooking, cleaning, and caring for their masters' children and received only part of their wages in cash, the rest being "paid" in the form of room and board. Their jobs offered them little personal or financial independence.

Now, women were taking different kinds of jobs. The jobs tended to be either industrial (as in garment shops or canneries) or clerical (in the rapidly expanding service sector). In both cases, women worked both with one another and in proximity to men. Their places of work were distant from their homes and from parental supervision. They received all their pay in the form of wages, which, though low, heightened their sense of economic independence. These were indeed "new women" in what had once been exclusively a man's world. Their ranks, however, included few black women, who, like black men, were largely excluded from the expanding job opportunities in the economy's manufacturing and clerical sectors. Black women's concentration in domestic service jobs actually increased in the early 20th century, as they took the places vacated by white women.

Once the barriers against white women in the workforce had fallen, other barriers also began to weaken—especially the Victorian ban on close associations with men outside of marriage. Young women and men flocked to the dance halls that were opening in every major city. They rejected the stiff formality of earlier ballroom dances like the cotillion or the waltz for the freedom and intimacy of newer forms, like the fox trot, tango, and bunny-hug. They went to movies and to amusement parks together, and they engaged, far more than their parents had, in premarital sex. It is estimated that the proportion of women having sex before marriage rose from 10 percent to 25 percent in the generation that was coming of age between 1910 and 1920.

The Rise of Feminism

This movement toward sexual equality was one expression of women's dissatisfaction with their subordinate place in society. By the second decade of the 20th century, eloquent spokeswomen had emerged to make the case for full female equality. The writer Charlotte Perkins Gilman called for the release of women from domestic chores through the collectivization of housekeeping. Social activist Margaret Sanger insisted, in her lectures on birth control, that women should be free to enjoy sexual relations without having to worry about unwanted motherhood. The anarchist Emma Goldman denounced marriage as a kind of prostitution and embraced the ideal of "free love"—love unburdened by contractual commitment. Alice Paul, founder of the National Women's Party, brought a new militancy to the campaign for woman suffrage (see Chapter 2).

These women were among the first to use the term "feminism" to describe their desire for complete equality with men. Some of them came together in Greenwich

Village, a community of radical artists and writers in lower Manhattan, where they found a supportive environment in which to express and live by their feminist ideals. Crystal Eastman, a leader of the feminist Greenwich Village group called Heterodoxy, defined the feminist challenge as "how to arrange the world so that women can be human beings, with a chance to exercise their infinitely varied gifts in infinitely varied ways, instead of being destined by the accident of their sex to one field of activity."

The movement for sexual and gender equality aroused considerable anxiety in the more conservative sectors of American society. Parents worried about the promiscuity of their children. Conservatives were certain that the "new women" would transform American cities into dens of iniquity. Vice commissions sprang up in every major city to clamp down on prostitution, drunkenness, and pornography. The campaign for prohibition—a ban on the sale of alcoholic beverages—gathered steam. Movie theater owners were pressured into excluding "indecent" films from their screens. Many believed the lurid tales of international vice lords scouring foreign lands for innocent girls who could be delivered to American brothel owners. This "white slave trade" inspired passage of the 1910 Mann Act, which made the transportation of women across state lines for immoral purposes a federal crime.

Nor did it escape the attention of conservatives that Greenwich Village was home not only to the dangerous exponents of "free love" but also to equally dangerous

Equal Pay for Equal Work, Regardless of Sex • A demand for equal pay, made here in 1910 by female trade unionists in San Diego, illustrates the quest for full equality that fueled an early 20th-century feminist movement.

advocates of class warfare. Prominent IWW organizer Elizabeth Gurley Flynn was a member of Heterodoxy; her lover, Carlo Tresca, was a leading IWW theoretician. "Big Bill" Haywood also frequented Greenwich Village, where he was lionized as a working-class hero. When Greenwich Village radicals began publishing an avant-garde artistic journal in 1914, they called it *The Masses;* its editor was Max Eastman, the brother of Crystal. This convergence of labor and feminist militancy intensified conservative feeling that the nation had strayed too far from its roots.

Cultural conservatism was strongest in those areas of the country least involved in the ongoing industrial and sexual revolutions—in farming communities and small towns; in the South, where industrialization and urbanization were proceeding at a slower rate than elsewhere; and among old social elites, who felt pushed aside by the new corporate men of power.

What conservatives shared with radicals was a conviction that the country could not afford to ignore its social problems—the power of the corporations; the poverty and powerlessness of wage earners; the role of women and African Americans. Conservatives were as determined to restore a Victorian morality as radicals were determined to achieve working-class emancipation and women's equality. But in politics, neither would become the dominant force. That role would fall to the so-called progressives, a widely diverse group of reformers who confidently and optimistically believed that they could bring both order and justice to the new society.

Conclusion

Between 1890 and 1920, corporate power, innovation, and demands had stimulated the growth of cities, attracted millions of immigrants from southern and eastern Europe, enhanced commercial opportunities, and created the conditions for a vibrant urban culture. Many Americans thrived in this new environment, taking advantage of business opportunities or, as in the case of women, discovering liberties for dress, employment, dating, and sex that they had not known. But millions of Americans were impoverished, unable to rise in the social order or to earn enough in wages to support their families. Many also resented the monotony and regimentation of industrial work. African Americans who had migrated to the North in search of economic opportunity suffered more than any other single group, as they found themselves shut out of most industrial and commercial employment.

Henry Ford, whose generous $5-a-day wage drew tens of thousands to his Detroit factories, was an exceptional employer. Although other employers had learned to restrain their crass displays of wealth and had turned toward philanthropy in search of a better public image, they were reluctant to follow Ford's lead in improving the conditions in which their employees labored.

Working-class Americans proved resourceful in creating self-help institutions to attend to their own and each other's needs. In some cities, they gained a measure of power through the establishment of political machines. Labor unions arose and, against great odds, fought for a society of greater equality and justice. But it remained unclear how successful these institutions would be in their efforts to inject greater equality and opportunity into an industrial society in which the gap between rich and poor had reached alarming proportions.

Chronology

1897   Depression ends; prosperity returns

1899   Theodore Roosevelt urges Americans to live the "strenuous life"

1890s   Football becomes sport-of-choice in Ivy League • Young women put away their corsets

1900–1914   Immigration averages more than 1 million per year

1901   U.S. Steel is formed from 200 separate companies • Andrew Carnegie devotes himself to philanthropic pursuits • 1 of every 400 railroad workers dies on the job

1904   20 percent of the North's industrial population lives below poverty line

1905   *Lochner* v. *New York:* Supreme Court declares unconstitutional a New York state law limiting the workday of bakery employees • Industrial Workers of World (IWW) founded

1907   Henry Ford unveils his Model T

1907–1911   73 of every 100 Italian immigrants return to Italy

1909   Immigrants and their children comprise more than 96 percent of labor force building and maintaining railroads

1910   Black skilled tradesmen in northern cities reduced to 10 percent of total skilled trades workforce • 20,000 nickelodeons dot northern cities

1911   Triangle Shirtwaist Company fire kills 146 workers • Frederick Winslow Taylor publishes *The Principles of Scientific Management*

1913   Henry Ford introduces the first moving assembly line; employee turnover reaches 370 percent a year • 66 men, women, and children killed in "Ludlow massacre" • John D. Rockefeller establishes Rockefeller Foundation

1914   Henry Ford introduces the $5-a-day wage • Theda Bara, movies' first sex symbol, debuts • *The Masses,* a radical journal, begins publication

1919   Japanese farmers in California sell $67 million in agricultural goods, 10 percent of state's total

1920   Nation's urban population outstrips rural population for first time

1921   1,250,000 Model Ts sold, a sixteenfold increase over 1912

Suggested Readings

For a general overview of the period, Alan Dawley, *Struggles for Justice: Social Responsibility and the Liberal State* (1991), and Nell Irvin Painter, *Standing at Armageddon: The United States, 1877–1919* (1987), are excellent accounts that are particularly strong on issues of social history.

Economic Growth and Technological Innovation

On economic growth in the late 19th and early 20th centuries, see Harold G. Vatter, *The Drive to Industrial Maturity: The United States Economy, 1860–1914* (1975); Elliot Brownlee, *Dynamics of Ascent: A History of the American Economy,* 2nd ed. (1979); David Hounshell, *From the American System to Mass Production, 1800–1932: The Development of Manufacturing Technology in the United States* (1984); Nathan Rosenberg, *Technology and American Economic Growth* (1972); Charles Singer et al., eds., *History of Technology,* vol. 5: *The Late Nineteenth Century* (1958); and Harold I. Sharlin, *The Making of the Electrical Age* (1963). David Nye, *Electrifying America: Social Meanings of a New Technology, 1890–1940* (1990), is a fascinating account of the social consequences of technological change. For an older but lively history on this theme, see Frederick Lewis Allen, *The Big Change: America Transforms Itself, 1900–1950* (1952). Robert Conot, *A Streak of Luck* (1979), and Matthew Josephson, *Edison* (1959), assess Thomas Edison's contributions to the electrical revolution.

The Rise of the Modern Corporation

Alfred D. Chandler Jr., *The Visible Hand: The Managerial Revolution in American Business* (1977), is the classic work. See also Richard Tedlow, *The Rise of the American Business Corporation* (1991); Naomi Lamoreaux, *The Great Merger Movement in American Business, 1895–1904* (1985); and Glenn Porter, *The Rise of Big Business, 1860–1910* (1973). On the emerging alliance between corporations and science, see David F. Noble, *America by Design: Science, Technology and the Rise of Corporate Capitalism* (1977); Frederick A. White, *American Industrial Research Laboratories* (1961); and Leonard S. Reich, *The Making of Industrial Research: Science and Business at GE and Bell, 1876–1926* (1985). On the legal and political changes that undergirded the corporation's triumph, see Martin J. Sklar, *The Corporate Reconstruction of American Capitalism, 1890–1916: The Market, the Law and Politics* (1988). Olivier Zunz, *Making America Corporate, 1870–1920* (1990), is one of the first social histories to focus on the middle managers who comprised the new corporate middle class. A provocative exploration of the paths to economic development shut off by the triumph of mass production is found in Michael J. Piore and Charles F. Sabel, *The Second Industrial Divide: Possibilities for Prosperity* (1984). For an equally provocative critique of this interpretation, consult Philip Scranton, *Endless Novelty: Specialty Production and American Industrialization, 1865–1925* (1997).

Scientific Management

Any examination of this topic must start with Frederick Winslow Taylor, *The Principles of Scientific Management* (1911) and Robert Kanigel, *The One Best Way: Frederick Winslow Taylor and the Enigma of Efficiency* (1997). Daniel Nelson, *Frederick W. Taylor and the Rise of Scientific Management* (1980), and David Montgomery, *The Fall of the House of Labor: The Workplace, the State, and American Labor Activism, 1865–1925* (1987), are important. For its broader political ramifications, see Samuel Haber, *Efficiency and Uplift: Scientific Management in the Progressive Era* (1964). Allan Nevins and Frank E. Hill, *Ford* (1954–1963), is still the best biography of Henry Ford, but on Ford's labor policies, Stephen Meyer III, *The Five Dollar Day: Labor Management and Social Control in the Ford Motor Company, 1908–1921* (1981), and Nelson Lichtenstein and Stephen Meyer III, eds., *On the Line: Essays in the History of Auto Work* (1989), are essential reading. For a general perspective on the changes in work and management in this period, consult Sanford M. Jacoby, *Employing Bureaucracy: Managers, Unions, and the Transformation of Work in American Industry, 1900–1945* (1985).

Robber Barons and the Turn to Philanthropy

The classic work on the robber barons themselves is Matthew Josephson, *The Robber Barons* (1934). On the industrialists' turn to philanthropy, see Andrew Carnegie, *The Gospel of Wealth* (1889), and *Autobiography* (1920); Robert H. Bremner, *American Philanthropy* (1988); George E. Pozzetta, ed., *Americanization, Social Control and Philanthropy* (1991); Barry D. Karl and Stanley N. Katz, "The American Private Philanthropic Foundation and the Public Sphere, 1890–1930," *Minerva* 19 (Summer 1981): 236–270; and Ellen Condliffe Lagemann, *The Politics of Knowledge: The Carnegie Corporation, Philanthropy, and Public Policy* (1989). On Rockefeller, see Ron Chernow, *Titan: The Life of John D. Rockefeller Sr.* (1998).

"Racial Fitness" and Social Darwinism

On America's growing obsession with physical and racial fitness during this period, see John Higham, "The Reorientation of American Culture in the 1890s," in John Horace Weiss, ed., *The Origins of Modern Consciousness*, pp. 25–48 (1965), and Higham, *Strangers in the Land: Patterns of American Nativism*, rev. ed. (1992). For an assessment of the influence of Darwinist thinking on American culture, see Richard Hofstadter, *Social Darwinism in American Thought*, rev. ed. (1955); Robert Bannister, *Social Darwinism: Science and Myth in Anglo-American Social Thought* (1979); and Carl N. Degler, *In Search of Human Nature: The Decline and Revival of Darwinism in American Social Thought* (1991).

Immigration: General Histories

The best single-volume history of European immigrants is John Bodnar, *The Transplanted: A History of Immigrants in Urban America* (1985). Maldwyn Allen Jones, *American Immigration* (1974), and Alan M. Kraut, *The Huddled Masses: The Immigrant in American Society, 1880–1921* (1982), are also useful. Ronald Takaki, *A Different Mirror: A History of Multicultural America* (1993), Roger Daniels, *Coming to America: A History of Immigration and Ethnicity in American Life* (1990), and Leonard Dinnerstein, Roger L. Nichols, and David Reimers, *Natives and Strangers: Ethnic Groups and the Building of America* (1979), integrate the story of European immigrants with that of African, Asian, and Latin American newcomers. Stephan Thernstrom, ed., *Harvard Encyclopedia of American Ethnic Groups* (1980), is indispensable on virtually all questions pertaining to immigration and ethnicity. Frank Thistlewaite, "Migration from Europe Overseas," in Stanley N. Katz and Stanley I. Kutler, eds., *New Perspectives on the American Past* (1969), Vol. 2, pp. 152–181, is a pioneering article on patterns of European migration.

Histories of Particular Immigrant Groups

Irving Howe, *World of Our Fathers: The Journey of the East European Jews to America and the Life They Found and Made* (1976), is the best work on Jewish immigration, although it must be supplemented by Susan A. Glenn, *Daughters of the Shtetl: Life and Labor in the Immigrant Generation* (1990). For work on the Irish, see Kerby A. Miller, *Emigrants and Exiles: Ireland and the Irish Exodus to North America* (1985), and Hasia A. Diner, *Erin's Daughters in America: Irish Immigrant Women in the Nineteenth Century* (1983). Other excellent works on particular ethnic groups include Ewa Morawska, *For Bread with Butter: The Life-Worlds of East Central Europeans in Johnstown, Pennsylvania, 1890–1940* (1985); John J. Bukowczyk, *And My Children Did Not Know Me: A History of Polish Americans* (1987); Virginia Yans-McLaughlin, *Family and Community: Italian Immigrants in Buffalo, 1880–1930* (1977); Yusi Ichioka, *The Issei: The World of the First Japanese Immigrants, 1895–1924* (1988); Sucheng Chan, *Asian Americans: An Interpretive History* (1991); and Mario T. Garcia, *Desert Immigrants: The Mexicans of El Paso, 1880–1920* (1981). Olivier Zunz, *The Changing Face of Inequality: Urbanization, Industrial Development and Immigrants in Detroit, 1880–1920* (1982), and S. J. Kleinberg, *The Shadow of the Mills: Working-Class Families in Pittsburgh, 1870–1907* (1989), compare the experiences of several European American groups in one city.

Immigrant Labor

Essential sources on both immigrant and nonimmigrant labor are Herbert Gutman, *Work, Culture and Society in Industrializing America* (1976); Montgomery, *The Fall of the House of Labor* (previously cited); and Alice Kessler-Harris, *Out of Work: A History of Wage-Earning Women in the United States* (1982). For a brief but incisive survey of working conditions in this period, consult Melvyn Dubofsky, *Industrialism and the American Worker, 1865–1920,* 2nd ed. (1985). Tamara Hareven, *Family Time and Historical Time: The Relationship between the Family and Work in a New England Industrial Community* (1982), and James R. Barrett, *Work and Community in the Jungle: Chicago's Packinghouse Workers, 1894–1922* (1990), are excellent local studies. Leon Stein, *The Triangle Fire* (1962), and John F. McClymer, *The Triangle Strike and Fire* (1998), chronicle that industrial disaster; and Alexander Keyssar, *Out of Work: The First Century of Unemployment in Massachusetts* (1986), offers the best analysis of unemployment in this period.

Immigrants, African Americans, and Social Mobility

Good sources on this topic include Stephan Thernstrom, *The Other Bostonians: Poverty and Progress in the American Metropolis* (1973); Joel Perlman, *Ethnic Differences: Schooling and Social Structure among the Irish, Italians, Jews, and Blacks in an American City, 1880–1935* (1988); Thomas Kessner, *The Golden Door: Italian and Jewish Mobility in New York City, 1880–1915* (1977); Edna Bonacich and John Modell, *The Economic Basis of Ethnic Solidarity: Small Businessmen in the Japanese-American Community* (1980); Stephen Steinberg, *The Ethnic Myth: Race, Ethnicity, and Class in America* (1981); Thomas Sowell, *Ethnic America: A History* (1981); and Stanley Lieberson, *A Piece of the Pie: Blacks and White Immigrants Since 1880* (1980).

Immigrants, Political Machines, and Organized Crime

Steven P. Erie, *Rainbow's End: Irish Americans and the Dilemmas of Urban Machine Politics, 1840–1945* (1988), insightfully examines the benefits and costs of big city machines. See also Harold Zink, *City Bosses in the United States: A Study of Twenty Municipal Bosses* (1930); M. Craig Brown and Charles

N. Halaby, "Machine Politics in America, 1870–1945," *Journal of Interdisciplinary History* 8 (1987): 587–612; John M. Allswang, *Bosses, Machines, and Urban Voters* (1977); Alexander B. Callow, ed., *The City Boss in America* (1976); and William L. Riordon, *Plunkitt of Tammany Hall: A Series of Very Plain Talks on Very Practical Politics* (1994). On organized crime, consult Joseph Albini, *The American Mafia* (1971); Humbert Nelli, *The Business of Crime* (1976); and Jenna Weissman Joselit, *Our Gang: Jewish Crime and the New York Jewish Community* (1983). Doris Kearns Goodwin, *The Fitzgeralds and the Kennedys* (1987), chronicles the history of President John F. Kennedy's family.

African Americans

John Hope Franklin and Alfred A. Moss Jr., *From Slavery to Freedom: A History of Negro Americans*, 7th ed. (1994), offers a masterful overview. Gavin Wright, *Old South, New South: Revolutions in the Southern Economy Since the Civil War* (1986), analyzes the southern sharecropping economy, while William H. Harris, *The Harder We Run: Black Workers Since the Civil War* (1982), assesses the experiences of black industrial workers, South and North. On black female workers, consult Jacqueline Jones, *Labor of Love, Labor of Sorrow: Black Women, Work and the Family from Slavery to the Present* (1985). Kenneth L. Kusmer, *A Ghetto Takes Shape: Black Cleveland, 1870–1930* (1978), is the best work on the formation of urban black communities in the North prior to the Great Migration (1916–1920), but it should be supplemented with Elizabeth Hafkin Pleck, *Black Migration and Poverty: Boston, 1865–1900* (1979); Allan H. Spear, *Black Chicago: The Making of a Negro Ghetto, 1890–1920* (1967); and Theodore Hershberg et al., *Philadelphia: Work, Space, Family, and Group Experience in the Nineteenth Century* (1981). On the rise of a new black middle class, see Evelyn Brooks Higginbotham, *Righteous Discontent: The Women's Movement in the Black Baptist Church, 1880–1920* (1993), and Kevin K. Gaines, *Uplifting the Race: Black Leadership, Politics, and Culture in the Twentieth Century* (1996).

Workers and Unions

Indispensable sources are Montgomery, *The Fall of the House of Labor* (previously cited); David Brody, *Workers in Industrial America: Essays on the Twentieth Century Struggle* (1980); and Melvyn Dubofsky, *We Shall Be All: A History of the Industrial Workers of the World* (1969). Samuel Gompers's career can be traced through Stuart Kaufman, *Samuel Gompers and the Origins of the American Federation of Labor* (1973), and Gompers's own *Seventy Years of Life and Labor: An Autobiography*, ed. Nick Salvatore (1984). Michael Kazin, *Barons of Labor: The San Francisco Building Trades and Union Power in the Progressive Era* (1987), is a sterling study of AFL craftsmen at work and in local politics; and Gwendolyn Mink, *Old Labor and New Immigrants in American Political Development: Union, Party, and State, 1875–1920* (1986), offers a provocative interpretation of the AFL's role in national politics. Christopher Tomlins, *The State and the Unions: Labor Relations, Law, and the Organized Labor Movement in America, 1880–1960* (1985), carefully analyzes the effect of law on the labor movement's development.

David A. Corbin, *Life, Work, and Rebellion in the Coal Fields: The Southern West Virginia Miners, 1880–1922* (1981), examines the rise of the United Mine Workers; and Howe, *World of Our Fathers* (previously cited), treats the early years of the ILGWU in New York City. Sterling D. Spero and Abram L. Harris, *The Black Worker: The Negro and the Labor Movement* (1931), and James R. Grossman, *Land of Hope: Chicago, Black Southerners, and the Great Migration* (1989), analyze AFL attitudes toward black workers. Eric Arnesen, *Waterfront Workers of New Orleans: Race, Class and Politics, 1863–1923* (1991), probes that city's remarkable experiment in biracial unionism. Graham Adams Jr., *Age of Industrial Violence, 1910–1915: The Activities and Findings of the United States Commission on Industrial Relations* (1966), chronicles the Ludlow massacre and other labor-capital confrontations in these years. See also J. Anthony Lukas, *Big Trouble: A Murder in a Small Western Town Sets Off a Struggle for the Soul of America* (1997), a remarkable study of class conflict in the West during the early years of the 20th century.

The Rise of Mass Culture

On the rise of mass culture, see David Nasaw, *Going Out: The Rise and Fall of Public Amusements* (1993); William Leach, *Land of Desire: Merchants, Power, and the Rise of a New American Culture*

(1993); Roy Rosenzweig, *Eight Hours for What We Will: Workers and Leisure in an Industrial City, 1870–1920* (1983); and Lewis A. Erenberg, *Steppin' Out: New York Night-life and the Transformation of American Culture, 1890–1930* (1981). Warren I. Susman, *Culture as History: The Transformation of American Society in the Twentieth Century* (1984), is essential reading for any student of this subject. Excellent studies of the rise of movies are Rosenzweig, *Eight Hours for What We Will* (previously cited); Lary May, *Screening Out the Past: The Birth of Mass Culture and the Motion Picture Industry* (1980); Robert Sklar, *Movie-Made America: A Social History of the American Movies* (1975); and Steven J. Ross, *Working-Class Hollywood: Silent Film and the Shaping of Class in America* (1998).

The "New Woman"

On the emergence of the "new woman," see Kathy Peiss, *Cheap Amusements: Working Women and Leisure in Turn-of-the-Century New York* (1986); Elaine Tyler May, *Great Expectations: Marriage and Divorce in Post-Victorian America* (1980); Leslie Woodcock Tentler, *Wage-Earning Women: Industrial Work and Family Life in the United States, 1900–1930* (1979); Joanne Meyerowitz, *Women Adrift: Independent Wage-Earners in Chicago, 1870–1930* (1988); and Elizabeth Lunbeck, *The Psychiatric Persuasion: Knowledge, Gender and Politics in Modern America* (1994).

Feminism

Nancy F. Cott, *The Grounding of Modern Feminism* (1987), is the most important study of the movement's origins. Linda Gordon, *Woman's Body, Woman's Right: A Social History of Birth Control in America* (1976), and James Reed, *The Birth Control Movement and American Society: From Private Vice to Public Virtue* (1983), are important works on the history of birth control. Also see the following first-rate biographies: David M. Kennedy, *Birth Control in America: The Career of Margaret Sanger* (1970); Alice Wexler, *Emma Goldman: An Intimate Life* (1984); and Christine A. Lunardini, *From Equal Suffrage to Equal Rights: Alice Paul and the National Women's Party, 1912–1928* (1986). For a brief biography of Charlotte Perkins Gilman, see Gary Scharnhorst, *Charlotte Perkins Gilman* (1985). Leslie Fishbein, *Rebels in Bohemia: The Radicals of the Masses, 1911–1917* (1982), deftly recreates the politics and culture of Greenwich Village.

Progressivism

Progressivism was a reform movement that sought to reinvigorate American politics and society in an age convulsed by industrialization. The movement took its name from individuals who left the Republican Party in 1912 to join Theodore Roosevelt's new party, the Progressive Party. But the term "progressive" refers to a much larger and more varied group of reformers than those who gathered around Roosevelt in 1912.

Progressives wanted to cleanse politics of corruption, tame the power of the "trusts" and, in the process, inject more liberty into American life. They fought against prostitution, gambling, drinking, and other forms of vice. They first appeared in municipal politics, organizing movements to oust crooked mayors and to break up local gas or streetcar monopolies. They then carried their fights to the states and finally to the nation. Two presidents, Theodore Roosevelt and Woodrow Wilson, placed themselves at the head of this movement.

Progressivism was popular among a variety of groups who brought to the movement distinct, and often conflicting, aims. But on one issue most progressives agreed: the need for an activist government to right political, economic, and social wrongs. Some progressives wanted government to become active only for a limited period—long enough to clean up the political process, end drinking, upgrade the electorate, and break up trusts. But these problems were so difficult to solve that many progressives endorsed the notion of a permanently active government—with the power to tax income, regulate industry, supervise trade, protect consumers from fraud, empower workers, safeguard the environment, and provide social welfare. Progressives, in other words, came to see the federal government as the institution best equipped to solve social problems.

Such positive attitudes toward government power marked an important change in American politics. Americans had long been suspicious of centralized government, viewing it as the enemy of liberty. The Populists had broken with that view, but they had been defeated. So the progressives had to build a new case for strong government as the protector of liberty and equality. Although their own success would be limited, their influence on 20th-century reform would endure.

Progressivism and the Protestant Spirit

Progressivism emerged first and most strongly among young, mainly Protestant, middle-class Americans who felt alienated from their society. Many, such as Jane

Addams (the settlement house pioneer), John R. Commons (a progressive policy-maker), and Woodrow Wilson, had been raised in devout Protestant homes—Presbyterian, Baptist, Methodist, Quaker—in which religious conviction had often been a spur to social action. They were expected to become ministers or missionaries or to serve their church in some other way. They had abandoned this path, for they were plagued by doubt concerning God's purposes and covenant. But they never lost their zeal for righting moral wrongs and for uplifting the human spirit. They were distressed by the immorality and corruption rampant in American politics, and by the gap that separated rich from poor. For them, progressivism was in part an expression of their religiously rooted social conscience. They became, to use the evocative phrase of one historian, "ministers of reform."

Other Protestant reformers retained their faith. This was true of William Jennings Bryan, the former Populist leader who became an ardent progressive (serving as Woodrow Wilson's secretary of state) and a prominent Presbyterian and evangelical. Throughout his political career, Bryan always insisted that Christian piety and American democracy were integrally related, and that both were revealed in divine law. Billy Sunday, a former major league baseball player who became the most theatrical evangelical preacher of his day, elevated opposition to saloons and the "liquor trust" into a righteous crusade. And Walter Rauschenbusch led a movement known as the Social Gospel, which emphasized the duty of Christians to work for the social good. Not all these groups saw eye-to-eye; in fact they often battled each other over how much to alter their beliefs in order to reconcile divine revelations with scientific truth. Eventually these fights would diminish Protestant authority in America. But that authority remained strong throughout the Progressive Era, and as long as it did, the Protestant spirit burned bright in the ranks of reformers.

Protestants, of course, formed a large and diverse population, large sections of which showed little interest in reform. Thus, it is important to identify smaller and more cohesive groups of reformers. Of the many that arose, three were of particular importance, especially in the early years: investigative journalists, who were called "muckrakers"; the founders and supporters of settlement houses; and socialists.

Muckrakers, Magazines, and the Turn toward "Realism"

The term "muckraker" was coined by Theodore Roosevelt, who had intended it as a criticism of newspaper and magazine reporters who, for no purpose other than monetary reward, wrote stories about scandalous situations. But it became a badge of honor among journalists who were determined to expose the seedy, sordid side of life in the United States. During the first decade of the century, at the height of their influence, they presented the public with one startling revelation after another. Ida Tarbell revealed the shady practices by which John D. Rockefeller had transformed his Standard Oil Company into a monopoly. Lincoln Steffens unraveled the webs of bribery and corruption that were strangling local governments in the nation's great cities. George Kibbe Turner documented the extent of prostitution and family disintegration in the ethnic ghettos of those cities. David Graham Phillips, in a sensational nine-month series entitled "The Treason of the Senate," castigated senators as "eager, resourceful, indefatigable agents of interests as hostile to the American people as any invading army could be." These muckrakers wanted to shock the public into recognizing the shameful state of political, economic, and social affairs and to prompt "the people" to take action.

The tradition of investigative journalism reached back at least to the 1870s, when newspaper and magazine writers exposed the corrupt practices of New York City's Boss Tweed and his well-oiled Tammany Hall machine. But the rise of the muckrakers reflected two factors, one economic and the other intellectual, which transformed investigative reporting into something of national importance.

Increased Newspaper and Magazine Circulation

A dramatic expansion in newspaper and magazine circulation was the economic factor underlying the rise of the muckrakers. From 1870 to 1909 the number of daily newspapers rose from 574 to 2,600, and their circulation increased from less than 3 million to more than 24 million. During the 1890s magazines also underwent a revolution. Cheap, 10-cent periodicals such as *McClure's Magazine* and *Ladies Home Journal,* with circulations of 400,000 to 1 million, displaced genteel and relatively expensive 35-cent publications such as *Harper's* and *The Atlantic Monthly.* The expanded readership brought journalists considerably more money and prestige and attracted many talented and ambitious men and women to the profession. It also made magazine publishers more receptive to stories that might appeal to their newly acquired millions of readers. The muckrakers were ready to supply these stories. Once Sam McClure, the shrewd publisher of *McClure's,* had recognized the

Editorial Room of the *New York American,* 1917 • The *New York American* was part of the vast expansion in daily newspapers that occurred between 1870 and 1920. Started by Ambrose Pulitzer in 1882, it was purchased by newspaper mogul William Randolph Hearst in 1895 and made an integral part of his effort to lure millions of new readers to his empire of print.

draw of muckraking journalism, he filled his magazine with sensational stories of ill-gotten economic power, government corruption, and urban vice.

The Turn toward "Realism"

The intellectual factor favoring the muckrakers was the turn toward "realism" among the nation's middle class. "Realism" was a way of thinking that prized detachment, objectivity, and skepticism. It arose in the 1890s in response to a widespread sense that prevailing attitudes were no longer relevant to the radical transformation that society was undergoing. Many people, for example, felt that constitutional theory, with its emphasis on citizenship, elections, and democratic procedures, had little to do with the way government in the United States actually worked. What could one learn about bosses, machines, and graft from studying the Constitution? There was also a sense that the nation's glorification of the "self-made man" and of "individualism" was preventing Americans from coping effectively with the sudden centrality of large-scale organizations—corporations, banks, labor unions—to the nation's economy and to society. And finally, many people felt that American artists and writers were too preoccupied with emulating European styles and were oblivious to the rich materials visible throughout industrial and urban America.

In the 1890s this impatience reached a crisis point. Intellectuals and artists of all sorts—philosophers John Dewey and William James; social scientists Thorstein Veblen and Charles Beard; novelists Frank Norris, Theodore Dreiser, and Upton Sinclair; painters John Sloan, George Bellows and other members of the "Ashcan

Photographic Realism • Photography proved to be an essential new medium for demonstrating how, to use the words of the reformer-photographer Jacob Riis, "the other half lives." Riis and his associates traveled throughout New York City to document the living conditions of the city's poor. Here, a family of seven lives in a tenement room that serves as their bedroom and kitchen.

school"; photographers Jacob Riis and Lewis Hine; architects Louis Sullivan and Frank Lloyd Wright; jurists Oliver Wendell Holmes and Louis Brandeis—all set about creating truer, more realistic ways of representing and analyzing American society. Many of these intellectuals and artists were inspired by the work of investigative journalists; some had themselves been newspapermen. Years of firsthand observation enabled these and other writers to describe American society as it "truly was." They brought shadowy figures vividly to life. They pictured for Americans the captain of industry who ruthlessly destroyed his competitors; the con artist who tricked young people new to city life; the innocent immigrant girl who fell prey to the white slave traders; the corrupt policeman under whose protection urban vice flourished.

A vast middle class, uneasy about the state of American society, applauded the muckrakers for telling these stories, and became interested in reform. Members of this class put pressure on city and state governments to send crooked government officials to jail and to stamp out the sources of corruption and vice. Between 1902 and 1916 more than 100 cities launched investigations of the prostitution trade. At the federal level, all three branches of government felt compelled to address the question of "the trusts"—the concentration of power in the hands of a few industrialists and financiers. Progressivism began to crystallize into a political movement centered on the abuses the muckrakers had exposed.

Settlement Houses and Women's Activism

Established by middle-class reformers, settlement houses were intended to help the largely immigrant poor cope with the harsh conditions of city life. Much of the inspiration for settlement houses came from young, college-educated, Protestant women from comfortable but not particularly wealthy backgrounds. Many of them had inherited a commitment to social justice from parents and grandparents who had fought their own reform battles, especially the battle to abolish slavery. Growing up in these reform-minded families, such women were troubled by the problems of industrialization. Highly educated and talented, they rebelled against being relegated solely to the roles of wife and mother. For them, the settlement houses provided a way to assert their independence and apply their talents in socially useful ways.

Hull House

Jane Addams and Ellen Gates Starr, graduates of Illinois's Rockford Female Seminary, established the nation's first settlement house, in Chicago, in 1889. The two women had been inspired by a visit the year before to London's Toynbee Hall, where a small group of middle-class men had been living and working with that city's poor since 1884. Addams and Starr hoped to reproduce the spirit of Toynbee Hall in Chicago. They bought a decaying mansion that had once been the country home of a prominent Chicagoan, Charles J. Hull. By 1889 "Hull House" had been surrounded by factories, churches, saloons, and tenements inhabited by very poor, largely foreign-born working-class families.

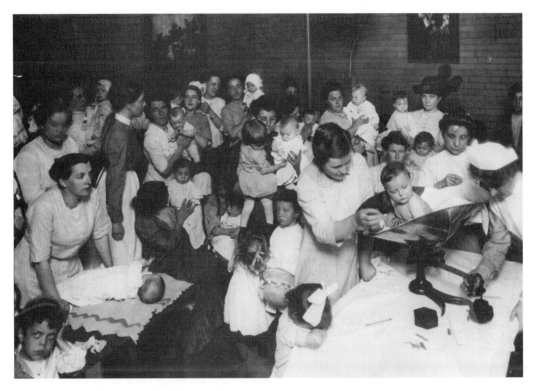

Women and Reform • Women played a key role in progressive reform, especially in terms of providing services to the urban poor. Here, the Infant Welfare Society operates a baby clinic for the poor in Chicago.

Addams quickly emerged as the guiding spirit of Hull House. She moved into the building and demanded that all workers there do the same. She and Starr enlisted extraordinary women such as Florence Kelley, Alice Hamilton, and Julia Lathrop, who quickly made Hull House a hub of social, cultural, and intellectual activity. They set up a nursery for the children of working mothers, a penny savings bank, and an employment bureau, soon followed by a baby clinic, a neighborhood playground, and social clubs. Determined to minister to cultural as well as economic needs, Hull House sponsored an orchestra, reading groups, and a lecture series. Members of Chicago's widening circle of reform-minded intellectuals, artists, and politicians contributed their energies to the enterprise. John Dewey taught philosophy and Frank Lloyd Wright lectured on architecture. Clarence Darrow, the workingman's lawyer, and Henry Demarest Lloyd, Chicago's radical muckraker, spent considerable time at Hull House. In 1893 Illinois Governor John P. Altgeld named Hull House's Florence Kelley as the state's chief factory inspector. Her investigations led to Illinois's first factory law, which prohibited child labor, limited the employment of women to eight hours a day, and authorized the state to hire inspectors to enforce the law.

There seemed to be no limit to the energy, imagination, and commitment of the Hull House principals. Julia Lathrop used her appointment to the State Board of

Charities to agitate for improvements in the care of the poor, the handicapped, and the delinquent. With Edith Abbott and Sophonisba Breckinridge, she established the Department of Social Research at the University of Chicago (which would evolve into the nation's first school of social work). Alice Hamilton, who had overcome sex discrimination to become a doctor, pioneered in the field of public health.

The Hull House leaders did not command the instant fame accorded the muckrakers. They were less interested in sensational exposés or engaging in highly publicized crusades on the poor's behalf. Rather, they set a higher value on teaching the poor to help themselves. Nevertheless, they were steadily drawn into the public arena. Thousands of women across the country were inspired to build their own settlement houses on the Hull House model (there would eventually be more than 400 settlement houses nationwide). By 1910 Jane Addams had become one of the nation's most famous women. She and other settlement house workers played a critical role in fashioning the progressive agenda and in drafting pieces of progressive legislation.

The Cultural Conservatism of Progressive Reformers

In general, settlement house workers were much more sympathetic toward the poor, the illiterate, and the downtrodden than the muckrakers were. Jane Addams, though she disapproved of machine politics as heartily as Lincoln Steffens, saw firsthand the benefits machine politicians delivered to their constituents. She respected the cultural inheritance of the immigrants and admired their resourcefulness. Although she wanted them to become Americans, she encouraged them to preserve their "immigrant gifts" in their new identity. Those attitudes were more liberal than the attitudes of other reformers, who considered most immigrants culturally, even racially, inferior and a threat to American civilization.

But there were limits even to Addams's sympathy for the immigrants. In particular, she disapproved of the new working-class entertainments—movies, amusement parks, dance halls—that gave adolescents extensive and unregulated opportunities for intimate association. She was also troubled by the emergence of the "new

Women Enrolled in Institutions of Higher Education, 1870–1930

Year	Women's Colleges (thousands of students)	Coed Institutions (thousands of students)	Total (thousands of students)	Percentage of All Students Enrolled
1870	6.5	4.6	11.1	21.0%
1880	15.7	23.9	39.6	33.4
1890	16.8	39.5	56.3	35.9
1900	24.4	61.0	85.4	36.8
1910	34.1	106.5	140.6	39.6
1920	52.9	230.0	282.9	47.3
1930	82.1	398.7	480.8	43.7

Source: From Mabel Newcomer, *A Century of Higher Education for American Women* (New York: Harper and Row, 1959), p. 46.

woman" and her frank sexuality (see Chapter 1). Addams tended to equate female sexuality with prostitution. Such attitudes revealed the extent to which she still adhered to Victorian notions of "pure," asexual womanhood.

In fact, a good many champions of progressive reform were cultural conservatives. In addition to their position on women's sexuality, their conservatism was evident in their attitudes toward alcohol. Drinking was a serious problem in poor, working-class areas. Many men wasted their hard-earned money on drinks at the local saloon, and that drain on meager family resources created tension between husbands and wives at home. Domestic fights and family violence sometimes ensued. Settlement house workers were well aware of the ill-effects of alcoholism (there were 250 saloons in Chicago's 19th Ward alone) and sought to combat it. In their campaign for social hygiene, they called on working people to refrain from drink and worked for legislation that would shut down the saloons. The progressives joined forces with the Women's Christian Temperance Union (245,000 members strong by 1911) and the Anti-Saloon League. By 1916, through their collective efforts, these groups had won prohibition of the sale and manufacture of alcoholic beverages in 16 states. In 1919 their crowning achievement was the Eighteenth Amendment to the U.S. Constitution, making Prohibition the law of the land (see Chapter 4).

In depicting alcohol and saloons as unmitigated evils, however, the prohibition movement ignored the role saloons played in ethnic, working-class communities. On Chicago's South Side, for example, where the city's huge meatpacking industry was concentrated, saloons provided tens of thousands of packinghouse workers with the only decent place to eat lunch. There were no cafeterias in the meatpacking plants, and few workers could stomach eating their lunch where animals were slaughtered, dressed, and packed. Some saloons catered to particular ethnic groups: They served traditional foods and drinks, provided meeting space for fraternal organizations, and offered camaraderie to men longing to speak in their native tongue. Saloonkeepers sometimes functioned as informal bankers, cashing checks and making small loans.

Alcohol figured in ethnic life in other ways, too. For Catholics, wine was central to Communion. Jews greeted each Sabbath and religious festival with a blessing over wine. For both groups, the sharing of wine or beer marked the celebration of births, marriages, deaths, and other major family events. Understandably, most of the nation's immigrants shunned the prohibition movement. They had no interest in being "uplifted" and "reformed" in quite that way. Here was a gulf separating the immigrant masses from the Protestant middle class that even compassionate reformers such as Jane Addams could not bridge.

A Nation of Clubwomen

Settlement house workers comprised only one part of a vast network of female reformers. Hundreds of thousands of women belonged to local women's clubs that sprouted throughout the country in the late 19th century. Conceived as self-help organizations in which women would be encouraged to sharpen their minds, refine their domestic skills, and strengthen their moral faculties, these clubs began taking on tasks of social reform. Clubwomen typically focused their energies on improving schools, building libraries and playgrounds, expanding educational and vocational opportunities for girls, and securing fire and sanitation codes for tenement houses. In so doing, they made traditional female concerns—the nurturing of children, the care of the home—questions of public policy. Few individual women could match the remarkable dedication and innovation shown by the settlement house pioneers. Still, clubwomen as a group significantly increased public awareness of the problems afflicting children and families.

Socialism and Progressivism

While issues such as women's sexuality and men's alcoholism drew progressives in a conservative direction, other issues drew them to socialism. In the early part of the 20th century, socialism stood for the transfer of control over industry from a few industrialists to the laboring masses. Socialists believed that such a transfer, usually defined in terms of government ownership and operation of economic institutions, would make it impossible for wealthy elites to control society. Government control meant popular control. It would make America a genuinely democratic society.

Socialism attracted a substantial and diverse following in the United States. The Socialist Party of America, founded in 1901, became a political force during the first 16 years of the century, and socialist ideas influenced progressivism. In 1912, at the peak of its influence, the Socialist Party enrolled more than 115,000 members. Its presidential candidate, the charismatic Eugene Victor Debs of Terre Haute, Indiana, attracted almost 1 million votes—6 percent of the total votes cast that year. In that same year, 1,200 Socialists held elective office in 340 different municipalities. Of these, 79 were mayors of cities as geographically and demographically diverse as Schenectady, New York; Milwaukee, Wisconsin; Butte, Montana; and Berkeley, California. More than 300 newspapers and periodicals, with a combined circulation exceeding 2 million, spread the socialist gospel. The most important socialist publication was *Appeal to Reason,* published by the Kansan Julius Wayland and sent out each week to 750,000 subscribers. In 1905 Wayland published, in serial form, a novel by an obscure muckraker named Upton Sinclair, which depicted the scandalous working conditions in Chicago's meatpacking industry. When it was later published in book form in 1906, *The Jungle* created such an outcry that the federal government was forced to regulate the meat industry.

The Many Faces of Socialism

Socialists during this period came in many varieties. In Milwaukee, they consisted of predominantly German working-class immigrants and their descendants; in New York City, their numbers were strongest among Jewish immigrants from eastern Europe, especially among garment workers living and laboring in the city's Lower East Side. In the Southwest, tens of thousands of disgruntled native-born farmers who had been Populists in the 1890s now flocked to the socialist banner. In Oklahoma alone, by 1912 these erstwhile Populists were numerous enough to support 11 socialist weeklies. In that same year, Oklahoma voters gave a higher percentage

Eugene V. Debs, Socialist • During the 1908 presidential election, Eugene Debs campaigned aboard "The Red Special," a train chartered by the Socialist Party to take him throughout the country. Debs's influence would peak in the election of 1912, when he received nearly a million votes.

of their votes, over 16 percent, to the Socialist candidate Debs than did the voters of any other state. In the West socialism was popular among miners, timber cutters, and others who labored in isolated areas where industrialists enjoyed extraordinary power, not just at work sites but in the hastily constructed towns or camps where the workers were obliged to live. These radicals gravitated to the militant labor union, the Industrial Workers of the World (IWW) (Chapter 1), which from 1905 to 1913 found a home in the Socialist Party.

Socialists differed not only in their occupations and ethnic origins but also in their politics. The IWW was the most radical socialist group, with its incessant calls for revolution, its contempt for electoral politics, and its refusal to accommodate any aspect of the capitalist order. By contrast, mainstream socialism, as articulated by Debs, called for revolution but was more deeply rooted in and respectful of American political, cultural, and religious traditions. Mainstream socialists saw themselves as the saviors rather than the destroyers of the American republic—as the true heirs of Thomas Jefferson. Their confidence that the nation could be redeemed through conventional politics—through the election of Debs as president—is evidence of their affection for the American experiment in democracy.

And their faith in redemption reveals the degree to which Protestant religious beliefs underlay their quest for social justice and what they called a "cooperative commonwealth." Evolutionary socialists, led by Victor Berger of Milwaukee, abandoned talk of revolution altogether and chose instead an aggressive brand of reform politics. They were dubbed "gas and water socialists" because of their interest in improving city services.

These differences would, after 1912, fragment the socialist movement. But for a decade or so, all these divergent groups managed to coexist in a single political party. That was due in no small measure to the eloquence of Debs, who in his speeches was able to impart to the socialist ideal a passion, a power, and a distinctly American accent. When he was released from a Chicago jail in 1895, where he had been imprisoned for his role in leading the strike against the Pullman Company, (see the Prologue), Debs declared to the 100,000 admirers who had gathered to celebrate his release: "Manifestly the spirit of '76 still survives. The fires of liberty and noble aspirations are not yet extinguished. . . . The vindication and glorification of American principles of government, as proclaimed to the world in the Declaration of Independence, is the high purpose of this convocation."

Socialists and Progressives

Debs's speeches both attracted and disturbed progressives. On the one hand, he spoke compellingly about the economic threats that concerned progressives—unregulated capitalism and the excessive concentration of wealth in "trusts." And his confidence that a strong state could bring the economic system under control mirrored the progressives' own faith in the positive uses of government. Indeed, progressives often worked hand-in-hand with socialists to win economic and political reforms, especially at the municipal and state levels, and many intellectuals and reformers moved easily back and forth between socialism and progressivism. Florence Kelley, Hull House reformer and Illinois factory inspector, was one such person; Clarence Darrow, a Chicago trial lawyer who successfully defended the IWW's William Haywood in 1907 against charges that he had murdered a former Idaho governor, was another. Walter Lippmann, a brilliant Harvard student who would become a close adviser to President Wilson during the First World War, began his political career in 1912 as an assistant to the Socialist mayor of Schenectady. Several of the era's outstanding intellectuals, including John Dewey, Richard Ely, and Thorstein Veblen, also traveled back and forth between the socialist and progressive camps. So did Helen Keller, the country's leading spokesperson for the disabled.

On the other hand, Debs's talk of revolution scared progressives, as did his efforts to organize a working-class political movement independent of middle-class involvement or control. Although progressives wanted to tame capitalism, they did not want to eliminate it altogether. They wanted to improve the working and living conditions of the masses but not cede political control to them. The progressives hoped to contain socialism: to offer a political program with enough socialist elements to counter the appeal of Debs's more radical movement. In this, they were successful.

Municipal Reform

The cities were the testing grounds for progressive reform. The first battles were over control of municipal transportation networks and utilities. Street railways were typically owned and operated by private corporations, as were electrical and gas systems. Many of the corporations used their monopoly power to charge exorbitant fares and rates, and often they won that power by bribing city officials who belonged to one of the political machines. Corporations achieved generous reductions in real estate taxes in the same way.

The assault on private utilities and their protectors in city government gained momentum in the mid-1890s. In Detroit, reform-minded Mayor Hazen S. Pingree led successful fights (in the years from 1890 to 1896) to control the city's gas, telephone, and trolley companies. In Chicago in 1896 and 1897, a group of middle-class reformers ousted a corrupt city council that had bestowed favors on the utilities tycoon Charles T. Yerkes and elected a mayor, Carter Harrison Jr., who promised to protect Chicago's streetcar riders from exploitation. In St. Louis in 1900, middle-class consumers and small businessmen joined hands with striking workers to challenge the "streetcar trust." In Cleveland, the crusading reformer Tom Johnson won election as mayor in 1901, curbed the power of the streetcar interests, and brought honest and efficient government to the city. Journalist Lincoln Steffens believed that Cleveland, under Johnson, was the best-governed city in the country.

Occasionally, a reform politician of Johnson's caliber would rise to power through one of the regular political parties. But this path to power was a difficult one, especially in cities where the political parties were controlled by machines. Consequently, progressives worked for reforms that would strip the parties of their power. Two of their favorite reforms were the city commission and the city manager forms of government, designed to transfer municipal power from party politicians to nonpartisan experts.

The City Commission Plan

First introduced in Galveston, Texas, in 1900, in the wake of a devastating tidal wave, the city commission shifted municipal power from the mayor and his aldermen to five city commissioners, each responsible for a different department of city government. In Galveston and elsewhere, the impetus for this reform came from civic-minded businessmen determined to rebuild government on the same principles of efficient and scientific management that had energized the private sector. The results were often impressive. The Galveston commissioners restored the city's credit after a close brush with bankruptcy, improved the city's harbor, and built a massive seawall to protect the city from future floods. And they accomplished all that on budgets only two-thirds the size of what they had been in the past. In Houston, Texas; Des Moines, Iowa; Dayton, Ohio; Oakland, California; and elsewhere, commissioners similarly improved urban infrastructures, expanded city services, and strengthened the financial health of the cities. Many commissions established publicly owned utilities. By 1913 more than 300 cities, most of them small to middling in size, had adopted the city commission plan.

The City Manager Plan

The city commission system did not always work to perfection, however. Sometimes the commissioners used their position to reward electoral supporters with jobs and contracts; at other times, they pursued power and prestige for their respective departments, without regard for city welfare. The city manager plan was meant to overcome such problems. Under this plan, the commissioners continued to set policy, but the implementation of policy—and all day-to-day administrative tasks—now rested with a "chief executive." This official, who was appointed by the commissioners, was to be insulated from the pressures of running for office. The city manager would curtail rivalries between commissioners and ensure that no outside influences interfered with the expert, businesslike management of the city. The job of city manager was explicitly modeled after that of a corporation executive. First introduced in Sumter, South Carolina, in 1911 and then in Dayton, Ohio, in 1913, by 1919 the city manager plan had been adopted in 130 cities.

The Costs of Reform

Although these reforms limited corruption and improved services, they were not universally popular. Poor and minority voters, in particular, found that their influence in local affairs was weakened by the shift to city commissioners and city managers. Previously, candidates for municipal office (other than the mayor) competed in ward elections rather than in citywide elections. Voters in working-class wards commonly elected workingmen to represent them, and voters in immigrant wards made sure that fellow ethnics represented their interests on city councils. Citywide elections diluted the strength of these constituencies. Candidates from poor districts often lacked the money needed to mount a citywide campaign, and they were further hampered by the nonpartisan nature of such elections. Denied the support of a political party or platform, they had to make themselves personally known to voters throughout the city. That was a much easier task for the city's "leading citizens"—manufacturers, merchants, and lawyers—than it was for workingmen. In Dayton, the resulting tilt of the electoral system toward the city's wealthier citizens prompted a coalition of working-class groups to publish a pamphlet entitled *Dayton's Commission Manager Plan: Why Big Manufacturers, Bond Holders, and Public Franchise Grabbers Favor It, and Workingmen and Common People Oppose.* Dayton's Socialists had good reason to be upset. In the years following the introduction of the commission-manager system, the proportion of Dayton citizens voting Socialist rose from 25 to 44 percent, while the number of Socialists elected to office declined from five to zero. Progressive political reforms thus frequently had the effect of reducing the influence of radicals, minorities, and the poor in elections.

Political Reform in the States

Political reform in the cities quickly spread to the states. As at the local level, political parties at the state level were often dominated by corrupt, incompetent politicians who did the bidding of powerful private lobbies. In New Jersey in 1903, for example, large industrial and financial interests, working through the Republican Party machine, controlled numerous appointments to state government, including the chief justice of the state supreme court, the attorney general, and the commissioner of banking and insurance. Such webs of influence ensured that New Jersey would provide large corporations such as the railroads with favorable political and economic legislation.

Restoring Sovereignty to "The People"

Progressives introduced reforms designed to undermine the power of party bosses, restore sovereignty to "the people," and encourage honest, talented individuals to enter politics. One such reform was the direct primary, a mechanism that enabled voters themselves, rather than party bosses, to choose party candidates. Mississippi introduced this reform in 1902 and Wisconsin in 1903. By 1916 all but three states (New Mexico, Rhode Island, and Connecticut) had adopted the direct primary. Closely related was a movement to strip state legislatures of their power to choose U.S. senators. State after state enacted legislation that permitted voters to choose Senate candidates in primary elections. In 1912 a reluctant U.S. Senate was obliged to approve the Seventeenth Amendment to the Constitution, mandating the direct election of senators. The state legislatures ratified this amendment in 1913.

The direct election of U.S. senators had first been proposed by the Populists back in the 1890s; so too had two other reforms, the initiative and the referendum, both of which were adopted first by Oregon in 1902 and then by 18 other states between 1902 and 1915. The initiative allowed reformers to put before voters in general elections legislation that state legislatures had yet to approve. The referendum gave voters the right in general elections to repeal an unpopular act that a state legislature had passed. Less widely adopted but important nevertheless was the recall, a device that allowed voters to remove from office any public servant who had betrayed their trust. As a further control over the behavior of elected officials, numerous states enacted laws that regulated corporate campaign contributions and restricted lobbying activities in state legislatures.

These laws did not eliminate corporate privilege or destroy the power of machine politicians, as their proponents had claimed they would. Nevertheless, they curbed the worst abuses of the "interests," made politics more honest, and strengthened the influence of ordinary voters.

Creating a Virtuous Electorate

Progressive reformers focused as well on creating a responsible electorate that understood the importance of the vote and that resisted efforts by the "interests" to manipulate elections. To create this ideal electorate, reformers had to see to it that all those citizens who were deemed virtuous could cast their votes free of coercion and intimidation. At the same time, reformers sought to disfranchise all citizens who were considered irresponsible and corruptible. In pursuing these goals, progressives substantially altered the composition of the electorate and strengthened government regulation of voting. The results were contradictory. On the one hand, progressives enlarged the electorate by extending the right to vote to women; on the other hand, they either initiated or tolerated laws that barred large numbers of minority and poor voters from the polls.

The Australian Ballot

Government regulation of voting had begun back in the 1890s when virtually every state adopted the Australian, or secret, ballot. This reform required voters to vote in private rather than in public. It also required the government, rather than political parties, to print the ballots and supervise the voting. Prior to this time, each political party had printed its own ballot with only its candidates listed. At election time, each party mobilized its loyal supporters, put the correct ballot in their hands, and, if necessary, marched them to the polls. The competition between rival parties was intense and lively, and voter turnouts were invariably high. But the system lent itself to corruption. Party workers offered liquor, free meals, and other bribes to get voters to the polls and to "persuade" them to cast the right ballot. Because the ballots were cast in public, few voters who had accepted gifts of liquor and food dared to cross watchful party officials. Critics argued that the system corrupted the electoral process. They also pointed out that it made "ticket-splitting"—dividing one's vote between candidates of two or more parties—virtually impossible.

The Australian ballot solved these problems. Although it predated progressivism, its enactment depended on the support of many who would later label themselves progressives. More to the point, it reflected the progressives' determination to use government power to encourage citizens to cast their votes responsibly and wisely.

Personal Registration Laws

That same determination was apparent in the progressives' support for the personal registration laws that virtually every state passed between 1890 and 1920. These laws required prospective voters to appear at a designated government office with proper identification; only then would they be allowed to register to vote. Frequently, these laws also mandated a certain period of residence in the state prior to registration and a certain interval between registration and actual voting. Personal registration laws were meant to disfranchise citizens who showed no interest in voting until election day when a party worker arrived with a few dollars and offered a free ride to the polls.

Although these laws reduced the participation of countless such citizens, they also excluded many hard-working, responsible, poor people who wanted to vote but had failed to register, either because their work schedules made it impossible or because they were intimidated by the complex regulations. The laws were particularly frustrating for immigrants whose knowledge of American government and of the English language were limited.

Disfranchisement

Some election laws promoted by the progressives were expressly designed to keep noncitizen immigrants from voting. In the 1880s, 18 states had passed laws allowing immigrants to vote without first becoming citizens. Progressives reversed this trend, so that by the time of the First World War, only seven states—all with tiny immigrant populations—still allowed alien suffrage. At the same time, the newly formed Bureau of Immigration and Naturalization (1906) made it more difficult to become a citizen than it had been in the 19th century. Applicants for citizenship now had to appear before a judge who interrogated them, in the English language, on American history and civics. In addition, immigrants were required to provide two witnesses to vouch for their "moral character" and their "attachment to the principles of the Constitution." Finally, immigrants had to swear (and, if necessary, prove) that they were not anarchists or polygamists and that they had resided continuously in the United States for five years.

Most progressives defended the new rigor of the process. U.S. citizenship, they believed, carried great responsibilities; it was not to be bestowed lightly, certainly not on anyone who might abuse its privileges. This position was understandable, given the electoral abuses progressives had exposed. Moreover, progressives were proud of the efficiency they brought to the complex process of sorting out those who deserved citizenship from those who did not. Nevertheless, their franchise and naturalization reforms also had the effect of denying the vote to a large proportion of the population. In cities and towns where immigrants dominated the workforce, the numbers of registered voters fell alarmingly. Nowhere was exclusion more startling than in the South, where between 1890 and 1904 every ex-Confederate state passed laws designed to strip blacks of their right to vote. Because laws explicitly barring blacks from voting would have violated the Fifteenth Amendment, this exclusion had to be accomplished indirectly—through literacy tests, property qualifications, and poll taxes. Any citizen who failed a reading test, or who could not sign his name, or who did not own a minimum amount of property, or who could not pay a poll tax, lost his right to vote. The citizens who failed these tests most frequently were blacks, who formed the poorest and least educated segment of the southern population, but a large portion of the region's poor whites also failed the tests. The effects of disfranchisement were stark. In 1900 only 1,300 blacks voted in Mississippi elections, down from 130,000 in the 1870s. In Virginia voter turnout dropped from 60 percent of adult men (white and black) in 1900 to 28 percent in 1904.

Many progressives in the North, such as Governor Robert La Follette of Wisconsin, bitterly criticized southern disfranchisement. Others, including Jane Addams and John Dewey, joined in 1910 with the black intellectual W. E. B. Du Bois and others to found the National Association for the Advancement of Colored People (NAACP), an interracial political organization that made the struggle for black equality its primary and uncompromisable goal. But in the South, white progressives rarely challenged disfranchisement, either because to do so would be to risk defeat for their political agenda or because they believed that former slaves and their offspring were ill-adapted to citizenship. They had little difficulty using progressive ideology to justify disfranchisement. Because progressives everywhere believed that the franchise was a precious gift that was to be granted only to those who could handle its responsibilities, it obviously had to be withheld from any who were deemed racially or culturally unfit. Progressives in the North excluded many immigrants on just those grounds. Progressives in the South saw the disfranchisement of African Americans in the same light.

Disillusionment with the Electorate

In the process of identifying those groups "unfit" to hold the franchise, some progressives soured on the electoral process altogether. The more they looked for

Voter Participation in Presidential Elections, 1876–1920

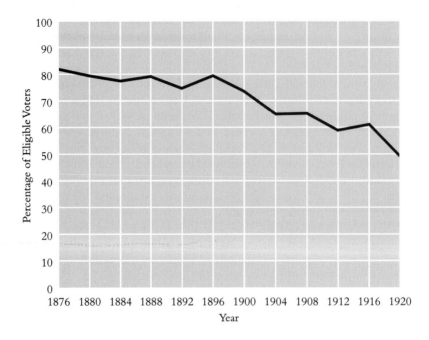

Source: Data from *Historical Statistics of the United States, Colonial Times to 1970* (White Plains, N.Y.: Kraus International, 1989).

rational and virtuous voters, the fewer they found. In *Drift and Mastery* (1914), Walter Lippmann developed a theory that ordinary people had been overwhelmed by industrial and social changes. Because these changes seemed beyond their comprehension or control, they clung to outworn customs and traditions; they "drifted," unable to "master" the circumstances of modern life or take charge of their own destiny. Lippmann did not suggest that such ordinary people should be barred from voting. But he did argue that more political responsibility should be placed in the hands of experts endowed by training and knowledge with the tools necessary to make government effective and just. Like the proponents of the city manager movement, Lippmann wanted to increase the influence of appointed, as opposed to elected, officials. The growing disillusionment with the electorate, in combination with intensifying restrictions on the franchise, created an environment in which fewer and fewer Americans actually went to the polls. Voting participation rates fell from 79 percent in 1896 to only 49 percent in 1920.

Woman Suffrage

The major exception to this trend was the enfranchisement of women. This momentous reform was accepted by several states during the 1890s and the first two decades of the 20th century and then became federal law with the ratification of the Nineteenth Amendment to the Constitution in 1920.

Launched in 1848 at the famous Seneca Falls convention, the women's rights movement had floundered in the 1870s and 1880s. In 1890 suffragists came together in a new organization, the National American Woman Suffrage Association (NAWSA), led by such venerable figures as Elizabeth Cady Stanton and Susan B. Anthony. Thousands of young, college-educated women reinvigorated the movement at the grassroots. They campaigned door-to-door, held impromptu rallies, and pressured state legislators.

Wyoming, which attained statehood in 1890, became the first state to grant women the right to vote, followed in 1893 by Colorado and in 1896 by Idaho and Utah. The main reason for success in these sparsely populated western states was not egalitarianism but rather the conviction that women's supposedly gentler and more nurturing nature would tame and civilize the rawness of the frontier.

This notion reflected a subtle but important change in the thrust of the suffrage movement. Earlier generations had insisted that women were fundamentally equal to men, but the new suffragists argued that women were different from men. Women, they stressed, possessed a moral sense and a nurturing quality that men lacked. Consequently, they understood the civic obligations implied by the franchise and could be trusted to vote virtuously. Their votes would hasten to completion the progressive task of cleansing the political process of corruption. Their experience as mothers and household managers, moreover, would enable them to guide local and state governments in efforts to improve education, sanitation, family wholesomeness, and the condition of women and children in the workforce. In other words, the enfranchisement of women would enhance the quality of both public and private life.

Suffragists were slow to ally themselves with blacks, Asians, and other disfranchised groups. In fact, many suffragists, especially those in the South and West, vehemently opposed the franchise for Americans of color. They, like their male counterparts, believed that members of these groups lacked moral strength and

Woman Suffrage Before 1920

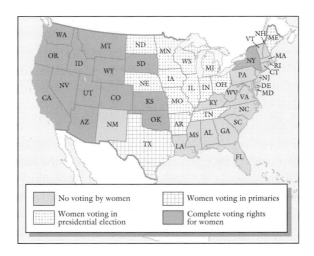

thus did not deserve the franchise. Unlike the suffrage pioneers of the 1840s and 1850s, many Progressive Era suffragists were little troubled by racial discrimination and injustice.

Washington, California, Kansas, Oregon, and Arizona followed the lead of the other western states by enfranchising women in the years from 1910 to 1912. After a series of setbacks in eastern and midwestern states, the movement regained momentum under the leadership of the strategically astute Carrie Chapman Catt, who became president of NAWSA in 1915, and the radical Alice Paul, who founded the militant National Women's Party in 1916. Aided by a heightened enthusiasm for democracy generated by America's participation in the First World War (see Chapter 4) and by the decision to shift the movement's focus from individual states to the nation at large, the suffragists achieved their goal of universal woman suffrage in 1920.

Predictions that suffrage for women would radically alter politics turned out to be false. The political system was not cleansed of corruption, and the government did not rush headlong to address the private needs of women and their families. Although the numbers of voters increased after 1920, voter participation rates continued to decline. Still, the extension of the vote to women, 144 years after the founding of the nation, was a great political achievement.

Economic and Social Reform in the States

In some states, progressive reform extended well beyond political parties and the electorate. Progressives also wanted to limit the power of the corporations, strengthen organized labor, and offer social welfare protection to the weak. State governments were pressured into passing such legislation by progressive alliances of middle-class and working-class reformers, and by dynamic state governors.

Robert La Follette and Wisconsin Progressivism

Nowhere else did the progressives' campaign for social reform flourish as it did in Wisconsin. The movement arose first in the 1890s, in hundreds of Wisconsin cities and towns, large and small, as citizens began to mobilize against the state's corrupt Republican Party and the special privileges the party had granted to private utilities and railroads. These reform-minded citizens came from varied backgrounds. They were middle-class and working-class, urban and rural, male and female, intellectual and evangelical, Protestant Scandinavian and German Catholic. Wisconsin progressivism had already gained considerable momentum by 1897, when Robert La Follette assumed its leadership.

La Follette was born into a prosperous farming family in 1855. He entered politics as a Republican in the 1880s and embraced reform in the late 1890s, when he became convinced that large corporations and their henchmen were destroying the American dream. Elected governor in 1900, he secured for Wisconsin both a direct primary and a tax law that stripped the railroad corporations of tax exemptions they had long enjoyed. In 1905 he pushed through a civil service law mandating that every state employee had to meet a certain level of competence.

Robert La Follette, Wisconsin Progressive • As this photograph suggests, Robert La Follette was a vigorous campaigner who carried his reform message to every part of the state.

A tireless campaigner and a spellbinding speaker, "Fighting Bob" won election to the U.S. Senate in 1906. Meanwhile, the statewide reform organization he had built while governor continued to thrive. The growing strength of Wisconsin's labor and socialist movements forced progressive reformers to focus their legislative efforts on issues of corporate greed and social welfare. By 1910 reformers had passed state laws that regulated railroad and utility rates, instituted the nation's first state income tax, and provided workers with compensation for injuries, limitations on work hours, restrictions on child labor, and minimum wages for women.

Many of these laws were written by social scientists at the University of Wisconsin, with whom reformers had close ties. Richard Ely, a Christian socialist, economist, and founder of the American Economic Association (1885), had originally laid the groundwork for cooperation between the university and the statehouse. In the first decade of the 20th century, John R. Commons, another University of Wisconsin economist, emerged as a progressive policymaker who drafted Wisconsin's civil service and public utilities laws. In 1911 Commons designed and won legislative approval for the Wisconsin Industrial Commission, which brought together employers, trade unionists, and disinterested professionals and gave them broad powers to investigate and regulate relations between capital and labor throughout the state. Because the powers granted to the commission were so broad and because it represented such a novel form of regulation, Commons and others hailed it as nothing less than a fourth branch of government. Indeed, the Wisconsin Industrial Commission was an innovation of utmost significance. Never before had a state government so plainly committed itself to the cause of industrial justice. For the first time, the rights of labor would be treated with the same respect as the rights of industry.

Equally important was the responsibility the commission delegated to nonelected professionals: social scientists, lawyers, engineers, and others. These professionals, Wisconsin reformers believed, would succeed where political parties had failed—namely, in providing the public with expert and honest government.

Progressives in many other states shared the faith expressed by Wisconsin reformers in industrial justice, in a strong government, and in the capacity of expert administrators to provide disinterested public service. The "Wisconsin idea" was quickly adopted in Ohio, Indiana, New York, and Colorado; and in 1913 the federal government established its own Industrial Relations Commission and hired Commons to direct its investigative staff. In areas other than capital-labor relations, too, reformers began urging state and federal governments to shift the policymaking initiative away from political parties and toward administrative agencies staffed by professionals. To those disillusioned with electoral politics, this shift appeared to be a brilliant method for improving government.

Progressive Reform in New York

New York was probably second only to Wisconsin in the vigor and breadth of its progressive movement. As in Wisconsin, progressives in New York focused first on fighting political corruption. Startling revelations of close ties between leading Republican politicians and life insurance companies vaulted the reform lawyer Charles Evans Hughes into the governor's mansion in 1907. Hughes immediately established several public service commissions to regulate railroads and utility companies. As in Wisconsin, the growing strength of labor had an effect. Successful strikes by New York City's garment workers forced state legislators to treat the condition of workers more seriously than they might have otherwise. With the establishment of the Factory Investigating Committee, New York, like Wisconsin, became a pioneer in labor and social welfare policy.

New York state legislators also were being pressured by middle-class reformers—settlement house workers such as Lillian Wald of the Henry Street Settlement, lawyers such as Louis Brandeis—whose work with the poor had convinced them that laws were needed to promote social justice. This combined pressure from working-class and middle-class constituencies impelled some state Democrats, including Assemblyman Alfred E. Smith and Senator Robert F. Wagner, to convert from machine to reform politics. Their appearance in the progressive ranks was an important development, for they brought with them a new reform sensibility. Wagner and Smith were both ethnic Catholics (Wagner was born in Germany, while Smith was the grandchild of Irish immigrants) who opposed prohibition, city commissions, voter registration laws, and other reforms whose intent seemed anti-immigrant and anti-Catholic. By contrast, they supported reforms meant to improve the working and living conditions of New York's urban poor. They agitated for a minimum wage, factory safety, workmen's compensation, the right of workers to join unions, and the regulation of excessively powerful corporations. Their participation in progressivism in New York, and their influence nationwide, accelerated the movement's shift away from preoccupation with political parties and electorates and toward questions of economic justice and social welfare.

A Renewed Campaign for Civil Rights

While politicians such as Smith and Wagner introduced an ethnic sensibility into progressivism, a new generation of African American activists began insisting that the issue of racial equality also be placed on the reform agenda.

The Failure of Accommodationism

Booker T. Washington's message—that blacks should accept segregation and disfranchisement as unavoidable and focus their energies instead on self-help and self-improvement—was increasingly criticized by black activists such as W. E. B. Du Bois, Ida B. Wells, Monroe Trotter, and others. Washington's accommodationist leadership (see the Prologue), in their eyes, brought blacks in the South no reprieve from the white racism that had poisoned race relations in the 1880s and 1890s. More than 100 blacks had been lynched in the year 1900 alone; between 1901 and 1914 at least 1,000 others would be hanged until death by groups of white vigilantes. Increasingly, unsubstantiated rumors of black assaults on whites became occasions for white mobs to rampage through black neighborhoods and indiscriminately destroy life and property. In 1908 a mob in Springfield, Illinois, attacked black businesses and individuals; a force of 5,000 state militia was required to restore order. The troops were too late, however, to stop the lynching of two black men, one a successful barber and the other an 84-year-old man who had been married to a white woman for over 30 years. There was a sad irony in the deaths of these African Americans. Murdered in Abraham Lincoln's hometown and within walking distance of his grave, they died just as black and white Americans everywhere were preparing to celebrate the centennial of the Great Emancipator's birth.

Washington had long believed that blacks who educated themselves or who succeeded in business would be accepted as equals by whites and welcomed into their society. But as Du Bois and other militants observed, white rioters in Springfield and elsewhere made no distinction between rich blacks and poor, or between solid citizens and petty criminals. All that had seemed to matter was the color of one's skin. Similarly, many black militants knew from personal experience that individual accomplishment was not enough to overcome racial prejudice. Du Bois himself was a brilliant scholar who became, in 1899, the first African American to receive a Ph.D. from Harvard University. Had he been white, Du Bois would have been asked to teach at Harvard or another elite academic institution. No prestigious white university, South or North, ever made him an offer.

From the Niagara Movement to the NAACP

Seeing no future in accommodation, Du Bois and other young black activists came together at Niagara Falls in 1905 to declare their independence of Washington and to fashion their own aggressive political agenda. They demanded that African Americans be given the right to vote in states where it had been taken away; that segregation be abolished; and that the many discriminatory barriers placed in the path of black advancement be removed. They declared their commitment to freedom of speech, the brotherhood of all men, and respect for the working man. Although their numbers were small, the members of the so-called Niagara movement were inspired by the example of the antebellum abolitionists. Meeting in Boston, Oberlin, and Harpers Ferry—all places of special significance to the abolitionist cause—they hoped to rekindle the militant, uncompromising spirit of that earlier crusade.

The 1908 Springfield riot had shaken a sizable number of whites. Some, especially those already involved in matters of social and economic reform, now joined in common cause with the Niagara movement. A conference was planned for Lincoln's birthday in 1909 to revive, in the words of the writer William English Walling, "the spirit of the abolitionists" and to "treat the Negro on a plane of absolute political and social equality." Oswald Garrison Villard, the grandson of William Lloyd Garrison, called on "all believers in democracy to join in a National conference for the discussion of present evils, the voicing of protests, and the renewal of the struggle for civil and political liberty." The conference brought together a number of distinguished progressives, white and black, including Mary White Ovington, Jane

W. E. B. Du Bois • W. E. B. Du Bois was a founder of the National Association for the Advancement of Colored People and the editor of its magazine, *The Crisis*. He went on to become one of the most important African American intellectuals and activists of the 20th century.

Addams, John Dewey, William Dean Howells, Ida B. Wells, and Du Bois. They drew up plans to establish an organization dedicated to fighting racial discrimination and prejudice. In May 1910 the National Association for the Advancement of Colored People (NAACP) was officially launched, with Moorfield Storey of Boston as president, Walling as chairman of the executive committee, and Du Bois as the director of publicity and research. The NAACP carried on the tasks begun by the Niagara movement.

The formation of the NAACP marked the beginning of the modern civil rights movement. The organization immediately launched a magazine, *The Crisis,* edited by Du Bois, to publicize and protest the lynchings, riots, and other abuses directed against black citizens. Equally important was the Legal Redress Committee, which initiated lawsuits against city and state governments for violating the constitutional rights of African Americans. The committee scored its first major success in 1915, when the U.S. Supreme Court ruled that the so-called "grandfather" clauses of the Oklahoma and Maryland constitutions violated the Fifteenth Amendment. (These clauses allowed poor, uneducated whites—but not poor, uneducated blacks—to vote, even if they failed to pay their state's poll tax or to pass its literacy test, by exempting the descendants of men who had voted prior to 1867.) NAACP lawyers won again in 1917 when the Supreme Court declared unconstitutional a Louisville, Kentucky, law that required all blacks to reside in predetermined parts of the city.

By 1914, the NAACP had enrolled thousands of members in scores of branches throughout the United States. The organization's success also stimulated the formation of other groups committed to the advancement of blacks. Thus, the National Urban League, founded in 1911, worked to improve the economic and social conditions of blacks in cities. The Urban League pressured employers to hire blacks, distributed lists of available jobs and housing in African American communities, and developed social programs to ease the adjustment of rural black migrants to city life.

Progress toward racial equality was slow. Attacking segregation and discrimination through lawsuits was, by its nature, a snail-paced strategy that would take decades to complete. The growing membership of the NAACP, although impressive, was not large enough to qualify it as a mass movement. And its interracial character made the organization seem dangerously radical to millions of whites, South and North. Storey, Villard, and other white NAACP leaders responded to this hostility by limiting the number and power of African Americans who worked for the organization. This conciliatory policy, in turn, outraged black militants such as Trotter and Wells, who argued that a civil rights organization should not be in the business of appeasing white racists.

Despite its limitations, the early work of the NAACP was significant. The NAACP gave Du Bois the security and visibility he needed to carry on his fight against Washington's accommodationism. Even before his death in 1915, Washington's enormous influence in black and white communities had begun to recede. The NAACP, more than any other organization, was responsible for resurrecting the issue of racial equality at a time when many white Americans had accepted as normal the practices of racial segregation and discrimination. And the NAACP's close links to influential groups of white progressives gave the advocates of racial equality reason to hope that their cause would benefit from the growing clamor for reform.

National Reform

The more progressives focused on economic and social matters, the more they sought to increase their influence in national politics. Certain problems demanded national solutions. A patchwork of state regulations, for example, was not enough to curtail the power of the trusts, protect workers, or monitor the quality of consumer goods. Moreover, state and federal courts were often hostile toward progressive goals: They repeatedly struck down as unconstitutional reform laws regulating working hours or setting minimum wages, on the grounds that they impinged on the freedom of contract and trade. With a national movement, progressives could force the passage of laws less vulnerable to judicial veto or elect a president who could overhaul the federal judiciary through the appointment and confirmation of progressive-minded judges.

National leadership was not going to emerge from Congress. The Democratic Party had been badly scarred by the Populist challenge of the 1890s. Divided between the radical Bryanites and the conservative followers of Grover Cleveland, and consequently unable to speak with one voice on questions of social and economic policy, after 1896 the Democrats seemed incapable of winning a national election or offering a national agenda. The Republican Party was more unified and popular, but it was controlled by a conservative "Old Guard." Led by Senator Nelson Aldrich of Rhode Island and House Speaker Joseph G. Cannon of Illinois, and closely tied to Marcus A. Hanna and other industrialists, the "Grand Old Party" (or G.O.P., a nickname Republicans gave the party in the 1880s) was resolutely pro-business and devoted to a 19th-century style of backroom patronage. It feared insurgency and turned a deaf ear to the popular clamor for change. When Robert La Follette arrived in the Senate from Wisconsin in 1907, the Republican Old Guard ostracized him as a dangerous radical.

National progressive leadership came from the executive rather than the legislative branch, and from two presidents in particular, the Republican Theodore Roosevelt and the Democrat Woodrow Wilson. These two presidents, the best-known progressives of their time, sponsored reforms that profoundly affected the lives of Americans and altered the nature of the American presidency.

The Roosevelt Presidency

When the Republican bosses chose Theodore Roosevelt as William McKinley's running mate in 1900, their purpose was more to remove this headstrong, unpredictable character from New York state politics than to groom him for national leadership. As governor of New York, Roosevelt had shown himself to be a moderate reformer. But even his modest efforts to rid the state's Republican Party of corruption and to institute civil service reform were too much for the state party machine, led by Thomas C. Platt. Consigning Roosevelt to the vice presidency seemed like a safe solution. McKinley was a young, vigorous politician, fully in control of his party and his presidency. Then in September 1901, less than a year into his second term, McKinley was shot by an anarchist assassin. The president clung to life for nine days, and then died. Upon succeeding McKinley, Theodore Roosevelt, aged 42, became the youngest chief executive in the nation's history.

Roosevelt was a study in contrasts. Born to an aristocratic New York family, Roosevelt nevertheless developed an uncommon affection for "the people." Asthmatic, sickly, and nearsighted as a boy, he remade himself into a vigorous adult. With an insatiable appetite for high-risk adventure and confrontation—everything from "dude ranching" in the Dakota Territory, to big-game hunting in Africa, to wartime combat—he was also a voracious reader and an accomplished writer. Aggressive and swaggering in his public rhetoric, he was a skilled, patient negotiator in private. A devout believer in the superiority of his Anglo-Saxon race, he nevertheless appointed members of "inferior" races to important posts in his administration. Rarely has a president's personality so enthralled the American public. He is the only 20th-century president immortalized on Mount Rushmore.

Regulating the Trusts

It did not take long for Roosevelt to reveal his flair for the dramatic. In 1902 he ordered the Justice Department to prosecute the Northern Securities Company, a $400 million monopoly that had been set up by leading financiers and railroad tycoons to control all railroad lines and traffic in the Northwest from Chicago to Washington state. Never before had an American president sought to use the Sherman Antitrust Act to break up a monopoly. The news shocked J. P. Morgan, the banker who had brokered the Northern Securities deal. Morgan rushed to the White House, where he is said to have told Roosevelt, "If we have done anything wrong, send your man to my man and they can fix it up." Roosevelt would have none of this "fixing." In 1903 a federal court ordered Northern Securities dissolved, and the U.S. Supreme Court upheld the decision the next year. Roosevelt was hailed as the nation's "trust-buster."

But that was not quite how Roosevelt viewed himself. Although his administration initiated proceedings against more than 40 corporations, Roosevelt did not believe in breaking up all, or even most, large corporations. Industrial concentration, Roosevelt believed, brought the United States wealth, productivity, and a rising standard of living. The role of government should be to regulate these industrial giants, to punish those that used their power improperly, and to protect citizens who were at a disadvantage in their dealings with industry. This new role would require the federal government to expand its powers to include the monitoring of economic developments, the prosecution of corporate misdeeds, and the adjudication of disputes between capital and labor. The *strengthening* of the federal government—not a return to small-scale industry—was the true aim of Roosevelt's antitrust campaign. And this newly fortified government—the centerpiece of a political program that Roosevelt would later call the "New Nationalism"— was to be led by a forceful president, willing to use all the powers at his disposal to achieve prosperity and justice.

Toward a "Square Deal"

Roosevelt displayed his willingness to use government power to protect the economically weak in a long and bitter 1902 coal miners' strike. Miners in the anthracite fields of eastern Pennsylvania wanted recognition for their union, the United Mine Workers (UMW). They also wanted a 10 to 20 percent increase in wages and an eight-hour day. When their employers, led by the uncompromising George F. Baer of the Reading Railroad, refused to negotiate, they went on strike. In October, the fifth month of the strike, Roosevelt summoned the mine owners and John Mitchell, the UMW president, to the White House. Baer expected Roosevelt to act as presidents had acted in similar disputes in the past: threaten the striking workers with arrest by federal troops if they failed to return to work. Instead, Roosevelt supported Mitchell's request for arbitration and warned the mine owners that if they refused to go along, 10,000 federal troops would seize their property. Coal production would then resume under government control. Stunned, the mine owners agreed to submit the dispute to arbitrators, who awarded the unionists a 10 percent wage increase and a nine-hour day.

The mere fact that the federal government, under White House pressure, had ordered employers to compromise with their workers carried great symbolic weight. Roosevelt enjoyed a surge of support from ordinary Americans convinced that he shared their dislike for ill-gotten wealth and privilege. He also raised the hopes of African Americans when, only a month into his presidency, he dined with Booker T. Washington at the White House. Rarely had an American president so honored an African American leader. Blacks were impressed, too, by how easily Roosevelt brushed off the bitter protests of white southerners who accused him of striking a blow against segregation.

In his 1904 election campaign, Roosevelt promised that, if reelected, he would offer every American a "square deal." The slogan resonated with voters and helped carry Roosevelt to a victory (57 percent of the popular vote) over the lackluster, conservative Democrat Alton B. Parker. To the surprise of many observers, Roosevelt had aligned the Republican Party with the cause of reform.

Expanding Government Power: The Economy

Emboldened by his victory, the president intensified his efforts to extend government regulation of economic affairs. His most important proposal was to give the government power to set railroad shipping rates and thereby to eliminate the industry's discriminatory marketing practices. The government, in theory, already possessed this power through the Interstate Commerce Commission (ICC), a national regulatory body established by Congress in 1887. But the courts had so weakened the oversight and regulatory functions of the ICC as to render it virtually powerless. Roosevelt achieved his goal in 1906. Congress passed the Hepburn Act, which significantly increased the ICC's powers of rate review and enforcement and established an important precedent for future government efforts to regulate private industry. Roosevelt supported the Pure Food and Drug Act, passed by Congress that same year, which protected the public from fraudulently marketed and dangerous foods and medications. The uproar created by the publication of Sinclair's *The Jungle* in 1906 prompted Roosevelt to order a government investigation of conditions in the meatpacking industry. When the investigation corroborated Sinclair's findings, Roosevelt supported the Meat Inspection Act (1906), which committed the government to monitoring the quality and safety of meat being sold to American consumers.

Packinghouses and Reform • Once Upton Sinclair exposed the working conditions and dangers of contamination in Chicago packinghouses, where cattle and hogs were killed and turned into dinner meat for millions of Americans, the public cried out for government regulation of the industry. This photo of a Chicago packinghouse creates an image of a clean, orderly, and regulated industry.

Expanding Government Power: The Environment

Roosevelt also did more than any previous president to extend federal control over the nation's physical environment. In his youth, Roosevelt had developed a profound love for wilderness, an affection that would stay with him for life. He was not a "preservationist" in the manner of John Muir, founder of the Sierra Club, who insisted that the beauty of the land and the well-being of its wildlife should be protected from all human interference. Roosevelt, unlike Muir, was a hunter. He viewed the wilderness as a place to live strenuously, to test oneself against rough natural elements, and to match wits against strong and clever game. Here, Americans could reenact the evolutionary struggle that, over the course of millions of years, had shown man to be supreme among all of earth's animals. Roosevelt further believed that in the West—that land of ancient forests, lofty mountain peaks, and magnificent canyons—Americans could learn something important about their nation's roots and destiny. To preserve this West, Roosevelt oversaw the creation of 5 new national parks, 16 national monuments, and 53 wildlife reserves. The work of his administration led directly to the formation of the National Park Service in 1916.

Roosevelt also emerged a strong supporter of the "conservationist" movement. Conservationists cared little for national parks or grand canyons. They wanted to manage the environment, so as to ensure the most efficient use of the nation's resources for economic development. Roosevelt shared the conservationists' belief

Theodore Roosevelt, Outdoorsman • Throughout his life Theodore Roosevelt emphasized the virtues of a "strenuous life" and the importance of maintaining wilderness areas where men could test themselves against nature. Here he poses with John Muir, the era's leading preservationist, against a spectacular western backdrop.

that the plundering of western timberlands, grazing areas, water resources, and minerals had reached crisis proportions, and that the future of the West as a source of economic growth and area of settlement was at risk. Only the institution of broad regulatory controls would avert that crisis and restore the West's economic potential.

To that end, Roosevelt appointed a Public Lands Commission in 1903 to survey public lands, inventory them, and establish permit systems to regulate the kinds and numbers of users. Soon after, the Departments of Interior and Agriculture decreed that certain western lands rich in natural resources and waterpower could not be used for agricultural purposes. Government officials also limited waterpower development by requiring companies to acquire permits and then to pay fees for the right to generate electricity on their sites. When political favoritism and corruption within the Departments of the Interior and Agriculture threatened these efforts at regulation, Roosevelt authorized the hiring of bureaucrats who had been trained in universities to replace state and local politicians. Scientific expertise, rather than political connections, would now determine the distribution and use of western lands.

Gifford Pinchot, a European-trained specialist in forestry management and Roosevelt's close friend, led the drive for expert and scientific management of natural resources. In 1905 he persuaded Roosevelt to relocate jurisdiction for the national forests from the Department of the Interior to the Department of Agriculture, which, Pinchot argued, was the most appropriate department to oversee the efficient "harvest" of the nation's forest crop. The newly created National Forest Service, under Pinchot's control, quickly instituted a system of competitive bidding for the right to harvest timber on national forest lands. Pinchot and his expanding staff of college-educated foresters also implemented a new policy that exacted user fees from livestock ranchers who had previously used national forest grazing lands for free. Armed with new legislation and bureaucratic authority, Pinchot and fellow conservationists in the Roosevelt administration also declared vast stretches of federal land in the West off-limits to mining and dam construction.

The Old Guard in the Republican Party did not take kindly to these initiatives. When Roosevelt recommended the prosecution of cattlemen and lumbermen who were illegally using federal land for private gain, congressional conservatives struck back with legislation (in 1907) that curtailed the president's power to create new government land reserves. Roosevelt responded by seizing another 17 million acres for national forest reserves before the new law went into effect. To his conservative opponents, excluding commercial activity from public land—a program they regarded as socialistic—was bad enough. But flouting the will of Congress with a 17-million-acre land grab was a violation of hallowed constitutional principles governing the separation of powers. Yet, to millions of American voters, Roosevelt's willingness to defy western cattle barons, mining tycoons, and other "malefactors of great wealth" added to his popularity.

Progressivism: A Movement for the People?

Historians have long debated how much Roosevelt's economic and environmental reforms altered the balance of power between the "interests" and the people. Some have demonstrated that many corporations were eager for federal government regulation—that railroad corporations wanted relief from the ruinous rate wars that were driving them to the brink of bankruptcy, for example, and that the larger meatpackers believed that the costs of government food inspections would drive smaller meatpackers out of business. So, too, historians have shown that large agribusinesses, timber companies, and mining corporations in the West believed that government regulation would aid them and hurt smaller competitors. According to this view, government regulation benefited the corporations more than it benefited workers, consumers, and small businessmen.

This revisionist view has much to commend it. These early reforms did not go far enough in curtailing corporate power. Corporations, working through lobbying organizations such as the National Civic Federation and through Old Guard Republicans in the Senate, fought with some success to turn the final versions of the reform laws to their advantage. But that does not mean (as some historians have argued) that the corporations were the sponsors of reform, or that they dictated the content of reform measures.

Popular anger over the power of the corporations and over political corruption remained a driving force of progressivism. After 1906, the presence in the Senate of La Follette, Albert Beveridge of Indiana, and other anticorporate Republicans gave that anger a powerful national voice. Before he left office in 1909, Roosevelt would expand his reform program to include income and inheritance taxes, a national workmen's compensation law, abolition of child labor, and the eight-hour workday. Those proposals widened the rift between Roosevelt and the Old Guard, as did his public attacks on the courts for declaring unconstitutional important pieces of progressive legislation. In 1907 the progressive program was still evolving. Whether the corporations or the people would benefit most remained unclear.

The Republicans: A Divided Party

What was clear was that progressivism was tearing the Republican Party apart. The financial panic of 1907 further strained relations between Roosevelt reformers and Old Guard conservatives. A failed speculative effort by several New York banks to corner the copper market triggered a run on banks, a short but severe dip in industrial production, and widespread layoffs. Everywhere, people worried that a devastating depression, like that of the 1890s, was in the offing. Indeed, only the timely decision of J. P. Morgan and his fellow bankers to pour huge amounts of private cash into the collapsing banks saved the nation from a disastrous economic crisis. Prosperity quickly returned, but the jitters caused by the panic lingered. Conservatives blamed Roosevelt's "radical" economic policies for the fiasco. To Roosevelt and his fellow progressives, however, the panic merely pointed up how little impact their reforms had actually made on the reign of "speculation, corruption, and fraud."

Roosevelt now committed himself even more strongly to a reform agenda that included a drastic overhaul of the banking system and the stock market. The Republican Old Guard, meanwhile, was more determined than ever to run the "radical" Roosevelt out of the White House. Sensing that he might fail to win his party's nomination, and mindful of a rash promise he had made in 1904 not to run again in 1908, Roosevelt decided not to seek reelection. It was a decision that would soon come back to haunt him. Barely 50, he was too young and energetic to end his political career. He loved power too much. And much of his reform program had yet to win Congressional approval.

The Taft Interregnum

Roosevelt thought he had found in William Howard Taft, his secretary of war, an ideal successor. Taft had worked closely with Roosevelt on foreign and domestic policies. He had supported Roosevelt's progressive reforms and offered him shrewd advice on countless occasions. He was a genial, honest, and superbly competent man, and Roosevelt believed he possessed both the ideas and the skills to complete the reform Republican program.

To reach that conclusion, however, Roosevelt had to ignore some obvious differences between Taft and himself. Taft neither liked nor was particularly adept at the rough-and-tumble game of electoral and congressional politics. With the exception of a judgeship in an Ohio superior court, he had never held elective office. His greatest love was for the law, and his greatest political asset was an ability to debate thorny constitutional questions. His respect for the Constitution and its separation of powers made him suspicious of the powers, formal and informal, that Roosevelt had arrogated to the presidency. His training as a jurist made him averse to risk, to public displays of emotion, and to symbolic gestures. He was by nature a cautious and conservative man, qualities that endeared him to the Republican Old Guard.

As Roosevelt's anointed successor, Taft easily won the election of 1908, defeating the Democrat William Jennings Bryan with 52 percent of the vote. But his conservatism soon revealed itself in his choice of staid corporation lawyers, rather than freethinking reformers, for cabinet positions.

Taft's Battles with Congress

Taft's troubles began when he appeared to side with the Old Guard and against progressives in two acrimonious congressional battles. The first was over tariff legislation, the second over the dictatorial powers of House Speaker "Uncle Joe" Cannon.

Progressives had long desired tariff reduction, believing that competition from foreign manufacturers would benefit American consumers and check the economic power of American manufacturers. Taft himself had raised expectations for tariff reduction when he called Congress into special session to consider a reform bill that called for a modest reduction of tariffs and an inheritance tax. The bill passed the House but was gutted in the Senate when the Old Guard killed the inheritance tax and eliminated most of the tariff reductions. When congressional progressives pleaded with Taft to use his power to whip conservative senators into line, he pressured the Old Guard into including a 2 percent corporate income tax in their version of the bill, but he did not insist on the tariff reductions. As a result, the Payne-Aldrich Tariff he signed into law on August 5, 1909, did nothing to encourage foreign imports. Progressive Republicans, bitterly disappointed, held Taft responsible.

They were further angered when Taft withdrew his support of their efforts to strip Speaker Cannon of his legislative powers, which (they felt) he was putting to improper use. By 1910 Republican insurgents no longer looked to Taft for leadership; instead they entered into an alliance with reform-minded congressional Democrats. This bipartisan coalition of insurgents first curbed Cannon's powers and then, over Taft's objections, diluted the pro-business nature of a railroad regulation bill. Relations between Taft and the progressive Republicans then all but collapsed in a bruising controversy over Taft's conservation policies.

The Ballinger-Pinchot Controversy

Richard A. Ballinger, a corporate lawyer and Taft's secretary of the interior, had aroused progressives' suspicions by reopening for private commercial use 1 million acres of land that the Roosevelt administration had previously brought under federal protection. Then, Gifford Pinchot, still head of the National Forest Service, obtained information implicating Ballinger in the sale of Alaskan coal deposits to a syndicate headed up by J. P. Morgan and the mining magnate David Guggenheim. Pinchot showed the information, including an allegation that Ballinger had personally profited from the sale, to Taft. When Taft defended Ballinger, Pinchot leaked the story to the press and publicly called on Congress to investigate the matter. Pinchot's insubordination cost him his job, but it riveted the nation's attention once again on corporate greed and government corruption. Taft's Old Guard allies controlled the investigation that followed, and Congress exonerated Ballinger. But Louis D. Brandeis, lawyer for the congressional reformers, kept the controversy alive by accusing Taft and his attorney general of tampering with information that had been sent to congressional investigators. Whatever hope Taft may have had of escaping political damage disappeared when Roosevelt, returning from an African hunting trip by way of Europe in the spring of 1910, staged a highly publicized rendezvous with Pinchot in England. In so doing, Roosevelt signaled his continuing support for his old friend Pinchot and his sharp displeasure with Taft.

Roosevelt's Return

When Roosevelt arrived in the United States later that summer, he was still insisting that his political career was over. But his craving for the public eye and his conviction that the reform insurgency needed his leadership prompted a quick return from retirement. In September, Roosevelt embarked on a speaking tour, the high point of which was his elaboration at Osawatomie, Kansas, of his "New Nationalism," a far-reaching reform program that called for a strong federal government to stabilize the economy, protect the weak, and restore social harmony.

The 1910 congressional elections confirmed the popularity of Roosevelt's positions. Insurgent Republicans trounced conservative Republicans in primary after primary, and the embrace of reform by the Democrats brought them a majority in the House of Representatives for the first time since 1894. When Robert La Follette, the standard-bearer of congressional reform who was challenging Taft for the Republican presidential nomination, seemed to suffer a nervous breakdown during a campaign speech in February 1912, Roosevelt announced his own candidacy.

Although La Follette quickly recovered his health and resumed his campaign, there was little chance that he could beat Roosevelt in the fight for the Republican nomination. Taft, too, would have lost to Roosevelt had the decision been in the hands of rank-and-file Republicans. In the 13 states sponsoring preferential primaries, Roosevelt overwhelmed both La Follette and Taft and won nearly 75 percent of the delegates. But the party's national leadership and nominating machinery remained in the hands of the Old Guard, and they were determined to deny Roosevelt the Republican nomination. Taft, angered by Roosevelt's behavior, refused to step aside. At the Republican convention in Chicago, Taft won renomination on the first ballot, largely because the Republican National Committee, disregarding popular sentiment, had awarded Taft 235 of the 254 contested delegate seats.

The Bull Moose Campaign

Roosevelt had expected this outcome. The night before the convention opened, he had told a spirited assembly of 5,000 supporters that the party leaders would not succeed in derailing their movement. "We stand at Armageddon," he declared, and "we battle for the Lord." The next day, Roosevelt and his supporters withdrew from the convention and from the Republican Party. In August, the reformers reassembled as the new Progressive Party, nominated Roosevelt for president and the California governor Hiram W. Johnson for vice president, and hammered out the far-reaching reform platform they had long envisioned: sweeping regulation of the corporations, extensive protections for workers (minimum wage, workmen's compensation, the prohibition of child labor), a sharply graduated income tax, and woman suffrage. The new party constituted a remarkable assemblage of reformers—social workers, suffragists, muckrakers, conservationists, and others—all exhilarated by their defiance of party bosses. "I am as strong as a bull moose," Roosevelt roared as he readied for combat; his proud followers took to calling themselves "Bull Moosers."

Some of them, however, probably including Roosevelt himself, knew that their mission was futile. Their party was poorly organized. They had failed to enroll many of the Republican insurgents who had supported Roosevelt in the primaries but who now refused to abandon the GOP. Consequently, the Republican vote would be split between Roosevelt and Taft. And Roosevelt could not even be assured of a united progressive vote. The Democrats had nominated a powerful reform candidate of their own.

The Rise of Woodrow Wilson

Few would have predicted in 1908 that the distinguished president of Princeton University, Woodrow Wilson, would be the 1912 Democratic nominee for president of the United States. Prior to 1910 Wilson had never run for elective office, nor had he ever held an appointed post in a local, state, or federal administration. The son of a Presbyterian minister from Virginia, Wilson had practiced law for a short time after graduating from Princeton (then still the College of New Jersey) in 1879 before settling on an academic career. Earning his doctorate in political science from Johns Hopkins in 1886, he taught history and political science at Bryn Mawr and Wesleyan (Connecticut) before returning to Princeton in 1890. He became president of Princeton in 1902, a post he held until he successfully ran for the governorship of New Jersey in 1910.

Throughout his almost 30 years in academe, however, Wilson had aspired to a career in politics. As a scholar, he focused largely on the workings of government institutions and on how they might be improved. In 1885 he published *Congressional Government,* a brilliant analysis and critique of Congress that would long remain the most important work in its field. He thrived on his association with students, faculty, and other members of the university community. He enjoyed his role as a leader and admired the powerful leadership style of such British parliamentary giants as Benjamin Disraeli and William Gladstone. "I feel like a new prime minister getting ready to address his constituents," he remarked to his wife as he prepared for the Princeton presidency in 1902. The national reputation he won in that office rested less on his originality as an educator than on the leadership he displayed in transforming the humdrum College of New Jersey into a world-class university.

Wilson's public stature as a university president afforded him new opportunities to comment on political as well as educational matters. Identifying himself with the anti-Bryan wing of the Democratic Party, he attracted the attention of wealthy conservatives, such as George Harvey of *Harper's Weekly,* who saw him as a potential presidential candidate. It was Harvey and his associates who convinced the bosses of the New Jersey Democratic machine to nominate Wilson for governor in 1910. Beset by growing opposition to his aggressive style of leadership from trustees and faculty members at Princeton, and eager to test his talents in a new arena, Wilson accepted the nomination and won the governorship handily. He then shocked his conservative backers by declaring his independence from the state's Democratic machine and moving New Jersey into the forefront of reform.

The Unexpected Progressive

Wilson's embrace of reform was partly a matter of expediency. Aspiring to the White House, he sensed that an alliance with reformers rather than with standpatters would best further his political career. But his turn toward progressivism also reflected an impulse that Wilson's conservative supporters had failed to detect. Wilson's Presbyterian upbringing had instilled in him a strong sense that society should be governed by God's moral law. As a young man in the 1880s, he had come to believe—along with many other young Protestants—that the social consequences of unregulated industrialization were repugnant to Christian ethical principles. "The modern industrial organization," he wrote at the time, had "so distorted competition as to put it into the power of some to tyrannize over many, as to enable the rich and strong to combine against the poor and weak." And therefore, Wilson asked, "must not government lay aside all timid scruple and boldly make itself an agency for social reform as well as political control?" As a young man, Wilson had been drawn to socialism because of its plans to build a strong government that would tame the "captains of industry" and reinvigorate American democracy.

Wilson's early socialist sympathies had dissolved amid the anger, chaos, and violence of the agrarian and labor uprisings of the 1890s. Wilson wanted reform to occur in an orderly, peaceful way; he recoiled from the labor and populist agitators who, in his eyes, showed no respect for existing social and political institutions. The more Wilson stressed the values of order, harmony, and tradition in his public speeches as president of Princeton, the more he attracted the attention of conservatives such as George Harvey. But although Wilson's reform impulses had receded, they had not disappeared. Their presence in his thought helps to explain his emergence in 1911 and 1912 as one of the most outspoken progressives in the nation.

The Election of 1912

At the Democratic convention of 1912, Wilson was something of a dark horse, running a distant second to House Speaker Champ Clark of Missouri, a personable but undistinguished (and alcoholic) candidate with solid support among Bryanite Democrats in the Midwest and West. When the New York delegation, still ruled by Tammany Hall, gave Clark a simple majority of delegates, virtually everyone assumed that he would soon command the two-thirds majority needed to win the nomination. But Wilson's managers held onto Wilson's delegates and began chipping away at Clark's lead. On the fourth day, on the 46th ballot, Wilson finally won the nomination. The exhausted Democrats then closed ranks behind a candidate who pledged to renew the national campaign for reform.

The stage was now set for the momentous 1912 election. Given the split in Republican ranks, Democrats had their best chance in 20 years of regaining the White House. A Wilson victory, moreover, would give the country its first southern-born president in almost 50 years and would restore the South to national power. Finally, whatever its outcome, the election promised to deliver a hefty vote for reform. Both Roosevelt and Wilson were running on reform platforms, and the Socialist Party candidate, Eugene V. Debs, was attracting larger crowds and generating greater enthusiasm than had been expected. Taft was so certain of defeat that he barely campaigned.

Debate among the candidates focused on the trusts. All three reform candidates agreed that corporations had acquired too much economic power. Debs argued that the only way to ensure popular control of that power was for the federal government to assume ownership of the trusts. That solution was anathema to Roosevelt and Wilson. Roosevelt called for the establishment of a powerful government that would regulate and, if necessary, curb the power of the trusts. This was the essence of his New Nationalism, the program he had been advocating since 1910.

Wilson, however, was too suspicious of centralized government to countenance such a program. Rather than regulate the trusts, he wanted to break them up. He argued that monopolies were choking the competition and commerce that had brought prosperity to most Americans in the 19th century. He wanted to reverse the tendency toward economic concentration and thus restore opportunity to the people. This philosophy, which Wilson labeled the "New Freedom," called for a temporary concentration of governmental power in order to dismantle the trusts. But once that was accomplished, Wilson promised, the government would relinquish its power.

Wilson won the November election with 42 percent of the popular vote to Roosevelt's 27 percent and Taft's 23 percent; Debs made a strong showing with 6 percent, the largest in his party's history. The three candidates who had pledged themselves to sweeping reform programs—Wilson, Roosevelt, and Debs—together

Presidential Election, 1912

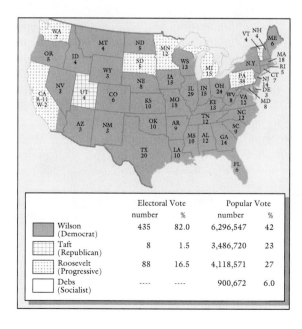

	Electoral Vote		Popular Vote	
	number	%	number	%
Wilson (Democrat)	435	82.0	6,296,547	42
Taft (Republican)	8	1.5	3,486,720	23
Roosevelt (Progressive)	88	16.5	4,118,571	27
Debs (Socialist)	----	----	900,672	6.0

won a remarkable 75 percent of the vote. Never before had a president come into office with such an overwhelming popular mandate for reform. Wilson rose to the challenge.

The Wilson Presidency

The new president immediately put into practice the parliamentary-style leadership he had long admired. He assembled a cabinet of talented men who could be counted on for wise counsel, loyalty, and influence over vital Democratic constituencies. He cultivated a public image of himself as a president firmly in charge of his party and as a faithful tribune of the people.

Tariff Reform and a Progressive Income Tax

Like his predecessor, Wilson first turned his attention to tariff reform. Immediately after his inauguration, he called Congress into special session to consider the matter. To dramatize the gulf separating himself from the reclusive Taft, Wilson personally appeared before Congress—the first president to do so since John Adams—to press his case. The House passed a tariff reduction bill within a month. But the bill ran into trouble in the Senate, chiefly because of the pressure that protectionist lobbyists applied to key Democratic senators. Wilson outflanked them by appealing directly to the American people to destroy the influence of private

Woodrow Wilson • American politics requires its presidents to develop a common touch. Here, Woodrow Wilson throws out the first ball of the 1916 baseball season and simultaneously launches his reelection campaign that, in November, will return him to office for a second term.

interests on lawmakers. Wilson's plea to the public, together with an ensuing investigation of senator-lobbyist relations, humbled the Senate into complying with the president's wishes. Rarely had Washington seen such a dazzling display of presidential leadership in legislative matters.

The resulting Underwood-Simmons Tariff of 1913 achieved the long-sought progressive aim of significantly reducing tariff barriers (from approximately 40 to 25 percent). Then, partly as a matter of expediency (new funds had to be found to make up for revenue lost to tariff reductions), another progressive ambition was achieved with passage of a law calling for an income tax. The Sixteenth Amendment to the Constitution, ratified by the states in 1913, had already given the government the right to impose an income tax; the income tax law passed by Congress made good on the progressive pledge to reduce the power and privileges of wealthy Americans by requiring them to pay taxes on a greater *percentage* of their income than the poor.

The Federal Reserve Act

Wilson continued to demonstrate his leadership by keeping Congress in session through the summer to consider various plans to overhaul the nation's aged and ailing financial system, unchanged since the Civil War. With the memory of the Panic of 1907 still fresh, virtually everyone in both parties agreed on the need for greater federal regulation of banks and currency. But there were sharp differences over how to proceed. The banking interests and their congressional supporters wanted the government to give the authority to regulate credit and currency flows either to a single bank or to several regional banks. Bryanite Democrats and Republican progressives opposed the vesting of so much financial power in private hands and insisted that any reformed financial system must be publicly controlled. Wilson worked out a compromise plan that included both private and public controls and marshaled the votes to push it through both the House and the Senate. Before the year 1913 ended, Wilson had signed the Federal Reserve Act, the most important law passed in his first administration.

The Federal Reserve Act established 12 regional banks, each controlled by the private banks in its region. Every private bank in the country was required to deposit an average of 6 percent of its assets in its regional Federal Reserve bank. The reserve would be used to make loans to member banks and to issue paper currency (Federal Reserve notes) to facilitate financial transactions. The regional banks were also instructed to use their funds to shore up member banks in distress and to respond to sudden changes in credit demands by easing or tightening the flow of credit. A Federal Reserve Board appointed by the president and responsible to the public rather than to private bankers would set policy and oversee activities within the 12 reserve banks.

The Federal Reserve system did a great deal to strengthen the nation's financial structure and was in most respects an impressive political achievement for Wilson. In its final form, however, it revealed that Wilson was retreating from his New Freedom pledge. The Federal Reserve Board was a less powerful and less centralized federal authority than a national bank would have been, but it nevertheless represented a substantial increase in government control of banking. Moreover, the bill authorizing the system made no attempt to break up private financial institutions that had grown too powerful or to prohibit the interlocking directorates that large banks used to augment their power. Because it sought to work with large banks rather than to break them up, the Federal Reserve system seemed more consonant with the principles of Roosevelt's New Nationalism than with those of Wilson's New Freedom.

From the New Freedom to the New Nationalism

Wilson's failure to mount a vigorous antitrust campaign confirmed his drift toward the New Nationalism. For example, in 1914 Wilson swung his full support behind the Federal Trade Commission Act, which created a government agency by that name to regulate business practices. Because the act gave the Federal Trade Commission (FTC) wide powers to collect information on corporate pricing policies and on cooperation and competition among businesses, the FTC might have been used to prosecute trusts for "unfair trade practices." But the Senate stripped the FTC Act's companion legislation, the Clayton Antitrust Act, of virtually all provisions that would have allowed vigorous government prosecution of the trusts. Wilson supported this weakening of the Clayton Act, having decided that the breakup of large-scale industry was no longer practical or preferable. The purpose of the FTC, in Wilson's eyes, was to help businesses, large and small, to regulate themselves in ways that contributed to national well-being. In accepting giant industry as an inescapable feature of modern life and in seeking to regulate industrial behavior by means of government agencies like the FTC, Wilson had become, in effect, a New Nationalist.

But what kind of New Nationalist was he? Would he use government merely to assist businessmen and bankers to regulate themselves? Or would he use government to balance the claims of industry and finance against the claims of labor, farmers, and other disadvantaged groups?

In 1914 and 1915 Wilson favored the first approach: He intended the FTC to become as much a friend to business as a policeman. His nominations to the Federal Reserve Board were generally men who had worked for powerful Wall Street firms and large industrial corporations. At this time, Wilson usually refused to use government powers to aid organized groups of workers and farmers. Court rulings had earlier made worker and farmer organizations vulnerable to prosecution under the terms of the Sherman Antitrust Act of 1890. AFL president Samuel Gompers and other labor leaders tried but failed to convince Wilson to insert into the Clayton Antitrust Act a clause that would unambiguously grant labor and farmer organizations immunity from further antitrust prosecutions.

Nor did Wilson, at this time, view with any greater sympathy the campaign for African Americans' political equality. He supported efforts by white southerners in his cabinet, such as Postmaster General Albert Burleson and Treasury Secretary William McAdoo, to segregate their government departments, and he ignored pleas from the NAACP to involve the federal government in a campaign against lynching.

In late 1915, however, Wilson changed his tune, in part because he feared losing his reelection in 1916. The Bull Moosers of 1912 were retreating back to the

Republican Party. Wilson remembered how much his 1912 victory, based on only 42 percent of the popular vote, had depended on the Republican split. To halt the progressives' rapprochement with the GOP, he made a stunning bid for their support. In January 1916 he nominated Louis Brandeis to the Supreme Court. Not only was Brandeis one of the country's most respected progressives, he was also the first Jew nominated to serve on the country's highest court. Congressional conservatives did everything they could to block the confirmation of a man they regarded as dangerously radical. But Wilson, as usual, was better organized, and by June his forces in the Senate had emerged victorious.

Wilson followed up this victory by pushing through Congress the first federal workmen's compensation law (the Kern-McGillicuddy Act, which covered federal employees), the first federal law outlawing child labor (the Keating-Owen Act), and the first federal law guaranteeing workers an eight-hour day (the Adamson Act, which covered the nation's 400,000 railway workers). The number of Americans affected by these acts was in fact rather small; the U.S. government had a long way to go to protect the interests of the poor and the weak. But Wilson had, nevertheless, reoriented the Democratic Party to a New Nationalism that cared as much about the interests of the powerless as the interests of the powerful.

Trade unionists flocked to Wilson, as did most of the prominent progressives who had followed the Bull Moose in 1912. Meanwhile, Wilson had appealed to the supporters of William Jennings Bryan by supporting legislation that made large amounts of federal credit available to farmers in need. He had put together a reform coalition capable of winning a majority at the polls. In the process, he had transformed both the constituencies and the programs of the Democratic Party. From 1916 on, the Democrats, rather than the Republicans, became the chief guardians of the American reform tradition.

That Wilson did so is a sign of the strength of the reform and radical forces in American society. By 1916 the ranks of middle-class progressives had grown broad and

Growth in Federal Employees, 1891–1917

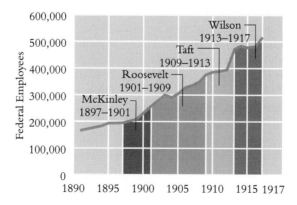

Source: Reprinted by permission from *The Federal Government Service*, ed. W. S. Sayre (Englewood Cliffs, N. J.: Prentice-Hall, 1965), p. 41, The American Assembly.

deep. Working-class protest had also accelerated in scope and intensity. In Lawrence, Massachusetts, in 1912, and in Paterson, New Jersey, in 1913, for example, the IWW organized strikes of textile workers that drew national attention, as did the 1914 strike by Colorado mine workers that ended with the infamous Ludlow massacre (see Chapter 1). These protests reflected the mobilization of those working-class constituencies—immigrants, women, the unskilled—long considered inconsequential both to American labor and party politics. Assisted by radicals, these groups had begun to fashion a more inclusive and politically contentious labor movement. Wilson and other Democrats understood the potential strength of this new labor movement, and the president's pro-labor legislative agenda in 1916 can be understood, in part, as an effort to channel labor's new constituents into the Democratic Party. It was a successful strategy and contributed to Wilson's reelection in 1916.

Conclusion

By 1916, the progressives had accomplished a great deal. They demonstrated that traditional American concerns with democracy and liberty could be adapted to an industrial age. They exposed and curbed some of the worst abuses of the American political system. They enfranchised women and took steps to protect the environment. They broke the hold of laissez-faire economic policies on national politics and replaced them with the idea of a strong federal government committed to economic regulation and social justice. They transformed the presidency into a post of legislative and popular leadership. They enlarged the executive branch by establishing new commissions and agencies charged with administering government policies.

The progressives, in short, had presided over the emergence of a new national state, one in which power increasingly flowed away from municipalities and states and toward the federal government. There was a compelling logic to this reorientation: A national government stood a better chance of solving the problems of capitalist instability, growing economic inequality, mismanagement of natural resources, and consumer fraud than did local and state governments. Although this new state, in 1916, was still small, it offered a blueprint for further reform.

The promise of effective remedies, however, brought threats of new political dangers. In particular, the new national state was giving rise to a bureaucratic elite whose power rested on federal authority rather than private wealth or political machines. The progressives glorified the university-educated experts and scientific managers who staffed the new federal agencies. These new government men (and a few women), progressives argued, would bring to the political process the very qualities that party politicians allegedly lacked: knowledge, dedication, and honesty. But many of these new public servants were not entirely disinterested and unassuming. Some had close ties to the corporations and businesses that their agencies were expected to regulate. Others allowed their prejudices against women, immigrants, and minorities to shape social policy. Still others believed that "the people" could not be trusted to evaluate the government's work intelligently. For these reasons, the progressive state did not always enhance democracy or secure the people's sovereignty. America's involvement in imperial expansion and world war would further demonstrate how a powerful state could serve illiberal ends.

Chronology

1889   Hull House established

1890–1904   All ex-Confederate states pass laws designed to disfranchise black voters • Virtually all states adopt the Australian (secret) ballot

1900   La Follette elected governor of Wisconsin • City commission plan introduced in Galveston, Texas

1901–1914   More than 1,000 African Americans lynched

1901   Johnson elected reform mayor of Cleveland • McKinley assassinated; Roosevelt becomes president

1902   Direct primary introduced in Mississippi • Initiative and referendum introduced in Oregon • Roosevelt sides with workers in coal strike

1903   *McClure's Magazine* publishes Standard Oil exposé • Federal court dissolves Northern Security Company

1904   Roosevelt defeats Alton B. Parker for presidency

1905   National Forest Service established

1906   La Follette elected to U.S. Senate • Congress passes Hepburn Act • Upton Sinclair publishes *The Jungle* • Congress passes Pure Food and Drug Act and Meat Inspection Act

1907   Reformer Hughes elected New York governor • Financial panic shakes economy

1908   Taft defeats Bryan for presidency

1909   Congress passes Payne-Aldrich tariff bill

1910   Ballinger-Pinchot controversy • NAACP founded • Wilson elected governor of New Jersey

1911   National Urban League founded • City manager plan introduced in Sumter, South Carolina

1912   Roosevelt forms Progressive Party • Wilson defeats Roosevelt, Taft, and Debs for presidency

1913   Sixteenth and Seventeenth Amendments ratified • Congress passes Underwood-Simmons Tariff • Congress establishes Federal Reserve system • Wisconsin Industrial Commission established

1914   Congress establishes Federal Trade Commission • Congress passes Clayton Antitrust Act

1916   Louis Brandeis appointed to Supreme Court • Kern-McGillicuddy Act, Keating-Owen Act, and Adamson Act passed • National Park Service formed • National Women's Party founded

1919   Eighteenth Amendment ratified

1920   Nineteenth Amendment ratified

Suggested Readings

No topic in 20th century American history has generated as large and rapidly changing a scholarship as has progressivism. Today, few scholars treat this political movement in the terms set forth by the progressives themselves: as a movement of "the people" against the "special interests." In *The Age of Reform: From Bryan to FDR* (1955), Richard Hofstadter argues that progressivism was the expression of a declining Protestant middle class at odds with the new industrial order. In *The Search for Order, 1877–1920* (1967), Robert Wiebe finds the movement's core in a rising middle class, closely allied to the corporations and bureaucratic imperatives that were defining this new order. Gabriel Kolko, *The Triumph of Conservatism: A Reinterpretation of American History* (1963), and

James Weinstein, *The Corporate Ideal in the Liberal State, 1900–1918* (1969), both argue that progressivism was the work of industrialists themselves, who were eager to ensure corporate stability and profitability in a dangerously unstable capitalist economy. Without denying the importance of this corporate search for order, Nell Irvin Painter, *Standing at Armageddon: The United States, 1877–1919,* (1987), and Alan Dawley, *Struggles for Justice: Social Responsibility and the Liberal State* (1991), insist on the role of the working class, men and women, whites and blacks, in shaping the progressive agenda. James T. Kloppenberg, *Uncertain Victory: Social Democracy and Progressivism in European and American Thought, 1870–1920* (1986), and Thomas J. Knock, *To End All Wars: Woodrow Wilson and the Quest for a New World Order* (1992), emphasize the influence of socialism on progressive thought, while Martin J. Sklar, *The Corporate Reconstruction of American Capitalism, 1900–1916: The Market, the Law and Politics* (1988), stresses the role of progressivism in "containing" or taming socialism. Paul Boyer, *Urban Masses and Moral Order in America, 1820–1920* (1978), treats progressivism as a cultural movement to enforce middle-class norms on an unruly urban and immigrant population. Theda Skocpol, *Protecting Soldiers and Mothers: The Political Origins of Social Policy in the United States* (1992), reconstructs the central role of middle-class Protestant women in shaping progressive social policy, while Robert M. Crunden, *Ministers of Reform: The Progressives' Achievement in American Civilization, 1889–1920* (1982), stresses the religious roots of progressive reform. Summaries of some of these various interpretations of progressivism—but by no means all—can be found in Arthur S. Link and Richard L. McCormick, *Progressivism* (1983).

Muckrakers, Settlement Houses, and Women Reformers

On the muckrakers, see Walter M. Brasch, *Forerunners of Revolution: Muckrakers and the American Social Conscience* (1990); Harold S. Wilson, *McClure's Magazine and the Muckrakers* (1970); and Justin Kaplan, *Lincoln Steffens* (1974). On the settlement houses and women reformers, consult Jane Addams, *Twenty Years at Hull House* (1910); Kathryn Kish Sklar, *Florence Kelley and the Nation's Work: The Rise of Women's Political Culture, 1830–1900* (1995); Allen F. Davis, *Spearheads for Reform: The Social Settlements and the Progressive Movement, 1890–1914* (1967); Mina Julia Carson, *Settlement Folk: Social Thought and the American Settlement Movement, 1885–1930* (1990); and Rivka Shpak Lissak, *Pluralism and the Progressives: Hull House and the New Immigrants, 1890–1919* (1989). Ruth Borden, *Women and Temperance* (1980), is useful on the role of women in the prohibition movement. Paula Baker, "The Domestication of Politics: Women and American Political Society, 1780–1920," *American Historical Review* 89 (June 1984): 620–647, and Robyn Muncy, *Creating a Female Dominion in American Reform, 1890–1935* (1991), are important for understanding women's political activism in the years before they gained the vote.

Socialism

For general histories, see James Weinstein, *The Decline of Socialism in America, 1912–1925* (1967), and Irving Howe, *Socialism in America* (1985). Mari Jo Buhle, *Women and American Socialism, 1870–1920* (1981), expertly analyzes the experiences of women who became socialists. Nick Salvatore, *Eugene V. Debs: Citizen and Socialist* (1982), is a superb biography of the charismatic Debs; Melvyn Dubofsky, *We Shall Be All: A History of the Industrial Workers of the World* (1969), offers the most thorough treatment of the IWW. James R. Green, *Grass-Roots Socialism: Radical Movements in the Southwest, 1895–1943* (1978), and Elliott Shore, *Talkin' Socialism: J. A. Wayland and the Role of the Press in American Radicalism, 1890–1912* (1988), analyze socialist movements in the Southwest.

Political Reform in the Cities

Melvin Holli, *Reform in Detroit: Hazen S. Pingree and Urban Politics* (1969), is an exemplary study of a progressive mayor. On efforts to reform municipal governments, see David C. Hammack, *Power and Society: Greater New York at the Turn of the Century* (1982); Bradley R. Rice, *Progressive Cities: The Commission Government Movement in America, 1901–1920* (1977); and Martin J. Schiesl, *The Politics of Efficiency: Municipal Administration and Reform in America* (1977).

Reform in the States

Richard L. McCormick, *The Party Period and Public Policy* (1986), is indispensable on the roots of state reform. Thomas E. Cronin, *Direct Democracy: The Politics of Initiative, Referendum and Recall*

(1989), examines the various movements to limit the power of party bosses and private interests in state politics. David P. Thelen, *The New Citizenship: Origins of Progressivism in Wisconsin, 1885–1900* (1972) and *Robert M. La Follette and the Insurgent Spirit* (1976), offer the best introduction to Wisconsin progressivism. For New York progressivism, consult Richard L. McCormick, *From Realignment to Reform: Political Change in New York State, 1893–1910* (1981); J. Joseph Huthmacher, *Senator Robert F. Wagner and the Rise of Urban Liberalism* (1971); Oscar Handlin, *Al Smith and His America* (1958); and Irvin Yellowitz, *Labor and the Progressive Movement in New York State* (1965). On social and economic reform movements more generally, see John D. Buenker, *Urban Liberalism and Progressive Reform* (1973). George E. Mowry, *The California Progressives* (1951), and Michael Kazin, *Barons of Labor: The San Francisco Building Trades and Union Power in the Progressive Era* (1987), examine the complexities of progressivism in California. On progressivism in the South, consult Sheldon Hackney, *Populism to Progressivism in Alabama* (1969); Jack Temple Kirby, *Darkness at the Dawning: Race and Reform in the Progressive South* (1972); and Dewey Grantham, *Southern Progressivism: The Reconciliation of Progress and Tradition* (1983).

Reconfiguring the Electorate and the Regulation of Voting

On progressive efforts to reform and reconfigure the electorate, see Michael E. McGerr, *The Decline of Popular Politics: The American North, 1865–1928* (1986); L. E. Fredman, *The Australian Ballot: The Story of an American Reform* (1968); Paul Kleppner, *Who Voted? The Dynamics of Electoral Turnout, 1870–1980* (1982); and John Francis Reynolds, *Testing Democracy: Electoral Behavior and Progressive Reform in New Jersey, 1880–1920* (1988). J. Morgan Kousser, *The Shaping of Southern Politics: Suffrage Restriction and the Establishment of the One-Party South, 1880–1910* (1974), is indispensable on black disfranchisement. On the campaign for woman suffrage, see Anne Firor Scott and Andrew MacKay Scott, *One Half the People: The Fight for Woman Suffrage* (1982); Aileen Kraditor, *Ideas of the Woman Suffrage Movement* (1965); David Morgan, *The Suffragists and Democrats: The Politics of Woman's Suffrage in America* (1972); and Christine Lunardini, *From Equal Suffrage to Equal Rights: Alice Paul and the National Women's Party, 1912–1920* (1986).

Civil Rights

On the renewed campaign for black civil rights, see Charles F. Kellogg, *NAACP: The History of the National Association for the Advancement of Colored People* (1967); Louis R. Harlan, *Booker T. Washington: Wizard of Tuskegee, 1901–1915* (1983); David Levering Lewis, *W.E.B. Du Bois: Biography of a Race, 1868–1919* (1993); and Nancy Weiss, *The National Urban League, 1910–1940* (1974).

National Reform

George E. Mowry, *The Era of Theodore Roosevelt* (1958), and Arthur Link, *Woodrow Wilson and the Progressive Era* (1954), are comprehensive overviews of progressivism at the national level. On the conservation movement, see Samuel P. Hays, *The Gospel of Efficiency: The Progressive Conservation Movement, 1890–1920* (1962); Stephen R. Fox, *The American Conservation Movement: John Muir and His Legacy* (1981); and Alfred Runte, *National Parks: The American Experience* (1979). On conflicts within the Republican Party, consult Horace S. Merrill and Marion G. Merrill, *The Republican High Command* (1971). On the Federal Reserve Act, see Robert T. McCulley, *Banks and Politics during the Progressive Era: The Origins of the Federal Reserve System* (1992) and James Livingston, *Origins of the Federal Reserve System: Money, Class and Corporate Capitalism, 1890–1913* (1986). On Louis Brandeis, consult Phillippa Strum, *Louis D. Brandeis* (1984), and Melvin Urofsky, *Louis D. Brandeis and the Progressive Tradition* (1981).

Theodore Roosevelt

Good biographies of Roosevelt include Henry F. Pringle, *Theodore Roosevelt* (1931); William H. Harbaugh, *The Life and Times of Theodore Roosevelt* (1975); G. Wallace Chessman, *Theodore Roosevelt and the Politics of Power* (1969); Robert V. Friedenberg, *Theodore Roosevelt and the Rhetoric of Militant Decency* (1990); and H. W. Brands, *TR: The Last Romantic* (1997). John M. Blum, *The Republican Roosevelt* (1954), is a brief but interpretively significant account of Roosevelt's career, and Edmund Morris, *The Rise of Theodore Roosevelt* (1979), is a lively account of Roosevelt's early years.

William Howard Taft

The fullest biography is still Henry F. Pringle, *The Life and Times of William Howard Taft*, 2 vols. (1939). For more critical views of Taft, see Paolo E. Coletta, *The Presidency of Taft* (1973), and Donald E. Anderson, *William Howard Taft* (1973). On the Pinchot-Ballinger affair, consult James Penich Jr., *Progressive Politics and Conservation: The Ballinger-Pinchot Affair* (1968), and Harold T. Pinkett, *Gifford Pinchot: Private and Public Forester* (1970).

Woodrow Wilson

The premier biography and chronicle of Wilson's life from birth until the First World War is Arthur S. Link, *Woodrow Wilson*, 5 vols. (1947–1965). Other important biographies include Arthur Walworth, *Woodrow Wilson*, 2 vols. (1958); John M. Blum, *Woodrow Wilson and the Politics of Morality* (1962); August Heckscher, *Woodrow Wilson* (1991); Kendrick A. Clements, *The Presidency of Woodrow Wilson* (1992); and John Milton Cooper Jr., *The Warrior and the Priest: Woodrow Wilson and Theodore Roosevelt* (1983).

Becoming a World Power, 1898–1917

For much of the 19th century, most Americans were preoccupied by continental expansion. They treasured their distance from European societies, monarchs, and wars. Elections rarely turned on international events, and presidents rarely made their reputations as statesmen in the world arena. The diplomatic corps, like most agencies of the federal government, was small and inexperienced. The government projected its limited military power westward and possessed virtually no capacity or desire for involvement overseas.

The nation's rapid industrial growth in the late 19th century forced a turn away from such continentalism. Technological advances, especially the laying of transoceanic cables and the introduction of steamship travel, diminished America's physical isolation. The babel of languages one could hear in American cities testified to how much the Old World had penetrated the New. Then, too, Americans watched anxiously as England, Germany, Russia, Japan, and other industrial powers intensified their competition for overseas markets and colonies, and some believed America also needed to enter this contest. The voices making this argument grew more insistent and persuasive as the long economic depression of the 1890s stripped the United States of its prosperity and pride.

A war with Spain in 1898 gave the United States an opportunity to upgrade its military and acquire colonies and influence in the Western Hemisphere and Asia. Under Presidents William McKinley and Theodore Roosevelt, the United States pursued these initiatives, with impressive results. But subjugating the peoples of Cuba, Puerto Rico, and the Philippines, denying them the right to be free and self-governing, did not sit well with all Americans. It seemed as though the United States was becoming the kind of nation that Americans had once despised—one that valued power more than liberty. Exercising imperial power did not trouble Roosevelt, who wanted to create an international system in which a handful of industrial nations—led by the United States—pursued their global economic interests, dominated world trade, and kept the world at peace. It did concern Woodrow Wilson, however, who sought, as a result, to devise a policy toward postrevolutionary Mexico that restrained American might and respected Mexican desires for liberty. It was a worthy ambition but one that proved exceedingly difficult to achieve.

The United States Looks Abroad

By the late 19th century, sizable numbers of Americans had become interested in extending their country's influence abroad. The most important groups were Protestant missionaries, businessmen, and imperialists.

Protestant Missionaries

Protestant missionaries were among the most active promoters of American interests abroad. Integration of the world economy made evangelical Protestants, like most Americans, more conscious of the diversity of the world's peoples. Overseas missionary activity grew quickly between 1870 and 1900, most of it directed toward China. Between 1880 and 1900 the number of women's missionary societies doubled, from 20 to 40; by 1915 these societies enrolled 3 million women. Convinced of the superiority of the Anglo-Saxon race, Protestant missionaries considered it their Christian duty to teach the Gospel to the "ignorant" Asian masses and save their souls. Missionaries also believed that their efforts would free those masses from their racial destiny, enabling them to become "civilized." In this "civilizing" effort, missionaries resembled progressive reformers who sought to uplift America's immigrant masses at home.

Businessmen

For different reasons, industrialists, traders, and investors also began to look overseas, sensing that they could make fortunes in foreign lands. Exports of American manufactured goods rose substantially after 1880. By 1914 American foreign investment already equaled 7 percent of the nation's gross national product—the same level that was achieved in the 1960s, a time when the American economy was far more internationally oriented than it had been before the First World War. Companies such as Kodak Camera, Singer Sewing Machine, Standard Oil, American Tobacco, and International Harvester had become multinational corporations with overseas branch offices.

Some industrialists became entranced by the prospect of clothing, feeding, housing, and transporting the 400 million people of China. James B. Duke, who headed American Tobacco, was selling 1 billion cigarettes a year in East Asian markets. Looking for ways to fill empty boxcars heading west from Minnesota to Tacoma, Washington, the railroad tycoon James J. Hill imagined stuffing them with wheat and steel destined for China and Japan. He actually published and distributed wheat cookbooks throughout East Asia to convince the population there to shift from a rice-based to a bread-based diet. Although export trade with East Asia during this period never fulfilled the expectations of Hill and other industrialists, their talk about the "wealth of the Orient" convinced politicians that this part of the world was important to national well-being.

The shocks of the 1890s only intensified the appeal of foreign markets. First, the 1890 U.S. census announced that the frontier had disappeared; America had completed the task of westward expansion. Then, in 1893 a young historian named Frederick Jackson Turner published an essay, "The Significance of the Frontier in American History," that articulated what many Americans feared: that the frontier had been essential to the growth of the economy and to the cultivation of democracy. It was the wilderness, Turner argued, that had transformed the Europeans who settled the New World into Americans. They shed their European clothes, tools, social customs, and political beliefs, and acquired distinctively "American" characteristics—rugged individualism, egalitarianism, and a democratic faith. How, Turner wondered, could the nation continue to prosper now that the frontier had gone?

In recent years, historians of the American West have criticized Turner's "frontier thesis." They have argued that the very idea of the frontier as uninhabited wilderness overlooked the tens of thousands of Indians who occupied the region and that much else of what Americans believe about the West is based more on myth than on reality. They have also pointed out that it makes little sense to view the 1890s as a decade in which opportunities for economic gain dried up in the West.

Even though all these points are valid, they would have meant little to Americans living in Turner's time. For them, as for Turner, concern about the disappearing frontier expressed a fear that the increasingly urbanized and industrialized nation had lost its way. Turner's essay appeared just as the country was entering the deepest, longest, and most conflict-ridden depression in its history (see the Prologue). What could the republic do to regain its economic prosperity and political stability? Where would it find its new frontiers? One answer to these questions focused on the pursuit of overseas expansion. As Senator Albert J. Beveridge of Indiana declared in 1899: "We are raising more than we can consume. . . . We are making more than we can use. Therefore, we must find new markets for our produce, new occupation for our capital, new work for our labor."

Imperialists

Eager to assist in the drive for overseas economic expansion was a third group of politicians, intellectuals, and military strategists who viewed such expansion as a key ingredient in the pursuit of world power. They wanted the United States to take its place alongside Britain, France, Germany, and Russia as a great imperial nation. They believed that the United States should join the intensifying competition among European powers; it should build a strong navy, solidify a sphere of influence in the Caribbean, and extend markets into Asia. Their desire to control ports and territories beyond the continental borders of their own country made them imperialists. Many of them were also Social Darwinists, who believed that success in international competition and conquest reflected the laws of nature. America's destiny required that it prove itself the military equal of the strongest European nations and the master of the "lesser" peoples of the world.

Perhaps the most influential imperialist was Admiral Alfred Thayer Mahan. In the 1880s Mahan had become convinced that all the world's great empires, beginning with Rome, had relied on their capacity to control the seas. In an influential book, *The Influence of Sea Power upon History, 1660–1783* (1890), Mahan laid out a program to transform the United States into a great world power. He called for the construction of a first-class navy with enough ships and firepower to make its presence felt everywhere in the world. To be effective, that global fleet would require a canal across Central America through which U.S. warships could pass swiftly from the Atlantic to the Pacific Oceans. It would also require a string of far-flung service bases from the Caribbean to the southwestern Pacific. Mahan recommended that the U.S. government take possession of Hawaii and other strategically located Pacific islands with superior harbor facilities.

Presidents William McKinley and Theodore Roosevelt would eventually make almost the whole of Mahan's vision a reality. But in the early 1890s Mahan doubted that Americans would accept the responsibility and costs of empire. Although the

THE WORLD'S CONSTABLE.

Imperial Visions • This cartoon offers an admiring look at President Theodore Roosevelt's expansionist foreign policy. A dominating Roosevelt is both the physical enforcer of world order and a skillful arbitrator, willing to use negotiation and compromise to settle disputes.

imperialists counted in their ranks such prominent figures as Theodore Roosevelt and Senator Henry Cabot Lodge of Massachusetts, many Americans still insisted that the United States should not aspire to world power by acquiring overseas bases and colonizing foreign peoples.

Mahan's pessimism was misplaced, however. He had, in fact, underestimated the government's alarm over the scramble of Europeans to extend their imperial control. Every administration from the 1880s on committed itself to a "big navy" policy. By 1898 the U.S. Navy ranked fifth in the world and by 1900 it ranked third. Already in 1878, the United States had secured rights to Pago Pago, a superb deep-water harbor in Samoa (a collection of islands in the southwest Pacific inhabited by Polynesians), and in 1885 it had leased Pearl Harbor from the Hawaiians. Both harbors were expected to serve as fueling stations for the growing U.S. fleet.

These attempts to project U.S. power overseas had already deepened the government's involvement in the affairs of distant lands. In 1889, the United States established a protectorate over part of Samoa, a move meant to forestall German and British efforts to weaken American influence on the islands. In the early 1890s, President Grover Cleveland's administration was increasingly drawn into Hawaiian affairs, as tensions between American sugar plantation owners and native Hawaiians upset the islands' economic and political stability. The American plantation owners succeeded in deposing one Hawaiian king in 1891 and putting into power Queen Liliuokalani, a ruler beholden to them. But when Liliuokalani strove to establish her independence, the planters, assisted by U.S. sailors, overthrew her too. Cleveland declared Hawaii a protectorate in 1893, but he resisted the imperialists in Congress who wanted to annex the islands. He failed in his efforts to develop an alternative policy that would both assure the United States of continued access to Pearl Harbor and bring an end to the islands' social unrest.

By this time, imperialist sentiment in Congress and throughout the nation was being fueled by "jingoism." Jingoists—the word was coined in England in the 1870s and quickly entered American discourse—were nationalists who thought that a swaggering foreign policy and a willingness to go to war would enhance their nation's glory. They were constantly on the alert for insults to their country's honor and swift to call for military retaliation. This predatory brand of nationalism emerged not only in Britain and the United States, but in France, Germany, and Japan as well. The anti-imperialist editor of *The Nation,* E. L. Godkin, exclaimed in 1894: "The number of men and officials of this country who are now mad to fight somebody is appalling." Spain's behavior in Cuba in the 1890s gave those men and officials the war they sought.

The Spanish-American War

By the 1890s the islands of Cuba and Puerto Rico were virtually all that remained of the vast Spanish empire in the Americas. Relations between the Cubans and their Spanish rulers had long been deteriorating. A revolt in 1868 had taken the Spanish 10 years to subdue. In 1895 the Cubans staged another revolt, sparked by their continuing resentment of Spanish control and by a depressed economy caused in part by an 1894 U.S. tariff law that made Cuban sugar too expensive for the U.S. market. The fighting was brutal. Cuban forces destroyed large areas of the island to make it uninhabitable by the Spanish. The Spanish army, led by General Valeriano Weyler, responded in kind, forcing large numbers of Cubans into concentration camps. Denied adequate food, shelter, and sanitation, an estimated 200,000 Cubans—one-eighth of the island's population—died of starvation and disease.

Such tactics, especially those ascribed to "Butcher" Weyler (as he was known in much of the U.S. press), inflamed American opinion. Many Americans sympathized with the Cubans, who seemed to be fighting the kind of anticolonial war Americans themselves had waged over 100 years earlier. Americans were kept well informed about the atrocities by accounts in the *New York Journal,* owned by William Randolph Hearst, and the *New York World,* owned by Joseph Pulitzer. Hearst and Pulitzer were transforming newspaper publishing in much the same way Sam McClure and others had revolutionized the magazine business (see Chapter 2). To boost circulation they sought out the most sensational and shocking stories and then described them in lurid detail. They were accused of engaging in "yellow journalism"—embellishing stories with titillating details when the true reports did not seem dramatic enough. Ironically, Hearst and Pulitzer were catering to the same hunger for "real life" accounts that would soon vault the muckrakers to national fame.

The sensationalism of the yellow press and its frequently jingoistic accounts were not sufficient to bring about American intervention in Cuba, however. In the final days of his administration, President Cleveland resisted mounting pressure to intervene. William McKinley, who succeeded him in 1897, denounced the Spanish even more harshly, but still made no move to send U.S. troops to Cuba. McKinley's aim was not to prompt a war but to force Spain into concessions that would satisfy the Cuban rebels and bring an end to the conflict. Initially, this strategy seemed to be working: Spain relieved "Butcher" Weyler of his command, stopped incarcerating Cubans in concentration camps, and granted Cuba limited autonomy. But the Spaniards who lived on the island refused to be ruled by a Cuban government, even one with modest powers. The Cuban rebels, for their part, continued to demand full independence. Late in 1897, when riots broke out in Havana, McKinley ordered the battleship *Maine* into Havana harbor to protect U.S. citizens and their $50 million worth of property. Two unexpected events then set off a war.

The first was the February 9, 1898, publication in Hearst's *New York Journal* of a letter stolen from Depuy de Lôme, the Spanish minister to Washington, in which he described McKinley as "a cheap politician" and a "bidder for the admiration of the crowd." The de Lôme letter also implied that the Spanish were not serious about resolving the Cuban crisis through negotiation and reform. The news embarrassed Spanish officials and outraged U.S. public opinion. Then, only six days later, the *Maine* exploded in Havana harbor, killing 260 American sailors. Although subsequent investigations revealed that the most probable cause of the explosion was a malfunctioning boiler, Americans were certain that it had been the work of Spanish agents. "Remember the Maine!" screamed the headlines in the yellow press. On March 8, Congress responded to the clamor for war by authorizing $50 million to mobilize U.S. forces. In the meantime, McKinley notified Spain of his conditions for avoiding war: Spain would pay an indemnity for the *Maine,* abandon its concentration camps, end the fighting with the rebels, and commit itself to Cuban independence. On April 9, Spain accepted all the demands but the last. Nevertheless, on April 11, McKinley asked Congress for authority to go to war. Three days later Congress approved a war resolution, which included a declaration (spelled out in the Teller Amendment) that the United States would not use the war as an opportunity to acquire territory in Cuba. On April 24, Spain responded with a formal declaration of war against the United States.

"A Splendid Little War"

Secretary of State John Hay called the fight with Spain "a splendid little war." Begun in April, it ended in August. More than 1 million men volunteered to fight, while fewer than 500 were killed or wounded in combat. The American victory over Spain was complete, not just in Cuba but in the neighboring island of Puerto Rico and in the Philippines, Spain's strategic possession in the Pacific.

Actually, the war was more complicated than it seemed. The main reason for the easy victory was U.S. naval superiority. In the war's first major battle, a naval engagement in Manila harbor in the Philippines on May 1, a U.S. fleet commanded by Commodore George Dewey destroyed an entire Spanish fleet while losing only one sailor (to heat stroke). On land, the story was different. On the eve of war the U.S.

The Sinking of the *Maine* • An explosion aboard the battleship *Maine* in Havana harbor on February 15, 1898, killed 260 American sailors and drove the United States into war with Spain. Two days later, William Randolph Hearst's *New York Journal* declared on its front page that a Spanish mine had caused the explosion and subsequent sinking—a charge that would later be disputed.

Army consisted of only 26,000 troops, skilled at skirmishing with Indians but ill-prepared and ill-equipped for all-out war. A force of 80,000 Spanish regulars awaited them in Cuba, with another 50,000 in reserve in Spain. Congress immediately increased the Army to 62,000 and called for an additional 125,000 volunteers. The response to this call was astounding, but outfitting, training, and transporting the new recruits overwhelmed the Army's capacities. Its standard-issue, blue flannel uniforms proved too heavy for fighting in Cuba. Rations were so poor that soldiers referred to one choice item as "embalmed beef." Most of the volunteers had to make do with ancient Civil War rifles that still used black, rather than smokeless,

The Storming of San Juan Hill • This painting by Frederick Remington depicts the exhausted but valiant Rough Riders who, under Theodore Roosevelt's leadership, played a key role in the assault on San Juan Hill.

powder. It took more than five days in June to ship an invasion force of 16,000 men the short distance from Tampa, Florida, to Daiquiri, Cuba. Moreover, the Army was unprepared for the effects of malaria and other tropical diseases.

That the Cuban revolutionaries were predominantly black also came as a shock to the U.S. forces. In their attempts to arouse support for the Cuban cause, U.S. newspapers had portrayed the Cuban rebels as fundamentally similar to white Americans. They were described as intelligent, civilized, and democratic, possessing an "Anglo-Saxon tenacity of purpose." And, they were white—"fully nine-tenths" white, according to one report. The Spanish oppressors, by contrast, were depicted as dark complexioned—"dark cruel eyes, dark swaggering men" is how the writer Sherwood Anderson imagined them—and as possessing the characteristics of their "dark race": barbarism, cruelty, and indolence. The U.S. troops' first encounters with Cuban and Spanish forces dispelled these myths. Their Cuban allies appeared poorly outfitted, rough in their manners, and primarily black-skinned. The Spanish soldiers appeared well-disciplined, tough in battle, and light-complexioned.

The Cuban rebels were actually skilled guerrilla fighters, but racial prejudice prevented most U.S. soldiers and reporters from crediting their military accomplishments. Instead, they judged the Cubans harshly—as primitive, savage, and

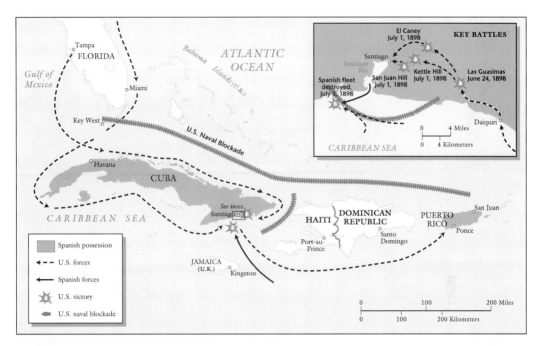

Spanish-American War in Cuba, 1898

incapable of self-control or self-government. White U.S. troops shrank from too close an association with their black Cuban allies. They preferred not to fight along-side the Cubans; increasingly, they refused to coordinate strategy with them.

At first, the U.S. Army's ineptitude and its racial misconceptions did little to diminish the soldiers' hunger for a good fight. No one was more eager for battle than Theodore Roosevelt who, along with Colonel Leonard Wood, led a volunteer cavalry unit comprised of Ivy League gentlemen, western cowboys, sheriffs, prospectors, Indians, and small numbers of Hispanics and ethnic European Americans. Roosevelt's "Rough Riders," as the unit came to be known, landed with the invasion force and played an active role in the three battles fought in the hills surrounding Santiago. Their most famous action, the one on which Roosevelt would build his lifelong reputation as a military hero, was a furious charge up Kettle Hill into the teeth of Spanish defenses. Roosevelt's bravery was stunning, though his judgment was faulty. Nearly 100 men were killed or wounded in the charge. Reports of Roosevelt's bravery overshadowed the equally brave performance of other troops, notably the 9th and 10th Negro Cavalries, which played a pivotal role in clearing away Spanish fortifications on Kettle Hill and allowing Roosevelt's Rough Riders to make their charge. One Rough Rider commented: "If it had not been for the Negro cavalry, the Rough Riders would have been exterminated." Another added: "I am a Southerner by birth, and I never thought much of the colored man. But . . . I never saw such fighting as those Tenth Cavalry men did. They didn't seem to know what fear was, and their battle hymn was 'There'll be a hot time in the old town tonight.'" The 24th and 25th Negro Infantry Regiments performed equally vital tasks in the U.S. Army's conquest of the adjacent San Juan Hill.

African American Troops • The U.S. forces that invaded Cuba included four African American units: the 9th and 10th Negro Cavalries and the 24th and 25th Negro Infantries. Three of the four played vital roles in the taking of Kettle and San Juan Hills, a fact ignored by Frederick Remington when he depicted the storming of San Juan Hill as the work of white soldiers alone.

African American soldiers risked their lives despite the segregationist policies that confined them to all-black regiments. At the time, Roosevelt gave them full credit for what they had done. He praised the black troops as "an excellent breed of Yankee," and declared that no "Rough Rider will ever forget the tie that binds us to the Ninth and Tenth Cavalry." But soon after returning home, he began minimizing their contributions, even to the point of calling their behavior cowardly. Like most white American officers and enlisted men of the time, Roosevelt had difficulty believing that blacks could fight well. By the start of the First World War, the U.S. military had excluded black troops from combat roles altogether.

The taking of Kettle Hill, San Juan Hill, and other high ground surrounding Santiago gave the U.S. forces a substantial advantage over the Spanish defenders. Nevertheless, logistical and medical problems nearly did them in. The troops were short of food, ammunition, and medical facilities. Their ranks were devastated by malaria, typhoid, and dysentery; more than 5,000 soldiers died from disease. Even the normally ebullient Roosevelt was close to despair: "We are within measurable distance of a terrible military disaster," he wrote his friend Henry Cabot Lodge on July 3.

Fortunately, the Spanish had lost the will to fight. On the very day Roosevelt wrote to Lodge, Spain's Atlantic fleet tried to retreat from Santiago harbor and was promptly destroyed by a U.S. fleet. The Spanish army in Santiago surrendered on July 16; on July 18 the Spanish government asked for peace. While negotiations for an armistice proceeded, U.S. forces overran the neighboring island of Puerto Rico. On August 12 the U.S. and Spanish governments agreed to an armistice. But before the news could reach the Philippines, the United States had captured Manila and had taken prisoner 13,000 Spanish soldiers.

The armistice required Spain to relinquish its claim to Cuba, cede Puerto Rico and the Pacific island of Guam to the United States, and tolerate the American occupation of Manila until a peace conference could be convened in Paris on October 1, 1898. At that conference, American diplomats startled their Spanish counterparts by demanding that Spain also cede the Philippines to the United States. After two months of stalling, the Spanish government agreed to relinquish their coveted Pacific colony for $20 million, and the transaction was sealed by the Treaty of Paris on December 10, 1898. The "splendid little war" seemed to have given way to a splendid peace.

The United States Becomes a World Power

The acquisition of the Philippines, Guam, and Puerto Rico had nothing to do with the reasons the United States had gone to war. America's initial war aim had been to oust the Spanish from Cuba—an aim supported by both imperialists and anti-imperialists, but for different reasons. Imperialists hoped to incorporate Cuba into a new American empire; anti-imperialists hoped to see the Cubans gain their independence. But only the imperialists condoned the U.S. acquisition of Puerto Rico, Guam, and particularly the Philippines, which they viewed as integral to the extension of American interests into Asia. Soon after the war began, President McKinley had cast his lot with the imperialists. First, he annexed Hawaii, giving the United States permanent control of its first-rate, deep-water port facility at Pearl Harbor. Then, he set his sights on setting up a U.S. naval base at Manila. Never before had the United States sought such a large military presence outside the Western Hemisphere.

In a departure of equal importance, McKinley announced his intent to administer much of this newly acquired territory as U.S. colonies. Virtually all the territory previously acquired by the United States had been settled by Americans, who had eventually petitioned for statehood and been admitted to the Union with the same rights as existing states. In the case of these new territories, however, only Hawaii would be allowed to follow a traditional path toward statehood. There, the powerful American sugar plantation owners prevailed on Congress to pass an act in 1900 extending U.S. citizenship to all Hawaiian citizens and putting Hawaii on the road to statehood. But no influential group of Americans resided in the Philippines. The United States had little interest in those islands beyond controlling Manila harbor. The decision to make the whole country an American colony was taken mainly to prevent other powers, such as Japan and Germany, from gaining a foothold somewhere in the 400-island archipelago and launching attacks on the American naval base in Manila.

The McKinley administration might have taken a different course. A broadly based anticolonial movement had coalesced in the Philippines during the war. This

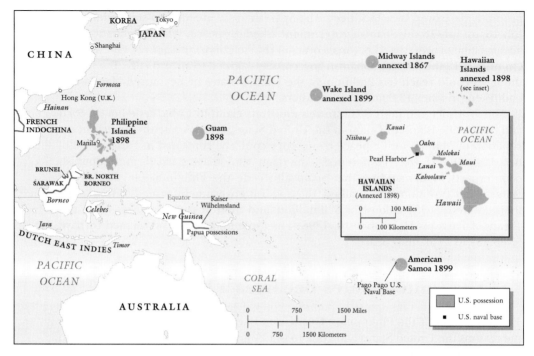

American South Pacific Empire, 1900

movement had supported American efforts to defeat the Spanish oppressors. The United States might have negotiated a deal with Emilio Aguinaldo, the leader of the movement, that would have given the Philippines independence in exchange for a U.S. naval base at Manila. An American fleet stationed there would have been able to protect both American interests and the fledgling Philippine nation from predatory assaults by Japan, Germany, or Britain. Alternatively, the United States might have annexed the Philippines outright and offered Filipinos U.S. citizenship as the first step toward statehood. But McKinley believed that self-government was beyond the capacity of the "inferior" Filipino people, as were the other responsibilities associated with U.S. citizenship. The United States, according to McKinley, would undertake a solemn mission to "civilize" the Filipinos and thereby prepare them for independence. But until that mission was complete, the Philippines would be ruled by American governors appointed by the president.

The Debate over the Treaty of Paris

The proposed acquisition of the Philippines aroused opposition both in the United States and in the Philippines. Anti-imperialist sentiment was evident even before the Treaty of Paris was signed in December 1898. The Anti-Imperialist League, based in the Northeast, enlisted the support of several elder statesmen in McKinley's own party, as well as the former Democratic President Grover Cleveland, the industrialist Andrew Carnegie, and the labor leader Samuel Gompers. William Jennings Bryan, meanwhile, marshaled a vigorous anti-imperialist protest among Democrats in the

South and West, while Mark Twain, William James, William Dean Howells, and other men of letters lent the cause their prestige. Some of these anti-imperialists believed that the subjugation of the Filipinos would violate the nation's most precious principle: the right of all people to independence and self-government. Moreover, they feared that the large military and diplomatic establishment that would be required to administer the colony would threaten political liberties at home.

Other anti-imperialists were motivated more by self-interest than by democratic ideals. U.S. sugar producers, for example, feared competition from Filipino producers. Trade unionists worried that poor Filipinos would flood the U.S. labor market and depress wage rates. Some businessmen warned that the costs of maintaining an imperial outpost would exceed any economic benefits that the colony might produce. Many Democrats, meanwhile, simply wanted to gain partisan advantage by opposing the Republican administration's foreign policy. Still other anti-imperialists were most concerned about the racial implications of colonization. Social Darwinists to the core, they feared the contaminating effects of contact with "inferior" Asian races.

The contrasting motivations of the anti-imperialists ultimately weakened their opposition. Even so, they almost dealt McKinley and his fellow imperialists a defeat in the U.S. Senate, where the Treaty of Paris had to be ratified. On February 6, 1899, the Senate voted 57 to 27 in favor of the treaty, only one vote beyond the minimum two-thirds majority required for ratification. McKinley was unsure about the outcome until the final hours. Two last-minute developments may have brought victory. First, William Jennings Bryan, in the days just before the vote, abandoned his opposition and announced his support for the treaty. (He would later explain that he had decided for ratification in order to end the war with Spain and that he intended to work for Filipino independence through diplomatic means.) Second, on the eve of the vote, Filipinos rose in revolt against the U.S. army of occupation. With another war looming and the lives of American soldiers imperiled, a few senators who had been reluctant to vote for the treaty may have felt obligated to support the president.

The American-Filipino War

The acquisition of the Philippines immediately embroiled the United States in a long, brutal war to subdue the Filipino rebels. In four years of fighting, more than 120,000 American soldiers served in the Philippines and more than 4,200 of them died. The war cost $160 million, or eight times what the United States had paid Spain to acquire the archipelago. The war brought Americans face-to-face with an unpleasant truth: that American actions in the Philippines were virtually indistinguishable from Spain's actions in Cuba. Like Spain, the United States refused to acknowledge a people's aspiration for self-rule. Like "Butcher" Weyler, American generals permitted their soldiers to use savage tactics. Whole communities suspected of harboring guerrillas were driven into concentration camps (of the sort that Americans had condemned the Spanish for using in Cuba), while their houses, farms, and livestock were destroyed. American soldiers executed so many Filipino rebels (whom they called "goo-goos") that the ratio of Filipino dead to wounded reached 15 to 1, a statistic that made the American Civil War, in which one soldier had died for every five wounded, seem relatively humane. One New York infantry-man wrote home that his unit had killed 1,000 Filipinos—men, women, and children—in retaliation for the murder of a single American soldier: "I am in my glory when I can sight my gun on some dark skin and pull the trigger," he exclaimed. A total of 15,000 Filipino soldiers died in the fighting. Estimates of total Filipino deaths from gunfire, starvation, and disease range from 50,000 to 200,000.

The United States finally gained the upper hand after General Arthur MacArthur (father of Douglas) was appointed commander of the islands in 1900. MacArthur did not lessen the war's ferocity, but he understood that it could not be won by guns alone. He offered amnesty to Filipino guerrillas who agreed to surrender, and he cultivated close relations with the islands' wealthy elites. McKinley supported this effort to build a Filipino constituency sympathetic to the U.S. presence. To that end, he sent William Howard Taft to the islands in 1900 to establish a civilian government. In 1901 Taft became the colony's first "governor-general" and declared that he intended to prepare the Filipinos for independence. He transferred many governmental functions to Filipino control and sponsored a vigorous program of public works (roads, bridges, schools) that would give the Philippines the infrastructure necessary for economic development and political independence. By 1902 this dual strategy of ruthless war against those who had taken up arms and concessions to those who were willing to live under benevolent American rule had crushed the revolt. Though sporadic fighting continued until 1913, American control of the Philippines was secure. The explicit commitment of the United States to Philippine independence (a promise that was deferred until 1946), together with an extensive program of internal improvements, eased the nation's conscience.

Controlling Cuba and Puerto Rico

Helping the Cubans achieve independence had been one of the major rationalizations for the war against Spain. But in 1900, when General Leonard Wood, now commander of American forces in Cuba, authorized a constitutional convention to write the laws for a Cuban republic, the McKinley administration made clear it would not easily relinquish control of the island. At McKinley's urging, the U.S. Congress attached to a 1901 army appropriations bill the Platt Amendment (Orville Platt was the Republican senator from Connecticut), delineating three conditions for Cuban independence. First, Cuba would not be permitted to make treaties with foreign powers. Second, the United States would have broad authority to intervene in Cuban political and economic affairs. Third, Cuba would sell or lease land to the United States for naval stations. The delegates to Cuba's constitutional convention were so outraged by these conditions that they refused even to vote on them. But the dependence of Cuba's vital sugar industry on the U.S. market and the continuing presence of a U.S. army on Cuban soil rendered resistance futile. In 1901, by a vote of 15 to 11, the delegates reluctantly wrote the Platt conditions into their constitution. "There is, of course, little or no independence left Cuba under the Platt Amendment," Wood candidly admitted to his friend Theodore Roosevelt, who had recently succeeded the assassinated McKinley as president. Cuba's status, in truth, differed little from that of the Philippines. Both were colonies of the United States. In the case of Cuba, economic dependence

Controlling Cuba • The United States intervened in Cuban affairs five times between 1906 and 1921 to protect its economic interests and to keep its Cuban allies in power. Here U.S. Marines fire at Cuban insurgents.

closely followed political subjugation. Between 1898 and 1914, American trade with Cuba increased more than tenfold (from $27 million to $300 million), while investments more than quadrupled (from $50 million to $220 million). The United States intervened in Cuban political affairs a total of five times between 1906 and 1921 to protect its economic interests and those of the indigenous ruling class with whom it had become closely allied. The economic, political, and military control that the United States imposed on Cuba would fuel anti-American sentiment there for years to come.

Puerto Rico received somewhat different treatment. The United States did not think independence appropriate, even though under Spanish rule the island had enjoyed a large measure of political autonomy and a parliamentary form of government. Nor did the United States follow its Cuban strategy by granting Puerto Rico nominal independence under informal economic and political controls. Instead, the United States annexed the island outright with the Foraker Act (1900). This act, unlike every previous annexation authorized by Congress since 1788, contained no provision for making the inhabitants citizens of the United States. Puerto Rico was designated an "unincorporated" territory, which meant that Congress would dictate the island's government and specify the rights of its inhabitants. Puerto Ricans were allowed no role in designing their government, nor was their consent requested. With the Foraker Act, Congress had, in effect, invented a new, imperial mechanism for ensuring sovereignty over lands deemed vital to U.S.

economic and military security. The U.S. Supreme Court upheld the constitutionality of this mechanism in a series of historic decisions, known as the Insular Cases, in the years from 1901 to 1904.

In some respects Puerto Rico fared better than "independent" Cuba. Puerto Ricans were granted U.S. citizenship in 1917 and won the right to elect their own governor in 1947. Still, Puerto Ricans enjoyed fewer political rights than Americans in the 48 states. Moreover, throughout the 20th century they endured a poverty rate far exceeding that of the mainland. In 1948, for example, three-fourths of Puerto Rican households subsisted on $1,000 or less annually, a figure below the U.S. poverty line. In its skewed distribution of wealth and its lack of industrial development, Puerto Rico resembled the poorly developed nations of Central and South America more than it did the affluent country that took over its government in 1900.

The subjugation of Cuba and the annexation of Puerto Rico troubled Americans far less than the U.S. takeover in the Philippines. Since the first articulation of the Monroe Doctrine in 1823, the United States had, in effect, claimed the Western Hemisphere as its sphere of influence. Within that sphere, many Americans believed, the United States possessed the right to act unilaterally to protect its interests. Before 1900 most of its actions (with the exception of the Mexican War) had been designed to limit the influence of European powers—Britain, France, Russia and Spain—on the countries of the hemisphere. After 1900, however, it assumed a more aggressive role, seizing land, overturning governments it did not like, forcing its economic and political policies on weaker neighbors in order to turn the Caribbean Sea into what policymakers called an "American Mediterranean."

China and the "Open Door"

Except for the Philippines and Guam, the United States made no effort to take control of Asian lands. Such a policy might well have triggered war with other world powers already well established in the area. Nor were Americans prepared to tolerate the financial and political costs Asian conquest would have entailed. The United States opted for a diplomatic rather than a military strategy to achieve its foreign policy objectives. In China, in 1899 and 1900, it proposed the policy of the "Open Door."

The United States was concerned that the actions of the other world powers in China would block its own efforts to open up China's markets to American goods. Britain, Germany, Japan, Russia, and France—each coveted their own chunk of China, where they could monopolize trade, exploit cheap labor, and establish military bases. By the 1890s each of these powers was building a sphere of influence, either by wringing economic and territorial concessions from the weak Chinese government or by seizing outright the land and trading privileges they desired.

To prevent China's breakup and to preserve American economic access to the whole of China, McKinley's secretary of state, John Hay, sent "Open Door" notes to the major world powers. The notes asked each power to open its Chinese sphere of influence to the merchants of other nations and to grant them reasonable harbor fees and railroad rates. Hay also asked each power to respect China's sovereignty by enforcing Chinese tariff duties in the territory it controlled.

None of the world powers was eager to endorse either of Hay's requests, though Britain and Japan gave provisional assent. France, Germany, Russia, and Italy responded evasively, indicating their support for the Open Door policy in theory but insisting that they could not implement it until all the other powers had done so. Hay then put the best face on their responses by declaring that all the powers had agreed to observe his Open Door principles and that he regarded their assent as "final and definitive." Americans took Hay's bluff as evidence that the United States had triumphed diplomatically over its rivals. The rivals themselves may have been impressed by Hay's diplomacy, but whether they intended to uphold the United States' Open Door policy was not at all clear.

The first challenge to Hay's policy came from the Chinese themselves. In May 1900 a nationalist Chinese organization, colloquially known as the "Boxers," sparked an uprising to rid China of all "foreign devils" and foreign influences. Hundreds of Europeans were killed, as were many Chinese men and women who had converted to Christianity. When the Boxers laid siege to the foreign legations in

Putting Down the Boxer Rebellion • U.S. troops stand guard over captured Chinese rebels, who, as part of the 1900 Boxer uprising, had sought to rid China of foreign peoples and cultural influences. The U.S. troops were part of a multinational expeditionary force that was sent to China to defeat the movement.

Beijing and cut off communication between that city and the outside world, the imperial powers raised an expeditionary force to rescue the diplomats and punish the Chinese rebels. The force, which included 5,000 U.S. soldiers rushed over from the Philippines, broke the Beijing siege in August, and ended the Boxer Rebellion soon thereafter.

Hay feared that other major powers would use the rebellion as a reason to demand greater control over Chinese territory. He sent out a second round of Open Door notes, now asking each power to respect China's political independence and territorial integrity, in addition to guaranteeing unrestricted access to its markets. Impressed by America's show of military strength and worried that the Chinese rebels might strike again, the imperialist rivals responded more favorably to this second round of notes. Britain, France, and Germany endorsed Hay's policy outright. With that support, Hay was able to check Russian and Japanese designs on Chinese territory. Significantly, when the powers decided that the Chinese government should pay them reparations for their property and personnel losses during the Boxer Rebellion, Hay convinced them to accept payment in cash rather than in territory. By keeping China intact and open to free trade, the United States had achieved a major foreign policy victory. Americans began to see themselves as China's savior as well.

Theodore Roosevelt, Geopolitician

Roosevelt had been a driving force in the transformation of U.S. foreign policy during the McKinley administration. As assistant secretary of the navy, as a military hero, as a vigorous speaker and writer, and then as vice president, Roosevelt worked tirelessly to remake the country into one of the world's great powers. He fervently believed that the Anglo-Saxon character of the nation destined it for supremacy in both economic and political affairs. He did not assume, however, that international supremacy would automatically accrue to the United States. A nation, like an individual, had to strive for greatness. It had to demand of its citizens physical and mental fitness. It had to build a military force that could convincingly project power overseas. And it had to be prepared to fight. All great nations, Roosevelt declared, ultimately depended on the skill and dedication of their warriors.

Roosevelt's appetite for a good fight caused many people to rue the ascension of this "cowboy" to the White House after McKinley's assassination in 1901. But behind his blustery exterior was a shrewd analyst of international relations. Roosevelt intended to maximize his country's advantages in the world political economy but not at the sacrifice of world order. As much as he craved power for himself and the nation, he understood that the United States could not rule every portion of the globe through military or economic means. Consequently, he sought to bring about a balance of power among the great industrial nations through negotiation rather than war. Such a balance would enable each imperial power to safeguard its key interests and contribute to world peace and progress.

Absent from Roosevelt's geopolitical thinking was concern for the interests of less powerful nations. Roosevelt had little patience with the claims to sovereignty of small countries or the human rights of weak peoples. In his eyes, the peoples of

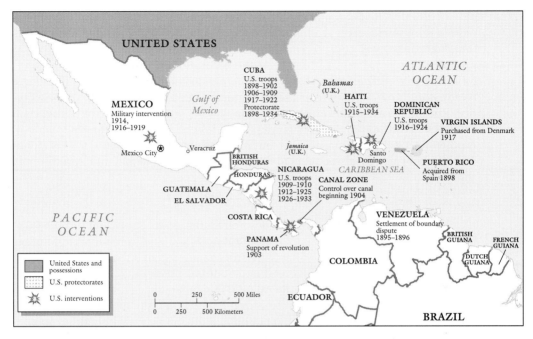

United States Presence in Latin America, 1895–1934

Latin America, Asia (with the exception of Japan), and Africa were racially inferior and thus incapable of self-government or industrial progress. They were better suited to subservience and subsistence than to independence and affluence.

The Roosevelt Corollary

Ensuring U.S. dominance in the Western Hemisphere ranked high on Roosevelt's list of foreign policy objectives. In 1904 he issued a "corollary" to the Monroe Doctrine, which had asserted the right of the United States to keep European powers from meddling in hemispheric affairs. In his corollary Roosevelt declared that the United States possessed a further right: the right to intervene in the domestic affairs of hemispheric nations to quell disorder and forestall European intervention. The Roosevelt corollary formalized a policy that the United States had already deployed against Cuba and Puerto Rico in 1900 and 1901. Subsequent events in Venezuela and the Dominican Republic had further convinced Roosevelt of the need to expand the scope of U.S. intervention in hemispheric affairs.

The governments of both Venezuela and the Dominican Republic were controlled by corrupt dictators. Both had defaulted on debts owed to European banks. Their delinquency prompted a German-led European naval blockade and bombardment of Venezuela in 1902 and a threatened invasion of the Dominican Republic by Italy and France in 1903. The United States forced the German navy to retreat from the Venezuelan coast in 1903. In the Dominican Republic, after a revolution had chased the dictator from power, the United States assumed control of the nation's customs collections in 1905 and refinanced the Dominican national debt through U.S. bankers.

The prevalence of corrupt, dictatorial regimes in Latin America and the willingness of European bankers to loan these regimes money had provided ideal conditions for bankruptcy, social turmoil, and foreign intervention. The United States now took aggressive actions to correct those conditions. But rarely in Roosevelt's tenure did the United States show a willingness to help the people who had suffered under these regimes to establish democratic institutions or achieve social justice. Roosevelt was only interested in reestablishing order and control. Thus, when Cubans seeking genuine national independence rebelled against their puppet government in 1906, the United States sent in the Marines to silence them. U.S. troops remained in Cuba for three years to guard against further democratic revolts.

The Panama Canal

In addition to maintaining order, Roosevelt's interest in Latin America also embraced the building of a canal across Central America. The president had long believed, along with Admiral Mahan, that the nation's pursuit of imperial stature required a strong global navy. The United States needed a way of moving its ships swiftly from the Pacific Ocean to the Atlantic Ocean, and back again. Central America's narrow width, especially in its southern half, made it the logical place to build a canal. In fact, a French company had obtained land rights and had begun construction of a canal across the Colombian province of Panama in the 1880s. But even though a "mere" 40 miles of land separated the two oceans, the French were stymied by technological difficulties and financial costs of literally moving mountains. Moreover, French doctors found they were unable to check the spread of malaria and yellow fever among their workers. By the time Roosevelt entered the White House in 1901, the French Panama Company had gone bankrupt.

Roosevelt was not deterred by the French failure. He first presided over the signing of the Hay-Pauncefote Treaty with Great Britain in 1901, releasing the United States from an 1850 agreement that prohibited either country from building a Central American canal without the other's participation. He then instructed his advisers to develop plans for a canal across Nicaragua. The Panamanian route chosen by the French was shorter than the proposed Nicaraguan route and the canal begun by the French was 40 percent complete, but the company that possessed the rights to it *(Compagnie Universelle du Canal Interocéanique)* wanted $109 million for it, more than the United States was willing to pay. In 1902, however, the company reduced the price to $40 million, a sum that Congress approved. Secretary of State Hay quickly negotiated an agreement with Tomas Herran, the Colombian chargé d'affaires in Washington. The agreement, formalized in the Hay-Herran Treaty, accorded the United States a 6-mile-wide strip across Panama on which to build the canal. Colombia was to receive a onetime $10 million payment and annual rent of $250,000.

The Colombian legislature, however, rejected the proposed payment as insufficient and sent a new ambassador to the United States with instructions to ask for a onetime payment of $20 million and a share of the $40 million being paid to the French company. Actually, the Colombians (not unreasonably) were hoping to stall negotiations until 1904, when they would regain the rights to the canal zone and consequently to the $40 million sale price promised to the French company.

Roosevelt Inspects Work on the Panama Canal • Theodore Roosevelt's 1906 visit to the Panama Canal made him the first U.S. president to travel overseas while in office. Here he poses in a giant, steam-powered earth mover.

Although Colombia was acting within its rights as a sovereign nation, Roosevelt would not tolerate the delay. Unable to get what he wanted through diplomatic means, he resorted to military action. Along with Philippe Bunau-Varilla, a French director of the *Compagnie Universelle,* Roosevelt encouraged the Panamanians to revolt against Colombian rule. The Panamanians had staged several rebellions in the previous 25 years, all of which had failed. But the 1903 rebellion succeeded, mainly because a U.S. naval force, under Roosevelt's instructions, prevented Colombian troops from landing in Panama. Meanwhile, the U.S.S. *Nashville* put U.S. troops ashore to help the new nation secure its independence. The United States formally recognized Panama as a sovereign state only two days after the rebellion against Colombia began.

Bunau-Varilla declared himself the new state's diplomatic representative, even though he was a French citizen operating out of a Wall Street law firm and hadn't set foot in Panama in 15 years. Even as the duly appointed Panamanian delegation embarked for the United States for negotiations over the canal, Bunau-Varilla rushed to Washington, where he and Secretary of State Hay signed the Hay-Bunau-Varilla Treaty (1903). It granted the United States a 10-mile-wide canal zone in return for the package Colombia had rejected—$10 million down, and $250,000 annually. Thus, the United States secured its canal, not by dealing with the newly installed Panamanian government, but with Bunau-Varilla's French company. When the Panamanian delegation arrived in Washington and read the treaty, one of them became so enraged that he knocked Bunau-Varilla cold. Under the circumstances, however, the Panamanian delegation's hands were tied. If it objected to the counterfeit treaty, the United States might withdraw its troops from Panama, leaving the new country at the mercy of Colombia. The instrument through which the United States secured the Canal Zone is known in Panamanian history as "the treaty which no Panamanian signed" and it bedeviled relations between the two countries for much of the 20th century.

Roosevelt's severing of Panama from Colombia prompted angry protests in Congress. The Hearst newspapers decried the Panama foray as "nefarious" and "a quite unexampled instance of foul play in American politics." But Roosevelt was not perturbed. Elihu Root (secretary of state in Roosevelt's second administration), after hearing Roosevelt defend his action before a meeting of his cabinet, jokingly told the president, "You have shown that you were accused of seduction and you have conclusively proved that you were guilty of rape." Roosevelt later gloated, "I took the Canal Zone and let Congress debate!"

Roosevelt turned the building of the canal into a test of American ingenuity and will power. Engineers overcame every obstacle; doctors developed drugs to combat malaria and yellow fever; armies of construction workers "made the dirt fly." The canal remains a testament to the labor of some 30,000 workers, imported mainly from the West Indies, who, over a 10-year period, labored 10 hours a day, six days a week, for 10 cents an hour. Roosevelt visited the canal site in 1906, the first American president to travel overseas while in office. When the canal opened to great fanfare in 1914, the British ambassador James Bryce described it as "the greatest liberty Man has ever taken with Nature." The canal shortened the voyage from San Francisco to New York by more than 8,000 miles and significantly enhanced the international prestige of the United States. Moreover, the strategic importance of the canal further strengthened U.S. resolve to preserve political order in Central America and the Caribbean.

In 1921 the United States paid the Colombian government $25 million as compensation for its loss of Panama. It took Panama more than 70 years, however, to regain control of the 10-mile-wide strip of land that Bunau-Varilla, in connivance with the U.S. government, had bargained away in 1902. President Jimmy Carter signed a treaty in 1977 providing for the reintegration of the Canal Zone into Panama and the transfer of the canal itself to Panama by the year 2000.

Keeping the Peace in East Asia

Roosevelt's foreign policy in Asia, in sharp contrast to his policy in the Caribbean and Latin America, was characterized by a refusal to use military force. His main

Anti-Japanese Sentiment in California • Despite Theodore Roosevelt's negotiation of a "gentlemen's agreement" in 1907, anti-Japanese feeling remained a potent force in California. This 1923 photo conveys one white woman's determination to keep Japanese people out of her neighborhood.

objective was to preserve the Open Door policy in China and the balance of power throughout East Asia. The chief threats came from Russia and Japan, both of whom wanted to seize large chunks of China. At first, Russian expansion into Manchuria and Korea prompted Roosevelt to support Japan when in 1904 it launched a devastating attack on the Russian Pacific fleet anchored at Port Arthur, China. But once the ruinous effects of the war on Russia became clear—not only on the battlefield, where Russia's losses to the Japanese were mounting, but also on the home front where a revolution erupted in 1905—Roosevelt entered into secret negotiations to arrange a peace. He invited representatives of Japan and Russia to Portsmouth, New Hampshire, and prevailed on them to negotiate a compromise. The settlement favored Japan by perpetuating its control over most of the territories it had won during the brief Russo-Japanese War. Its chief prize was Korea, which became a protectorate of Japan, but Japan also acquired the southern part of Sakhalin Island, Port Arthur, and the South Manchurian Railroad. Russia avoided having to pay Japan a huge indemnity and it retained Siberia, thus preserving its role as an East Asian power. Finally, Roosevelt protected China's territorial integrity by inducing the armies of both Russia and Japan to leave Manchuria. Roosevelt's success in ending the Russo-Japanese War won him the Nobel Prize for Peace in 1906; he was the first American to earn that award.

Although Roosevelt succeeded in negotiating a peace between these two world powers, he subsequently ignored, and even encouraged, challenges to the sovereignty of weaker Asian nations. In a secret agreement with Japan (the Taft-Katsura Agreement of 1905), for example, the United States agreed that Japan could dominate Korea in return for a Japanese promise not to attack the Philippines. And in the Root-Takahira Agreement of 1908, the United States tacitly reversed its earlier stand on the inviolability of Chinese borders by recognizing Japanese expansion into southern Manchuria.

In Roosevelt's eyes the overriding need to maintain peace with Japan justified ignoring the claims of Korea and, increasingly, of China. Roosevelt believed that the Japanese bid for world-power status could not be stopped. He admired Japan's industrial and military might and regarded Japanese expansion into East Asia as a natural expression of its imperial ambition. The task of American diplomacy, Roosevelt believed, was first to allow the Japanese to build a secure sphere of influence in East Asia (much as the United States had done in Central America), and second to encourage them to join the United States in pursuing peace rather than war. This was a delicate diplomatic task that required both sensitivity and strength, especially when anti-Japanese agitation broke out in California in 1906.

White Californians had long feared the presence of Asian immigrants. They had pressured Congress into passing the Chinese Exclusion Act of 1882, which ended most Chinese immigration to the United States. Then, in the early years of the 20th century, they turned their racism on Japanese immigrants, whose numbers in California had reached 24,000. In 1906 the San Francisco school board ordered the segregation of Asian schoolchildren so that they would not "contaminate" white children. In 1907 the California legislature debated a law to bar any more Japanese immigrants from entering the state. Anti-Asian riots erupted in San Francisco and Los Angeles, encouraged in part by hysterical stories in the press about the "Yellow Peril."

Tokyo was outraged by the treatment of its citizens in California. Japanese militarists began talking of a possible war with the United States. Roosevelt, putting his own racist attitudes aside, assured the Japanese government that he too was appalled by the Californians' behavior. In 1907 he reached a "gentlemen's agreement" with the Japanese, by which the Tokyo government promised to halt the immigration of Japanese adult male laborers to the United States in return for Roosevelt's pledge to end anti-Japanese discrimination. Roosevelt did his part by persuading the San Francisco school board to rescind its segregation ordinance.

At the same time, Roosevelt worried that the Tokyo government would interpret his sensitivity to Japanese honor as weakness. So he ordered the main part of the U.S. fleet, consisting of 16 battleships, to embark on a 45,000-mile world tour, including a splashy stop in Tokyo Bay. Many Americans, including influential congressmen, deplored the cost of the tour and feared that the appearance of the U.S. Navy in a Japanese port would provoke military retaliation. But Roosevelt brushed his critics aside, and, true to his prediction, the Japanese were impressed by the "Great White Fleet's" show of strength. Their response seemed to lend validity to the African proverb Roosevelt often invoked as a guiding principle of his foreign policy: "Speak softly and carry a big stick."

In fact, Roosevelt's handling of Japan was the most impressive aspect of his foreign policy. Unlike many other Americans, he refused to let racist attitudes cloud

The "Great White Fleet" • To demonstrate America's growing international might, Theodore Roosevelt dispatched a fleet of 16 battleships in 1907 on a 15-month, 45,000-mile world tour that included a celebrated stop in Japan. Here the powerful fleet steams toward home.

his thinking. He knew when to make concessions and when to stand firm. His policies lessened the prospect of a war with Japan while preserving a strong U.S. presence in East Asia.

William Howard Taft, Dollar Diplomat

William Howard Taft brought impressive credentials to the job of president. He had gained valuable experience in colonial administration as the first governor-general of the Philippines. As Roosevelt's secretary of war and chief negotiator for the delicate Taft-Katsura agreement of 1905, he had learned a great deal about conducting diplomacy with imperialist rivals. Yet Taft lacked Roosevelt's grasp of balance-of-power politics and capacity for leadership in foreign affairs. Further, Taft's secretary of state, Philander C. Knox, a corporation lawyer from Pittsburgh, was without diplomatic expertise. Knox's conduct of foreign policy seemed to be directed almost entirely toward expanding opportunities for corporate investment overseas, a disposition that prompted critics to deride his policies as "dollar diplomacy."

Taft and Knox believed that U.S. investments would effectively substitute "dollars for bullets," and thus offer a more peaceful and less coercive way of maintaining stability and order. Taking a swipe at Roosevelt's "big stick" policy, Taft announced that "modern diplomacy is commercial."

U.S. Global Investments and Investments in Latin America, 1914

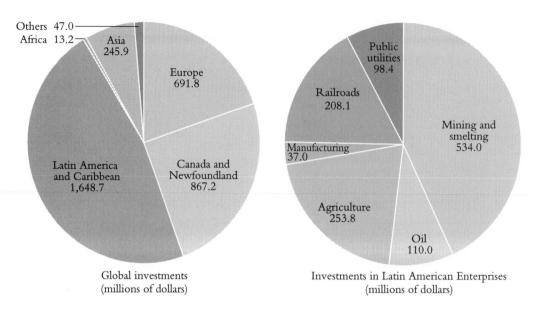

Global investments
(millions of dollars)

Investments in Latin American Enterprises
(millions of dollars)

Source: From Cleona Lewis, *America's Stake in International Investments* (Washington, D.C.: The Brookings Institute, 1938), pp. 576–606.

The inability of Taft and Knox to grasp the complexities of power politics led to a diplomatic reversal in East Asia. Knox, prodded by his banker friends, sought to expand American economic activities throughout China—even in Manchuria, where they encroached on the Japanese sphere of influence. In 1911 Knox proposed that a syndicate of European and American bankers buy the South Manchurian Railroad (then under Japanese control) to open up North China to international trade. Japan reacted by signing a friendship treaty with Russia, its former enemy, which signaled their joint determination to exclude American, British, and French goods from Manchurian markets. Knox's plans for a syndicate collapsed. The United States' Open Door policy had been dealt a serious blow. Similar efforts by Knox to increase American trade with Central and South China triggered further hostile responses from the Japanese and the Russians and contributed to the collapse of the Chinese government and the onset of the Chinese Revolution in 1912. Taft and Knox had unleashed a series of unanticipated events that they did not like and could not control.

Dollar diplomacy worked better in the Caribbean, where no major power contested U.S. policy. Knox encouraged American investment in the region, both to provide corporations with opportunities for profit and to weaken the power of European investors. During the Taft administration, fully half of the rapidly growing portfolio of U.S. overseas investments went to Latin America. Companies such as United Fruit of Boston, which established extensive banana plantations in Costa Rica and Honduras, grew so powerful that they were able to influence both the economies and the governments of Central American countries. When political turmoil threatened their investments, the United States simply sent in its troops. Thus, when Nicaraguan dictator José Santos Zelaya reportedly began negotiating with a European country to build a second trans-Isthmian canal in 1910, a force of U.S. Marines toppled his regime. Marines landed again in 1912 when Zelaya's successor, Adolfo Diaz, angered Nicaraguans with his pro-American policies. This time the Marines were instructed to keep the Diaz regime in power. Except for a brief period in 1925, U.S. troops would remain in Nicaragua continuously from 1912 until 1933. Under Taft, then, the United States continued to do whatever American policymakers deemed necessary to bolster friendly governments and maintain order in Latin America.

Woodrow Wilson, Struggling Idealist

Woodrow Wilson's foreign policy in the Caribbean initially appeared to be no different from that of his Republican predecessors. In 1915 the United States sent troops to Haiti to put down a revolution; they remained as an army of occupation for 21 years. In 1916, when the people of the Dominican Republic (who shared the island of Hispaniola with the Haitians) refused to accept a treaty making them more or less a protectorate of the United States, Wilson forced them to accept the rule of a U.S. military government. When German influence in the Danish West Indies began to expand, Wilson purchased the islands from Denmark, renamed them the Virgin Islands, and added them to the U.S. Caribbean empire. By the time Wilson left office in 1921, he had intervened militarily in the Caribbean more often than any American president before him.

Wilson's relationship with Mexico in the wake of its revolution, however, reveals that Wilson was troubled by a foreign policy that took no account of a less powerful nation's right to determine its own future. He deemed the Mexicans capable of making democracy work and, in general, showed a concern for morality and justice in foreign affairs—matters to which Roosevelt and Taft had paid scant attention. So he felt that U.S. foreign policy should help to advance democratic ideals and institutions in Mexico.

In his dealings with Mexico, however, Wilson was not motivated solely by his fondness for democracy. He also feared that political unrest in Mexico, and elsewhere in Latin America, could lead to violence, social disorder, and revolutionary governments hostile to U.S. economic interests. He therefore believed that the export of American-style democracy was a way of introducing orderly, controlled change to areas of social unrest. If a democratic government could be put in place in Mexico, Wilson believed, property rights would be respected and U.S. investments would remain secure. His desire both to encourage democracy and to limit the extent of social change made it difficult to devise a consistent foreign policy toward Mexico.

The Mexican Revolution broke out in 1910 when dictator Porfirio Diaz, who had ruled for 34 years, was overthrown by democratic forces led by Francisco Madero. Madero's talk of democratic reform frightened many foreign investors, especially those in the United States and Great Britain, who owned more than half of all

Mexican real estate, 90 percent of its oil reserves, and practically all of its railroads. Thus, when Madero himself was overthrown early in 1913 by Victoriano Huerta, a conservative general who promised to protect foreign investments, the dollar diplomatists in the Taft administration and in Great Britain breathed a sigh of relief. Henry Lane Wilson, the U.S. ambassador to Mexico, had helped to engineer Huerta's coup. Before close relations between the United States and Huerta could be worked out, however, Huerta's men murdered Madero.

Woodrow Wilson, who became president shortly after Madero's assassination in 1913, might have overlooked it (as did the European powers) and entered into close ties with Huerta on condition that he protect American property. Instead, Wilson refused to recognize Huerta's "government of butchers" and demanded that Mexico hold democratic elections. Wilson favored Venustiano Carranza and Francisco ("Pancho") Villa, two enemies of Huerta who commanded rebel armies and who claimed to be democrats. In April 1914 Wilson seized upon the arrest of several U.S. sailors by Huerta's troops to send a fleet into Mexican waters. He then ordered the U.S. Marines to occupy the Mexican port city of Veracruz and to prevent a German ship there from unloading munitions meant for Huerta's army. In the resulting action between U.S. and Mexican forces, 19 Americans and 126

A Baffled Uncle Sam • Between 1913 and 1917, the United States allied itself with President Venustiano Carranza's government in Mexico, later opposed it, and then resumed its support. The indecisiveness weakened America's hand, enabling a diminutive Carranza (as depicted in this cartoon) to impose his will on a much larger, but uncertain, Uncle Sam. Objecting to the U.S. pursuit of Pancho Villa, Carranza demands that all U.S. troops be removed from Mexican territory.

Mexicans were killed. The battle brought the two countries dangerously close to war, something Wilson did not want. Although Huerta briefly wore the mantle of the defender of Mexico's honor, American control over Veracruz weakened and embarrassed his regime to the point where Carranza was able to take power.

But Carranza did not behave as Wilson had expected. He rejected Wilson's efforts to shape a new Mexican government and announced a bold land-reform program. That program called for the distribution of some of Mexico's agricultural land to impoverished peasants and the transfer of developmental rights on oil lands from foreign corporations to the Mexican government. If the program went into effect, U.S. petroleum companies would lose control of their Mexican properties, a loss that Wilson deemed unacceptable. So Wilson now threw his support to Pancho Villa, who seemed more willing than Carranza to protect U.S. oil interests. When Carranza's forces defeated Villa's forces in 1915, Wilson reluctantly withdrew his support of Villa and prepared to recognize the Carranza government.

Events continued to spin out of Wilson's control, however. Furious that Wilson had abandoned him, Villa and his soldiers pulled 18 U.S. citizens from a train in northern Mexico and murdered them, along with another 17 in an attack on Columbus, New Mexico. Determined to punish Villa, Wilson got permission from Carranza to send a U.S. expeditionary force under General John J. Pershing into Mexico to hunt down Villa's hated "bandits." Pershing's troops pursued Villa's forces 300 miles into Mexico but failed to catch them. The U.S. troops did, however, clash twice with Mexican troops under Carranza's command, bringing the countries to the brink of war once again. Because the United States was about to enter the First World War, Wilson could not afford a fight with Mexico. So, in 1917, he quietly ordered Pershing's troops home and grudgingly recognized the Carranza government.

Wilson's policies toward Mexico in the years from 1913 to 1917 seemed to have produced few concrete results, except to reinforce an already deep antagonism among Mexicans toward the United States. His repeated changes in strategy, moreover, seemed to indicate a lack of skill and decisiveness in foreign affairs. Actually, however, Wilson recognized something that Roosevelt and Taft had not: that more and more peoples of the world were determined to control their own destinies. The United States, he believed, could not remain oblivious to their quest. Somehow the nation had to find a way to support their democratic aspirations while also safeguarding its own economic interests. The First World War would make this quest for a balance between democratic principles and national self-interest all the more urgent.

Conclusion

We can assess the dramatic turn in U.S. foreign policy after 1898 either in relation to the foreign policies of rival world powers or against America's own democratic ideals. By the first standard, U.S. foreign policy looks impressive. The United States achieved its major objectives in world affairs: It tightened its control over the Western Hemisphere and projected its military and economic power into Asia. It did so while sacrificing relatively few American lives and while constraining the jingoistic appetite for truly extensive military adventure and conquest. The United States added only 125,000 square miles to its empire in the years from 1870 to 1900, while Great Britain, France, and Germany were enlarging their empires by 4.7, 3.5, and 1.0 million square miles, respectively. Relatively few foreigners were subjected to American colonial rule. By contrast, in 1900 the British Empire extended over 12 million square miles and embraced one-fourth of the world's population. At times, American rule could be brutal, as it was to Filipino soldiers and civilians alike, but on the whole it was no more severe than British rule and significantly less severe than that of the French, German, Belgian, or Japanese imperialists. McKinley, Roosevelt, Taft, and Wilson all placed limits on American expansion and avoided, prior to 1917, extensive foreign entanglements and wars.

If measured against the standard of America's own democratic ideals, however, U.S. foreign policy after 1898 must be judged more harshly. It demeaned the peoples of the Philippines, Puerto Rico, Guam, Cuba, and Colombia as inferior, primitive, and barbaric and denied them the right to govern themselves. In choosing to behave like the imperialist powers of Europe, the United States abandoned its long-standing claim that it was a different kind of nation—one that valued liberty more than power.

Many Americans of the time judged their nation by both standards and thus faced a dilemma that would extend throughout the 20th century. On the one hand, they believed with Roosevelt that the size, economic strength, and honor of the United States required it to accept the role of world power and policeman. On the other hand, they continued to believe with Wilson that they had a mission to spread the values of 1776 to the farthest reaches of the earth. The Mexico example demonstrates how hard it was for the United States to reconcile these two very different approaches to world affairs.

Chronology

1893 Frederick Jackson Turner publishes an essay announcing the end of the frontier

1898 Spanish-American War (April 14–August 12) • Treaty of Paris signed (December 10), giving U.S. control of Philippines, Guam, and Puerto Rico • U.S. annexes Hawaii

1899–1902 American-Filipino War

1899–1900 U.S. pursues "Open Door" policy toward China

1900 U.S. annexes Puerto Rico • U.S. and other imperial powers put down Chinese Boxer Rebellion

1901 U.S. forces Cuba to adopt constitution favorable to U.S. interests

1903 Hay-Bunau-Varilla Treaty signed, giving U.S. control of Panama Canal Zone

1904 "Roosevelt corollary" to Monroe Doctrine proclaimed

1905 Roosevelt negotiates end to Russo-Japanese War

1906–1917 U.S. intervenes in Cuba, Nicaragua, Haiti, Dominican Republic, and Mexico

1907 Roosevelt and Japanese government reach a "Gentlemen's Agreement" restricting Japanese immigration to U.S. and ending discrimination against Japanese schoolchildren in California

1907–1909 Great White Fleet circles the earth

1909–1913   William Howard Taft conducts "dollar diplomacy"

1910   Mexican Revolution

1914   Panama Canal opens

1914–1917   Wilson struggles to develop a policy toward Mexico

1917   U.S. purchases Virgin Islands from Denmark

Suggested Readings

General works on America's imperialist turn in the 1890s and early years of the 20th century include John Dobson, *America's Ascent: The United States Becomes a Great Power, 1880–1914* (1978); H. Wayne Morgan, *America's Road to Empire* (1965); David F. Healy, *U.S. Expansionism: Imperialist Urge in the 1890s* (1970); Ernest R. May, *Imperial Democracy: The Emergence of America as a Great Power* (1961); Robert L. Beisner, *From the Old Diplomacy to the New, 1965–1900* (1986); and Walter LaFeber, *The Cambridge History of Foreign Relations: The Search for Opportunity, 1865–1913* (1993).

Motives for Expansion

Patricia Hill, *The World Their Household: The American Woman's Foreign Mission Movement and Cultural Transformation, 1870–1920* (1984), and Jane Hunter, *The Gospel of Gentility: American Women Missionaries in Turn-of-the-Century China* (1984), are very good on the overseas work of female Protestant missionaries. William Appleman Williams, *The Tragedy of American Diplomacy,* rev. ed. (1972), is still indispensable on the economic motives behind imperialism, but it should be supplemented with Emily Rosenberg, *Spreading the American Dream: American Economic and Cultural Expansion, 1890–1945* (1982). For an important critique of Frederick Jackson Turner's notion that the year 1890 marked the end of the frontier, consult Patricia Nelson Limerick, *The Legacy of Conquest: The Unbroken Past of the American West* (1987). William E. Livezey, *Mahan on Sea Power* (1981), analyzes Admiral Mahan's strategy for transforming the United States into a world power, and Walter R. Herrick, *The American Naval Revolution* (1966), examines the emergence of a "Big Navy" policy. Julius W. Pratt, *Expansionists of 1898* (1936), is an important account of mounting jingoist fever in the 1890s.

The Spanish-American War

David F. Trask, *The War with Spain in 1898* (1981), is a comprehensive study of the Spanish-American War, but it should be supplemented with Philip S. Foner, *The Spanish-Cuban-American War and the Birth of American Imperialism,* 2 vols. (1972). See also James E. Bradford, *Crucible of Empire: The Spanish-American War and Its Aftermath* (1993). Joyce Milton, *The Yellow Journalists* (1989), discusses the role of the press in whipping up war fever, and Michael Blow, *A Ship to Remember: The Maine and the Spanish-American War* (1992), analyzes the battleship sinking that became the war's catalyst. Graham A. Cosmas, *An Army for Empire: The United States Army in the Spanish-American War* (1971), examines the achievements and failures of the army. Edmund Morris, *The Rise of Theodore Roosevelt* (1979), captures the daring of Roosevelt's Rough Riders and their charge up Kettle Hill, while William B. Gatewood Jr., *"Smoked Yankees": Letters from Negro Soldiers, 1898–1902* (1971), examines the important and unappreciated contributions of black soldiers. Gerald F. Linderman, *The Mirror of War: American Society and the Spanish-American War* (1974), brilliantly recaptures the shock that overtook Americans who discovered that their Cuban allies were black and the Spanish enemies were white.

Building an Empire

Julius W. Pratt, *America's Colonial Empire* (1950), analyzes steps the United States took to build itself an empire in the wake of the Spanish-American War. The annexation of Hawaii can be followed in Merze Tate, *The United States and the Hawaiian Kingdom* (1965), and William A. Russ Jr., *The Hawaiian Republic, 1894-1898, and Its Struggle to Win Annexation* (1961). The acquisition of Guam and

Samoa is examined in Paul Carano and Pedro Sanchez, *A Complete History of Guam* (1964), and Paul M. Kennedy, *The Samoan Tangle* (1974). The anti-imperialist movement is analyzed in E. Berkeley Tompkins, *Anti-Imperialism in the United States, 1890–1920: The Great Debate* (1970); Robert L. Beisner, *Twelve Against Empire: The Anti-Imperialists, 1898–1900* (1968); and Daniel B. Schirmer, *Republic or Empire? American Resistance to the Philippine War* (1972). Richard E. Welch Jr., *Response to Imperialism: The United States and the Philippine War, 1899–1902* (1979), and Stuart Creighton Miller, *"Benevolent Assimilation": The American Conquest of the Philippines, 1899–1903* (1982), analyze the Filipino-American war, while Peter Stanley, *A Nation in the Making: The Philippines and the United States, 1899–1921* (1974), examines the fate of the Philippines under the first 20 years of U.S. rule. James H. Hitchman, *Leonard Wood and Cuban Independence, 1898–1902* (1971), and Louis A. Perez, *Cuba under the Platt Amendment, 1902–1934* (1986), analyze the extension of U.S. control over Cuba, while Raymond Carr, *Puerto Rico: A Colonial Experiment* (1984), examines the history of Puerto Rico following its annexation by the United States. For the unfolding of the Open Door policy toward China, consult Marilyn B. Young, *The Rhetoric of Empire: American China Policy, 1895–1901* (1968); Warren I. Cohen, *America's Response to China* (1971); and Thomas J. Mc-Cormick, *China Market: America's Quest for Informal Empire, 1890–1915* (1971).

Theodore Roosevelt

Howard K. Beale, *Theodore Roosevelt and the Rise of America to World Power* (1956), is still a crucial work on Roosevelt's foreign policy, although it should be supplemented with David H. Burton, *Theodore Roosevelt: Confident Imperialist* (1968), and Frederick Marks III, *Velvet on Iron: The Diplomacy of Theodore Roosevelt* (1979). Richard H. Collin, *Theodore Roosevelt's Caribbean: The Panama Canal, the Monroe Doctrine and the Latin American Context* (1990), examines Roosevelt's Caribbean policy. Of the many books written on the Panama Canal, two stand out: Walter LaFeber, *The Panama Canal* (1978), and David McCullough, *The Path between the Seas* (1977), a lively account of the canal's construction. See also Michael L. Conniff, *Black Labor on a White Canal: Panama, 1904–1981* (1985). For Roosevelt's policy in East Asia, consult Akira Iriye, *Pacific Estrangement: Japanese and American Expansion, 1897–1911* (1972); Charles Neu, *An Uncertain Friendship: Theodore Roosevelt and Japan, 1906–1909* (1967); and Charles Neu, *The Troubled Encounter* (1975). On the treatment of the Japanese in California, see Jules Becker, *The Course of Exclusion, 1882–1924: San Francisco Newspaper Coverage of the Chinese and Japanese in the United States* (1991).

William Howard Taft

Ralph E. Minger, *William Howard Taft and American Foreign Policy* (1975), and Walter V. Scholes and Marie V. Scholes, *The Foreign Policies of the Taft Administration* (1970), are the standard works on William Howard Taft's foreign policies. For a comprehensive look at his "dollar diplomacy" and its effects on the Caribbean, see Dana G. Munro, *Intervention and Dollar Diplomacy in the Caribbean, 1900–1920* (1964).

Woodrow Wilson

Two books by Arthur Link, *Wilson the Diplomatist* (1957) and *Woodrow Wilson: Revolution, War, and Peace* (1979), sympathetically treat Wilson's struggle to fashion an idealistic foreign policy. These works must be supplemented with Thomas J. Knock, *To End All Wars: Woodrow Wilson and the Quest for a New World Order* (1992). Lloyd C. Gardner, *Safe for Democracy: The Anglo-American Response to Revolution, 1913–1923* (1984), offers a more critical appraisal of Wilson's policies. On U.S. responses to the Mexican Revolution, see John S. D. Eisenhower, *Intervention: The United States and the Mexican Revolution, 1913–1917* (1993); Peter Calvert, *The Mexican Revolution, 1910–1914* (1968); Kenneth J. Grieb, *The United States and Huerta* (1969); and Robert E. Quirk, *An Affair of Honor: Woodrow Wilson and the Occupation of Veracruz* (1962).

4

War and Society, 1914–1920

The First World War broke out in Europe in August 1914. The Triple Alliance of Germany, Austria-Hungary, and the Ottoman Empire squared off against the Triple Entente of Great Britain, France, and Russia. The United States entered the war on the side of the Entente (the Allies, or Allied Powers, as they came to be called) in 1917. Over the next year and a half, the United States converted its immense and sprawling economy into a disciplined war production machine, raised a 5-million-man army, and provided both the war matériel and troops that helped propel the Allies to victory. The United States emerged from the war as the world's mightiest country. In these and other respects, the war had been a great triumph.

But the war also convulsed American society more deeply than any event since the Civil War. This war was the first "total" war, meaning that it required combatants to devote virtually all their resources to the fight. Thus the United States government had no choice but to pursue a degree of industrial control and social regimentation without precedent in American history. Needless to say, the ensuing government buildup was itself a controversial measure in a society that had long distrusted state power. Moreover, significant numbers of Americans from a variety of constituencies opposed the war. To overcome this opposition, Wilson couched American war aims in disinterested and idealistic terms: The United States, he claimed, wanted a "peace without victory," a "war for democracy," and liberty for the world's oppressed peoples. Because these words drew deeply on American political traditions, Wilson believed that Americans would be inspired by them, put aside their suspicions, and lend him their support.

Many people in the United States and abroad responded enthusiastically to Wilson's ideals. But his idealism also backfired. Wilson could not deliver a "peace without victory" without the support of the other victors (England and France), and this support was never forthcoming. At home, disadvantaged groups stirred up trouble by declaring that American society had failed to live up to its democratic and egalitarian ideals. Wilson supported repressive policies to silence these rebels and to enforce unity and conformity on the American people. In the process, he tarnished the ideals for which America had been fighting. Only a year after the war had triumphantly ended, Wilson's hopes for a "peace without victory" abroad had been destroyed, and America was being torn apart by violent labor disputes and race riots at home.

Europe's Descent into War

Europe began its descent into war on June 28, 1914, in Sarajevo, Bosnia, when a Bosnian nationalist assassinated Archduke Franz Ferdinand, heir to the Austro-Hungarian throne. This act was meant to protest the Austro-Hungarian imperial presence in the Balkans, and to encourage the Bosnians, Croatians, and other

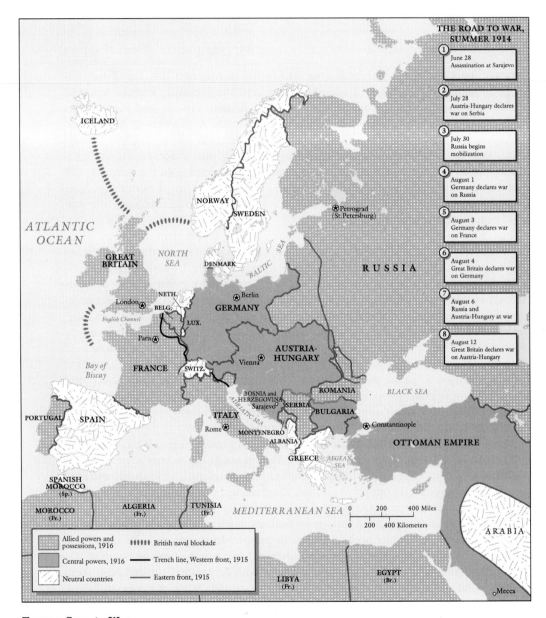

THE ROAD TO WAR, SUMMER 1914

1. June 28 — Assassination at Sarajevo
2. July 28 — Austria-Hungary declares war on Serbia
3. July 30 — Russia begins mobilization
4. August 1 — Germany declares war on Russia
5. August 3 — Germany declares war on France
6. August 4 — Great Britain declares war on Germany
7. August 6 — Russia and Austria-Hungary at war
8. August 12 — Great Britain declares war on Austria-Hungary

Legend:
- Allied powers and possessions, 1916
- Central powers, 1916
- Neutral countries
- British naval blockade
- Trench line, Western front, 1915
- Eastern front, 1915

Europe Goes to War

Balkan peoples to join the Serbs in establishing independent nations. Austria-Hungary responded to this provocation on July 28 by declaring war on Serbia, holding it responsible for the archduke's murder.

The conflict might have remained local had not an intricate series of treaties divided Europe into two hostile camps. Germany, Austria-Hungary, and Italy, the so-called Triple Alliance, had promised to come to each other's aid if attacked. Italy would soon opt out of this alliance, to be replaced by the Ottoman Empire. Arrayed against the nations of the Triple Alliance were Britain, France, and Russia in the Triple Entente. Russia was obligated by another treaty to defend Serbia against Austria-Hungary, and consequently on July 30 it mobilized its armed forces to go to Serbia's aid. That brought Germany into the conflict to protect Austria-Hungary from Russian attack. On August 3 German troops struck not at Russia itself but at France, Russia's western ally. To reach France, German troops had marched through neutral Belgium. On August 4 Britain reacted by declaring war on Germany. Within the space of only a few weeks, Europe found itself engulfed in war.

Complicated alliances and defense treaties of the European nations undoubtedly hastened the rush toward war. But equally important was the fierce competition that existed among the larger powers to build the strongest economies, the largest armies and navies, and the grandest colonial empires. Britain and Germany, in particular, were engaged in a bitter struggle for European and world supremacy. Few Europeans had any idea that these military buildups might lead to a terrible war that would kill nearly an entire generation of young men and expose the barbarity lurking in their civilization. Historians now believe that several advisers close to the German emperor, Kaiser Wilhelm II, were actually eager to engage Russia and France in a fight for supremacy on the European continent. They expected that a European war would be swift and decisive—in Germany's favor. But England and France also believed in their own superiority. Millions of young men, rich and poor, rushed to join the armies on both sides and share in the expected glory.

But there was to be no quick victory. The two camps were evenly matched. Moreover, the first wartime use of machine guns and barbed wire made it easier to defend against attack than to go on the offensive. (Both tanks and airplanes had also been invented by this time, but military strategists on both sides were slow to put them to offensive use.) On the western front, after the initial German attack narrowly failed to take Paris in 1914, the two opposing armies confronted each other along a battle line stretching from Belgium in the north to the Swiss border in the southeast. Troops dug trenches to protect themselves from artillery bombardment and poison gas attacks. Commanders on both sides mounted suicidal ground assaults on the enemy by sending tens of thousands of infantry, armed only with rifles, bayonets, and grenades, out of the trenches and directly into enemy fire. Barbed wire further retarded forward progress, enabling enemy artillery and machine guns to cut down appalling numbers of men. In 1916, during one 10-month German offensive at Verdun (France), 600,000 German troops died; 20,000 British troops were killed during only the first day of an Entente assault on the Somme River (also in France). Many of those who were not killed in combat succumbed to disease that spread rapidly in the cold, wet, and rat-infested trenches. In eastern Europe the armies of Germany and Austria-Hungary squared off against those of Russia and Serbia. Though trench warfare was not employed there, the combat was

U.S. Soldiers in Battle on the Western Front • The bleak landscape surrounding these American troops points to the devastation wrought by the First World War.

no less lethal. By the time the First World War ended, an estimated 8.5 million soldiers had died and more than twice that number had been wounded. Total casualties, both military and civilian, had reached 37 million. Europe had lost a generation of young men, as well as its confidence, stability, and global supremacy.

American Neutrality

Soon after the fighting began, Woodrow Wilson told Americans that this was a European war and that the United States wanted no role in the hostilities. Neither side was threatening a vital American interest, nor was either side fighting for a lofty principle. The United States would therefore proclaim its neutrality and maintain normal relations with both sides while seeking to secure a peace. Normal relations meant that the United States would continue trading with both camps. Wilson's neutrality policy was greeted by lively opposition, especially from Theodore Roosevelt, who was convinced that the United States should join the Entente to check German power and expansionism. But a majority of Americans applauded Wilson's determination to keep the country out of war.

It was easier to proclaim neutrality than it was to achieve it, however. Many Americans, especially those with economic and political power, identified culturally more with Britain than with Germany. They shared with the English a language, a common ancestry, and a commitment to liberty. Wilson himself revered the British parliamentary system of government. His closest foreign policy adviser, Colonel Edward M. House, was decidedly pro-British, as was Robert Lansing, a trusted counselor in the State Department. Only William Jennings Bryan, Wilson's secretary of state, was immune to the appeal of the English.

Germany had no such attraction for U.S. policymakers. On the contrary, Germany's acceptance of monarchical rule, the prominence of militarists in German politics, and the weakness of democratic traditions inclined U.S. officials to judge Germany harshly.

The United States was tied to Great Britain by economics as well as culture, and Great Britain was more important than Germany to American manufacturers and investors. In 1914 the United States exported more than $800 million in goods to Britain and its allies, compared with $170 million to Germany and Austria-Hungary (which came to be known as the Central Powers), a disparity of almost 5 to 1. As soon as the war began, the British and then the French turned to the United States for food, clothing, munitions, and other war supplies. Orders from the Allies quadrupled during the first two years of war to $3.2 billion. The U.S. economy, which had been languishing in 1914, enjoyed a great boom. Bankers began to issue loans to the Allied Powers, once Wilson permitted them to do so in 1915, further knitting together the American and British economies and giving American investors a direct stake in an Allied victory. Moreover, the British navy had blockaded German ports, which further limited U.S. trade with Germany. By 1916 U.S. exports to the Central Powers had plummeted to barely $1 million, a fall of more than 99 percent in two years.

The British blockade of German ports clearly violated American neutrality. The Wilson administration vigorously protested the search and occasional seizure of American merchant ships by the British navy. But it never suspended loans or the export of goods to Great Britain in retaliation for the blockade. To do so would have plunged the U.S. economy into a severe recession. In failing to protect its right to trade with Germany, however, the United States compromised its neutrality and allowed itself to be drawn slowly into war.

Submarine Warfare

To combat British control of the seas and to check the flow of U.S. goods to the Allies, Germany unveiled a terrifying new weapon, the *Unterseeboot,* or U-boat, the first militarily effective submarine. Early in 1915 Germany announced its intent to use its U-boats to sink on sight enemy ships en route to the British Isles. On May 7, 1915, without warning, a German U-boat torpedoed the British passenger liner *Lusitania,* en route from New York to London. The ship sank in 22 minutes, killing 1,198 men, women, and children, 128 of them U.S. citizens. Americans were shocked by the sinking. Innocent civilians who had been given no warning of attack, no chance to surrender, had been murdered in cold blood. The attack appeared to confirm what anti-German agitators were saying: that the Germans were by nature barbaric and uncivilized. The circumstances surrounding the sinking of the *Lusitania,* however, were more complicated than most Americans realized.

Prior to its sailing, the Germans had alleged that the *Lusitania* was secretly carrying a large store of munitions to Great Britain (a charge later shown to have been true) and that it therefore was subject to U-boat attack. Germany had explicitly warned American passengers not to travel on British passenger ships that carried munitions. Moreover, Germany claimed, with some justification, that the purpose of the U-boat attacks—the disruption of Allied supply lines—was no different from Britain's purpose in blockading German ports. Because its surface ships were outnumbered by the British navy, Germany claimed it had no alternative but to choose the underwater strategy. If a submarine attack seemed more reprehensible than a conventional sea battle, the Germans argued, it was no more so than the British attempt to starve the German people into submission with a blockade.

American political leaders might have used the *Lusitania* incident to denounce both Germany's U-boat strategy and Britain's blockade as actions that violated the rights of citizens of neutral nations. Only Secretary of State Bryan had the courage to say so, however, and his stand proved so unpopular in Washington that he resigned from office; Wilson chose the pro-British Lansing to take his place. Wilson denounced the sinking of the *Lusitania* in harsh, threatening terms and demanded that Germany pledge never to launch another attack on the citizens of neutral nations, even when they were traveling in British or French ships. Germany acquiesced to Wilson's demand.

The resulting lull in submarine warfare was short-lived, however. In early 1916 the Allies began to arm their merchant vessels with guns and depth charges capable of destroying German U-boats. Considering this a provocation, Germany renewed its campaign of surprise submarine attacks. In March 1916 a German submarine torpedoed the French passenger liner *Sussex,* causing a heavy loss of life and injuring several Americans. Again Wilson demanded that Germany spare civilians from attack. In the so-called *Sussex* pledge, Germany once again relented but warned that it might resume unrestricted submarine warfare if the United States did not prevail upon Great Britain to permit neutral ships to pass through the naval blockade.

The German submarine attacks strengthened the hand of Theodore Roosevelt and others who had been arguing that war with Germany was inevitable and that the United States must prepare itself to fight. By 1916 Wilson could no longer ignore these critics. Between January and September of that year, he sought and won congressional approval for bills to increase the size of the Army and Navy, tighten federal control over National Guard forces, and authorize the building of a merchant fleet. In October he established the Council of National Defense to advise him on matters of war mobilization. But although Wilson, through his preparedness campaign, had conceded ground to the pro-war agitators, he did not share their belief that war with Germany was either inevitable or desirable. To the contrary, he accelerated his diplomatic initiatives to forestall the necessity of American military involvement. He dispatched Colonel House to London in January 1916 to draw up a peace plan with the British foreign secretary, Lord Grey. This initiative resulted in the House-Grey memorandum of February 22, 1916, in which Britain agreed to ask the United States to negotiate a settlement between the Allies and the Central Powers. The British believed that the terms of such a peace settlement would be favorable to the Allies and would include substantial American economic aid to Britain and France. Thus, they were furious when Wilson revealed that he wanted an impartial, honestly negotiated peace in which the claims of the Allies and Central Powers would be treated with equal respect and consideration. Britain now rejected U.S. peace overtures, and relations between the two countries grew unexpectedly tense.

The Peace Movement

Underlying Wilson's 1916 peace initiative was a vision of a new world order in which relations between nations would be governed by negotiation rather than war and in which justice would replace power as the fundamental principle of diplomacy. Wilson had been developing his views on a "New Diplomacy" for some time, but only in 1916 did he commit his presidency to their implementation. In a major foreign policy address on May 27 of that year, Wilson formally declared his support for what he would later call a League of Nations, an international parliament dedicated to the pursuit of peace, security, and justice for all the world's peoples.

In this effort to keep the United States out of war and to commit national prestige to the cause of international peace rather than conquest, Wilson enjoyed the support of a large number of Americans. Carrie Chapman Catt, president of the National American Woman Suffrage Association, and Jane Addams, founder of

Women for Peace • Women were in the forefront of the movement to keep the United States out of war, as was made clear on this billboard by the Organization of American Women for Strict Neutrality.

the Women's Peace Party, actively opposed the war. In 1915 an international women's peace conference at The Hague (in the Netherlands) had drawn many participants from the United States. A substantial pacifist group emerged among the nation's Protestant clergy. Midwestern progressives such as Robert La Follette, Bryan, and George Norris urged that the United States steer clear of this European conflict, as did prominent socialists such as Eugene V. Debs. In April 1916 many of the country's most prominent progressives and socialists joined hands in the American Union Against Militarism and pressured Wilson to continue pursuing the path of peace.

Wilson's peace campaign also attracted support from the country's sizable Irish and German ethnic populations, who were determined to block any formal military alliance with Great Britain. That many German ethnics, who continued to feel affection for their native land and culture, would oppose U.S. entry into the war is hardly surprising. And the Irish viewed England as an arrogant imperial power that kept Ireland under subjugation. That view was confirmed when England crushed the "Easter Rebellion" that Irish nationalists had launched on Easter Monday 1916 to win their country's independence. The Irish in America, like those in Ireland, wanted to see Britain's strength sapped (and Ireland's prospects for freedom enhanced) by a long war.

Wilson's Vision: "Peace without Victory"

The 1916 presidential election revealed the breadth of peace sentiment. At the Democratic convention, Governor Martin Glynn of New York, the Irish American keynote speaker who renominated Wilson for a second term, praised the president for keeping the United States out of war. His portrayal of Wilson as the "peace president" electrified the convention and made "He kept us out of war" a campaign slogan. The slogan proved particularly effective against Wilson's Republican opponent, Charles Evans Hughes, whose close ties to Theodore Roosevelt seemed to place him in the pro-war camp. Combining the promise of peace with a pledge to push ahead with progressive reform, Wilson won a narrow victory.

Emboldened by his electoral triumph, Wilson intensified his quest for peace. On December 16, 1916, he sent a peace note to the belligerent governments, entreating them to consider ending the conflict and, to that end, to state their terms for peace. Although Germany refused to specify its terms and Britain and France announced a set of conditions too extreme for Germany ever to accept, Wilson pressed ahead, initiating secret peace negotiations with both sides. To prepare the American people for what he hoped would be a new era of international relations, Wilson appeared before the Senate on January 22, 1917, to outline his plans for peace. In his speech, he reaffirmed his commitment to a League of Nations as an institution capable of preserving world peace. But for such a league to succeed in its difficult mission, Wilson argued, it would have to be handed a sturdy peace settlement. This entailed, in Wilson's memorable phrase, a "peace without victory," a peace that would both deny belligerents the joy of triumph and spare them the humiliation of defeat. A peace settlement that made no allowance for winners or losers would ensure the equality of the combatants, and "only a peace between equals can last."

Wilson then listed the crucial principles of a lasting peace: freedom of the seas; disarmament; and the right of every people to self-determination, democratic self-government, and security against aggression. Wilson was proposing not simply to end the war in ways that ensured peace between the Allies and the Central Powers. He was also advocating a revolutionary change in world order, one that would allow all the earth's peoples, regardless of their size or strength, to achieve political independence and to participate as equals in world affairs. These were uncommon views coming from the leader of a world power, and they stirred the despairing masses of Europe and elsewhere who were caught in a deadly conflict.

German Escalation

But Wilson's oratory came too late to serve the cause of peace. In early January, the German government had secretly embarked on a bold strategy to overpower the Allies, even at the risk of bringing the United States into the war. Sensing the imminent collapse of Russian forces on the eastern front, Germany had decided to throw its full military might at France and Britain. On land it planned to launch a massive assault on the trenches, and at sea it prepared to unleash its submarines to attack all vessels, belligerent and neutral, heading for British ports. Germany knew that this last action would compel the United States to enter the war, but it was gambling on being able to strangle the British economy and leave France isolated before significant numbers of American troops could reach European shores.

The United States learned of Germany's intention to resume unrestricted submarine warfare on February 1 and immediately broke off diplomatic relations. Wilson continued to hope for a negotiated settlement, however, until February 25, when the British intercepted and passed on to the president a telegram from Germany's foreign secretary, Arthur Zimmermann, to the German minister in Mexico. The infamous "Zimmermann telegram" instructed the minister to ask the Mexican government to attack the United States in the event of war between Germany and the United States. In return, Germany would pay the Mexicans a large fee and regain for them the "lost provinces" of Texas, New Mexico, and Arizona. Wilson, Congress, and the American public were outraged by the story, which had been given banner headlines in the nation's press. The United States was on the verge of declaring war.

In March news arrived that Tsar Nicholas II's autocratic regime in Russia had collapsed and had been replaced by a liberal-democratic government under the leadership of Alexander Kerensky. As long as the tsar ruled Russia and stood to benefit from the Central Powers' defeat, Wilson could not honestly claim that America's going to war against Germany would bring democracy to Europe. The fall of the tsar and the need of Russia's fledgling democratic government for support gave Wilson the rationale he needed to justify American intervention.

Appearing before a joint session of Congress on April 2, Wilson declared that the United States must enter the war because "the world must be made safe for democracy." He continued:

> We shall fight for the things which we have always carried nearest our hearts—for democracy, for the right of those who submit to authority to have a voice in their own

Governments, for the rights and liberties of small nations, for a universal dominion of right by such a concert of free peoples as shall bring peace and safety to all nations and make the world itself at last free. To such a task we dedicate our lives and our fortunes.

Inspired by his words, Congress broke into thunderous applause. Most members—although not all—had been persuaded to put aside their doubts. On April 6, Congress voted to declare war by a vote of 373 to 50 in the House and 82 to 6 in the Senate.

The United States thus embarked on a grand experiment to reshape the world. Wilson had given millions of people around the world reason to hope, both that the terrible war would soon end and that their strivings for freedom and social justice would be realized. Although he was taking America to war on the side of the Allies, he stressed that America would not itself become an "ally." It would fight as an "Associated Power" instead, a phrase meant to underscore America's independence and its determination to keep its war aims pure and disinterested.

Still, there was ample cause to worry. Many Americans remained opposed to the war and would refuse to join Wilson's crusade. And Wilson himself understood all too well the risks of his undertaking. A few days before his speech to Congress, he had confided to a journalist the likely impact of war on the American public. If he took the American people to war, Wilson feared, "they'll forget there ever was such a thing as tolerance. To fight you must be brutal and ruthless, and the spirit of ruthless brutality will enter into the very fibre of our national life, infecting Congress, the courts, the policeman on the beat, the man in the street."

American Intervention

The entry of the United States into the war gave the Allies the muscle they needed to defeat the Central Powers, but it almost came too late. Germany's resumption of unrestricted submarine warfare took a frightful toll on Allied shipping. From February through July 1917, German subs sank almost 4 million tons of shipping, more than one-third of Britain's entire merchant fleet. One of every four large freighters departing Britain in those months never returned; at one point, the British Isles were down to a mere four weeks of provisions. American intervention ended Britain's vulnerability in dramatic fashion. U.S. and British naval commanders now grouped merchant ships into convoys and provided them with warship escorts through the most dangerous stretches of the North Atlantic. Destroyers armed with depth charges were particularly effective as escorts. Their shallow draft made them invulnerable to torpedoes, and their great acceleration and speed allowed them to pursue slow-moving U-boats. The U.S. and British navies had begun to use sound waves (later called "sonar") to pinpoint the location of underwater craft, and this new technology increased the effectiveness of destroyer attacks. By the end of 1917, the tonnage of Allied shipping lost each month to U-boat attacks had declined by two-thirds, from almost 1 million tons in April to 350,000 tons in December. The increased flow of supplies stiffened the resolve of the exhausted British and French troops.

The French and British armies had bled themselves white by taking the offensive in 1916 and 1917 and had scarcely budged the trench lines. The Germans had been content in those years simply to hold their trench position in the West, for they were engaged in a huge offensive against the Russians in the East. The Germans intended first to defeat Russia and then to shift their eastern armies to the West for a final assault on the weakened British and French lines. Their opportunity came in the winter and spring of 1918.

A second Russian revolution in November 1917 had overthrown Kerensky's liberal-democratic government and had brought to power a revolutionary socialist government under Vladimir Lenin and his Bolshevik Party. Believing that the war was not in the best interests of the working classes, that it was a conflict between rival capitalist elites interested only in wealth and power (and indifferent to the slaughter of the masses in the trenches), Lenin pulled Russia out of the war. In March 1918 he signed a treaty at Brest-Litovsk that added to Germany's territory and resources and enabled Germany to shift its eastern forces to the western front.

Russia's exit from the war hurt the Allies. Not only did it expose French and British troops to a much larger German force, it also challenged the Allied claim that they were fighting a just war against German aggression. Lenin had published the texts of secret Allied treaties showing that Britain and France, like Germany, had plotted to enlarge their nations and empires through war. The revelation that the Allies were fighting for land and riches rather than democratic principles outraged large numbers of people in France and Great Britain, demoralized Allied troops, and threw the French and British governments into disarray. The treaties also embarrassed Wilson, who had brought America into the war to fight for democracy, not territory. But Wilson quickly restored the Allies' credibility by unveiling, in January 1918, a concrete program for peace. Wilson's Fourteen Points reaffirmed the American commitment to the "New Diplomacy" and renounced territorial aggrandizement as a legitimate war aim. This document provided the ideological cement that held the Allies together at a critical moment, persuading doubters that the war could yet serve progressive ends.

In March and April 1918, Germany launched its huge offensive against British and French positions, sending Allied troops reeling. A ferocious assault against French lines on May 27 met with little resistance; German troops advanced 10 miles a day—a pace not seen on the western front since the earliest days of the war—until they reached the Marne River, within striking distance of Paris. The French government prepared to evacuate the city. Its War Cabinet considered asking the Germans for an armistice. At this perilous moment, a large American army—fresh, well-equipped, and oblivious to the horrors of trench warfare—arrived to reinforce what remained of the French lines.

In fact, these American troops, part of the American Expeditionary Force (AEF) commanded by General John J. Pershing, had begun landing in France almost a year earlier. But it took many months to build up a sizable and disciplined force. The United States had had to create a modern army from scratch, because its existing force was small, ranking only 17th in the world, and largely untested. Men had to be drafted, trained, supplied with the necessary food and equipment; ships for transporting them to Europe had to be found or built. In France, Pershing put his troops through additional training before committing them to battle. He was determined that the American soldiers—or "doughboys," as they were called—should acquit themselves well on the battlefield, both to bring a decisive end to the war and

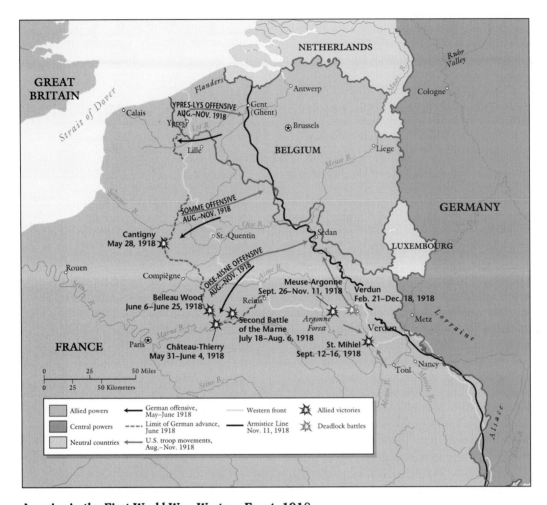

America in the First World War: Western Front, 1918

to counter the perception, held by Germans and Allies alike, that American troops were soft. Pershing would not be disappointed. The army he ordered into battle to counter the German spring offensive of 1918 fought well, with enthusiasm and bravery. Many American soldiers fell, but the German offensive ground to a halt. Paris was saved, and Germany's best chance for victory slipped from its grasp.

Buttressed by this show of AEF strength, the Allied troops staged a major offensive of their own in late September. Millions of Allied troops (including more than a million from the AEF) advanced across the 200-mile-wide Argonne forest in France, cutting German supply lines. By late October, they had reached the German border. Faced with an invasion of their homeland and with rapidly mounting popular dissatisfaction with the war, German leaders asked for an armistice, to be followed by peace negotiations based on Wilson's Fourteen Points. Having forced the Germans to agree to numerous concessions, the Allies ended the war on November 11, 1918. The carnage was finally over.

Mobilizing for "Total" War

Compared to Europe, the United States suffered little from the war. The deaths of 112,000 American soldiers paled in comparison to European losses: 900,000 by Great Britain, 1.2 million by Austria-Hungary, 1.4 million by France, 1.7 million by Russia, and 2 million by Germany. The U.S. civilian population was also spared most of the war's ravages—the destruction of homes and industries, the shortages of food and medicine, the spread of disease—that afflicted millions of Europeans. Only with the flu epidemic that swept across the Atlantic from Europe in 1919 to claim approximately 500,000 American lives did Americans briefly experience wholesale suffering and death.

Still, the war had a profound effect on American society. Every military engagement the United States had fought since the Civil War—the Indian wars, the Spanish-American War, the American-Filipino War, the Boxer Rebellion, the Latin American interventions—had been limited in scope. Even the troop mobilizations that seemed large at the time—the more than 100,000 needed to fight the Spanish and then the Filipinos—did not severely tax American resources. The First World War was different. It was a "total" war to which every combatant had committed virtually all its resources. The scale of the effort for the United States became apparent early in 1917 when Wilson asked Congress for a conscription law that would permit the federal government to raise a multimillion-man army. The United States would also have to devote much of its agricultural, transportation, industrial, and population resources to the war effort if it wished to end the European stalemate. Who would organize this massive effort? Who would pay for it? Would Americans accept the sacrifice and regimentation it would demand? These were vexing questions for a nation long committed to individual liberty, small government, and a weak military.

Organizing Industry

The question of how to organize the economy for war reopened a debate that Wilson and Roosevelt had engaged in during the presidential campaign of 1912 (see Chapter 2). Southern and midwestern Democrats, fearing the centralization of governmental authority, pushed for a decentralized, or New Freedom, approach to mobilization. Northeastern progressives, on the other hand, saw the war as an opportunity to realize their New Nationalist dream of establishing a strong state to regulate the economy, boost efficiency, and achieve social harmony. Siding at first with the New Freedom faction, Wilson delegated the chore of mobilization to local defense councils throughout the country. When that effort failed, however, Wilson moved to a New Nationalist position and created several centralized federal agencies—the War Industries Board, the National War Labor Board, the Aircraft Production Board, the U.S. Railroad Administration, the Emergency Fleet Corporation, the

Fuel Administration, and the Food Administration—each charged with supervising nationwide activity in its assigned economic sector.

The agencies exhibited varying success. The Food Administration, headed by mining engineer Herbert Hoover, was able to increase production of basic food-stuffs substantially through the use of economic incentives. Hoover also put in place an efficient distribution system that delivered food to millions of troops and European civilians. Under Hoover, a tireless and innovative administrator, the Food Administration was the federal government's most stunning achievement. Treasury Secretary William McAdoo, as head of the U.S. Railroad Administration, also per-formed well in shifting the rail system from private to public control, coordinating dense train traffic, and making capital improvements that allowed goods to move rapidly to eastern ports, where they were loaded onto ships and sent to Europe. At the other extreme, the Aircraft Production Board and Emergency Fleet Corpora-tion did a poor job of supplying the Allies with combat aircraft and merchant ves-sels. On balance, the U.S. economy performed wonders in supplying troops with uniforms, food, rifles, munitions, and other basic items; it failed badly, however, in producing more sophisticated weapons and machines such as artillery, aircraft, and ships.

At the time, the new government war agencies were thought to possess awesome power over the nation's economy and thus to represent a near-revolution in gov-ernment. But most of them were more powerful on paper than in fact. Consider, for example, the War Industries Board (WIB), an administrative body established by Wilson in July 1917 to harness the might of manufacturing to the needs of the military. The WIB floundered for the first nine months of its existence, as it lacked the statutory authority to force manufacturers and the military to adopt its plans. But the appointment of Wall Street investment banker Bernard Baruch as WIB chairman in March 1918 turned the agency around. Rather than attempting to force manufacturers to do the government's bidding, Baruch made war production too lucrative an activity to resist. He permitted industrialists to charge high prices for their products, thus significantly increasing their profits. He won exemptions from antitrust laws for corporations that complied with his requests, thereby strengthening their economic power. And Baruch filled the WIB with investment bankers and corporate lawyers from Wall Street, experienced capitalists whom man-ufacturers would instinctively trust. Baruch, however, did not hesitate to unleash his wrath upon corporations that resisted WIB enticements or to expose their recalci-trance to the furies of congressional and public opinion.

Baruch's forceful leadership worked reasonably well throughout his nine months in office. War production increased substantially, and manufacturers dis-covered the financial benefits of cooperation between the public and private sec-tors. But Baruch's approach created problems, too. His favoritism toward the large corporations hurt smaller competitors. Moreover, the cozy relationship between government and corporate America violated the progressive pledge to protect the people against the "interests." Achieving cooperation by boosting corporate profits was a costly way for the government to do business. Indeed, the costs of the war soared beyond anyone's expectations. When the United States entered the war, $10 billion was considered an extravagant estimate of what the war would cost (the federal government's annual budget prior to the war averaged only $700 million). By the time the war ended, its total cost had reached $33 billion.

Organizing Civilian Labor

The government worried as much about labor's cooperation as about industry's compliance, for the best-laid production plans could be disrupted by a labor shortage or an extended strike. The outbreak of war in 1914 had strengthened the market power of workers, because war orders from Europe prompted manufacturers to expand their production facilities and workforces. Meanwhile, the number of European immigrants plummeted—from more than 1 million in 1914, to 200,000 in 1915, to 31,000 in 1918. That meant that 3 million potential workers were lost to U.S. industry. The economy lost another 5 million workers to military service in 1917 and 1918.

Manufacturers responded to the shortage by encouraging potential workers around the country to come to their factories in the North. From the rural South, 500,000 African Americans migrated to the industrial centers of New York, Chicago, Detroit, Cleveland, Philadelphia, and St. Louis between 1916 and 1920. Another half-million white southerners followed the same path during that period.

The "Great Migration" • Job opportunities in northern industries prompted hundreds of thousands of African American sharecroppers and tenant farmers to leave the South between 1916 and 1920. Here, one migrating family travels north.

Hundreds of thousands of Mexicans fled their revolution-ridden homeland for agriculture, mining, and railroad jobs in the Southwest; some of them made their way to Kansas City, Chicago, and other manufacturing centers of the Midwest. Approximately 40,000 northern women found work as streetcar conductors, railroad workers, metalworkers, munitions makers, and in other jobs customarily reserved for men. The number of female clerical workers doubled between 1910 and 1920, with many of these women finding work in the government war bureaucracies. Altogether, a million women toiled in war-related industries.

These workers alleviated but did not eliminate the nation's acute labor shortage. Unemployment, which had been hovering around 8.5 percent in 1915, plunged to 1.2 percent in 1918. Workers were quick to recognize the benefits to be won from the tight labor market. White male workers quit jobs they did not like, confident that they could do better (opportunities for blacks, Mexicans, and women were more limited). Workers took part in strikes and other collective actions in unprecedented numbers. From 1916 to 1920 more than 1 million workers went on strike every year. Union membership almost doubled, from 2.6 million in 1915 to 5.1 million in 1920. Workers commonly sought higher wages and shorter hours through strikes and unionization. Wages rose an average of 137 percent from 1915 to 1920, although postwar inflation largely negated these gains. Between 1916 and 1920 the average workweek declined from 55 to 51 hours. Many workers achieved the 48-hour week. Workers also struck in response to managerial attempts to speed up production and tighten discipline. As time passed, increasing numbers of workers

Women Doing "Men's" Work • Labor shortages during the war years allowed thousands of women to take industrial jobs customarily reserved for men. The Union Pacific railroad hired these women in Cheyenne, Wyoming.

began to wonder why the war for democracy in Europe was not being matched by democratization of power in their factories at home. "Industrial democracy" became the battle cry of an awakened labor movement.

Wilson's willingness to include labor in his 1916 progressive coalition reflected his awareness of labor's potential power (see Chapter 2). In 1917 he was the first U.S. president to address a convention of the American Federation of Labor (AFL). And in 1918 he bestowed prestige on the newly formed National War Labor Board (NWLB) by appointing former president William Howard Taft as one of its two cochairmen. The NWLB brought together representatives of labor, industry, and the public to resolve labor disputes. AFL president Samuel Gompers' presence on the board gave unions a strong national voice in government affairs. In return for his appointment, Gompers was expected to mobilize workers behind Wilson, discredit socialists who criticized the war, and discourage strikes that threatened war production. The support Gompers received from the NWLB's public representatives—men like Frank Walsh and Felix Frankfurter, who firmly believed that working conditions needed improvement and that workers had a right to organize themselves into unions—gave the NWLB a pro-labor slant. Although, like most other federal wartime agencies, the NWLB lacked the ability to impose its will, it managed to pressure many manufacturers into improving wages and hours, reducing wage discrimination, and allowing their workers to join unions.

Organizing Military Labor

Only when it came to raising an army did the federal government use its full power without hesitation. From the very start, the Wilson administration rejected the idea of a volunteer army. Instead, Wilson committed himself to conscription—to the drafting of most men of a certain age, irrespective of their family's wealth, ethnic background, or social standing. The Selective Service Act of May 1917 empowered the administration to do just that. By war's end, local Selective Service boards had registered 24 million young men age 18 and older, and had drafted nearly 3 million of them into the military. Another 2 million volunteered for service.

There was relatively little resistance to the draft, even among recently arrived immigrants. The Selective Service Administration may have defused the potential resistance of immigrants by exempting from military service all males who had not filed naturalization papers. Even with that exemption, foreign-born men constituted 18 percent of the armed forces—a percentage greater than their share of the total population. Almost 400,000 African Americans served, representing approximately 10 percent, the same as the percentage of African Americans in the total population. Many more would undoubtedly have served had southern draft boards permitted more of them to register and had the Marines and other service branches been willing to accept African Americans into their ranks.

The U.S. Army, under the command of Chief of Staff Peyton March and General John J. Pershing, faced the difficult task of fashioning these ethnically and racially diverse millions into a professional fighting force. Teaching raw recruits to fight was hard enough, Pershing and March observed; teaching them to put aside their racial and ethnic prejudices was a task they refused to tackle. Rather than integrate the armed forces, they segregated black soldiers from white. Virtually all African

OUR
REGULAR DIVISIONS

Honored and Respected by All
Enlist for the Infantry –
or in one of the other 12 branches.
Nearest Recruiting Office :

Recruiting Soldiers • This poster played a part in the government's campaign to attract young men to the Army. Here soldiering is depicted as an opportunity to dress in a smart uniform, protect one's country, and earn the devotion of the nation's women.

Americans were assigned to all-black units that were barred from combat. Being stripped of a combat role was particularly galling to blacks, who, in previous wars, had proven themselves to be among the best American fighters. Pershing was fully aware of the African American contribution. He himself had commanded African American troops in the 10th Cavalry, the all-black regiment that had distinguished itself in the Spanish-American War (Chapter 3). Pershing's military reputation had depended so heavily on the black troops who fought for him that he had acquired the nickname "Black Jack."

For a time, the military justified its intensified discrimination against blacks by referring to the results of rudimentary "IQ" (intelligence quotient) tests administered by psychologists to 2 million AEF soldiers. These tests allegedly "proved" that native-born Americans and immigrants from the British Isles, Germany, and Scandinavia were well endowed with intelligence, while African Americans and immigrants from southern and eastern Europe were poorly endowed. But these tests were scientifically so ill-conceived that their findings revealed nothing about the true distribution of intelligence in the population. The tests' most sensational revelation was that more than half of the soldiers in the AEF—white and black—were "morons," men who had failed to reach the mental age of 13. After trying to absorb the apparent news that most U.S. soldiers were feeble-minded, the military sensibly rejected the pseudo-science on which these intelligence findings were based. In 1919 it discontinued the IQ testing program.

Given the sharp racial and ethnic differences among American troops and the short time Pershing and his staff had to train recruits, the performance of the AEF was impressive. The United States increased the size of the Army from a mere 100,000 to 5 million in little more than a year. No troop ships were sunk by the Germans, nor were any soldiers killed during the dangerous Atlantic crossing. In combat, U.S. troops became known for their sharpshooting skills. The most decorated soldier in the AEF was Sergeant Alvin C. York of Tennessee, who captured 35 machine guns and 132 prisoners and who killed 17 German soldiers with 17 bullets. York had learned his marksmanship hunting wild turkeys in the Tennessee hills. "Of course, it weren't no trouble nohow for me to hit them big [German] army targets," he later commented. "They were so much bigger than turkeys' heads."

One of the most decorated AEF units was New York's 369th Regiment, a black unit recruited in Harlem. Bowing to pressure from civil rights groups like the NAACP that some black troops be allowed to fight, Pershing had offered the 369th to the French army. The 369th entered the French front line, served in the forward Allied trenches for 191 days (longer than any other U.S. regiment), and scored one major success after another. In gratitude for its service, the French government decorated the entire unit with one of its highest honors—the *Croix de Guerre.*

Paying the Bills

Raising and maintaining a 5-million-man military force and securing the cooperation of employers, farmers, and workers contributed to the cost of the war. As chief purchaser of food, uniforms, munitions, weapons, vehicles, and sundry other items for the U.S. military, the government incurred huge debts. To help pay its bills, it sharply increased tax rates and launched a high-pressure campaign to sell war bonds. The new taxes hit the wealthiest Americans the hardest: The richest were slapped with a 67 percent income tax and a 25 percent inheritance tax. Corporations were ordered to pay an "excess profits" tax. Proposed by the Wilson administration and backed by Robert La Follette and other congressional progressives who feared that the "interests" would use the war to enrich themselves, these taxes were meant to ensure that all Americans would sacrifice something for the war.

The revenues brought in by the taxes, however, provided only about one-third of the $33 billion that the government ultimately spent on the war. The rest came from the sale of "Liberty Bonds." These were 30-year bonds the government sold to individuals with a return of 3½ percent in annual interest. The government offered five bond issues between 1917 and 1920 and all were quickly sold out. Their success was due in no small measure to a high-powered sales pitch, orchestrated by Treasury Secretary William G. McAdoo, that equated bond purchases with patriotic duty. McAdoo's agents blanketed the country with posters, sent bond "salesmen" into virtually every American community to speak to unionists, businessmen, fraternal orders, ethnic societies, and women's clubs, enlisted Boy Scouts to go door-to-door, and staged rallies at which movie stars such as Mary Pickford, Douglas Fairbanks, and Charlie Chaplin stumped for the war.

Arousing Patriotic Ardor

The Treasury's bond campaign was only one aspect of an extraordinary government effort to arouse public support for the war. In 1917 Wilson set up a new agency, the Committee on Public Information (CPI), to publicize and popularize the war. Under the chairmanship of George Creel, a midwestern progressive and a muckraker, the CPI conducted an unprecedented propaganda campaign. The CPI distributed 75 million copies of pamphlets explaining U.S. war aims in several languages. It trained a force of 75,000 "Four Minute Men" to deliver succinct, uplifting war speeches to numerous groups in their home cities and towns. It papered the walls of virtually every public institution (and many private ones) with posters, placed advertisements in mass-circulation magazines, sponsored exhibitions, and peppered newspaper editors with thousands of press releases on the progress of the war.

Faithful to his muckraking past, Creel wanted to give the people "the facts" of the war, believing that well-informed citizens would see the wisdom of Wilson's policies. He also felt his work gave him an opportunity to achieve the progressive goal of uniting all Americans into a single moral community. Consequently, CPI propaganda appealed to Americans' highest ideals—their faith in democracy, their yearning for community, their belief in justice. Americans everywhere were told that the United States had entered the war "to make the world safe for democracy," to help the world's weaker peoples achieve self-determination, to bring a measure of social justice into the conduct of international affairs. Americans were asked to affirm those ideals by doing everything they could to support the war.

This uplifting message had a profound effect on the American people, although not always in ways anticipated by CPI propagandists. It imparted to many a deep love of country and a sense of participation in a grand democratic experiment. Among others it sparked a new spirit of independence, in particular among those who were experiencing poverty, powerlessness, and discrimination. Workers, women, European ethnics, and African Americans began demanding that America live up to its democratic ideals at home as well as abroad. Workers by the hundreds of thousands, and then by the millions, rallied to the cry of "industrial democracy." Women seized upon the democratic fervor to bring their fight for suffrage to a successful conclusion (see Chapter 2). African Americans began to dream that the war might deliver them from second-class citizenship. European ethnics believed that Wilson's support of their countrymen's rights abroad would improve their own chances for success in the United States.

Although the CPI had helped to unleash it, this new democratic enthusiasm troubled Creel and others in the Wilson administration who were charged with maintaining national unity. The United States, after all, was still deeply divided along class, ethnic, and racial lines. During the war, as before, workers and industrialists regarded each other with suspicion. Cultural differences compounded this class division, for the working class was overwhelmingly ethnic in composition, while the industrial and political elites consisted mainly of the native-born whose families had been "Americans" for generations. Progressives had fought hard to overcome these divisions. They had tamed the power of capitalists, improved the condition of workers, encouraged the Americanization of immigrants, and articulated a new, more inclusive idea of American nationhood. But their work was far from complete when

Unifying a Heterogenous People • This multilingual poster urging coal miners to work harder for "the boys in the trenches" illustrates the magnitude of the problem confronting government officials charged with achieving a unified home front: How could they successfully unite workers who could not understand each other?

the war broke out, and the war itself opened up new social and cultural divisions. German immigrants still formed the largest foreign-born group—2.3 million—in the population. Another 2.3 million immigrants came from some part of the Austro-Hungarian Empire. And more than 1 million Americans—native-born and immigrants—supported the Socialist Party and the Industrial Workers of the World, both of which had opposed the war. The decision to authorize the CPI's massive unity campaign is evidence that the progressives understood how widespread the discord was. Still, they had not anticipated that the promotion of democratic ideals at home would exacerbate, rather than lessen, the nation's social and cultural divisions.

Wartime Repression

By early 1918 the CPI's campaign had developed a darker, more coercive side. Now its hymns to national unity were accompanied by accusations of ethnic disloyalty and working-class subversion. Inflammatory advertisements called on patriots to report on neighbors, coworkers, and ethnics whom they suspected of subverting the war effort. Propagandists called on all immigrants, especially those from central, southern, and eastern Europe, to pledge themselves to "100 percent Americanism" and to repudiate all ties to their homeland, native language, and ethnic customs. Those who resisted were warned that they might be forcibly stripped of the foreign cultural traits they were unwilling to shed voluntarily. The CPI aroused hostility to Germans, for example, by spreading lurid tales of German atrocities and encouraging the public to see movies like *The Prussian Cur* and *The Beast of Berlin*. The Department of Justice arrested thousands of German and Austrian immigrants whom it suspected of subversive activities. Congress passed the Trading with the Enemy Act, which required foreign-language publications to submit all war-related stories to post office censors for approval.

German Americans became the objects of popular hatred. American patriots sought to expunge every trace of German influence from American culture. In Boston, performances of Beethoven's symphonies were banned, and the German-born conductor of the Boston Symphony Orchestra was forced to resign. Although Americans would not give up the German foods they had grown to love, they would no longer call them by their German names. Sauerkraut was rechristened "liberty

Anti-German Hysteria • As appeals to patriotism failed to engender unity, the government turned to tales of German atrocities. In this still image from a government-produced "Liberty Loan" movie, a brutal German soldier is about to ravish a beautiful and innocent young woman beneath a crucifix. As a result of this and related efforts, anti-German feelings reached a fevered pitch.

Renamed German American Words

Original	"Patriotic" Name
hamburger	salisbury steak, liberty steak, liberty sandwich
sauerkraut	liberty cabbage
Hamburg Avenue, Brooklyn, New York	Wilson Avenue, Brooklyn, New York
Germantown, Nebraska	Garland, Nebraska
East Germantown, Indiana	Pershing, Indiana
Berlin, Iowa	Lincoln, Iowa
pinochle	liberty
German shepherd	Alsatian shepherd
Deutsches Hans of Indianapolis	Athenaeum of Indiana
Germania Maennerchor of Chicago	Lincoln Club
Kaiser Street	Maine Way

Source: From La Vern J. Rippley, *The German Americans* (Boston: Twayne Publishers, 1976), p. 186; and Robert H. Ferrell, *Woodrow Wilson and World War I, 1917–1921* (New York: Harper and Row, 1985), pp. 205–206.

cabbage," hamburgers became "liberty sandwiches." Libraries removed works of German literature from their shelves, while Theodore Roosevelt and others urged school districts to prohibit the teaching of the German language. Patriotic school boards in Lima, Ohio, and elsewhere burned the German books in their districts.

German Americans were at risk of being fired from work, losing their businesses, and being assaulted on the street. A St. Louis mob lynched an innocent German immigrant whom they suspected of subversion. After only 25 minutes of deliberation, a St. Louis jury acquitted the mob leaders, who had brazenly defended their crime as an act of patriotism. German Americans began hiding their ethnic identity, changing their names, speaking German only in the privacy of their homes, celebrating their holidays only with trusted friends. This experience devastated the once-proud German American community; many would never recover from the shame and vulnerability they experienced in those years.

The anti-German campaign escalated into a general anti-immigrant crusade. Congress passed the Immigration Restriction Act of 1917, over Wilson's veto, which declared that all adult immigrants who failed a reading test would be denied admission to the United States. The act also banned the immigration of laborers from India, Indochina, Afghanistan, Arabia, the East Indies, and several other countries within an "Asiatic Barred Zone." This legislation marked the beginning of a movement in Congress that, four years later, would close the immigration door to virtually all transoceanic peoples. Congress also passed the Eighteenth Amendment to the Constitution, which prohibited the manufacture and distribution of alcoholic beverages (see Chapter 2). The crusade for Prohibition was not new, but anti-immigrant feelings generated by the war gave it added impetus. Prohibitionists pictured the nation's urban ethnic ghettos as scenes of drunkenness, immorality, and disloyalty. They also accused German American brewers of operating a "liquor trust" to sap people's will to fight. The Eighteenth Amendment was quickly ratified by the states, and in 1919 Prohibition became the law of the land.

More and more, the Wilson administration relied on repression to achieve domestic unity. In the Espionage, Sabotage, and Sedition Acts passed in 1917 and 1918, Congress gave the administration sweeping powers to silence and even imprison dissenters. These acts went far beyond outlawing behavior that no nation at war could be expected to tolerate, such as spying for the enemy, sabotaging war production, destroying war matériel, and calling for the enemy's victory. By making it illegal to write or utter any statement that could be construed as profaning the flag, the Constitution, or the military, they constituted the most drastic restriction of free speech at the national level since enactment of the Alien and Sedition Acts of 1798.

Government repression fell most heavily on the IWW and the Socialist Party, which viewed the war as a cruel game staged by U.S. and European capitalists to make money. Both groups had opposed intervention before 1917. Although they subsequently muted their opposition, they continued to insist that the true enemies of American workers were to be found in the ranks of American employers, not in Germany or Austria-Hungary. The government responded by banning many socialist materials from the mails and by disrupting socialist and IWW meetings. By the spring of 1918 government agents had raided every IWW office in the country and had arrested 2,000 IWW members, including its entire executive board. Most of those arrested would be sentenced to long jail terms. William Haywood, the IWW president, fled to Europe and then to the Soviet Union rather than go to jail. Eugene V. Debs, the head of the Socialist Party, received a 10-year jail term for making an antiwar speech in Canton, Ohio, in the summer of 1918.

This official repression, carried out in an atmosphere of supercharged patriotism, unleashed wave after wave of repression carried out by the people themselves. In the mining town of Bisbee, Arizona, a sheriff with an eager force of 2,000 deputized citizens kidnapped 1,200 IWW members, herded them into cattle cars, and dumped them onto the New Mexico desert with hardly any food or water. Vigilantes in Butte, Montana, chained an IWW organizer to a car and let his body scrape the pavement as they drove the vehicle through city streets. Then they strung him up to a railroad trestle, castrated him, and left him to die.

Citizens who judged federal action to be inadequate organized groups to enforce patriotism. The largest of these, the American Protective League, functioned as an agency of surveillance. Its 250,000 members, most of them businessmen and professionals, routinely spied on fellow workers and neighbors, opened the mail and tapped the phones of those suspected of disloyalty, and harassed—sometimes to the point of assault—young men who were thought to be evading the draft. Attorney General Thomas Gregory publicly endorsed the group and sought federal funds to support its "police" work.

The spirit of coercion even infected institutions that had long prided themselves on tolerance. In July 1917 Columbia University fired two professors for speaking out against U.S. intervention in the war. The National Americanization Committee, which prior to 1917 had pioneered a humane approach to the problem of integrating immigrants into American life, now supported surveillance, internment, and deportation of aliens suspected of anti-American sentiments. The intolerance that Wilson had feared the war would unleash had materialized.

Wilson himself bore significant responsibility for this climate of repression. On the one hand, he did attempt to block certain pieces of repressive legislation; for example, he vetoed both the Immigration Restriction Act and the Volstead Act (the act passed by Congress to enforce Prohibition), only to be overridden by Congress. But on the other hand Wilson did little to halt Attorney General Gregory's prosecution of radicals or Postmaster General Burleson's campaign to exclude Socialist Party publications from the mail. He ignored pleas from progressives that he intervene in the Debs case to prevent the ailing 62-year-old from going to jail. His acquiescence in these matters cost him dearly among progressives and socialists, groups that had given Wilson critical support in the 1916 election. Wilson did not regard the damage as fatal, however. He believed that once the Allies, with U.S. support, won the war and arranged a just peace in accordance with the Fourteen Points, his administration's wartime actions would be forgiven and the progressive coalition would be restored.

The Failure of the International Peace

In the month following Germany's surrender on November 11, 1918, Wilson was confident about the prospects of achieving a just peace. Both Germany and the Allies had publicly accepted the Fourteen Points as the basis for negotiations. Wilson's international prestige was enormous. People throughout the world were inspired by his dream of a democratic, just, and harmonious world order free of poverty, ignorance, and war. Poles, Lithuanians, and other eastern Europeans whose pursuit of nationhood had been frustrated for 100 years or more now believed that independence might be within their reach. Zionist Jews in Europe and the United States dared to dream of a Jewish homeland within their lifetimes. Countless African and Asian peoples imagined achieving their freedom from colonial domination.

To capitalize on his fame and to maximize the chances for a peace settlement based on his Fourteen Points, Wilson broke sharply with diplomatic precedent and decided to head the American delegation to the Paris Peace Conference in January 1919 himself. Enormous crowds of wildly enthusiastic Europeans turned out to hail Wilson's arrival on the continent in December. Some 2 million French citizens— the largest throng ever assembled on French soil—lined the parade route in Paris to catch a glimpse of "Wilson, *le juste* [the just]." In Rome, Milan, and La Scala near-delirious Italians acclaimed him "The Savior of Humanity" and "The Moses from Across the Atlantic."

In the Fourteen Points, Wilson had translated his principles for a new world order into specific proposals for world peace and justice. The first group of points called for all nations to abide by a code of conduct that embraced free trade, freedom of the seas, open diplomacy, disarmament, and the resolution of disputes through mediation. A second group, based on the principle of self-determination, proposed redrawing the map of Europe to give the subjugated peoples of the Austro-Hungarian, Ottoman, and Russian empires national sovereignty. The last point called for establishing a League of Nations, an assembly in which all nations

"Savior of Humanity" • Wherever he traveled in Europe, Woodrow Wilson was greeted by huge, delirious crowds that were eager to thank him for ending Europe's terrible war and to endorse his vision of a peaceful, democratic world. Here millions of Italians greet Wilson's 1919 arrival in Milan.

would be represented and in which all international disputes would be given a fair hearing and an opportunity for peaceful solutions.

The Paris Peace Conference and the Treaty of Versailles

Although representatives of 27 nations began meeting in Paris on January 12, 1919, to discuss Wilson's Fourteen Points, negotiations were controlled by the "Big Four": Wilson, Prime Minister David Lloyd George of Great Britain, Premier Georges Clemenceau of France, and Prime Minister Vittorio Orlando of Italy. When Orlando quit the conference after a dispute with Wilson, the Big Four became the Big Three. Wilson quickly learned that his negotiating partners' support for the Fourteen Points was much weaker than he had believed. The cagey Clemenceau mused: "God gave us the Ten Commandments, and we broke them. Wilson gives us Fourteen Points. We shall see." Indeed, Clemenceau and Lloyd George refused to include most of Wilson's points in the peace treaty. The points having to do with freedom of the seas and free trade were omitted, as were the proposals for open diplomacy and Allied disarmament. Wilson won partial endorsement of the principle of self-determination: Belgian sovereignty was restored, Poland's status as a nation was affirmed, and the new nations of Czechoslovakia, Yugoslavia, Finland, Lithuania, Latvia, and Estonia were created. Some lands of the former Ottoman Empire—Armenia, Palestine, Mesopotamia, and Syria—were to be placed under League of

Nations' trusteeships with the understanding that they would some day gain their independence. But Wilson failed in his efforts to block a British plan to transfer former German colonies in Asia to Japanese control, an Italian plan to annex territory inhabited by 200,000 Austrians, and a French plan to take from Germany its valuable Saar coal mines.

Nor was Wilson able to blunt the drive to punish Germany for its wartime aggression. In addition to awarding the Saar basin to France, the Allies gave portions of northern Germany to Denmark and portions of eastern Germany to Poland and Czechoslovakia. Germany was stripped of virtually its entire navy and air force, and forbidden to place soldiers or fortifications in western Germany along the Rhine. It was allowed to keep an army of only 100,000 men. In addition, Germany was forced to admit its responsibility for the war. In accepting this "war guilt," Germany was, in effect, agreeing to compensate the victors in cash ("reparations") for the pain and suffering it had inflicted on them.

Lloyd George and Clemenceau brushed off the protests of those who viewed this desire to prostrate Germany as a cruel and vengeful act that would lower the chances of a genuine peace. That the German people, after their nation's 1918 defeat, had overthrown the monarch (Kaiser Wilhelm II) who had taken them to war, and had reconstituted their nation as a democratic republic—the first in their country's history—won them no leniency. In 1921 an Allied commission notified the Germans that they were to pay the victors $33 billion, a sum well beyond what a defeated and economically ruined Germany could muster. In insisting that Germany bear total responsibility for the loss of life and property, the Allies conveniently—and disingenuously—denied the role of their own governments in bringing on the war. The Treaty of Versailles was signed by Great Britain, France, the United States, Germany, and other European nations on June 28, 1919.

The League of Nations

The Allies' single-minded pursuit of self-interest disillusioned many liberals and socialists in the United States. But Wilson seemed not to be dismayed, for he had won approval of the most important of his Fourteen Points—the point that called for the creation of the League of Nations. The League, whose structure and responsibilities were set forth in the Covenant attached to the peace treaty, would usher in Wilson's new world order. Drawing its membership from the signatories to the Treaty of Versailles (except, for the time being, Germany), the League would function as an international parliament and judiciary, establishing rules of international behavior and resolving disputes between nations through rational and peaceful means. A nine-member executive council—the United States, Britain, France, Italy, and Japan would have permanent seats on the council, while the other four seats would rotate among the smaller powers—was charged with administering decisions.

The League, Wilson believed, would redeem the failures of the Paris Peace Conference. Under its auspices, free trade and freedom of the seas would be achieved, reparations against Germany would be reduced or eliminated, disarmament of the Allies would proceed, and the principle of self-determination would be extended to peoples outside Europe. Moreover, the League would have the power to punish

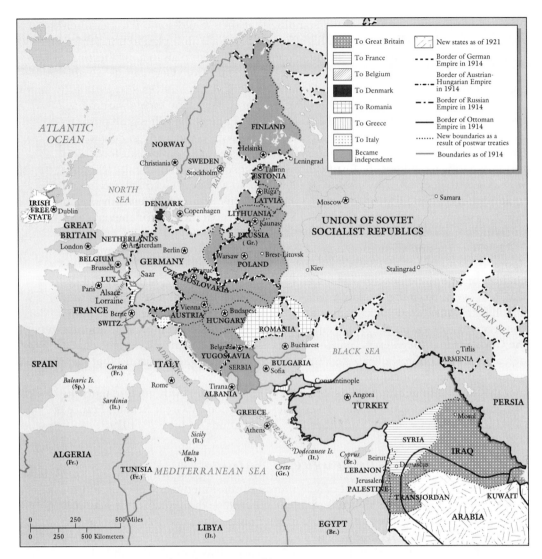

Europe and the Near East after the First World War

aggressor nations—those who violated "the territorial integrity and existing political independence" of League members. Such aggressors, Article X of the Covenant made clear, would be subject to economic isolation and military retaliation.

Wilson versus Lodge: The Fight over Ratification

For the League to succeed, however, Wilson had to convince the U.S. Senate to ratify the Treaty of Versailles. Wilson knew that this would be no easy task. The Republicans had gained a majority in the Senate in 1918, and two groups within their ranks were determined to frustrate Wilson's ambitions. One group was a caucus of 14 midwesterners and westerners known as the "irreconcilables." Most of them were conservative isolationists who wanted the United States to preserve its separation from Europe, but a few were prominent progressives—Robert La Follette, William Borah, and Hiram Johnson—who had voted against the declaration of war in 1917. The blatant self-interest displayed at the peace conference confirmed this group's suspicion that the European Allies were cunning and ruthless and incapable of decent behavior in international matters. Under no circumstances would they support a plan that would embroil the United States in European affairs.

The second opposition group was led by Senator Henry Cabot Lodge of Massachusetts. These Republicans rejected the principles that underlay the very creation of the League. They did not subscribe to Wilson's belief that every group of people on earth had a right to form their own nation; that every state, regardless of its size, its economic condition, and the vigor and intelligence of its people, should have a voice in world affairs; and that disputes between nations could be settled in open, democratic forums. They subscribed instead to Theodore Roosevelt's vision of a world controlled by a few great nations, each militarily strong, secure in its own sphere of influence, and determined to avoid war through a carefully negotiated balance of power. In other words, these Republicans were internationalists, but of a sort much different from Wilson. They preferred to let Europe return to the power politics that had prevailed before the war rather than experiment with a new world order that might constrain and compromise U.S. power and autonomy.

This Republican critique was a cogent one that merited extended discussion. Of particular importance were the questions raised about the power given the League by Article X to undertake military actions against aggressor nations. Did Americans want to authorize an international organization to decide when the United States would go to war? Was this not a violation of the Constitution, which vested war-making power solely in the Congress? Even if the constitutional problem could be solved, how could the United States ensure that it would not be forced into a military action that might damage its national interest?

It soon became clear, however, that a number of the Republicans, especially Lodge, were more interested in humiliating Wilson than in engaging in debate. They had never liked his domestic reform policies, and they now accused him of promoting socialism through his wartime expansion of government power. They were angry that he had failed to include any distinguished Republicans, such as Lodge, Elihu Root, or William Howard Taft, on the Paris peace delegation. And they were still bitter about the 1918 congressional elections, when Wilson, in an effort to win votes for Democratic candidates, had argued that a Republican victory would embarrass the nation abroad in a critical moment in world affairs. Though Wilson's electioneering had failed to sway the voters (the Republicans won a majority in both Houses), his suggestion that a Republican victory would injure national honor had infuriated Theodore Roosevelt and his supporters. Roosevelt died in 1919, but his close friend Lodge kept his rage alive. "I never thought I could hate a man as much as I hate Wilson," Lodge conceded in a moment of candor.

As chairman of the Senate Foreign Relations Committee, which was charged with considering the treaty before reporting it to the Senate floor, Lodge had considerable power, and he did everything possible to obstruct ratification. He packed the committee with senators likely to oppose the treaty. He delayed action by reading every one of the treaty's 300 pages aloud and by subjecting it to endless criticism in six long weeks of public hearings. When his committee finally reported the treaty to the full Senate, it came encumbered with nearly 50 amendments whose adoption Lodge made a precondition of his support. Some of the amendments expressed reasonable concerns—namely, that participation in the League not diminish the role of Congress in determining foreign policy, or compromise the sovereignty of the nation, or involve the nation in an unjust or ill-advised war. But many were meant only to complicate the task of ratification.

Despite Lodge's obstructionism, the treaty's chances for ratification by the required two-thirds majority of the Senate were still good. In most parts of the country, public sentiment was running heavily in favor of the treaty. And, within the Senate itself, many Republicans were prepared to vote for ratification if Wilson indicated his willingness to accept some of the proposed amendments. Wilson, who had handled Congress brilliantly during his first term, possessed the political savvy to salvage the treaty and, along with it, U.S. participation in the League of Nations. But at this crucial moment in national and world history, his political skills deserted him. He refused to compromise. He announced that he would carry his case directly to the people. In September 1919 he undertook a whirlwind cross-country tour that covered more than 8,000 miles with 37 stops. He addressed as many crowds as he could reach, sometimes speaking for an hour at a time, four times a day. Although his audiences grew larger and more responsive, their enthusiasm was of little consequence. In thinking that this "appeal to the country" would force Republican senators to change their votes, Wilson had gravely miscalculated. All he achieved was his own physical exhaustion.

On September 25, after giving a speech at Pueblo, Colorado, Wilson suffered excruciating headaches throughout the night. His physician ordered him back to Washington, where on October 2 he suffered a near-fatal stroke. Wilson hovered near death for two weeks and remained seriously disabled for another six. His condition improved somewhat in November, but his left side remained paralyzed, his speech was slurred, his energy level low, and his emotions dangerously unstable. Wilson's wife, Edith Bolling Wilson, and his doctor isolated him from Congress and the press, withholding news they thought might upset him and preventing the public from learning how much his body and mind had deteriorated.

Many historians believe that Wilson's stroke intensified his tendency toward self-righteousness, petulance, and rigidity. It is likely that the stroke impaired Wilson's political judgment. If so, that may explain his refusal to consider any of the Republican amendments to the treaty, even after it had become clear that compromise offered the only chance of winning U.S. participation in the League of Nations. When Lodge presented an amended treaty for a ratification vote on November 19, Wilson ordered Senate Democrats to vote against it; 42 (of 47) Democratic senators complied, and with the aid of 13 Republican irreconcilables, the Lodge version was defeated. Only moments later, the unamended version of the treaty—Wilson's version—received only 38 votes.

The Treaty's Final Defeat

As the magnitude of the calamity became apparent, supporters of the League in Congress, the nation, and the world urged the Senate and the president to reconsider.

The British government, groups representing millions of League supporters throughout the United States, prominent Democrats—all pushed for compromise. Wilson would not budge. A bipartisan group of senators desperately tried to work out a compromise without consulting him. When that effort failed, the Senate put to a vote, one more time, the Lodge version of the treaty. Because 23 Democrats, most of them southerners, still refused to break with Wilson, this last-ditch effort at ratification failed on March 8, 1920, by a margin of 7 votes. Wilson's dream of a new world order died that day. The crumpled figure in the White House seemed to bear little resemblance to the hero who, barely 15 months before, had been greeted in Europe as the world's savior. Wilson filled out his remaining 12 months in office as an invalid, presiding over the interment of progressivism. He died in 1924.

The judgment of history lies heavily upon these events, for the flawed treaty and the failure of the League are thought by many to have contributed to Adolf Hitler's rise and the outbreak of a second world war even more terrifying than the first. It is necessary to ask, then, whether American participation in the League would have significantly altered the course of world history.

The mere fact of U.S. membership in the League would not have magically solved Europe's postwar problems. The U.S. government was inexperienced in diplomacy and prone to mistakes. Its freedom to negotiate solutions to international disputes would have been limited by the large number of American voters who remained strongly opposed to American entanglement in European affairs. Even if such opposition could have been overcome, the United States would still

---

Woodrow Wilson's Fourteen Points, 1918: Record of Implementation

1. Open covenants of peace openly arrived at	Not fulfilled
2. Absolute freedom of navigation upon the seas in peace and war	Not fulfilled
3. Removal of all economic barriers to the equality of trade among nations	Not fulfilled
4. Reduction of armaments to the level needed only for domestic safety	Not fulfilled
5. Impartial adjustments of colonial claims	Not fulfilled
6. Evacuation of all Russian territory; Russia to be welcomed into the society of free nations	Not fulfilled
7. Evacuation and restoration of Belgium	Fulfilled
8. Evacuation and restoration of all French lands; return of Alsace-Lorraine to France	Fulfilled
9. Readjustment of Italy's frontiers along lines of Italian nationality	Compromised
10. Self-determination for the former subjects of the Austro-Hungarian Empire	Compromised
11. Evacuation of Romania, Serbia, and Montenegro; free access to the sea for Serbia	Compromised
12. Self-determination for the former subjects of the Ottoman Empire; secure sovereignty for Turkish portion	Compromised
13. Establishment of an independent Poland with free and secure access to the sea	Fulfilled
14. Establishment of a League of Nations affording mutual guarantees of independence and territorial integrity	Compromised

Source: From G. M. Gathorne-Hardy, *The Fourteen Points and the Treaty of Versailles,* Oxford Pamphlets on World Affairs, no. 6 (1939), pp. 8–34; and Thomas G. Paterson et al., *American Foreign Policy: A History,* 2nd ed. (Lexington, Mass.: D. C. Heath, 1983), vol. 2, pp. 282–293.

have confronted European countries determined to go their own way. And, as we have learned from United Nations policies in Bosnia and elsewhere in the 1990s, international organizations can fail in their peacekeeping responsibilities.

Nevertheless, one thing is clear: No stable international order could have arisen after the First World War without the full involvement of the United States. The United States emerged from the war as both the greatest economic power in the world and as a leading military power. The League of Nations required American authority and prestige in order to operate effectively as an international parliament. We cannot know whether the League, with American involvement, would have offered the Germans a less humiliating peace, allowing them to rehabilitate their economy and salvage their national pride; nor whether an American-led League would have stopped Hitler's expansionism before it escalated into full-scale war in 1939. Still, it seems fair to suggest that American participation would have strengthened the League and improved its ability to bring a lasting peace to Europe.

The Postwar Period: A Society in Convulsion

The end of the war brought no respite from the forces that were convulsing American society. Workers were determined to regain the purchasing power they had lost to inflation. Employers were determined to halt or reverse the wartime gains labor had made. Radicals saw in this conflict between capital and labor the possibility of a socialist revolution. Conservatives were certain that the revolution (led by American Bolsheviks) had already begun. Returning white servicemen were nervous about regaining their civilian jobs and looked with hostility on the black, Hispanic, and female workers who had been recruited to take their places. Black veterans were in no mood to return to segregation and subordination. The federal government, meanwhile, uneasy over the centralization of power during the war, quickly dismantled such agencies as the War Industries Board and the National War Labor Board. By so doing, it deprived itself of mechanisms that might have enabled it to intervene in social conflicts and keep them from erupting into rage and violence.

Labor-Capital Conflict

Nowhere was the escalation of conflict more evident than in the workplace. In 1919, 4 million workers—one-fifth of the nation's manufacturing workforce—went on strike. In January 1919, a general strike paralyzed the city of Seattle when 60,000 workers walked off their jobs. By August, walkouts had been staged by 400,000 eastern and midwestern coal miners, 120,000 New England textile workers, and 50,000 New York City garment workers. Then came two strikes that turned public opinion sharply against labor. In September, Boston policemen walked off their jobs after the police commissioner refused to negotiate with their newly formed union. Rioting and looting soon broke out. University students, businessmen, and veterans tried to patrol the streets but failed. Other Boston unions debated whether to come to the strikers' aid, but, in the end, they were reluctant to support a walkout of policemen. Massachusetts Governor Calvin Coolidge, outraged by the policemen's

The Seattle General Strike • Some 60,000 Seattle workers walked off their jobs in January 1919 during the first of several massive labor demonstrations that year.

betrayal of their sworn public duty, refused to negotiate with them, called out the National Guard to restore order, and then fired the entire police force. His tough stand would bring him national fame and the Republican vice presidential nomination in 1920.

Hard on the heels of the policemen's strike came a strike by more than 300,000 steelworkers in the Midwest. Led by U.S. Steel, the largest corporation in the world, the mighty steel industry symbolized the economic power of the United States. No union had established a footing in this industry since the 1890s, when Andrew Carnegie had ousted the ironworkers' union from his Homestead, Pennsylvania, mills. Most steelworkers labored long hours (the 12-hour shift was still standard) for low wages in workplaces where they were exposed to serious injury. The organizers of the 1919 strike had somehow managed to persuade steelworkers with varied skill levels and ethnic backgrounds to put aside their differences and demand an eight-hour day and union recognition. When the employers rejected those demands—and refused even to meet with union committees—the workers walked off their jobs. The employers responded by procuring armed guards to beat up the strikers and by hiring nonunion labor to keep the plants running. In many areas, local and state police enlisted by the employers prohibited union meetings, ran strikers out of town, and opened fire on those who disobeyed orders. In Gary, Indiana, a confrontation between unionists and armed guards left 18 strikers dead. To arouse public support for their antiunion campaign, industry leaders painted the strike leaders as dangerous and violent radicals bent on the destruction of political liberty and economic freedom. They succeeded in arousing public opinion against the steelworkers, and the strike collapsed in January 1920. The defeat was shattering for unionists.

Radicals and the Red Scare

The steel companies succeeded in putting down the strike by fanning the public's fear that revolutionary sentiment was spreading among the workers. Radical sentiment was indeed on the rise. Mine workers and railroad workers had begun calling for the permanent nationalization of coal mines and railroads. Longshoremen in San Francisco and Seattle refused to load ships carrying supplies to the White Russians who had taken up arms against Lenin's Bolshevik government. Socialist trade unionists mounted the most serious challenge to Gompers' control of the AFL in 25 years. In 1920, nearly a million Americans voted for the Socialist presidential candidate Debs, who ran his campaign from the Atlanta Federal Penitentiary. Small groups of anarchists contemplated, and occasionally carried out, bomb attacks on businessmen and public officials.

This radical surge did not mean, however, that leftists had fashioned themselves into a single movement or political party. On the contrary, the Russian Revolution had split the American Socialist Party. One faction, which would keep the name Socialist and would continue to be led by Debs, insisted that radicals follow a democratic path to socialism rather than the dictatorial path taken by Lenin's Bolsheviks. The other group, which would take the name Communist, wanted to establish a Lenin-style "dictatorship of the proletariat" in the United States. Small groups of anarchists, some of whom advocated campaigns of terror to speed the revolution, represented yet a third radical tendency; by and large, the anarchists refused to make common cause with either the socialists or the communists.

The fact that the radical camp was in such disarray escaped the notice of most Americans, who assumed that radicalism was a single, coordinated movement bent on establishing a communist government on American soil. They saw the nation's vast immigrant communities as breeding grounds for Bolshevism. Beginning in 1919, this perceived "Red Scare" prompted government officials and private citizens to embark on yet another campaign of repression.

The postwar repression of radicalism closely resembled the wartime repression of dissent. Thirty states passed sedition laws to punish people who advocated revolution. Numerous public and private groups intensified Americanization campaigns designed to strip foreigners of their "subversive" ways and remake them into loyal citizens. Universities fired radical professors, and vigilante groups wrecked the offices of socialists and tortured IWW agitators. A newly formed veterans' organization, the American Legion, took on the American Protective League's role of identifying seditious individuals and organizations and making sure that the public's devotion to "100 percent Americanism" did not abate.

The Red Scare reached its climax on New Year's Day 1920 when federal agents broke into the homes and meeting places of thousands of suspected revolutionaries in 33 cities across the country. Directed by Attorney General A. Mitchell Palmer, these widely publicized "Palmer raids" were meant to expose the extent of revolutionary activity and to establish the ambitious Palmer as the chief guardian of national security and traditional values. Palmer's agents, expecting to find evidence that radicals were arming themselves for revolution, uncovered three pistols, no rifles, and no explosives. Nevertheless, they arrested 6,000 people and kept many of them in jail for weeks without formally charging them with a crime. Finally, those who were not citizens (approximately 500) were deported and the rest were released.

Palmer's failure to expose a revolutionary plot blunted support for him in official circles. But that did not deter Palmer, who now alleged that revolutionaries were planning a series of assaults on government officials and government buildings for May 1, 1920. When nothing happened on that date, his credibility suffered another serious blow.

As Palmer's exaggerations of the Red threat became known, many Americans began to reconsider their near-hysterical fear of dissent and subversion. But the political atmosphere remained hostile to radicals, as the Sacco and Vanzetti case revealed. In May 1920, two Italian-born anarchists, Nicola Sacco and Bartolomeo Vanzetti, were arrested in Brockton, Massachusetts, and charged with armed robbery and murder. Both men proclaimed their innocence and insisted that they were being punished for their political beliefs. Indeed, their foreign accents and their defiant espousal of anarchist doctrines in the courtroom inclined many Americans, including the judge who presided at their trial, to view them harshly. Although the case against them was weak, they were convicted of first-degree murder and sentenced to death. Their lawyers attempted numerous appeals, all of which failed. Anger over the verdicts began to build, first among Italian Americans, then among radicals, and finally among liberal intellectuals. Protests compelled the governor of Massachusetts to appoint a commission to review the case, but no new trial was ordered. On August 23, 1927, Sacco and Vanzetti were executed, still insisting that they were innocent.

Racial Conflict and the Rise of Black Nationalism

The hundreds of thousands of African Americans who came north during the war carried with them dreams of deliverance from southern servitude. In northern industries, many of them found their first well-paying jobs. The more than 400,000 blacks who served in the armed forces believed that a victory for democracy abroad would help them achieve democracy for themselves at home. At first, the discrimination they encountered in the military did not weaken their conviction that they would be treated as full-fledged citizens upon their return. Many began to talk about the birth of a "New Negro"—independent and proud. Thousands joined the NAACP, which was at the forefront of the fight for black equality. By 1918, there were 100,000 African Americans subscribing to the NAACP's magazine, *The Crisis,* whose editor, W. E. B. Du Bois, had urged them to support the war.

That wartime optimism made the discrimination and hatred African Americans encountered after the war hard to endure. Many black workers who had found jobs in the North were fired to make way for returning white veterans. Returning black servicemen, meanwhile, had to scrounge for poorly paid jobs as unskilled laborers. In the South, lynch mobs targeted black veterans who were no longer willing to tolerate the usual insults and indignities; 10 of the 70 blacks lynched in the South in 1919 were veterans.

The worst antiblack violence that year occurred in the North, however, in a series of urban race riots. Crowded conditions during the war had forced black and white ethnic city dwellers into uncomfortably close proximity. Ethnic whites had themselves been the target of discrimination by native-born Americans. But that experience had not made all of them advocates of racial equality; instead, many regarded blacks with a mixture of fear and prejudice. They resented having to share neighborhoods, trolleys, parks, streets, and workplaces with blacks. They also wanted blacks barred from unions, seeing them as threats to their job security rather than as fellow workers.

Racial tensions escalated into race riots. The deadliest explosion occurred in Chicago in July 1919, when a black teenager who had been swimming in Lake Michigan was killed by whites after coming too close to a whites-only beach. Rioting soon broke out throughout the city, with white mobs invading black neighborhoods, torching homes and stores, and attacking innocent residents. Led by war veterans, some of whom were armed, the blacks fought back, turning the border areas between white and black neighborhoods into battle zones. Fighting raged for five days, leaving 38 dead (23 black, 15 white) and more than 500 injured. Race rioting in other cities pushed the death total to 120 before the summer of 1919 ended.

The riots made it clear to blacks that the North was not the Promised Land. Confined to unskilled jobs and to segregated neighborhoods with substandard housing and exorbitant rents, black migrants in Chicago, New York, and other northern cities suffered severe economic hardship throughout the 1920s. The NAACP carried on its campaign for civil rights and racial equality, but many blacks no longer shared its belief that they would one day be accepted as first-class citizens. They turned instead to a compelling leader from Jamaica, Marcus Garvey, who gave voice to their bitterness. "The first dying that is to be done by the black man in the future," Garvey declared in 1918, "will be done to make himself free. And then when we are finished, if we have any charity to bestow, we may die for the white man. But as for me, I think I have stopped dying for him."

Garvey called on blacks to give up their hopes for integration and to set about forging a separate black nation. He argued that racial mixing would never work, and reminded blacks that they possessed a rich culture stretching back over the centuries that would enable them to achieve greatness as a nation. Garvey's grand vision was to build a black nation in Africa that would bring together all the world's people of African descent. In the short term, he wanted to help American and Caribbean blacks to achieve economic and cultural independence.

Garvey's call for black separatism and self-sufficiency—or, black nationalism, as it came to be called—elicited a remarkable response among blacks in the United States. In the early 1920s, the Universal Negro Improvement Association (UNIA), which Garvey had founded, enrolled millions of members in 700 branches in 38 states. His newspaper, *The Negro World,* reached a circulation of 200,000. The New York chapter of UNIA embarked on an ambitious economic development program and set up grocery stores, restaurants, and factories. Garvey's most visible economic venture was the Black Star Line, a shipping company with three ships that proudly flew the UNIA flag from their masts.

Marcus Garvey, Black Nationalist • A Jamaican native, Marcus Garvey became a popular figure among African Americans, many of whom, by 1919 and 1920, had lost faith in America's commitment to racial equality.

This black nationalist movement did not endure for long, however. Garvey entered into bitter disputes with other black leaders, including W. E. B. Du Bois, who regarded him as a flamboyant, self-serving demagogue. Garvey sometimes showed poor judgment, as when he expressed support for the Ku Klux Klan on the grounds that it shared his pessimism about the possibility of racial integration. Inexperienced in economic matters as well, Garvey squandered a great deal of UNIA money on abortive business ventures. The U.S. government regarded his rhetoric as inflammatory and sought to silence him. In 1923 he was convicted of mail fraud involving the sale of Black Star stocks and was sentenced to five years in jail. In 1927 he was deported to Jamaica and the UNIA folded. But Garvey's philosophy of black nationalism endured.

Conclusion

The resurgence of racism in 1919 and the consequent turn to black nationalism among African Americans were signs of how the high hopes of the war years had been dashed. Industrial workers, immigrants, and radicals also learned through bitter experience that the fear, intolerance, and repression unleashed by the war interrupted their pursuit of liberty and equality. They came to understand as well that Wilson's commitment to these ideals counted for less than did his administration's and Congress's determination to discipline a people whom they regarded as dangerously heterogeneous and unstable. Of the reform groups, only woman suffragists made enduring gains—especially the right to vote—but, for the feminists in their ranks, these steps forward did not compensate for the collapse of the progressive movement and, with it, their program of achieving equal rights for women across the board.

A similar disappointment engulfed those who had embraced and fought for Wilson's dream of creating a new and democratic world order. The world in 1919 appeared as volatile as it had been in 1914. More and more Americans—perhaps even a majority—were coming to believe that U.S. intervention had been a colossal mistake.

In other ways, the United States benefited a great deal from the war. By 1919, the American economy was by far the world's strongest. Many of the nation's leading corporations had improved productivity and management during the war. U.S. banks were poised to supplant those of London as the most influential in international finance. The nation's economic strength triggered an extraordinary burst of growth in the 1920s, and millions of Americans rushed to take advantage of the prosperity that this "people's capitalism" had put within their grasp. But the joy generated by affluence did not dissolve the class, ethnic, and racial tensions that the war had exposed. And the failure of the peace process added to Europe's problems, delayed the emergence of the United States as a leader in world affairs, and created the preconditions for another world war.

Chronology

1914   First World War breaks out (July–August)

1915   German submarine sinks *Lusitania* (May 7)

1916   Woodrow Wilson unveils peace initiative • Wilson reelected as "peace president"

1917   Germany resumes unrestricted submarine warfare (February) • Tsar Nicholas II overthrown in Russia (March) • U.S. enters the war (April 6) • Committee on Public Information established • Congress passes Selective Service Act, Espionage Act, Immigration Restriction Act • War Industries Board established • Lenin's Bolsheviks come to power in Russia (Nov.)

1918   Lenin signs treaty with Germany, pulls Russia out of war (March) • Germany launches offensive on western front (March–April) • Congress passes Sabotage Act and Sedition Act • French, British, and U.S. troops repel Germans, advance toward Germany (April–October) • Eugene V. Debs jailed for making antiwar speech • Germany signs armistice (Nov. 11)

1919   Treaty of Versailles signed (June 28) • Chicago race riot (July) • Wilson suffers stroke (September 25) • Police strike in Boston

1919–1920   Steelworkers strike in Midwest • Red Scare prompts "Palmer raids" • Senate refuses to ratify Treaty of Versailles • Universal Negro Improvement Association grows under Marcus Garvey's leadership

1920   Anarchists Sacco and Vanzetti convicted of murder

1923   Marcus Garvey convicted of mail fraud

1924   Woodrow Wilson dies

1927   Sacco and Vanzetti executed

Suggested Readings

On the factors leading to the outbreak of war in Europe in 1914, see James Joll, *The Origins of the First World War* (1984), and Fritz Fisher, *Germany's War Aims in the First World War* (1972). On the horrors of trench warfare, see John Keegan, *The Face of Battle* (1976), and Erich Maria Remarque's classic novel, *All Quiet on the Western Front* (1929). Paul Fussell, *The Great War and Modern Memory* (1973), is indispensable for understanding the effects of the First World War on European culture.

American Neutrality and Intervention

On American neutrality, see Arthur S. Link, *Woodrow Wilson: Revolution, War and Peace* (1979); John Milton Cooper Jr., *The Vanity of Power: American Isolationism and the First World War, 1914–1917* (1969); and Ernest R. May, *The World War and American Isolation, 1914–1917* (1959). Roland C. Marchand, *The American Peace Movement and Social Reform, 1898–1918* (1972), reconstructs the large and influential antiwar movement, while Ross Gregory, *The Origins of American Intervention in the First World War* (1971), analyzes the events that triggered America's intervention. Daniel R. Beaver, *Newton D. Baker and the American War Effort, 1917–1919* (1966), and John W. Chambers, *To Raise an Army: The Draft Comes to Modern America* (1987), analyze efforts to raise a multimillion-man fighting machine. Russell Weigley, *The American Way of War* (1973), examines the combat experiences of the American Expeditionary Force, while David F. Trask, *The AEF and Coalition Warmaking, 1917–1918* (1973), looks at relations between the AEF and the Allied armies. On the soldiers themselves, consult J. Garry Clifford, *The Citizen Soldiers* (1972), and A. E. Barbeau and Florette Henri, *The Unknown Soldiers: Black American Troops in World War I* (1974). Frank E. Vandiver, *Black Jack: The Life and Times of John J. Pershing* (1977), chronicles the life of the AEF's commander. Daniel H. Kevles, "Testing the Army's Intelligence: Psychologists and the Military in World War I," *Journal of American History* 55 (December 1968): 565–582, examines the military's use and misuse of IQ tests.

The Home Front

David Kennedy, *Over Here: The First World War and American Society* (1980), is a superb account of the effects of war on American society, but it should be supplemented with Robert H. Ferrell, *Woodrow Wilson and World War I, 1917–1921* (1985), and Ronald Schaffer, *America in the Great War: The Rise of the War Welfare State* (1991). On industrial mobilization, see Robert D. Cuff, *The War Industries Board: Business-Government Relations during World War I* (1973), and the pertinent sections of Jordan Schwarz, *The Speculator* (1981), an excellent biography of Bernard Baruch. Efforts to secure labor's cooperation are examined in Valerie J. Connor, *The National War Labor Board* (1983); Keith Grieves, *The Politics of Manpower, 1914–1918* (1988); and Frank L. Grubb, *Samuel Gompers and the Great War* (1982). On the migration of African Americans to northern industrial centers and the movement of women into war production, see Florette Henri, *Black Migration: Movement North, 1900–1920* (1975); Joe William Trotter Jr., ed., *The Great Migration in Historical Perspective: New Dimensions of Race, Class, and Gender* (1991); James R. Grossman, *Land of Hope: Chicago, Black Southerners, and the Great Migration* (1989); and Maurine W. Greenwald, *Women, War and Work* (1980). David Montgomery, *The Fall of the House of Labor: The Workplace, the State, and American Labor Activism, 1865–1925* (1987), expertly reconstructs the escalation of labor-management tensions during the war, but it should be read alongside Joseph A. McCartin, *Labor's Great War: The Struggle for Industrial Democracy and the Origins of Modern Labor Relations, 1912–1921* (1997). Charles Gilbert, *American Financing of World War I* (1970), is indispensable on wartime tax and bond policies. See also Sidney Ratner, *Taxation and Democracy in America* (1967), and Dale N. Shook, *William G. McAdoo and the Development of National Economic Policy, 1913–1918* (1987).

Government Propaganda and Repression

Stephen Vaughn, *Holding Fast the Inner Lines: Democracy, Nationalism, and the Committee on Public Information* (1980), is an important account of the CPI, the government's central propaganda agency. See also George Creel, *How We Advertised America* (1920); John A. Thompson, *Reformers and War: Progressive Publicists and the First World War* (1987); and Walton Rawls, *Wake Up, America! World War I and the American Poster* (1987). The government's turn to repression as a way of achieving social unity can be followed in Zechariah Chafee Jr., *Free Speech in the United States* (1941); Harry N. Scheiber, *The Wilson Administration and Civil Liberties, 1917–1921* (1960); Harold C. Peterson and Gilbert Fite, *Opponents of War, 1917–1918* (1968); and William Preston Jr., *Aliens and Dissenters: Federal Suppression of Radicals, 1903–1933* (1966). John Higham, *Strangers in the Land: Patterns of American Nativism, 1865–1925* (1955), and Frederick C. Luebke, *Bonds of Loyalty: German-Americans and World War I* (1974), analyze the effects of this repression on European ethnic communities. Carol S. Gruber, *Mars and Minerva: World War I and the Uses of Higher Learning in America* (1975), discusses the effect of war on universities.

Woodrow Wilson and the League of Nations

The best introduction is Thomas J. Knock, *To End All Wars: Woodrow Wilson and the Quest for a New World Order* (1992). For a more critical view of Wilson's motives, however, consult Arno Mayer, *The Politics and Diplomacy of Peacemaking: Containment and Counterrevolution at Versailles, 1918–1919* (1967); N. Gordon Levin Jr., *Woodrow Wilson and World Politics: America's Response to War and Revolution* (1968); and Lloyd C. Gardner, *Safe for Democracy: The Anglo-American Response to Revolution, 1913–1923* (1984). On Republican opposition to the League of Nations, see Ralph Stone, *The Irreconcilables: The Fight against the League of Nations* (1970), and William C. Widenor, *Henry Cabot Lodge and the Search for an American Foreign Policy* (1980).

Postwar Strikes and Radicalism

Nell Irvin Painter, *Standing at Armageddon: The United States, 1877–1919* (1987), offers a good overview of the class and racial divisions that convulsed American society in 1919. Consult Dana Frank, *Purchasing Power: Consumer Organizing, Gender, and the Seattle Labor Movement, 1919–1929* (1994), on the Seattle general strike; Francis Russell, *A City in Terror* (1975), on the Boston police strike; and David Brody, *Labor in Crisis: The Steel Strike of 1919* (1965), on the steel strike. James Weinstein, *The Decline of Socialism in America, 1912–1925* (1967), and Theodore Draper, *The Roots of American Communism* (1957), analyze the effects of the Bolshevik Revolution on American socialism. On the Red Scare, consult Robert K. Murray, *Red Scare: A Study in National Hysteria* (1955); Stanley Coben, *A. Mitchell Palmer: Politician* (1963); and Richard Polenberg, *Fighting Faiths: The Abrams Case, the Supreme Court, and Free Speech* (1987). Roberta Strauss Feuerlicht, *Justice Crucified* (1977), and Francis Russell, *Tragedy in Dedham* (1962), offer divergent interpretations of the Sacco-Vanzetti affair. Paul Avrich, *Sacco-Vanzetti: The Anarchist Background* (1991), reconstructs the anarchist milieu from which Sacco and Vanzetti emerged.

Race Riots and Black Nationalism

William Tuttle Jr., *Race Riot: Chicago in the Red Summer of 1919* (1970), and Elliott M. Rudwick, *Race Riot at East St. Louis* (1964), examine the two most notorious race riots of 1919. On the emergence of Marcus Garvey and the Universal Negro Improvement Association, see Judith Stein, *The World of Marcus Garvey: Race and Class in Modern Society* (1986), and David Cronon, *Black Moses* (1955).

5

The 1920s

Americans elected a president in 1920, Warren G. Harding, who could not have been more different from his predecessor, Woodrow Wilson. A Republican, Harding boasted of his "Main Street" origins and presented himself as a common man with common desires. In his 1920 campaign he called for a "return to normalcy." Although he died in office in 1923, his carefree spirit is thought to characterize the 1920s.

To many Americans, indeed, the decade was one of fun rather than reform, of good times rather than high ideals. It was, in the words of novelist F. Scott Fitzgerald, the "Jazz Age," a time when the quest for personal gratification seemed to replace the quest for public welfare.

Despite Harding's call for a return to a familiar past, America seemed to be rushing headlong into the future. The word "modern" began appearing everywhere: modern times, modern women, modern technology, the modern home, modern marriage. Although the word was rarely defined, it connoted certain beliefs: that science was a better guide to life than religion; that people should be free to choose their own lifestyles without fear of community or divine censure; that sex should be a source of pleasure for women as well as men; that women and minorities should be equal to and enjoy the same rights as white men.

Many other Americans, however, deplored this embrace of the new and tried to revive the values of traditional America. They reaffirmed their belief that God's word transcended science; that people should obey the moral code set forth in the Bible; that women were not equal to men; and that blacks, Mexicans, and eastern European immigrants were inferior to Anglo-Saxon whites. They made their voices heard in a resurgent Ku Klux Klan and the fundamentalist movement, and on issues such as evolution and immigration. In seeking to restore an older America, they found themselves arguing against their nation's commitment to liberty and equality.

Modernists and traditionalists confronted each other in party politics, in legislatures, in courtrooms, and in the press. Their battles make it impossible to think of the 1920s merely as a time for the pursuit of leisure. Nor were the 1920s free of economic and social problems that had troubled Americans for decades.

Prosperity

Despite the strains placed on the U.S. economy after the First World War, it remained strong and innovative during the 1920s. The nation had not suffered the loss of factories, roads, and electrical lines that Germany and France had experienced. Its industries had emerged intact, even strengthened, from the war. The war needs of the Allies had created an insatiable demand for American goods and capital. Manufacturers and bankers, with prodding and promises of profits by the government, had exported so many goods and extended so many loans to the Allies that by war's end the United States was the world's leading creditor nation. New York City challenged London as the hub of world finance. At home, the government had helped the large corporations and banks to consolidate their power. Corporate America had responded by lifting productivity and efficiency to new heights through advances in technology and management.

For a time after the war ended, the country did experience economic turmoil and depression. From 1919 to 1921, it struggled to redirect industry from wartime production to civilian production, a process slowed by the government's hasty withdrawal from its wartime role as economic regulator and stabilizer. Workers went on

The "Jazz Age" in Paris • African American artists who had moved to Europe played an important role in exporting innovations in American music, dance, and theater. This 1920s poster advertises an event starring Josephine Baker, the African American cabaret star who became one of the most celebrated cultural figures in Paris.

strike to protest wage reductions or increases in the workweek. Farmers were hit by a severe depression as the overseas demand for American foodstuffs fell from its peak of 1918 and 1919. Disgruntled workers and farmers even joined forces to form statewide farmer-labor parties, which for a time threatened to disrupt the country's two-party system in the upper Midwest. In 1924 the two groups formed a national Farmer-Labor Party. Robert La Follette, their presidential candidate, received an impressive 16 percent of the vote that year. But then the third-party movement fell apart.

Its collapse reflected a rising public awareness of how vigorous and productive the economy had become. Beginning in 1922, the nation embarked on a period of remarkable growth. From 1922 to 1929, gross national product grew at an annual rate of 5.5 percent, rising from $149 billion to $227 billion. The unemployment rate never exceeded 5 percent—and real wages rose about 15 percent.

A Consumer Society

The rate of economic growth was matched by the variety of products being produced. In the 19th century economic growth had rested primarily on the production of capital goods, such as factory machinery and railroad tracks, that made production and distribution more efficient. In the 1920s, however, growth rested more on the proliferation of consumer goods. Some products, such as cars and telephones, had been available since the early 1900s, but in the 1920s their sales reached new levels. In 1920, just 12 years after Ford introduced the Model T, there were 8 million cars on the road. By 1929, there were 27 million—one for every five Americans. Other consumer goods became available for the first time—tractors, washing machines, refrigerators, electric irons, radios, and vacuum cleaners. The term "consumer durable" was coined to describe such goods, which, unlike food, clothing, and other "perishables," were meant to last. Even "perishables" took on new allure. Scientists had discovered the importance of vitamins in the diet and began urging Americans to consume more fresh fruits and vegetables. The agricultural economy of southern California grew rapidly as urban demand for the region's fresh fruits and vegetables skyrocketed. Improvements in refrigeration and in packaging, meanwhile, made it possible to transport fresh produce long distances and to extend its shelf life in grocery stores. And more and more stores were being operated by large grocery chains that could afford the latest refrigeration and packaging technology.

The public responded to these innovations with excitement. American industry had made fresh food and stylish clothes available to the masses. It had put within the reach of ordinary people an array of machines meant to make their work easier and their leisure more fun. Refrigerators, vacuum cleaners, and washing machines would spare women much of the drudgery of housework. Radios would expand the public's cultural horizons. Automobiles, asphalt roads, service stations, hot dog stands, "tourist cabins" (the forerunners of motels), and traffic lights seemed to herald a wholly new civilization. By the middle of the decade the country was a network of paved roads. City dwellers now had easy access to the country and made a ritual of day-long excursions. Camping trips and long-distance vacations became routine.

Farmers and their families could now hop into their cars and head for the nearest town with its stores, movies, amusement parks, and sporting events. Suburbs proliferated, billed as the perfect mix of urban and rural life. Young men and women everywhere discovered that cars were a place where they could "make out," and even make love, without fear of reproach by prudish parents or prying neighbors.

In the 1920s Americans also discovered the excitement of owning stocks. The number of stockholders in AT&T, the nation's largest corporation, rose from 140,000 to 568,000. The number holding stock in U.S. Steel grew from 96,000 to 146,000. By 1929, as many as 7 million Americans owned stock, most of them people of ordinary, middle-class means. This widespread ownership of stocks reflected the need of the nation's corporations for working capital. Because privately held wealth was not enough to satisfy that need, corporations sought to sell their stocks and bonds to the general public. They were assisted in that endeavor by a New York Stock Exchange that was able to process complicated transactions.

A People's Capitalism

Capitalists boasted that they had created a "people's capitalism" in which virtually all Americans could participate. Gone were the days in which capitalism had enriched only a lucky few. Now, everyone could own a piece of corporate America. Now, everyone could have a share of luxuries and amenities. Poverty, capitalists claimed, had been banished, and the gap between rich and poor had been closed. If every American could own a car and house, buy quality clothes, own stock, take vacations, and go to the movies, then clearly there was no longer any significant inequality in society.

Actually, not everyone was participating in the people's capitalism. Although wages were rising, millions of Americans still did not earn enough income to partake fully of the marketplace. Robert and Helen Lynd were social scientists who studied the people of Muncie, Indiana, a small industrial city of 35,000, and published their findings in a classic study entitled *Middletown*. They discovered that working-class families who bought a car often did not have enough money left for other goods. One housewife admitted, "We don't have no fancy clothes when we have the car to pay for. . . . The car is the only pleasure we have." Another declared, "I'll go without food before I'll see us give up the car." But many industrialists resisted any increase in wages, and workers lacked the organizational strength to force them to pay more.

One solution came with the introduction of consumer credit. Car dealers, home appliance salesmen, and other merchants began to offer installment plans that enabled consumers to purchase a product by making a down payment and promising to pay the rest in installments. That was an important innovation. Before the 1920s houses were just about the only thing ordinary consumers could purchase on credit. By 1930, however, 15 percent of all purchases—60 percent of all cars and 75 percent of all radios—were made on the installment plan.

Even so, many poor Americans benefited little from the consumer revolution. Middle-class Americans acquired a disproportionate share of cars, refrigerators, washing machines, and other consumer durables. They also were the main consumers of fresh vegetables and the main buyers of stock.

The Rise of Advertising and Mass Marketing

But even middle-class consumers had to be wooed. How could they be persuaded to buy another car only a few years after they had bought their first one? General Motors had the answer: Make the new one seem more attractive than the old one, or make consumers feel embarrassed for not having the latest model. So, in 1926, General Motors introduced the concept of the annual model change. In each of its five divisions—Buick, Oldsmobile, Pontiac, Cadillac, and Chevrolet—cars were given a different look every year as GM engineers changed headlights and chassis colors, streamlined bodies, and added new features. The strategy worked. GM leaped past Ford and became the world's largest car manufacturer.

In response, Henry Ford reluctantly introduced his Model A in 1927 to provide customers with a colorful alternative to the drab Model T, but he was not convinced that consumers would spend money on changes he regarded as trivial and irrelevant to a car's utility. Having spent his lifetime selling a product renowned for its utility and reliability, Ford could not believe that sales could be increased by appealing to the intangible hopes and fears of consumers. He was wrong. The desire to be beautiful, handsome, or sexually attractive; to exercise power and control; to demonstrate competence and success; to escape anonymity, loneliness, and boredom; to experience pleasure—all such desires, once activated, could motivate a consumer to buy a new car at a time when the old one was still serviceable, or to spend money on goods that might have once seemed frivolous to some.

Arousing such desires required more than producing cleverly designed commodities that beckoned to consumers with their bright colors, sleek lines, and attractive packaging. It called for advertising campaigns intended to make a product seem to be the answer to the consumer's desires. To create those campaigns, corporations turned to a new kind of company: professional advertising firms. They were led by such people as Edward Bernays, Doris Fleischmann, and Bruce Barton—well-educated, sensitive to public taste, and understanding of human psychology. The new advertising entrepreneurs believed that many Americans felt buffeted by forces they could not control, bewildered by bureaucratic workplaces and the anonymity of urban living. This modern anomie, they argued, left consumers susceptible to suggestion.

In their campaigns, advertisers played upon the emotions and vulnerabilities of their target audiences. One cosmetics ad decreed: "Unless you are one woman in a thousand, you must use powder and rouge. Modern living has robbed women of much of their natural color." A perfume manufacturer's ad pronounced: "The first duty of woman is to attract. . . . It does not matter how clever or independent you may be, if you fail to influence the men you meet, consciously or unconsciously, you are not fulfilling your fundamental duty as a woman." A mouthwash ad warned about one unsuspecting gentleman's bad breath—"the truth that his friends had been too delicate to mention"—which stood between him and the success he so obviously otherwise deserved, while a tobacco ad matter-of-factly declared: "Men at the top are apt to be pipe-smokers. . . . It's no coincidence— pipe-smoking is a calm and deliberate habit—restful, stimulating. His pipe helps a man think straight. A pipe is back of most big ideas."

Bernays, Fleischmann, Barton, and the other new advertising professionals felt that their ads amounted to more than manipulation. They believed they were helping people to manage their lives in ways that would increase their satisfaction and pleasure. By enhancing one's appearance and personality with the help of goods to be found in the marketplace, one would have a better chance of achieving success and happiness. Their goal was to help consumers free their true selves through the acquisition of certain products.

American consumers responded enthusiastically. Their interest in fashion, their eagerness to fill their homes with the latest products, their alacrity to take up the craze of the moment (mah-jongg, crossword puzzles, miniature golf) all evidenced Americans' preoccupation with self-improvement and personal pleasure. The most enthusiastic of all were middle-class Americans, who could afford to buy what the advertisers were selling. Many of them were newcomers to middle-class ranks, searching for ways to affirm—or even create—their new identity. The aforementioned ad for pipe tobacco, for example, was certainly targeted at the new middle-class man—who held a salaried position in a corporate office or bank, or worked as a commission salesman, or owned a small business.

As male wage earners moved into the new middle class, their wives were freed from the necessity of outside work. Advertisers appealed to the new middle-class woman, too, as she refocused her attention toward dressing in the latest fashion, managing the household, and raising the children. Vacuum cleaners and other consumer durables would make her more efficient, and books on child-rearing, many imbued with a popularized Freudianism, would enable her to mold her children for future success in work and marriage. Cosmetics would aid women in their "first duty"—to be beautiful for the men in their lives—a beauty that would lead to sexual arousal and fulfillment for both men and women.

"New Women" • Young, middle-class women were in the forefront of a 1920s movement to win more freedom for all women in matters of dress, sexuality, and public behavior. Here two fashionable women playfully declare independence from their men by placing themselves in the driver's seat of the "Rambling Wreck from Georgia Tech."

Changing Attitudes toward Marriage and Sexuality

That husbands and wives were encouraged to pursue sexual satisfaction together was one sign of how much prescriptions for married life had changed since the 19th century, when women were thought to lack sexual passion and men were tacitly expected to satisfy their drives through extramarital liaisons. Modern husbands and wives were expected to share other leisure activities as well—dining out, playing cards with friends, going to the movies, attending concerts, and discussing the latest selection from the newly formed Book-of-the-Month Club. Husbands and wives now aspired to a new ideal—to be best friends, full partners in the pursuit of happiness.

The public pursuit of pleasure was also noticeable among young and single middle-class women. The so-called "flappers" of the 1920s wore their dresses short, rolled their stockings down, painted their faces with red lipstick, and smoked in public. They took their inspiration from depictions of saucy, working-class women of the previous decade, whom moviemakers had popularized and refined. Flappers were signaling their desire for independence and equality; but they had no thought of achieving those goals through politics, as had their middle-class predecessors in the woman suffrage movement. Rather, those goals were to be achieved through the creation of a new female personality endowed with self-reliance, outspokenness, and a new appreciation for the pleasures of life.

Celebrating a Business Civilization

Industrialists, advertisers, and merchandisers now began to claim that what they were doing was at the heart of American civilization. It was business, they argued, that made America great, and it was businessmen who provided the nation with its wisest, most vigorous leadership. In 1924 President Calvin Coolidge declared that "the business of America is business." Even religion became a business. Bruce Barton, in his best-seller *The Man That Nobody Knows* (1925), depicted Jesus as a sort-of business executive "who picked up twelve men from the bottom ranks of business and forged them into an organization that conquered the world." Elsewhere, Barton hailed Jesus as an early "national advertiser," and proclaimed that Peter and Paul were really not so different from Americans who sold vacuum cleaners.

Some corporate leaders tried to live up to Barton's evangelistic image of them. Posing as benevolent employers, they set up employee cafeterias, hired doctors and nurses to staff on-site medical clinics, and engaged psychologists to counsel troubled employees. They built ball fields and encouraged employees to join industry-sponsored leagues. They published employee newsletters and gave awards to employees who did their jobs well and with good spirit. Some employers set up profit-sharing plans and offered stock options to reward employees for their efforts. And some even gave employees a voice in determining working conditions. The real purpose of these measures—collectively known as welfare capitalism—was to encourage employee loyalty to the firm and to the capitalist system. The original motivation behind them was management's fear of union power and its memory of the paralyzing strikes of 1919. But as the decade proceeded and as prosperity rolled on, the programs reflected the confidence that capitalism had indeed become humane.

Welfare Capitalism at Work • In 1920, the Sayles Finishing Plants, Inc., a textile corporation in Saylesville, Rhode Island, built this attractive housing development for its employees. By providing their workforces with first-rate homes and other such amenities, large corporations hoped to win the loyalty of their employees.

Industrial Workers

Many industrial workers benefited from the nation's prosperity. A majority of them enjoyed rising wages and a reasonably steady income. Skilled craftsmen in the older industries of construction, railroad transportation, and printing fared especially well. Their real wages rose by 30 to 50 percent over the decade. The several million workers employed in the large mass-production industries (like automobile and electrical equipment manufacture) also did well. Their wages were relatively high, and they enjoyed unprecedented benefits—paid sick leave, paid vacations, life insurance, stock options, subsidized mortgages, and retirement pensions. Although all workers in companies with these programs were eligible for such benefits, skilled workers were in the best position to claim them. Semiskilled and unskilled workers were subject to seasonal and business-cycle layoffs and thus often failed to complete the minimum periods of continuous employment required to qualify for benefits.

Semiskilled and unskilled industrial workers also had to contend with a labor surplus throughout the decade. Although industrial output rose impressively, the number of industrial workers failed to rise above 8.6 million. This was because as employers replaced workers with machines, the aggregate demand for industrial labor increased at a far lower rate than it had in the preceding 20 years. The declining need for labor was one of the reasons employers supported immigration restriction in 1924. Despite a weakening demand for labor, rural whites, rural blacks, and Mexicans continued their migration to the cities, stiffening the competition for factory jobs. Employers could hire and fire as they saw fit and were therefore able to keep wage increases lagging behind increases in productivity.

This softening demand for labor helps to explain why many working-class families did not benefit much from the decade's prosperity or from its consumer revolution. An estimated 40 percent of workers remained mired in poverty, unable to afford a healthy diet or adequate housing, much less any of the more costly consumer goods. In 1930, for instance, 75 percent of American households did not own a washing machine, 70 percent were without a vacuum cleaner, 60 percent had no radio, and 50 percent did without a car.

The million or more workers who labored in the nation's two largest industries, coal and textiles, suffered the most during the 1920s. Throughout the decade, both industries experienced severe overcapacity. By 1926 only half of the coal mined each year was being sold. New England textile cities, especially those that relied on cotton manufacture, experienced levels of unemployment that sometimes approached 50 percent. One reason was that many textile industrialists had shifted their operations to the South, where taxes and wages were lower. But the southern textile industry also suffered from excess capacity, and prices and wages continued to fall. Plant managers put constant pressure on their workers to speed up production. Workers loathed the frequent "speed-ups" of machines and the "stretch-outs" in the number of spinning or weaving machines each worker was expected to tend. By the late 1920s, labor strife and calls for unionization were rising sharply among disgruntled workers in both the South and the North. In battles reminiscent of those of the 1890s and early 1900s, strikers confronted private police forces hired by employers or National Guardsmen called out by governors to keep the peace. As before, the show of force usually put an end to the strikes.

Unionization of textiles and coal, and of more prosperous industries as well, would have brought workers a larger share of the decade's prosperity. Moreover, progressive labor leaders, such as Sidney Hillman of the Amalgamated Clothing Workers, argued that unionization would actually increase corporate profits by compelling employers to observe uniform wage and hour schedules that would restrain ruinous competition. Hillman pointed out—as Henry Ford had in the preceding decade—that rising wages would enable workers to purchase more consumer goods and thus increase corporate sales and revenues. But Hillman's views were ignored outside the garment industry.

Elsewhere, unions lost ground as business and government, backed by middle-class opinion, remained hostile to labor organization. Employers painted a picture of unions as unpatriotic and un-American. Neither was the government supportive. In 1922 the Justice Department broke a strike of 400,000 railroad workers. A conservative Supreme Court, meanwhile, whittled away at labor's legal protections. In 1921 it ruled that lower courts could issue injunctions against union members, prohibiting them from striking or picketing an employer. State courts also enforced what union members called "yellow dog" contracts, written pledges by which employees promised not to join a union while they were employed. Any employee who violated that pledge was subject to immediate dismissal.

These measures crippled efforts to organize trade unions. Membership fell from a high of 5 million in 1920 to less than 3 million in 1929, a mere 10 percent of the nation's industrial workforce. Not all of that decline was the result of the hostile political climate, though. Many workers, especially those who were benefiting from welfare capitalist programs, decided they no longer needed trade unions. And the labor movement hurt itself by moving too slowly to open its ranks to semiskilled and unskilled factory workers.

The Politics of Business

Republican presidents governed the country from 1921 to 1933. In some respects, their administrations resembled those of the Gilded Age, when presidents were mediocre, corruption was rampant, and the government's chief objective was to remove obstacles to capitalist development. But in other respects, the state-building tradition of Theodore Roosevelt lived on, although in somewhat altered form.

Harding and the Politics of Personal Gain

Warren Gamaliel Harding defeated the Democrat James M. Cox for the presidency in 1920. A strikingly handsome and personable man, Harding, in fact, possessed few qualifications for the presidency. From modest origins as a newspaper editor in the small town of Marion, Ohio, he had risen to the U.S. Senate chiefly because the powerful Ohio Republican machine, controlled by Harry M. Daugherty, knew it could count on him to do its bidding. His election to the presidency occurred for the same reason. The Republican Party bosses believed that almost anyone they nominated in 1920 could defeat the Democratic opponent. Rather than nominate someone like General Leonard Wood, who might turn out to be as independent, reformist, and volatile as his recently deceased friend, Theodore Roosevelt, they chose a man they could control. Harding's good looks and geniality made him a favorite with voters, and he swept into office with 61 percent of the popular vote, the greatest landslide since 1820.

Harding was not a bad man. Soon after taking office he released the 66-year-old Socialist Party leader, Eugene V. Debs, from jail. Aware of his own intellectual limitations, Harding included talented men in his cabinet. Indeed, his choice of Herbert Hoover as secretary of commerce, Charles Evans Hughes as secretary of state, and Andrew Mellon as secretary of the treasury were particularly impressive appointments. But Harding did not possess the will to alter his ingrained political habits. He had built his political career on a willingness to please the lobbyists who came to his Senate office asking for favors and deals. He had long followed Harry Daugherty's advice and would continue to do so, now that he had made Daugherty his attorney general. Harding apparently did not think of men such as Daugherty as self-serving or corrupt. They were his friends; they had been with him since the beginning of his political career. He made sure the "boys" had jobs in his administration, and he continued to socialize with them. Many a night he could be found drinking (despite Prohibition), gambling, and womanizing with the "Ohio Gang" at its K Street hangout. Sometimes the gang convened in the White House itself. Alice Roosevelt Longworth, Theodore Roosevelt's daughter, once came into the White House study and found the air "heavy with tobacco smoke," its tables cluttered with "bottles containing every imaginable brand of whiskey, . . . [and] cards and poker chips at hand."

Americans averted their eyes from these questionable activities, and the press portrayed Harding as a capable, compassionate president. It seems, too, that Harding kept himself blind to the widespread use of public office for private gain that characterized his administration. The K Street house was not just a place to carouse. It was also a place of business where the Ohio Gang got rich selling government appointments, judicial pardons, and police protection to bootleggers. By 1923 the corruption could no longer be concealed. Journalists and senators began to focus public attention on the actions of Secretary of the Interior Albert Fall, who had persuaded Harding to transfer control of large government oil reserves at Teapot Dome, Wyoming, and Elk Hills, California, from the Navy to the Department of the Interior. Fall had then immediately leased the deposits to two oil tycoons, Harry F. Sinclair and Edward L. Doheny, who were allowed to pump oil from the wells in exchange for providing the Navy with a system of fuel tank reserves. Fall had issued the leases secretly, without allowing other oil corporations to compete for them, and he had accepted almost $400,000 from Sinclair and Doheny.

Fall would pay for this shady deal with a year in jail. He was not the only Harding appointee to do so. Charles R. Forbes, head of the Veterans' Bureau, would go to Leavenworth Prison for swindling the government out of $200 million in hospital supplies. The exposure of Forbes's theft prompted his lawyer, Charles Cramer, to commit suicide; Jesse Smith, Attorney General Daugherty's close friend and housemate, also killed himself, apparently to avoid being indicted and brought to trial. Daugherty himself managed to escape conviction and incarceration for bribery by burning incriminating documents held by his brother's Ohio bank. Still, Daugherty was forced to leave government service in disgrace. This shocking record of wrongdoing prompted one observer to remark that the Harding administration was "responsible in its short two years and five months for more concentrated robbery and rascality than any other in the whole history of the Federal Government."

Harding grew depressed when he finally realized what had been going on. In the summer of 1923, in poor spirits, he left Washington for a West Coast tour. He fell ill in Seattle and died from a heart attack in San Francisco. At the time of his death, the corruption within Harding's administration had not yet been revealed to the American public. The train returning his body to Washington attracted crowds of grief-stricken mourners who little suspected the web of corruption and bribery in which Harding had been caught. But even as the revelations poured forth in 1924 and 1925, many Americans seemed not to care. Some of this insouciance reflected the carefree atmosphere of the 1920s, but much of it had to do with the character of the man who succeeded Harding.

Coolidge and the Politics of Laissez-Faire

Calvin Coolidge rarely smiled. At the many dinners he attended as vice president, he said hardly a word. Silence was his public creed, much to the chagrin of Washington's socialites. He was never enticed into carousing with the "boys," nor did he ever stand by as liquor was being served. He believed that the best government was the government that governed least, and he took a long nap every afternoon. The welfare of the country hinged on the character of its people—their willingness to work hard, to be honest, to live within their means. Coolidge quickly put to rest the anxiety aroused by the Harding scandals.

Born in Vermont and raised in Massachusetts, he gained national visibility in September 1919, when as governor of Massachusetts he took a firm stand against Boston's striking policemen (see Chapter 4). His reputation as a man who battled labor radicals earned him a place on the 1920 national Republican ticket. His

A Stern Yankee • In sharp contrast to Warren Harding, Calvin Coolidge did not enjoy informality, banter, or carousing. Here he strikes a formal pose while standing at his White House desk.

image as an ordinary man helped convince voters in 1920 that the Republican Party would return the country to its commonsensical ways after eight years of reckless reforms. Coolidge won his party's presidential nomination handily in 1924 and easily defeated his Democratic opponent, John W. Davis. Coolidge's popularity remained strong throughout his first full term, and he probably would have been renominated and reelected in 1928. But he chose not to run.

Coolidge took greatest pride in those measures that reduced the government's control over the economy. The Revenue Act of 1926 slashed the high income and estate taxes that progressives had pushed through Congress during the First World War. Once again, Americans could dispose of their wealth as they saw fit. Coolidge twice vetoed the McNary-Haugen Bill, passed by Congress in 1926 and again in 1928, which would have compelled the government to pay subsidies to farmers when domestic farm prices fell below certain levels. He stripped the Federal Trade Commission of the powers it needed to regulate business affairs. He supported Supreme Court decisions rendered between 1918 and 1923 invalidating Progressive Era laws that had strengthened organized labor and protected children and women from exploitation. For Coolidge, as for a majority of the Supreme Court justices, such laws constituted illegal government intervention in the free market. Coolidge's strong stand against government meddling in economic affairs prompted a later Republican president, Ronald Reagan, to substitute a portrait of the laissez-faire Yankee for one of Harry Truman on a White House wall.

Hoover and the Politics of "Associationalism"

Republicans in the 1920s did more than simply lift government restraints and regulations from the economy. Some Republicans, led by Secretary of Commerce Herbert Hoover, conceived of government as a dynamic, even progressive, economic force. Hoover shared Coolidge's regard for such old-fashioned virtues as hard work, independence, and individualism. But, unlike Coolidge, he did not believe that the United States could return to the simplicities of the past. Industry had become too powerful and too predatory. Removing government controls would not restore opportunity to the common man; it would simply permit corporations to continue their wasteful, selfish ways. Although Hoover was not anticorporate or anticapitalist, he wanted corporations to abandon their profligacy and turn to cooperation and public service. He envisioned an economy built on the principle of association. Industrialists, wholesalers, retailers, operators of railroad and shipping lines, small businessmen, farmers, workers, doctors—each of these groups would form a trade association whose members would share economic information, discuss problems of production and distribution, and seek ways of achieving greater efficiency and profit. Hoover believed that the very act of associating in this way—an approach that historian Ellis Hawley has called "associationalism"—would convince participants of the superiority of cooperation over competition, of negotiation over conflict, of public service over selfishness.

Trained as a geologist at Stanford University, Hoover had worked first as a mining engineer and then as a manager of large mining operations in Australia, China, Latin America, and Russia. During the war, he had directed the government's Food Administration and had made it an outstanding example of public management. From that experience, he had come to appreciate the advantages of coordinating the activities of thousands of producers and distributors scattered across the country. He learned too that the government could play a role in bringing about that coordination.

Hoover's ambition as secretary of commerce was to make the department the grand orchestrator of economic cooperation. During his eight years in that post, from 1921 to 1929, he organized over 250 conferences around such themes as unemployment or the problems of a particular industry or economic sector. He brought together government officials, representatives of business, policymakers, and others who had a stake in strengthening the economy.

Hoover achieved some notable successes. He convinced steel executives to abandon the 12-hour day. His support of labor's right to organize contributed to the passage of the 1926 Railway Labor Act, one of the few acts of the 1920s that endorsed

Preparing for the Presidency • Herbert Hoover addresses voters via radio during his 1928 campaign for the presidency. Hoover's success as a mining businessman, wartime food administrator, and secretary of commerce made him an overwhelming favorite against Democratic candidate Alfred E. Smith.

labor's right to bargain collectively. His efforts to persuade farmers to join together in marketing cooperatives, which he believed would solve problems of inefficiency and overproduction, led to the Cooperative Marketing Act of 1926. He worked to standardize the size and shape of a great variety of products—everything from nuts and bolts to automobile tires, from toilet paper to pipes—so as to increase their usefulness and strengthen their sales. When the Mississippi River overflowed its banks in 1927, Hoover was the man Coolidge appointed to organize the relief effort. Hoover used this disaster as an opportunity to place credit operations in flood-affected areas on a sounder footing and to organize local banks into associations with adequate resources and expertise. He also persuaded local public and private groups to engage in farsighted plans for future flood control.

Hoover's dynamic conception of government brought him into conflict with Republicans whose economic philosophy began and ended with laissez-faire. Hoover found himself increasingly at odds with Coolidge, who declared in 1927: "That man has offered me unsolicited advice for six years, all of it bad."

The Politics of Business Abroad

Republican domestic policy disagreements between laissez-faire and association-alism spilled over into foreign policy as well. Hoover had lived many years abroad and had consulted with the heads of European governments on matters of famine relief during the First World War. He believed he had special expertise in foreign affairs and had accepted the post of secretary of commerce thinking he would represent the United States in negotiations with foreign companies and governments. In fact, he intended to apply his concept of "associationalism" to international relations. He wanted the world's leading nations to meet regularly in conferences, to limit military buildups, and to foster an international environment in which capitalism—especially U.S. capitalism—could flourish. Aware that the United States would have to contribute to the creation of such an environment, especially in devastated Europe, Hoover hoped to persuade American bankers to adopt investment and loan policies that would aid European recovery. If they refused to do so, he was prepared to urge the government to take an activist, supervisory role in foreign investment.

In 1921 and 1922 Hoover had some influence on the design of the Washington Conference on the Limitation of Armaments. Although he did not serve as a negotiator at the conference—Secretary of State Charles Evans Hughes reserved that role for himself and his subordinates—he did supply Hughes's team with a wealth of economic information. And he helped Hughes to use that information to design forceful, detailed proposals for disarmament. Those proposals gave U.S. negotiators a decided advantage over their European and Asian counterparts and helped them win a stunning accord, the Five-Power Treaty, by which the United States, Britain, Japan, France, and Italy agreed to scrap more than 2 million tons of their warships. Never before had world powers agreed to such a vast program of disarmament. Hughes also obtained pledges from all the signatories that they would respect the "Open Door" in China, long a U.S. foreign policy objective (see Chapter 3).

These triumphs redounded to Hughes's credit but not to Hoover's, and Hughes used it to consolidate his control over foreign policy. He rebuffed Hoover's efforts to put international economic affairs under the direction of the Commerce Department and rejected Hoover's suggestion to intervene in the international activities of U.S. banks. In so doing, Hughes revealed his affinity for the laissez-faire rather than the associational school of Republican politics. Hughes was willing to urge bankers to participate in Europe's economic recovery, and he was willing to use the power of government to protect their investments once they were made, but the bankers would be free to decide which loans would be appropriate.

Hughes put his policy into action in 1923 to resolve a crisis in Franco-German relations. The victorious Allies had imposed on Germany an obligation to pay $33 billion in war reparations (see Chapter 4). In 1923, when the impoverished German government suspended its payments, France sent troops to occupy the Ruhr valley, whose industry was vital to the German economy. German workers retaliated by going on strike, and the crisis threatened to undermine Europe's precarious economic recovery.

Hughes understood that the only way to relieve the situation was to convince the French to reduce German reparations to a reasonable level. To help them come to that decision, he demanded that France repay in full the money it had borrowed from the United States during the First World War. The only way France could pay off those loans was to get additional credit from U.S. bankers, but Hughes made it clear that this would not happen until France had agreed to reduce German reparations. At last France relented and sent representatives to a U.S.-sponsored conference in 1924 to restructure Germany's obligation.

Up to this point, Hughes had been dexterous in using his powers as secretary of state. But he suddenly withdrew the government from the conference proceedings and turned over negotiations to a group of American bankers. The conference produced the Dawes Plan (after the Chicago banker and chief negotiator, Charles G. Dawes), which sharply reduced German reparations from $542 million to $250 million annually and called on U.S. and foreign banks to stimulate the German economy with a quick infusion of $200 million in loans. Within a matter of days, banker J. P. Morgan Jr. raised more than $1 billion from eager American investors. Money poured into German financial markets, and the German economy was apparently stabilized.

The Dawes Plan reveals the degree to which the Coolidge administration was determined to have the private sector participate in U.S. foreign policy. In the short term, the plan won applause on both sides of the Atlantic. But it soon became apparent that the U.S. money flooding into Germany was creating its own problems. American investors were so eager to lend to Germany that their investments became speculative and unsound. At this point, a stronger effort by the U.S. government to direct loans to sound investments might have helped. That is what Hoover had been urging since the early 1920s. But Hughes's successor as secretary of state, Frank Kellogg, was interested in no such initiatives; nor was Secretary of the Treasury Mellon. Laissez-faire reigned abroad even more firmly than it did at home.

In only two areas did Republicans depart from their hands-off approach to foreign affairs. The first was in their pursuit of disarmament and world peace. The Five-Power Treaty, negotiated by Hughes in 1921 and 1922, was a major success. Secretary of State Kellogg followed in Hughes's footsteps by drawing up a treaty with Aristide Briand, the French foreign minister, outlawing war as a tool of national policy. In 1928, representatives of the United States, France, and 13 other nations met in Paris to sign the Kellogg-Briand pact, in which the signatories pledged to avoid war and to settle all international disputes through "pacific means." Hailed as a great stride toward world peace, the pact soon attracted the support of 48 other nations. In the United States, it energized a broad peace movement born of disillusionment with Woodrow Wilson's belief that America could save humanity by going to war. The pact gave these pacifists hope that the United States would never again commit the grievous Wilsonian error.

Coolidge viewed the treaty as an opportunity to further reduce the size of the U.S. government. With the threat of war removed, the United States could scale back its military forces and eliminate much of the bureaucracy needed to support a large standing army and navy. Unfortunately for both Coolidge and the peace movement, the pact contained no enforcement mechanism. It would do nothing to slow the next decade's descent into militarism and war.

The other area in which the Republican administrations of the 1920s took a hands-on approach was Latin America. U.S. investments in the region more than doubled from 1917 to 1929, and the U.S. government continued its policy of intervening in the internal affairs of Latin America to protect U.S. interests. Republican administrations did attempt to curtail American military involvement in the Caribbean, in part to cut costs and in part to appease congressional critics, such as William E. Borah of Idaho, who were arguing vociferously against the use of troops there. Indeed, the Coolidge administration pulled American troops out of the Dominican Republic in 1924 and Nicaragua in 1925. But, in the case of Nicaragua, U.S. Marines were sent back in 1926 to end a war between liberal and conservative

Nicaraguans and to protect American property; this time they stayed until 1934. U.S. troops, meanwhile, occupied Haiti continuously between 1919 and 1934, keeping in power governments friendly to U.S. interests. Opposition to such heavy-handed tactics continued to build in the United States, but they would not yield a significant change in U.S. policy until the 1930s (see Chapter 6).

Farmers, Small-Town Protestants, and Moral Traditionalists

Although many Americans benefited from the prosperity of the 1920s, others did not. Overproduction was impoverishing substantial numbers of farmers. Beyond these economic inequalities, many white Protestants, especially those in rural areas and small towns, believed that the country was being overrun by racially inferior and morally suspect foreigners.

Agricultural Depression

The 1920s brought hard times to the nation's farmers after the boom period of the war years. During the war, domestic demand for farm products had risen steadily, and foreign demand had exploded as the war disrupted agricultural production in France, Ukraine, and other European food-producing regions. Herbert Hoover, who through his Food Administration made large quantities of American agricultural commodities available to the Europeans, also ensured that U.S. farmers would reap ample profits. Soon after the war, however, Europe's farmers quickly resumed their customary levels of production. Foreign demand for American foodstuffs fell precipitously, creating an oversupply and depressing prices in the United States.

Contributing further to the plight of U.S. farmers was the sharp rise in agricultural productivity made possible by the tractor, which greatly increased the acreage that each farmer could cultivate. The number of tractors in use almost quadrupled in the 1920s, and 35 million new acres came under cultivation. Produce flooded the market. Prices fell even further, as did farm incomes. By 1929, the annual per capita income of rural Americans was only $223, one-quarter that of the nonfarm population. Millions were forced to sell their farms. Their choices were then to scrape together a living as tenants or to abandon farming altogether. More than 3 million of them chose to pull out, packing their belongings into jalopies or loading them onto trains headed for the city.

Those who stayed on the land grew increasingly vociferous in their demands. In the first half of the decade, radical farmers working through such organizations as the Nonpartisan League of North Dakota and farmer-labor parties in Minnesota, Wisconsin, and other midwestern states led the movement. By the second half of the decade, however, leadership of the farm movement had passed from farming radicals to farming moderates, and from small farmers in danger of dispossession to larger farmers and agribusinesses seeking to extend their holdings. By lobbying through such organizations as the Farm Bureau Federation, the more powerful agricultural interests brought pressure on Congress to set up economic controls that would protect them from failure. Their proposals, embodied in the McNary-Haugen

Bill, called on the government to erect high tariffs on foreign produce and to purchase surplus U.S. crops at prices that enabled farmers to cover their production costs. The government would then sell the surplus crops in the world market for whatever prices they fetched. Any money lost in international sales would be absorbed by the government rather than by the farmers. The McNary-Haugen Bill passed Congress in 1926 and in 1928, only to be vetoed by President Coolidge both times. That it passed Congress at all in these laissez-faire years testifies to the seriousness of the farmers' plight and to the strength of the farm bloc in Congress.

Cultural Dislocation

Added to the economic plight of the farmers was a sense of cultural dislocation. Farmers had long perceived themselves as the backbone of the nation—hardworking, honest, God-fearing yeomen, guardians of independence and liberty.

The 1920 census challenged the validity of that view. For the first time, a slight majority of Americans now lived in urban areas. That finding did not in itself signify very much, for the census classified as "urban" those towns with a population as small as 2,500 (by other standards, such towns could have been classified as rural). But the census figures did reinforce the widespread perception that both the economic and cultural vitality of the nation had shifted from the countryside to the metropolis. Industry, the chief engine of prosperity, was an urban phenomenon. Leisure—the world of amusement parks, department stores, professional sports, movies, cabarets, and theaters—was to be enjoyed in cities; so too were flashy fashions and open sexuality. Catholics, Jews, and African Americans, who together outnumbered white Protestants in many cities, seemed to be the principal creators of this new world. They were also thought to be the purveyors of Bolshevism, hedonism, and other modes of radicalism. Cities, finally, were the home of secular intellectuals who had scrapped their belief in Scripture and in God and had embraced science as their new, unimpeachable authority.

All through the Progressive Era rural Americans had believed that the cities could be redeemed, that city dwellers could be reformed, that the values of rural America—the values of Protestantism—would triumph. War had crushed that confidence and had replaced it with the fear that urban culture and urban people would undermine all that "true" Americans held dear. Cities, they feared, were breeding grounds for atheism, sexual license, and Bolshevism.

These fears grew even more intense with the changes brought by prosperity. Urban-industrial America was obviously the most prosperous sector of society; its consumer culture and its commodities were penetrating the countryside as never before, helped along by the revolution in communications. Even small towns now sported movie theaters and automobile dealerships. Radio waves carried news of city life into isolated farmhouses. The growth in the circulation of national magazines also broke down the wall separating country from city. Mail-order catalogs—like those of Sears, Roebuck and Company—invited farmers to fantasize that they too could fill their homes with refrigerators, RCA victrolas, and Hoover vacuum cleaners.

Rural Americans were ambivalent about this cultural invasion. On the one hand, country dwellers were eager to participate in the consumer marketplace. On the

Buying Houses from a Catalog • By the 1920s, cars, Coca-Cola, radios, and other modern commodities had found their way to the country's smallest towns. Many rural residents did their shopping through the mail order catalogs of Sears, Roebuck and Co. From 1909 to 1930, the company even sold houses by mail order. This one arrived unassembled—with instructions, of course, about how to put it together.

other, they were terrified that by doing so they would expose the countryside to atheism, immorality, and radicalism. Their determination to protect their imperiled way of life was manifested by their support of Prohibition, the Ku Klux Klan, immigration restriction, and religious fundamentalism.

Prohibition

The Eighteenth Amendment to the Constitution, which prohibited the manufacture and sale of alcohol, went into effect in January 1920. At its inception it was supported by a large and varied constituency that included farmers, middle-class city dwellers, feminists, and progressive reformers who loathed the powerful "liquor trust" and who saw firsthand the deleterious effects of drink on the urban poor. It soon became apparent, however, that Prohibition was doing more to encourage law-breaking than abstinence. With only 1,500 federal agents to enforce the law, the government could not possibly police the drinking habits of 110 million people. With little fear of punishment, those who wanted to drink did so, either brewing liquor at home or buying it from speakeasies and bootleggers. Because the law prevented legitimate businesses from manufacturing liquor, organized crime simply added alcohol to its business portfolio. Mobsters procured much of their liquor from Canadian manufacturers such as Seagram. They supported small armies of lawbreakers to smuggle it across the border, protect it in warehouses, and distribute it to speakeasies. Al Capone's Chicago-based mob alone employed 1,000 men to protect its liquor trafficking, which was so lucrative that Capone became the richest (and most feared) gangster in America. Blood flowed in the streets of Chicago and other northern cities as rival mobs fought one another to enlarge their share of the market.

These unexpected consequences caused many early advocates of Prohibition, especially in the cities, to withdraw their support. That was not the response of Prohibition's rural, Protestant supporters, however. The violence spawned by liquor trafficking confirmed their view that alcohol was an agent of evil that had to be eradicated. The high-profile participation of Italian, Irish, and Jewish gangsters in the bootleg trade merely reinforced their view that Catholics and Jews were threats to law and morality. Many rural Protestants became more, not less, determined to rid the country of liquor once and for all; many resolved to rid the country of Jews and Catholics as well.

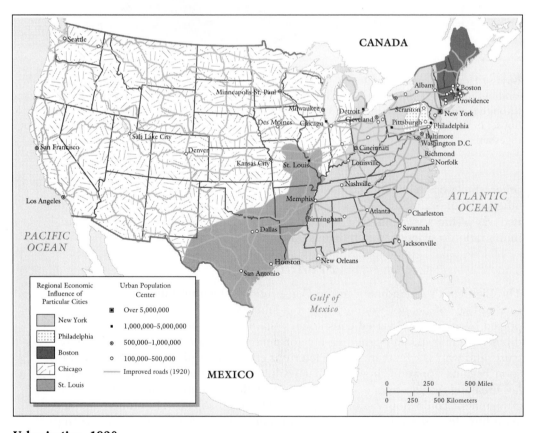

Urbanization, 1920

The Ku Klux Klan

The original Ku Klux Klan, formed in the South in the late 1860s, had died out with the defeat of Reconstruction and the reestablishment of white supremacy. The new Klan was created in 1915 by William Simmons, a white southerner who had been inspired by D. W. Griffith's racist film, *Birth of a Nation*, in which the early Klan was depicted as having saved the nation (and especially its white women) from predatory blacks. By the 1920s control of the Klan had passed from Simmons to a Texas dentist, Hiram Evans, and its ideological focus had expanded from a loathing of blacks to a hatred of Jews and Catholics as well. Evans's Klan propagated a nativist message that the country should contain—or better yet, eliminate—the influence of Jews and Catholics and restore "Anglo-Saxon" racial purity, Protestant supremacy, and traditional morality to national life. Evans's message swelled Klan ranks and expanded its visibility and influence in the North and South alike. By 1924, as many as 4 million Americans are thought to have belonged to the Klan, including the half-million members of its female auxiliary, Women of the Ku Klux Klan. Not only was the Klan strong in states of the Old Confederacy like Louisiana and Texas and in border states like Oklahoma and Kansas, it thrived, too, in such northern states as Indiana, Pennsylvania, Washington, and Oregon. It even drew significant membership from the cities of those states. Indiana, for example, was home to 500,000 Klansmen and women, many of them in the Indianapolis area. In 1924 Indiana voters elected a Klansman to the governorship and sent several other Klan members to the statehouse.

In some respects, the Klan functioned just as many other fraternal organizations did. It offered members friendship networks, social services, and conviviality. Its rituals, regalia, and mock-medieval language (the Imperial Wizard, Exalted Cyclops, Grand Dragons, King Kleagles, Klonvocations, etc.) gave initiates the same sense of

The Ku Klux Klan • In this eerie 1920 photo, Klan members in Richmond, Virginia, perform a charitable act—delivering food to the needy—even as their white sheets and hoods remind onlookers of the group's commitment to the politics of hate.

superiority, valor, and mystery that so many other fraternal societies, from the Masons to the Knights of Columbus, imparted to their members. But the Klan also stirred up hate. It thrived on lurid tales of financial extortion by Jewish bankers and sexual exploitation by Catholic priests. The accusations were sometimes general, as in the claim that an international conspiracy of Jewish bankers had caused the agricultural depression, or allegations that the pope had sent agents to the United States with instructions to destroy democracy. More common, and more incendiary, however, were the seemingly plausible, yet totally manufactured, tales of Jewish or Catholic depravity. Stories circulated of Jewish businessmen who had opened amusement parks and dance halls to which they lured innocent adolescents, tempting them with sexual transgression and profiting handsomely from their moral debasement. Likewise, Catholic priests and nuns were said to prey on Protestant girls and boys who had been forced into convents and Catholic orphanages. These outrageous stories sometimes provoked attacks on individual Jews and Catholics. More commonly, they prompted campaigns to boycott Jewish businesses and Catholic institutions, and to ruin reputations.

The emphasis on sexual exploitation in these stories reveals the anxiety Klan members felt about modern society's acceptance of sexual openness and sexual gratification. Many Klanspeople lived in towns like Muncie, Indiana, where, as the Lynds reported, life was suffused with modern attitudes. That such attitudes might reflect the yearnings of Protestant children rather than the manipulation of deceitful Jews and Catholics was a truth some Protestant parents found difficult to accept.

Immigration Restriction

Although the vast majority of Protestant Americans never joined the Klan, many of them did respond to the Klan's nativist argument that the country and its values would best be served by limiting the entry of outsiders. That was the purpose of the Johnson-Reed Immigration Restriction Act of 1924.

By the early 1920s most Americans believed that the country could no longer accommodate the million immigrants who had been arriving each year prior to the war and the more than 800,000 who arrived in 1921. Industrialists no longer needed unskilled European laborers to operate their factories, their places having been taken either by machines or by African American and Mexican workers. And most of the leaders of the labor movement were convinced that the influx of workers unfamiliar with English and with trade unions was weakening labor solidarity. Progressive reformers, who had been so keen on Americanization programs a decade earlier, no longer believed that immigrants could be easily Americanized or that harmony between the native-born and the foreign-born could be readily achieved. Congress responded to constituents' concerns by passing an immigration restriction act in 1921. Then, in 1924, the more comprehensive Johnson-Reed Act was passed into law. The 1924 law imposed a yearly quota of 165,000 immigrants from countries outside the Western Hemisphere, effectively reducing total immigration to only 20 percent of the prewar annual average.

The sponsors of the 1924 act believed that certain groups—British, Germans, and Scandinavians, in particular—were racially superior and that, consequently, these groups should be allowed to enter the United States in greater numbers.

However, because the Constitution prohibits the enactment of explicitly racist laws, Congress had to achieve this racist aim through subterfuge. Lawmakers established a formula to determine the annual immigrant quota for each foreign country, which was to be computed at 2 percent of the total number of immigrants from that country already resident in the United States in the year 1890. In 1890, immigrant ranks had been dominated by the British, Germans, and Scandinavians, so the new quotas would thus allow for a relatively larger cohort of immigrants from those countries. Immigrant groups that were poorly represented in the 1890 population—Italians, Greeks, Poles, Slavs, and eastern European Jews—were effectively locked out. The Johnson-Reed Act also reaffirmed the long-standing policy of excluding Chinese immigrants, and it added Japanese and other Asians to the list of groups that were altogether barred from entry. The act did not officially limit immigration from nations in the Western Hemisphere, chiefly because agribusiness interests in Texas and California had convinced Congress that cheap Mexican laborers were indispensable to their industry's prosperity. Still, the establishment of a

Annual Immigrant Quotas under the Johnson-Reed Act, 1925–1927

Northwest Europe and Scandinavia		Eastern and Southern Europe		Other Countries	
Country	*Quota*	*Country*	*Quota*	*Country*	*Quota*
Germany	51,227	Poland	5,982	Africa	
Great Britain		Italy	3,845	(other than	
and Northern		Czechoslovakia	3,073	Egypt)	1,100
Ireland	34,007	Russia	2,248	Armenia	124
Irish Free State		Yugoslavia	671	Australia	121
(Ireland)	28,567	Romania	603	Palestine	100
Sweden	9,561	Portugal	503	Syria	100
Norway	6,453	Hungary	473	Turkey	100
France	3,954	Lithuania	344	New Zealand and	
Denmark	2,789	Latvia	142	Pacific Islands	100
Switzerland	2,081	Spain	131	All others	1,900
Netherlands	1,648	Estonia	124		
Austria	785	Albania	100		
Belgium	512	Bulgaria	100		
Finland	471	Greece	100		
Free City					
of Danzig	228				
Iceland	100				
Luxembourg	100				
Total (number)	142,483	Total (number)	18,439	Total (number)	3,745
Total (%)	86.5%	Total (%)	11.2%	Total (%)	2.3%

Note: Total annual immigrant quota was 164,667
Source: From *Statistical Abstract of the United States* (Washington, D.C.: Government Printing Office, 1929), p. 100.

Border Patrol along the U.S.-Mexican border and the imposition of a $10 head tax on all prospective Mexican immigrants made entry into the United States more difficult for Mexicans than it had been.

The Johnson-Reed Act accomplished Congress's underlying goal. Annual immigration from transoceanic nations fell by 80 percent. The large number of available slots for English and German immigrants regularly went unfilled, while the smaller number of available slots for Italians, Poles, Russian Jews, and others prevented hundreds of thousands of them from entering the country. A "national origins" system put in place in 1927 reduced the total annual quota further, to 150,000, and reserved more than 120,000 of these slots for immigrants from northwestern Europe. Except for minor modifications in 1952, the Johnson-Reed Act would dictate U.S. immigration policy until 1965.

Remarkably few Americans, outside of the ethnic groups that were being discriminated against, objected to these laws at the time they were passed—an indication of how broadly acceptable racism and nativism had become. In fact, racism and religious bigotry enjoyed a resurgence during the Jazz Age. The pseudoscience of eugenics, based upon the idea that nations could improve the racial quality of their population by pruning away its weaker racial strains, found supporters not only in Congress but among prestigious scientists as well. Universities such as Harvard and Columbia set quotas similar to those of the Johnson-Reed Act to reduce the proportion of Jews among their undergraduates.

Fundamentalism

Of all the forces reacting against urban life, Protestant fundamentalism was perhaps the most enduring. Fundamentalists regard the Bible as God's word and thus the source of all "fundamental" truth. They believe that every event depicted in the Bible, from the creation of the world in six days to the resurrection of Christ, happened exactly as the Bible describes it. For fundamentalists, God is a deity whose presence is palpable, who intervenes directly in the lives of individuals and communities, and who makes known both his pleasure and his wrath to those who acknowledge his divinity. Sin must be actively purged, salvation actively sought.

The rise of the fundamentalist movement from the 1870s through the 1920s roughly paralleled the rise of urban-industrial society. Fundamentalists recoiled from the "evils" of the city—from what they perceived as its poverty, its moral degeneracy, its irreligion, and its crass materialism. Fundamentalism took shape in reaction against two additional aspects of urban society: the growth of liberal Protestantism and the revelations of science.

Liberal Protestants believed that religion had to be adapted to the skeptical and scientific temper of the modern age. No biblical story in which a sea opens up, the sun stands still, or a woman springs forth from a man's rib could possibly be true. The Bible was to be mined for its ethical values rather than for its literal truth. Liberal Protestants removed God from his active role in history and refashioned him into a distant and benign deity who watches over the world but does not intervene to punish or to redeem. They turned religion away from the quest for salvation and toward the pursuit of good deeds, social conscience, and love for one's neighbor. Although those with a liberal bent constituted only a minority of Protestants, they were highly articulate, visible, and influential in social reform movements. Fundamentalism arose in part to counter the "heretical" claims of the liberal Protestants.

Liberal Protestants and fundamentalists both understood that science was the source of most challenges to Christianity. Scientists privileged natural law over divine intervention. They believed that rational inquiry was a better guide to the past and to the future than prayer and revelation. Scientists even challenged the ideas that God had created the world and had fashioned mankind in his own image. These were beliefs that many religious peoples, particularly fundamentalists, simply could not accept. Their fundamentalism acquired sharper definition as they mobilized to restore God and the Bible to their proper place in American life. Conflict was inevitable. It came in 1925, in Dayton, Tennessee.

The Scopes Trial

No aspect of science aroused more anger among fundamentalists than Charles Darwin's theory of evolution. There was no greater blasphemy than to suggest that man emerged from lower forms of life instead of being created by God himself. In states where they were strong, fundamentalists pressured their legislatures to expunge any mention of evolution from the classroom. In Tennessee in 1925, they succeeded in getting a law passed forbidding the teaching of "any theory that denies the story of the divine creation of man as taught in the Bible."

For Americans who accepted the authority of science—liberal Protestants, natural and social scientists, the liberal elites of New York, Chicago, and other cities—denying the truth of evolution was as ludicrous as insisting that the sun revolved around the earth. In their newspapers, journals, and pulpits they ridiculed the fundamentalists, but they worried that the passage of the Tennessee law might signal the onset of a campaign to undermine First Amendment guarantees of free speech. The American Civil Liberties Union, founded by liberals during the Red Scare of 1919 and 1920, began searching for a teacher who would be willing to challenge the constitutionality of the Tennessee law. They found their man in John T. Scopes, a 24-year-old biology teacher in Dayton. After confessing that he had taught evolution to his students, Scopes was arrested. The case quickly attracted national attention. William Jennings Bryan, the former Populist, progressive, and secretary of state, announced that he would help to prosecute Scopes, and the famous liberal trial lawyer Clarence Darrow rushed to Dayton to lead Scopes's defense. That Bryan and Darrow had once been allies in the progressive movement only heightened the drama. A small army of journalists descended on Dayton, led by H. L. Mencken, an iconoclastic Baltimore-based journalist famous for his savage critiques of the alleged stupidity and prudishness of small-town Americans.

The trial dragged on, and most of the observers expected Scopes to be convicted. (He was.) But it took an unexpected turn when Darrow persuaded the judge to let Bryan testify as an "expert on the Bible." Darrow knew that Bryan's testimony would have no bearing on the question of Scopes's innocence or guilt. (The jury was not even allowed to hear it.) His aim was to expose Bryan as a fool for believing that the Bible was a source of literal truth and thus to embarrass the fundamentalists. In a brilliant confrontation, Darrow made Bryan's defense of the Bible look silly, and he then led Bryan to admit that the "truth" of the Bible was not always easy to accept. In that case, Darrow asked, how could fundamentalists be so sure that everything in the Bible was literally true? Bryan could not give a clear answer.

In his account of the trial, Mencken portrayed Bryan as a pathetic figure who had been devastated by his humiliating experience on the witness stand, a view popularized in the 1960 movie, *Inherit the Wind*. When Bryan died only a week after the trial ended, Mencken claimed that the trial had broken Bryan's heart. In Mencken's view, Darrow had delivered a mortal blow both to Bryan and fundamentalism.

Bryan deserved a better epitaph than the one Mencken had given him. He had survived worse battles during his long career. Far from being devastated by his encounter with Darrow, Bryan was preparing to take his case to the people when he died peacefully in his sleep. Diabetes caused his death, not a broken heart. Nor was Bryan the innocent fool that Mencken made him out to be. He remembered when social conservatives had used Darwin's phrase "survival of the fittest" to prove that the wealthy and politically powerful were racially superior to the poor and powerless (see Chapter 1). His rejection of Darwinism evidenced his democratic faith that all human beings were creatures of God and thus capable of striving for perfection and equality.

The public ridicule attendant on the Scopes trial did take its toll on fundamentalists. Many of them retreated from politics and refocused their attention on personal redemption, on purging sin from their own hearts rather than from the hearts of others. In the end, the fundamentalists were able to prevail on three more states to prohibit the teaching of evolution. But the controversy had even more far-reaching effects. Worried about losing sales, publishers quietly removed references to Darwin from their science textbooks, a policy that would remain in force until the 1960s. In this respect, the fundamentalists had scored a significant victory.

Ethnic and Racial Communities

The 1920s were a decade of change for ethnic and racial minorities. Government policy simultaneously discouraged the continued immigration of "new immigrants" from southern and eastern Europe and encouraged the migration of African Americans from the South to the North and of Mexicans across the Rio Grande and into the American Southwest. Some minorities benefited from the prosperity of the decade; others created and sustained vibrant subcultures. All, however, experienced a surge in religious and racial discrimination that made them uneasy in Jazz Age America.

European Americans

European American immigrants—and especially the southern and eastern European majority among them—were concentrated in the cities of the Northeast and Midwest. A large number were semiskilled and unskilled industrial laborers and suffered economic insecurity as a result. In addition, they faced cultural discrimination. Catholic ethnics and Jews were favorite targets of the Klan and its politics of hate. Catholics generally opposed Prohibition, viewing it as a crude attempt by Protestants to control their behavior. Southern and eastern Europeans, particularly

Jews and Italians, resented immigration restriction and the implication that they were unworthy of citizenship. Italians were outraged by the execution of Nicola Sacco and Bartolomeo Vanzetti in 1927 (Chapter 4), convinced that prejudice had led to their conviction. Had the two men been native-born Protestants, Italians argued, their lives would have been spared.

Southern and eastern Europeans everywhere were the objects of intensive Americanization campaigns meant to strip them of their foreign ways. State after state passed laws requiring public schools to instruct children in the essentials of citizenship. Several states, including Rhode Island, extended these laws to private schools as well, convinced that immigrants' children who attended Catholic parochial schools were spending too much time learning about their native religion, language, and country. An Oregon law tried to eliminate Catholic schools altogether by ordering all children aged 8 to 16 to enroll in public schools. But attending a public school was no guarantee of acceptance, either—a lesson learned by Jewish children who had excelled in their studies only to be barred from Harvard, Columbia, and other elite universities.

Southern and eastern European Americans responded to these insults and attacks by strengthening the very institutions and customs Americanizers were trying to undermine. Ethnic associations flourished in the 1920s—Catholic churches and Jewish synagogues, fraternal and mutual benefit societies, banks and charitable organizations, athletic leagues and youth groups. Children learned their native

The House that Ruth Built • When officials opened its doors in 1923, Yankee Stadium became the nation's most celebrated baseball park. Babe Ruth and his fellow New York Yankees did not disappoint their fans, many of whom were European immigrants and their children. Here "the Babe" approaches home plate after hitting his 50th home run during a game in 1927. Ruth would go on to hit 60 round-trippers that year, setting a record that stood until Roger Maris (61) broke it in 1961. In 1998, Mark McGwire (70) and Sammy Sosa (66) became only the second and third players to surpass Ruth's 1927 feat.

languages and customs at home and at church if not at school, and joined with their parents to celebrate their ethnic heritage. Among Italians and French Canadians, saints' days were occasions for parades, speeches, band concerts, games, and feasts, all serving to solidify ethnic bonds and affirm ethnic identity.

These immigrants and their children were not oblivious to the new consumer culture, however. They flocked to movies and amusement parks, to baseball games and boxing matches. Children usually entered more enthusiastically into the world of American mass culture than did their immigrant parents, a behavior that often set off family conflicts. The famed New York Yankee, Lou Gehrig, had to fight to convince his German-born mother that playing baseball was honorable work. But many ethnics found it possible to reconcile their own culture with American culture. Youngsters who went to the movies did so with friends from within their community. Ethnics also played sandlot baseball, but their leagues were customarily organized around churches or ethnic associations. In these early days of radio, ethnics living in large cities could always find programs in their native language and music from their native lands. In the 1920s, their mass culture and ethnic culture comfortably coexisted.

European American ethnics also resolved to develop the political muscle needed to defeat the forces of nativism, to repeal state and federal laws designed to denigrate them and their traditions, and to turn government policy in a more favorable direction. One sign of this determination was a sharp rise in the number of immigrants who became U.S. citizens. The number of immigrant Poles, Slavs, Italians, Lithuanians, and Hungarians who became naturalized citizens nearly doubled during the decade; the number of naturalized Greeks almost tripled. Armed with the vote, ethnics turned out on election day to defeat unsympathetic city councilmen, mayors, state representatives, and even an occasional governor. Their growing national strength first became apparent at the Democratic national convention of 1924, when urban-ethnic delegates almost won approval of planks calling for the repeal of Prohibition and condemnation of the Klan. Then, after denying the presidential nomination to William G. McAdoo, Woodrow Wilson's treasury secretary, son-in-law, and heir apparent, they nearly secured it for their candidate, Alfred E. Smith, the Irish American governor of New York. McAdoo represented the rural and southern constituencies of the Democratic Party. His forces ended up battling Smith's urban-ethnic forces for 103 ballots, until the two men gave up and supporters from each camp switched their votes to a compromise candidate, the corporate lawyer John W. Davis.

The nomination fight devastated the Democratic Party in the short term, and the popular Coolidge easily defeated the little-known Davis. This split between the party's rural Protestant and urban-ethnic constituencies would keep the Democrats from the White House for nearly a decade. But the convention upheaval of 1924 also marked an important milestone in the bid by European Americans for political power. They would achieve a second milestone at the Democratic national convention of 1928 when, after another bitter nomination struggle, they were finally successful in securing the presidential nomination for Al Smith. Never before had a major political party nominated a Catholic for that high office. Herbert Hoover crushed Smith in the general election, as nativists stirred up anti-Catholic prejudice yet again, and as large numbers of southern Democrats either stayed home or voted Republican. But there were encouraging signs in the campaign, none more so than

Smith's beating Hoover in the nation's 12 largest cities. European Americans would yet have their day.

African Americans

Despite the urban race riots of 1919 (see Chapter 4), African Americans continued to leave their rural homes for the industrial centers of the South and the North. In the 1920s alone, nearly a million blacks traveled North. In New York City and Chicago, their numbers grew so large—300,000 in New York and 234,000 in Chicago—that they formed cities unto themselves. When word of New York City's urban black enclave reached the Caribbean, thousands of West Indian blacks set off for Harlem. Within these black metropolises, complex societies emerged consisting of workers, businessmen, professionals, intellectuals, artists, and entertainers. Social differentiation intensified as various groups—long-resident northerners and newly arrived southerners, religious conservatives and cultural radicals, African Americans and African Caribbeans—found reason to disapprove of one another's ways. Still, the diversity and complexity of urban black America were thrilling, nowhere more so than in Harlem, the "Negro capital." The black writer James Weldon Johnson described Harlem in the 1920s:

> Throughout colored America Harlem is the recognized Negro capital. Indeed, it is Mecca for the sightseer, the pleasure-seeker, the curious, the adventurous, the enterprising, the ambitious, and the talented of the entire Negro world. . . . Not merely a colony or a community or a settlement—not at all a "quarter" or a slum or a fringe—[Harlem is] . . . a black city, located in the heart of white Manhattan, and containing more Negroes to the square mile than any other spot on earth. It strikes the uninformed observer as a phenomenon, a miracle straight out of the skies.

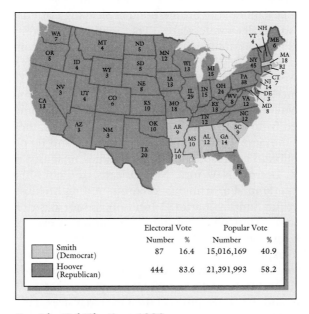

		Electoral Vote		Popular Vote	
		Number	%	Number	%
	Smith (Democrat)	87	16.4	15,016,169	40.9
	Hoover (Republican)	444	83.6	21,391,993	58.2

Presidential Election, 1928

Not even the glamour of Harlem could erase the reality of racial discrimination, however. Most African Americans could find work only in New York City's least-desired and lowest-paying jobs. Because they could rent apartments only in areas that real estate agents and banks had designated as "colored," African Americans suffered the highest rate of residential segregation of any minority group. Although there were fashionable districts in Harlem, where affluent blacks lived, most of the housing stock was poor and rents were high.

Harlem became a black ghetto, an area set apart from the rest of the city by the skin color of its inhabitants, by its higher population density and poverty rate, by its higher incidence of infectious diseases, and by the lower life expectancy of its people. At the same time, substantial numbers of New York City's European ethnics were leaving their lower Manhattan ghettos for the "greener" pastures of Brooklyn and the Bronx. That the Harlem ghetto crystallized at the very moment when European ethnics were able to break out of their crowded urban neighborhoods for more roomy and airy locations on the urban periphery reveals the particularly harsh form of antiblack racism.

Blacks did enjoy some important economic breakthroughs in the 1920s. Henry Ford, for example, hired large numbers of African Americans to work in his Detroit auto factories. But even here a racist logic was operating, for Ford believed that black and white workers, divided along racial lines, would not challenge his authority. Until the 1940s, in fact, unions made less headway at Ford plants than at the plants of other major automobile manufacturers.

African Americans grew pessimistic about achieving racial equality. After Marcus Garvey's black nationalist movement collapsed in the mid-1920s (see Chapter 4), no comparable organization arose to take its place. The NAACP continued to fight racial discrimination, and the Urban League carried on quiet negotiations with industrial elites to open up jobs to African Americans. Black socialists led by A. Philip Randolph built a strong all-black union, the Brotherhood of Sleeping Car Porters. But the victories were small; white allies were scarce. The political initiatives emerging among European ethnics had no counterpart in the African American community.

In terms of black culture, however, the 1920s were remarkably vigorous and productive. Black musicians coming north to Chicago and New York brought with them their distinctive musical styles, most notably the blues and ragtime. Influenced by the harmonies and techniques of European classical music, which black musicians learned from their European ethnic counterparts, these southern styles metamorphosed into jazz. Urban audiences, first black and then white, found this new music irresistible. They responded to its melodies, its sensuality, its creativity, its savvy. In Chicago, Detroit, New York, New Orleans, and elsewhere, jazz musicians came together in cramped apartments, cabarets, and nightclubs to jam, compete, and entertain. Willie Smith, Charles P. Johnson, Count Basie, Fats Waller, Duke Ellington, and Louis Armstrong were among the most famous musicians of the day. By the late 1920s they were being hailed in Europe as well.

Jazz seemed to express something quintessentially modern. Jazz musicians broke free of convention, improvised freely, and produced new sounds that gave rise to new sensations. Both blacks and whites found in jazz an escape from the routine, the predictability, and the conventions of their everyday lives. That they could listen to it in nightclubs where they could drink and enjoy the company of attractive partners intensified their pleasure.

The Harlem Renaissance

Paralleling the emergence of jazz was a black literary and artistic awakening known as the Harlem Renaissance. Black novelists, poets, painters, sculptors, and playwrights set about creating works rooted in their own culture instead of imitating the styles of white Europeans and Americans. The movement had begun during the war, when blacks sensed that they might at last be advancing to full equality. It was symbolized by the image of the "New Negro," who would no longer be deferential to whites but who would display his or her independence through talent and determination. The "New Negro" would be assertive in every field—at work, in politics, in the military, and in arts and letters. As racial discrimination intensified after the war, cultural activities took on special significance. The world of culture was the one place where blacks could express their racial pride and demonstrate their talent.

Langston Hughes, a young black poet, said of the Harlem Renaissance: "We younger Negro artists who create now intend to express our individual dark-skinned selves without fear or shame. If white people are pleased, we are glad. If they are not, it doesn't matter. We know we are beautiful. And ugly, too." The writers Claude McKay, Jean Toomer, and Zora Neale Hurston, the poet Countee Cullen, and the painter Aaron Douglas were other prominent Renaissance participants. In 1925, *Survey Graphic,* a white liberal magazine, devoted an entire issue to "Harlem—the Mecca of the New Negro." Alain Locke, an art and literary critic and

The Cotton Club Orchestra • This popular orchestra, led by Andy Preer (sixth from left), played in one of the premier jazz clubs in 1920s Harlem. The Cotton Club, like most of its counterparts, hired black musicians but refused to admit black customers. Orchestra members included (left to right) Depriest Wheeler, trombone; Leroy Maxey, drums; Andy Brown, tenor sax; Harry Cooper, trumpet; Earres Prince, piano; Preer, director/violinist; David Jones, C Melody Sax; Jimmy Smith, tuba; R. Q. Dickerson, trumpet; Charlie Stamps, banjo; and Eli Logan, alto sax.

professor of philosophy at Howard University in Washington, D.C., was editor of the issue and of the book *The New Negro,* published later that year. Locke became the movement's leading visionary and philosopher.

But even these cultural advances did not escape white prejudice. The most popular jazz nightclubs in Harlem, most of which were owned and operated by whites, refused to admit black customers. The only African Americans who were permitted inside were the jazz musicians, singers and dancers, prostitutes, and kitchen help. Moreover, the musicians had to play what the white patrons wanted to hear. Duke Ellington, for example, featured "jungle music," which for whites revealed the "true" African soul—sensual, innocent, primitive. Such pressures curtailed the artistic freedom of musicians and reinforced racist stereotypes of African Americans as inferior people who were closer to nature than the "more civilized" white audiences who came to hear their music.

Artists and writers experienced similar pressures. Many of them depended for their sustenance on the support of wealthy white patrons. Those patrons were generous, but they wanted a return on their investment. Charlotte Mason, the New York City matron who supported Hughes and Hurston, for example, felt free to judge their work and expected them to entertain her friends by demonstrating "authentic Negritude." Hurston accepted this role, but for Hughes it became intolerable. Both Hughes and Hurston paid a dear price for their patron's support, including the collapse of their once-close friendship.

Mexican Americans

After the Johnson-Reed Act of 1924, Mexicans became the country's chief source of immigrant labor. A total of 500,000 Mexicans came north in the 1920s. Some headed for the steel, auto, and meatpacking plants of the Midwest, but most settled in the Southwest, where they worked on the railroads and in construction, agriculture, and manufacturing. In Texas three of every four construction workers and eight of every 10 migrant farm workers were Mexicans. An official of the San Antonio Chamber of Commerce declared: "Mexican farm labor is rapidly proving the making of this State." In California, Mexican immigrants made up 75 percent of the state's agricultural workforce.

Mexican farm laborers in Texas worked long hours for little money. As a rule, they were paid from 50 cents to a dollar less per day than Anglo workers. They were usually barred from becoming machine operators or assuming other skilled positions. Forced to follow the crops, they had little opportunity to develop settled homes and communities. For shelter, Mexican farm workers were dependent on the facilities offered by farm owners. Farm owners rarely required the services of Mexican workers for more than several days or weeks, and few were willing to spend the money required to provide decent homes and schools. Houses typically lacked even wooden floors or indoor plumbing. Mexican laborers found it difficult to protest these conditions. Their knowledge of English and American law was limited. Few owned cars or trucks that would have allowed them to escape a bad employer and search for a good one. Many were in debt to employers who had advanced them money and who threatened them with jail if they failed to fulfill the terms of their contract. Others feared deportation; they lacked visas, having slipped

Mexican American Poverty • These adobe shacks along the Rio Grande between El Paso and Juarez illustrate the difficult circumstances in which many rural Mexican migrants lived.

into the United States illegally rather than pay the immigrant tax or endure harassment from the Border Patrol.

Increasing numbers of Mexican immigrants, however, found their way to California, where daily wages for agricultural work sometimes exceeded those in Texas by as much as 80 percent. Some escaped agricultural labor altogether for construction and manufacturing jobs in midwestern and southwestern cities. Thousands had worked on building military installations in San Antonio during the war, and by 1920 the 40,000 immigrants who lived there comprised the largest Mexican community in the United States. As the decade progressed, that distinction shifted to Los Angeles, where a rapidly growing Mexican population reached 100,000 by 1930. Mexican men in Los Angeles worked in the city's large railroad yards, at the city's numerous construction sites, as unskilled workers in local factories, and as agricultural workers in the fruit and vegetable fields of Los Angeles County. Mexican women labored in the city's garment shops, fish canneries, and food processing plants.

The Los Angeles Mexican American community increased in complexity as it grew in size. By the mid-1920s it included a growing professional class, a proud group of *californios* (Spanish-speakers who had been resident in California for generations), a large number of musicians and entertainers, a small but energetic band of entrepreneurs and businessmen, conservative clerics and intellectuals who had fled or been expelled from revolutionary Mexico, and Mexican government officials who had been sent to counter the influence of the conservative exiles and to strengthen the ties of the immigrants to their homeland. This diverse mix gave rise

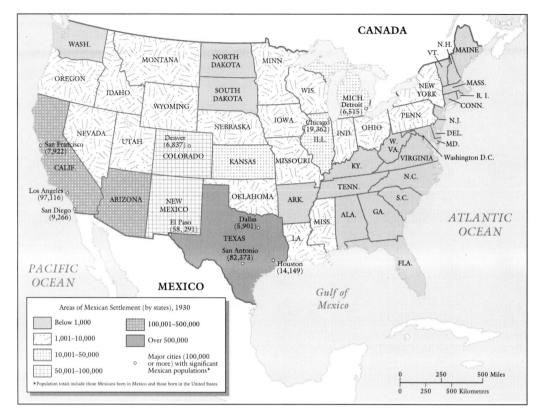

Mexican Population in the United States, 1930

to much internal conflict, but it also generated considerable cultural vitality. Indeed, Los Angeles became the same kind of magnet for Mexican Americans that Harlem had become for African Americans. Mexican musicians flocked to Los Angeles, as did Mexican playwrights. The city supported a vigorous Spanish-language theater. Mexican musicians performed on street corners, at ethnic festivals and weddings, at cabarets, and on the radio. Especially popular were folk ballads, called *corridos,* that spoke to the experiences of Mexican immigrants. Although very different in form and melody from the African American blues, *corridos* resembled the blues in their emphasis on the suffering, hope, and frustrations of ordinary folk.

This flowering of Mexican American culture in Los Angeles could not erase the low wages, high rates of infant mortality, racial discrimination, and other hardships Mexicans faced; nor did it encourage Mexicans, in Los Angeles or elsewhere, to mobilize themselves as a political force. Unlike European immigrants, Mexican immigrants showed little interest in becoming American citizens and acquiring the vote. Yet, the cultural vibrancy of the Mexican immigrant community did sustain many individuals who were struggling to survive in a strange, and often hostile, environment.

The "Lost Generation" and Disillusioned Intellectuals

Many native-born, white artists and intellectuals also felt uneasy in America in the 1920s. Their unease arose not from poverty or discrimination but from alienation. They despaired of American culture and regarded the average American as anti-intellectual, small-minded, materialistic, and puritanical. Many fled to Europe, and those who remained walled themselves off from contact with the masses. H. L. Mencken once described the American people as "a timorous, sniveling, poltroonish, ignominious mob." The novelist Sinclair Lewis ridiculed small-town Americans in *Main Street* (1920), "sophisticated" city dwellers in *Babbitt* (1922), physicians in *Arrowsmith* (1925), and evangelicals in *Elmer Gantry* (1927).

Before the First World War intellectuals and artists had been deeply engaged with "the people," some as progressive reformers, some as radicals. Although they were critical of many aspects of American society, they believed that they could help bring about a new politics and improve social conditions. Some of them joined the war effort before the United States had officially intervened. Ernest Hemingway, John Dos Passos, and e. e. cummings, among others, sailed to Europe and volunteered their services to the Allies, usually as ambulance drivers carrying wounded soldiers from the front. They found little idealism in the trenches, however—only disease and death.

America's intellectuals were further shocked by the effect the war had on American society. The wartime push for consensus created intolerance of radicals, immigrants, and blacks. Intellectuals had been further dismayed by Prohibition, the rebirth of the Ku Klux Klan, the rise of fundamentalism, and the executions of Sacco and Vanzetti. Not only had many Americans embraced conformity for themselves, but they seemed determined to force conformity on others. The young critic Harold Stearns wrote in 1921 that "the most moving and pathetic fact in the social life of America today is emotional and aesthetic starvation." Before these words were published, Stearns had sailed for France. So many alienated young men like Stearns showed up in Paris that Gertrude Stein, an American writer whose Paris apartment became a gathering place for them, took to calling them the "Lost Generation."

The indictment of America by these writers and intellectuals was not always justified. Most of them were young and inexperienced, with little knowledge of how most Americans lived. Few expressed sympathy for the plight of farmers or the working-class poor. Few knew much about the rich cultural heritage of immigrant communities. Still, they managed to convert their disillusionment into a new literary sensibility. The finest works of the decade focused on the psychological toll of living in what the poet T. S. Eliot referred to as *The Waste Land* (1922). F. Scott Fitzgerald's novel *The Great Gatsby* (1925) told of a man destroyed by his desire to be accepted into a world of wealth, fancy cars, and fast women. In the novel *A Farewell to Arms* (1929), Ernest Hemingway wrote of an American soldier overwhelmed by the sense-lessness and brutality of war who deserts the army for the company of a woman he loves. The playwright Eugene O'Neill created characters haunted by despair, loneliness, and unfulfilled longing. Writers created innovations in style as well as in content. Sherwood Anderson, in his novel *Winesburg, Ohio* (1919), blended fiction and autobiography. John Dos Passos, in *Manhattan Transfer* (1925), mixed journalism with more traditional literary methods. Hemingway wrote in an understated, laconic prose that somehow drew attention to his characters' rage and vulnerability.

White southern writers found a tragic sensibility surviving from the South's defeat in the Civil War that spoke to their own loss of hope. One group of writers, calling themselves "the Agrarians," argued that the enduring agricultural character of their region offered a more hopeful path to the future than did the mass-production and mass-consumption regime that had overtaken the North. In 1929 William Faulkner published *The Sound and the Fury,* the first in a series of novels set in northern Mississippi's fictional Yoknapatawpha County. Faulkner explored the violence and terror that marked relationships among family members and towns-people, while at the same time maintaining compassion and understanding. Faulkner, Lewis, Hemingway, O'Neill, and Eliot each received the Nobel Prize for Literature.

Democracy on the Defensive

Their disdain for the masses led many intellectuals to question democracy itself. If ordinary people were as stupid, prejudiced, and easily manipulated as they seemed, how could they be entrusted with the fate of the nation? Although few intellectuals were as frank as Mencken, who dismissed democracy as "the worship of jackals by jackasses," their distrust of democracy ran deep. Walter Lippmann, a former radical and progressive, declared that modern society had rendered democracy obsolete. In his view, average citizens, buffeted by propaganda emanating from powerful opinion-makers, could no longer make the kind of informed, rational judgments that were needed to make democracy work. They were vulnerable to demagogues determined to keep them in irrational and dangerous mobs. Lippmann's solution, and that of many other political commentators, was to shift government power from the people to educated elites. Those elites, who would be appointed rather than elected, would conduct foreign and domestic policy in an informed, intelligent way. Only then, in Lippmann's view, could government in the United States be effective and just.

The influence and prestige of Mencken and Lippmann was especially strong among university students, whose ranks and political significance were growing. But the antidemocratic views of Mencken, Lippmann, and their ilk did not go uncontested. The philosopher John Dewey, who taught at Columbia University but whose reputation and influence extended well beyond academia, was the most articulate spokesman for the "prodemocracy" position. He acknowledged that the concentration of power in a few giant organizations had eroded the authority of Congress, the presidency, and other democratic institutions. But democracy was not doomed, he insisted. The people could reclaim their freedom by making big business subject to government control. The government could then use its power to democratize corporations and to regulate the communications industry to ensure that every citizen had access to the facts needed to make reasonable, informed political decisions.

Dewey's views attracted the support of a wide range of liberal intellectuals and reformers, including Robert and Helen Lynd, the authors of *Middletown;* Rexford Tugwell, professor of economics at Columbia; and Felix Frankfurter, a rising star at Harvard's law school. These people had ties to labor leaders such as Sidney Hillman and to reformers in philanthropic foundations such as Mary Van Kleeck of the

Al Smith, Democratic Presidential Candidate • Herbert Hoover crushed Al Smith, the governor of New York, in the 1928 elections, generating pessimism in Democratic ranks about the possibilities for a renewal of progressive politics. But Smith did carry the nation's 12 largest cities, a sign that a new urban, and liberal, constituency was taking shape.

Russell Sage Foundation. Some were gaining experience as policymakers in reform administrations like that of New York Governor Franklin D. Roosevelt. They formed the vanguard of a new liberal movement that was committed to taking up the work the progressives had left unfinished.

But these reformers were utterly without power, except in a few states. The Republican Party had driven reformers from its ranks. The Democratic Party was a fallen giant, crippled by a split between its principal constituencies—rural Protestants and urban ethnics—over Prohibition, immigration restriction, and the Ku Klux Klan. The labor movement was moribund. The Socialist Party had never recovered from the trauma of war and Bolshevism. La Follette's Farmer-Labor Party, after a promising debut, had stalled. John Dewey and his friends tried to launch yet another third party, but they failed to raise money or arouse mass support.

Reformers took little comfort in the presidential election of 1928. Hoover's smashing victory suggested that the trends of the 1920s—the dominance of the Republicans, the centrality of Prohibition to political debate, the paralysis of the Democrats, the growing economic might of capitalism, and the pervasive influence of the consumer culture—would continue unabated.

Conclusion

Signs abounded in the 1920s that Americans were creating a new and bountiful society. The increased accessibility of cars, radios, vacuum cleaners, and other consumer durables; rising real wages, low unemployment, and installment buying; the widening circle of stock owners; and the spread of welfare capitalism—all these pointed to an economy that had become more prosperous, more consumer-oriented, even somewhat more egalitarian. Moves to greater equality within marriage and to enhanced liberty for single women in terms of dress, activities, and aspirations suggested that economic change was propelling social change as well.

But the changes unfolded unevenly. Many working-class and rural Americans benefited little from the decade's prosperity. And the changes aroused resistance, especially from farmers and small-town Americans who feared that the rapid growth of cities and the large urban settlements of European and Mexican Catholics, Jews, and African Americans were rendering their white, Protestant America unrecognizable.

In the Democratic Party, farmers, small-town Americans, and moral traditionalists fought bitterly against the growing power of urban, ethnic constituencies. Elsewhere, the traditionalists battled hard to protect religion's authority against the inroads of science and to purge the nation of "inferior" population streams. In the process they arrayed themselves against American traditions of liberty and equality, even as they posed as the defenders of the best that America had to offer.

Their resistance to change caused many of the nation's most talented artists and writers to turn away from their fellow Americans in disgust. Meanwhile, although ethnic and racial minorities experienced high levels of discrimination, they nevertheless found enough freedom to create vibrant ethnic and racial communities and to launch projects—as in the case of African Americans in Harlem and Mexican Americans in Los Angeles—of cultural renaissance.

The Republican Party, having largely shed its reputation for reform, took credit for engineering the new economy of consumer plenty. It looked forward to years of political dominance. A steep and unexpected economic depression, however, would soon dash that expectation, revive the Democratic Party, and destroy Republican political power for a generation.

Chronology

1920 Prohibition goes into effect • Warren G. Harding defeats James M. Fox for presidency • Census reveals a majority of Americans live in urban areas • 8 million cars on road

1922 United States, Britain, Japan, France, and Italy sign Five-Power Treaty, agreeing to reduce size of their navies

1923 Teapot Dome scandal lands Secretary of the Interior Albert Fall in jail • Harding dies in office; Calvin Coolidge becomes president

1924 Dawes Plan to restructure Germany's war debt put in effect • Coolidge defeats John W. Davis for presidency • Ku Klux Klan membership approaches 4 million • Immigration Restriction Act cuts immigration by 80 percent and discriminates against Asians and southern and eastern Europeans

1925 Scopes trial upholds right of Tennessee to bar teaching of evolution in public schools • *Survey Graphic* publishes a special issue, *The New Negro*, announcing the Harlem Renaissance • F. Scott Fitzgerald publishes *The Great Gatsby* • U.S. withdraws Marines from Nicaragua

1926 Revenue Act cuts income and estate taxes • Coolidge vetoes McNary-Haugen bill, legislation meant to relieve agricultural distress • U.S. sends Marines back to Nicaragua to end civil war and protect U.S. property

1928   15 nations sign Kellogg-Briand pact, pledging to avoid war • Coolidge vetoes McNary-Haugen bill again • Herbert Hoover defeats Alfred E. Smith for presidency

1929   Union membership drops to 3 million • 27 million cars on road • William Faulkner publishes *The Sound and the Fury*

1930   Los Angeles's Mexican population reaches 100,000

Suggested Readings

Overviews

See William Leuchtenberg, *The Perils of Prosperity, 1914–1932* (1958); Geoffrey Perrett, *America in the Twenties* (1982); and Ellis Hawley, *The Great War and the Search for a Modern Order: A History of the American People and Their Institutions, 1917–1933* (1979). Frederick Lewis Allen, *Only Yesterday* (1931), remains the most entertaining account of the Jazz Age.

Prosperity and a Consumer Society

George Soule, *Prosperity Decade: From War to Depression, 1917–1929* (1947), offers a thorough analysis of the decade's principal economic developments. Alfred D. Chandler Jr., *Strategy and Structure: Chapters in the History of the American Enterprise* (1962), and Adolph A. Berle Jr. and Gardiner F. Means, *The Modern Corporation and Private Property* (1932), examine changes in the structure and management of corporations. Important works on the consumer revolution include Robert S. Lynd and Helen Merrell Lynd, *Middletown: A Study in Modern American Culture* (1929); Warren I. Susman, *Culture as History: The Transformation of American Society in the Twentieth Century* (1984); Stewart Ewen, *Captains of Consciousness: Advertising and the Social Roots of the Consumer Culture* (1976); Roland Marchand, *Advertising the American Dream: Making Way for Modernity, 1920–1940* (1985); Richard Wightman Fox and T. J. Jackson Lears, eds., *The Culture of Consumption: Critical Essays in American History, 1880–1980* (1983); and Jackson Lears, *Fables of Abundance: A Cultural History of Advertising in America* (1994). The ways in which consumer ideals reshaped gender roles and family life can be followed in Ruth Schwartz Cowan, *More Work for Mother* (1982); William Chafe, *The American Woman: Her Changing Social, Economic, and Political Role* (1972); Dorothy M. Brown, *Setting a Course: American Women in the 1920s* (1987); Paula S. Fass, *The Damned and the Beautiful: American Youth in the 1920s* (1977); and Ben B. Lindsay and Wainright Evans, *The Companionate Marriage* (1927).

Republican Politics

John D. Hicks, *Republican Ascendancy, 1921–1933* (1960), and Arthur M. Schlesinger Jr., *The Crisis of the Old Order* (1957), are excellent introductions to national politics during the 1920s. On Harding, see Robert K. Murray, *The Politics of Normalcy: Governmental Theory and Practice in the Harding-Coolidge Era* (1973), and Eugene Trani and David Wilson, *The Presidency of Warren G. Harding* (1977). William Allen White, *A Puritan in Babylon* (1939), is a colorful portrait of Calvin Coolidge; but see also Donald McCoy, *Calvin Coolidge: The Quiet President* (1967), and Thomas B. Silver, *Coolidge and the Historians* (1982). On Hoover's efforts to substitute "associational" politics for laissez-faire, two indispensable sources are Ellis Hawley, ed., *Herbert Hoover as Secretary of Commerce: Studies in New Era Thought and Practice* (1974), and Joan Hoff Wilson, *Herbert Hoover: Forgotten Progressive* (1975); see also David Burner, *Herbert Hoover: A Public Life* (1979). On Republican foreign policy, see Thomas Buckley, *The United States and the Washington Conference* (1970); Dexter Perkins, *Charles Evans Hughes and American Democratic Statesmanship* (1953); Joan Hoff Wilson, *American Business and Foreign Policy, 1920–1933* (1971); Warren I. Cohen, *Empire without Tears* (1987); Derek A. Aldcroft, *From Versailles to Wall Street, 1919–1929* (1977); and Robert H. Ferrell, *Peace in Their Time* (1952).

Agricultural Distress and Prohibition

On agricultural distress and protest, see Gilbert Fite, *George Peek and the Fight for Farm Parity* (1954), and Theodore Saloutos and John D. Hicks, *Twentieth Century Populism: Agricultural Discontent in the*

Middle West, 1900–1939 (1951). For an examination of the economic and social effects of Prohibition, consult Andrew Sinclair, *The Era of Excess* (1962); Norman Clark, *Deliver Us from Evil: An Interpretation of American Prohibition* (1976); Mark Thornton, *The Economics of Prohibition* (1991); and John C. Burnham, *Bad Habits: Drinking, Smoking, Taking Drugs, Gambling, Sexual Misbehavior, and Swearing in American History* (1993).

Nativism, Ku Klux Klan, and Immigration Restriction

John Higham, *Strangers in the Land: Patterns of American Nativism, 1865–1925* (1955), remains the best work on the spirit of intolerance that gripped America in the 1920s. On the 1920s resurgence of the Ku Klux Klan, consult David Chalmers, *Hooded Americanism: The History of the Ku Klux Klan* (1965); Kenneth Jackson, *The Ku Klux Klan in the City* (1965); Nancy MacLean, *Behind the Mask of Chivalry: The Making of the Second Ku Klux Klan* (1994); Leonard J. Moore, *Citizen Klansmen: The Ku Klux Klan in Indiana, 1921–1928* (1991); Katherine M. Blee, *Women of the Klan: Racism and Gender in the 1920s* (1991); and Shawn Lay, ed., *The Invisible Empire in the West: Toward a New Historical Appraisal of the Ku Klux Klan of the 1920s* (1992). The movement for immigration restriction is examined in William S. Bernard, *American Immigration Policy: A Reappraisal* (1950); Robert A. Divine, *American Immigration Policy* (1957); and Henry B. Leonard, *The Open Gates: The Protest Against the Movement to Restrict Immigration, 1896–1924* (1980).

Liberal and Fundamentalist Protestantism

Ferenc Morton Szasz, *The Divided Mind of Protestant America, 1880–1930* (1982), expertly analyzes the split in Protestant ranks between liberals and fundamentalists. On the fundamentalist movement itself, consult George S. Marsden, *Fundamentalism in American Culture* (1980); Norman Furniss, *The Fundamentalist Controversy, 1918–1931* (1954); and William G. McLoughlin, *Modern Revivalism* (1959). Ray Ginger, *Six Days or Forever? Tennessee versus John Thomas Scopes* (1958), is a colorful account of the Scopes trial, while Lawrence Levine, *Defender of the Faith: William Jennings Bryan: The Last Decade, 1915–1925* (1965), offers a sympathetic portrait of Bryan during his final years. For a provocative reading of the Scopes trial, see Garry Wills, *Under God: Religion and American Politics* (1990).

Industrial Workers

Irving Bernstein, *The Lean Years: A History of the American Worker, 1920–1933* (1960), remains the most thorough examination of 1920s workers, but it should be supplemented with Robert H. Zeiger, *American Workers, American Unions, 1920–1985* (1986); Melvyn Dubofsky and Warren Van Tine, *John L. Lewis: A Biography* (1977); Leslie Tentler, *Wage-Earning Women* (1979); and Jacquelyn Hall et al., *Like a Family: The Making of a Southern Cotton Mill World* (1987). Siegfried Giedion, *Mechanization Takes Command: A Contribution to Anonymous History* (1948), is an insightful account of the effects of mechanization.

European American Ethnic Communities

On ethnic communities and Americanization in the 1920s, see Gary Gerstle, *Working-Class Americanism: The Politics of Labor in a Textile City, 1914–1960* (1989); Lizabeth Cohen, *Making a New Deal: Industrial Workers in Chicago, 1919–1939* (1990); and Stephen J. Shaw, *The Catholic Parish as a Way-Station of Ethnicity and Americanization: Chicago's Germans and Italians, 1903–1939* (1991). Leonard Dinnerstein, *Antisemitism in America* (1994), analyzes the resurgence of anti-Semitism in the 1920s and the use of quotas by universities to limit the enrollment of Jews. On the growing political strength of European American ethnics, see David Burner, *The Politics of Provincialism* (1967); Oscar Handlin, *Al Smith and His America* (1958); Paula Elder, *Governor Alfred E. Smith: The Politician as Reformer* (1983); and Kristi Andersen, *The Creation of a Democratic Majority, 1928–1936* (1979).

African Americans

Good studies of the African American experience in the 1920s include Gilbert Osofsky, *Harlem: The Making of a Ghetto: Negro New York, 1890–1930* (1963); Kenneth L. Kusmer, *A Ghetto Takes Shape:*

Black Cleveland, 1870–1930; Joe William Trotter Jr., *Black Milwaukee: The Making of an Industrial Proletariat, 1915–1945* (1985); and August Meier and Elliott Rudwick, *Black Detroit and the Rise of the UAW* (1979). Kathy H. Ogren, *The Jazz Revolution: Twenties America and the Meaning of Jazz* (1989), offers a probing analysis of jazz's place in 1920s culture. On the Harlem Renaissance, see Nathan Huggins, *Harlem Renaissance* (1971); Cary D. Mintz, *Black Culture and the Harlem Renaissance* (1988); and Jervis Anderson, *This Was Harlem: A Cultural Portrait, 1900–1950* (1981). Arnold Rampersand, *The Life of Langston Hughes,* 2 vols. (1986–1988), and Robert E. Hemenway, *Zora Neale Hurston: A Literary Biography* (1977), are important biographical works on two leading African American literary figures.

Mexican Americans

On the 1920s experience of Mexican immigrants and Mexican Americans, see George J. Sánchez, *Becoming Mexican American: Ethnicity, Culture and Identity in Chicano Los Angeles, 1900–1945* (1993); David Montejano, *Anglos and Mexicans in the Making of Texas, 1836–1986* (1987); Ricardo Romo, *East Los Angeles: History of a Barrio* (1983); Mark Reisler, *By the Sweat of Their Brow: Mexican Immigrant Labor in the United States, 1900–1940* (1976); and Manuel Gamio, *The Life Story of the Mexican Immigrant* (1931).

The "Lost Generation" and Disillusioned Intellectuals

Malcolm Cowley, *Exiles Return* (1934), is a marvelous account of the writers and artists who comprised the "lost generation." See also Arlen J. Hansen, *Expatriate Paris* (1990), and William Wiser, *The Great Good Place: American Expatriate Women in Paris* (1991). On the southern "Agrarians," see John Stewart, *The Burden of Time* (1965), and Paul K. Conkin, *Southern Agrarians* (1988). Frederick J. Hoffman, *The Twenties: American Writing in the Postwar Decade,* rev. ed. (1962), is a fine sampler of the decade's best fiction. For biographical treatments of some of the decade's notable writers, consult Cleanth Brooks, *William Faulkner: The Yoknapathwapha County* (1963); Joel Williamson, *William Faulkner and Southern* History (1993); Carlos Baker, *Hemingway: The Writer as Artist* (1965); Kim Townshend, *Sherwood Anderson* (1987); and Virginia S. Carr, *Dos Passos: A Life* (1984). For a provocative interpretation of the intertwined character of white and black literary cultures in 1920s New York, see Ann Douglas, *Terrible Honesty: Mongrel Manhattan in the 1920s* (1995).

Political Thought

Robert Crunden, *From Self to Society: Transition in American Thought, 1919–1941* (1972), and Roderick Nash, *The Nervous Generation: American Thought, 1917–1930* (1969), are superior analyses of intellectual thought during the decade. On Mencken, see George H. Douglas, *H. L. Mencken* (1978), and Edward A. Martin, *H. L. Mencken and the Debunkers* (1984). Ronald Steel, *Walter Lippmann and the American Century* (1980), and Robert Westbrook, *John Dewey and American Democracy* (1991), are the best biographies of these two critical thinkers. On the new reform vanguard that began to form around Sidney Hillman, Franklin Roosevelt, and others, see Steven Fraser, *Labor Will Rule: Sidney Hillman and the Rise of American Labor* (1991), and Kenneth S. Davis, *FDR: The New York Years, 1928–1933* (1985).

6

The Great Depression
and the New Deal, 1929–1939

T he Great Depression began on October 29, 1929—"Black Tuesday"—with a spectacular stock market crash. On that one day, the value of stocks plummeted $14 billion. By the end of that year, stock prices had fallen 50 percent from their September highs. By 1932, the worst year of the depression, they had fallen another 30 percent. In three years, $74 billion of wealth had simply vanished. Meanwhile the unemployment rate had soared to 25 percent.

Many Americans who lived through the Great Depression were never able to forget the scenes of misery that they saw on every hand. In cities, the poor meekly awaited their turn for a piece of stale bread and thin gruel at ill-funded soup kitchens. Scavengers poked through garbage cans for food, scoured railroad tracks for coal that had fallen from trains, and sometimes ripped up railroad ties for fuel. Hundreds of thousands of Americans built makeshift shelters out of cardboard, scrap metal, and whatever else they could find in the city dump. They called their towns "Hoovervilles," after the president whom they despised for his apparent refusal to help them.

The Great Depression brought cultural crisis as well as economic crisis. In the 1920s the leaders of American business had successfully redefined the national culture in business terms, as Americans' values became synonymous with the values of business: economic growth, freedom of enterprise, and acquisitiveness. But the swagger and bluster of American businessmen during the 1920s made them vulnerable to attack in the 1930s, as jobs, incomes, and growth all disappeared. With the prestige of business and business values in decline, how could Americans regain their hope and recover their confidence in the future? In 1930 and 1931 there were no convincing answers.

The gloom broke in early 1933 when Franklin Delano Roosevelt became president and unleashed the power of government to regulate capitalist enterprises, to restore the economy to health, and to guarantee the social welfare of Americans unable to help themselves. Roosevelt called his pro-government program a "new deal for the American people," and it would dominate national politics for the next 40 years. Hailed as a hero, Roosevelt became (and remains) the only president to serve more than two terms. In the short term, the New Deal did not restore prosperity to America. But the "liberalism" that the New Deal championed found acceptance among millions, who agreed with Roosevelt that only a large and powerful government could guarantee Americans their liberty.

Causes of the Great Depression

There had been other depressions, or "panics," in American history, and no one would have been surprised had the boom of the 1920s been followed by an economic downturn lasting a year or two, not unlike the one that had followed the First World War. No one was prepared, however, for the economic catastrophe of the 1930s.

Stock Market Speculation

Any explanation of the depth and longevity of the Great Depression must begin with the collapse of the stock market. In 1928 and 1929 the New York Stock Exchange had undergone a remarkable run-up in prices. In less than two years, the Dow Jones Industrial Average had doubled. Money had poured into the market. Everybody expected to get rich quick. But many of these investors were buying on 10 percent "margin"—putting up only 10 percent of the price of a stock and borrowing the rest from brokers or banks. Few thought they would ever have to repay these loans with money out of their own pockets. Instead, investors expected to be able to resell their shares within a few months at dramatically higher prices, pay back their loans from the proceeds, and still clear a handsome profit. And, for a while, that is exactly what they did. In 1928 alone, for example, the value of RCA stock soared 400 percent. But the possibility of making a fortune with an investment of only a few thousand dollars only intensified investors' greed. Eventually, stock prices were bid up to irrational levels. Money flowed indiscriminately into all kinds of risky enterprises, as speculation became rampant. The stock market spiraled upward, out of control. When confidence in future earnings finally faltered, in October 1929, creditors began demanding that investors who had bought stocks on margin repay their loans. The market crashed from its dizzying heights.

Still, the crash, by itself, does not explain why the Great Depression lasted as long as it did. Poor decision making by the Federal Reserve Board, an ill-advised tariff that took effect soon after the depression hit, and a lopsided concentration of wealth in the hands of the rich deepened the economic collapse and made recovery more difficult.

Mistakes by the Federal Reserve Board

In 1930 and 1931, the Federal Reserve curtailed the amount of money in circulation and raised interest rates, thereby making credit more difficult for the public to secure. Although such a tight money policy might have restrained the stock market and strengthened the economy if it had been used during the boom years of 1928 or 1929, it was disastrous once the market had crashed. What the economy needed in 1930 and 1931 was an expanded money supply, lower interest rates, and easier credit. Such a course would have enabled debtors to pay their creditors. Instead, by choosing the opposite course, the Federal Reserve plunged an economy starved for credit deeper into depression. Higher interest rates also triggered an international crisis, as the banks of Germany and Austria, heavily dependent on U.S. loans, went bankrupt. The German-Austrian collapse, in turn, spread financial panic through

Europe and ruined many U.S. manufacturers and banks specializing in European trade and investment.

An Ill-Advised Tariff

The Tariff Act of 1930, also known as the Hawley-Smoot Tariff, accelerated economic decline abroad and at home. Throughout the 1920s, agricultural interests had been seeking higher tariffs as a way of protecting American farmers against foreign competition. But Hawley-Smoot not only raised tariffs on 75 agricultural goods, it also raised tariffs on 925 manufactured products. Industrialists had convinced their supporters in the Republican-controlled Congress that such protection would give American industry much needed assistance. But, as a thousand American economists had warned, the legislation, which raised ad valorem duties from 32 to 40 percent (the highest rate in American history), was a disaster. Angry foreign governments retaliated by raising their own tariff rates to keep out American goods. International trade, already weakened by the tight credit policies of the Federal Reserve, was dealt another blow at the very moment when it desperately needed a boost. The shortsighted monetary and trade policies of the U.S. government had spread economic crisis throughout the western industrialized world.

A Maldistribution of Wealth

A serious maldistribution in the nation's wealth that had developed in the 1920s also stymied economic recovery. Although average income rose in the 1920s, the income of the wealthiest families rose higher than the rest. Between 1918 and 1929 the share of the national income that went to the wealthiest 20 percent of the population rose by more than 10 percent, while the share that went to the poorest 60 percent fell by almost 13 percent. The Coolidge administration contributed to this maldistribution by lowering taxes on the wealthy, thereby increasing the proportion of the national wealth concentrated in their hands. The deepening inequality of income distribution slowed consumption and held back the growth of consumer-oriented industries (cars, household appliances, processed and packaged foods, recreation), the most dynamic elements of the U.S. economy. Even when the rich spent their money lavishly—building huge mansions, buying expensive cars, vacationing on the French Riviera—they still spent a smaller proportion of their total incomes on consumption than wage earners did. For the average wage earner in the 1920s, the purchase of a car might take one-quarter to one-half of annual earnings. Had more of the total increase in national income found its way into the pockets of average Americans during the 1920s, the demand for consumer goods would have been steadier and the newer consumer industries would have been correspondingly stronger. Such an economy might have recovered relatively quickly from the stock market crash of 1929. But recovery from the Great Depression did not come until 1941, more than a decade later.

Hoover: The Fall of a Self-Made Man

In 1928 Herbert Hoover seemed to represent living proof that the American dream could be realized by anyone who was willing to work for it. Circumstances that would have deterred others—the loss of both parents at an early age, being raised by relatives with little money—seemed only to intensify Hoover's ambition. At Stanford University he majored in geology. After graduation, he took part in mining expeditions to many parts of the world. As he rose quickly through corporate ranks, Hoover's managerial skills brought him more demanding and more handsomely rewarded tasks. By the age of 40, he had become a millionaire. Hoover's government service began during the First World War, when he won an international reputation for his expert management of agricultural production in the United States and his success in feeding millions of European soldiers and civilians. Then, in the 1920s, he served as an active and influential secretary of commerce (see Chapters 4 and 5). As the decade wound down, no American seemed better qualified to become president of the United States, an office that Hoover assumed in March 1929, after soundly defeating his Democratic opponent, Alfred E. Smith, in the 1928 presidential election. One of the architects of Coolidge prosperity, Hoover was certain he could make prosperity a permanent feature of American life. "We in America today are nearer to the final triumph over poverty than ever before in the history of any land," he declared in August 1928. A little more than a year later, and only six months after Hoover had taken office, the Great Depression struck.

Hoover's Program

Within a short time after the stock market collapse, the depression had spread to nearly every sector of the economy. To cope with the crisis, Hoover first turned to the "associational" principles he had followed as secretary of commerce (see Chapter 5). He encouraged organizations of farmers, industrialists, and bankers to share information, bolster one another's spirits, and devise policies to aid economic recovery. Farmers would restrict output, industrialists would hold wages at predepression levels, and bankers would help each other remain solvent. The federal government would provide them with information, strategies of mutual aid, occasional loans, and morale-boosting speeches.

Hoover, to his credit, pursued a more aggressive set of economic policies once he realized that associationalism, despite a brief moment of success in 1931, had failed to improve economic conditions. To ease the European crisis, Hoover secured a one-year moratorium on loan payments that European governments owed American banks. He steered through Congress the Glass-Steagall Act of 1932, intended to help American banks meet the demands of European depositors who wished to convert their dollars to gold. And to ease the crisis at home he began to expand the government's economic role. The Reconstruction Finance Corporation (RFC), created in 1932, made $2 billion available in loans to ailing banks and to corporations willing to build low-cost housing, bridges, and other public works. The RFC was the biggest federal peacetime intervention in the economy to that point in American history. The Home Loan Bank Board, set up that same year, offered funds to savings and loans, mortgage companies, and other financial institutions that lent money for home construction.

Despite this new government activism, Hoover was uncomfortable with the idea that the government was responsible for restoring the nation's economic welfare. In 1932 RFC expenditures gave rise to the largest peacetime deficit in U.S. history, prompting Hoover to try to balance the federal budget. He supported the Revenue Act of 1932, which tried to increase government revenues by raising taxes, thus erasing the deficit. He also insisted that the RFC issue loans only to relatively healthy institutions that were capable of repaying them and that it favor public works, such as toll bridges, that were likely to become self-financing. As a result of these constraints, the RFC spent considerably less than Congress had mandated. For example, it expended only about 20 percent of its $1.5 billion budget for public works.

Hoover was especially reluctant to engage the government in providing relief to unemployed and homeless Americans. Every citizen, he believed, must rely for survival on his or her own efforts. To give money to the poor, he insisted, would destroy their desire to work, undermine their sense of self-worth, and erode their capacity for citizenship.

But Hoover saw no similar peril in extending government assistance to ailing banks and businesses. Critics pointed to the seeming hypocrisy of Hoover's policies. For example, in 1930 Hoover refused a request of $25 million to help feed Arkansas farmers and their families but approved $45 million to feed the same farmers' livestock. And in 1932, shortly after rejecting an urgent request from Chicago for aid to help pay its teachers and municipal workers, Hoover approved a $90 million loan to rescue that city's Central Republic Bank.

The Bonus Army

In the spring of 1932 a group of army veterans mounted a particularly emotional challenge to Hoover's policies. In 1924 Congress had authorized a $1,000 bonus for First World War veterans in the form of compensation certificates that would mature in 1945. Now the veterans were demanding that the government pay the bonus immediately. A group of them from Portland, Oregon, decided to take action. Calling themselves the Bonus Expeditionary Force, they hopped onto empty boxcars of freight trains heading east, determined to stage a march on Washington. As the impoverished "army" moved eastward, many surviving on the handouts of sympathizers along the way, their ranks multiplied, so that by the time they reached Washington their number had swelled to 20,000, including wives and children. The so-called Bonus Army set up camp in the Anacostia Flats, southeast of the Capitol, and petitioned Congress for early payment of the promised bonus. The House of Representatives agreed, but the Senate turned them down. Hoover flatly refused to meet with them. When he learned that they were planning to confront him as he arrived at the Capitol to adjourn Congress in July, he secluded himself in the White House. Later that month, after a group of veterans who had been staying in abandoned Washington apartments had scuffled with the police, federal troops led by Army Chief of Staff Douglas MacArthur and 3rd Cavalry Commander George Patton attacked the veterans' Anacostia encampment, set the tents and shacks ablaze, and dispersed the protestors. In the process, more than 100 veterans were wounded and one infant was killed.

News that impoverished veterans and their families had been attacked in the nation's capital served only to harden anti-Hoover opinion. In the 1932 elections, the discredited Republicans were voted out of office after having dominated national politics (excepting Woodrow Wilson's two terms) for 36 years. Hoover received only 39.6 percent of the popular vote and just 59 (of 531) electoral votes. When he left the presidency in 1933 Hoover was a bewildered man, reviled by Americans for what they took to be his indifference to their suffering and his ineptitude in dealing with the economy's collapse.

The Democratic Roosevelt

The voters who swept Franklin D. Roosevelt into office in 1932 were determined to punish Hoover, even though they knew little about the man they were electing or what he would do as president.

An Early Life of Privilege

Roosevelt was born in 1882 into a patrician family. On his father's side, he was descended from Dutch gentry who in the 17th century had built large estates on the fertile land along the Hudson River. By the 1880s the Hyde Park manor where Roosevelt grew up had been in the family for over 200 years. His mother's family—the Delanos—were no less distinguished; several of her ancestors had come over on the Mayflower. In short, Roosevelt was raised among people who were convinced of their superiority in matters of ancestry, intelligence, and leadership. His education at Groton, Harvard College, and Columbia Law School was typical of the path followed by the sons of America's elite.

The Roosevelt family was wealthy, although not spectacularly so by the standards of the late 19th century. His parents' net worth of more than $1 million was relatively small in comparison to the fortunes being amassed by the rising class of industrialists and railroad tycoons. By the early 20th century, the Rockefellers, Carnegies, Vanderbilts, Stanfords, Harrimans, and Huntingtons each commanded fortunes of $50 to $100 million or more. This widening gap between the wealth of the old landed gentry and that of the new industrial tycoons disturbed families like the Roosevelts, who were concerned that the new economic elite would dislodge them from their social position. Moreover, they were offended by the habits of these newcomers—their vulgar displays of wealth, their lack of taste and etiquette, their indifference to the natural environment, their hostility toward those less fortunate than themselves. In 1899 Theodore Roosevelt, an older cousin of Franklin Roosevelt, had remarked that such people were "sunk in a scrambling commercialism, heedless of the higher life." He classified the highest type of man as "a statesman like Lincoln, a soldier like Grant"—men committed to national glory and national well-being. In his career as president and as a progressive, Theodore Roosevelt strove to become such a statesman through his willingness to challenge the trusts, his commitment to national parks, and his sympathies with the poor and powerless (see Chapter 2).

Theodore was young Franklin's hero. In 1907, as a 25-year-old law clerk, Franklin imagined a career for himself that would duplicate that of his world-famous cousin. First, he would win a seat in the New York State Assembly, then he would be appointed assistant secretary of the navy, and then he would become governor of New York, vice president, and then president of the United States. Incredibly, this is almost exactly what happened (except that he became a state senator rather than an assemblyman and he lost his 1920 race for the vice presidency).

The New York governorship and the U.S. presidency might have eluded him had he not been transformed by personal calamity. In 1921, at the age of 39, he was stricken by polio and permanently lost the use of his legs. Before becoming paralyzed, Roosevelt had not distinguished himself either at school or in the practice of law, nor could he point to many significant political achievements. He owed his political ascent more to his famous name than to actual accomplishments or hard work. He was charming, gregarious, and popular among his associates in the New York Democratic Party. He enjoyed a good time and devoted a great deal of energy to sailing, partying, and enjoying the company of women other than his wife, Eleanor. After his illness, Roosevelt spent the next two years bedridden, and he seemed to acquire a new determination and seriousness. He developed a compassion for those suffering misfortune that would later enable him to reach out to the millions caught in the Great Depression.

Roosevelt's physical debilitation also transformed his relationship with Eleanor, with whom he had shared a testy and increasingly loveless marriage. Eleanor's dedication to nursing Franklin back to health forged a new bond between them. More conscious of his dependence on others, he now welcomed her as a partner in his career. Eleanor soon displayed a talent for political organization and public speaking, a talent that surprised those who knew her only as a shy, awkward woman. She would become an active, eloquent First Lady, her husband's trusted ally, and an architect of American liberalism.

Roosevelt Liberalism

As governor of New York for four years (1929–1933), Roosevelt had initiated various reform programs, and his success made him the front-runner in the contest for the 1932 Democratic presidential nomination. It was by no means certain, however, that he would be the party's choice. Since 1924 the Democrats had been sharply divided between southern and midwestern agrarians on the one hand and northeastern ethnics (European immigrants and their descendants) on the other. The agrarians, heirs to William Jennings Bryan and now led by John Nance Garner of Texas and William Gibbs McAdoo of Georgia and California, favored government regulation—both of the nation's economy and of the private affairs of its citizens. Their support of government intervention in the pursuit of social justice marked them as economic progressives, while their advocacy of Prohibition revealed a deep cultural conservatism as well as a nativistic strain. By contrast, urban ethnics, led by Al Smith, an Irish Catholic, former governor of New York, and the 1928 Democratic presidential candidate, opposed Prohibition and other forms of government interference in the private lives of its citizens. On the issue of whether the government should regulate the economy, urban ethnics were divided, with Smith increasingly committed to a policy of laissez-faire and Senator Robert Wagner of New York and others supporting more federal control.

Roosevelt understood the need to carve out a middle ground, around which these factions could unite as a majority party. As governor of New York, and then as a presidential candidate in 1932, he surrounded himself with men and women who embraced the new reform movement called liberalism. Frances Perkins, Harry

Hopkins, Raymond Moley, Rexford Tugwell, Adolph Berle, Samuel Rosenman—all were interventionist in economic matters and libertarian on questions of personal behavior. They shared with the agrarians and Wagner's supporters a desire to regulate capitalism, but agreed with Al Smith that the government had no business telling people how to behave. This was the liberalism that Roosevelt championed.

But it by no means assured Roosevelt of the presidential nomination in 1932. At the Democratic convention in July, Smith worked to secure the nomination of the more conservative Newton Baker. McAdoo, hoping to deadlock the convention so that he could take the nomination himself, initially supported Speaker of the House Garner. As the balloting entered its third round, Roosevelt began to fall behind. At that point, however, McAdoo and Garner reevaluated their strategy. Recognizing that party unity and a victory in the general election might be more important than their own ambitions, they swung their support to Roosevelt, putting him over the top. Roosevelt, in gratitude, chose Garner as his vice presidential running mate. In a move designed to dramatize the party's new vigor, Roosevelt flew from the governor's mansion in Albany to Chicago to deliver his acceptance speech in person, the first nominee in party history to do so. In a rousing call to action, he declared: "Ours must be the party of liberal thought, of planned action, of enlightened international outlook, and of the greatest good for the greatest number of citizens." He promised "a new deal for the American people."

In his campaign, however, Roosevelt did not always emphasize this call to activism. He sometimes spoke of using government programs to stabilize the economy, but he also spent much of his time wooing conservative Democrats and rebutting Republican allegations that a Democratic victory would destroy all that was sacred in American life. In point of fact, Roosevelt only made two outright promises during his presidential campaign: to repeal Prohibition and to balance the budget. Thus, the nation had to wait until March 4, 1933—the day Roosevelt was sworn in as president—to learn what the New Deal would bring.

The First New Deal, 1933–1935

By the time Roosevelt assumed office, the economy lay in shambles. From 1929 to 1932 industrial production fell by 50 percent, while new investment declined from $16 billion to a mere fraction of $1 billion. In those same years more than 100,000 businesses went bankrupt. The nation's banking system was on the verge of collapse; in 1931 alone, more than 2,000 banks with deposits of $1.7 billion had shut their doors. The unemployment rate was soaring. Some Americans feared that the opportunity for reform had already passed.

But not Roosevelt. "This nation asks for action, and action now," Roosevelt declared in his inaugural address. "We must act, and act quickly." Roosevelt was true to his word. In his first "Hundred Days," from early March through early June 1933, Roosevelt persuaded Congress to pass 15 major pieces of legislation to help bankers, farmers, industrialists, workers, homeowners, the unemployed, and the hungry. He also prevailed on Congress to repeal Prohibition. Not all the new laws helped to relieve distress and promote recovery. But, in the short term, that seemed not to matter. Roosevelt had brought excitement and hope to the nation. He was confident, decisive, and defiantly cheery. He seemed to have no fear—either of the presidency itself or of the perilous state of the nation. "The only thing we have to fear is fear itself," he declared. He would not be discouraged. He used the radio to reach out to ordinary Americans. On the second Sunday after his inaugural, he launched a series of radio addresses known as "fireside chats." Whereas Hoover had behaved like a distant autocrat, upbraiding Americans for their lack of fortitude, Roosevelt behaved like a kindly grandfather, speaking in a plain, friendly, and direct voice to the forlorn and discouraged. In his first chat, he explained the banking crisis in simple terms, but without condescension. "I want to take a few minutes to talk with the people of the United States about banking," he began. An estimated 20 million Americans listened.

To hear the president speaking warmly and conversationally—as though he were actually there in the room—was riveting. An estimated 500,000 Americans wrote letters to Roosevelt within days of his inaugural address. Millions more, many of them barely literate, would write to him and to Eleanor Roosevelt over the next few years. Many of the letters were simply addressed to "Mr. or Mrs. Roosevelt, Washington, D.C." Democrats began to hang portraits of Franklin Roosevelt in their homes, often next to a picture of Jesus or the Madonna.

Franklin D. Roosevelt and the CCC • President Roosevelt poses with young men during a 1933 inspection visit to a Civilian Conservation Corps camp in Virginia's Shenandoah National Park. The CCC, which eventually put more than 2 million young men to work on environmental projects, was always one of Roosevelt's favorite programs.

Roosevelt was never the benign father figure he made himself out to be. His public image was skillfully crafted. Compliant news photographers agreed not to show him in a wheelchair or struggling with the leg braces and cane he used to take even small steps. For his part, Roosevelt often sought to hide the true content of legislation he proposed with diverting rhetoric. These media campaigns worked. Policy failures seemed not to diminish his appeal.

To his credit, Roosevelt used his popularity and executive power to strengthen American democracy at a time when democracy was crumbling around the world. During his long tenure in office, however, he set in motion tendencies that would long plague American politics: a drift of power to the executive branch, a steady expansion of the size and reach of federal bureaucracies, and a widening gap between political appearance and political reality.

Saving the Banks

Roosevelt's first order of business was to save the nation's financial system. By inauguration day, several states had already shut their banks. This was the crisis within the crisis—the event that made Congress willing to give Roosevelt broad powers to take some kind of action. Roosevelt immediately ordered all the nation's banks closed—a bold move he brazenly called a "bank holiday." He then had Congress rush through an Emergency Banking Act (EBA) that made federal loans available to private bankers. He followed that with an Economy Act (EA) that committed the government to balancing the budget.

Both the EBA and the EA were fiscally conservative programs that Hoover had proposed earlier. The EBA made it possible for private bankers to retain financial control of their institutions, and the EA announced the government's intention of pursuing a fiscally prudent course. Only after the financial crisis had eased did Roosevelt turn to the structural reform of banking. A second Glass-Steagall Act (1933) separated commercial banking from investment banking. It also created the Federal Deposit Insurance Corporation (FDIC), which assured depositors that the government would protect up to $5,000 of their savings (this was a far more sweeping piece of banking legislation than the first Glass-Steagall Act, passed by Congress during the Hoover presidency). The Securities Act (1933) and the Securities Exchange Act (1934) imposed long overdue regulation on the New York Stock Exchange, both by reining in buying on the margin (and other speculative practices) and by establishing the Securities and Exchange Commission to enforce federal law.

Saving the People

Although a fiscal conservative at heart, Roosevelt understood the need to temper financial prudence with compassion. Congress responded swiftly in 1933 to Roosevelt's request to establish the Federal Emergency Relief Administration (FERA), granting it $500 million for relief to the poor. To head it, Roosevelt appointed a brash young reformer, Harry Hopkins, who disbursed $2 million during his first two hours on the job. Roosevelt then won congressional approval for the Civilian Conservation Corps (CCC), which put more than 2 million single young men to work planting trees, halting erosion, and otherwise improving the environment. The following winter, Roosevelt launched the Civil Works Administration (CWA), an ambitious work-relief program, also under Harry Hopkins's direction, that hired 4 million unemployed at $15 a week and put them to work on 400,000 small-scale government projects. For middle-class Americans threatened with the loss of their homes, Roosevelt won Congressional approval for the Homeowners' Loan Corporation (1933) to refinance mortgages. These direct subsidies to millions of jobless and home-owning Americans lent credibility to Roosevelt's claim that the New Deal would set the country on a new course.

Repairing the Economy: Agriculture

In 1933 Roosevelt expected economic recovery to come not from relief, but through agricultural and industrial cooperation. He regarded the Agricultural Adjustment Act, passed in May, and the National Industrial Recovery Act (NIRA), passed in June, as the most important legislation of his Hundred Days. Both were based on the idea that curtailing production would trigger economic recovery. By shrinking the supply of agricultural and manufactured goods, Roosevelt's economists reasoned, they could restore the balance of normal market forces. Then, as demand for scarce goods exceeded supply, prices would rise and revenues would climb. Farmers and industrialists, earning a profit once again, would increase their

Legislation Enacted during the "Hundred Days," March 9–June 16, 1933

Date	Legislation	Purpose
March 9	Emergency Banking Act	Provide federal loans to private bankers
March 20	Economy Act	Balance the federal budget
March 22	Beer-Wine Revenue Act	Repeal Prohibition
March 31	Unemployment Relief Act	Create the Civilian Conservation Corps
May 12	Agricultural Adjustment Act	Establish a national agricultural policy
May 12	Emergency Farm Mortgage Act	Provide refinancing of farm mortgages
May 12	Federal Emergency Relief Act	Establish a national relief system, including the Civil Works Administration
May 18	Tennessee Valley Authority Act	Promote economic development of the Tennessee Valley
May 27	Securities Act	Regulate the purchase and sale of new securities
June 5	Gold Repeal Joint Resolution	Cancel the gold clause in public and private contracts
June 13	Home Owners Loan Act	Provide refinancing of home mortgages
June 16	National Industrial Recovery Act	Set up a national system of industrial self-government and establish the Public Works Administration
June 16	Glass-Steagall Banking Act	Create Federal Deposit Insurance Corporation; separate commercial and investment banking
June 16	Farm Credit Act	Reorganize agricultural credit programs
June 16	Railroad Coordination Act	Appoint federal coordinator of transportation

Source: Arthur M. Schlesinger Jr., *The Coming of the New Deal* (Boston: Houghton Mifflin, 1959), pp. 20–21.

investment in new technology and hire more workers, and prosperity and full employment would be the final result.

To curtail farm production, the Agricultural Adjustment Administration (AAA), set up by the Agricultural Adjustment Act, began paying farmers to keep a portion of their land out of cultivation and to reduce the size of their herds. The program was controversial, as many farmers, proud of their work ethic, did not readily accept the idea that they were to be paid more money for working less land and husbanding fewer livestock. But few refused to accept government payments. As one young Kansas farmer reported:

> There were mouthy individuals who seized every opportunity to run down the entire program . . . condemning it as useless, crooked, revolutionary, or dictatorial; but . . . when the first AAA payments were made available, shortly before Christmas, these same wordy critics made a beeline for the courthouse. They jostled and fell over each other in their mad scramble to be the first in line to receive allotment money.

The AAA had made no provision, however, for the countless tenant farmers and farm laborers who would be thrown out of work by the reduction in acreage. In the South, the victims were disproportionately black. A Georgia sharecropper wrote Harry Hopkins of his misery: "I have Bin farming all my life But the man I live with Has Turned me loose taking my mule [and] all my feed. . . . I can't get a Job so

Dustbowl Refugees on Their Way to Los Angeles • This photo juxtaposes the poverty of the Okies, forced to walk or hitch rides to California, with the luxury available to those mythical Americans who had made it (and who could afford a relaxing ride on the train).

Some one said Rite you." New Dealers within the Department of Agriculture, such as Rexford Tugwell and Jerome Frank, were sympathetic to the plight of share-croppers, but they were not successful during the First New Deal in extending to them the government's helping hand.

The programs of the AAA also proved inadequate to Great Plains farmers, whose economic problems had been compounded by ecological crisis. Just as the depression rolled in, the rain stopped falling on the plains. The land, stripped of its native grasses by decades of excessive plowing, dried up and turned to dust. And then the dust began to blow, sometimes traveling 1,000 miles across open prairie. Dust became a fixed feature of daily life on the plains (which soon became known as the "Dust Bowl"), covering furniture, floors, and stoves, and penetrating people's hair and lungs. The worst dust storm occurred on April 14, 1935, when a great mass of dust, moving at speeds of 45 to 70 miles an hour, roared through Colorado, Kansas, and Oklahoma, blackening the sky, suffocating cattle, and dumping thousands of tons of topsoil and red clay on homes and streets.

The government responded to this calamity by establishing the Soil Conservation Service (SCS) in 1935. Recognizing that the soil problems of the Great Plains could not be solved simply by taking land out of production, the SCS began an ambitious program to teach farmers how to minimize soil erosion. SCS experts urged plains farmers to plant soil-conserving grasses and legumes in place of wheat. They taught them how to plow along contour lines and how to build terraces—techniques that had been proven effective in slowing the runoff of rainwater and improving its absorption into the soil. Plains farmers were open to these suggestions, especially when the government offered to subsidize those willing to implement them. Bolstered by the new assistance, plains agriculture began to recover.

Still, the government offered little to the rural poor—the tenant farmers and sharecroppers. Nearly 1 million had left their homes by 1935, and another 2.5 million would leave after 1935. Most headed west, piling their belongings onto their jalopies, snaking along Route 66 until they reached California. They became known as Okies, because many, although not all, had come from Oklahoma. Their dispossession and forced migration disturbed many Americans, for whom the plight of these once-sturdy yeomen became a symbol of how much had gone wrong with the American dream.

In 1936 the Supreme Court ruled that AAA-mandated limits on farm production constituted illegal restraints of trade. Congress responded by passing the Soil Conservation and Domestic Allotment Act, which justified the removal of land from cultivation for reasons of conservation rather than economics. This new act also called upon landowners to share their government subsidies with sharecroppers and tenant farmers, although landowners managed to evade this and subsequent laws that required them to share federal funds.

The use of subsidies, begun by the AAA, did eventually bring stability and prosperity to agriculture. But the costs were high. Agriculture became the most heavily subsidized sector of the U.S. economy, and the Department of Agriculture grew into one of the government's largest bureaucracies. And the rural poor, black and white, never received a fair share of federal benefits. Beginning in the 1930s, and continuing in the 1940s and 1950s, they would be forced off the land and into the cities of the North and West.

Repairing the Economy: Industry

American industry was so vast that paying individual manufacturers direct subsidies to reduce, or even halt, production was never contemplated. Instead, the government decided to limit production through persuasion and association—two techniques that Hoover had also favored. To head the National Recovery Administration (NRA), authorized under the National Industrial Recovery Act, Roosevelt chose General Hugh Johnson, who had participated in experiments in industrial planning during the First World War. Johnson's first task was to persuade industrialists and businessmen, large and small, to agree to raise employee wages to a minimum of 30 to 40 cents an hour and to limit employee hours to a maximum of 30 to 40 hours a week. The intent was to reduce the quantity of goods that any factory or business could produce.

Johnson launched a high-powered publicity campaign, using techniques first developed by the Committee of Public Information during the First World War (see Chapter 4). He distributed pamphlets and pins to publicize his program throughout the country. He used the radio to exhort all Americans to do their part. He staged an elaborate NRA celebration in Yankee Stadium and organized a massive parade down New York City's Fifth Avenue. He sent letters to millions of employers asking them to place a "blue eagle"—the logo of the NRA—on storefronts, at factory entrances, and on company stationery to signal their participation in the campaign to limit production and restore prosperity. Blue eagles soon sprouted everywhere, usually accompanied by the slogan "We Do Our Part." Americans everywhere joined the campaign and morale soared.

Johnson understood, however, that his propaganda campaign could not by itself guarantee recovery. So he brought together the largest producers in every sector of manufacturing and asked each group (or conference) to work out a code of fair competition that would specify prices, wages, and hours throughout the sector. He also asked each conference to restrict production.

In the summer and fall of 1933, the NRA codes drawn up for steel, textiles, coal mining, rubber, garment manufacture, and other industries seemed to be working. The economy picked up and people began to hope that an end to the depression might be near. But in the winter and spring of 1934, economic indicators plunged downward once again and manufacturers began to evade the provisions of the codes. Government committees set up to enforce the codes were powerless to punish violators. By the fall of 1934, it was clear that the NRA had failed. When the Supreme Court declared the NRA codes unconstitutional in May 1935, the Roosevelt administration allowed the agency to die. By then, New Dealers had given up on the idea that limiting production would promote recovery.

Rebuilding the Nation

In addition to establishing the NRA, the National Industrial Recovery Act also launched the Public Works Administration (PWA). The PWA was given a $3.3 billion budget to sponsor internal improvements that would strengthen the nation's infrastructure of roads, bridges, sewage systems, hospitals, airports, and schools. The labor needed for these projects would shrink relief rolls and reduce unemployment. But the projects themselves could be justified in terms that conservatives approved: economic investment rather than short-term relief.

The PWA authorized the building of three major dams in the West—the Grand Coulee, Boulder, and Bonneville—that opened up large stretches of Arizona, California, and Washington to industrial and agricultural development. It funded the construction of the Triborough Bridge in New York City and the 100-mile causeway linking Florida to Key West. It also appropriated money for the construction of thousands of new schools between 1933 and 1939.

The TVA Alternative

There was one piece of legislation passed during Roosevelt's First New Deal that specified a strategy for economic recovery very different from the one promoted by the NRA. The Tennessee Valley Authority Act (1933) called for the government itself—rather than private corporations—to promote economic development throughout the Tennessee Valley, a vast river basin winding through parts of Kentucky, Tennessee, Mississippi, Alabama, Georgia, and North Carolina. The act created the Tennessee Valley Authority (TVA) to control flooding on the Tennessee River, harness its water power to generate electricity, develop local industry (such as fertilizer production), improve river transportation, and ease the poverty and isolation of the area's inhabitants. In some respects the TVA's mandate resembled that of the PWA, but the TVA enjoyed even greater authority. The extent of its control over economic development reflected the influence of Rexford Tugwell and other New Dealers who were committed to a government-planned and government-operated economy. Although they rarely said so, these reformers were drawn to socialism.

The accomplishments of the TVA were many. It built, completed, or improved more than 20 dams, including the huge Wheeler Dam near Muscle Shoals in Alabama. At several of the dam sites, the TVA built hydroelectric generators and soon became the nation's largest producer of electricity. Its low rates compelled private utility companies to reduce their rates as well. The TVA also constructed waterways to bypass unnavigable stretches of the river, reduced the danger of flooding, and taught farmers how to prevent soil erosion and use fertilizers.

Although the TVA was one of the New Deal's most celebrated successes, it generated little support for more ambitious experiments in national planning. For the government to have assumed control of established industries and banks would have been quite a different matter from bringing prosperity to an impoverished region. Like Roosevelt, few members of Congress or the public favored the radical growth of governmental power that such programs would entail. Thus, little thought was given to replacing the NRA with a nationwide TVA, for instance. The New Deal never embraced the idea of the federal government as a substitute for private enterprise, notwithstanding the scope and success of the TVA experiment.

The New Deal and Western Development

As the example of the TVA suggests, New Deal programs could make an enormous difference to a particular region's welfare. Other regional beneficiaries of the New Deal included the New York City area, which prospered from the close links of local

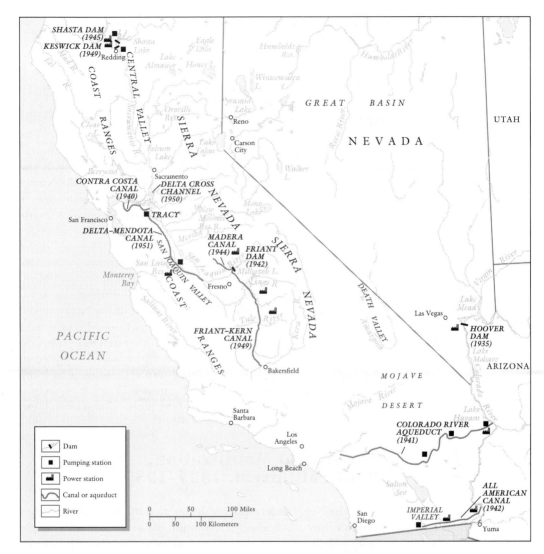

Federal Water Projects in California Built or Funded by the New Deal

politicians to the Roosevelt administration. But the region that benefited most from the New Deal was the West. Between 1933 and 1939, per capita payments for public works projects, welfare, and federal loans in the Rocky Mountain and Pacific Coast states outstripped those of any other region.

Central to this western focus was the program of western dam building that became one of the New Deal's most enduring legacies. Western real estate and agricultural interests wanted to dam the West's major rivers to provide water and electricity for urban and agricultural development. But the costs were prohibitive, even to the largest capitalists, until the New Deal offered to defray the expenses with federal dollars. Western interests found a government ally in the Bureau of

Reclamation, a hitherto small federal agency (in existence since 1902) that became, under the New Deal, a prime dispenser of infrastructural funds. Drawing on PWA monies, the bureau oversaw the building of the Boulder Dam (later renamed Hoover Dam), which provided drinking water for southern California, irrigation water for California's Imperial Valley, and electricity for Los Angeles and southern Arizona. It also authorized the Central Valley Project and the All-American Canal, vast water-harnessing projects in central and southern California meant to provide irrigation, drinking water, and electricity to California farmers and towns. The greatest construction project of all was the Grand Coulee Dam on the Columbia River in Washington, which created a lake 150 miles long. Together with the Bonneville Dam (also on the Columbia), the Grand Coulee gave the Pacific Northwest the cheapest electricity in the country and created the potential for huge economic and population growth. Not surprisingly, these two dams also made Washington state the largest per capita recipient of New Deal aid.

These developments did not attract as much attention in the 1930s as did the TVA. The benefits of this dam building program, in terms of economic development and population growth, were not fully realized until after the Second World War. Also, dam building in the West was not seen as a radical experiment in government planning and management. Unlike the TVA, the Bureau of Reclamation did not actually build the dams itself; it hired private contractors to do the work and made them rich. Moreover, the benefits of these dams were intended to flow first to large agricultural and real estate interests, not to the poor; they were intended to aid private enterprise, rather than bypass it. In political terms, then, dam building in the West was more conservative than it was in the Tennessee Valley. Even so, this activity made the federal government a key architect of the modern American West.

Political Mobilization, Political Unrest, 1934–1935

Although Roosevelt and the New Dealers quickly dismantled the NRA in 1935, they could not stop the political forces it had set it in motion. By mobilizing the people and giving them reason to believe that recovery was on its way, the NRA had freed Americans from their torpor. They now believed that they themselves could make a difference. If the New Dealers could not achieve economic recovery, the people would find others who could. Popular criticism of the New Deal was directed not at Roosevelt but at his advisers and at the Democratic Congress. Still, Roosevelt was worried by the breadth and depth of the insurgency, which seemed to threaten his political survival.

Populist Critics of the New Deal

Some critics were disturbed not only by the New Deal's failure to bring recovery but also by what they perceived as the conservative bent of New Deal programs. Banking reforms, the AAA, and the NRA, they alleged, all seemed to favor large economic interests. Ordinary people, "the forgotten Americans" whom Roosevelt had pledged to protect, had been ignored.

In the South and Midwest, millions listened regularly to the radio addresses of Louisiana Senator Huey Long, a former governor of that state and a spellbinding orator. Heir to a populist tradition, Long lampooned the rich as "pigs swilling in the trough of luxury." In attacks on New Deal programs, he alleged that "not a single thin dime of concentrated, bloated, pompous wealth, massed in the hands of a few people has been raked down to relieve the masses." Long offered a simple alternative: "Break up the swollen fortunes of America and . . . spread the wealth among all our people." He called for a redistribution of wealth that would guarantee each American family a $5,000 estate.

Long's rhetoric inspired hundreds of thousands of Americans to join the Share the Wealth clubs his supporters organized. A majority came from middle-class ranks: independent proprietors who operated their own farms, businesses, and shops; self-employed doctors and lawyers; plumbers, carpenters, electricians, and other contractors. Each of these groups worried that the big business orientation of New Deal programs might undermine their economic and social status. Substantial numbers of Share the Wealth club members also came from highly skilled and white-collar sections of the working class—railroad workers, bricklayers, postal workers, teachers, department store salesclerks, and others who aspired to a middle-class income and lifestyle. By 1935 Roosevelt regarded Long as the man most likely to unseat him in the presidential election of 1936. But before that campaign began, Long was murdered by an assassin who apparently harbored a grudge against him dating back to his days as governor.

Meanwhile, in the Midwest, Father Charles Coughlin, the "radio priest," delivered a message similar to Long's. Coughlin's weekly radio audience in 1933 and 1934 is estimated to have been between 30 and 40 million listeners. Like Long, Coughlin appealed to anxious middle-class Americans and to privileged groups of workers who believed that middle-class status was slipping from their grasp. A devoted Roosevelt supporter at first—he had once called the New Deal "Christ's Deal"—Coughlin had become a harsh critic. The New Deal was run by bankers, he claimed. The NRA was a program to resuscitate corporate profits. Coughlin called for a strong government to set national priorities and to compel capital, labor, agriculture, professionals, and other interest groups to do its bidding. He founded the National Union of Social Justice (NUSJ) in 1934 as a precursor to a political party that would challenge the Democrats in 1936. Coughlin admired leaders, such as Italy's Benito Mussolini, who built strong states through decree rather than through democratic consent. If necessary, he admitted in 1936, he would "'dictate' to preserve democracy."

As Coughlin's disillusionment with the New Deal deepened, his admiration for Hitler and Mussolini grew more pronounced. A strain of anti-Semitism became apparent in his radio talks, as in his accusation that Jewish bankers were masterminding a world conspiracy to dispossess the toiling masses. Although Coughlin was a compelling speaker, he failed to build the NUSJ into an effective force. Its successor, the Union Party, attracted only a tiny percentage of voters in 1936. Embittered, Coughlin moved further and further to the political right. By 1939 his denunciations of democracy and Jews had become so extreme that some radio stations refused to carry his addresses. But millions of ordinary Americans continued to believe that the "radio priest" was their savior.

Another popular figure was Francis E. Townsend, a California doctor who claimed that the way to end the depression was to give every senior citizen $200 a month. The Townsend Plan briefly garnered the support of an estimated 20 million Americans.

None of these self-styled reformers—Long, Coughlin, and Townsend—showed much skill at transforming his popularity into disciplined political parties that could compete in elections. Still, their attacks on New Deal programs deepened popular discontent and helped to legitimate other insurgent movements. The most important of them was the labor movement.

Labor's Rebirth

The ranks of the working class were diverse: immigrant radicals and ethnic conservatives, northerners and southerners, blacks and whites, skilled and unskilled, factory workers and farm workers, men and women. But labor's diversity was not as great as it had been during the Progressive Era. Mass immigration had ended in 1921, and the trend toward Americanization at school, at work, and in popular entertainment (including the movies) had broadened throughout the decade. The Great Depression itself further heightened the sense of shared experience. Few working-class families escaped the distress and despair of the early depression years.

This commonality of working-class sentiment first became apparent in 1932, when many workers voted for Roosevelt. Following his election, the NRA helped to transform their despair into hope. It set guidelines for wages and work hours that, if implemented by employers, would improve working conditions. Moreover, Clause 7(a) of the National Industrial Recovery Act granted workers the right to join labor unions of their own choosing, and obligated employers to recognize unions and bargain with them in good faith.

Millions of workers joined labor unions in 1933 and early 1934, encouraged by John L. Lewis, president of the United Mine Workers, who often declared in his rousing speeches and radio addresses: "The president wants you to join a union." Actually, Roosevelt did not favor the rapid growth of unions. But Lewis reckoned that Roosevelt would not disavow a key clause in his celebrated recovery program. And Lewis also believed that by repeatedly invoking the president's name he could transform working-class support for Roosevelt into union strength.

The demands of union members were quite modest at first. They wanted employers to observe the provisions of the NRA codes. They wanted to be treated fairly by their foremen. And they wanted employers to recognize their unions. But few employers were willing to grant them any say in their working conditions. Many ignored the NRA's wage and hour guidelines altogether, and even used their influence over NRA code authorities to get worker requests for wage increases and union recognition rejected.

Workers flooded Washington with letters addressed to President Roosevelt, Labor Secretary Frances Perkins, and General Hugh Johnson asking them to force employers to comply with the law. A Rhode Island textile worker who had been fired for joining a union asked why the NRA had not responded to his complaint or punished the company that had fired him. "If people can be arrested for violating certain laws," he wondered, "why can't this company?"

John L. Lewis • The president of the United Mine Workers and the principal founder of the Congress of Industrial Organizations (CIO), John L. Lewis was the most famous and charismatic labor leader of the 1930s.

When their pleas went unanswered, workers began to take matters into their own hands. In 1934 they staged 2,000 strikes in virtually every industry and region of the country. Many of the strikes grew out of local disputes and attracted little attention. But a few escalated into armed confrontations between workers and police that shocked the nation. In Toledo in May, 10,000 workers surrounded the Electric Auto-Lite plant, declaring that they would block all exits and entrances until the company agreed to shut down operations and negotiate a union contract. A seven-hour pitched battle between strikers and police waged with water hoses, tear gas, and gunfire failed to dislodge the strikers. Ultimately, the National Guard was summoned, and two strikers were killed in an exchange of gunfire. In Minneapolis, unionized truckdrivers and warehousemen fought police, private security forces, and the National Guard in a series of street battles from May through July that left four dead and hundreds wounded. In San Francisco in July, longshoremen fought employers and police in street skirmishes in which two were killed and scores wounded. Employers there had hoped that the use of force would break a two-month-old strike, but the violence provoked more than 100,000 additional workers in the transportation, construction, and service industries to walk off their jobs in a general strike. From July 5 to July 19, the city of San Francisco was virtually shut down. In both Minneapolis and San Francisco, the intervention of evenhanded municipal and state authorities eventually enabled strikers to win important concessions from employers.

The largest and most violent confrontation began on September 1, 1934, with the strike of 400,000 textile workers at mills from Maine to Alabama. Workers who had never acknowledged a common bond with their fellows—Catholic Euro-Americans in New England and white Protestants in the Southeast—now joined hands. They insisted that they were Americans bound together by class and national loyalties that transcended ethnic and religious differences. In the first two weeks of September, the strikers brought cotton production to a virtual standstill. Employers recruited replacement workers and hired private security forces to protect them. At many of the mills, the arrival of strikebreakers prompted violent confrontations between strikers and police. In northern communities, such as Saylesville and Woonsocket, Rhode Island, full-scale riots erupted. The result was several deaths, hundreds of injuries, and millions of dollars in property damage. Similar confrontations took place throughout the South, where vigilante bands helped local police and National Guardsmen beat up strikers, kill union organizers or run them out of the state, and incarcerate hundreds of strikers in barbed-wire camps.

Anger at the Polls

By late September, textile union leaders had lost their nerve and called off the strike. But workers took their anger to the polls. In Rhode Island, they elected scores of new Democrats to municipal and state offices and broke the Republican Party's 30-year domination of state politics. In the South Carolina gubernatorial race, working-class voters rejected a conservative Democrat, Coleman Blease, and chose instead Olin T. Johnston, a former mill worker and an ardent New Dealer. In the country as a whole, Democrats won 70 percent of the contested seats in the Senate and House in what the *New York Times* called the "most overwhelming victory in the history of American politics." The Democrats increased their majority, from 310 to 319 (out of 432) in the House, and from 60 to 69 (out of 96) in the Senate. No sitting president's party had ever done so well in an off-year election.

But the victory was not an unqualified victory for Roosevelt and the First New Deal. The 74th Congress would include the largest contingent of radicals ever sent to Washington: Tom Amlie of Wisconsin, Ernest Lundeen of Minnesota, Maury Maverick of Texas, Vito Marcantonio of New York, and some 30 others. Their support for the New Deal depended on whether Roosevelt delivered more relief, more income security, and more political power to farmers, workers, the unemployed, and the poor.

The Rise of Radical Third Parties

Radical critics of the New Deal also made an impressive showing in state politics in 1934 and 1936. They were particularly strong in states gripped by labor unrest. In Wisconsin, for example, Philip La Follette, the son of Robert La Follette (see Chapter 2), was elected governor in 1934 and 1936 as the candidate of the radical Wisconsin Progressive Party. In Minnesota, discontented agrarians and urban workers organized the Minnesota Farmer-Labor (MFL) Party and elected their candidate to the governorship in 1930, 1932, 1934, and 1936. In Washington, yet another radical third party, the Commonwealth Builders, elected both senators and almost half the state legislators in 1932 and 1934. And in California, the socialist and novelist Upton Sinclair and his organization, End Poverty in California (EPIC), came closer to winning the governorship than anyone had expected.

The impressive showings of the Wisconsin Progressive Party, Minnesota Farmer-Labor Party, Upton Sinclair's EPIC, and Washington state's Commonwealth Builders made it clear that many voters were prepared to abandon Democrats who refused to endorse a more comprehensive program of reform. A widespread movement to form local labor parties offered further evidence of voter volatility, as did the growing appeal of the Communist Party.

The American Communist Party (CP) had emerged in the early 1920s with the support of radicals who wanted to adopt the Soviet Union's path to socialism. Their numbers were insignificant throughout the decade, but they began to attract attention in the desperate years of the early 1930s. Confident that the Great Depression signaled the death throes of capitalism, party members dedicated themselves to marshaling the forces of socialism.

CP organizers spread out among the poorest and most vulnerable populations in America—homeless urban blacks in the North, black and white sharecroppers in the South, Chicano and Filipino agricultural workers in the West—and mobilized them in unions and unemployment leagues. CP members also played significant roles in the Minneapolis, San Francisco, and textile workers' strikes, and they were influential in the Minnesota Farmer-Labor Party and in Washington's Commonwealth Builders. Once they stopped preaching world revolution in 1935 and began calling instead for a "popular front" of democratic forces against fascism, their ranks grew even more. By 1938, approximately 80,000 Americans were thought to have been members of the Communist Party.

Although the Communist Party proclaimed its allegiance to democratic principles beginning in 1935, it nevertheless remained a dictatorial organization that took its orders from the Soviet Union. Many Americans feared the growing strength of the Communist Party and began to call for its suppression. Actually, the CP was never strong enough to pose a real political threat. Membership turnover was high, as many left the party after learning about its undemocratic character. Its chief role in 1930s politics was to channel popular discontent into unions and political parties that would, in turn, force New Dealers to respond to the demands of the nation's dispossessed.

The Second New Deal, 1935–1937

The labor unrest of 1934 had taken Roosevelt by surprise, and for a time he kept his distance from the masses mobilizing in his name. But in the spring of 1935, with the presidential election coming up in 1936, he decided to place himself at their head. Roosevelt's rhetoric suddenly took on an anticorporate tone. He called for the "abolition of evil holding companies." He attacked the wealthy for their profligate and unpatriotic ways. He called for new programs to aid the poor and downtrodden. Roosevelt had not become a socialist, as his critics have charged. Rather, he sought to reestablish his contact with the people and turn them away from radical solutions. He also hoped to win reelection.

Philosophical Underpinnings

To point the New Deal in a more populist direction, Roosevelt turned increasingly to reform-minded businessmen, investment bankers, lawyers, economists, and labor leaders who subscribed to a relatively new economic theory, underconsumptionism. Advocates of this theory held that underconsumption, or a chronic weakness in consumer demand, had caused the Great Depression. Individual consumers simply had not possessed enough money to purchase what American industries had produced. The path to recovery lay, therefore, not in restricting the output of producers, as the architects of the First New Deal had tried to do, but in boosting consumer expenditures through a variety of government policies. These policies included government support for strong labor unions (to force up wages), higher social welfare expenditures (to put more money in the hands of the poor), and vast public works projects (to create hundreds of thousands of new jobs).

Underconsumptionists did not worry that new welfare and public works programs might strain the federal budget. If the government found itself short of revenue, it could always borrow additional funds from private sources. Government borrowing, in fact, was viewed as a crucial antidepression tool. Those who lent the government money would receive a return on their investment; those who received government assistance would have additional income to spend on consumer goods; and manufacturers would profit from increases in consumer spending. Government borrowing, in short, would stimulate the circulation of money throughout the economy and would put an end to the depression. This fiscal policy, a reversal of the conventional wisdom that government should always balance its budget, would in the 1940s come to be known as Keynesianism, after John Maynard Keynes, the British economist who had been its most forceful advocate.

Many politicians and economists rejected the notion that increased government spending and the deliberate buildup of federal deficits would lead to prosperity. Roosevelt himself remained committed to fiscal restraint and balanced budgets. But in 1935, as the nation entered its sixth year of the depression, he was willing to give the new ideas a try. Reform-minded members of the 1934 Congress were themselves eager for a new round of legislation directed more to the needs of ordinary Americans than to the needs of big business.

Legislation of the Second New Deal

Much of that legislation was passed by Congress from January to June 1935—a period that came to be known as the Second New Deal. Two of the acts were of historic importance. The Social Security Act, passed in May, created the nation's first comprehensive system of social insurance. It required the states to set up welfare funds from which money would be disbursed to the elderly poor, the unemployed, unmarried mothers with dependent children, and the disabled. It also enrolled a majority of working Americans in a pension program that guaranteed them a steady income upon retirement. A federal system of employer and employee taxation was set up to fund the pensions. Despite limitations on coverage and inadequate pension levels,

Public Art • Through direct and indirect subsidies, the New Deal encouraged a vast program of public art to decorate libraries, post offices, museums, and other buildings with sculptures, paintings, and murals. This image reproduces a portion of Mexican artist Diego Rivera's vast modernist fresco, "Detroit Industry," from the Detroit Museum of Art. In it, Rivera depicts production of the 1932 Ford V-8 motor at the automaker's massive River Rouge plant.

the Social Security Act of 1935 provided a sturdy foundation upon which future presidents and congresses would erect the American welfare state.

Equally historic was the passage, in June, of the National Labor Relations Act (NLRA). This act delivered what the NRA had only promised: the right of every worker to join a union of his or her own choosing, and the obligation of employers to bargain with that union in good faith. The NLRA, also called the Wagner Act after its sponsor in the Senate, Robert Wagner of New York, set up a National Labor Relations Board (NLRB) to supervise union elections and to investigate claims of unfair labor practices. The NLRB was to be staffed by federal appointees, who would have the power to impose fines on employers who violated the law. Never before had the government sided so strongly with labor. Union leaders hailed the act as their "Magna Carta."

Congress also passed the Holding Company Act to break up the 13 utility companies that controlled 75 percent of the nation's electric power. It passed the Wealth Tax Act, which increased tax rates on the wealthy from 59 to 75 percent, and on corporations from 13¾ to 15 percent; and it passed the Banking Act, which strengthened the power of the Federal Reserve Board over its member banks. Congress also created the Rural Electrification Administration (REA) to bring electric power to rural households. Finally, it passed the Emergency Relief Appropriation Act, a $5 billion act that dwarfed similar legislation passed during the First New Deal. Roosevelt funneled part of this sum to the PWA and the CCC and used another part to create the National Youth Administration (NYA), which provided work and guidance to the nation's youth.

Roosevelt directed most of the new relief money, however, to the Works Progress Administration (WPA) under the direction of the irrepressible Harry Hopkins, who was now known as the New Deal's "minister of relief." Continuing the infrastructure program begun by the PWA, the WPA built or improved thousands of schools, playgrounds, airports, and hospitals. WPA crews were put to work raking leaves, cleaning streets, and landscaping cities. In the process, the WPA provided jobs to approximately 30 percent of the nation's jobless.

By the time the decade ended, the WPA, in association with an expanded Reconstruction Finance Corporation, PWA, and other agencies, had brought about the building of 500,000 miles of roads, 100,000 bridges, 100,000 public buildings, and 600 airports. The New Deal had transformed America's urban and rural landscapes. Everywhere Americans turned they found concrete examples of its accomplishments. The awe generated by those great public works projects helped Roosevelt retain popular support at a time when the success of the New Deal's economic policies was uncertain. The WPA also funded a vast program of public art, supporting the work of thousands of painters, architects, writers, playwrights, actors, and intellectuals. Beyond extending relief to struggling artists, it fostered the creation of art that spoke to the concerns of ordinary Americans, adorned public buildings with colorful murals, and boosted public morale.

Victory in 1936: The New Democratic Coalition

Roosevelt described his Second New Deal as a program to limit the power and privilege of the wealthy few and to increase the security and welfare of ordinary citizens. In his 1936 reelection campaign, he excoriated the corporations as "economic royalists" who had "concentrated into their own hands an almost complete control over other people's property, other people's money, other people's labor—other people's lives." He called on voters to strip the economic royalists of their power and "save a great and precious form of government for ourselves and the world." American voters responded by handing Roosevelt the greatest landslide victory in the history of American politics to that time. He received 61 percent of the popular vote; Alf Landon of Kansas, his Republican opponent, received only 36 percent. Only two states, Maine and Vermont, representing a mere 8 electoral votes, went for Landon.

The 1936 election won for the Democratic Party its reputation as the party of reform and the party of the "forgotten American." Of the 6 million Americans who went to the polls for the first time, many of them European ethnics, 5 million voted for Roosevelt. Among the poorest Americans, Roosevelt received 80 percent of the vote. Black voters in the North deserted the Republican Party—the "Party of Lincoln"—in droves, calculating that their interests would best be served by the "Party

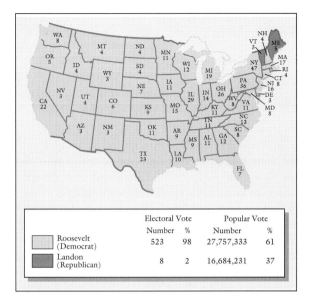

	Electoral Vote		Popular Vote	
	Number	%	Number	%
Roosevelt (Democrat)	523	98	27,757,333	61
Landon (Republican)	8	2	16,684,231	37

Presidential Election, 1936

of the Common Man." Roosevelt also did well among white middle-class voters, many of whom were grateful to him for pushing through the Social Security Act. These constituencies would constitute the "Roosevelt coalition" for most of the next 40 years, helping to solidify the Democratic Party as the new majority party in American politics.

Rhetoric versus Reality

Although many of those who voted for Roosevelt in 1936 viewed his victory as the first step toward the establishment of a social democracy in the United States, Roosevelt himself had never set that as his goal. His anticorporate rhetoric in 1935 and 1936 was more radical than the laws he supported. The Wealth Tax Act took considerably less out of wealthy incomes and estates than was advertised, and the utility companies that were to have been broken up by the Holding Company Act remained largely intact. Moreover, Roosevelt promised more than he delivered to the nation's poor. Farm workers, for example, were not covered by the Social Security Act or by the National Labor Relations Act. Consequently, thousands of African American sharecroppers in the South, along with substantial numbers of Chicano farm workers in the Southwest, were excluded from their protections and benefits. The sharecroppers were shut out because southern Democrats would not have voted for an act that was meant to improve the economic or social condition of southern blacks. For the same reason, the New Deal made little effort to restore voting rights to southern blacks or to protect their basic civil rights. White supremacy lived on in New Deal democracy.

Roosevelt's populist stance in 1935 and 1936 also obscured the enthusiastic support that some capitalists were according the Second New Deal. In the West, Henry

J. Kaiser headed a consortium of six companies that built the Hoover, Bonneville, and Grand Coulee dams; and in Texas, building contractors Herman and George Brown were bankrolling a group of elected officials that included a young Democratic congressman named Lyndon Johnson. In the Midwest and the East, Roosevelt's corporate supporters included real estate developers, mass merchandisers (such as Bambergers and Sears, Roebuck), clothing manufacturers, and the like. These firms, in turn, had financial connections with recently established investment banks such as Lehman Brothers and Goldman Sachs, competitors of the House of Morgan and its allies in the Republican banking establishment, and with consumer-oriented banks such as the Bank of America and the Bowery Savings Bank. All of these New Deal supporters, convinced that prosperity depended on high and stable levels of consumer spending, were willing to tolerate strong labor unions, welfare programs, and high levels of government spending. But they had no intention of surrendering their wealth or power. The Democratic Party had become, in effect, the party of the masses and one section of big business; from one constituency came votes, from the other came money to finance electoral campaigns. But the conflicting interests of these two constituencies would create tensions within the Democratic Party throughout all the years of its political domination.

New Deal Men, New Deal Women

For the academics, policymakers, and bureaucrats who designed and administered the rapidly growing roster of New Deal programs and agencies, 1936 and 1937 were exciting years. Fired by idealism and dedication, they were confident they could make the New Deal work. In the euphoria that set in after the 1936 election victory, they devised countless schemes to expand the role of government in economic life. They planned and won congressional approval for the Farm Security Administration (FSA), an agency designed to improve the economic lot of tenant farmers, sharecroppers, and farm laborers. They drafted and got passed laws that outlawed child labor, set minimum wages and maximum hours for adult workers, and committed the federal government to building low-cost housing. They investigated and tried to regulate concentrations of corporate power.

Although they worked on behalf of "the people," the New Dealers themselves had little desire to share the lot of common men and women. They were, in fact, a new class of technocrats. But they did have noble aspirations. What fired their imagination was the prospect of building a strong state committed to prosperity and justice. They delighted in the intellectual challenge and the technical complexity of social policy. They did not welcome interference from those they regarded as less intelligent or motivated by outworn ideologies.

This was particularly true of the men, who far outnumbered women among New Deal policymakers. Many of the male New Dealers had earned advanced degrees in law and economics at elite universities such as Harvard, Columbia, and Wisconsin. Not all had been raised among wealth and privilege, however, as was generally the case with earlier generations of reformers. To his credit, Franklin Roosevelt was the first president since his cousin Theodore Roosevelt to welcome Jews and Catholics into his administration. Some became members of Roosevelt's inner circle of advisers—men like Thomas "Tommy the Cork" Corcoran, Jim Farley, Ben Cohen, and

Women and the New Deal • Following the example set by Eleanor Roosevelt, women played an important role in the New Deal. Here Roosevelt meets with Mary McLeod Bethune who, as director of the Division of Negro Affairs for the National Youth Administration, was the first African American woman to head a federal agency.

Samuel Rosenman. These were men who had to struggle to make their way, first on the streets and then in school and at work. They brought to the New Deal intellectual aggressiveness, quick minds, and mental toughness. They were young men in a hurry and represented a new kind of Washington insider.

The profile of New Deal women was different. Although a few, notably Eleanor Roosevelt and Secretary of Labor Frances Perkins, were more visible than women in previous administrations had been, many of the female New Dealers worked in relative obscurity, in agencies like the Women's Bureau or the Children's Bureau (both in the Department of Labor). And women who worked on major legislation, as did Mary Van Kleeck on the Social Security Act, or who directed major programs, as did Jane Hoey, chief of Social Security's Bureau of Public Assistance, received less credit than men in comparable positions. Moreover, female New Dealers tended to be a generation older than their male colleagues and were more likely to be Protestant than Catholic or Jewish. Many of them had known each other since the days of Progressive Era reform and woman suffrage (see Chapter 2).

The New Deal offered these women little opportunity, however, to advance the cause of women's equality. Demands for greater economic opportunity, sexual freedom, and full equality for women were heard less often in the 1930s than they had been in the preceding two decades. One reason was that the suffrage movement, after its 1920 triumph, had lost its momentum. Another was that prominent New Deal women such as Perkins did not vigorously pursue a campaign for equal rights. They concentrated instead on "protective legislation"—laws that safeguarded female workers, who were thought to be more fragile than men. Those who insisted that women needed special protections could not easily argue that women were the equal of men in all respects.

But feminism was hemmed in on all sides by a male hostility that the depression had only intensified. Men in all walks of life experienced the Great Depression as a kind of emasculation. They had built their male identities on the value of hard work and the ability to provide economic security for their families. For them, the loss of work unleashed feelings of inadequacy. That the unemployment rates of men—most of whom labored in blue-collar industries—tended to be higher than those of women, many of whom worked in white-collar occupations less affected by job cutbacks, exacerbated male vulnerability. Many fathers and husbands resented wives and daughters who had taken over their breadwinning roles.

This male anxiety had political and social consequence. Several states passed laws outlawing the hiring of married women. New Deal relief agencies were reluctant to authorize aid for unemployed women. The labor movement made the protection of the male wage earner one of its principal goals. The Social Security pension system did not cover waitresses, domestic servants, and other largely female occupations. Some commentators even proposed ludicrous gender remedies to the problem of unemployment. Norman Cousins of the *Saturday Evening Post,* for example, suggested that the depression could be ended simply by firing 10 million working women and giving their jobs to men. "Presto!" he declared. "No unemployment, no relief roles. No Depression."

Rates of Unemployment in Selected Male and Female Occupations, 1930

Male Occupations	Percentage Male	Percentage Unemployed
Iron and steel	96%	13%
Forestry and fishing	99	10
Mining	99	18
Heavy manufacturing	86	13
Carpentry	100	19
Laborers (road and street)	100	13

Female Occupations	Percentage Female	Percentage Unemployed
Stenographers and typists	96%	5%
Laundresses	99	3
Trained nurses	98	4
Housekeepers	92	3
Telephone operators	95	3
Dressmakers	100	4

Source: U.S. Department of Commerce, Bureau of the Census, *Fifteenth Census of the United States, 1930, Population* (Washington, D.C.: Government Printing Office, 1931).

Many artists introduced a strident masculinism into their painting and sculpture, favoring male figures with muscle-bulging physiques that, 40 years later, would come to be associated with Arnold Schwarzenegger. Mighty Superman, the new comic-strip hero of 1938, reflected the spirit of the times. Superman was depicted as a working-class hero who, on several occasions, saved workers from coal mine explosions and other disasters caused by the greed and negligence of villainous employers.

Superman's greatest vulnerability, however, other than kryptonite, was his attraction to the sexy and aggressive *working* woman, Lois Lane. He was never able to resolve his female dilemma by marrying Lois and tucking her away in a safe domestic sphere, because the continuation of the comic strip demanded that Superman repeatedly be exposed to kryptonite and female danger. But the producers of male and female images in other mass media, like the movies, faced no such technical obstacles. Anxious men could take comfort from the conclusion of the movie *Woman of the Year,* in which Spencer Tracy persuades the ambitious Katharine Hepburn to exchange her successful newspaper career for the bliss of motherhood and homemaking. From a thousand different points, 1930s politics and culture

Manhood and Womanhood in the Great Depression • In this 1937 mural done for a Huntsville, Alabama courtroom, Xavier Gonzalez celebrates traditional gender roles. Shapely women gather fruit, nurse children, and engage in home handicrafts while muscular men labor in the fields and factories. The presence of a TVA dam in the background suggests that the New Deal was helping to restore gender roles to their proper and "natural" state. Gonzalez titled the mural "Tennessee Valley Authority."

made it clear that woman's proper place was in the home. Faced with such obstacles, it is not surprising that women activists failed to make feminism a part of New Deal reform.

Labor Ascendant

In 1935 John L. Lewis of the United Mine Workers, Sidney Hillman of the Amalgamated Clothing Workers, and the leaders of six other unions that had seceded from the American Federation of Labor (AFL) had cobbled together a new labor organization. The Committee for Industrial Organization (CIO—later renamed the Congress of Industrial Organizations) took as its goal the organization of millions of nonunion workers into effective unions that would strengthen labor's influence in politics. In 1936 Lewis and Hillman created a second organization, Labor's Non-Partisan League (LNPL), to develop a labor strategy for the 1936 elections. Although professing the league's nonpartisanship, Lewis intended from the start that LNPL's role would be to channel labor's money, energy, and talent into Roosevelt's reelection campaign. Roosevelt welcomed the league's help, and labor would become one of the most important constituencies of the new Democratic coalition. The passage of the Wagner Act and the creation of the NLRB in 1935 enhanced the labor movement's status and credibility. Membership in labor unions climbed steadily, and in short order union members began flexing their new muscles.

In late 1936 the United Auto Workers (UAW) took on General Motors, widely regarded as the mightiest corporation in the world. Workers occupied key GM factories in Flint, Michigan, declaring that their "sit-down" strike would continue until GM agreed to recognize the UAW and negotiate a collective bargaining agreement. Frank Murphy, the pro-labor governor of Michigan, refused to use National Guard troops to evict the strikers, and Roosevelt declined to send federal troops. The 50-year-old practice of using soldiers to break strikes came to an end, and General Motors capitulated after a month of resistance. Soon, the U.S. Steel Corporation, which had defeated unionists in the bloody strike of 1919 (see Chapter 4), announced that it was ready to negotiate a contract with the newly formed CIO steelworkers union.

The labor movement's public stature grew along with its size. Many writers and artists, whose work was funded through the WPA, depicted the labor movement as America's first and best hope—the voice of the people and the embodiment of the nation's values. Murals sprang up in post offices and other public buildings featuring portraits of blue-collar Americans at work. Broadway's most celebrated play in 1935 was Clifford Odets's *Waiting for Lefty,* a raw drama about taxi drivers who confront their bosses and organize an honest union. Audiences were so moved by the play that they often spontaneously joined in the final chorus of "Strike, Strike, Strike," the words that ended the play. *Pins and Needles,* a 1937 musical about the hopes and dreams of garment workers that was performed by actual members of the International Ladies Garment Workers Union, became the longest-running play in Broadway history (until *Oklahoma* broke its record of 1,108 performances in 1943).

Similarly, many of the most popular novels and movies of the 1930s celebrated the decency, honesty, and patriotism of ordinary Americans. In *Mr. Deeds Goes to Town* (1936) and *Mr. Smith Goes to Washington* (1939) Frank Capra delighted movie

Strike! • Autoworkers in Michigan celebrate a 1937 victory over General Motors.

audiences with fables of simple, small-town heroes vanquishing the evil forces of wealth and decadence. Likewise, in *The Grapes of Wrath,* the best-selling novel of 1939, John Steinbeck told an epic tale of an Oklahoma family's fortitude in surviving eviction from their land, migrating westward, and suffering exploitation in the "promised land" of California. In 1940 John Ford used Steinbeck's novel as the basis for one of that year's highest-grossing and most acclaimed movies. Moviegoers found special meaning in the declaration of one of the story's main characters, Ma Joad: "We're the people, we go on." In themselves and in one another, Americans seemed to discover the resolve they needed to rebuild a culture that had surrendered its identity to corporations and business.

America's Minorities and the New Deal

The New Deal, on the whole, paid little attention to the particular needs of racial or ethnic minorities. Reformers generally believed that issues of capitalism's viability, economic recovery, and the inequality of wealth and power outweighed problems of racial and ethnic discrimination; only in the case of Native Americans did New Dealers pass legislation specifically designed to improve a minority's social and economic position. Because they were disproportionately poor, most minority groups did profit from the populist and pro-labor character of New Deal reforms. But the gains were distributed unevenly. Eastern and southern European ethnics benefited the most while African Americans and Mexican Americans advanced the least.

Eastern and Southern European Ethnics

Eastern and southern European immigrants and their children had begun mobilizing politically in the 1920s in response to religious and racial discrimination (see Chapter 5). By the early 1930s, they had made themselves into a formidable political force in the Democratic Party in the urban North and West, and no Democratic politician with presidential aspirations could afford to ignore their power. Roosevelt understood their importance well, for he was a product of New York Democratic politics where men such as Robert Wagner and Al Smith had begun to organize the "ethnic vote" even before 1920 (see Chapter 2). He made sure that a significant portion of New Deal monies for welfare, infrastructural improvements, and unemployment relief reached the urban areas where most European ethnics lived. As a result, Jewish and Catholic Americans, especially those descended from southern and eastern European immigrants, voted for Roosevelt in overwhelming numbers. The New Deal did not eliminate anti-Semitism and anti-Catholicism from American society, but it did allow millions of European ethnics to believe, for the first time, that they would overcome the second-class status they had long endured. From their ranks came many ardent New Dealers and staunch American patriots.

Southern and eastern European ethnics also benefited from their strong working-class presence. Forming one of the largest groups in the mass-production industries of the Northeast, Midwest, and West, they made crucial contributions to the labor movement's 1934 rebirth and to the CIO's formation in 1935. Roosevelt accommodated himself to their wishes not simply out of beneficence, but because he understood and feared the power they wielded through their labor organizations.

African Americans

The New Deal did more to reproduce patterns of racial discrimination than to advance the cause of racial equality. African Americans who belonged to CIO unions or who lived in northern cities benefited from New Deal programs; they deserted the Republican Party and began voting Democratic in large numbers. But the vast majority of blacks lived in rural areas of the South where they were barred from voting, largely excluded from AAA programs, and denied federal protection in their efforts to form agricultural unions. The CCC ran separate camps for black and white youth. The TVA hired few blacks. Those enrolled in the CWA and other work-relief programs frequently received less pay than whites doing the same jobs. Roosevelt consistently refused to support legislation to make lynching a federal crime—a key objective of civil rights activists at the time.

This failure to push a strong civil rights agenda did not mean that New Dealers were themselves racist or oblivious to racism's effects. Eleanor Roosevelt spoke out frequently against racial injustice. In 1939 she resigned from the Daughters of the American Revolution when the organization refused to allow black opera singer Marian Anderson to perform in its concert hall. With the support of Secretary of the Interior Harold Ickes, she then pressured the federal government into granting Anderson permission to sing from the steps of the Lincoln Memorial. On Easter Sunday, 75,000 people gathered to hear Anderson and to demonstrate their support for racial equality. But the president did not attend.

Evicted Sharecroppers, 1937 • In response to criticism that the original Agricultural Adjustment Administration did little for farm tenants and sharecroppers, Congress passed additional legislation in 1936 mandating that landowners share federal benefits with those who worked their land. But a group of Missouri landowners chose to evict their sharecropper tenants rather than share the benefits, compelling hundreds of sharecropping families, such as this one, to set up makeshift camps along highways from Sikeston, Missouri, to the Arkansas border.

Roosevelt did eliminate segregationist practices in the federal government that had been in place since Woodrow Wilson's presidency. He appointed Mary McLeod Bethune, Robert Weaver, William Hastie, and other African Americans to important second-level posts in his administration. Working closely with each other in what came to be known as the "Black Cabinet," these officials fought hard against discrimination in New Deal programs and enjoyed occasional successes.

But Roosevelt was never willing to make the fight for racial justice a priority. He refused to support his black cabinet if it meant alienating white southern senators who controlled key congressional committees. This refusal revealed Roosevelt's belief that economic issues were more important than racial ones. It revealed, too, Roosevelt's pragmatism. His decisions to support particular policies often depended on his calculation of their potential political cost or gain. He offered little support to the labor movement until its rising strength in 1934 and 1935 threatened his reelection prospects in 1936. Because he needed the electoral support of European ethnics in the North and the white supremacist Democratic Party in the South, he made sure that New Deal programs offered both constituencies ample benefits. By the same token, he calculated that his failure to eliminate racial discrimination from New Deal agencies or to support an antilynching bill would not damage his political power. African Americans were not yet strong enough as an electoral constituency or as a reform movement to force Roosevelt to accede to their wishes.

Mexican Americans

Owing to a repatriation policy begun during the Hoover administration and continued during the early years of the New Deal, the experience of Mexicans during the Great Depression was particularly harsh. Repatriation meant the return of immigrants to their land of origin. In 1931, Hoover's secretary of labor, William N. Doak, announced a plan for repatriating illegal aliens and giving their jobs to American citizens. The federal campaign quickly focused on Mexican immigrants in California and the Southwest, where local governments were eager to eliminate the minority poor from relief rolls. The U.S. Immigration Service swooped in on businesses and homes in a number of highly publicized raids, rounded up large numbers of Mexicans and Mexican Americans, and demanded that each detainee prove his or her legal status. Those who failed to produce the necessary documentation were deported. Altogether, the federal government repatriated 82,000 Mexican immigrants between 1929 and 1935.

Local governments pressured many more into leaving. Los Angeles County officials, for example, "persuaded" 12,000 unemployed Mexicans to leave by threatening to remove them from the relief rolls and offering them free railroad tickets to Mexico; Colorado officials secured the departure of 20,000 Mexicans through the use of similar techniques. The combined efforts of federal, state, and local governments created a climate of fear in Mexican communities that prompted 500,000 to return to Mexico by 1935. This total equaled the number of Mexicans who had come to the United States in the 1920s. Los Angeles lost one-third of its Mexican population. Included in repatriate ranks, in Los Angeles and elsewhere, were a significant number of legal immigrants who were unable to produce their immigration papers, the American-born children of illegals, and some Mexican Americans who had lived in the Southwest for generations.

The advent of the New Deal in 1933 eased but did not eliminate pressure on Chicano communities. New Deal agencies made more money available for relief, thereby lightening the burden on state and local governments. Some federal programs, moreover, prohibited the removal of illegal aliens from relief rolls. But federal laws, more often than not, failed to dissuade local officials from continuing their campaign against Mexican immigrants. Where Mexicans gained access to relief rolls, they received payments lower than those given to "Anglos" (whites) or were compelled to accept tough agricultural jobs that did not pay living wages. These circumstances caused thousands more to relinquish hopes of making it in America and to return to Mexico.

Life grew harder for immigrant Mexicans who stayed behind. The Mexican cultural renaissance that had arisen in 1920s Los Angeles (see Chapter 5), and that depended on immigrant musicians, actors, and other artists, could not continue. Hounded by government officials, Mexicans everywhere sought to escape public attention and scrutiny. In Los Angeles, where their influence had been felt throughout the city in the 1920s, they retreated into the separate community of East Los Angeles. To many, they became the "invisible minority."

Mexicans and Mexican Americans who lived in urban areas and worked in blue-collar industries did benefit from New Deal programs. In Los Angeles, for example, Chicanos employed in canneries, in garment and furniture shops, and on the docks responded to the New Deal's pro-labor legislation by joining unions in large numbers and winning concessions from their employers. These Mexicans and Mexican Americans shared the belief of southern and eastern Europeans that the New Deal would bring them economic improvement and cultural acceptance. But most Chicanos lived in rural areas and labored in agricultural jobs. The National Labor Relations Act did not protect their right to organize unions, while the Social Security Act excluded them from the new federal welfare system. The New Deal, in short, offered the rural Chicano majority little.

Native Americans

The New Deal, by contrast, promised Native Americans dramatic improvements. From the 1880s until the early 1930s, federal policy had contributed to the elimination of Native Americans as a distinctive population. The Dawes Act of 1887 (see the Prologue) had called for tribal lands to be broken up and allotted to individual owners in the hope that Indians would adopt the work habits of white farmers. But Native Americans had proved stubbornly loyal to their languages, religions, and other cultures. Few of them succeeded as farmers, and many of them lost land to white speculators. By 1933, nearly half the Indians living on reservations whose land had been allotted were landless while many who retained allotments held land that was largely desert or semidesert.

The shrinking land base in combination with a growing population deepened Native American poverty. The assimilationist pressures on Native Americans, meanwhile, reached a climax in the intolerant 1920s when the Bureau of Indian Affairs (BIA), prodded by Protestant missionaries, outlawed Indian religious ceremonies, forced children from tribal communities into federal boarding schools, banned polygamy, and imposed limits on the length of men's hair.

Government officials working in the Hoover administration began to question this draconian assimilationist policy, but its reversal had to await the New Deal and Roosevelt's appointment of John Collier as the commissioner of the BIA. Collier brought the kind of energy and administrative efficiency to Indian matters that Harry Hopkins had injected into New Deal relief programs. He set a furious pace during the New Deal's early years, pressuring the CCC (which established a full Indian Division), AAA, and other New Deal agencies to employ Indians on projects that improved reservation land and trained Indians in land conservation methods. He prevailed on Congress to pass the Pueblo Relief Act of 1933, which compensated Pueblos for land taken from them in the 1920s, and the Johnson-O'Malley Act of 1934, which funded states to provide for Indian health care, welfare, and education. As part of his campaign to make the BIA more responsive to Native Americans needs, Collier increased the number of Indian employees of the BIA from a paltry few hundred in 1933 to a respectable 4,600 in 1940.

Collier took steps to abolish federal boarding schools, encourage enrollment in local public schools, and establish community day schools—the number of which increased 70 percent between 1933 and 1941. Collier insisted that Native Americans be allowed to practice their traditional religions, despite angry opposition from Protestant missionaries, and he created the Indian Arts and Crafts Board in 1935 to nurture traditional Indian artists and to help them market their works.

Native Americans and the New Deal • From the National Recovery Administration to the Indian Reorganization Act, the New Deal attempted to assist Native American populations in a variety of ways. Here, 110-year-old Chief Little John and his great-great-grandson work together on an NRA project.

The centerpiece of Collier's reform strategy was the Indian Reorganization Act (also known as the Wheeler-Howard Act) of 1934, which revoked the allotment provisions of the Dawes Act. The IRA restored land to tribes, granted Indians the right to establish constitutions and bylaws for self government, provided support for new tribal corporations that would regulate the use of communal lands, and appropriated funds for economic development. This was a landmark act that signaled the government's abandonment of an assimilationist policy and its recognition that Native American tribes possessed the right to chart their own political, cultural, and economic futures. It reflected Collier's commitment to "cultural pluralism," a doctrine that celebrated the diversity of peoples and cultures in American society and sought to protect that diversity against the pressures of assimilation. Collier hoped that the IRA would invigorate traditional Indian cultures and tribal societies, and sustain both for generations. Cultural pluralism was not a popular creed in America during the depression years, making its acceptance as the rationale for the IRA all the more remarkable.

Collier encountered opposition everywhere: from Protestant missionaries and cultural conservatives who wanted to continue an assimilationist policy; from white farmers and businessmen who feared that the new legislation would restrict their access to Native American land; and even from a sizable number of Indian groups, some of which had embraced assimilation while others viewed the IRA as one more attempt by the federal government to impose "the white man's will" on the Indian peoples. This opposition made the IRA a more modest bill than the one Collier had originally championed.

A vocal minority of Indians continued to oppose the act even after its passage. The most crushing blow to Collier came when the Navajo Indians, the nation's largest tribe, voted to reject its terms. They voted as the BIA was forcing them to reduce their livestock herds in order to halt the erosion of reservation land. For a variety of reasons, 76 other tribes joined the Navajo in opposition. Still, a large majority of tribes—181, nearly 70 percent of the total—supported Collier's reform and began organizing new governments under the IRA. Although their quest for independence would suffer setbacks, as Congress and the BIA continued to interfere with their economic and political affairs, these tribes gained significant measures of freedom and autonomy. The New Deal, then, showed considerably more sensitivity to the needs and aspirations of Native Americans than had previous administrations.

The New Deal Abroad

When he first entered office, Roosevelt seemed to favor a nationalist approach to international relations. The United States, he believed, should pursue foreign policies to benefit its domestic affairs, without regard for the effects of those policies on world trade and international stability. Thus, in June 1933, Roosevelt abruptly pulled the United States out of the World Economic Conference in London, a meeting called by leading nations to strengthen the gold standard and thereby stabilize the value of their currencies. Roosevelt feared that the other nations would force the United States into an agreement designed to keep the gold content of the dollar high and commodity prices in the United States low. This would then frustrate the efforts of just-established New Deal agencies (the AAA and NRA in particular) to inflate the prices of agricultural and industrial goods.

Soon after his withdrawal from the London conference, however, Roosevelt put the United States on a more internationalist course. In November 1933, he became the first president to recognize the Soviet Union and to establish diplomatic ties with its Communist rulers. In December 1933, he inaugurated a "Good Neighbor Policy" toward Latin America by formally renouncing the right of the United States to intervene in the affairs of Latin American nations. To back up his pledge, Roosevelt ordered home the Marines stationed in Haiti and Nicaragua, scuttled the Platt Amendment that had given the United States control over the Cuban government since 1901, and granted Panama more political autonomy and a greater administrative role in operating the Panama Canal.

None of this, however, meant that the United States had given up its influence over Latin America. When a 1934 revolution brought a radical government to power in Cuba, the United States ambassador there worked with conservative Cubans to put a regime more favorable to U.S. interests in its place. The United States did refrain from sending its troops to Cuba. It also kept its troops at home in 1936 when a radical government in Mexico nationalized a number of U.S.-owned and British-owned petroleum companies. The United States merely demanded that the new Mexican government compensate the oil companies for their lost property—a demand

The "Good Neighbor Policy" in Action • President Franklin D. Roosevelt, seated on left, and President Anastasio Somoza of Nicaragua, seated on right, sign an agreement extending Export-Import Bank credits to Nicaragua. Through such agreements, the United States hoped to bolster its image in Latin America and stabilize the region's economy for American traders and investors.

that Mexico eventually met. Although the United States was still the dominant power in hemispheric affairs, its newfound restraint inspired hopes throughout Latin America that a new era had dawned.

The Roosevelt administration's recognition of the Soviet Union and embrace of the Good Neighbor Policy can be seen as an international expression of the liberal principles that guided its domestic policies. But these diplomatic initiatives also reflected Roosevelt's interest in stimulating international trade. American businessmen wanted access to the Soviet Union's market. Latin America was already a huge market for the United States, but one in need of greater stability. To win the support of American traders and investors, Roosevelt stressed how the Good Neighbor Policy would improve the region's business climate.

Roosevelt's interest in building international trade was also evident in his support for the Reciprocal Trade Agreement, passed by Congress in 1934. This act allowed his administration to lower U.S. tariffs by as much as 50 percent in exchange for similar reductions by other nations. By the end of 1935, the United States had negotiated reciprocal trade agreements with 14 countries. Roosevelt's turn to free trade—a move consonant with the Second New Deal's program of increasing the circulation of goods and money through the economy—further solidified support for the New Deal in parts of the business community. By the time of the 1936 election, the Democratic Party had attracted the support of top executives of Standard Oil of California and New Jersey, American Tobacco, Coca-Cola, General Electric, United Fruit, Manufacturers Trust, Chase National Bank, and of other corporations and banks with large stakes in foreign trade.

Actually increasing the volume of international trade turned out to be more difficult than passing legislation to encourage it. The supporters of free trade encountered vociferous opposition to tariff reduction both within the United States and abroad. In Germany and Italy, belligerent nationalists Adolf Hitler and Benito Mussolini told their people that the solution to their ills lay not in trade but in military strength and conquest. Throughout the world, similar appeals to national pride proved to be more popular than calls for tariff reductions and international trade. In the face of this historical current, the New Deal's internationalist economic policies made little headway.

Stalemate, 1937–1940

By 1937 and 1938 the New Deal had begun to lose momentum. One reason was an emerging split between working-class and middle-class Democrats. After the UAW's victory over General Motors in 1937, other workers began to imitate the successful tactics pioneered by the Flint militants. The sit-down strike became ubiquitous across the nation. Many middle-class Americans, meanwhile, were becoming disturbed by labor's growing power and by what appeared to be a turn toward radicalism. To many, it seemed, Roosevelt had gone too far.

The Court-Packing Fiasco

The president's proposal on February 5, 1937, to alter the makeup of the Supreme Court exacerbated middle-class fears. Roosevelt asked Congress to give him the power to appoint one new Supreme Court justice for every member of the court who was over the age of 70 and who had served for at least 10 years. His stated reason was that the current justices were too old and feeble to handle the large volume of cases coming before them. But his real purpose was to prevent the conservative justices on the court—a majority of whom had been appointed by Republican presidents—from dismantling his New Deal. Roosevelt had not minded when, in 1935, the court had declared the NRA unconstitutional, but he was not willing to see the Wagner Act and the Social Security Act invalidated. His proposal, if accepted, would have given him the authority to appoint six additional justices, thereby securing a pro–New Deal majority.

What seems remarkable about this episode is Roosevelt's willingness to tamper with an institution that many Americans considered sacred. Although he had not consulted members of Congress beforehand, the president seemed genuinely surprised by the storm of indignation, both on Capitol Hill and in the country at large, that greeted his "court-packing" proposal. Roosevelt's political acumen had apparently been dulled by the victory he had won in 1936, which he believed had given him a mandate to do whatever he deemed necessary to keep the New Deal alive. This inflated sense of power infuriated many who had previously been New Deal

Unemployment in the Nonfarm Labor Force, 1929–1945

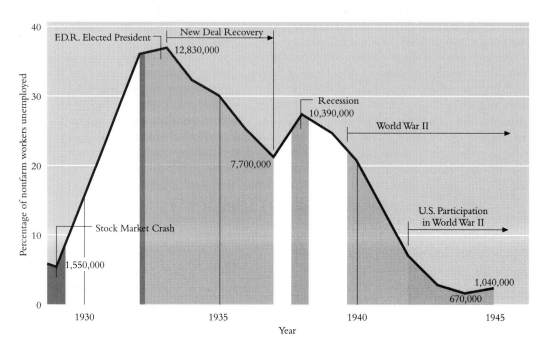

Source: Data from *Historical Statistics of the United States, Colonial Times to 1970* (White Plains, N.Y.: Kraus International, 1989), p. 126.

enthusiasts. Although working-class support for Roosevelt remained strong, many middle-class voters turned away from the New Deal, convinced that the president was moving in a radical, dictatorial, and un-American direction. In 1937 and 1938 a conservative opposition took shape, uniting Republicans, conservative Democrats (many of them southerners), and civil libertarians determined to protect private property and government integrity.

Ironically, Roosevelt's court-packing scheme may not have been necessary. In March 1937, just one month after he proposed his plan, Supreme Court Justice Owen J. Roberts, who had formerly opposed New Deal programs, decided to support them. In April and May, the Court upheld the constitutionality of the Wagner Act and Social Security Act, both by a 5-to-4 margin. The principal reforms of the New Deal would endure. Roosevelt allowed his ill-advised and now superfluous court-reform proposal to die in Congress that summer. Within three years, five of the aging justices had retired, giving Roosevelt the opportunity to fashion a court more to his liking. But nonetheless, Roosevelt's reputation had suffered.

The Recession of 1937–1938

Whatever hope Roosevelt may have had for a quick recovery from the court-packing fiasco was dashed by a sharp recession that struck the country in late 1937 and 1938. Again, Roosevelt had mostly himself to blame. The New Deal programs of 1935 had stimulated the economy. In 1937 production surpassed the highest level of 1929, and unemployment fell to 14 percent. Believing that the depression was easing at last, Roosevelt began to scale back relief programs. WPA rolls were slashed, PWA projects were shut down, and the Federal Reserve tightened credit. New payroll taxes took $2 billion dollars from wage earners' salaries to finance the Social Security pension fund. That withdrawal would not have hurt the economy had the money been returned to circulation as pensions for retirees. But no Social Security pensions were scheduled to be paid until 1941. Once again, the economy became starved for money, and once again the stock market crashed. By October 1937, the market fell by almost 40 percent from its August high. By March 1938, the unemployment rate had soared to 20 percent. In the off-year elections later that year, voters elected many conservative Democrats and Republicans opposed to the New Deal. These conservatives were not strong enough to dismantle the New Deal reforms already in place, but they were able to block the passage of new programs. A political stalemate ensued. And the economy limped along.

Conclusion

Despite the court fiasco, the New Deal reinvigorated American democracy. Roosevelt first assumed the presidency in the same week that Adolf Hitler established a Nazi dictatorship in Germany. Some feared that Roosevelt, by accumulating more power into the hands of the federal government than had ever been done in peacetime, aspired to autocratic rule. But nothing of the sort happened. Roosevelt and the New Dealers did not weaken democracy; they strengthened it. They inspired millions of Americans who had never before voted to go to the polls. Groups that had been marginalized—southern and eastern Europeans, unskilled workers, Native Americans—now felt that their political activism could make a difference.

Not everyone benefited to the same degree from the broadening of American democracy. Northern factory workers, farm owners, European ethnics, and middle-class consumers (especially homeowners) were among the groups who benefited most. In contrast, the socialist and communist elements of the labor movement failed to achieve their radical demands. Southern industrial workers, black and white, benefited little from New Deal reforms; so did farm laborers. Feminists made no headway. African Americans and Mexican Americans gained meager influence over public policy.

Of course, New Deal reforms might not have mattered to any group had not the Second World War rescued the New Deal economic program. With government war orders flooding factories from 1941 on, the economy grew vigorously, unemployment vanished, and prosperity finally returned. The architects of the Second New Deal, who had argued that large government expenditures would stimulate consumer demand and trigger economic recovery, were vindicated.

The war also solidified the political reforms of the 1930s: an increased role for the government in regulating the economy and in ensuring the social welfare of those unable to help themselves; strong state support of unionization, agricultural subsidies, and progressive tax policies; the use of government power and money to develop the West and Southwest. In sharp contrast to progressivism, the reforms of the New Deal endured. Voters returned Roosevelt to office for unprecedented third and fourth terms. And these same voters remained wedded for the next 40 years to Roosevelt's central idea: that a powerful state would enhance the pursuit of liberty and equality.

Chronology

1929 Herbert Hoover assumes the presidency • Stock market crashes on "Black Tuesday"

1930 Tariff Act (Hawley-Smoot) raises tariffs

1931 2,000 U.S. banks fail • Austrian bank failure triggers European depression

1932 Unemployment rate reaches 25 percent • Reconstruction Finance Corporation established • Bonus Army marches on Washington • Roosevelt defeats Hoover for presidency

1933 Roosevelt assumes presidency • "Hundred Days" legislation defines First New Deal (March–June) • Roosevelt administration recognizes the Soviet Union • "Good Neighbor Policy" toward Latin America launched • Reciprocal Trade Agreement lowers tariffs

1934 Father Charles Coughlin and Huey Long challenge conservatism of First New Deal • 2,000 strikes staged across country • Democrats overwhelm Republicans in off-year election • Radical political movements emerge in Wisconsin, Minnesota, Washington, and California • Indian Reorganization Act restores tribal land, provides funds, and grants limited right of self-government to Native Americans

1935 Committee for Industrial Organization (CIO) formed • Supreme Court declares NRA unconstitutional • Roosevelt unveils his Second New Deal • Congress passes Social Security Act • National Labor Relations Act (Wagner Act) guarantees workers' right to join unions • Holding Company Act breaks up utilities' near-monopoly • Congress passes Wealth Tax Act • Emergency Relief Administration Act passed; funds Works Progress Administration and other projects • Rural Electrification Administration established • Number of Mexican immigrants returning to Mexico reaches 500,000

1936 Roosevelt defeats Alf Landon for second term • Supreme Court declares AAA unconstitutional • Congress passes Soil Conservation and Domestic Allotment Act to replace AAA • Farm Security Administration established

1937 United Auto Workers defeat General Motors in sit-down strike • Roosevelt attempts to "pack" the Supreme Court • Supreme Court upholds constitutionality of Social Security and National Labor Relations acts • Severe recession hits

1938 Conservative opposition to New Deal does well in off-year election • Superman comic debuts

1939 75,000 gather to hear Marian Anderson sing at Lincoln Memorial

Suggested Readings

T. H. Watkins, *The Great Depression: America in the 1930s* (1993), provides a broad overview of society and politics during the 1930s. No work better conveys the tumult and drama of that era than Arthur M. Schlesinger Jr.'s three-volume *The Age of Roosevelt: The Crisis of the Old Order* (1957), *The Coming of the New Deal* (1958), and *The Politics of Upheaval* (1960).

Causes of the Great Depression

On causes of the depression, consult John Kenneth Galbraith, *The Great Crash* (1955); Milton Friedman and Anna J. Schwartz, *The Great Contraction, 1929–1933* (1965); Michael A. Bernstein, *The Great Depression: Delayed Recovery and Economic Change in America, 1929–1939* (1987); Charles Kindelberger, *The World in Depression* (1973); and John A. Garraty, *The Great Depression* (1986).

Herbert Hoover

On Hoover's failure to restore prosperity and popular morale, see Albert U. Romasco, *The Poverty of Abundance: Hoover, the Nation, the Depression* (1965), and David Burner, *Herbert Hoover: A Public Life* (1979). Roger Daniels, *The Bonus March* (1971), analyzes the event that became a symbol of Hoover's indifference to the depression's victims. More sympathetic treatments of Hoover's efforts to cope with the depression can be found in Harris G. Warren, *Herbert Hoover and the Great Depression* (1959); Joan Hoff Wilson, *Herbert Hoover: Forgotten Progressive* (1975); and Martin L. Fausold, *The Presidency of Herbert C. Hoover* (1985). Hoover offered his own spirited defense of his policies and a critique of the New Deal in his *Memoirs: The Great Depression* (1952).

Franklin D. Roosevelt and Eleanor Roosevelt

No 20th century president has attracted more scholarly attention than Franklin Roosevelt. The most detailed biography is Frank Freidel, *Franklin D. Roosevelt* (1952–1973), four volumes that cover Roosevelt's life from birth through the Hundred Days of 1933. The most complete biography, and one that is remarkably good at balancing Roosevelt's life and times, is Kenneth S. Davis, *FDR* (1972–1993), also in four volumes. Anyone interested in Roosevelt's youth and prepresidential career should consult Geoffrey Ward's *Before the Trumpet: Young Franklin Roosevelt, 1882–1905* (1985) and *A First-Class Temperament: The Emergence of Franklin Roosevelt* (1989). James McGregor Burns, *Roosevelt: The Lion and the Fox* (1956), offers an intriguing portrait of Roosevelt as president.

On Eleanor Roosevelt, see Lois Scharf, *Eleanor Roosevelt: First Lady of American Liberalism* (1987); Joseph P. Lash, *Eleanor and Franklin* (1981); and, most importantly, Blanche Wiesen Cook, *Eleanor Roosevelt*, vol. 1 (1992), which chronicles her life from birth until she moved into the White House in 1933.

New Deal Overviews

William E. Leuchtenberg, *Franklin D. Roosevelt and the New Deal, 1932–1940* (1963), is still an authoritative account of the New Deal, although it should be supplemented with Robert S. McElvaine, *The Great Depression* (1984). Both books treat the New Deal as a transformative moment in American politics and economics. For more critical interpretations of the New Deal, stressing the limited nature of the era's reforms, see Barton J. Bernstein, "The New Deal: The Conservative Achievements of Liberal Reform," in Barton J. Bernstein, ed., *Toward a New Past: Dissenting Essays in American History* (1968); Paul K. Conkin, *The New Deal* (1975); and Anthony J. Badger, *The New Deal: The Depression Years, 1933–1940* (1989). Barry D. Karl, *The Uneasy State: The United States from 1915–1945* (1983), and the essays in Steve Fraser and Gary Gerstle, eds., *The Rise and Fall of the New Deal Order, 1930–1980* (1989), offer new perspectives on the achievements and limitations of the New Deal.

First New Deal

See Susan E. Kennedy, *The Banking Crisis of 1933* (1973), and Michael Parrish, *Securities Regulation and the New Deal* (1970), on the First New Deal's efforts to restructure the nation's financial institutions. On New Deal relief efforts, consult George T. McJimsey, *Harry Hopkins: Ally of the Poor and Defender of Democracy* (1987); John Salmond, *The Civilian Conservation Corps, 1933–42* (1967); Percy H. Merrill, *Roosevelt's Forest Army: A History of the Civilian Conservation Corps, 1933–1942* (1981); and Bonnie Fox Schwartz, *The Civilian Works Administration: The Business of Emergency Employment in the New Deal 1933–1934* (1984). James T. Patterson, *America's Struggle against Poverty, 1900–1980* (1981), contains a substantial section on New Deal poor relief. For the New Deal's role in rebuilding the nation's infrastructure, see T. H. Watkins, *Righteous Pilgrim: The Life and Times of Harold Ickes, 1874–1952* (1990), and James S. Olson, *Saving Capitalism: The Reconstruction Finance Corporation and the New Deal, 1933–1940* (1988). Albert V. Romasco, *The Politics of Recovery: Roosevelt's New Deal* (1983), provides a useful overview of the First New Deal's efforts to restore prosperity.

First New Deal, Agricultural Policy

Van Perkins, *Crisis in Agriculture* (1969), and Theodore M. Saloutos, *The American Farmer and the New Deal* (1982), examine efforts to revive agriculture; David E. Conrad, *The Forgotten Farmers: The Story of Sharecroppers in the New Deal* (1965), and Paul Mertz, *The New Deal and Southern Rural Poverty* (1978), focus on groups ignored by New Deal programs. Donald Worster, *Dust Bowl: The Southern Plains in the*

1930s (1979), and James N. Gregory, *American Exodus: The Dust Bowl Migration and Okie Culture in California* (1989), are indispensable on the crisis in plains agriculture and the ensuing "Okie" migration.

First New Deal, Industrial Policy

Ellis Hawley, *The New Deal and the Problem of Monopoly* (1966), is essential to understand the First New Deal's industrial policy. See also Bernard Bellush, *The Failure of the NRA* (1975); Michael Weinstein, *Recovery and Redistribution under the NRA* (1980); and Donald R. Brand, *Corporatism and the Rule of Law: A Study of the National Recovery Administration* (1988). On the TVA alternative, see Thomas K. McCraw, *TVA and the Power Fight, 1933–1939* (1971), and Walter L. Creese, *TVA's Public Planning: The Vision, the Reality* (1990).

Popular Unrest

On populist critics of the New Deal, see Alan Brinkley, *Voices of Protest: Huey Long, Father Coughlin and the Great Depression* (1982); Michael Kazin, *The Populist Persuasion: An American History* (1995); and Abraham Holtzman, *The Townsend Movement* (1963). For the rebirth of the labor movement, consult Irving Bernstein, *The Turbulent Years: A History of the American Worker, 1933–1941* (1969); Lizabeth Cohen, *Making a New Deal: Industrial Workers in Chicago, 1919–1939* (1990); Gary Gerstle, *Working-Class Americanism: The Politics of Labor in a Textile City, 1914–1960* (1989); Jacquelyn Hall et al., *Like a Family: The Making of a Southern Cotton Mill World* (1987); Bruce Nelson, *Workers on the Waterfront: Seamen, Longshoremen, and Unionism in the 1930s* (1988); and Joshua B. Freeman, *In Transit: The Transport Workers Union in New York City, 1933–1966* (1989).

Radical Politics

Richard M. Vallely, *Radicalism in the States: The Minnesota Farmer-Labor Party and the American Political Economy* (1989), and Greg Mitchell, *The Campaign of the Century: Upton Sinclair's EPIC Race for Governor of California and the Birth of Media Politics* (1992), analyze the upheaval in state politics that followed closely upon labor's resurgence. Irving Howe and Lewis Coser, *The American Communist Party: A Critical History (1919–1957)* (1957), is still the best single-volume history of the Communist Party during the 1930s. On the work of communists among the nation's dispossessed, see Mark Naison, *Communists in Harlem during the Depression* (1983); Robin D. G. Kelley, *Hammer and Hoe: Alabama Communists during the Great Depression* (1990); Dorothy Ray Healey and Maurice Isserman, *California Red: A Life in the American Communist Party* (1990); and Vicki Ruiz, *Cannery Women/Cannery Lives: Mexican Women, Unionization, and the California Food Processing Industry, 1930–1950* (1987).

The Second New Deal

Steven Fraser, *Labor Will Rule: Sidney Hillman and the Rise of American Labor* (1991), is indispensable for understanding the ideology, programs, and personalities of the Second New Deal. On the forging of the 1936 Democratic coalition, see Kristi Andersen, *The Creation of a Democratic Majority, 1928–1936* (1979), and Nancy J. Weiss, *Farewell to the Party of Lincoln: Black Politics in the Age of FDR* (1983). Roy Lubove, *The Struggle for Social Security* (1968), and J. Joseph Huthmacher, *Senator Robert Wagner and the Rise of Urban Liberalism* (1968), provide in-depth analyses of the Social Security Act, Wagner Act, and other crucial pieces of Second New Deal legislation. For critical perspectives on these reforms that stress their limitations as well as their achievements, consult Christopher Tomlins, *The State and the Unions: Labor Relations, Law and the Organized Labor Movement in America, 1880–1960* (1985), and Mark Leff, *The Limits of Symbolic Reform: The New Deal and Taxation, 1933–1939* (1984). Important for understanding the role of capitalists and money in the New Deal coalition are Jordan A. Schwarz, *The New Dealers: Power Politics in the Age of Roosevelt* (1993); Robert A. Caro, *The Years of Lyndon Johnson: The Path to Power* (1981); and Colin Gordon, *New Deals: Business, Labor, and Politics in America, 1920–1935* (1994).

New Deal Men, New Deal Women

On the political and cultural style of New Deal men, see Peter H. Irons, *The New Deal Lawyers* (1982); Samuel I. Rosenman, *Working with Roosevelt* (1952); Joseph P. Lash, *Dealers and Dreamers: A*

New Look at the New Deal (1988); and Katie Louchheim, ed., *The Making of the New Deal: The Insiders Speak* (1983). On New Deal women, consult Susan Ware, *Beyond Suffrage: Women in the New Deal* (1981), and *Partner and I: Molly Dewson, Feminism and New Deal Politics* (1987); also see Linda Gordon, *Pitied But Not Entitled: Single Mothers and the History of Welfare, 1890–1935* (1994). On feminist weakness and male anxiety during the depression, see Lois Scharf, *To Work and to Wed: Female Employment, Feminism, and the Great Depression* (1980); Winifred Wandersee, *Women's Work and Family Values: 1920–1940* (1981); and Alice Kessler-Harris, *Out to Work: A History of Wage-Earning Women in the United States* (1982). Elizabeth Faue, *Community of Suffering and Struggle: Women, Men, and the Labor Movement in Minneapolis, 1915–1945* (1991), is illuminating on the strident masculinism that dominated 1930s labor and popular culture.

Labor and the CIO

Melvyn Dubofsky and Warren Van Tine, *John L. Lewis: A Biography* (1977), is important on the birth of the CIO and labor's growing power in 1936 and 1937. Sidney Fine, *Sit-Down: The General Motors Strike of 1936–1937* (1967), is the most complete study of that pivotal event, but Nelson Lichtenstein, *"The Most Dangerous Man in Detroit": Walter Reuther and the Fate of American Labor* (1995), should be consulted for the broader industrial and union context in which it occurred. The best work on the centrality of labor and the "common man" to literary and popular culture in the 1930s is that of Michael Denning, *The Cultural Front: The Laboring of American Culture in the Twentieth Century* (1996); see also Richard H. Pells, *Radical Visions and American Dreams: Culture and Social Thought in the Depression Years* (1973). On the government's role in supporting public art through the WPA and other federal agencies, see William F. McDonald, *Federal Relief Administration and the Arts* (1968); Richard D. McKinzie, *The New Deal for Artists* (1973); and Barbara Melosh, *Engendering Culture: Manhood and Womanhood in New Deal Public Art and Theater* (1991).

Minorities and the New Deal

Harvard Sitkoff, *A New Deal for Blacks* (1978), is a wide-ranging examination of the place of African Americans in New Deal reform. See also John B. Kirby, *Black Americans in the Roosevelt Era: Liberalism and Race* (1980); Robert L. Zangrando, *The NAACP Crusade against Lynching, 1909–1950* (1980); and James Goodman, *Stories of Scottsboro* (1994). Abraham Hoffman, *Unwanted Mexican Americans in the Great Depression: Repatriation Pressures, 1929–1939* (1974), is the best introduction to the repatriation campaign. George J. Sánchez, *Becoming Mexican American: Ethnicity, Culture and Identity in Chicano Los Angeles, 1900–1945* (1993), reconstructs the experience of the largest Mexican urban settlement in 1930s America; and Cletus E. Daniel, *Bitter Harvest: A History of California Farmworkers, 1870–1941* (1981), shows how little Chicanos and other groups of agricultural laborers benefited from New Deal reform. On Native Americans, consult Francis Paul Prucha, *The Great Father: The United States Government and the American Indians* (1984), and Christine Bolt, *American Indian Policy and American Reform* (1987). The importance of John Collier and the Indian Reorganization Act are treated well in Lawrence C. Kelly, *The Assault on Assimilation: John Collier and the Origins of Indian Policy Reform* (1983), and Graham D. Taylor, *The New Deal and American Indian Tribalism: The Administration of the Indian Reorganization Act, 1934–1945* (1980). For more detailed examinations of particular tribes' encounters with the New Deal, see Donald L. Parman, *The Navajos and the New Deal* (1976), and Harry A. Kersey Jr., *The Florida Seminoles and the New Deal, 1933–1942* (1989).

Ebbing of New Deal

James T. Patterson, *Congressional Conservatism and the New Deal* (1967), expertly analyzes the growing congressional opposition to the New Deal in the late 1930s. See also Frank Freidel, *FDR and the South* (1965). Leonard Baker, *Back to Back: The Duel between FDR and the Supreme Court* (1967), chronicles the court-packing fight. Alan Brinkley, *The End of Reform: New Deal Liberalism in Recession and War* (1995), provocatively examines the efforts of New Dealers to adjust their beliefs and programs as they lost support, momentum, and confidence in the late 1930s.

7

America during the
Second World War

T he Second World War, a struggle of unprecedented destruction that
brought death to some *60 million* people worldwide, vastly changed American life. During a decade-long process, the United States abandoned isolationism, moved toward military engagement on the side of the Allies, and emerged
triumphant in a global war in which U.S. forces fought and died in North Africa,
Europe, and Asia.

To succeed militarily, the United States greatly expanded the power of its national government. The mobilization for war finally brought the country out of the
Great Depression and produced significant economic and social change. The nation's productive capacity—spurred by new technologies and by a new working relationship among government, business, labor, and scientific researchers—dwarfed
that of every other nation and provided the economic basis for military victory.

At home, while fighting a war against the Axis Powers, citizens considered the
meaning of liberty and equality both in the international order and in their own
lives. Although a massive propaganda effort to bolster popular support for wartime
sacrifice heralded the war as a struggle to protect and preserve "the American way of
life," the war inevitably raised significant challenges to defining "the American way."
How would America, while striving for victory, reorder its economy, its culture, and
the social patterns that had shaped racial, ethnic, and gender relationships during
the 1930s? What process of international reconstruction might be required to build
a prosperous and lasting peace?

The Road to War: Aggression and Response

The road to the Second World War began at least a decade before U.S. entry in 1941.
The worldwide depression of the 1930s contributed to international political instability. In Japan, Italy, and Germany, economic collapse and rising unemployment created
political conditions that nurtured ultranationalistic movements promising recovery
through military buildup and territorial expansion. Elsewhere in Europe and in the
United States itself, economic problems made governments turn inward, concentrating upon domestic recovery and avoiding expensive foreign entanglements. As
international economic and political stability deteriorated, Americans tried to decide
how to respond to acts of aggression overseas.

The Rise of Aggressor States

The war began first in the Far East. On September 18, 1931, Japanese military forces seized Manchuria and created a puppet state called Manchukuo. This action violated the League of Nations charter, the Washington treaties, and the Kellogg-Briand Pact (see Chapter 5). Japanese military leaders, who had urged their nation to accumulate an empire, won their gamble: The international community was too preoccupied with domestic economic ills to counter Japan's move. In the United States, the Hoover-Stimson Doctrine declared a policy of "nonrecognition" of Manchukuo, and the League of Nations also condemned Japan's action; but these stands were not backed by force, and Japan ignored them.

Meanwhile, ultranationalist states in Europe also sought to alleviate domestic ills through military aggression. Adolf Hitler's National Socialist (Nazi) Party came to power in Germany in 1933, instituting a fascist regime, a one-party dictatorial state. Hitler denounced the Versailles peace settlement of 1919, blamed Germany's plight on a Jewish conspiracy, claimed a genetic superiority for the "Aryan" race of German-speaking peoples, and promised to build a new empire (the "Third Reich"). The regime withdrew from the League of Nations and reinstituted compulsory military service. Nearly doubling Germany's military expenditures (a blatant violation of the Treaty of Versailles), Hitler sought to create an air force and an army that would out-number those of France, Germany's major European rival. Another fascist government in Italy, headed by Benito Mussolini, also launched a military buildup and dreamed of empire. In October 1935 Mussolini's armies invaded Ethiopia, a proud and independent African kingdom that had never before succumbed to colonialist rule. After meeting fierce resistance, Italy prevailed over Ethiopian forces.

Isolationist Sentiment and American Neutrality

Many Americans wished to isolate their country from these foreign troubles. Revisionist historians, writing after the First World War, had maintained that Woodrow Wilson manipulated the country into a war that had not been in the nation's best interests. Antiwar movies, such as *All Quiet on the Western Front* and *The Big Parade,* popularized the notion that war was a power game played by business and governmental elites who used appeals to nationalism to dupe common people into serving as cannon fodder. Between 1934 and 1936 a Senate investigating committee headed by Republican Gerald P. Nye of North Dakota held well-publicized hearings. The Nye committee underscored claims that American bankers and munitions makers had developed a huge financial stake in an Anglo-French victory and that the nation had been maneuvered into the First World War to preserve their profits. By 1935 public opinion polls suggested that Americans overwhelmingly opposed involvement in foreign conflicts and feared being manipulated by what one writer called "merchants of death."

To prevent a repetition of the circumstances that had supposedly drawn the United States into the First World War, Congress enacted neutrality legislation to prohibit the growth of financial or emotional connections to belligerents. The Neutrality Acts of 1935 and 1936 mandated an arms embargo against belligerents, prohibited loans to them, and curtailed Americans' travel on ships belonging to nations at war. The Neutrality Act of 1937 further broadened the embargo to cover all trade with belligerents, unless the nation at war paid in cash and carried the products away in its own ships. This "cash-and-carry" provision minimized damage to America's export sector while it reduced the risk that loans or the presence of American commerce in a war zone might entangle the country in a conflict.

The isolationist mood in the United States, matched by British policies of non-involvement, encouraged Hitler's expansionist designs. In March 1936 Nazi troops again violated the Versailles agreement and seized the Rhineland. And a few months later, Hitler and Mussolini extended aid to General Francisco Franco, a fellow fascist who was seeking to overthrow Spain's republican government. By lending Franco sophisticated weaponry and soldiers, Italy and Germany used the Spanish civil war as a training ground for fascist forces. Republicans in Spain appealed to antifascist nations for assistance, but only the Soviet Union responded. Britain, France, and the United States, fearing that the conflict would flare into world war if more nations took sides, adopted policies of noninvolvement. The United States even extended its arms embargo to cover civil wars, a move that aided the well-armed fascist forces and crippled republican resistance.

Growing Interventionist Sentiment

Although the United States remained officially uninvolved, the Spanish Civil War did precipitate a major debate over foreign policy. Many conservative groups in the United States applauded Franco as a strong anticommunist whose fascist state would support religion and a stable social order in Spain. In contrast, many on the political left, particularly writers and intellectuals, championed the cause of republican Spain and denounced the fascist repression that was sweeping Europe. Cadres of Americans, including the famed "Abraham Lincoln battalion," crossed the Atlantic and joined Soviet-organized, international brigades, which fought alongside republican forces. American peace groups, which had been so strong during the 1920s and early 1930s, now split over how peace could be best maintained. Some continued to advocate neutrality and isolation, but others argued for a strong stand against fascist militarism and aggression. Increasingly, Americans separated into camps of isolationists and interventionists.

Tilting cautiously toward the interventionist side, the administration of President Franklin Roosevelt tried to influence the debate. In October 1937 Roosevelt called for international cooperation to "quarantine" aggressor states, and he gingerly suggested some modification of America's neutrality legislation. But congressional leaders were adamant in maintaining the policy of noninvolvement.

Japan's Invasion of China

As Americans were debating strict neutrality versus cautious engagement, Japan once again launched an attack, this time on China itself. In the summer of 1937, after an exchange of gunfire between Japanese and Chinese troops at the Marco Polo Bridge southwest of Beijing, Japanese armies invaded southward, capturing Beijing, Shanghai, Nanjing, and Shandong. The Japanese government demanded that China become subservient politically and economically to Tokyo. It also announced a plan for a greater East Asia Co-Prosperity Sphere, which would supposedly liberate peoples throughout Asia from Western colonialism and create a self-sufficient economic zone under Japanese leadership. Toward the end of 1937 Japanese planes sank the *Panay*, an American gunboat that was evacuating American officials from Nanjing, but Japan's quick apology defused the potential crisis. Even so, the *Panay* incident and Japanese brutality in occupying Nanjing, where perhaps 300,000 Chinese were killed in a sustained assault against civilians, alarmed Roosevelt. The president began to consult with Britain about planning for a possible war in Asia.

Further aggression heightened the sense of alarm among interventionists in the United States, especially when the expansionist states began cooperating with each other. In October 1936 Germany and Italy agreed to cooperate as the "Axis Powers," and Japan joined them to form an alliance against the Soviet Union in November 1936. Italy followed Japan and Germany in withdrawing from the League of Nations. In March 1938 Hitler annexed Austria to the Third Reich and then announced his intention to annex the Sudetenland, a portion of Czechoslovakia inhabited by 3.5 million people of German descent. In May, Roosevelt announced a program of naval rearmament that would increase the American Navy beyond the treaty limits that Japan had already violated.

The Outbreak of War in Europe

The leaders of France and Britain, wishing to avoid a confrontation with Germany, met with Hitler in Munich in September of 1938. They acquiesced to Germany's seizure of the Sudetenland in return for Hitler's promise to seek no more territory. Roosevelt expressed relief that the Munich Conference seemed to promise future peace in Europe.

The promise of peace did not last. In March 1939 Germans marched into Prague and, within a few months, annexed the rest of Czechoslovakia. In August 1939 Hitler secured Germany's eastern flank by signing a nonaggression pact with the Soviet Union. The bitterest of enemies, Stalin and Hitler nonetheless agreed to cooperate in carving up territory: In a secret protocol they plotted to divide Poland and the Baltic states. By the fall of 1939 Germany was clearly preparing for an attack on Poland.

Britain and France were finally ready to draw the line. Both countries pledged to defend Poland, and on September 1, 1939, Hitler's invasion forced them into action. Two days after Hitler's armies stormed into Poland, Britain and France declared war on Germany. The Allies, however, were unable to mobilize in time to help the Poles. Outnumbered and outgunned, Polish forces fought valiantly but could not withstand Germany's unrelenting strikes on land and from the air. With Soviet troops moving in simultaneously from the east, Poland fell within weeks. Once the occupation of Poland was completed, Hitler's troops waited out the winter of 1939–1940. Some observers dubbed this period a *sitzkrieg*, or "sitting war."

The lull proved only temporary. In April 1940 a German *blitzkrieg*, or "lightning war," began moving swiftly and suddenly, overrunning Denmark, Norway, the Netherlands, Belgium, Luxembourg, and then France. The speed with which Hitler's well-trained army moved shocked Allied leaders in Paris and London; Britain barely managed to evacuate its troops, but not its equipment, from the French coastal town of Dunkirk, just before it fell before the German onslaught

German Expansion at Its Height

that began in late May. Early in June, Italy joined Germany by declaring war on the Allies. In June 1940, France fell, and Hitler installed a pro-Nazi government at Vichy in southern France. French officials were forced to surrender to Hitler in the same railway car used for the German surrender to France at the end of the First World War. In only six weeks, Hitler's army had seized complete control of Europe's Atlantic coastline, from the North Sea south to Spain, where Franco remained officially neutral but decidedly pro-Axis.

America's Response to War in Europe

In a somber, six-minute speech delivered on the day that Britain and France entered the war against Germany, President Roosevelt declared U.S. neutrality. But the tone of his speech was hardly neutral. Unlike Woodrow Wilson when the European war had broken out in 1914, Roosevelt did not urge Americans to be impartial. From 1939 to 1941 Roosevelt tried to mobilize public opinion against Congress's Neutrality Acts and in favor of what he called "measures short of war" that would bolster the Allied fight against the Axis.

At Roosevelt's urging, late in 1939 Congress lifted the Neutrality Act's ban on selling arms to either side and substituted a "cash-and-carry" provision that permitted arms sales to belligerents who could pay cash for their purchases and carry them away in their own ships. Because Britain and France controlled the Atlantic sea lanes, they clearly benefited from this change in U.S. policy. Congress responded further to Roosevelt's requests, appropriating additional funds for rearmament and passing the Selective Training and Service Act of 1940, the first peacetime draft in U.S. history. Abandoning any further pretense of neutrality, the United States began supplying war matériel directly to Great Britain. The appointment of two Republicans to the cabinet—Henry Stimson as secretary of war and Frank Knox as secretary of the Navy—gave the new policies bipartisan overtones, if not full bipartisan support.

Meanwhile, Hitler was concentrating his attention on Great Britain. From August through October 1940 Germany's *Luftwaffe* subjected British air bases to daily raids, coming close to knocking Britain's Royal Air Force (RAF) out of the war. Just as he was on the verge of success, however, Hitler lost patience with this strategy and ordered instead the bombing of London and other cities—first by day and then by night. In addition to giving the RAF time to recover, Germany's nighttime bombings of Britain's cities also aroused a sense of urgency about the war in the United States. The use of airpower against civilians in the Battle of Britain, as it was called, shocked Americans, who heard the news in dramatic radio broadcasts from London. As writer Archibald MacLeish phrased it, radio journalist Edward R. Murrow had "skillfully burned the city of London in our homes and we felt the flames."

In September 1940 the president ignored any possible constitutional questions about the limits of his authority and agreed to transfer 50 First World War–era naval destroyers to the British navy. In return, the United States gained the right to build eight naval bases in British territory in the Western Hemisphere. This "destroyers-for-bases" deal infuriated isolationist members of Congress. Even within the president's own party, opposition was strong. Democratic Senator Burton K. Wheeler of Montana distributed more than a million antiwar postcards, at government expense, an action that Secretary of War Stimson characterized as "very near the line of subversion activities . . . if not treason."

Resistance to Roosevelt's pro-Allied policies extended beyond Congress. The most formidable opposition came from the America First Committee, organized by General Robert E. Wood, head of Sears, Roebuck, and Company, the giant department store chain. Included among its members was the aviation hero Charles Lindbergh, who campaigned vigorously at mass rallies across the country against aid to the Allies.

Although the people who tried to keep the United States out of the war were generally lumped together as "isolationists," this single term obscures their ideological diversity. Some pacifists, including members of religious groups committed to nonviolence, opposed all wars as immoral, even those against evil regimes. Some political progressives disliked fascism but feared even more the growth of centralized power that the conduct of war would require in the United States; they also distrusted the elites who dominated international decision making. On the other hand, some conservatives sympathized with fascism, viewing Germany not as an enemy but as the future. Finally, some Americans opposed Roosevelt's pro-Allied policies because they shared Hitler's anti-Semitism.

Indeed, a strong current of anti-Semitism existed in the country at large. An organization called the German American Bund, for example, defended Hitler's anti-Semitic policies and denounced Roosevelt's "Jew Deal," a reference to the presence of Jewish advisers in FDR's New Deal administration. In 1939 congressional leaders had quashed the Wagner-Rogers Bill, which would have boosted immigration quotas in order to allow for the entry of 20,000 Jewish children otherwise slated for Hitler's concentration camps. Bowing to anti-Semitic prejudices, the United States adopted a restrictive refugee policy that did not permit even the legal quota of Jewish immigrants from Eastern Europe to enter the country during the Second World War. The consequences of these policies became even graver after June of 1941, when Hitler established the death camps that would systematically exterminate millions of Jews, gypsies, homosexuals, and anyone else whom the Nazis deemed "unfit" for life in the Third Reich and its occupied territories.

To counteract the isolationists, with Roosevelt's encouragement, those who favored supporting the Allies also organized. The Military Training Camps Association, for example, lobbied on behalf of the Selective Service Act. The Committee to Defend America by Aiding the Allies, headed by William Allen White, who was a Republican and a well-known Kansas newspaper editor, organized more than 300 local chapters in just a few weeks. Like the isolationists, interventionist organizations drew from an ideologically diverse group of supporters. All, however, sounded alarms about the dangerous possibility that fascist brutality, militarism, and racism might overrun Europe as Americans watched passively.

Presidential election politics in 1940 forced Roosevelt to tone down his pro-Allied rhetoric. Republicans nominated Wendell Willkie, a lawyer and business executive with ties to the party's liberal, internationalist wing. Democrats broke with the practice of limiting presidents to two terms in office and nominated Roosevelt for a third. To overcome the disadvantages of the third-term issue, and to differentiate his policies from Willkie's, the president played to the popular opposition to war. He promised not to send American boys to fight in "foreign wars." Once he had defeated Willkie and won an unprecedented third term in November, however, Roosevelt produced his most ambitious plan yet to support Britain's war effort.

An "Arsenal of Democracy"

Britain was nearly out of money, so the president proposed an additional provision to the Neutrality Act. The United States would now loan, or "lend-lease," rather than sell munitions to the Allies. By making the United States a "great arsenal of democracy," FDR assured Americans, he would "keep war away from our country and our people." But not everyone in Congress felt as Roosevelt did. During the bitter debate over the Lend-Lease Act, Senator Wheeler evoked Roosevelt's unpopular destruction of farm surpluses during the early years of the New Deal by charging that the act would result in the "plowing under" of every fourth American boy. Nevertheless, the symbolically numbered House Resolution 1776 was passed by Congress on March 11, 1941. When Germany turned its attention away from Britain and suddenly attacked its recent ally the Soviet Union in June, Roosevelt extended lend-lease to Joseph Stalin's communist regime, even though it had earlier cooperated with Hitler.

Wheeler continued his opposition. In September 1941 he created a special Senate committee to investigate whether Hollywood movies were being used to sway people in a pro-war direction. Some isolationists, pointing out that many Hollywood producers were Jewish, expressed blatantly anti-Semitic opinions.

Still maintaining his stated policy of nonbelligerence, Roosevelt next took steps to coordinate military strategy with Britain. Should the United States be drawn into a two-front war against both Germany and Japan, the president pledged to follow a Europe-first strategy. And to back up his promise, Roosevelt deployed thousands of marines to Greenland and Iceland to relieve British troops, which had occupied these strategic Danish possessions after Germany's seizure of Denmark.

Then, in August 1941, Roosevelt and British Prime Minister Winston Churchill, meeting on the high seas off the coast of Newfoundland, worked out the basis of what would shortly become a formal wartime alliance. An eight-point declaration of common principles, the so-called Atlantic Charter, disavowed territorial expansion, endorsed free trade and self-determination, and pledged the postwar creation of a new world organization that would ensure "general security." Roosevelt agreed to Churchill's request that the U.S. Navy convoy American goods as far as Iceland. This step, aimed at ensuring the safe delivery of lend-lease supplies to Britain, inched the United States even closer to belligerence. Soon, in an undeclared naval war, Germany was using its formidable submarine "wolfpacks" to attack U.S. ships.

By this time, Roosevelt and his advisers understood that in order to defeat Hitler the United States would have to enter the war, but public support for such a move was still lacking. The president urged Congress to repeal the Neutrality Act altogether to allow U.S. merchant ships to carry munitions directly to Britain. Privately, he may have hoped that Germany would commit some provocative act in the North Atlantic that would move public opinion toward further involvement. The October 1941 sinking of the U.S. destroyer *Reuben James* did just that, and Congress did repeal the Neutrality Act—but the vote was so close and the debate so bitter that Roosevelt knew he could not yet seek a formal declaration of war. Having insisted that aid to the Allies was an alternative to U.S. involvement in the war rather than a way into it, the president now found himself caught in the web of his own rhetoric. By avoiding any further provocations at sea, Hitler made Roosevelt's task no easier. In addition, Hitler was now concentrating his attacks on the Soviet Union, a country for which Americans felt far less sympathy than they did for Britain.

The Attack at Pearl Harbor

As it turned out, America's formal entry into the war came about as a result of escalating tensions with Japan rather than Germany. In response to Japan's invasion of China in 1937, the United States extended economic credits to China to bolster its efforts to defend itself, and sales of some types of U.S. equipment to Japan were halted. Then, in 1939 the United States abrogated its Treaty of Commerce and Navigation with Japan, an action that allowed for the possible future curtailment or even the outright prohibition of U.S. exports to the island nation.

These measures did little to deter Japanese aggression, and by 1940 Germany's successes in Europe had further raised the stakes in Asia. As the European war sapped the strength of France, Britain, and the Netherlands, the links between those countries and their Southeast Asian colonies grew more tenuous. Japan quickly mobilized to exploit the vacuum created by a weakened Europe. Japanese expansionists called for the incorporation of Southeast Asia into their East Asian Co-Prosperity Sphere.

The president hoped that a 1940 ban on the sale of aviation fuel and high-grade scrap iron to Japan would slow Japan's imminent military advance into Southeast Asia. But this act only intensified Japanese militancy. After joining the Axis alliance in September 1940, Japan pushed deeper into Indochina to secure strategic positions and access to raw materials it could no longer buy from the United States. When Japan's occupation of French Indochina went unopposed, its military forces prepared to launch attacks on Singapore, the Netherlands East Indies (Indonesia), and the Philippines. Roosevelt expanded the trade embargo against Japan, promised further assistance to China, and accelerated the U.S. military buildup in the Pacific. Then, in mid-1941, Roosevelt played his most important card. He froze Japanese assets in the United States, effectively bringing under presidential control all commerce between the two countries, including trade in the petroleum that was vital to the Japanese economy. With this action, Roosevelt hoped to bring Japan to the bargaining table. But faced with impending economic strangulation, the leaders of Japan began planning for a preemptive attack on the United States.

On December 7, 1941, nearly the entire U.S. Pacific fleet, stationed at Pearl Harbor in Hawaii, was destroyed by Japanese bombers that swooped down without warning. Only the fleet's aircraft carriers, which were out to sea at the time, were spared. Altogether, 19 ships were sunk or severely damaged; 188 planes were destroyed on the ground; and more than 2,200 Americans were killed. In a war message broadcast by radio on December 8, Roosevelt decried the Japanese attack and labeled December 7 "a date which will live in infamy," a phrase that served as a rallying cry throughout the war. Secretary of War Stimson remembered: "My first feeling was of relief that the indecision was over and that a crisis had come that would unite all our people."

For the Japanese, the attack on Pearl Harbor was an act of desperation. The U.S. embargoes, especially on petroleum, had narrowed Japan's options. Negotiations between the two countries proved fruitless: Japan was unwilling to abandon its designs on China, the only concession that might have brought a lifting of the embargoes. With limited supplies of raw materials, Japan had little hope of winning a prolonged war. Japanese military strategists gambled that a crippling blow would so weaken U.S. military power that a long war would be avoided. Japanese leaders decided to risk a surprise attack. "Sometimes a man has to jump with his eyes closed," remarked General Hideki Tojo, who became Japan's prime minister.

A few Americans charged that Roosevelt had intentionally provoked Japan in order to open a "backdoor" to war. They pointed out that the fleet at Pearl Harbor, the nation's principal Pacific base, lay vulnerable at its docks, not even in a state of full alert. In actuality, the American actions and inactions that led to Pearl Harbor were more confused than they were devious. Beginning in 1934 the United States had gradually enlarged its Pacific fleet, and Roosevelt had also increased the number of B-17 bombers based in the Philippines. The president hoped that the possibility of aerial attacks would intimidate Japan and slow its expansion. But the strategy of deterrence failed. It may also have contributed to the lack of vigilance at Pearl Harbor. American leaders doubted that Japan would risk a direct attack, and intelligence experts, who had broken MAGIC, the Japanese secret code, expected Japan to move toward Singapore or other British or Dutch possessions. Intercepted messages, along with visual sightings of Japanese transports, seemed to confirm preparations for a strike in Southeast Asia (a strike that did occur). A warning that Japan might also be targeting Pearl Harbor was not sent with sufficient urgency and was lost under a mountain of intelligence reports. Confusion and error, not official duplicity, explain America's lack of preparedness at Pearl Harbor. Roosevelt's priorities had been, and would remain, focused on Europe and Hitler.

On December 8, 1941, Congress declared war against Japan. There was only one dissenting vote, that of Representative Jeannette Rankin, a longtime peace activist from Montana. Japan's allies, Germany and Italy, declared war on the United States three days later, on December 11. Hitler, whose eastern offensive had been stalled within sight of Moscow, mistakenly assumed that war with Japan would keep the United States preoccupied in the Pacific. The three Axis Powers drastically underestimated America's ability to mobilize swiftly and effectively. And they utterly failed to perceive how their own actions, more than anything Roosevelt himself could have done, would now unite Americans behind the war.

Fighting the War in Europe

The first few months after America's entry into the war proved to be discouraging. German forces already controlled most of Europe from Norway to Greece and had pushed rapidly eastward into the Soviet Union. Now they were rolling across North Africa, threatening the strategically important Suez Canal and the Middle East, which remained under British control. In the Atlantic, German submarines were sinking hundreds of thousands of tons of Allied shipping, endangering Allied supply lines. Japan seemed unstoppable in the Pacific. Following the attack on Pearl Harbor, Japanese forces overran Malaya, the Dutch East Indies, and the Philippines and drove against the British in Burma and the Australians in New Guinea.

Long before December 7, 1941, the Roosevelt administration had expected war and had vainly tried to prepare for it. The challenge had been to train personnel and mobilize resources without, as Henry Stimson noted, "any declaration of war by Congress and with the country not facing the danger before it." When war came,

Army morale was low, industrial production was still on a peacetime footing, and labor-management relations were contentious. As the country faced the need for rapid economic and military mobilization, new government bureaucracies began to spring up everywhere. A proliferation of new agencies, new faces, and new procedures plunged wartime Washington into confusion. In March 1943, Stimson confided in his diary: "The president is the poorest administrator I have ever worked under. . . . [H]e has constituted an almost innumerable number of new administrative posts." These positions were filled with generally inexperienced people, all of whom now laid claim to the president's time.

Indeed, the wartime growth in the size of government transformed American foreign policymaking. Military priorities—acquiring naval bases, securing landing rights for aircraft, ensuring points for radio transmissions, and gaining access to raw materials—superseded all other demands. The administration was being forced to settle on new policies overnight and then implement them on a global scale the following day. The newly formed Joint Chiefs of Staff, consisting of representatives from each of the armed services, became Roosevelt's major source of guidance on military strategy. In Washington, where architecture symbolizes political power, the War Department's new Pentagon complex dwarfed the State Department's cramped quarters at "Foggy Bottom." The giant five-story, five-sided building was completed in January 1943, after 16 months of round-the-clock work.

In the Atlantic, German submarines sank 7 million tons of Allied shipping in the first 16 months after Pearl Harbor. Aircraft equipped with radar, a new technology developed with the encouragement of the war department and in collaboration with Britain, proved effective against submarines in 1942, but the Army and Navy engaged in months of bickering over who should conduct the antisubmarine warfare. Finally, the Navy was given official responsibility, and after developing effective radar strategies, it performed well. During 1943 Germany's submarine capability faded "from menace to problem," in the words of Admiral Ernest King.

Campaigns in North Africa and Italy

Military strategy, however, became a contentious issue among the Allied Powers, now consisting principally of the United States, Britain, and the Soviet Union. All advisers agreed that their primary focus would be the European theater, and Roosevelt and his military strategists immediately established a unified command with the British. The Soviet Union, facing 200 German divisions just west of Moscow and suffering hundreds of thousands of casualties, pleaded with Roosevelt and Churchill to open a second front in western Europe to relieve pressure on the USSR. Many of Roosevelt's advisers, including Stimson and General George C. Marshall, agreed. They feared that if German troops forced the Soviet Union out of the war, Germany would then turn its full attention to defeating Britain. Churchill, however, urged instead the invasion of French North Africa, which was under the control of Vichy France. Churchill's strategy sought to peck away at the edges of enemy power rather than strike at its heart. At a meeting between Roosevelt and Stalin at Casablanca, Morocco, in January 1943, Roosevelt sided with Churchill, and the promised invasion of France was postponed. The risks of a cross-Channel assault were great, Roosevelt reasoned, and the home front needed some rapid victories. To assuage Stalin's fears that his two allies might sign a separate peace with Hitler, the two leaders did announce that they would stay in the fight until Germany agreed to nothing less than unconditional surrender. Continuing disagreements over the timing of the cross-Channel invasion, however, still strained the alliance.

The North African operation, code-named TORCH, began with Anglo-American landings in Morocco and Algeria in November 1942. To ease resistance against the Allies' North African invasion, U.S. General Dwight D. Eisenhower struck a deal with French Admiral Jean Darlan, a Nazi sympathizer, an anti-Semite, and the Vichy officer who controlled France's colonies in North Africa. Darlan agreed to break with the Vichy regime and stop resisting the Allied operation in return for Eisenhower's pledge that the United States would support him. The deal outraged some Americans who believed that it compromised the moral purpose of the war. Darlan's assassination in December 1942, called an "act of Providence" by one of Eisenhower's deputies, put an end to the embarrassment. But the antagonism that Eisenhower's action had created between Americans and the Free French movement, led by General Charles de Gaulle, had lasting consequences after the war.

As TORCH progressed, the Soviets managed to turn the tide of battle at Stalingrad. They cut off and destroyed one German army in the city and sent other German armies reeling backward. Despite this defeat in the East, Hitler poured reinforcements into North Africa, but they were not enough to stop both TORCH and the British, who were driving west from Egypt. About 200,000 Axis soldiers surrendered to the Allies in April and May 1943.

In the summer of 1943 Allied troops followed up the successful North African campaign by overrunning the island of Sicily and then fighting their way slowly north through Italy's mountains. Their successes boosted morale in the United States. But the Italian campaign drained resources that would be needed for the cross-Channel invasion of France, while scarcely denting the German stranglehold on Europe.

Some American officials increasingly worried about the postwar implications of wartime strategy. Stimson, for example, warned that the peripheral campaigns through Africa and Italy might leave the Soviets dominating central Europe. Unless the western democracies confronted Germany in the heart of Europe, he argued, Germany would be left holding "the leg for Stalin to skin the deer and I think that will be dangerous business for us at the end of the war." Acting on such advice, Roosevelt finally agreed to set a date for the cross-Channel invasion that Stalin had long been promised.

Operation OVERLORD

Operation OVERLORD, directed by Supreme Allied Commander Dwight Eisenhower, finally began on June 6, 1944, D-Day. During the months preceding D-Day, probably the largest invasion force in history had been assembled in England. Disinformation and diversionary tactics had led the Germans to expect a landing at the narrowest part of the English Channel rather than in the Normandy region. Allied intelligence officers knew from monitoring the cables sent to Tokyo by Japan's ambassador in Berlin that their ruse had worked. After several delays, due to the

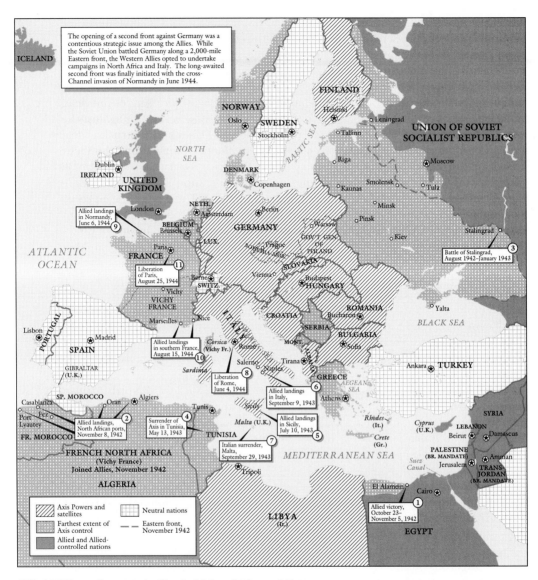

The opening of a second front against Germany was a contentious strategic issue among the Allies. While the Soviet Union battled Germany along a 2,000-mile Eastern front, the Western Allies opted to undertake campaigns in North Africa and Italy. The long-awaited second front was finally initiated with the cross-Channel invasion of Normandy in June 1944.

Allied Military Strategy in North Africa, Italy, and France

Channel's unpredictable weather, nervous commanders finally ordered the daring plan to begin. The night before, as naval guns pounded the Normandy shore, three divisions of paratroopers were dropped behind enemy lines to disrupt German communications. Then, at dawn, more than 4,000 Allied ships landed troops and supplies on Normandy's beaches. The first American troops to land at Omaha Beach met especially heavy German fire and took enormous casualties. But the waves of invading troops continued throughout the day and indeed through the weeks that followed. Within three weeks, over 1 million people had landed, secured the Normandy coast, and opened the long-awaited second front.

Troops Land on Omaha Beach, June 6, 1944 • The long-delayed, cross-Channel invasion from England to Nazi-occupied France was the largest military operation of its kind in history. Although more than 1,000 Allied troops were killed at Omaha Beach on the initial day, the invasion force established a secure beachhead from which to move eastward against German troops.

Just as the Battle of Stalingrad had reversed the tide of the war in the East, so operation OVERLORD turned the tide in the West. Within three months, U.S., British, and Free French troops entered Paris. After turning back a desperate German counteroffensive in Belgium, at the Battle of the Bulge in December and January, Allied armies swept eastward, crossing the Rhine and heading toward Berlin.

The Allies had conflicting views on how the defeat of Germany should be orchestrated. British strategists favored a swift drive, so as to meet up with Soviet armies in Berlin or even farther east. General Eisenhower favored a strategy that was militarily less risky and politically less provocative to the Soviets. Eisenhower doubted that Allied troops could reach Berlin from the west before the Soviet armies arrived, and he knew that stopping short of Berlin would save lives among the troops under his command. He was also eager to end the war on a note of trust and believed that racing the Soviets to Berlin would undermine the basis for postwar Soviet-American cooperation. In the end, Eisenhower's views prevailed. He

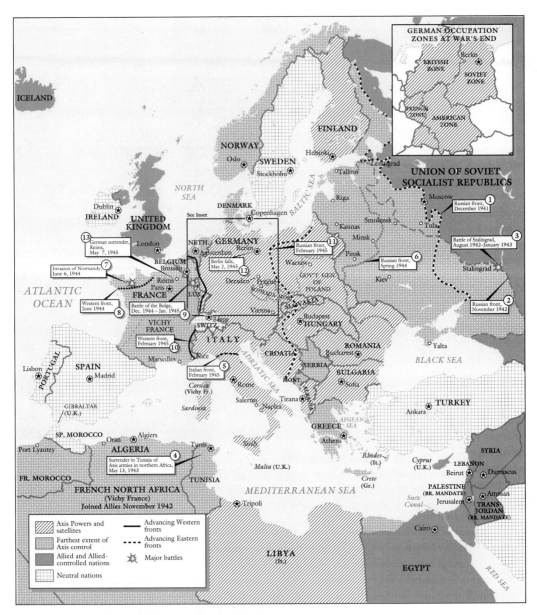

Allied Advances and Collapse of German Power

moved cautiously along a broad front, halting his troops at the Elbe River, west of Berlin, and allowing Soviet troops to roll into the German capital. Although the Soviet armies suffered staggering casualties in taking Berlin, they nevertheless worked with the other Allies to establish joint administration of the city.

As the war in Europe drew to a close, the horrors perpetrated by the Third Reich became visible to the world. Almost from the beginning of U.S. participation in the war, many Americans were aware that Hitler was bent on genocide against Jews,

President Franklin Roosevelt and General Dwight Eisenhower • Franklin Roosevelt watched over Allied military leaders, including the popular General Dwight Eisenhower, throughout the Second World War. White House photographers were careful to picture Roosevelt, who died of a cerebral hemorrhage before the war's end, in ways that concealed both his longtime paralysis and his increasingly frail health. Here FDR and Eisenhower review troops in Sicily in 1943.

gypsies, and other targeted groups. Although only a military victory could put an end to German death camps, the Allies could have saved thousands of Jews by encouraging them to emigrate and helping them to escape. Allied leaders, however, worried about the impact large numbers of Jewish refugees would have on their countries, and they were also reluctant to use scarce ships to transport Jews to neutral sanctuaries. In 1943, after Romania proposed permitting an evacuation of 70,000 Jews from its territory, Allied leaders avoided any serious discussion of the plan. The United States even refused to relax its strict policy on visas to admit Jews who might have escaped on their own. With no way of crossing the Atlantic and with few places in Europe that would accept them, hundreds of thousands of Jews who might have been saved went to Nazi death camps.

Hitler's campaign of extermination, now called the Holocaust, killed between 5 and 6 million Jews out of Europe's prewar population of 10 million; hundreds of thousands more from various other groups were also murdered, especially gypsies, homosexuals, intellectuals, communists, and the physically and mentally handicapped. The Allies would, in 1945 and 1946, bring 24 high German officials to trial at Nuremburg for "crimes against humanity." Large quantities of money, gold, and jewelry that Nazi leaders stole from victims of the Holocaust and deposited in Swiss banks, however, remained largely hidden from view for more than 50 years. Not until 1997 did Jewish groups and the U.S. government, seeking some restitution for victim's families, begin to force investigations of the Swiss banking industry and its relationship to stolen "Nazi gold."

With Hitler's suicide in April and Germany's surrender on May 8, 1945, the military foundations for peace in Europe were complete. Soviet armies controlled Eastern Europe; British and U.S. forces predominated in Italy and the rest of the Mediterranean; Germany and Austria fell under divided occupation. Governmental leaders now needed to work out a plan for transforming these military arrangements into a comprehensive political settlement for the postwar era, a challenge as great as winning the war itself. Meanwhile, the war in the Pacific was still far from over.

The Pacific Theater

For six months after Pearl Harbor, nearly everything in the Pacific went Japan's way. Britain's supposedly impregnable colony at Singapore fell easily. American naval garrisons in the Philippines and on Guam and Wake islands were overwhelmed, and American and Filipino armies were forced to surrender at Bataan and Corregidor in the Philippines. Other Japanese forces steamed southward to menace Australia. Then the tide turned.

Seizing the Initiative in the Pacific

When Japan finally suffered its first naval defeat at the Battle of the Coral Sea in May 1942, Japanese naval commanders decided to hit back hard. They amassed 200 ships and 600 planes to destroy what remained of the U.S. Pacific fleet and to take Midway Island, a strategic location for Hawaii's security. U.S. intelligence, however, was monitoring Japanese codes and warned Admiral Chester W. Nimitz of the plan. Surprising the Japanese navy, U.S. planes sank four Japanese carriers, destroyed a total of 322 planes, and preserved American presence at Midway. The U.S. Navy's losses were substantial, but Japan's were so much greater that its offensive capabilities were crippled.

Two months later, American forces splashed ashore at Guadalcanal in the Solomon Islands and successfully relieved the pressure on Australia and its military supply lines. The bloody engagements in the Solomons continued for months on both land and sea, but they accomplished one major objective: seizing the initiative against Japan. This success, combined with the delay in opening a second front in Europe, also affected grand strategy. According to prewar plans, the war in Europe was to have received highest priority. But by 1943 the two theaters were receiving roughly equal resources.

The bloody engagements in the Pacific dramatically illustrated that the war was, in historian John Dower's phrase, a "war without mercy." It was a war in which racial prejudices reinforced brutality. For Japan, the Pacific conflict was a war to establish forever the superiority of the divine Yamato race. Prisoners taken by the Japanese, mostly on the Asian mainland, were brutalized in unimaginable ways, and survival rates were low. The Japanese army's Unit 731 tested bacteriological weapons in China and, like the Nazi doctors, conducted horrifying medical experiments on live subjects. American propaganda images also played upon themes of racial superiority, portraying the Japanese as animalistic subhumans. American troops often rivaled Japan's forces in their disrespect for the enemy dead and sometimes killed the enemy rather than take prisoners. The longer the Pacific war lasted, the more it seemed to loosen the boundaries of acceptable violence against combatants and civilians alike.

China Policy

U.S. policymakers hoped that China would fight Japan more effectively and then emerge after the war as a strong and united nation. Neither hope was realized.

General Joseph W. Stilwell, who had worked with the Chinese armies resisting the Japanese invasion in the late 1930s, undertook the job of turning China into an effective military force. Jiang Jieshi (formerly spelled Chiang Kai-shek) headed China's government and appointed the prickly Stilwell his chief of staff. But the hatred between "Vinegar Joe" Stilwell and Jiang, fueled by disputes over military priorities in the Chinese theater, became so intense that in May 1943 Roosevelt bowed to Jiang's demand for Stilwell's dismissal. Meanwhile, Japan's advance into China continued, and in 1944 its forces captured seven of the principal U.S. air bases in China.

These disagreements took place within the context of an even more disruptive situation: China was beset by civil war. Jiang's Nationalist government was incompetent, corrupt, and unpopular. It avoided engaging the Japanese invaders and still made extravagant demands for U.S. assistance. Meanwhile, a growing communist movement led by Mao Zedong was fighting effectively against the Japanese and enjoyed widespread support among Chinese peasants. Stilwell urged Roosevelt to cut off support to Jiang unless he fought with more determination. Roosevelt, however, feared that such actions would create even greater chaos and was unwilling to strengthen Mao's position. He continued to provide moral support and matériel to Jiang's armies and successfully pressed Stalin to support Jiang rather than Mao. Moreover, pressed by a powerful "China lobby" of domestic conservatives, he insisted that Jiang's China be permitted to stand with the major powers after victory had been won. By tying U.S. policy to Jiang's leadership and entertaining the myth that China was a stable power, Roosevelt and the "China lobby" prepared the way for great difficulties in forging a China policy in the postwar period.

Pacific Strategy

In contrast to the war in Europe, there was no unified command to guide the war in the Pacific, and top military commanders continually disagreed on matters of strategy. Consequently, military actions often emerged from compromise. General Douglas MacArthur, commander of the army in the South Pacific, favored an offensive launched from his headquarters in Australia through New Guinea and the Philippines and on to Japan. After Japan drove him out of the Philippines in May 1942, he promised to return, and he was determined to keep his word. He argued that the United States must be in control of the Philippines at war's end in order to

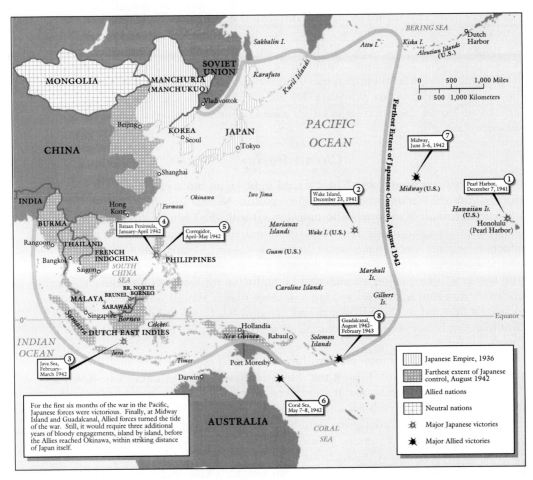

For the first six months of the war in the Pacific, Japanese forces were victorious. Finally, at Midway Island and Guadalcanal, Allied forces turned the tide of the war. Still, it would require three additional years of bloody engagements, island by island, before the Allies reached Okinawa, within striking distance of Japan itself.

Japanese Expansion and Early Battles in the Pacific

preserve its strategic position in Asia. Admiral Nimitz disagreed. He favored an advance across the smaller islands of the central Pacific, pointing out that a route that bypassed the Philippines would provide more direct access to Japan. Unable to decide between the two strategies, the Joint Chiefs of Staff authorized both.

Marked by fierce fighting and heavy casualties, both offensives moved forward. MacArthur took New Guinea, and Nimitz's forces liberated the Marshall Islands and the Marianas in 1943 and 1944. An effective radio communication system conducted in the Navajo language by a special Marine platoon of Navajo Indians made a unique contribution. Navajo-speaking squads arrived with the first assault contingents on hundreds of Pacific beaches and set up radio contact with headquarters and with supporting units. Navajo, a language unfamiliar to both the Japanese and the Germans, provided a secure medium for sensitive communications. In late 1944 the fall of Saipan brought American bombers within range of Japan. The capture of the island of Iwo Jima—18 square miles taken at the cost of 27,000 American casualties—and of Okinawa further shortened that distance during the spring of 1945.

Okinawa illustrated the nearly unbelievable ferocity of the island campaigns: 120,000 Japanese soldiers died; 48,000 Americans. U.S. military planners extrapolated from these numbers when considering the dreaded prospect of an invasion of the home islands of Japan itself.

As the seaborne offensive proceeded, the United States brought its airpower into play. Before the war, Roosevelt had become convinced that aerial bombing produced almost magical power. At one time, he even had hoped that the mere threat of bombing would be so frightening that airpower would serve as a substitute for war rather than as a means of conducting it. The effects of strategic bombing in Europe, however, had been ambiguous. The Nazi bombardment of British cities in 1940 and 1941 only steeled British resolve, uniting the nation and boosting civilian morale. The Allies' strategic bombing of German cities, including the destruction of such large cities as Hamburg and Dresden, produced equally mixed results. Indeed, military historians still debate the relative merits of the strategic bombing in Europe, wondering whether the gains against military targets really offset the huge civilian casualties and the unsustainable losses of American pilots and aircraft. Still, Roosevelt continued to believe that airpower might provide the crucial advantage over the Japanese, and strategic bombing once more became a major tactic for victory.

In February 1944 General Henry Harley ("Hap") Arnold, commander of the newly formed 20th Army Air Force, presented Roosevelt with a plan for strategic air assaults on Japanese cities. His proposal included a systematic campaign of destruction through the firebombing of urban targets, "not only because they are greatly congested but because they contain numerous war industries." Roosevelt approved the plan. In the month before bombing began, the Office of War Information lifted its ban on atrocity stories about Japan's treatment of American prisoners. The effort was designed to prepare the public for the massive killing of Japanese civilians that was expected. As grisly reports and racist anti-Japanese propaganda swept across the country, it was thought the public would become more accepting of what was permissible in war. Arnold's original air campaign, operating from bases in China, turned out to be cumbersome and ineffective; it was replaced by an even more lethal operation, running from Saipan, under the aegis of General Curtis LeMay.

The official position on the incendiary raids on Japanese cities was that they constituted "precision" rather than "area" bombing. In actuality, the success of a mission was measured in terms of the number of square miles that had been left scorched and useless. Destroying Japan's industrial capacity by firebombing the workers who ran the factories sounded like a focused strategy, but the systematic burning of entire cities brought unprecedented civilian casualties. The number of Japanese civilians killed in the raids is estimated to have been greater than the number of Japanese soldiers killed in battle. An attack on Tokyo on the night of March 9–10, 1945, inaugurated the new policy by leveling 16 square miles (one-fourth) of the city, destroying 267,000 buildings and inflicting 185,000 casualties. One by one, LeMay torched other cities. In his memoirs, LeMay summarized his strategy: "Bomb and burn them until they quit."

By the winter of 1944–1945, a combined sea and air strategy had emerged: The United States would seek "unconditional surrender" by blockading Japan's seaports, continuing its bombardment of Japanese cities from the air, and perhaps invading Japan itself. Later critics of the policy of unconditional surrender have suggested that it may have hardened the determination with which Japan fought the war after its imminent defeat had become obvious. These critics have pointed out that many Japanese assumed that unconditional surrender would mean the death of the emperor; moreover, the policy prevented U.S. negotiators from vigorously pursuing peace feelers, which some Japanese leaders were trying to send through third parties. With the unconditional surrender policy in place and Japan's determination to fight even in the face of certain defeat, the strategy of American leaders seemed to require massive destruction to achieve victory.

Atomic Power and Japanese Surrender

At Los Alamos, New Mexico, scientists from all across the United States had been secretly working on a weapon that promised just such massive destruction. Advances

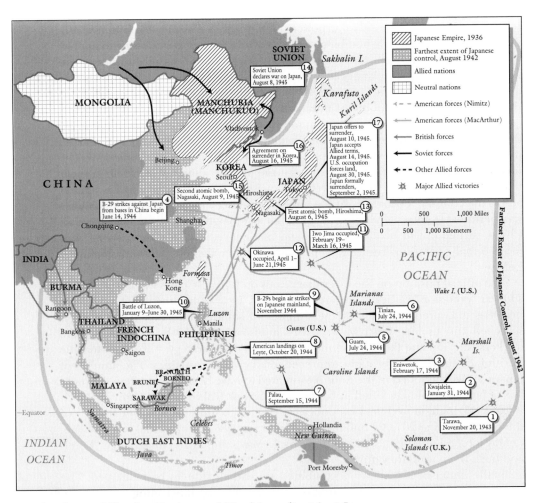

Pacific Theater Offensive Strategy and Final Assault against Japan

in theoretical physics during the 1930s had suggested that splitting the atom (fission) would release a tremendous amount of energy. Fearful that Germany was racing ahead in this effort, Albert Einstein, a Jewish refugee from Germany, urged President Roosevelt to launch a secret program to build a bomb based on atomic research. The government subsequently enlisted top scientists in the Manhattan Project, the largest and most secretive military project yet undertaken. On July 16, 1945, after a succession of breakthroughs in physics research, the first atomic weapon was successfully tested at Trinity Site, near Alamagordo, New Mexico. The researchers then notified the new president, Harry S. Truman, that the terrifying new weapon was ready.

Truman and his top policymakers assumed that the weapon should be put to immediate military use. They were eager to end the war, both because a possible land invasion of Japan might have cost so many American lives and also because the Soviet Union was planning to enter the Pacific theater, and Truman wished to limit Soviet power in that region. Secretary of War Stimson wrote: "It was our common objective, throughout the war, to be the first to produce an atomic weapon and use it. The possible atomic weapon was considered to be a new and tremendously powerful explosive, as legitimate as any other of the deadly explosive weapons of modern war." Churchill called the bomb a "miracle of deliverance" and a peace-giver. Truman later said that he had never lost a night's sleep over its use.

Other advisers had more qualms, and there was some disagreement over where and how the bomb should be deployed. A commission of atomic scientists, headed by Jerome Franck, recommended a "demonstration" that would impress Japan with

Hiroshima, Japan, August 1945 • The terrible destruction of total war was most dramatically demonstrated when the United States dropped two atomic bombs on Japan.

the bomb's power yet cause no loss of life. General Marshall suggested using the bomb only on military installations or on some large manufacturing area from which people would be warned away in advance. But most of Truman's advisers agreed that simply demonstrating the bomb's power might not be enough. The purpose of the bomb, Stimson said, was to make "a profound psychological impression on as many inhabitants as possible." They believed that it would take massive destruction to bring unconditional surrender.

In the context of the earlier brutal aerial bombardment of Japanese cities, dropping atomic bombs on the previously unbombed cities of Hiroshima and Nagasaki on August 6 and 9, 1945, seemed simply an acceleration of existing policy rather than a departure from it. "Fat Man" and "Little Boy," as the two bombs were nicknamed, were merely viewed as bigger, more effective firebombs. Of course, atomic weapons did produce yet a new level of violence. Colonel Paul Tibbets, who piloted the plane that dropped the first bomb, reported that "the shimmering city became an ugly smudge . . . a pot of bubbling hot tar." Teams of U.S. observers who entered the cities in the aftermath were stunned at the immediate devastation, including the instantaneous incineration of both human beings and man-made structures, as well as the longer-lasting horror of radiation disease. The mushroom clouds over

The War Is Over • Tired revelers take a curbside rest on VJ Day in San Diego, a city that experienced dramatic economic growth during the Second World War. Feelings of exhilaration—and exhaustion—are apparent at the conclusion of a day of celebration and the end of years of war.

Hiroshima and Nagasaki would inaugurate a new "atomic age," in which dreams of peace were mingled with nightmares of Armaggedon. But in those late summer days of 1945, most Americans sighed with relief. News reports on August 15 proclaimed Japan's surrender, VJ Day.

The War at Home: The Economy

The success of the U.S. military effort in both Europe and Asia depended on mobilization at home. Ultimately, it was this mobilization, first to help the Allies and then to support America's own war effort, that finally brought the depression of the 1930s to an end and helped Roosevelt win reelection to two more terms as president. But the war did more than restore prosperity. From 1941 to 1945, as America's people and productivity bent toward the single aim of victory, the war transformed the nation's entire political economy—its government, its business and financial institutions, and its labor force.

Government's Role in the Economy

The federal bureaucracy nearly quadrupled in size during the war, as new economic agencies proliferated. The most powerful of these, the War Production Board, oversaw the conversion and expansion of factories, allocated resources, and enforced production priorities and schedules. The War Labor Board had jurisdiction over labor-management disputes, and the War Manpower Commission allocated labor to various industries. The Office of Price Administration regulated prices to control inflation and rationed such scarce commodities as gasoline, rubber, steel, shoes, coffee, sugar, and meat. All these agencies, and others, intruded into the workings of the market economy by imposing government controls on economic decisions, both in business and in the home. Although most of the controls were abandoned after the war, the concept of greater governmental regulation of the economy survived.

From 1940 to 1945 the U.S. economy expanded rapidly, accelerating from a decade of sluggishness to one of full-speed, even force-fed, production. In each year of the war, GNP rose by 15 percent or more. According to a War Production Board report, "A country that . . . could produce in 1944 $199,000,000,000 in goods and services was an invincible opponent." When Roosevelt called for the production of 60,000 planes, shortly after Pearl Harbor, skeptics jeered. Yet within the next few years the nation produced nearly 300,000 planes—in a dazzling range of designs. The Maritime Commission oversaw construction of more than 53 million tons of shipping, turning out ships faster than German submarines could sink them. The previously dormant economy spewed out prodigious quantities of other supplies, including 2.5 million trucks and 50 million pairs of shoes. This was a "war of massed machines," as journalist Hanson Baldwin described it.

Striving to increase production, industry entered into an unprecedented relationship with government to promote scientific and technological research and development, "R&D." Government money subsidized new industries, such as electronics, and enabled others, such as rubber and chemicals, to transform their processes and products. Annual expenditures on R&D doubled prewar levels, with the government providing most of the funds. The newly established Office of Scientific Research and Development, headed by Vannevar Bush, entered into contracts for a variety of projects with universities and scientists. Under this program, radar and penicillin (both British breakthroughs), rocket engines, and other new products were rapidly perfected for wartime use. Refugees from Nazi tyranny brought added strength to the scientific and academic establishments, contributing to advances in physics, astronomy, psychiatry, and architecture. In the four decades after 1930, they won no fewer than 24 Nobel Prizes.

The Manhattan Project was perhaps the most dramatic example of the new connections among science, national defense, and the federal goverment. The project employed nearly 130,000 people by mid-1944 and eventually cost more than $2 billion. Many of the émigré scientists who had fled Nazi regimes participated in the conceptualization and implementation of the project at the highest levels.

Business and Finance

To finance the war effort, government spending rose from $9 billion in 1940 to $98 billion in 1944. In 1941 the national debt stood at $48 billion; by VJ Day it was $280 billion. With few goods to buy, Americans invested in war bonds, turning their savings into tanks and planes. Although war bonds provided a relatively insignificant contribution to the war, they did help drive the level of personal saving up to 25 percent of consumer income. The purchase of war bonds also played an important psychological role by giving millions of Americans an even larger stake in victory.

As production shifted from autos to tanks, from refrigerators to guns, many consumer goods became scarce. Essentials such as food, fabrics, and gasoline were rationed and, consequently, were shared more equitably than they had been before the war. Higher taxes on wealthier Americans tended to redistribute income and narrow the gap between the poor and the well-to-do. War bonds, rationing, and progressive taxation gave Americans a sense of shared sacrifice and helped ease the class tensions of the 1930s.

As the war fostered an increase in personal savings and promoted a measure of income redistribution, however, it also facilitated the dismantling of many of the New Deal agencies most concerned with the interests of the poor. A Republican surge in the off-year elections of 1942—the GOP gained 44 seats in the House and 7 new senators—helped strengthen an anti–New Deal, conservative coalition in Congress. In 1943 Congress abolished the job creation programs run by the Works Progress Administration (WPA), the Civilian Conservation Corps (CCC), and the National Youth Administration (NYA) (see Chapter 6). It also shut down the Rural Electrification Administration (REA) and Farm Security Administration (FSA), agencies that had assisted impoverished rural areas. And the budget for the National Recovery Planning Board, which represented an attempt to introduce comprehensive national planning into America's market economy, was drastically reduced. As dollar-a-year business executives flocked to Washington to run the new wartime bureaus, the Roosevelt administration shifted its attitude toward big business from one of guarded hostility to one of cooperation. Although many in the business community never fully trusted Roosevelt, the war nevertheless nudged the president's New Deal to the right.

In win-the-war Washington, social programs withered as big businesses that were considered essential to victory flourished under government subsidies. What was "essential," of course, became a matter of definition. Coca-Cola and Wrigley's chewing gum won precious sugar allotments by arguing that GIs overseas "needed" to enjoy their products. Both companies prospered. The Kaiser Corporation, whose spectacular growth in the 1930s had been spurred by federal dam contracts, now turned its attention to the building of ships, aircraft, and military vehicles, such as the famous "jeep." By 1943 the company was handling nearly one-third of the nation's military construction, establishing a new industrial base for southern California's previously agricultural economy. Federal subsidies, low-interest loans, and tax breaks enabled factories to expand and retool. A cost-plus formula built into government contracts guaranteed that manufacturers would make a profit.

The war concentrated power in the largest corporations. The enforcement of antitrust laws was postponed at Roosevelt's request. Legal challenges that had been years in preparation, such as the case against America's great oil cartel, were now tucked away. The renewal of some antitrust activity in 1944, when victory seemed assured, helped keep the concept of trust-busting alive, but it did little to curtail the growing power of giant enterprises. Congressional efforts to investigate alleged collusion in the awarding of government contracts and to increase assistance to small businesses similarly made little progress in Washington's crisis atmosphere. The top 100 companies, which had provided 30 percent of the nation's total manufacturing output in 1940, were providing 70 percent by 1943. Small businesses were left catering mainly to the civilian economy, which was plagued by erratic allocations, shortages, and stagnation.

The Workforce

During the first two years of military buildup, as factories began to step up production, many workers who had been idled during the depression were called back to work. Employment in heavy industry invariably went to men, and most of the skilled jobs went to whites. Initially, administrators of newly established, government-sponsored vocational training centers focused their efforts on the training of white males. They refused to set up courses for women or, especially in the South, to admit minority workers. Employers, they said, would never hire from these groups. But as military service drained the supply of white male workers, women and minorities became more attractive as candidates for production jobs. Soon, both private employers and government were encouraging women to go to work, southern African Americans to move to northern industrial cities, and Mexicans to enter the United States under the *bracero* guest worker program. As the country responded to labor shortages, the composition of the workforce changed dramatically.

Women were hired for jobs that had never been open to them before. They became welders, shipbuilders, lumberjacks, miners. For the first time, women won places in prestigious symphony orchestras. As major league baseball languished from a lack of players, female teams sprang up to give new life to the national pastime; the owner of the Chicago Cubs organized a woman's league in 1943 that eventually fielded 10 teams. Many employers hired married women, who, before the war, were often banned even from such traditionally female occupations as

Women Drive Taxis in Wartime • With so many men serving in the Armed Forces during the Second World War, women found employment opportunities—if only for the duration of the conflict—in job sectors that had previously been reserved strictly for men.

teaching. Minority women, who before the war had worked mostly on farms or as domestic servants, moved into clerical or secretarial jobs, where they had not previously been welcome. Most workplaces, however, continued to be segregated by sex—women working with other women and men working with other men. Still, the range of jobs open to women grew wider.

The character of unpaid labor, long provided mostly by women, also underwent significant change. Volunteer activities such as Red Cross projects, civil defense work, and recycling drives claimed more and more of the time of women, children, and older people. In the home, conservation was emphasized. Government propaganda exhorted homemakers: "Wear it out, use it up, make it do, or do without." "Work in a garden this summer." "Save waste fats for explosives." Most depression-era Americans were already used to scarcity and to "getting by," but the war now equated parsimonious lifestyles with patriotism rather than with poverty. Both in the home and in the factory, women's responsibilities and work-loads increased.

The new labor market improved the economic position of African Americans generally, as many moved into labor-scarce cities and into jobs that had previously been the preserve of whites. By executive order in June 1941, the president created the Fair Employment Practices Commission (FEPC), which tried to ban discrimination in hiring. In 1943 the government announced that it would not recognize as collective bargaining agents any unions that denied admittance to minorities. The War Labor Board outlawed the practice of paying different wages to whites and nonwhites doing the same job. Before the war, the African American population had been mainly southern, rural, and agricultural; within a few years, a substantial percentage of African Americans had become northern, urban, and industrial.

Although employment discrimination was hardly eliminated, twice as many African Americans held skilled jobs at the end of the war as at the beginning.

For both men and women, the war brought higher wages and longer work hours. Although in 1943 the government got labor unions to limit demands for wage increases to 15 percent, overtime often raised paychecks far more. During the war, average weekly earnings rose nearly 70 percent. Farmers, who had suffered through many years of low prices and overproduction, doubled their income and then doubled it again.

Labor Unions

The scarcity of labor during the war substantially strengthened the labor union movement. Union membership rose by 50 percent. Women and minority workers joined unions in unprecedented numbers (women accounted for 27 percent of total union membership by 1944), but the main beneficiaries of labor's new power were the white males who still provided the bulk of union membership.

Especially on the national level, the commitment of organized labor to female workers was weak. Not a single woman served on the executive boards of either the AFL or the CIO. The International Brotherhood of Teamsters even required women to sign a statement that their union membership could be revoked when the war was over. Unions did fight for contracts stipulating equal pay for men and women in the same job, but these benefited women only as long as they held "male" jobs. The unions' primary purpose in advocating equal pay was to maintain wage levels for the men who would return to their jobs after the war. During the first year of peace, as employers trimmed their workforces, both business and unions gave special consideration to returning veterans and worked to ease women out of the labor force. During the war, women held 25 percent of all jobs in automobile factories; by mid-1946 they held only 7.5 percent of those jobs. Older patterns of sex segregation returned to the workplace. Unions based their wage demands on the goal of securing male workers a "family wage," one that would be sufficient to support an entire family.

Some unions, reflecting the interests of their white male members, also supported racial discrimination. Union members believed that the hiring of lower-paid, nonwhite workers would jeopardize their own, better-paid positions. Early in the war, most AFL affiliates in the aircraft and shipbuilding industries—where the highest-paid jobs were to be found—had refused to accept African Americans as members. They quarreled with the FEPC over this policy throughout the war, some even claiming that the effort to advance blacks was the work of subversive, pro-communist "agitators." As growing numbers of African Americans were hired, tensions in the workplace ran high. In a Baltimore munitions factory, whites suspended work rather than integrate their washrooms and cafeterias. In Beaumont, Texas, martial law was declared to protect black workers from attacks by whites. All across the country—in a defense plant in Lockland, Ohio, at a transit company in Philadelphia, at a shipbuilding company in Mobile—white workers walked off the job to protest the hiring of African Americans. Beyond revealing deep-seated racism, such incidents reflected the union leaders' fears of losing the economic gains and recognition they had fought so hard to win during the 1930s. They wanted to prevent management from using the war as an excuse to erode their power and their wages.

The labor militancy of the 1930s was muted by a wartime no-strike pledge, but it nonetheless persisted. Despite no-strike assurances, for example, the United Mine Workers union called a strike in the bituminous coal fields in 1943. When the War Labor Board took a hard line against the union's demands, the strike was prolonged, prompting Secretary of the Interior Harold L. Ickes to blast both sides. He called the impasse "a black and stupid chapter in the history of the home front." In Detroit, disgruntled aircraft workers roamed the factory floors, cutting off the neckties of their supervisors; wildcat strikes erupted among bus drivers in St. Louis, Dodge assembly-line employees in Detroit, and streetcar conductors in Philadelphia. The increasingly conservative Congress responded by passing the Smith-Connally Act of 1943, which empowered the president to seize plants or mines if strikes interrupted war production. Even so, the war helped to strengthen organized labor's place in American life. By the end of the war, union membership was at an all-time high.

Assessing Economic Change

Overall, the impact of the war on America's political economy was varied. During the war, the workplace became more inclusive in terms of gender and race than ever before, and so did labor unions. More people entered the paid labor force, and many of them earned more money than rationing restrictions allowed them to spend. In a remarkable and welcome change from the decade of the Great Depression, jobs were plentiful and savings piled up. Although some of these changes proved to be short-lived, the new precedents and expectations arising from the wartime experience could not be entirely effaced at war's end.

More than anything else, the institutional scale of American life was transformed. Big government, big business, and big labor all grew even bigger during the war years. Science and technology forged new links of mutual interest among these three sectors. The old America of small farms, small businesses, and small towns did not disappear. But urban-based, bureaucratized institutions, in both the public and private sectors, increasingly organized life in postwar America.

The War at Home: Social Issues

Dramatic social changes accompanied the wartime mobilization. By the end of the war, 16 million Americans had served in the military. Ordered by military service or attracted by employment, many people moved away from the communities where they had grown up. Even on the home front, the war involved constant sacrifice— rationing, recycling, volunteer work. The war, most Americans believed, was being fought to preserve democracy and individual freedom against political systems that trampled on both.

Yet America hardly had an unblemished record in according full and equal access to the promise of American life. For many, wartime ideals highlighted everyday inequalities. As mobilization created new economic opportunities and demanded new sacrifices, many groups engaged in defining and redefining the American way of life.

Wartime Propaganda

During the First World War, government propagandists had asked Americans to fight for a more democratic world and a permanent peace. But such idealistic goals had little appeal for the skeptical generation of the 1930s and 1940s, who had witnessed the failures of Woodrow Wilson's promises. Only 20 years after Wilson's "war to end all wars," Americans were now embroiled in another worldwide conflict. Sensitive to popular cynicism about high-minded goals, the Roosevelt administration asked Americans to fight to preserve the "American way of life"—not to save the world. Artist and illustrator Norman Rockwell and movie director Frank Capra, masters of nostalgia, became the most celebrated and successful of the wartime propagandists.

Hollywood studios and directors eagerly answered the government's call by shaping inspiring and sentimental representations of American life. "The American film is our most important weapon," proclaimed one Hollywood producer. During the 1930s Frank Capra had become the champion of the self-made man in his box office winners such as *Mr. Deeds Comes to Town* and *Mr. Smith Goes to Washington.* Now called to make a series of government films entitled *Why We Fight,* Capra set Rockwell-type characters in motion and contrasted them with harrowing portrayals of the mass obedience and militarism in Germany, Italy, and Japan. (In this, he used footage from the enemy's own propaganda films.) A hundred or so Hollywood personalities received commissions to make films for the Army's Pictorial Division. Commissioned as a lieutenant colonel, Darryl Zanuck, chairman of Twentieth Century Fox, filmed Allied troops in North Africa and the Aleutian Islands. John Ford produced a gripping combat documentary of the Battle of Midway.

Print advertising also contributed to the wartime propaganda effort. Roosevelt encouraged advertisers to sell the benefits of freedom. Most obliged, and "freedom" often appeared in the guise of new washing machines, ingenious kitchen appliances, improved automobiles, a wider range of lipstick hues, and automation in a hundred forms. As soon as the war was over, the ads promised, American technological know-how would usher in a consumer's paradise. Ads sometimes suggested that Americans were fighting to restore the consumer society of the 1920s (see Chapter 5).

The president initially resisted the creation of an official propaganda bureau, preferring to rely on a newly created Office of Facts and Figures (OFF) to disseminate information to the public. Poet Archibald MacLeish, who headed the OFF, however, acknowledged that his office most often resembled a "Tower of Babel" when it came to setting forth the aims and progress of the war. So, in the spring of 1942, Roosevelt created the Office of War Information (OWI) to coordinate policies related to propaganda and censorship. Liberals charged that the OWI was dominated by advertising professionals who dealt in slogans rather than substance. Conservatives blasted it as a purveyor of crass political advertisements for causes favored by Roosevelt and liberal Democrats. Despite such sniping, the OWI established branches throughout the world; published a magazine called *Victory,* and produced hundreds of films, posters, and radio broadcasts.

The Home Front • The Roosevelt administration's Office of War Information (OWI) successfully portrayed the Second World War as a global struggle in which everyone, including homemakers, should participate.

Gender Equality

Paradoxically, nostalgic propaganda for an "American way of life" often clashed with the socioeconomic changes that wartime mobilization brought. Nowhere was this more apparent than in matters affecting the lives and status of women. As women took over jobs traditionally held by men, many people began to take more seriously the idea of gender equality. Some 350,000 women volunteered for military duty during the war; more than 1,000 women served as civilian pilots with the WASPs (Women's Airforce Service Pilots). Although they comprised only 2 percent of all military personnel, these women broke gender stereotypes. Not everyone approved. One member of Congress asked: "What has become of the manhood of America, that we have to call on our women?" But most in Congress came to support a women's corps, with full status, for each branch of the military, a step that had been thwarted during the First World War.

The military service of women, together with their new importance in the labor market, strengthened arguments for laws to guarantee equal treatment. Congress seriously considered, but did not pass, an Equal Rights Amendment (ERA) to the Constitution and a national equal-pay law. But women's organizations themselves

Join the WAC

... this is
my war, too.

THIS POSTER CONTRIBUTED TO THE WAC BY WAMSUTTA MILLS, NEW BEDFORD, MASS.

Women in the Military • In addition to the millions of women who "served" on the home front, beginning in 1942 more than 50,000 joined the military and served in noncombat roles. The kind of glamor photography that typically depicted Hollywood stars was also employed in pictures of female service personnel.

disagreed over how to advance women's opportunities. Organizations representing middle-class women strongly backed passage of the ERA, but other groups, more responsive to the problems of poor women, opposed its passage. They saw it as a threat to the protective legislation, regulating hours and hazardous conditions, that women's rights crusaders had struggled to win earlier in the century. Should women continue to be accorded "protected" status in view of their vulnerability to exploitation in a male-directed workplace? Or should they fight for "equal" status? This dilemma, evident particularly in the disagreement over the ERA, divided women long into the postwar era.

Even as the war temporarily narrowed gender differences in employment, government policies and propaganda frequently framed changes in women's roles in highly traditional terms. Women's expanded participation in the workplace was often portrayed as a short-term sacrifice, necessary to preserve women's "special" responsibilities—hearth and home. Feminine stereotypes abounded. A typical ad suggesting that women take on farm work declared: "A woman can do anything if she knows she looks beautiful doing it." Despite the acceptance of women into the armed services, most were assigned to stateside clerical and supply jobs; only a relatively few women served overseas. Day care programs for mothers working outside their homes received reluctant and inadequate funding. The 3,000 centers set up during the war filled only a fraction of the need and were swiftly shut down after the war. Leading social scientists and welfare experts, mostly male, blamed working mothers for the apparent rise in juvenile delinquency and in the divorce rate during the war years.

The war also widened the symbolic gap between "femininity" and "masculinity" by fostering the portrayal of women as sexual commodities. Military culture encouraged men to adopt a "pin-up" mentality toward women. Service publications contained pin-up sections, and tanks and planes were decorated with symbols of female sexuality. Wartime fiction often associated manliness with brutality and casual sex. After the war, tough-guy fiction with a violent and misogynist edge, like Mickey Spillane's "Mike Hammer" series of detective novels, became one of the most successful formulas of popular culture.

Racial Equality

Messages about race were as ambiguous as those related to gender; wartime culture both propelled yet firmly resisted change. Before the Second World War, America had been a sharply segregated society, with racial inequality enforced by law and custom. African Americans, disfranchised in the South and only beginning to achieve voting power in the North, had only limited access to the political, legal, or economic systems. The fight against fascism, however, challenged this old order in a number of ways.

Nazism, a philosophy based on the idea of racial inequality, exposed the racist underpinnings of much of 20th-century social science theory. "The Huns have wrecked the theories of the master race with which we were so contented so long," Frank Dixon, ex-governor of Alabama, remarked in 1944. The view that racial difference was not a function of biology but a function of culture—a view most American anthropologists had been advancing for a generation—gained wider popular acceptance during the war. The implication was that a democratic and pluralistic society could accommodate racial difference. This new thinking helped to lay the foundation for the postwar struggle against discrimination.

The northward migration of African Americans accelerated demands for equality. Drawn by the promise of wartime jobs, nearly 750,000 African Americans relocated to northern cities, where many sensed the possibility of political power for the first time in their lives. They found an outspoken advocate of civil rights within the White House itself. First Lady Eleanor Roosevelt repeatedly antagonized southern Democrats and members of her husband's administration (often including the president himself) by her advocacy of civil rights and her participation in integrated social functions. The writer Clare Boothe Luce once remarked that Mrs. Roosevelt "enjoyed comforting the afflicted and afflicting the comfortable." Although the president often ignored her appeals for federal action against discrimination, her advocacy nevertheless dramatized the need for reform.

African Americans understood the irony of fighting for a country that denied them equality and challenged the government to live up to its own rhetoric about freedom and democracy. The *Amsterdam News,* a Harlem newspaper, called for a "Double V" campaign—victory at home as well as abroad. In January 1941, even before the United States entered the war, labor leader A. Philip Randolph threatened to lead tens of thousands of frustrated black workers in a march on Washington to

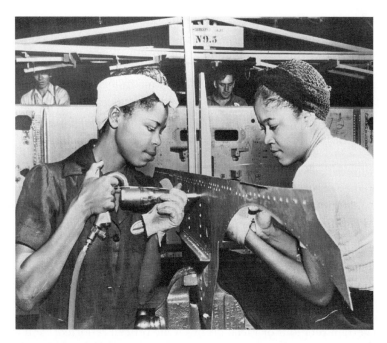

Women Find Industrial Work during Wartime • The Second World War provided an opportunity for African American workers to leave the rural South and find well-paying jobs in defense plants in the North and in California.

demand more defense jobs and integration of the military forces. With the support of major black organizations and other prestigious African American leaders, Randolph invited Roosevelt to address the planned gathering. But the president viewed the march as potentially embarrassing to his administration and urged that it be canceled. Randolph's persistence, however, forced Roosevelt to make concessions. In return for Randolph's canceling the march, the president created the FEPC in June of that year. The FEPC initially seemed a victory for equal rights, but Roosevelt gave the agency little power over discriminatory employers, who continued to argue that integrating the workforce would impair war production. During the war, the agency lost as many antidiscrimination cases as it won. Still, it provided an important precedent for federal action in civil rights.

Roosevelt also let stand the policy of segregation in the armed forces. "A jim crow army cannot fight for a free world," proclaimed the NAACP newspaper *The Crisis.* Yet General Marshall, Secretary of War Stimson, and others remained opposed to change. The Army and the Red Cross even went so far as to follow the scientifically absurd practice of segregating donated blood into "white plasma" and "black plasma." African Americans were relegated to inferior jobs in the military and excluded from combat status, practices that Roosevelt supported out of deference to his white southern constituency who feared that participation in combat might give African Americans new claims on full civil rights. Toward the end of the war, when manpower shortages forced the administration to put African American troops into combat, they performed with distinction.

Complaints about discrimination in the military reached a peak when an explosion at a naval ammunition depot near Vallejo, California, killed 300 stevedores, most of them black, who were loading ammunition. When the Navy assigned another group of black sailors to similar duty nearby, some of them refused, citing the danger. The resulting court-martial of 50 African American men was the largest mass trial in naval history. All of the sailors were found guilty of disobeying orders and received prison terms ranging from 8 to 15 years.

Racial Tensions

Racial tensions arose, especially in urban centers throughout the country. In industrial cities, the wartime boom threw already overcrowded, working-class neighborhoods into turmoil. Many of the residents of these neighborhoods came from European immigrant backgrounds or had migrated from rural areas. Wartime work provided their first real opportunity to escape from poverty, and they viewed the minority newcomers as unwelcome rivals for jobs and housing. In 1943, for example, it was estimated that between 6,000 and 10,000 African Americans arrived in Los Angeles every month. Once there, their living options were effectively limited to a few overcrowded neighborhoods segregated by landlords' practices and by California's restrictive housing covenants—legal agreements prohibiting the sale of homes to certain religious or racial groups. One official reported: "You will see life as no human is expected to endure it. Conditions are pitiful, and health problems are prevalent." Under such conditions, racial tensions festered.

Around the country, public housing projects presented a particularly explosive dilemma to federal officials charged with administering the supply of desperately needed housing. Should they follow local practice and keep housing segregated, or

Racial Tensions Flare into Violence • Clashes between African Americans and whites in Detroit on June 21, 1943, ended with 35 people dead, hundreds injured, more than a thousand under arrest, and millions of dollars in property damage.

should they integrate people of color into hostile white neighborhoods? Whites resisted the forced integration of public housing; nonwhites denounced the government for vacillating. In Buffalo, New York, threats of violence caused the cancellation of one housing project. In Detroit in June 1943, when police escorted African American tenants into a new complex, a full-scale race riot erupted. In several cities where integration was attempted, it took the intervention of federal troops to restore order.

Racial disturbances were not restricted to confrontations between whites and blacks. In Los Angeles, the so-called "zoot suit" incidents of 1943 pitted whites against Mexican Americans. Minor incidents between young Mexican American men wearing "zoot suits"—flamboyant outfits that featured oversized coats and trousers—and soldiers and sailors from nearby military bases escalated into virtual warfare between the zoot-suiters and local police. The Los Angeles City Council, recognizing that the zoot suit was becoming a symbol of rebellion for Mexican American youths, even tried to make it a crime to wear one. The Roosevelt administration feared that the zoot suit violence might have a negative effect on the Good Neighbor Policy in Latin America. The president's Coordinator of Inter-American Affairs, therefore, implemented a series of programs to ameliorate conditions contributing to tension. He allocated federal money to train Spanish-speaking Americans for wartime jobs, to improve education in barrios, and to open up more opportunities in colleges throughout the American Southwest.

American Indians comprised a significant group of new migrants to urban areas during the war. Although New Deal Indian policies (see Chapter 6) had attempted to restore tribal communities and Indian traditions, the Second World War introduced powerful pressures for migration and assimilation. By the end of the war, approximately 25,000 Indian men and several hundred Indian women had served in the armed forces, where Indians were fully integrated with whites. Some 40,000 other Indians found war work in nearby cities, many leaving their reservation for the first time. For Indians, the white-dominated towns and cities tended to be strange and hostile places. Rapid City, South Dakota, for example, attracted more than 2,000 Sioux from the Pine Ridge Reservation; most settled in informal camps at the outskirts of the city. Especially in smaller towns near reservations, such as Gallup, New Mexico, Flagstaff, Arizona, or Billings, Montana, established white residents often constructed formalized systems of discrimination against the newcomers. Many Indians moved back and forth between city and reservation, holding their urban jobs for only a few months at a time while seeking to live between two quite different worlds. Economic opportunities continued to be scarce on most reservations.

For African Americans, Latinos, and Indians, fighting for the "American way of life" represented a commitment not to the past but to the future. Demographic trends and a new militancy pointed the way to change. Increasingly, Americans of all backgrounds were realizing that racial grievances had to be addressed. In Detroit, for example, the local NAACP chapter emerged from the wartime years with a strong base from which to fight for jobs and political power. The Committee (later, Congress) on Racial Equality (CORE), an organization founded in 1942 and composed of whites and blacks who advocated nonviolent resistance to segregation, devised new strategies during the war. CORE activists staged sit-ins to integrate restaurants, theaters, and even prison dining halls in Washington, D.C. These same tactics would later be used in the 1950s and 1960s to force the desegregation of interstate buses and public accommodations. As the Swedish sociologist Gunnar Myrdal predicted in his influential study of American racial issues, *An American Dilemma* (1944), "fundamental changes" would soon have to come throughout the nation. Or, as the prominent African American novelist Richard Wright put it, America had to do something about its "white problem."

However, of all the minority groups in the United States, Japanese Americans suffered most grievously during the war. In the two months following the attack on Pearl Harbor, West Coast communities became engulfed in hysteria against people of Japanese descent. Fear of saboteurs gripped the white population. One military report concluded that a "large, unassimilated, tightly knit racial group, bound to an enemy nation by strong ties of race, culture, custom, and religion . . . constituted a menace" that justified extraordinary action.

Despite lack of evidence of disloyalty, government officials in February 1942 issued Executive Order 9066, directing the relocation and internment of first- and second-generation Japanese Americans (called Issei and Nisei, respectively) at inland camps. Curiously, in Hawaii where the presumed danger of subversion might have been much greater, no such internment took place; there, people of Japanese ancestry comprised 37 percent of the population and were essential to the economy. Forced to abandon their possessions or sell them for a pittance, nearly 130,000 Japanese Americans were confined in flimsy barracks, enclosed by barbed wire and

Japanese American Internment Camps • Throughout the 1930s, famed photographer Dorothea Lange portrayed the bleakness of the Dust Bowl. Here she captures an equally barren vista at the Manzanar War Relocation Center in California's Owens Valley, where—under the authority of Executive Order 9066 (1942)—the U.S. government interned some of more than 100,000 people of Japanese descent, two-thirds of whom were American citizens.

under armed guard. Two-thirds of the detainees were native-born U.S. citizens. Many had been substantial landowners in California's agricultural industries. In December 1944 a divided Supreme Court upheld the constitutionality of Japanese relocation in *Korematsu* v. *U.S.* (In 1988, however, Congress officially apologized for the injustice, concluding that it was "not justified by military necessity, and . . . not driven by analysis of military conditions." Congress authorized the payment of a cash indemnity to any affected person who was still living.)

Despite the internment, the suffering and sacrifice of Japanese American soldiers became legendary: The 100th Battalion, comprised of Nisei from Hawaii, was nearly wiped out; 57 percent of the famed 442nd Regimental Combat Team were killed or wounded in the mountains of Italy; and 6,000 members of the Military Intelligence Service provided invaluable service in the Pacific theater.

Racial hostilities reflected the underlying strains in America's social fabric, but there were other tensions pulling at Americans as well. Rifts developed between city dwellers and migrants from rural areas. Californians derided the "Okies," people who had fled the Dust Bowl of Oklahoma, as ignorant and dirty. In Chicago, migrants from Appalachia were met with a similar reception. Many ethnic communities, by preserving the language and culture of their homelands, also reflected social rivalries and divisions. At the beginning of the war, more than a third of white Americans were still either first- or second-generation immigrants.

Despite the underlying fragmentation of American society, the symbol of the "melting pot," together with appeals to nationalism, remained powerful. The war heightened racial and ethnic tensions precisely because the population was becoming less segmented geographically, ethnically, and racially. Wartime propaganda stressed the theme of national unity. The Second World War was called a "people's war," and America's "melting pot" was purposefully contrasted with the German and Japanese obsessions with racial purity. Wartime movies, plays, and music reinforced a sense of national community by building on cultural nationalism and expressing pride in American historical themes. Many foreign-language broadcasts and publications ceased to exist during the war, and naturalization applications nearly doubled from what they had been only five years earlier.

The great movements of population during the war—rural to urban, south to north, east to west—eroded geographical distinctions, and wartime demands for additional labor weakened the barriers to many occupations. As each of America's racial and ethnic minorities established records of distinguished military service, the claim of equality—"Americans All," in the words of a wartime slogan—took on greater moral force. The possibility for more equitable participation in the mainstream of American life, together with rhetoric extolling social solidarity and freedom, provided a foundation for the civil rights movements of the decades ahead. The war for "the American way of life," it turned out, carried many different meanings.

Shaping the Peace

On April 13, 1945, newspaper headlines across the country mourned, "President Roosevelt Dead." It was just a month before Germany's formal surrender and five months before Japan's. Difficult questions about demobilization and peace lay ahead.

Sorrow and shock were profoundly felt—in the armed forces, where many young men and women had hardly known any other president; in the diplomatic conference halls, where Roosevelt's magnetism had often brought unity, if not clarity; and among factory workers, farmers, and bureaucrats, for whom Roosevelt had symbolized optimism and unity through depression and war. Roosevelt had accumulated a host of critics and enemies. Indeed, he had defeated Republican Thomas E. Dewey in the 1944 presidential election by the smallest popular vote margin in nearly 30 years. Still, he had been the most popular president in modern history, and he left an enduring imprint on American life. "He was Commander-in-Chief, not only of the Armed Forces, but of our generation," wrote an editor of *Yank* magazine.

Compared with the legacy of Roosevelt, Vice President Harry S. Truman's stature seemed impossibly small. Born on a farm near Independence, Missouri, Harry Truman had served in France during the First World War. After the war, he went into politics under the auspices of Thomas J. Pendergast's Democratic Party machine in Kansas City. He was elected to the Senate in 1934, where he made his reputation in the early years of the Second World War, fighting waste in spending programs, and was chosen as Roosevelt's running mate in 1944. In contrast to Roosevelt, who was upper-class, elite-educated, and worldly, Truman was simply a "little man from Missouri." He prided himself on plain, direct talk. And he was poorly prepared for the job of president. Truman knew little about international affairs. Roosevelt had not included him in high-level policy discussions, and he knew little about any informal understandings that Roosevelt may have made with foreign leaders. In fact, during the period between the inauguration following the 1944 election and the president's death, Truman had met with Roosevelt only three times.

Despite his seeming limitations, Truman built on Roosevelt's many wartime conferences and agreements to shape the framework of international relations for the next half-century. Truman participated in the establishment of the United Nations, the creation of new international economic institutions, and the settlement of global political issues involving territory and governance.

The United Nations and International Economic Organizations

In the Atlantic Charter of 1941 and at a conference in Moscow in October 1943, the Allies had already pledged to create an international organization to replace the defunct League of Nations. The new United Nations (UN) fulfilled Woodrow Wilson's vision of collective security—his concept of an international body to deter aggressor nations. At the Dumbarton Oaks Conference in Washington in August 1944 and a subsequent meeting in San Francisco in April 1945, the Allies worked out the organizational structure of the UN. It would have a General Assembly, in which each member nation would be represented and have one vote. And it would have a Security Council, whose makeup would include five permanent members—the United States, Great Britain, the Soviet Union, France, and China—and six rotating members. The Security Council would have primary responsibility for maintaining peace, but any individual member of the council could exercise an absolute veto over any council decision. The inclusion of China in the Security Council was a victory for the United States. It was assumed that Jiang's government would remain in power and would continue to be a close U.S. ally. Finally, a UN Secretariat would handle day-to-day business, and an Economic and Social Council would promote social and economic advancement throughout the world.

The U.S. Senate accepted the UN charter in July 1945 with only two dissenting votes. This resounding victory for internationalism contrasted sharply with the Senate's rejection of membership in the League of Nations after the First World War. Americans of an earlier generation had worried that international isolationist policies might impinge on their country's ability to follow its own national interests. But following the Second World War, because U.S. power clearly dominated emerging organizations such as the UN, Americans thought it less likely that decisions of international bodies would clash with their nation's own foreign policies. In addition, Americans recognized that the war had partly resulted from the lack of a coordinated, international response to aggression during the 1930s and wanted to avoid the same mistake again.

Postwar economic settlements also illustrated a growing acceptance of new international organizations. In dealing with the world economy, U.S. policymakers endeavored to establish stable exchange rates for currency, create an international lending authority, and eliminate discriminatory trade practices. All these goals reflected their desire to avoid the chaotic conditions and economic protectionism that had unsettled the world economy during the 1930s.

At the Bretton Woods (New Hampshire) Conference of 1944, Americans had worked toward these objectives. The Soviet Union, whose state-directed economic policies challenged the assumptions of western capitalism, did not participate. The agreements reached at Bretton Woods created the International Monetary Fund (IMF), designed to maintain a stable system of international exchange by ensuring that each national currency could be converted into any other currency at a fixed rate. Exchange rates could be altered only with the agreement of the fund. (This international system of fixed exchange rates was replaced in 1971 by a system of floating exchange rates.) The International Bank for Reconstruction and Development, later renamed the World Bank, was also created to provide loans to war-battered countries and to promote the resumption of world trade. In the postwar era, American capital and American policies have dominated both the IMF and the World Bank, even though they are international bodies financed by member nations throughout the world. In 1947 a General Agreement on Tariffs and Trade (GATT) created the institutional structure for implementing free and fair trade agreements. Breaking up closed trading blocs and promoting freer trade was a major postwar goal for U.S. policymakers.

Spheres of Interest and Postwar Political Settlements

In wartime conversations, Stalin, Churchill, and Roosevelt all had assumed that powerful nations would have special "spheres of influence" in the postwar world. As early as January 1942 the Soviet ambassador to the United States reported to Stalin that Roosevelt had tacitly assented to Soviet postwar control over the Baltic states of Lithuania, Latvia, and Estonia. The Soviets accepted the exclusion of communists from Italy's postwar government. In 1944 Stalin and Churchill agreed informally and secretly that Britain would continue its dominance in Greece and that the

Soviets could dominate Romania and Bulgaria. Roosevelt understood why the Soviets wanted friendly states on their vulnerable western border, and he implied that he accepted the idea of postwar spheres of influence. But, at the same time, he talked about self-determination for small nations. At the Teheran Conference of November 1943, held just a year before the 1944 presidential election, Roosevelt told Stalin that American voters of Polish, Latvian, Lithuanian, and Estonian descent expected their homelands to be independent after the war.

Precisely how Roosevelt intended to handle the issue of Soviet influence in the postwar world will never be known. A master of finessing contradictions, Roosevelt was confident that he could improvise and smooth over difficulties that arose. As long as Soviet armies were essential to Germany's defeat—and the president wanted the USSR to join the war against Japan as well—Roosevelt cooperated with Stalin whenever possible. Roosevelt's political strengths were his flexibility, his ability to take contradictory positions simultaneously, and his skill at holding together unlikely coalitions. On many critical international issues of the 1930s—the gold standard, tariff policy, and entry into the war—Roosevelt had managed to straddle both sides of seemingly irreconcilable positions. On postwar issues, for which he seemed to have only the vaguest policy ideas, Roosevelt likely thought he could perform a similar juggling act.

The implications of these contradictions became apparent after Roosevelt's death. Then, the military results of the war, particularly the USSR's powerful position in Eastern Europe, strongly influenced postwar settlements regarding territory. On issues of governance—particularly in Germany, Poland, and Korea—splits between U.S. and Soviet interests widened. Germany, especially, became a focus and a symbol of bipolar tensions.

Early in the war, both the United States and the Soviet Union had urged the dismemberment and deindustrialization of Nazi Germany after its defeat. Roosevelt endorsed a controversial plan proposed by Secretary of the Treasury Henry Morgenthau that would have turned Germany into a pastoral, agricultural country. At a conference held at Yalta, in Ukraine, in early February 1945, the three Allied powers agreed to divide Germany into four zones of occupation (with France as the fourth occupation force). Later, as relations among the victors cooled, this temporary division of Germany permanently solidified into a Soviet-dominated zone in the East and the three Allied zones in the West. Berlin, the German capital, also was divided, even though it lay totally within the Soviet zone. As fear of the Soviets began to replace earlier concerns of a revived Germany, Truman abandoned the Morganthau plan in favor of efforts to rebuild the western zones of Germany.

Postwar rivalries also centered on Poland. During the war, Poland had two governments, a government-in-exile based in London and a communist-backed one in Lublin. At Yalta, the Soviets agreed to permit free elections in Poland after the war and to create a government "responsible to the will of the people," but Stalin also believed that the other Allied leaders had tacitly accepted the idea that Poland would fall within the Soviet's postwar sphere of influence. The agreement at Yalta was ambiguous at best, as many on the negotiating teams realized at the time. During Yalta, the war was still at a critical stage, and the western Allies chose to sacrifice clarity over the Polish issue in order to encourage cooperation with the Soviets. After Yalta, the Soviets assumed that Poland would be in their sphere of influence, but many Americans charged the Soviets with bad faith for failing to hold free elections and for not relinquishing control.

In Asia, military realities also influenced postwar settlements. Roosevelt had long wanted to bring the USSR into the war against Japan to relieve U.S. forces fighting in the Pacific. At Teheran in November 1943 and again at Yalta, Stalin pledged to send troops to Asia as soon as Germany had been defeated. But when U.S. policymakers learned that the atomic bomb was ready for use against Japan, they became eager to limit Soviet involvement in the Pacific theater. The first atomic bomb fell on Hiroshima just one day before the Soviets were to enter the war against Japan, and the United States took sole charge of the occupation and postwar reorganization of Japan. The Soviet Union and the United States split Korea, which had been occupied by Japan, into separate zones of occupation. Here, as in Germany, the zones later emerged as two antagonistic states (see Chapter 8).

The fate of the European colonies that had been seized by Japan in Southeast Asia was another issue that remained unresolved in the planning for peace. During the war, the United States had declared itself in favor of decolonization. The United States would have preferred to see the former British and French colonies become independent nations, with moderate governments friendly to the West and especially to American economic interests. But U.S. policymakers also worried about the left-leaning politics of many anticolonial nationalist movements. As the Cold War developed, the United States gradually moved to support Britain and France in their efforts to reassemble their colonial empires. Long struggles would ensue over the independence and political orientation of postwar governments throughout the colonized world.

In its own colony, the Philippines, the United States honored its long-standing pledge to grant independence. A friendly government that agreed to respect U.S. economic interests and military bases took power in 1946 and enlisted American advisers to help deal with leftist rebels. The Mariana, the Caroline, and the Marshall Islands, all of which had been captured by Japan during the war, were designated Trust Territories of the Pacific by the United Nations and placed under U.S. administration in 1947.

Although the countries of Latin America had not been very directly involved in the war or the peace settlements, U.S. relations with them were also profoundly affected by the war. Before 1941 the Roosevelt administration had sought to curb Nazi influence in Latin America. During the 1930s Roosevelt's Good Neighbor Policy, building upon a 1928 pledge to carry out no more military interventions in the hemisphere, had helped to improve U.S.–Latin American relations. The Office of Inter-American Affairs (OIAA), created in 1937, began an aggressive and successful policy of expanding cultural and economic ties. Just weeks after the German invasion of Poland in 1939, at the Pan American Conference in Panama City, Latin American leaders showed that the hemisphere was united on the side of the Allies. The conferees strengthened hemispheric economic cooperation and declared a 300-mile-wide band of neutrality in waters around the hemisphere (excepting Canada). After U.S. entry into the war, at a January 1942 conference in Rio de Janeiro, all the Latin American countries except Chile and Argentina broke off diplomatic ties with the Axis governments. When naval warfare in the Atlantic severed commercial connections between Latin America and Europe, Latin American countries became critical suppliers of raw materials to the United States, to the benefit of both. As economic and cultural ties increased, the United States consolidated its influence in Latin America.

Wartime conferences and settlements avoided clear decisions about creating a Jewish homeland in the Middle East, a proposal that England had supported, but not effected, after the First World War. The Second World War prompted survivors of the Holocaust and Jews from around the world to take direct action. Zionism, the movement to found a Jewish state in their ancient homeland, drew thousands of Jews to Palestine, where they began to carve out the new state of Israel. Middle Eastern affairs, which had been of small concern to U.S. policymakers before 1941, would take on greater urgency after 1948, when the Truman administration recognized the new state of Israel.

Conclusion

The world—and the United States along with it—changed dramatically during the era of the Second World War. Wartime mobilization ended the Great Depression and shifted the New Deal's focus away from domestic social reform and toward international concerns. It brought a historic victory over dictatorial, brutal regimes, and the United States emerged as the world's preeminent power, owning two-thirds of the world's gold reserves and controlling more than half of its manufacturing capacity.

At home, the war brought significant change. A more powerful national government, concerned with preserving national security, assumed nearly complete power over the nation's economy. New, cooperative ties were forged among government, business, labor, and scientific researchers. All sectors worked together to provide the seemingly miraculous growth in productivity that ultimately won the war.

The early 1940s sharpened debates over the nature of liberty and equality. Many Americans saw the Second World War as a struggle to protect and preserve the power and liberties they already enjoyed. Others, inspired by a struggle against racism and injustice abroad, insisted that a war for freedom should help expand equal rights at home.

News of Japan's surrender prompted the largest celebration in the nation's history. But questions remained about postwar policies. International conferences established a structure for the United Nations and for new, global economic institutions. Still, Americans remained uncertain about post-war reconstruction of former enemies and about future relations with wartime allies, particularly the Soviet Union. Domestically, the wrenching dislocations of war—psychic, demographic, and economic—took their toll. Postwar adjustments would be difficult for all Americans. And, of course, the nation now faced the future without the charismatic leadership of Franklin D. Roosevelt, the only president that many Americans had ever known.

Chronology

1931 Japanese forces seize Manchuria

1933 Hitler takes power in Germany

1936 Spanish Civil War begins • Germany and Italy agree to cooperate as the Axis Powers

1937 Neutrality Act broadens provisions of Neutrality Acts of 1935 and 1936 • Roosevelt makes "Quarantine" speech • Japan invades China

1938 France and Britain appease Hitler at Munich

1939 Hitler and Stalin sign Soviet-German nonaggression pact • Hitler invades Poland; war breaks out in Europe • Congress amends Neutrality Act to assist Allies

1940 Paris falls after German *blitzkrieg* (June) • Battle of Britain carried to U.S. by radio broadcasts • Roosevelt makes "destroyers-for-bases" deal with Britain • Selective Service Act passed • Roosevelt wins third term

1941 Lend-Lease established • Roosevelt creates Fair Employment Practices Commission • Atlantic Charter proclaimed by Roosevelt and Churchill • U.S. engages in undeclared naval war in North Atlantic • Congress narrowly repeals Neutrality Act • Japanese forces attack Pearl Harbor (December 7)

1942 Rio de Janeiro Conference (January) • President signs Executive Order 9066 for internment of Japanese Americans (February) • General MacArthur driven from Philippines (May) • U.S. victorious in Battle of Midway (June) • German army defeated at Battle of Stalingrad (August) • Operation TORCH begins (November)

1943 Axis armies in North Africa surrender (May) • Allies invade Sicily (July) and Italy (September) • "Zoot suit" incidents in Los Angeles; racial violence in Detroit • Allies begin drive toward Japan through South Pacific islands

1944 Allies land at Normandy (D-Day, June 6) • Allied armies reach Paris (August) • Allies turn back Germans at Battle of the Bulge (September) • Roosevelt reelected to fourth term • Bretton Woods Conference creates IMF and World Bank • Dumbarton Oaks Conference establishes plan for UN

1945 U.S. firebombs Japan • Yalta Conference (February) • Roosevelt dies; Truman becomes president (April) • Germany surrenders (May) • Potsdam Conference (July) • Hiroshima and Nagasaki hit with atomic bombs (August) • Japan surrenders (September) • United Nations established (December)

Suggested Readings

U.S. Entry into World War II

The U.S. entry into World War II is analyzed in Arnold A. Offner, *The Origins of the Second World War: American Foreign Policy and World Politics, 1917–1941* (1975); Waldo H. Heinrichs, *Threshold of War: Franklin D. Roosevelt and American Entry into World War II* (1988); Michael A. Barnhart, *Japan Prepares for Total War: The Search for Economic Security* (1987); Robert Dallek, *Franklin D. Roosevelt and American Foreign Policy, 1932–1945* (1979); Robert Divine, *The Reluctant Belligerent: American Entry into World War II* (1965); Akira Iriye, *The Origins of the Second World War in Asia and the Pacific* (1987); Ralph E. Schaffer, ed., *Towards Pearl Harbor: The Diplomatic Interchange between Japan and the United States, 1899–1941* (1991); and Sabura Ienaga, *The Pacific War: World War II and the Japanese* (1978). On isolationism, see Manfred Jonas, *Isolationism in America, 1935–1941* (1966); Wayne S. Cole, *Roosevelt and the Isolationists, 1932–45* (1983); and Goeffrey S. Smith, *To Save a Nation: American "Extremism," the New Deal, and the Coming of World War II* (1992).

Pearl Harbor

Pearl Harbor itself is the subject of several books by Gordon N. Prange, including *At Dawn We Slept: The Untold Story of Pearl Harbor* (1981); and *December 7, 1941: The Day the Japanese Attacked Pearl Harbor* (1988). See also John Toland, *Infamy: Pearl Harbor and its Aftermath* (1982), and Michael Slackman, *Target–Pearl Harbor* (1990).

Conduct and Diplomacy of the War

The conduct and diplomacy of the war can be surveyed in Alastair Parker, *The Second World War: A Short History* (1997); Gerhard L. Weinberg, *A World at Arms: A Global History of World War II* (1994); and Stephen E. Ambrose, *The American Heritage New History of World War II* (rev. ed., 1997) and *Citizen Soldiers* (1997). Other important studies include Martin Gilbert, *The Second World War: A Complete History* (1989); John Ellis, *Brute Force: Allied Strategy and Tactics in the Second World War* (1990); Michael J. Lyons, *World War II: A Short History* (1989); Gary R. Hess, *The United States at War, 1941–1945* (1986); Gaddis Smith, *American Diplomacy during the Second World War* (2nd ed., 1985); John Keegan, *The Second World War* (1989); Robert A. Divine, *Roosevelt and World War II* (1969) and *Second Chance: The Triumph of Internationalism in America during World War II* (1967); Mark Stoler, *The Politics of the Second Front: American Military Planning and Diplomacy in Coalition Warfare, 1941–1943* (1977); Ronald Schaffer, *Wings of Judgment: American Bombing in World War II* (1985); Michael S. Sherry, *The Rise of American Air Power: The Creation of Armageddon* (1987); D. Clayton James, *A Time for Giants: Politics of the American High Command in World War II,* (1987); Nathan Miller, *War at Sea: A Naval History of World War II* (1995). David Wyman, *The Abandonment of the Jews: America and the Holocaust, 1941–1945* (1984) and William B. Rubinstein, *The Myth of Rescue: Why the Democracies Could Not Have Saved More Jews from the Nazis* (1997) offer very different views of U.S. policy toward the Holocaust. See also Eric Markusen and David Kopf, *The Holocaust and Strategic Bombing: Genocide and Total War in the Twentieth Century* (1995) and Verne W. Newton, ed., *FDR and the Holocaust* (1996). Paul Fussell, *Wartime: Understanding and Behavior in the Second World War* (1989) examines life in the military, and David R. Segal, *Recruiting for Uncle Sam: Citizenship and Military Manpower Policy* (1989) discusses the selective service.

War in the Pacific

On the war in the Pacific, see Christopher Thorne, *Allies of a Kind: The United States, Britain, and the War against Japan, 1941–1945* (1978); Ronald Lewin, *The American Magic: Codes, Ciphers, and the Defeat of Japan* (1983); Ronald H. Spector, *Eagle against the Sun: The American War with Japan* (1985); John Dower, *War without Mercy: Race and Power in the Pacific War* (1986); Akira Iriye, *Power and Culture: The Japanese-American War, 1941–1945* (1981); Michael Schaller, *The U.S. Crusade in China, 1938–1945* (1979) and *Douglas MacArthur: The Far Eastern General* (1989); Sheldon H. Harris, *Factories of Death: Japan's Biological Warfare 1932–45 and the American Cover-Up* (1994); Edward J. Drea, *MacArthur's ULTRA: Code Breaking and the War against Japan* (1992); Bartlett E. Kerr, *Flames over Tokyo* (1991); Kenneth P. Werrell, *Blankets of Fire: U.S. Bombers over Japan During World War II* (1996); John D. Chappell, *Before the Bomb: How America Approached the End of the Pacific War* (1997); and Gunter Bischof and Robert L. Dupont, eds., *The Pacific War Revisited* (1997).

Individual Policymakers

Individual policymakers are treated in Warren Kimball, *The Juggler: Franklin Roosevelt as Wartime Statesman* (1991); Forrest C. Pogue, *George C. Marshall,* vols. II and III, (1966, 1973); Stephen E. Ambrose, *Eisenhower* (1983); Michael Schaller, *Douglas MacArthur: The Far Eastern General* (1989); and James Hershberg, *James B. Conant: Harvard to Hiroshima and the Making of the Nuclear Age* (1993).

The Home Front

The home front receives attention in John Morton Blum's *V Was for Victory: Politics and American Culture during World War II* (1976); William L. O'Neill, *A Democracy at War: America's Fight at Home and Abroad in World War II* (1993); Richard Polenberg's *War and Society: The United States 1941–1945* (1972); Allan M. Winkler, *Home Front U.S.A.: America during World War II* (1986); Gerald D. Nash, *The Great Depression and World War II: Organizing America, 1933–1945* (1979); William Tuttle, *Daddy's Gone to War: The Second World War in the Lives of America's Children* (1993); Michael C. C. Adams, *The Best War Ever: America and World War II* (1994); and John W. Jeffries, *Wartime America: The World War II Home Front* (1996). Geoffrey Perret, *Days of Sadness, Years of Triumph: The American People, 1939–1945* (1973) remains good reading; Studs Terkel, *"The Good War": An Oral History of World War II* (1984) is a classic. Helpful works on the economy and labor include Paul A. C. Koistinen, *The Military-Industrial Complex: A Historical Perspective* (1980); Stephen B. Adams, *Mr. Kaiser*

Goes to War (1998); James B. Atleson, *Labor and the Wartime State: Labor Relations and Law during World War II* (1998). Nelson Lichtenstein, *Labor's War at Home: The CIO in World War II* (1982); and Bartholomew H. Sparrow, *From the Outside In: World War II and the American State* (1996); and George Lipsitz, *Rainbow at Midnight: Labor and Culture in the 1940s* (1994).

Changing Gender Relations on the Home Front

Major studies on the changing gender relations on the home front include Leila J. Rupp, *Mobilizing Women for War: German and American Propaganda, 1939–1945* (1978), a comparative study of the United States and Germany; Karen Anderson, *Wartime Women: Sex Roles, Family Relations, and the Status of Women During World War II* (1981); D'Ann Campbell, *Women at War with America: Private Lives in a Patriotic Era* (1984); Susan Hartman *The Home Front and Beyond: American Women in the 1940s* (1982); Ruth Milkman, *Gender at Work: The Dynamics of Job Segregation during World War II* (1987); and Sherna Berger Gluck, *Rosie the Riveter Revisited: Women, the War, and Social Change* (1988). See also Glen Jeansonne, *Women of the Far Right: The Mothers' Movement and World War II* (1996). Judy Barrett Litoff and David C. Smith, eds., *Since You Went Away: World War II Letters from American Women on the Home Front* (1991) is a moving compilation. John Costello, *Virtue Under Fire: How World War II Changed Our Social and Sexual Attitudes* (1985), and Allan Berube, *Coming Out Under Fire: The History of Gay Men and Women in World War II* (1990) discuss changing sexual politics.

Race and the Home Front

On issues of race and the home front, see Peter Irons *Justice at War* (1993); Roger Daniels, *Concentration Camps U.S.A.: Japanese Americans and World War II* (1989); Mauricio Mazon, *The Zoot-Suit Riots: The Psychology of Symbolic Annihilation* (1984); Neil Wynn, *The Afro-American and the Second World War* (1993); Dominic J. Capeci, Jr., and Martha Wilkerson, *Layered Violence: The Detroit Rioters of 1943* (1991); Alison Bernstein, *American Indians and World War II: Toward a New Era in Indian Affairs* (1991); Clete Daniel, *Chicano Workers and the Politics of Fairness* (1991); and Merl E. Reed, *Seedtime for the Modern Civil Rights Movement: The President's Committee on Fair Employment Practice, 1941–1946* (1991).

The Peace Movement and Pacifism

The peace movement and pacifism are examined in Lawrence Wittner, *Rebels against War: The American Peace Movement, 1941–1960* (1969); Cynthia Eller, *Conscientious Objectors and the Second World War: Moral and Religious Arguments in Support of Pacifism* (1991); and Heather T. Frazier and John O'Sullivan, *"We Have Just Begun to Not Fight": An Oral History of Conscientious Objectors in Civilian Public Service during World War II* (1996); Rachel Waltner Goosen, *Women against the Good War* (1998).

Culture during the War

On culture during the war, see Lewis A. Erenberg and Susan E. Hirsch, eds., *The War in American Culture: Society and Consciousness during World War II* (1996); and Lawrence Samuel, *Pledging Allegiance: American Identity and the Bond Drive of World War II* (1997). Thomas Patrick Doherty, *Projections of War: Hollywood, American Culture, and World War II* (1993); Clayton Koppes and Gregory D. Black, *Hollywood Goes to War; How Politics, Profits & Propaganda Shaped World War II Movies* (1987); and John Whiteclay Chambers II and David Culbert, *World War II, Film, and History* (1996) concentrate on film. Allan M. Winkler, *The Politics of Propaganda: The Office of War Information, 1942–1945* (1978) covers propaganda; Frank W. Fox, *Madison Avenue Goes to War* (1975), describes wartime advertising; and Robin Winks *Cloak and Gown: Scholars in the Secret War, 1939–1961* (1987) describes academic ties to government policy. Karl Ann Marling and John Wetenhall, *Iwo Jima: Monuments, Memory, and the American Hero* (1991), and George H. Roeder, Jr., *The Censored War: American Visual Experience during World War II* (1993) both deal with the popular memory of the war.

Wartime Diplomacy and Postwar Settlements

On wartime diplomacy and postwar settlements, see Gabriel Kolko, *The Politics of War: The World and the United States Foreign Policy, 1943–1945* (1990); Remi Nadeau, *Stalin, Churchill and Roosevelt*

Divide Europe (1990); Randall B. Woods and Howard Jones, *Dawning of the Cold War: The United States' Quest for Order* (1991); Diane S. Clemens, *Yalta* (1970); Randall B. Woods, *A Changing of the Guard: Anglo-American Relations, 1941–1946* (1990); and Michael Schaller, *The American Occupation of Japan: The Origins of the Cold War in Asia* (1985).

Dropping of the Atomic Bomb

The dropping of the atomic bomb has attracted a large and impressive literature. Good starting places for understanding the various controversies are Michael J. Hogan, ed., *Hiroshima in History and Memory* (1996); Edward J. Linenthal and Tom Engelhardt, *History Wars: The Enola Gay and Other Battles for the American Past* (1996); and J. Samuel Walker, *Prompt and Utter Destruction: Truman and the Use of Atomic Bombs against Japan* (1997). Major works on this topic, from various perspectives, include Martin Sherwin, *A World Destroyed: The Atomic Bomb and the Grand Alliance* (1975); Barton J. Bernstein, *The Atomic Bomb: The Critical Issues* (1976); Michael Mandelbaum, *The Nuclear Revolution: International Politics before and after Hiroshima* (1981); John Ray Skates, *The Invasion of Japan: Alternative to the Bomb* (1994); Peter Wyden, *Day One: Before Hiroshima and After* (1984); Richard Rhodes, *The Making of the Atomic Bomb* (1986); Gar Alperowitz, *The Decision to Use the Bomb and the Architecture of an American Myth* (1995); Robert Jay Lifton, *Hiroshima in America: Fifty Years of Denial* (1995); Ronald Takaki, *Hiroshima: Why America Dropped the Atomic Bomb* (1995).

Videos

There are many video sources on World War II. *How Hitler Lost the War* (1990) and *The Call to Glory* (1991) are useful. The original *Why We Fight* series, produced by Frank Capra during the war, remains an important primary source. *WW II—The Propaganda Battle* is a fascinating entry in the "Walk Through the 20th Century Series," hosted by Bill Moyers. *Rosie the Riveter* (1980) is a documentary of women workers during the war. *Without Due Process* (1991) is a video account of the evacuation of Japanese-Americans. On the development of the atomic bomb, see *Day After Trinity* (1980) and *J. Robert Oppenheimer: Father of the Atomic Bomb* (1995). *The Promised Land* (1995) is a three-part documentary on the African-American migration from the Deep South to Chicago.

The Age of Containment, 1946–1954

T he Second World War, heralded as an effort to preserve and protect the
fabric of American life, had ended up transforming it. The struggle against
fascism had brought foreign policy issues to the center of political debate,
and the international struggles of the postwar period kept them there. As the Second
World War gave way to a "Cold War" between the United States and the Soviet Union,
Washington adopted global policies to "contain" the Soviet Union and to enhance
America's economic and military security. Preoccupation with national security
abroad, however, raised calls for limiting dissent at home. To fight communism overseas, might it also be necessary to institute "containment" policies at home?

The Cold War years from 1946 to 1954 also produced questions about government power. Should the activist, New Deal–style national government be abandoned? What role should Washington play in planning the postwar economy? What
should be its relationship to social policymaking, especially efforts to achieve equality? These broad questions first emerged during the presidency of Democrat Harry
Truman, from 1945 to 1953, as he struggled to define his Fair Deal programs. They
would remain central concerns during the administration of his Republican successor, Dwight David Eisenhower.

Creating a National Security State, 1945–1949

The wartime alliance between the United States and the Soviet Union had never
been anything but a marriage of convenience. Defeat of the Axis Powers had demanded that the two governments cooperate, but collaboration scarcely lasted beyond VE Day. Especially after President Franklin Roosevelt's death in April 1945,
relations between the United States and the Soviet Union steadily degenerated into
a Cold War of suspicion and growing tension.

Onset of the Cold War

Historians have discussed the origins of the Cold War from many different perspectives. The traditional interpretation, which gained new power after the collapse of
the Soviet Union in 1989, focuses on Soviet expansionism, stressing a traditional
Russian appetite for new territory, or an ideological zeal to spread international
communism, or some interplay between the two. The United States, proponents of
this view still insist, needed to take as hard a line as possible. Other historians—

generally called revisionists—view the Soviets' postwar behavior as primarily defensive. They argue that the Soviet Union's obsession with securing its borders was an understandable response to the invasion of its territory during both world wars. The United States, in this view, should have tried to reassure the Soviets by seeking accommodation, instead of pursuing policies that intensified Stalin's fears. Still other scholars maintain that assigning blame obscures the deep-seated clash of rival interests that made postwar tensions between the two superpowers inevitable.

In any view, the role of Harry Truman proved important. His brusk manner, in sharp contrast to Roosevelt's urbanity, brought a harsher tone to U.S.-Soviet meetings. Truman initially hoped that he could somehow cut a deal with Soviet Premier Joseph Stalin, much like his old mentor, "Boss" Tom Pendergast, struck bargains with rogue politicians back in Missouri. "I like Stalin," Truman once wrote his wife. "[He] knows what he wants and will compromise when he can't get it." However, as disagreements between the two former allies mounted, Truman came to rely on advisers hostile to Stalin's Soviet Union.

The atomic bomb provided an immediate source of friction. At the Potsdam Conference of July 1945, Truman had casually remarked to Stalin, "We have a new weapon of unusual destructive force." Calmly, Stalin had replied that he hoped the United States would make "good use" of it against Japan. Less calmly, Stalin privately ordered a crash program to develop atomic weapons of his own. After atomic bombs hit Japan, Stalin reportedly told his scientists that "the equilibrium has been destroyed. Provide the bomb. It will remove a great danger from us." Truman hoped that the bomb would scare the Soviets, and it did. Stalin grew even more concerned about Soviet security. Historians still debate whether "wearing the bomb ostentatiously on our hip," as Secretary of War Henry Stimson put it, frightened the Soviets into more cautious behavior or made them more fearful and aggressive.

In 1946 Truman authorized Bernard Baruch, a presidential adviser and special representative to the United Nations, to offer a plan for the international control of atomic power. The Baruch plan called for full disclosure by all UN member nations of nuclear research and materials, creation of an international authority to ensure concurrence, and destruction of all U.S. atomic weapons once these first steps were completed. Andrei A. Gromyko, the Soviet ambassador to the UN, argued that the Baruch plan would require other nations to halt their atomic research and disclose their secrets to the United Nations (dominated by the United States) before the United States itself was required to do anything. He complained that it would allow the United States to scrutinize Soviet progress in atomic research, while it maintained its own nuclear monopoly. Gromyko countered by proposing that the United States unilaterally destroy its atomic weapons first, with international disclosure and control to follow. The United States refused. Both sides used this deadlock to justify a stepped-up arms race.

Other sources of Soviet-American friction involved U.S. loan policies and the Soviet sphere of influence in Eastern Europe. Truman abruptly suspended lend-lease assistance to the Soviet Union in early September 1945, partly to pressure the Soviets into holding elections in Poland. Subsequently, Truman's administration similarly linked extension of U.S. reconstruction loans to its goal of rolling back Soviet power in Eastern Europe. This linkage strategy never worked. Lack of capital and signs of Western hostility provided the Soviets with excuses for tightening their grip on Eastern Europe, a course of action that further discouraged the United States from extending economic assistance to countries dominated by Moscow. A Soviet sphere of influence, which Stalin considered defensive and Truman labeled proof of communist expansionism, emerged in Eastern Europe. Suspicion steadily widened into mutual distrust. By 1946, the former allies were well on the way to becoming bitter adversaries.

From 1947 on, Harry Truman placed his personal stamp on the presidency by focusing on the fight against the Soviet Union. Dissenting voices were drowned out as the Truman administration pictured the United States and the Soviet Union engaged in a life-and-death struggle. The menace of an "international communist conspiracy" was said to justify extraordinary measures to ensure U.S. national security. The claim of protecting "national security"—an emotionally powerful term, whose meanings seemed infinitely expandable—allowed Truman to justify policy initiatives, in both foreign and domestic affairs, that extended the reach and power of the executive branch of government.

Containment Abroad: The Truman Doctrine

In March 1947, the president announced what became known as the Truman Doctrine when he addressed Congress on the civil war in Greece, a conflict in which communist-led insurgents were trying to topple a corrupt but pro-Western government. Historically, Greece had fallen within Great Britain's sphere of influence. But, badly weakened by the Second World War, Britain could no longer maintain its formerly strong presence there or in the Middle East. A leftist victory in Greece, Truman's advisers claimed, would open neighboring Turkey, which they considered crucial to U.S. interests, to Soviet subversion. But Truman's policymakers doubted they enjoyed broad support, either among the public or in Congress, for such a move. Seeking to justify U.S. aid to Greece and Turkey, Truman addressed Congress on March 12, 1947, in dramatic terms.

U.S. security interests, according to this Truman Doctrine, were now worldwide. Truman declared that the fate of "free peoples" everywhere, not simply the future of Greece and Turkey, hung in the balance. Unless the United States unilaterally aided countries "who are resisting attempted subversion by armed minorities or by outside pressures," totalitarian communism would spread around the world and threaten the security of the United States itself.

Initially, the Truman Doctrine's global vision of national security encountered skepticism. Henry Wallace, the president's most visible Democratic critic, chided Truman for exaggerating the expansive nature of Soviet foreign policy and its threat to the United States. Conservative Republicans looked suspiciously at the increase of executive power and the vast expenditures that the Truman Doctrine seemed to imply. If Truman wanted to win support for his position, Republican Senator Arthur Vandenberg had already advised, he would need to "scare hell" out of people, something that Truman proved quite willing to do.

The rhetorical strategy worked. With backing from both Republicans and Democrats, Truman's request for $400 million in assistance to Greece and Turkey, most of it in military aid, was passed by Congress in the spring of 1947. This vote signaled broad, bipartisan support for a national security policy that came to be called "containment."

The term "containment" was first used in a 1947 article in the influential journal *Foreign Affairs,* written under the pseudonym "X" by George Kennan, the State Department's leading expert on Soviet affairs. Kennan argued publicly for what he had already advised the Truman administration privately: The "main element" in any U.S. policy "must be that of a long-term, patient but firm and vigilant containment of Russian expansive tendencies." Although Kennan later insisted that he had meant containment to be a series of discrete responses to specific moves by the Soviets and never proposed an open-ended crusade, his broad prose lent itself to different interpretations. Whatever Kennan's intent, his "X" article quickly became associated with the alarmist tone of the Truman Doctrine.

Containment thus became the catchphrase for a global, anticommunist, national security policy. In the popular view, containment linked all leftist insurgencies, wherever they occurred, to a totalitarian movement controlled from Moscow that directly threatened, by heinous ideas as much as by military might, the United States. Although foreign policy debates regularly included sharp disagreements over precisely *how* to pursue the goal of containment, few Americans dared to question *why* the country needed a far-flung, activist foreign policy.

Truman's Loyalty Program

Nine days after proclaiming the Truman Doctrine, the president issued Executive Order 9835, which brought the containment of communism to the home front. Truman's order called for a system of loyalty boards empowered to determine whether there were "reasonable grounds" for believing that any government employee belonged to an organization or held political ideas that might pose a "security risk" to the United States. People judged to be security risks would lose their government jobs. The Truman loyalty program also authorized the attorney general's office to identify organizations it considered subversive, and in December 1947 the first Attorney General's List was released.

In developing the loyalty program, the Truman administration needed to gauge the extent of Soviet espionage activities in the United States. Although few historians ever doubted that the Soviets, even while a U.S. ally, carried on spy operations, scholars have disagreed about the scope and success of their operations. Were Soviet agents operating only at the fringes or had they penetrated the top levels of the U.S. government? Were they supplying information that might have been obtained almost anywhere or were they stealing vital national secrets? Although debates over these kinds of questions continue, they now take place against the backdrop of recently declassified evidence about Soviet espionage. As early as 1943, an Army counterintelligence unit had begun secretly intercepting transmissions between Moscow and the United States. Collected (and finally released to the public in 1995) as the "Venona files," these intercepted messages suggested that the USSR had several agents in wartime government agencies, including the Office of War Information and the top-secret OSS. Moscow began obtaining secret information about U.S. atomic work in 1944. The loyalty of government officials, in short, was a legitimate cause of concern. (Portions of the Venona intercepts became available on the World Wide Web in 1996.)

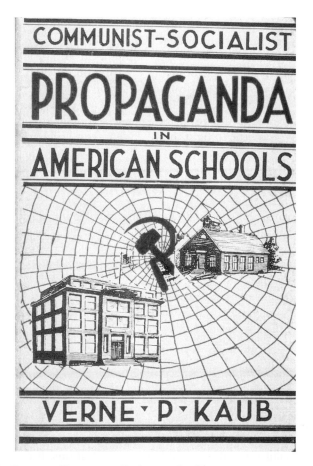

Anti-Communist Imagery Portrays a Nation under Siege • Pictures of communism spinning a kind of spider-like web over American institutions became a familiar metaphor of the Cold War era.

Curiously, the national security bureaucrats who intercepted the Soviet messages seem to have told neither the president nor his attorney general anything about their own super-secret operation or the intelligence being gathered. The mania for secrecy went so far that when it was discovered that a U.S. government employee working for the Soviet Union had informed Soviet intelligence about Venona, the project's leaders never sought to prosecute him because, in doing so, they would have had to reveal their own operation.

Truman's apparent lack of clear information may help to explain his inconsistent justification for the loyalty program. On the one hand, the president claimed that there were only a few security risks in the government but that their potential to do harm demanded a response that was unprecedented in peacetime. Framed in this way, the president's program repudiated Republican charges that hundreds, perhaps even thousands, of Communist Party members had been infiltrating the federal bureaucracy since the New Deal. On the other hand, it also clashed with the argument, championed by civil liberties groups, that a limited internal security threat logically demanded a limited, carefully crafted governmental response, one that distinguished between, say, an atomic scientist with suspicious ties to the Soviet embassy and a clerical worker in the Interior Department with leftist political leanings. Truman's muddled approach angered both civil libertarians, who charged the president with going too far, and staunch anticommunists, who accused him of doing too little to fight the Red Menace at home.

The National Security Act, the Marshall Plan, and the Berlin Crisis

The Truman Doctrine and the loyalty program only began the administration's national security initiatives. The National Security Act of 1947 created several new bureaucracies. It began the process that transformed the old Navy and War departments into a new Department of Defense, finally established in 1949. It instituted another new arm of the executive branch, the National Security Council, with broad authority over the planning of foreign policy. It established the Air Force as a separate service equal to the Army and Navy. And it created the Central Intelligence Agency (CIA) to gather information and to undertake covert activities in support of the nation's newly defined security interests.

The CIA proved the most flexible arm of the national security bureaucracy. Shrouded from public scrutiny, it used its secret funds to finance and encourage anticommunist activities around the globe. Between 1949 and 1952 the CIA's office for covert operations expanded its overseas stations from 7 to 47. The CIA cultivated ties with anti-Soviet groups in Eastern Europe and even within the Soviet Union itself, especially in Ukraine. It helped finance pro-U.S. labor unions in Western Europe to curtail the influence of leftist organizations. It orchestrated covert campaigns to prevent the Italian Communist Party from winning an electoral victory in 1948 and to bolster anticommunist parties in France, Japan, and elsewhere. From the beginning, the Truman administration encouraged the CIA to use its national security mandate broadly and aggressively.

Truman's administration also linked economic policies in Western Europe to the doctrine of containment. Concerned that the region's severe economic problems might embolden leftist, pro-Soviet political movements, Secretary of State George Marshall sought to strengthen the economies of Western Europe. Shortly after Congress approved funding for the Truman Doctrine, the secretary proposed the Marshall Plan, under which governments in Western Europe would coordinate their plans for postwar economic reconstruction with the help of funds provided by the United States. Between 1946 and 1951, nearly $13 billion in U.S. assistance was distributed to 17 Western European nations. The Soviets were also invited to participate in the Marshall Plan, but American policymakers correctly anticipated that Moscow would avoid any program whose major goal was rebuilding capitalism in Europe. Instead, Stalin responded to the Marshall Plan by further consolidating the Soviet's sphere of influence in Eastern Europe.

The Marshall Plan proved a stunning success. In response to charges by conservatives that the Marshall Plan was a "giveaway" program, the administration pointed out that it opened up both markets and investment opportunities in Western Europe to American businesses. Moreover, it helped stabilize the European economy by quadrupling industrial production within its first few years. Improved standards of living enhanced political stability and, along with the CIA's covert activities, helped undermine left-wing political parties in Europe.

American policymakers believed that to revitalize Europe under the Marshall Plan they would first have to restore the economy of Germany, which was still divided into zones of occupation. In June 1948 the United States, Great Britain, and France announced a plan for currency reform that would be the first step in merging their sectors of occupation into a federal German republic. Soviet leaders were alarmed by the prospect of a revitalized German state under Western auspices. Having twice been invaded by Germany during the preceding 35 years, they wanted a reunited but weak Germany. Hoping to sidetrack Western plans for Germany, in June 1948 the Soviets cut off all highways, railroads, and water routes linking West Berlin (which lay wholly within the Soviet sector of East Germany) to West Germany.

This Soviet blockade of Berlin failed. Air routes to the city remained open, and American and British pilots made 250,000 flights, round-the-clock, to deliver a total of 2 million tons of supplies to the city's beleaguered residents. Truman, hinting at a military response, reinstated the draft and sent two squadrons of B-29 bombers to Britain. Recognizing his defeat, Stalin abandoned the blockade in May 1949. The Soviets then created the German Democratic Republic out of their East German sector, and West Berlin survived as an enclave tied to the West. The "two Germanys" and the divided city of Berlin stood as symbols of Cold War tensions.

The Election of 1948

National security issues helped Harry Truman win the 1948 election, a victory that capped a remarkable political comeback. Truman had been losing the support of some Democrats, led by Henry A. Wallace, who thought his containment policies too militant; in September 1946, after Wallace criticized Truman's policies toward the Soviet Union, Truman had ousted him from the cabinet. Two months later, in the off-year national election of 1946, voters had given the Republicans control of Congress for the first time since 1928. Although his standing in public opinion polls had risen slowly in 1947 and 1948, most political pundits thought Truman had little chance to win the presidency in his own right in 1948. Challenged from the left by a new Progressive Party, which nominated Wallace, and from the right by both the Republican nominee Thomas E. Dewey and the southern segregationist candidacy of Strom Thurmond (running as the standard-bearer of the States' Rights Party, or "Dixiecrats"), Truman waged a vigorous campaign. He called the Republican-controlled Congress into special session, presented it with domestic policy proposals that were anathema to the GOP, and then denounced the "Republican Eightieth Congress, that do-nothing, good-for-nothing, worst Congress."

Thomas Dewey, who had been defeated by Franklin Roosevelt four years earlier, proved a cautious, lackluster campaigner in 1948. Even Republicans complained about his bland speeches and empty platitudes. A pro-Democratic newspaper caricatured Dewey's standard speech as four "historic sentences: Agriculture is important. Our rivers are full of fish. You cannot have freedom without liberty. The future lies ahead." When Dewey's campaign train, called "The Victory Special," reached Kansas City, Truman's old political base, Dewey was so confident of victory that he booked the same hotel suite the president used whenever he was in town.

Truman, for his part, conducted an old-style, stump-speaking campaign. He moved from town to town, stopping to denounce Dewey and Henry Wallace from the back of a railroad car. Dewey was plotting "a real hatchet job on the New Deal," and the Republican Party was controlled by a cabal of "cunning men" who were planning "a return of the Wall Street economic dictatorship," Truman charged. "Give 'em hell, Harry!" shouted enthusiastic crowds. In November, Truman won only 49.6 percent of the popular vote but gained a solid majority in the electoral college. He, and not Thomas Dewey, would be moving back into the presidential suite in Kansas City—and into the White House in Washington, D.C.

Truman's victory now seems less surprising to historians than it did to political analysts in 1948. Despite Republican electoral gains in the congressional elections of 1946, the Democratic Party was far from enfeebled. Indeed, the Democrats running for Congress in 1948, who identified themselves with Roosevelt rather than with Truman, generally polled a higher percentage of the popular vote in their districts than did Truman himself. Still, the loyalty of voters to the memory of Franklin Roosevelt and to his New Deal coalition—labor union members, farmers, people of color, and social justice activists—helped Truman.

Meanwhile, Truman commanded a constituency of his own by virtue of his anti-communist policies. In this sense, Truman's presidency established a pattern that

The "Little Man from Missouri" • Media politics during Harry Truman's presidency were still dominated by radio. In contrast to his predecessor, Franklin Roosevelt, Truman was not a particularly effective radio speaker. As he demonstrated during the 1948 presidential campaign, Truman's forte was the extemporaneous stump speech.

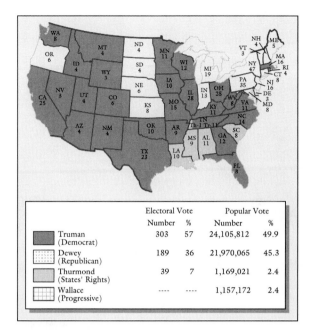

	Electoral Vote		Popular Vote	
	Number	%	Number	%
Truman (Democrat)	303	57	24,105,812	49.9
Dewey (Republican)	189	36	21,970,065	45.3
Thurmond (States' Rights)	39	7	1,169,021	2.4
Wallace (Progressive)	----	----	1,157,172	2.4

Presidential Election, 1948

would persist for several decades: If Democratic candidates could avoid appearing "soft" or "weak" on national security issues, they stood a good chance of being elected president. The candidacies of both George McGovern in 1972 and Jimmy Carter in 1980 faltered on the issue of national security. Conversely, Harry Truman stood "tough" in 1948. His hard-line national security credentials proved especially effective against his old nemesis Henry Wallace. After the election, Wallace's Progressive Party, which had challenged Truman's national security policies and had promised to revive the New Deal at home, lay in shambles. Hampered by his refusal to reject the support of Communist Party members, Wallace failed to win a single electoral vote and received less than 3 percent of the popular tally.

The Era of the Korean War, 1949–1952

To carry out the containment policy, the Truman administration marshaled the nation's economic and military resources. A series of Cold War crises in 1949 heightened its anticommunist fervor and deepened its focus on national security issues. These crises led ultimately to warfare in Korea.

NATO, China, and the Bomb

Building on the Truman Doctrine, the Marshall Plan, the Berlin Airlift, and the 1949 creation of the Federal Republic of Germany (West Germany), the United States set about creating a worldwide system of military alliances. In April 1949 the United States, Canada, and 10 European nations formed the North Atlantic Treaty

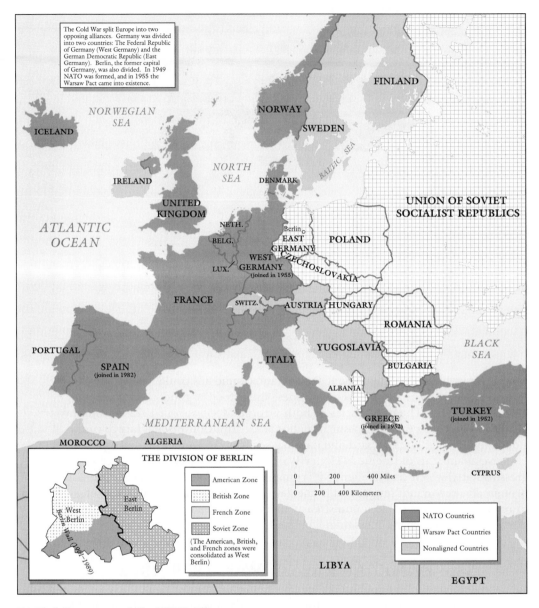

The Cold War split Europe into two opposing alliances. Germany was divided into two countries: The Federal Republic of Germany (West Germany) and the German Democratic Republic (East Germany). Berlin, the former capital of Germany, was also divided. In 1949 NATO was formed, and in 1955 the Warsaw Pact came into existence.

Divided Germany and the NATO Alliance

Organization (NATO). Members of NATO pledged that an attack against one would automatically be considered an attack against all and agreed to cooperate on economic and political, as well as military, matters. Some U.S. leaders worried about the implications of NATO. Republican Senator Robert Taft of Ohio declared that it was a provocation to the Soviet Union and an "entangling alliance" that defied common sense, violated the traditional U.S. foreign policy of nonentanglement, and threatened constitutional government by eclipsing Congress's power to declare war. The nation's use of military force, Taft warned, could be dictated by a response to events in other countries rather than shaped through its own policy-making processes. But the NATO concept prevailed, and the idea of pursuing containment through such "collective security" pacts expanded during the 1950s.

Meanwhile, events in China elevated Cold War tensions. Between 1945 and 1948 the United States extended to Jiang Jieshi's government a billion dollars in military aid and another billion in economic assistance. But Jiang steadily lost ground to the communist forces of Mao Zedong, who promised land reform and commanded wide support among China's peasantry. Experienced U.S. diplomats privately predicted that Jiang's downfall was inevitable, but the Truman administration continued publicly to portray Jiang as a respected leader of "free China" and to prop up his regime.

In 1949, when Mao's armies forced Jiang off the mainland to the offshore island of Formosa (Taiwan), many Americans wondered how communist forces could have triumphed. Republican opponents charged the Truman administration with a "sellout" to communism. Financed by conservative business leaders, a powerful "China lobby" excoriated Truman and his new secretary of state, Dean Acheson, for being "soft" on communism and, despite evidence of friction between Stalin and Mao, spoke of a global communist conspiracy directed from Moscow. Tainted by the "loss" of China, several state department officials who had criticized Jiang or merely predicted his downfall were dismissed and discredited, depriving the U.S. government of its most knowledgeable experts on China and Southeast Asia. Meanwhile, Acheson and Truman, responding to criticism, escalated their anticommunist rhetoric. For more than 20 years, even after friction between China and the Soviet Union became evident, the United States refused to recognize or deal with Mao's "Red China." Like Berlin, Jiang's anticommunist island of Formosa became a powerful symbol in the Cold War.

Late in 1949 the threat became even more alarming. Word reached Washington in September that the Soviets had exploded a crude atomic device, marking the end of the U.S. nuclear monopoly. Already besieged by critics who saw a world filled with Soviet gains and American defeats, Truman issued reassuring public statements but privately took the advice of hard-line advisers and authorized the development of a new bomb based upon the still unproven concept of nuclear fusion. The decision to build this "hydrogen bomb" wedded the doctrine of containment to the creation of ever more deadly nuclear technology.

NSC-68

Prompted by events of 1949, the Truman administration reviewed its foreign policy assumptions. George Kennan, worried that a simplistic and increasingly militaristic version of his containment concept was emerging, resigned from the State Department's policy planning staff. The task of conducting the foreign policy review fell to Paul Nitze, a hard-liner who produced a top-secret policy paper officially identified as National Security Council document number 68 (NSC-68). It provided a blueprint for both the rhetoric and the strategy of future Cold War foreign policy.

NSC-68 opened with an emotional account of a global ideological clash between "freedom," spread by U.S. power, and "slavery," promoted by the Soviet Union as the center of "international communism." Warning against any negotiations with the Soviets, the report urged a full-scale offensive to enlarge U.S. power. It endorsed covert action, economic pressure, more vigorous propaganda efforts, and a massive military buildup. Because Americans might oppose larger military spending and budget deficits, the report warned, U.S. actions should be labeled as "defensive" and be presented as a stimulus to the economy rather than as a drain on national resources. In NSC-68, "freedom" became redefined to mean simply "anticommunism."

The Korean War

The dire warnings of NSC-68 seemed confirmed in June 1950 when communist North Korea attacked South Korea. The Truman administration portrayed the move as a simple case of Soviet-inspired aggression against a "free" state. An assistant secretary of state remarked that the relationship of the Soviet Union to North Korea was "the same as that between Walt Disney and Donald Duck." Truman invoked once again the policy of containment: "If aggression is successful in Korea, we can expect it to spread through Asia and Europe to this hemisphere." The Korean situation, however, defied such simplistic analysis. Korea had been occupied by Japan between 1905 and 1945, and after Japan's defeat in the Second World War, Koreans had expected to establish their own independent state. Instead, the Soviet and U.S. zones of occupation resulting from the war were transformed into political entities. Against the desires of Koreans in both North and South, Korea became two states, split at the 38th parallel. The Soviet Union supported a communist government in the North under the dictatorial Kim Il-sung; the United States backed Syngman Rhee, who held a Ph.D. from Princeton University, to head the unsteady yet autocratic government in the South. Both leaders hoped that the patronage of a superpower might help to bolster their control and advance their respective notions of how Korean society should be organized.

But Korea could not be easily split along an arbitrary geographic line. It remained a single society, though it was riven by political factions as well as by ethnic and religious divisions. Rhee's oppressive regime, protective of upper-class landholders, generated opposition in the South, a movement that Kim's dictatorship encouraged. As discontent spread in the South, Kim moved troops across the 38th parallel on June 25, 1950, to attempt unification. Earlier, he had consulted both Soviet and Chinese leaders about his plans and received their support, after assuring them that a U.S. military response was highly unlikely.

The fighting in Korea soon escalated into an international conflict. The Soviets, uninformed about the precise details of Kim's plans, were boycotting the United Nations on the day the invasion was launched. Consequently, they were not present to veto a U.S. proposal to send a peacekeeping force to Korea. Under UN auspices, the United States rushed assistance to the dictatorial Rhee, who moved to eliminate disloyal civilians in the South as well as to repel the invading armies of the North.

U.S. goals in Korea were unclear. Should the United States seek to "contain" communism by driving the North Koreans back over the 38th parallel? Or should it try to reunify the country under Rhee's leadership? At first, that decision could be postponed because the war was going so badly. North Korean troops pushed their Soviet-made tanks rapidly southward; within three months, they took Seoul and reached the southern tip of the Korean peninsula. American troops seemed unprepared and, unaccustomed to the unusually hot Korean weather during these first months, fell sick. Fearing the worst, U.S. generals laid contingency plans for a large-scale American evacuation from Pusan. But American firepower gradually took its toll on the elite troops who had spearheaded North Korea's rapid move southward. North Korea had to send fresh, untrained recruits to replace seasoned fighters. As supply lines stretched out, the North Korean effort became more vulnerable.

General Douglas MacArthur then devised a plan that most other commanders considered crazy: an amphibious landing behind enemy lines at Inchon. MacArthur, now 70 years old, remained as bold and egotistical as he had been during the Second World War and as head of the occupation government of Japan. Rear Admiral James Doyle remarked, "If MacArthur had gone on the stage you never would have heard of John Barrymore." Those stunned by the riskiness of his proposed invasion, however, were even more astounded by its results. On September 15, 1950, the Marines successfully landed 13,000 troops at Inchon, suffered only 21 deaths, and moved back into Seoul within 11 days.

As MacArthur's troops drove northward, Truman faced a crucial decision. MacArthur, emboldened by success, urged moving beyond containment to an all-out war of "liberation" and reunification in Korea. Other advisers warned that China would retaliate if U.S. forces approached its border with Korea. Cautiously, Truman allowed MacArthur to carry the war into the North but ordered him to avoid antagonizing China.

UN Troops Counterattack in Korea, September 1950 • General Douglas MacArthur, a hero of the Second World War in the Pacific theater and the commander of United Nations forces in Korea, masterminded a daring amphibious landing at Inchon that resulted in the recapture of the South Korean capital of Seoul from North Korean forces. Here, U.S. Marines advance through Inchon.

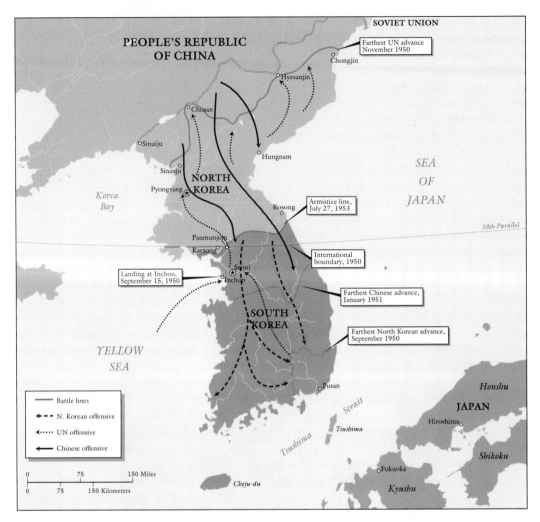

Korean War

MacArthur pushed too far. Downplaying a number of encounters between his troops and Chinese "volunteers," he continued to advance toward the Yalu River on the Chinese-Korean border. China responded by sending troops into North Korea and driving MacArthur back across the 38th parallel. With China now in the war, Truman again faced the question of military goals. When MacArthur's troops regained the initiative, Truman ordered his general to negotiate a truce at the 38th parallel. But MacArthur challenged the president, arguing instead for all-out victory over North Korea—and over China, too. Truman thereupon relieved him of his command in April 1951, pointing out that the Constitution specified that military commanders must obey the orders of the president, the commander in chief.

MacArthur returned home as a war hero. New York City greeted him with a ticker-tape parade that drew a crowd nearly twice as large as the one that had greeted General Dwight Eisenhower at the end of the Second World War. One poll reported that less than 30 percent of the U.S. public supported Truman's actions. The China lobby portrayed MacArthur as a martyr to Truman's "no-win," containment policy, and for a brief but intense moment MacArthur seemed a genuine presidential possibility for 1952. But this outpouring of admiration reflected MacArthur's personal charisma rather than any significant public support for a full-scale land war in Asia. During Senate hearings on the general's dismissal, military strategists expressed their opposition to such a war. And most Americans apparently preferred a negotiated settlement in Korea. Truman now set about convincing North Korea and South Korea to meet at the conference table. Eisenhower, the Republican candidate for president in 1952, promised to go to Korea to hasten the peace process. The negotiations that eventually reestablished the borderline at the 38th parallel emerged as a major foreign policy task for the new Eisenhower administration in 1953.

Korea and Containment

The Korean War had repercussions elsewhere. It focused American foreign policy ever more narrowly on anticommunism and justified the global offensive that NSC-68 had recommended. The United States announced a plan to rearm West Germany, scarcely five years after Germany's defeat, and increased NATO's military forces. In 1951 the United States signed a formal peace treaty with Japan, and a Japanese-American security pact granted the United States a base on Okinawa and permission for U.S. troops to be stationed in Japan. The United States also acquired bases in Saudi Arabia and Morocco, bolstering its strategic position in the Middle East. In 1950 direct military aid to Latin American governments, which had been voted down in the past, slid through Congress. By 1952 it had risen to nearly $52 million. In French Indochina, Truman provided assistance to strengthen French efforts to put down a communist-led movement that was fighting for independence. In the Philippines, the United States stepped up military assistance for the suppression of the leftist Huk rebels. And in 1951 the ANZUS collective security pact linked the United States strategically to Australia and New Zealand. Throughout the world, economic pressure, covert activities by the CIA, and propaganda campaigns helped to forge anticommunist alliances. Truman's global "Campaign of Truth," an intensive informational and psychological offensive, used mass media and cultural exchanges to counter Soviet claims with pro-American perspectives.

While the Truman administration fortified America's strategic position throughout the world, U.S. military budgets increased, approaching the level that NSC-68 had recommended. Strategic priorities linked Washington to ongoing weapons research and production. The Atomic Energy Commission had been created in 1946 to succeed the Manhattan Project in overseeing development of nuclear power; aviation had received special government funding for the first time in the 1946 budget; the Army had joined with aircraft manufacturers in an effort to develop surface-to-surface missiles. And to coordinate global strategy with the development of long-range weapons, a new "think tank"—RAND, an acronym for Research and Development—was created. Expensive contracts for the manufacture of military materials worried cost-conscious members of Congress, but the prospect that the contracts would create new jobs in their home districts muted their opposition. The Cold War, especially after Korea, brought what the historian Michael Sherry has called "the militarization of American life": a steady military buildup, an intermingling of military and economic policies, and an emphasis on anticommunism at home and abroad.

As the effort to contain communism intensified, U.S. policymakers became more suspicious of any movement that was supported by local communists or was even left-leaning in its political orientation. The U.S. occupation government in Japan, for example, increasingly restricted the activities of labor unions, suspended an antitrust program that American officials had earlier implemented, brought back conservative wartime leaders, and barred communists from government offices and universities. As in Germany, the United States tried to contain communism by strengthening industrial elites and promoting economic growth. U.S. war orders during the Korean conflict stimulated Japan's economy and provided the foundation for the procapitalist, anticommunist Japanese government that succeeded the American occupation in 1952.

In Africa, as well, anticommunism shaped U.S. policies, bringing the United States into an alliance with South Africa. In 1948 the all-white Nationalist Party instituted a legal system based on elaborate rules of racial separation and subordination of blacks (apartheid). State Department officials familiar with African affairs warned that supporting apartheid in South Africa would damage U.S. prestige, but the Truman administration decided to cement an alliance with South Africa nonetheless. That country, Truman reasoned, possessed important raw materials (especially, uranium for bombs and manganese for steel) and a cheap labor force. Moreover, South Africa's Nationalist Party was militantly anticommunist.

From 1947 to the early 1950s, U.S. citizens often felt embattled and insecure in the world. Containment relied on a rhetoric of defensiveness: The term "national security" replaced "national interest"; the "War Department" became the "Department of Defense." Yet the country was hardly on the defensive. The United States extended its power into the former British sphere of influence of Iran, Greece, and Turkey; initiated the Marshall Plan and NATO; transformed its former enemies—Italy, Germany, and Japan—into anti-Soviet bulwarks; assumed control of hundreds of Pacific islands; launched research for the development of the hydrogen bomb; winked at apartheid in order to win an anticommunist ally in South Africa; solidified its sphere of influence in Latin America; acquired bases around the globe; and devised a master plan for using military, economic, and covert action to achieve its goals. Beginning with the Truman Doctrine of 1947, the United States began to stake out global interests.

Containment at Home

Although containment abroad generally gained bipartisan support, Harry Truman's national security policies at home remained more divisive. A strident debate over how best to counter alleged communist influences in the United States raged from the late 1940s through the middle 1950s. Politicians, professional organizations, labor unions, business corporations, and individual citizens all strove to

"Duck and Cover!" • In order to mobilize the country for the Cold War crusade of the 1950s, the government actively promoted a civil defense drill called "duck and cover," in which people practiced what to do in the event of a nuclear attack. The drills were most common in school classrooms but were also conducted in businesses and communities, as is shown here in a 1951 exercise in San Diego.

demonstrate their anticommunist credentials. Conservative members of Congress and private watchdog groups, taking their cue from Truman's anticommunist rhetoric, launched their own search for evidence of internal communist subversion. Civil libertarians continued to complain that a "witch hunt" was being conducted against people whose only sins were dissent from the Truman administration's anticommunist measures or support for a leftist political agenda at home. Exaggerated charges of communist subversion became a familiar part of postwar political discourse. Indeed, witch-hunters increasingly charged Truman's own anticommunist administration with harboring people who were disloyal or "soft" on communism. In time, even devoted anticommunists began to complain that wild goose chases after unlikely offenders were hampering the search for authentic Soviet agents. Many of the country's most vocal anticommunists, as a commission on the role of Cold War intelligence-gathering later concluded, "clearly knew little or nothing" about internal security matters. Still, the search for supposed subversives affected many areas of postwar life, and a particularly vitriolic group of anticommunists emerged in Congress.

Anticommunism and the Labor Movement

The labor movement became a obvious target for anticommunist legislators. An unprecedented wave of labor strikes had swept across the country after the end of the Second World War. Militant workers had struck for increased wages and for a greater voice over workplace routines and production decisions. Strikes had brought both the auto industry and the electronics industry to a standstill. In

Stamford, Connecticut, and Lancaster, Pennsylvania, general strikes had led to massive work stoppages that later spread to Rochester, Pittsburgh, Oakland, and other large cities. By 1947, however, labor militancy had begun to subside as Truman took a hard line. He upbraided oil refinery strikers to "cut out all the foolishness." He also threatened to seize mines and railroads that had been shut down by strikes and ordered the strikers back to work.

Still, in 1947 congressional opponents of organized labor effectively tapped anticommunist sentiment to help pass the Labor-Management Relations Act, popularly known as the Taft-Hartley Act. The law negated some of the gains that unions had made during the 1930s by limiting a union's power to conduct boycotts, to compel employers to accept "closed shops" in which only union members could be hired, and to conduct any strike that the president judged against the national interest. In addition, the law strengthened the power of union leaders to discipline their own members. Finally, Taft-Hartley required that these same union officials sign affidavits stating that they did not belong to the Communist Party or to any other "subversive" organization. A union that refused to comply was effectively denied protection under national labor laws when engaged in conflict with management. Truman vetoed Taft-Hartley, but Congress swiftly overrode him. Trying to uncover communist infiltration of labor unions became a consistent quest of anticommunists in Congress and within the labor movement itself.

The place of communists in the labor movement, which had long been a contentious issue, was becoming a national security issue. Anticommunist unionists had long charged that communists, despite their energetic work in grass-roots organizing campaigns, were more loyal to their party than to their unions; now, in the context of the Cold War, they could cite communists for being disloyal to the nation itself. Differences over whether to support the Democratic Party or Henry Wallace's third-party effort in 1948 heightened tensions within many unions, and in the years following Truman's victory the Congress of Industrial Organizations (CIO) expelled 13 unions—and a full third of its membership—for allegedly following pro-Soviet, rather than pro-labor, policies. Meanwhile, many workers found their jobs at risk because of their political ideas, as red-hunters searched for so-called subversives in the workplace. By the end of the Truman era, some type of loyalty-security check had been conducted on about 20 percent of the American workforce, more than 13 million people. People who were especially outspoken on behalf of labor risked being labeled as pro-Communist.

HUAC and the Loyalty Program

Anticommunists carefully scrutinized the Hollywood film industry. In 1947, only three days after the unveiling of the Truman Doctrine, the House Committee on Un-American Activities (which became popularly known as HUAC) opened hearings in Hollywood to expose alleged communist infiltration. Long a bastion of anti–New Deal sentiment and extreme anticommunism, HUAC discovered a new national platform. Basking in the glare of newsreel cameras, its members seized on the refusal of 10 screen writers, producers, and directors who had been or still were Communist Party members to testify about their own political affiliations and those of other members of the film community. Known as "the Hollywood Ten," this group claimed that the First Amendment shielded their political activities from official scrutiny. But the federal courts upheld HUAC's inquisitional powers, and the Hollywood Ten eventually went to prison for contempt of Congress because of their defiance of HUAC.

Meanwhile, studio heads secretly drew up a "blacklist" of so-called subversives who could no longer work in Hollywood. Industry leaders denied the existence of such a list, but their disavowals were unconvincing. The actor John Wayne later explained, "The only thing our side did that was anywhere near blacklisting was just running a lot of people out of the business . . . ." By the mid-1950s hundreds of people in Hollywood and in the fledgling television industry—technicians who worked behind the scenes as well as performers who appeared in front of them—were unable to find jobs unless they would agree to appear before HUAC and ritualistically name people whom they had seen at some "communist meeting" at some time in the past.

Ronald Reagan and Richard Nixon first attracted the political spotlight through the HUAC hearings. Reagan, who was president of the Screen Actors Guild and also a secret informant for the FBI (identified as "T-10"), decried the presence of subversives in the movie industry. Nixon, then an obscure member of Congress from California, began his climb to national prominence in 1948 when Whittaker Chambers, a journalist who had once been active in the Communist Party, came before HUAC to charge Alger Hiss, a prominent liberal Democrat who had a long career in government, with having also been a party member and with passing classified documents to Soviet agents in the late 1930s.

The Hiss-Chambers-Nixon affair set off a raging controversy. Hiss maintained that he had been framed in an elaborate FBI plot, alleging that the Bureau rigged his typewriter so it would appear to be the source of incriminating evidence. Legal technicalities prevented Hiss from being prosecuted for espionage, but he was charged with lying to Congress about his activities. To Nixon and other leaders of the anticommunist campaign, the exposure of Hiss, who had been one of Franklin Roosevelt's advisers during the Yalta Conference of 1945 (see Chapter 7), proved the need to "clean house" in Washington, and to search out subversion with more vigor than was being shown by the Truman administration. But to civil libertarians, the cases of the Hollywood Ten and Alger Hiss suggested the consequences of overzealous witch-hunting. Debates over whether the Hiss case was an example of high-level espionage or anticommunist hysteria would continue for decades. The Venona files, which were not made public until the mid-1990s, suggested that U.S. intelligence experts were convinced that Hiss had indeed passed secrets to the Soviets. (Although some historians have cited this belief as proof of Hiss's guilt, others have argued that the Venona documents, by themselves, proved little because it was difficult to identify accurately the Soviet agents by the code names used in the files.)

Meanwhile, the Truman administration continued to pursue its own hard-line policies. Under the president's loyalty program, hundreds of government employees were dismissed. His attorneys general seemed to be competing for the honor of issuing the toughest policy statements on subversion or granting the broadest discretionary powers to J. Edgar Hoover, head of the FBI. Attorney General Tom Clark (whom Truman appointed to the Supreme Court in 1949) authorized Hoover to draw up his own list of alleged subversives and to detain them, without any legal hearing, in the event of a national security emergency. Clark's successor, Howard McGrath, proclaimed that communist subversives, each carrying "the germs of death for society," were lurking "in factories, offices, butcher stores, on street corners, in private business."

At the same time, the FBI was also accumulating dossiers on a wide range of artists and intellectuals, particularly prominent African Americans. Richard Wright (author of the novel *Native Son*), W. E. B. Du Bois (the nation's most celebrated African American intellectual), and Paul Robeson (one of America's most prominent entertainer-activists) became special targets. Robeson and Du Bois were harassed by State Department and immigration officials because of their ties to the Communist Party and their identification with anti-imperialist and antiracist struggles throughout the world.

Concern that people with subversive political affiliations and ideas might emigrate to the United States produced a new immigration law. In 1952 Congress passed the McCarran-Walter Act, which placed restrictions on immigration from areas outside northern and western Europe and on the entry of people whom immigration officials suspected might threaten national security.

Targeting Difference

Homosexuals became special targets of the antisubversive impulse. During the Second World War, with the disruption of many traditional social patterns, more visible and assertive gay and lesbian subcultures had begun to emerge, even within the armed forces. After the war, Dr. Alfred Kinsey's research on sexual behavior—the first volume, on male sexuality, was published in 1948—claimed that gays and lesbians could be found throughout American society. At about the same time, gays themselves formed the Mattachine Society (in 1950) and lesbians founded the Daughters of Bilitis (in 1955), organizations that cautiously began to push for recognition of rights for homosexuals. The *Kinsey Report*'s implicit claim that homosexuality was a normal form of sexuality that should be tolerated, together with the discreet militancy among gays and lesbians, produced a backlash that became connected to the broader antisubversion crusade. The fact that several founders of the Mattachine Society had also been members of the Communist Party, coupled with a belief that homosexuals could be blackmailed by Soviet agents more easily than heterosexuals, helped to link homosexuality with subversion.

A connection between antihomosexual and anticommunist rhetoric developed. Radical political ideas and homosexuality were both portrayed as "diseases" that could spread throughout the body politic by people who often looked no different from "ordinary" Americans. As a report from the U.S. Senate put it, "one homosexual can pollute a Government office" in much the same way as could a person with subversive ideas. According to this logic, homosexuality was an acceptable basis for denying people government employment.

The Rosenberg Case and "the Great Fear"

Harry Truman's last years as president were played out against a backdrop of public anxiety that the historian David Caute has called "the Great Fear." With their ceaseless warnings about hidden enemies, at home and abroad, the guardians of national security intensified that fear instead of allaying it.

Foreign policy events of 1949 and 1950, especially the Soviets' nuclear tests, highlighted the issue of whether subversives and spy rings were at work in the most sensitive recesses of the U.S. government. How had the Soviets so quickly developed atomic weaponry? Suspicions arose about the loyalty of foreign policy personnel, and stories about Soviet agents having stolen U.S. nuclear secrets spread rapidly. In 1949, as mentioned earlier, after two widely reported trials Alger Hiss went to prison for lying to Congress about his relationship with Whittaker Chambers. Then, in early 1950, Great Britain released evidence that a spy ring, long known to those with access to the Venona files, had been operating in the United States since the mid-1940s. Shortly afterward, the U.S. Justice Department arrested several alleged members of this ring, including two members of the Communist Party, Julius and Ethel Rosenberg.

The Rosenberg case became a Cold War melodrama. The trial, the verdicts of guilty, the sentences of death at Sing Sing prison, the numerous legal appeals, the worldwide protests, and the executions in 1953—all provoked intense controversy. Were the Rosenbergs guilty of having been involved in the theft of nuclear secrets? And even if they were guilty of passing information to the Soviets, were their death sentences on the charge of espionage the constitutionally appropriate punishment? To their supporters, the Rosenbergs (who steadfastly maintained their innocence) were not spies but left-leaning activists who had fallen victim to the Great Fear. Many believed that the entire government—from the White House to the FBI to the Supreme Court—seemed more intent on punishing scapegoats than in conducting a fair trial. To others, the evidence showed that some information had been channeled to the Soviets.

More than 45 years after the Rosenbergs' deaths, debates still rage over their case. Intelligence reports from the Cold War era not released until the 1990s strongly suggested that Julius Rosenberg had been engaged in espionage and that Ethel Rosenberg, though not directly involved, may have known of his activities. Yet, as the Commission on Protecting and Reducing Government Secrecy noted in 1997, the government declined to prosecute "a fair number of Americans who almost certainly were atomic spies." In some instances, it seems, a court trial could have compromised ongoing intelligence projects; in other cases, formal legal proceedings would have revealed illegal activities by Hoover's FBI and likely ended in a failed prosecution. Only Julius and Ethel Rosenberg were charged with a crime that carried the death penalty.

The manner in which the courts responded to the anticommunist crusade sparked controversy. During the Justice Department's 1949 prosecution of Communist Party leaders for sedition, for example, the trial judge allowed the government a wide latitude to introduce evidence against the defendants. In effect, he accepted the claim that, by definition, the American Communist Party was simply the arm of an international conspiracy. Its Marxist ideology and its theoretical publications, even in the absence of any proof of subversive *acts* against national security, justified convictions against the party's leaders. In contrast, civil libertarians insisted that the government lacked any evidence that the publications and speeches of Communist Party members, by themselves, posed any "clear and present danger" to national security. In this view, the Communist Party's abstract political beliefs, which should enjoy the protection of the First Amendment, were unconstitutionally put on trial.

When the convictions of the Communist Party leaders were appealed to the Supreme Court, in the case of *Dennis* v. *U.S.* (1951), civil libertarians renewed their arguments that this prosecution violated constitutional guarantees for the protection of speech. The Supreme Court, however, modified the "clear and present danger" doctrine and upheld the lower court. The defendants, a majority of the Court declared, had been constitutionally convicted.

By 1952, the Democrats who had created the national security state were no longer leading the anticommunist effort. Instead, the Truman administration itself had become a primary target of anticommunist zealots. In Congress, Republicans and conservative Democrats condemned the administration's handling of anticommunist initiatives and introduced their own legislation, the McCarran Internal Security Act of 1950. It authorized the detention, during any national emergency, of alleged subversives in special camps, and created the Subversive Activities Control Board (SACB) to investigate organizations suspected of being affiliated with the Communist Party and to administer the registration of organizations allegedly controlled by communists.

The Truman administration responded ambiguously to the McCarran Act. Although the president vetoed the law, a futile response that Congress quickly overrode, his administration secretly allowed the FBI's J. Edgar Hoover to continue a covert detention program that offered even fewer legal safeguards than the McCarran Act. There was never a national emergency to trigger the operation of either of these plans, but other anticommunist activities continued. Still, Truman could never defuse the charges leveled at his own administration.

McCarthyism

Republican Senator Joseph McCarthy of Wisconsin became Truman's prime accuser. Charging in 1950 that communists were at work in Truman's State Department, a totally unsubstantiated allegation that supposedly explained foreign policy "losses" such as China, McCarthy put the administration on the defensive. The nation was in a precarious position, according to McCarthy, "not because our only powerful potential enemy has sent men to invade our shores, but rather because of the traitorous actions of those who have been treated so well by this Nation." Among those people, McCarthy named Alger Hiss, Secretary of State Dean Acheson, and former Secretary of State George C. Marshall.

Truman's efforts to contain McCarthy failed. Although McCarthy never substantiated his charges, which grew more fantastic as the months passed, he lacked neither imagination nor targets. The main targets of McCarthy and his imitators were former members of the Communist Party of the United States and people associated with "communist front" organizations, supposedly legitimate political groups secretly manipulated by communists. In most of the cases McCarthy cited, the affiliations had been perfectly legal. He also made vague charges against the entertainment industry and academic institutions. And despite his claims that hundreds—and, later, dozens—of communist subversives were working in the State Department, he produced no credible evidence to support his case.

Still, McCarthy seemed unstoppable. In the summer of 1950, a subcommittee of the Senate Foreign Relations Committee, after examining State Department files in search of the damning material, concluded that McCarthy's charges amounted to "the most nefarious campaign of half-truths and untruths in the history of this republic." McCarthy simply charged that the files had been "raped," and he broadened his mudslinging to include Millard Tydings, the Maryland senator who had chaired the subcommittee and who had called McCarthy's charges "an effort to inflame the American people with a wave of hysteria and fear on an unbelievable scale." In the November 1950 elections, Tydings was defeated, in part, because of a fabricated photo that linked him to an alleged Communist Party member.

Despite McCarthy's recklessness, influential people tolerated, even supported, his crusade. Conservative, anticommunist leaders of the Roman Catholic Church endorsed McCarthy, himself a Catholic. Leading Republicans—including Senator Robert Taft, chair of the GOP policy committee in the Senate, and Kenneth Wherry, the Republican minority leader in the Senate—welcomed McCarthy's attacks on their Democratic rivals. Wherry cheered McCarthy on, urging people to get rid of "the alien-minded radicals and moral perverts" in the Truman administration. As head of a special Senate Subcommittee on Investigations, popularly known as the "McCarthy committee," McCarthy enjoyed broad subpoena power and legal immunity from libel suits. He bullied witnesses because of their alleged ties to communist organizations and encouraged self-styled "experts" to offer outlandish estimates of a vast Red Menace. Although McCarthy's contemporaries, historians now agree, overestimated his political power and personal appeal, the senator personified the kind of reckless demagoguery, "McCarthyism," that continues to bear his name.

In the long run, growing concern about national security subtly altered the nation's constitutional structure. Except for the Twenty-second and the Twenty-third Amendments (adopted in 1951 and 1961, respectively), which barred future presidents from serving more than two terms and allowed the District of Columbia a vote in presidential elections, there were no formal modifications of the written Constitution during these years. But legislative enactments, especially the National Security Act of 1947, and the growing power of the executive branch of government, particularly of agencies like the CIA and the FBI, brought important informal changes to the nation's unwritten constitution. As the Truman administration sought to contain communism and conduct a global foreign policy, older ideas about a constitutional structure of limited governmental powers gave way to the idea that broader executive authority was necessary to protect national security. During the 1960s, when Lyndon Johnson waged an undeclared war in Southeast Asia, and the 1970s, when Richard Nixon used claims of national security to cover up the illegal actions of his own administration, the implications of the broad executive power dating from the 1940s would become issues of controversy.

Domestic Policy: Truman's Fair Deal

Although the Truman administration placed its greatest priority on constructing a global policy of containment, it also reconstructed the domestic legacy of Franklin Roosevelt. Many supporters of FDR's New Deal still endorsed the "Second Bill of Rights" that FDR had proclaimed in his State of the Union address of 1944. According to this vision, all Americans had the "right" to a wide range of substantive liberties, including employment, food and shelter, education, and health care. Whenever people were unable to obtain these "rights," the national government was responsible for providing access to them. Such governmental largesse required constant economic and social planning—and government spending—for the general welfare.

In Europe, the idea of a "welfare state" that undertook economic planning in order to guarantee certain substantive rights won wide acceptance after the Second World War. However, talk about government planning and increased spending proved highly controversial in the United States. Even before the Second World War, the pace of domestic legislation in the United States had begun to slow, and throughout the war itself critics had assailed economic planning as meddlesome interference in private decision making. Government programs, Republicans charged, were an unconstitutional intrusion into people's private affairs and posed a threat to individual initiative and responsibility.

During Truman's presidency, opposition to dramatic innovations in social policymaking hardened. The National Association of Manufacturers (NAM) warned that new domestic programs would destroy the private, free enterprise system. Southern Democrats in Congress joined Republicans in blocking new programs that they feared might weaken white supremacy in their region. Even before Truman succeeded Roosevelt, these conservative forces had succeeded in abolishing several of the New Deal agencies that might have contributed to economic planning after the war and had flatly rejected FDR's Second Bill of Rights.

The Employment Act of 1946 and the Promise of Economic Growth

Faced with this kind of opposition to FDR's 1944 agenda, Truman needed to find a different approach to domestic policymaking. The 1946 debate over the Full Employment Bill helped identify one. The Full Employment Bill, as initially conceived, would have increased government spending and empowered Washington to intervene aggressively in the job market, so as to ensure employment for all citizens seeking work, a key goal of the Second Bill of Rights. To the bill's opponents, these provisions and the phrase "full employment" pointed toward something like the European welfare state, even socialism.

As the effort to enact this part of Roosevelt's Second Bill of Rights stalled, a scaled-down vision of domestic policymaking gradually emerged. The law that Congress finally passed, renamed the Employment Act of 1946, called for "maximum" (rather than for "full") employment and specifically acknowledged that private enterprise, not government, bore primary responsibility for economic decision making. The act, though it did not talk about full employment, nonetheless recognized that the national government would play an ongoing role in economic management. Rejecting the idea that economic involvement by Washington was automatically suspect, it created a new executive branch body, the Council of Economic Advisers, to help formulate long-range policy recommendations and signaled that government policymakers would assume some responsibility for the performance of the economy. How far that responsibility would extend remained to be determined.

A crucial factor in the gradual acceptance of Washington's new role was a growing faith that *advice* from economic experts, as an alternative to government *planning,* could help guarantee a constantly expanding economy. An influential group of theorists, many of them disciples of the British economist John Maynard Keynes, insisted that the United States no longer needed to endure the boom-and-bust cycles that had afflicted the nation during the 1920s and 1930s. Instead of leaving the economy to the uncoordinated decisions of private individuals and business firms, policymakers and citizens alike were urged to trust in the theoretical expertise of economists. Though these experts would not *impose* plans on their own, they would *advise* government and private business on the policies most likely to produce uninterrupted economic growth and an ever expanding array of consumer goods.

The promise of economic growth as a permanent condition of American life dazzled postwar business and government leaders. Corporate executives, many of whom had feared that the end of the war would intensify labor unrest and bring severe recession, viewed economic growth as a guarantee of social stability. Members of the Truman administration, seeking a domestic program that would not revive

Spreading the American Dream • A 1950 *Time* magazine cover depicts a world marketplace awash in consumer products from the United States. Note the relationship between the familiar Coca-Cola logo, in the background, and that of a consuming world in the foreground.

the political controversies of the 1930s, embraced the idea that the government should encourage economic growth not through centralized governmental planning but by updating, through measures such as the Employment Act of 1946, the cooperative relationship with both big business and organized labor that the Roosevelt administration had introduced during the Second World War.

In fact, Truman's closest advisers believed that such cooperation would actually make domestic policymaking easier. Economic growth would produce increased tax revenues and, in turn, give Washington the money to fund domestic programs. "With economic expansion, every problem is capable of solution," insisted George Soule, a celebrant of economic growth. Walter Heller, another leader of the postwar generation of economists, likened the promise of economic growth to finding both the rainbow and its proverbial pot of gold. Using the relatively new theory of a "gross national product" (or GNP), postwar experts could actually calculate the nation's growing economic bounty. Developed in 1939, the concept of GNP—defined as the total dollar value of all the goods and services produced in the nation during a given year—became the standard measure of economic health.

By the end of 1948 Truman and his advisers were preaching the gospel of economic growth. Indeed, that ideal fitted nicely with their foreign policy programs, such as the Marshall Plan, which were designed to create markets and investment

LOOK   JOHN DEMPSEY

"Merfson, I'm afraid I have some rather unpleasant news for you."

Automating the Workplace • The possibilities of replacing human labor with new technologies was no joke for industrial workers who faced the prospect that the job for which they had been trained would become a casualty of postwar automation.

opportunities overseas. Economic growth at home was linked to development in the world at large—and to the all-pervasive concern with national security.

Truman's Fair Deal

Convinced that constant economic growth was indeed possible, Truman unveiled, in his inaugural address of January 5, 1949, a domestic agenda he had briefly outlined during his 1948 presidential campaign. Truman's "Fair Deal" called for the extension of popular New Deal programs such as Social Security and minimum wage laws; enactment of long-stalled, Democratic-sponsored civil rights and national health care legislation; federal aid for education; and repeal of the Taft-Hartley Act of 1947. Charles Brannan, Truman's secretary of agriculture, proposed an ambitious new plan for supporting farm prices by means of additional governmental subsidies, and the president himself urged substantial spending on public housing projects.

The assumption on which Truman built his Fair Deal—namely, that domestic programs could be financed from economic growth—would dominate political discussions for years to come. Even most Democratic leaders refrained from the "tax the rich to aid the poor" rhetoric of the 1930s. Through the magic of constant economic growth, all Americans would enjoy progressively bigger pieces of an always expanding economic pie.

Two prominent government programs, both of which predated Truman's administration, suggested the approach to domestic policymaking that dominated the Fair Deal years. The first, the so-called GI Bill (officially entitled the Serviceman's Readjustment Act of 1944), had always enjoyed strong support in Congress. After previous wars, including the First World War, Congress had simply voted veterans cash pensions or bonuses. But, this time, Congress worked out a comprehensive program of benefits for the several million men and the 40,000 women who had served in the armed forces. The GI Bill, as it evolved with the endorsement of the Veterans Administration, encompassed several different programs, including immediate financial assistance for college and job-training programs for veterans of the Second World War. By 1947, the year of peak enrollment by former GIs, about half of the entire college and university population was receiving government assistance. In other provisions of the bill, veterans received preferential treatment when applying for government jobs; generous terms on loans when purchasing homes or businesses; and, eventually, comprehensive medical care in veterans' hospitals. The Veterans' Readjustment Assistance Act of 1952, popularly known as the "GI Bill of Rights," extended these programs to veterans of the Korean War. In essence, then, although the Truman administration did not enact FDR's Second Bill of Rights in its entirety, the Fair Deal did grant many of its social and economic protections to veterans.

Meanwhile, Social Security, the most popular part of Roosevelt's New Deal, expanded under Truman's Fair Deal. Fighting a rearguard attack by conservatives, the Social Security Administration defended its program, which also included support for the disabled and the blind, as a system that simply provided "income security" that older people had themselves earned through years of work and monetary contributions that had been withheld from their paychecks.

Returning Veterans Crowd College Classrooms • Taking advantage of the educational opportunities offered by the Servicemen's Readjustment Act (GI Bill) of 1944, approximately 8 million veterans studied at trade schools, technical institutes, and universities during the postwar period.

Under the Social Security Act of 1950 the level of benefits was increased significantly; the retirement portions of the program were expanded; and coverage was extended to more than 10 million people, including agricultural workers. As subsequent difficulties with the Social Security system would highlight, however, expansion of the program was not accompanied by any new plans for financing the system—a decision that reflected the postwar faith in the ability of steady economic growth to underwrite the cost of domestic programs.

The more expansive (and expensive) Fair Deal proposals either failed or were scaled back. For instance, Truman's plan for a comprehensive national health insurance program ran into opposition from conservatives in Congress and the powerful medical lobby. The American Medical Association (AMA) and the American Hospital Association (AHA) blocked any government intervention in the traditional fee-for-service medical system and steered Congress toward a less controversial alternative—federal financing of new hospitals under the Hill-Burton Act. Meanwhile, opinion polls suggested that most voters, many of whom were enrolling in private health insurance plans such as Blue Cross and Blue Shield, were simply apathetic, or confused, about Truman's national health proposals.

Because of the continued shortage of affordable housing in urban areas, polls showed greater support for home-building programs, another part of Truman's Fair Deal. Private construction firms and realtors welcomed extension of federal home loan guarantees, such as those established under the GI Bill and through the Federal Housing Administration, but they lobbied Congress against Truman's call for the construction of publicly financed housing projects. Yet even conservatives such as Senator Taft recognized the housing shortage and supported the Housing Act of 1949. This law promised "a decent home and a suitable living environment for every American family"; authorized construction of 810,000 public housing units (cutting back Truman's goal of 1.05 million); and, most important in the long run, provided federal funds for "urban renewal" zones, areas to be cleared of run-down dwellings and built up again with new construction. The Housing Act of 1949 set forth relatively bold goals but provided only modest funding for its public housing program.

Domestic policymaking during the Truman era, then, ultimately focused on specific groups, such as veterans of the Second World War and older Americans, rather than on more extensive programs for all, such as a national health care plan and a large-scale commitment to government-built, affordable housing projects. Opponents of economic planning and greater spending by government considered the broader proposals of the Fair Deal, especially comprehensive medical care and substantial spending for public housing, to be "welfare," and the Truman administration found it easier to defend more narrowly targeted programs, such as the GI Bill and Social Security, which could be hailed as economic "security" measures for specific groups. This approach to social policymaking under the Fair Deal significantly narrowed the approach of Roosevelt's Second Bill of Rights, which had envisioned a broad program of constitutionally guaranteed entitlements for all citizens.

Civil Rights

Truman, while modifying the New Deal's domestic policy assumptions, actually broadened its commitment to civil rights. In fact, he supported the fight against racial discrimination more strongly than any previous president, including FDR himself.

Truman had made a special appeal to African American voters during his 1948 presidential campaign. He had strongly endorsed proposals that had been advanced by a civil rights committee he established in 1946. The committee's report, entitled "To Secure These Rights," called for federal legislation against lynching; a special civil rights division within the Department of Justice; antidiscrimination initiatives in employment, housing, and public facilities; and desegregation of the military. Although these proposals prompted many white southern Democrats to bolt to the short-lived Dixiecrat Party in the 1948 election, they won Truman significant support from African Americans.

The Dixiecrat Party episode of 1948, a reaction to Truman's stance on civil rights, portended significant political change among southern whites who had voted overwhelmingly Democratic since the late 19th century. Strom Thurmond, the Dixiecrats' presidential candidate, denounced Truman for offering a "civil wrongs" program. Although Thurmond insisted that southern Democrats did not oppose all civil rights measures, he also argued that the Constitution required this kind of legislation to come from state governments and not from Washington. Moreover, white southern Democrats such as Thurmond pledged to fight any effort to end the pattern of racial segregation that had been part of southern social life for decades. Thurmond carried only four states in 1948, but his candidacy showed that, because of the issue of race, lifelong southern Democrats were willing to desert the party in national presidential elections.

Despite discord within his own party, Truman generally supported the efforts of the civil rights movement. When successive Congresses failed to enact any civil rights legislation—including an antilynching law and a ban on the poll taxes that prevented most southern blacks from voting—the movement turned to a sympathetic White House and to the federal courts. After A. Philip Randolph threatened to organize protests against continued segregation in the military, Truman issued an executive order calling for desegregation of the armed forces, a move that began to be implemented during the Korean War. Truman also endorsed the efforts of the Fair Employment Practices Commission (FEPC) to end racial discrimination in federal hiring, although many activists charged that the FEPC's actions too often failed to go far enough.

Meanwhile, Truman's Justice Department regularly appeared in court on behalf of litigants who were contesting government-backed segregation of public schools and "restrictive covenants" (legal agreements that prevented racial or religious minorities from acquiring real estate). In 1946, the Supreme Court declared restrictive covenants illegal and began chipping away at the "separate but equal" principle that had been used since *Plessy* v. *Ferguson* (1898) to justify segregated schools. In 1950,

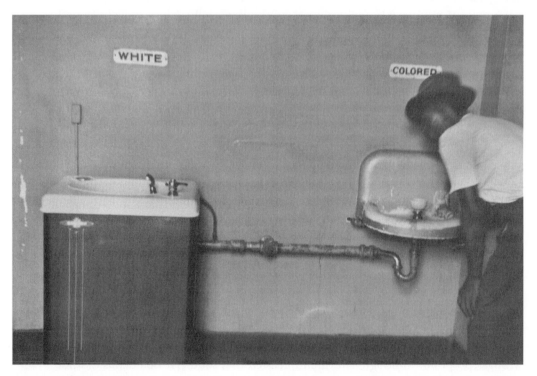

Separate and Equal? • Racial segregation of public facilities, including drinking fountains, remained the law throughout the South in the early 1950s. However, the separate facilities were rarely, if ever, equal. As part of the civil rights revolution of the late 1950s and 1960s, the Supreme Court would later rule that separate accommodations could never be equal because the core purpose of racial segregation was to label people of African descent as inferior to those of European ancestry.

the Court ruled that under the Fourteenth Amendment racial segregation in state-financed graduate and law schools was unconstitutional. In light of these decisions, all the traditional legal arguments that had been used since *Plessy* to legitimize racial segregation in all public schools seemed open to successful challenge—which would finally come in 1954 (see Chapter 9).

In summary, the years immediately after the Second World War marked a turning point in domestic policymaking. The New Deal's hope for comprehensive socioeconomic planning gave way to a view of social policy based on the assumption that, in contrast to the first half of the 20th century, the nation could expect uninterrupted economic growth. Henceforth, Washington could reap, through taxation, its own steady share of a growing economy, so the government could still finance a set of targeted programs to assist specific groups, such as military veterans and older people. As one supporter of this new approach argued, postwar policymakers were sophisticated enough to embrace "partial remedies," such as the GI Bill, rather than to wait for fanciful "cure-alls," such as FDR's Second Bill of Rights.

Social Change and Containment

The postwar years brought dramatic changes in the daily life of most Americans. Encouraged by the advertising industry, most people seemed, at one level, to believe that virtually any kind of change automatically meant "progress." (Hard-core southern segregationists, who were fighting against any change in their region's system of institutionalized racism, were an obvious exception.) And yet, at another level, the pace and scope of social change during these years brought a feeling of uneasiness into American life, prompting many people to try to contain the impact of new developments. Containment abroad sometimes paralleled a similar stance toward containing social innovation at home.

Jackie Robinson and the Baseball "Color Line"

The integration of organized baseball during the 1940s and 1950s powerfully symbolized the complex interplay between the celebration—and the containment—of change in the postwar United States. In 1947, major league baseball's policy of racial segregation finally changed when Jackie Robinson, who had played in the Negro National League, became the Brooklyn Dodgers' first baseman. A number of players, including several on Robinson's own club, had talked about boycotting any game in which Robinson appeared. Baseball's leadership, which recognized the need for new sources of players and the steady stream of African American fans coming out to the parks, crushed the opposition by threatening to suspend any player who refused to play with Robinson. (Baseball's moguls, though, did relatively little to protect Robinson himself; he was ordered to endure, without protest, racist insults, flying spikes, and brush-back pitches during his rookie season.)

The pressure to integrate the national pastime became inexorable. Several months after Robinson's debut, the Cleveland Indians signed center fielder Larry Doby, and a number of other African American stars quickly left the Negro leagues for the American and National circuits. Eventually, the talent of Robinson—named Rookie

The National Pastime Integrates, 1947 • Jackie Robinson, a star athlete at UCLA and a veteran of the Second World War, became the first African American to play Major League Baseball since the 19th century. Although Robinson faced considerable racist hostility when his team played on the road, most fans of the Brooklyn Dodgers welcomed their team's newest star.

of the Year in 1947 and the National League's Most Valuable Player in 1949—and of the other African American players carried the day. By 1960 every major league team fielded black players, and some had begun extensive recruiting in Puerto Rico and in the nations of the Caribbean. In 1997, the 50th anniversary of Robinson's debut, Major League Baseball staged elaborate memorial ceremonies for Robinson—and congratulated the sport for having led the fight against racial prejudice during the Cold War years.

Yet, during the late 1940s and early 1950s, baseball's leaders had worked to contain the participation of African Americans. Several teams, most notably the New York Yankees and the Boston Red Sox, waited for years before fielding any black players, claiming they could find no talented prospects. More commonly, teams restricted the number of nonwhite players they would take on and kept their managers, coaches, and front-office personnel solidly white. Even Jackie Robinson, a successful entrepreneur outside of baseball, never received an offer to return to the game in a management capacity after he retired as a player.

The Postwar Suburbs

Suburbia was another place where the celebration of change and efforts to contain its effects were both constant themes. Suburban living had long been a feature of the "American dream." The new Long Island, New York, suburb of Levittown, which welcomed its first residents in October 1947, seemed to make that dream a reality, at affordable prices, for middle-income families.

Nearly everything about Levittown seemed unprecedented. A construction company that had mass-produced military barracks during the Second World War, Levitt & Sons could complete a five-room bungalow every 15 minutes. Architectural critics sneered at these "little boxes," but potential buyers stood in long lines hoping to get one. By 1950, Levittown consisted of more than 10,000 homes and 40,000 residents. By then, bulldozers and construction crews were sweeping into other suburban developments across the country. One-quarter of all the houses that existed in 1960 had been built after 1949.

To keep up with the mass-production capabilities of builders, the lending industry streamlined its operations and called on government assistance. No longer were home loans simply a transaction between individual buyers and separate lending institutions. To help buyers purchase their first home, the government offered an extensive set of programs. The Federal Housing Administration (FHA), which had been established during the New Deal, helped private lenders extend credit to mass-production builders, who could then sell the houses they built on generous financing terms. Typically, people who bought FHA-financed homes needed only 5 percent of the purchase price as a down payment; they could then finance the rest with a long-term, government-insured mortgage. Millions of war veterans enjoyed even more favorable terms under the GI loan program operated by the Veterans Administration.

These government programs made it cheaper to buy a new house in the average suburb than to rent a comfortable apartment in most cities. Moreover, families could deduct from their federal income tax the interest they paid on their mortgages. This deduction was a disguised form of governmental subsidy for the building and lending industries and for homeowners. And, because construction never caught up with demand during the 1950s, many suburbanites could sell their first house at a profit and move up to a more spacious, more expensive dwelling.

Suburban homes promised greater privacy and more amenities than crowded city neighborhoods. Builders, quick to recognize the appeal of the new suburbs, soon began to offer larger houses, including the sprawling, one-level "ranch style" model. The joys of "easy and better" living often came with the house. Levitt homes, for example, contained an automatic washer and a built-in television set. By being attached to the house itself, even the TV qualified as a "structural" component and could be financed under federally guaranteed loan programs.

Suburbs enjoyed the reputation for being ideal places in which to raise children, and families were having babies in much larger numbers. After the war, a complex set of factors, including early marriages and rising incomes, helped produce a "baby boom" that would last well into the next decade. With houses generally occupying only about 15 percent of suburban lots, large lawns served as private playgrounds. Nearby schools were as new as the rest of the neighborhood, and suburban school boards used the lure of modern, well-equipped buildings to attract both skilled teachers and middle-income families.

In many respects, the new suburban lifestyle epitomized an optimistic spirit of new possibilities, confidence in the future, and acceptance of change. In other respects, though, it represented an effort to contain some of the effects of rapid change by creating a material and psychological refuge.

Most obviously, buying a new suburban home seemed a way of cushioning the impact of social and demographic changes. With African American families leaving the rural South in search of work in northern cities, "white flight" to suburbia quickened. Although Jackie Robinson, Larry Doby, and other talented athletes could find a place in professional baseball during the 1940s, not a single black person could find a home in Long Island's Levittown until well into the 1960s.

Segregation in postwar housing was not simply the result of individual choice. Government and private housing policies helped to structure and maintain the segregationist pattern of white suburbs and increasingly nonwhite urban neighborhoods. Federal laws allowed local groups to veto public housing projects in their communities. Although land and building costs would have been cheaper in the suburbs, public housing projects were concentrated on relatively expensive, high-density urban sites. More important, the lending industry channeled government loan guarantees away from most urban neighborhoods, and private lenders generally denied credit to nonwhites seeking new suburban housing.

The Baby Boom

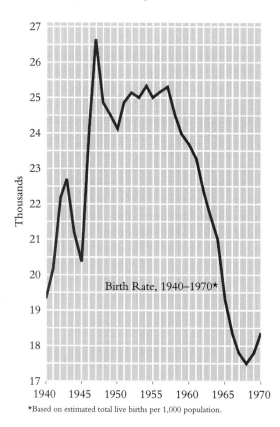

Birth Rate, 1940–1970★

★Based on estimated total live births per 1,000 population.

No one in the postwar housing industry admitted intentional complicity in these discriminatory patterns. William Levitt might identify his private housing projects with the public crusade against communism. "No man who owns his house and lot can be a Communist," he remarked in 1948. "He has too much to do." Levitt held himself blameless, however, for racial issues. He could help solve the nation's housing problem—and perhaps even the problem of domestic communism—but he deceptively claimed that his "private" construction had nothing to do with the public issue of race.

Similarly, the architects of suburbia saw nothing problematic with postwar gender patterns. William Levitt's confident identification of home ownership with men unconsciously reflected the fact that the lending industry made loan guarantees available only to men. Single women simply could not obtain FHA-backed loans, a policy that the agency justified on the grounds that men were the family breadwinners and that women rarely made enough money to qualify as good credit risks. As a result, home ownership in the new suburbs was invariably limited to white males, with wives as co-owners at best.

The Suburban Family and Gender Issues

Many suburban wives found their lives contained within the confines of their neighborhoods. Because the new suburbs generally lacked mass transit facilities, life revolved around the automobile. But if the male breadwinner needed the "family" car to commute to work, the wife spent the day at home. Until car ownership expanded in the mid-1950s, even a trip to the supermarket could prove difficult.

Still, wives and mothers found plenty of work at home. New appliances and conveniences—automatic clothes washers, more powerful vacuum cleaners, frozen foods, and home freezers—eased old burdens but created new ones. Contrary to what the ads promised, women were actually spending as much time on housework after the war as their grandmothers had spent at the turn of the century. The time spent on domestic tasks was reallocated but not reduced. Moreover, because child care facilities were not generally available in the new suburbs, mothers spent a great deal of time taking care of their children. In contrast to the urban neighborhoods or rural communities where many suburban housewives had grown up, the postwar Levittowns contained few older relatives or younger single women who could help with household and child care duties.

Daily life in the suburbs fell into a fairly rigid pattern of "separate spheres"—a public sphere of work and politics dominated by men and a private sphere of housework and child care reserved for women. Because few jobs of any kind initially were available in postwar suburbia, the distance between home and the workplace became greater for suburban men, and women who wanted to work found nearby job opportunities about as scarce as child care facilities.

Without mothers and grandmothers living close by, suburban mothers increasingly turned to child care manuals for advice. Dr. Benjamin Spock's *Baby and Child Care*, first published in 1946, sold millions of copies. Like earlier manuals, Spock's book assigned virtually all child care duties to women and underscored the importance of their nurturing role by stressing the need constantly to oversee a child's psychological growth. The future of the family and the nation itself, Spock implied, depended on the skill with which mothers handled the daily traumas of childhood.

Other manuals picked up where Dr. Spock left off and counseled mothers on the care and feeding of teenagers. The alarmist tone of many of these books reflected—and also helped to generate—widespread concern over "juvenile delinquency." The crusade against an alleged increase in juvenile crime, a nonphenomenon that subsequent evaluations of criminal justice statistics debunked, soon attracted the attention of government officials. J. Edgar Hoover, director of the FBI, and Attorney General Tom Clark coupled their pleas for containing communism with pleas for containing juvenile delinquency. In a 1953 report, Hoover claimed that the first of the war babies were about to enter their teenage years, "the period in which some of them will inevitably incline toward juvenile delinquency and, later, full-fledged criminal careers."

How could this threat be contained? Many authorities suggested cures that focused on the individual family. Delinquents, according to one study in the early 1950s, sprang from a "family atmosphere not conducive to development of emotionally well-integrated, happy youngsters, conditioned to obey legitimate authority."

So it was up to parents, especially mothers, to raise good kids. The ideal mother, according to most advice manuals, did not work outside the home but devoted herself to rearing her own segment of the baby boom generation. Women who sought careers outside the home risked being labeled, by amateur and professional psychologists alike, as lost, maladjusted, guilt-ridden, man-hating, or all of the above.

Versions of this message appeared elsewhere. Even the nation's prestigious women's colleges offered instruction that was assumed to lead to marriage, not to work or careers. In his 1955 commencement address at Smith, a women's college, Adlai Stevenson, the Democratic Party's urbane presidential candidate in 1952 and 1956, told the graduates that it was the duty of each to keep her husband "truly purposeful, to keep him whole." Postwar magazines, psychology, and popular culture were filled with concerns about the reintegration and stability of returned war veterans. Understanding, supportive wives and mothers seemed the antidote to social turmoil.

Discussions about the ideal postwar family did not always offer such a one-dimensional view of gender relationships. When interviewed by researchers, most men reported they did not want a "submissive, stay-at-home" wife. Even popular TV shows, such as *Father Knows Best* or *Leave It to Beaver,* suggested a hope that middle-class fathers would follow the lead of Jim Anderson and Ward Cleaver and become more involved in family life than their own fathers had been. And although experts on domestic harmony still envisioned suburban men earning their family's entire income, they also urged them to be "real fathers" at home. A 1947 article in *Parent's Magazine* declared that being a father was "the most important occupation in the world and for the world." Literature on parenting emphasized "family togetherness," and institutions like the YMCA began to offer courses on how to achieve it.

Calls for family togetherness responded, in one sense, to the belief that the problem of juvenile delinquency demanded that fathers work harder to achieve family harmony. In the movie *Rebel without a Cause* (1955), two teenagers begin to go astray, one because her father is unreasonably strict and the other because his father has left child-rearing entirely to his wife. This film, an otherwise bleak tale of

The Dating Game of the 1950s • A variety of new publications sought to prepare young men and women for stable marriages by encouraging the practice of "going steady." Notice the gender politics that are suggested in this cover from *Seventeen*, one of the first youth-oriented magazines of the Cold War era.

generational conflict, comes to a happy ending when the passive, ineffectual father suddenly promises his son "to be the kind of father that you can be proud of."

In another sense, the call for family togetherness was a reaction against what some cultural historians have seen as an incipient "male revolt" against "family values." Hugh Hefner's *Playboy* magazine, which first appeared in 1953, preached that men who neglected their own happiness in order to support a wife and children were not saints but suckers. In *Playboy*'s very first issue, Hefner proclaimed: "We aren't a 'family magazine.'" He told women to pass *Playboy* "along to the man in your life and get back to your *Ladies Home Companion*." In Hefner's version of the good life, the man rented a "pad" rather than owned a home; drove a sports car rather than a sedan or a station wagon; and courted the Playmate of the Month rather than the Mother of the Year.

Women's Changing Roles

Despite all of the media images that depicted the "average woman" as a homebound wife and mother, economic realities were propelling more and more women, suburban and nonsuburban, into the job market. Although female employment declined just after the war, it rose steadily during the late 1940s and throughout the 1950s. Moreover, increasing numbers of married women, white as well as nonwhite, were entering the labor force, many of them as part-time workers in the expanding clerical and service sectors. In 1948, about 25 percent of married mothers had jobs outside the home; at the end of the 1950s, nearly 40 percent did.

If more women were holding jobs outside their homes, their employment opportunities nevertheless remained largely contained within well-defined, sex-segregated areas. In 1950, for example, more than 90 percent of all nurses, telephone operators, secretaries, and elementary school teachers were women. Historically, pay scales in these "service" jobs were lower, labor unions were not as active, and chances for advancement were more limited than in male-dominated occupations. As low-paid jobs for women expanded, professional opportunities actually narrowed. Medical and law schools and many professional societies admitted few, if any, women; the number of women on college faculties shrank back even from the low levels of the 1920s and 1930s. Although the notion of the "family wage" was still invoked in order to excuse the disparity of pay and opportunity based on gender, more and more women were trying to support a family on their paychecks.

This was especially true for women of color; by 1960 slightly more than 20 percent of black families were headed by women. Recognizing that stereotypical images of domesticity hardly fit the experience of African American women, a large percentage of whom had always worked outside the home, *Ebony* magazine celebrated women who were able to combine success in parenting and in work. One story, for example, highlighted the only female African American mechanic at American Airlines; many others featured prominent educators and entertainers.

Postwar magazines targeted to white women also carried somewhat ambiguous messages about domesticity. Although pursuing activities outside the home was stigmatized by some social commentators as "unnatural," magazines that depended on a broad, popular readership generally gave more positive portrayals of women who were participating in public life, whether in politics or in the job market. Women's magazines, while being deferential to the dominant ideal of domesticity, still published articles that sensitively chronicled the difficulties of running a home and raising children and often ran stories on prominent career women. The immediate postwar era, in short, was a time of growing diversity in both the roles that women were assuming and the ways in which women were represented in mass culture.

The great fear of communism during the years from 1947 to 1954 accentuated pressures for conformity and often made it difficult to advocate significant social change. Yet, despite efforts to "contain" change at home, demographic shifts, new expectations stemming from the war, and robust prosperity inevitably transformed many social and cultural patterns. The everyday lives of Americans—racial patterns, child-rearing practices, living arrangements, and gender relationships—were inexorably changing.

From Truman to Eisenhower

Emphasis on anticommunism and containment continued into the presidency of Republican Dwight D. Eisenhower. The election of 1952 saw personnel changes in

Washington, but it marked few fundamental shifts in either foreign or domestic policies. Containing communism overseas and at home continued to be central issues, especially during the first two years of the Eisenhower presidency.

The Election of 1952

By 1952, Harry Truman and the Democrats were on the defensive. Denunciations of the communist threat remained the order of the day, for Democrats as well as for Truman's Republican critics. Adlai Stevenson of Illinois, the Democratic presidential candidate, denounced Joseph McCarthy but used McCarthy-like rhetoric in his own anticommunist pronouncements: "Soviet secret agents and their dupes" had "burrowed like moles" into governments throughout the world. "We cannot let our guard drop for even a moment." Stevenson approved of the prosecution of the Communist Party's leaders and the dismissal of schoolteachers who were party members.

But a strong anticommunist stance was not enough to save Stevenson or the Democratic Party in 1952. The GOP's vice presidential candidate, Senator Richard Nixon, called Stevenson "Adlai the appeaser" and claimed he held a Ph.D. from "Dean Acheson's Cowardly College of Communist Containment." Democrats faced criticism over Truman's handling of the Korean War and over revelations about favoritism and kickbacks on government contracts. Although these transgressions were minor when compared to the scandals of Warren Harding's administration in the 1920s (see Chapter 5), the Republicans used them effectively. Their successful election formula could be reduced to a simple equation, "K^1C^2": "Korea, corruption, and communism."

The Republicans turned for a presidential candidate to the hero of the Second World War, Dwight David Eisenhower, who was popularly known as "Ike." Eisenhower had neither sought elective office nor even been identified with a political party before 1952, but nearly a half-century of military service had made him a skilled politician. The last president to have been born in the 19th century, Ike grew up in Kansas; won an appointment to, and graduated from, West Point; rose through the Army ranks under the patronage of General George Marshall; directed the Normandy invasion of 1944 as Supreme Allied Commander; served as Army Chief of Staff from 1945 to 1948; and, after an interim period as president of Columbia University, returned to active duty as the commander of NATO, a post he held until May 1952.

Eisenhower seemed an attractive candidate. Although his partisan affiliations were vague—at one point, dissident Democrats had even hoped to persuade him to challenge Truman for their party's 1948 presidential nomination—Eisenhower finally declared himself a Republican. Initially reluctant to seek the presidency, he became convinced that Robert Taft, his main GOP rival, leaned too far to the right on domestic issues and, as a former isolationist, might abandon Truman's aggressive containment policies. Perceived as a middle-of-the-roader, Ike seemed able to lead the nation through a Cold War as firmly as he had during a hot one. Adlai Stevenson grumbled that the nation's press had embraced the old war hero even before knowing "what his party platform would be" or "what would be the issues of the campaign."

"I Like Ike!" • As Harry Truman's embattled presidency limped to a close, the nation warmly embraced his already popular successor, General Dwight David Eisenhower. While campaigning for the White House in 1952, Ike attracted large, enthusiastic crowds, including this one greeting his motorcade in southern California.

Ike achieved a great personal victory in the 1952 election. The Eisenhower-Nixon ticket received almost 7 million more popular votes than the Democrats and won in the Electoral College by a margin of 442 to 89. The Republican Party itself made less spectacular gains. The GOP gained only a one-vote majority in the Senate and an eight-vote majority in the House of Representatives. The electoral coalition Franklin Roosevelt had put together during the 1930s still survived, even though it showed signs of fraying, especially in the South. There, many of the white southern votes that had gone to the Dixiecrats in 1948 began swinging over to the Republicans, and Eisenhower carried four states in the Democratic Party's once "solid South."

Eisenhower Takes Command

Eisenhower's "moderate Republicanism" initially brought few fundamental changes in either foreign or domestic policies. Eisenhower honored his campaign pledge to travel to Korea as a means of bringing an end to U.S. military involvement there. However, armistice talks stalled when an impasse developed over whether North Korean and Chinese prisoners of war who had asked to remain in the South should be forcibly returned to North Korea and China. Hoping to end the diplomatic stalemate, Eisenhower began to threaten, in vague messages that quickly reached China and North Korea, the use of nuclear weapons if negotiations failed. Talks resumed, and on July 27, 1953, both sides signed a truce that established a special commission of neutral nations to rule on the POW cases. (The POWs themselves were subsequently allowed to determine whether they wished to be repatriated.) So finally ended the fighting in which more than 2 million Asians, mostly noncombatants, and

33,000 Americans had died. A formal peace treaty remained unsigned, however, and the 38th parallel remained one of the most heavily armed borders in the world. Not until 1997 did North Korea reluctantly agree to resume the treaty talks that had stalemated nearly 45 years earlier.

In both foreign and domestic policy, Eisenhower stood near the center—a stance that enabled him to imply that both those Republicans to his right and the Democrats to his left were straying from the political mainstream. This strategy not only helped Eisenhower pursue his foreign policies but eventually allowed him to wrest control of the issue of national security at home from Senator McCarthy and the other extreme anticommunists in Congress. The Republican-controlled Congress did go beyond the desires of the Eisenhower administration and pass the Communist Control Act of 1954, which barred the Communist Party from entering candidates in elections and extended the registration requirements established by the McCarran Act of 1950. But with a Republican administration now in charge of surveillance at home and covert operations abroad, many members of the GOP began to see McCarthy more as a liability than an asset.

McCarthy finally careened out of control when he claimed that the U.S. Army was harboring subversives within its ranks. During the spring of 1954, a televised Senate committee investigation into McCarthy's fantastic claim finally brought him down. Under the glare of TV lights during the Army-McCarthy hearings, the senator appeared as a crude, desperate bully who was flinging slanders in every direction. In December 1954 a majority of McCarthy's colleagues, including some who had once shielded him, voted to censure him for conduct "unbecoming" a member of the Senate. McCarthy faded from the limelight and died in obscurity in 1957, still a member of the Senate.

With McCarthyism discredited, Eisenhower could proceed with the expansion of the national security state that he had been quietly nurturing. Following the excesses of McCarthyism, Ike's low-key approach seemed eminently reasonable. Indeed, the demonstrated unreliability of Congress's anticommunist zealots strengthened Eisenhower's own position when he claimed the constitutional privilege to withhold from Congress secret information on national security matters. Relatively free from congressional oversight, the Eisenhower administration quietly proceeded to extend Truman's earlier programs of domestic surveillance, wiretapping, and covert action overseas.

Many historians now see Eisenhower as a skilled leader who increased the power of the executive branch while seeming to do the opposite. This revisionist view contrasts with the grandfatherly, slightly befuddled image that Eisenhower himself developed during the 1950s. According to one scholar, the crafty Eisenhower conducted a "hidden hand presidency." Mindful of how the mercurial Truman had become personally linked to unpopular policies, Ike tried to stay in the background and to project an air of calm steadiness. On matters of foreign policy, he usually had John Foster Dulles take center stage; on domestic issues, he let people assume that White House policies were being shaped by George Humphrey, his secretary of the treasury, and by Sherman Adams, his chief of staff.

Eisenhower's presidency helped to lower the pitch of the shrill anticommunist crusade that characterized American domestic and international policy from 1946 to 1954. With Eisenhower's presidency symbolizing tranquillity, a new sense of calm was settling over life in the United States in the middle 1950s—or so it seemed on the surface.

Conclusion

Efforts at "containing" communism dominated both domestic and foreign policy during the years after the Second World War. As worsening relations between the United States and the Soviet Union reached the stage of a Cold War, the Truman administration pursued policies that expanded the power of the government, particularly the executive branch, to counter the threat. The militarization of foreign policy intensified when the United States went to war in Korea in 1950. At home, anticommunism focused on containing the activities and ideas of alleged subversives. These initiatives raised difficult issues about how to protect the liberty of those who were suspected of being subversives or of simply being insufficiently zealous anticommunists.

Within this Cold War climate, struggles to achieve greater equality still emerged. Truman's Fair Deal promised that new economic wisdom would be able to guarantee economic growth and thereby provide the tax revenue to expand domestic programs. Truman himself pressed, more strongly than any previous president, for national measures to end racial discrimination.

The election of a Republican president, Dwight D. Eisenhower, in 1952 brought few immediate changes in the Cold War climate. A moderate on most issues and a skillful political strategist, Eisenhower projected the image of an elder statesperson who kept above day-to-day partisan battles. In time, his style of presidential leadership helped to lower the shrillness of anticommunist rhetoric and to offer the prospect of calmer times.

Chronology

1946 Baruch plan for atomic energy proposed • Employment Act passed • Republicans gain control of Congress in November elections

1947 Truman Doctrine announced • HUAC begins hearings on communist infiltration of Hollywood • George Kennan's "Mr. X" article published • National Security Act passed (CIA and NSC established) • Marshall Plan adopted • Truman's loyalty order announced • Taft-Hartley Act passed over Truman's veto • Jackie Robinson and Larry Doby break Major League Baseball's color line

1948 Berlin Airlift begins • Truman wins reelection • The *Kinsey Report* and Dr. Benjamin Spock's *Baby and Child Care* published

1949 NATO established • "Fall" of China to communism occurs • NSC-68 drafted • Soviet Union explodes atomic device • Truman outlines his Fair Deal

1950 Korean War begins • Senator Joseph McCarthy charges communist infiltration of State Department • McCarran Internal Security Act passed

1951 Truman removes General MacArthur as commander in Korea

1952 GI Bill of Rights passed • Dwight Eisenhower elected president

1953 Korean War ends • Julius and Ethel Rosenberg executed • *Playboy* magazine debuts

1954 Joseph McCarthy censured by U.S. Senate • Communist Control Act passed

Suggested Readings

U.S. Foreign Policy and the Origins of the Cold War

For overviews of U.S. foreign policy and the origins of the Cold War, see Thomas G. Paterson, *Meeting the Communist Threat: Truman to Reagan* (1988); Thomas J. McCormick, *America's Half-Century: United States Foreign Policy in the Cold War and After* (2nd ed., 1995); Warren I. Cohen, *America in the Age of Soviet Power* (1993); Fraser J. Harbutt, *The Iron Curtain: Churchill, America, and the Origins of the Cold War* (1986); John Lewis Gaddis, *Strategies of Containment: A Critical Appraisal of Postwar American National Security Policy* (1982), his *The Long Peace: Inquiries into the History of the Cold War* (1987); and his *We Now Know: Rethinking Cold War History* (1997); Thomas G. Paterson, *On Every Front: The Making and Unmaking of the Cold War* (rev. ed., 1992); Walter LaFeber, *America, Russia, and the Cold War, 1945–1992* (7th ed., 1993); Stephen Ambrose, *Rise to Globalism: American Foreign Policy Since 1938* (8th ed., 1997); H. W. Brands, *The Devil We Knew: Americans and the Cold War* (1993); Melvin Leffler, *The Specter of Communism* (1994); Deborah Welch Larson, *Anatomy of Mistrust: U.S.-Soviet Relations during the Cold War* (1997); and Ronald E. Powaksi, *The Cold War: The United States and the Soviet Union, 1917–1991* (1998).

Specific Issues and Incidents of the Cold War Era

For the history of specific issues and incidents of the Cold War era, see Gregg Herken, *The Winning Weapon: The Atomic Bomb in the Cold War, 1945–1950* (1980); Walter Hixson, *George F. Kennan: Cold War Iconoclast* (1989); Bruce R. Kuniholm, *The Origins of the Cold War in the Near East: Great Power Conflict and Diplomacy in Iran, Turkey, and Greece* (1980); Michael Schaller, *The American Occupation of Japan: The Origins of the Cold War in Asia* (1985); Frank Ninkovich, *Germany and the United States: The Transformation of the German Question since 1945* (1988); Robert A. Pollard, *Economic Security and the Origins of the Cold War, 1945–1950* (1985); Michael J. Hogan, *The Marshall Plan: America, Britain, and the Reconstruction of Western Europe, 1949–52* (1987); Louis Liebovich, *The Press and the Origins of the Cold War, 1944–1947* (1988); Howard Jones, *"A New Kind of War:" America's Global Strategy and the Truman Doctrine in Greece* (1989); Sallie Pisani, *The CIA and the Marshall Plan* (1991); Lawrence S. Wittner, *One World or None: A History of the World Nuclear Disarmament Movement through 1953* (1993); Steven Hugh Lee, *Outposts of Empire: Korea, Vietnam, and the Origins of the Cold War in Asia, 1949–84* (1995); Robert Accinelli, *Crisis and Commitment: United States Policy toward Taiwan, 1950–55* (1996); Michael L. Krenn, *The Chains of Interdependence: U.S. Policy toward Central America, 1945–1954* (1996); Richard Rhodes, *Dark Sun: The Making of the Hydrogen Bomb* (1995); and Justus D. Doenecke, *Not to the Swift: The Old Isolationists in the Cold War Era* (1979). A superb political history of the early Cold War years is James T. Patterson, *Grand Expectations: The United States, 1945–74* (1996).

National Security Policy

On national security policy during the late 1940s and early 1950s consult Daniel Yergin, *Shattered Peace: The Origins of the Cold War and the National Security State* (1977); Melvyn Leffler, *A Preponderance of Power: National Security, the Truman Administration, and the Cold War* (1992); and Michael S. Sherry, *In the Shadow of War: The United States Since the 1930s* (1995). See also Walter Isaacson and Evan Thomas, *The Wise Men: Six Friends and the World They Made: Acheson, Bohlen, Harriman, Kennan, Lovett, McCloy* (1986), and Evan Thomas, *The Very Best Men: Four Who Dared; The Early Years of the CIA* (1995).

Cultural Interpretations of National Security Policies

For cultural interpretations of national security policies see the relevant chapters of Richard Slotkin, *Gunfighter Nation: The Myth of the Frontier in Twentieth-Century America* (1992) and Robert J. Corber, *In the Name of National Security: Hitchcock, Homophobia, and the Political Construction of Gender in Postwar America* (1993). For broader views of the cultural climate of the early Cold War see Lary May, ed., *Recasting America: Culture and Politics in the Age of the Cold War* (1989); Stephen J. Whitfield, *The Culture of the Cold War* (2nd ed., 1996); William Graebner, *The Age of Doubt: American Thought and Culture in the 1940s* (1991); Paul Boyer, *By the Bomb's Early Light* (1985); Tom Englehardt, *The End of Victory Culture: Cold War America and the Disillusioning of a Generation* (1994); Guy Oakes, *The Imaginary War: Civil Defense and American Cold War Culture* (1994); Mark Jancovich, *Rational Fears: American Horror in the 1950s* (1996); Alan Nadel, *Containment Culture: American Narrative, Postmodernism, and the Atomic Age* (1995); and Margot A. Henriksen, *Dr. Strangelove's America: Society and Culture in the Atomic Age* (1997).

President Truman

Harry Truman enjoys a number of good biographical treatments. See Robert H. Ferrell, *Harry S Truman and the Modern American Presidency* (1983) and *Harry S. Truman: A Life* (1994); Donald R. McCoy, *The Presidency of Harry S. Truman* (1984); William E. Pemberton, *Harry S. Truman: Fair Dealer and Cold Warrior* (1988); David G. McCullough, *Truman* (1992), and Alonzo L. Hamby, *Man of the People: A Life of Harry S. Truman* (1995) and Sean J. Savage, *Truman and the Democratic Party* (1998). Michael J. Lacey, ed., *The Truman Presidency* (1989) offers interpretive essays, while Alonso L. Hamby, *Beyond the New Deal: Harry S Truman and American Liberalism* (1973) remains a useful look at Truman's Fair Deal that should be supplemented by the relevant chapter of the same author's *Liberalism and Its Challengers: Liberalism from FDR to Bush* (2nd ed., 1992). Steve Fraser and Gary Gerstle, eds., *The Rise and Fall of the New Deal Order, 1930–1980* (1989) takes a longer view of postwar themes.

Domestic Policymaking during the Fair Deal

On domestic policymaking during the Fair Deal, see R. Alton Lee, *Truman and Taft-Hartley: A Question of Mandate* (1966); Kevin Boyle, *The UAW and the Heyday of American Liberalism, 1945–1968* (1997). Allen J. Matusow, *Farm Policies and Politics in the Truman Years* (1967); Richard O. Davies, *Housing Reform during the Truman Administration* (1966); Susan M. Hartmann, *Truman and the 80th Congress* (1971); Monte M. Poen, *Harry S. Truman versus the Medical Lobby: The Genesis of Medicaire* (1979); Andrew J. Dunar, *The Truman Scandals and the Politics of Morality* (1984); the relevant chapters of Edward D. Berkowitz, *America's Welfare State: From Roosevelt to Reagan* (1991); and Sheryl R. Tynes, *Turning Points in Social Security: From "Cruel Hoax" to "Sacred Entitlement"* (1996).

Anticommunism

Anticommunism is the subject of M. J. Heale, *American Anticommunism: Combating the Enemy Within, 1880–1970* (1990) and Richard Gid Powers, *Not without Honor: The History of American Anticommunism* (1995), both of which take the long view. Fred Inglis, *The Cruel Peace: Everyday Life in the Cold War* (1991) offers an international perspective. Allen Weinstein's *Perjury: The Hiss Chambers Case* (rev. ed., 1997) is an important, once controversial study which is now bolstered by, among other recent works, Joseph Albright and Marcia Kunstel, *Bombshell: The Secret Story of America's Unknown Atomic Spy Conspiracy* (1997); Sam Tanenhaus, *Whittaker Chambers: A Biography* (1997); and *Secrecy: Report of the Commission on Protecting and Reducing Government Secrecy* (1997). Richard M. Fried, *Nightmare in Red: The McCarthy Era in Perspective* (1990) and Ellen Schrecker, *The Age of McCarthyism: A Brief History with Documents* (1994) are solid syntheses, but David Caute's *The Great Fear: The Anti-Communist Purge under Truman and Eisenhower* (1978) remains the most detailed account. See also Michael R. Belknap, *Cold War Political Justice: The Smith Act, the Communist Party, and American Civil Liberties* (1977); Stanley I. Kutler, *The American Inquisition: Justice and Injustice in the Cold War* (1982); Marjorie Garber and Rebecca L. Walkowitz, eds., *Secret Agents: The Rosenberg Case, McCarthyism, and Fifties America* (1995); and John F. Neville, *The Press, the Rosenbergs, and the Cold War* (1995).

Social Changes of the Early Cold War Years

The social changes of the early Cold War years have drawn the attention of many recent historical works. For an interesting view, see Wendy Kozol, *Life's America: Family and Nation in Postwar Photojournalism* (1994). The baby boom is the focus of Richard A. Easterlin, *Birth and Fortune: The Impact of Numbers on Personal Welfare* (2nd ed., 1987) and Landon Y. Jones, *Great Expectations: America and the Baby Boom Generation* (1980). See also the relevant chapters of John Modell, *Into One's Own: From Youth to Adulthood in the United States, 1920–1975* (1989). On women's issues, see the final chapters of Susan Strasser, *Never Done: A History of American Housework* (1982); Alice Kessler-Harris, *Out to Work: A History of Wage-Earning Women in the United States* (1982); Jacqueline Jones, *Labor of Love, Labor of Sorrow: Black Women, Work and the Family, From Slavery to the Present* (1985); Eugenia Kaledin, *Mothers and More: American Women in the 1950s* (1984); Leila Rupp and Verta Taylor, *Survival in the Doldrums: The American Women's Rights Movement, 1945 to the 1960s* (1990); Cynthia Harrison, *On Account of Sex: The Politics of Women's Issues, 1945–68* (1988). Family and gender issues are nicely tied to Cold War culture in Elaine Tyler May's *Homeward Bound: American Families in the Cold War Era* (1989) and in Stephanie Coontz, *The Way We Never Were: American Families and the Nostalgia Trip* (1992). On issues related to sexuality and gender, see the relevant chapters of John D'Emilio and Estelle B. Freedman, *Intimate Matters: A History of Sexuality in America* (1988); Wini Breines, *Young, White, and Miserable: Growing Up Female in the Fifties* (1992); Graham McCann, *Rebel Males: Clift, Brando and Dean* (1993); and Joanne Meyerowitz, ed., *Not June Cleaver: Women and Gender in Postwar America, 1945–1960* (1994).

Suburban and Urban Issues

On suburban and urban issues, see Robert A. Caro, *The Power Broker: Robert Moses and the Fall of New York* (1974); Mark Gelfand, *A Nation of Cities: The Federalist Government and Urban America, 1933–1945* (1975); Herbert Gans, *The Levittowners: Ways of Life and Politics in a New Suburban Community* (2nd ed., 1982); the relevant chapters of Kenneth T. Jackson, *Crabgrass Frontier: The Suburbanization of the United States* (1985); Barbara M. Kelly, *Expanding the American Dream: Building and Rebuilding Levittown* (1993); Rob Kling, Spencer Olin, and Mark Poster, *Postsuburban California: The Transformation of Orange County Since World War II* (1991). See also John M. Findlay, *Magic Lands: Western City Scapes and American Culture after 1940* (1992); David L. Kirp, John P. Dwyer, and Larry A. Rosenthal, *Our Town: Race, Housing and the Soul of Suburbia* (1995); John R., Gillis, *A World of their Own: Myth, Ritual, and the Quest for Family Values* (1996); Jon C. Teaford, *The Rough Road to Renaissance: Urban Revitalization in America, 1940–85* (1990) and *Post-Suburbia: Government and the Politics in the Edge Cities* (1997); Alan Ehrenhalt, *The Lost City: Discovering the Forgotten Virtues of Community in the Chicago of the 1950s* (1995); Michael F. Logan, *Fighting Sprawl and City Hall: Resistance to Urban Growth in the Southwest* (1995); James Hudnut-Beumler, *Looking for God in the Suburbs: the Religion of the American Dream and Its Critics, 1945–1965* (1994). Thomas J. Sugrue, *The Origins of the Urban Crisis: Race and Inequality in Postwar Detroit* (1996) is a recent, award-winning study.

The Korean War

On the Korean War, Burton I. Kaufman, *The Korean War: Challenges in Crisis, Credibility, and Command* (1986) is a brief synthesis. More detailed analyses may be found in several volumes by Bruce Cumings, *The Origins of the Korean War* (1981); *Child of Conflict: The Korean-American Relationship, 1943–53* (1983), a series of essays which he edited; and *Korea: The Unknown War* (coauthored with Jon Halliday) (1988); William Stueck, *The Korean War: An International History* (1995); Chen Jian, *China's Road to the Korean War: The Making of the Sino-American Confrontation* (1994); Shu Guang Zhang, *Mao's Military Romanticism: China and the Korean War, 1950–1953* (1995); William T. Bowers, William M. Hammond, and George L. MacGarrigle, *Black Soldier, White Army: The 24th Infantry Regiment in Korea* (1996).

The Eisenhower Years

The Eisenhower years received an early scholarly synthesis in Charles C. Alexander, *Holding the Line: The Eisenhower Era, 1952–1960* (1975) which can be updated with Chester Pach, Jr., and Elmo Richardson, *The Presidency of Dwight D. Eisenhower* (rev. ed., 1991); Robert F. Burk, *Dwight David Eisenhower* (1986); William B. Pickett, *Dwight David Eisenhower and American Power* (1995); the relevant chapter of Hamby, *Liberalism and Its Challengers* (2nd ed., 1992); and Jeff Broadwater, *Eisenhower and the Anti-Communist Crusade* (1992). Stephen E. Ambrose's massive two-volume study *Eisenhower* (1983, 1984) contains a wealth of information. *Adlai Stevenson and American Politics: The Odyssey of a Cold War Liberal* (1994), by Jeff Broadwater, is a solid biography of the man twice defeated by Eisenhower for the presidency. Fred I. Greenstein, *The Hidden-Hand Presidency: Eisenhower as Leader* (rev. ed., 1994) helped to begin the trend toward a new view of Eisenhower's presidency.

Videos

March of Time: American Lifestyles (1987) is a five-video compilation taken from newscasts of the period. *Post-War Hopes, Cold War Fears,* from the "Walk Through the 20th Century" series, offers an interesting overview. For a visual recounting of the beginning of U.S. involvement in the Vietnam War, see *The First Vietnam War* (1946–1954), a one-hour video documentary in the series "Vietnam: A Television History." *The Rise of J. Edgar Hoover* (1991) is a superb video documentary in the "American Experience" series. *The Forgotten War* (1987) is a three-part video documentary on Korea. *Truman* (1997) and *Ike,* formally titled *Eisenhower* (1993), are solid entries in PBS's "The White House Collection." *George Marshall and the American Century* (1993) offers a sweeping overview of Eisenhower's important military benefactor, while *The Marshall Plan: Against All Odds* (1997) covers Marshall's most important Cold War initiative. *Adlai Stevenson: The Man from Libertyville* (1992) is a video portrait of the Democrat who was twice defeated by Eisenhower for the presidency. *Seeing Red* (1993) looks, with considerable compassion, on the people who supported the Communist Party. The anti-communist crusade in Hollywood is the subject of *Hollywood on Trial* (1976) and *Legacy of the Hollywood Blacklist* (1987). *Point of Order: A Documentary of the Army-McCarthy Hearings* (1964) is a classic documentary on the congressional hearings that marked the beginning of McCarthy's demise.

9

Affluence and Its Discontents, 1954–1963

B eginning in 1954 the Cold War tensions that had prevailed since 1947 began to abate. President Dwight Eisenhower lowered the pitch of super-power rivalry. Yet he and his successor, John F. Kennedy, still directed a determined anticommunist foreign policy by combining a "New Look" military posture with expanded use of covert activities and economic leverage. At home, Eisenhower's relaxed presidential style and Kennedy's youthful charisma helped them cautiously extend some of the domestic programs initiated during the Roosevelt and Truman eras. The economic growth of the late 1950s and early 1960s encouraged talk, within most sectors of the country, about an age of affluence.

Nevertheless, these were not entirely "happy days." The era's general affluence also generated apprehension about a presumed conformity, the emergence of a "youth culture," and the impact of a mass commercial culture. At the same time, a broad-based movement against racial discrimination and new attention to economic inequities prompted renewed debate over the meaning of liberty, how to achieve equality, and the use of governmental power.

Foreign Policy, 1954–1960

By 1954 the shrill anticommunist rhetoric associated with McCarthyism and the Korean War era was beginning to subside. The dominant assumption of Cold War policy—that the United States had to protect the "free world" and fight communism everywhere—remained unchanged, but the focus of that policy shifted. Bipolar confrontations between the United States and the Soviet Union over European issues gave way to greater reliance on nuclear deterrence and to more subtle and complex power plays in the "Third World"—the Middle East, Asia, Latin America, and Africa.

The New Look and Summitry

One reason for this shift was a change of leadership in Moscow after the death of Joseph Stalin in 1953. Nikita Khrushchev, the new Soviet leader, talked of "peaceful coexistence" and denounced Stalin's police-state tactics during a speech in 1956. Seeking to free up resources to produce more consumer goods, Khrushchev began reducing Soviet armed forces.

The political climate in the United States also was changing. In December 1953, Admiral Arthur Radford, chairman of the Joint Chiefs of Staff, called for a reduction of the military budget and a revision of defense strategy. Radford's New Look reflected Eisenhower's belief that massive military expenditures would eventually impede the nation's economic growth. To limit military spending, now that the Korean War was over, Eisenhower sought a defense posture that relied less on expensive ground forces and more on airpower, advanced nuclear capabilities, and covert and psychological instruments of influence.

According to the Eisenhower administration's doctrine of "massive retaliation," the threat of U.S. atomic weaponry would hold communism in check. And to make America's nuclear umbrella more effective worldwide, Eisenhower expanded NATO to include West Germany in 1955 and added two other mutual defense pacts with noncommunist nations in Central and Southeast Asia. The Southeast Asia Treaty Organization (SEATO), formed in 1954, was a mutual defense pact among Australia, France, Great Britain, New Zealand, Pakistan, the Philippines, and Thailand. The weakly bonded Central Treaty Organization (CENTO), formed in 1959, linked Pakistan, Iran, Turkey, Iraq, and Britain.

The Eisenhower administration also elevated psychological warfare and "informational" programs into major Cold War weapons. The government-run Voice of America extended its radio broadcasts globally and programmed in more languages. Covertly, the government also funded Radio Free Europe, Radio Liberation (directly to the Soviet Union), and Radio Asia. In 1953 Eisenhower persuaded Congress to create the United States Information Agency (USIA) to coordinate anticommunist informational and propaganda campaigns.

In an effort to limit defense budgets, to score propaganda victories, and to improve relations with one another, the superpowers resumed high-level "summit" meetings. In May 1955 an agreement was reached to end the postwar occupation of Austria and to transform that country into a neutral state. Two months later the United States, the Soviet Union, Britain, and France met in Geneva. Making little progress on arms reduction, the future of Germany, and other matters, the meetings nonetheless inaugurated new cultural exchanges. Cold War tensions eased somewhat, and all sides hailed the conciliatory "spirit of Geneva." In the fall of 1959, to soothe a crisis that had developed over Berlin, Khrushchev toured the United States, met with Eisenhower, and paid well-publicized visits to farmers in Iowa and to Disneyland in California. But a summit scheduled for 1960 in Paris was canceled after the Soviets shot down an American U-2 spy plane over their territory. Still, the tone of Cold War rhetoric had grown less strident.

The superpowers even began to consider arms limitation. In Eisenhower's "open skies" proposal of 1955, the president proposed that the two nations verify disarmament efforts by reconnaissance flights over each other's territory. The Soviets, fearful of opening their land to inspection, refused. But some progress was made in limiting atomic tests. Responding to worries about the health hazards of atomic fallout, both countries slowed their above-ground testing and discussed entering into some form of test-ban agreement. For many Americans, concerns about the impact of nuclear testing came too late. Government documents declassified in the 1980s finally confirmed what antinuclear activists had long suspected: Many people who had lived "downwind" from rural nuclear test sites during the 1940s and 1950s had suffered an unusual number of atomic-related illnesses. Worse, in the 1990s it was revealed that Washington had conducted tests with radioactive materials on American citizens, who had no knowledge of these experiments.

Events in Eastern Europe accentuated American policymakers' caution about being drawn into a military confrontation with the Soviet Union. There, the reluctant satellites of the Soviet Union were chafing under the managed economy and police-state control imposed by the Soviets. Seizing on the post-Stalin thaw, Poland's insurgents staged a three-day rebellion in June 1956 and forced the Soviets to accept Wladyslaw Gomulka, an old foe of Stalin, as head of state. Hungarians then began to demonstrate in support of Imre Nagy, an anti-Stalinist communist, who formed a new government and pledged a multiparty democracy. Although the Soviets sought an accommodation that would both preserve their power and allow some reform, armed rebellion spread throughout Hungary.

In speeches, Secretary of State John Foster Dulles had talked of supporting "liberation" from communism rather than just "containment." Taking hope from such words, Hungarian revolutionaries appealed for American assistance, but the United States could hardly launch a military effort so close to Soviet power. Soviet armies crushed the uprising and killed thousands of Hungarians, including Nagy. U.S. policymakers learned that although advocating "liberation" from communism made good political rhetoric at home, it could lead to tragedy abroad.

Covert Action and Economic Leverage

Increasingly, the focus of the U.S. battle against communism began to shift from Europe to the Third World, with covert action and economic leverage replacing overt military confrontation as primary diplomatic tools. These techniques were less expensive than military action and provoked less public controversy because they were less visible.

During its first years, the CIA had concentrated its covert activities in Eastern Europe, where it sought to fan resistance to the Soviet Union by encouraging dissidents and supporting the broadcasts of Radio Free Europe. Gradually, however, the CIA broadened its role. In 1953 it helped to bring about the election of the anticommunist leader Ramón Magsaysay as president in the Philippines. That same year, the CIA helped plan and execute a coup to overthrow Mohammad Mossadegh's constitutional government in Iran, restoring to power Shah Reza Pahlavi. The increasingly dictatorial Shah remained a firm ally of the United States and a friend of American oil interests in Iran until his ouster by Moslem fundamentalists in 1979. In 1954 the CIA, working closely with the United Fruit Company, helped topple President Jacobo Arbenz Guzmán's elected government in Guatemala. Officials of the Eisenhower administration and officers of the fruit company regarded Arbenz as a communist because he sought to nationalize and redistribute large tracts of land, including some owned by United Fruit itself.

After these "successes" the CIA, under the direction of John Foster Dulles's brother Allen, grew in influence and power. In 1954 the National Security Council widened the CIA's mandate, and by 1960 it had approximately 15,000 agents (compared to about 6,000 when Eisenhower took office) deployed around the world.

Eisenhower also employed economic strategies—trade and aid—to fight communism and win converts in the Third World. Those strategies were aimed at opening more opportunities for American enterprises overseas, discouraging other countries from adopting state-directed economic systems, and encouraging expansion of commerce. U.S. policymakers came to identify "freedom" with "the free market" and regarded as a threat to "freedom" the efforts of Third World nations to break old colonial bonds by creating government-directed economies and nationalized industries. New governmental assistance programs offered economic aid to friendly nations, and military aid rose sharply as well. Under the Mutual Security Program and the Military Assistance Program, the United States spent $3 billion a year, and 225,000 representatives from nations around the world were trained in anticommunism and police tactics. The buildup of military forces in friendly Third World nations strengthened anticommunist forces but also contributed to the development of military dictatorships.

America and the Third World

In applying these new anticommunist measures, the Eisenhower administration employed a very broad definition of "communist." In many countries, communist political parties had joined other groups in fighting to bring about changes in labor laws and land ownership that would benefit the poor. Meanwhile, U.S. companies doing business abroad joined forces with local elites to resist the redistribution of power that such programs implied. Often economic elites and dictators abroad won U.S. support against their political opponents simply by whispering the word "communist." Consequently, the United States often found itself supporting "anticommunist" measures that simply suppressed political and social change.

Latin America

In Latin America, Eisenhower talked about encouraging democracy but regularly supported dictatorial regimes as long as they welcomed U.S. investment and suppressed leftist movements. Eisenhower awarded the Legion of Merit to unpopular dictators in Peru and Venezuela and privately confessed his admiration for the anticommunism of Paraguay's General Alfredo Stroessner, who sheltered ex-Nazis and ran his country as a private fiefdom. Vice President Richard Nixon toasted Cuban dictator Fulgencio Batista as "Cuba's Abraham Lincoln," and the CIA established a training program for Batista's repressive security forces. Surveying Eisenhower-era policies, America's disgruntled ambassador to democratic Costa Rica complained that Dulles had advised foreign service officers to "do nothing to offend the dictators; they are the only people we can depend on."

Such policies offended many Latin Americans, and "yankeephobia" spread. When Nixon traveled to South America in 1958, he met angry protesters. In Caracas, Venezuela, he was nearly killed when protesters stopped his motorcade and overturned the cars. The following year in Panama, protests against the United States flared into riots in which more than 100 people were injured.

Events in Cuba also dramatized the growing anti-American hostility. After Fidel Castro overthrew Batista in 1959 and tried to curtail Cuba's dependence on the United States, the Eisenhower administration imposed an economic boycott of the island. Castro turned to the Soviet Union, declared himself a communist, and pledged to support leftist insurgencies throughout Latin America. Although the CIA had begun to plot an invasion to unseat Castro, at the same time the Eisenhower administration ordered a review of the policies that had sparked such ill will throughout Latin America. The review recommended that policymakers should place more emphasis on democracy, human rights, and economic growth, recommendations that would soon find fruition in President John Kennedy's Alliance for Progress.

Nasserism and the Suez Crisis of 1956

In the Middle East, distrust of nationalism, neutralism, and social reform also influenced U.S. policy. In 1954, when Gamal Abdel Nasser overthrew a corrupt monarchy and took power in Egypt, he promised to rescue Arab nations from imperialist domination and guide them toward "positive neutralism." Exploiting anti-Israel sentiment and accepting aid from both the United States and the Soviet Union, Nasser strengthened Egypt's economic and military power. Then he purchased advanced weapons from communist Czechoslovakia and extended diplomatic recognition to communist China. Those actions prompted the United States to cancel loans for the building of the huge Aswan Dam, a project designed to improve agriculture along the Nile River and provide power for new industries. Nasser retaliated in July 1956 by nationalizing the British-controlled Suez Canal, arguing that canal tolls would provide substitute financing for the dam. Suez was of major economic and symbolic importance to Britain, and the British government, joined by France and Israel, attacked Egypt in October to retake the canal.

Although Eisenhower distrusted Nasser, he decried Britain's blatant attempt to retain its imperial position. The Soviets were, at just the same time, ruthlessly suppressing the Hungarian revolt, and Eisenhower could not effectively criticize the Soviets for maintaining a sphere of influence when Britain was engaged in a similar pursuit. Denouncing the Anglo-French-Israeli action, Eisenhower threatened to destabilize the British currency unless the invasion was terminated. In the end, a plan supported by the United States and the United Nations allowed Nasser to retain the Suez Canal. But American prestige and power in the area suffered as the Soviet Union took over financing of the Aswan Dam and cemented ties with Nasser.

With Nasser-style nationalism now more closely aligned with the Soviets, the Eisenhower administration feared the spread of "Nasserism" throughout the oil-rich Middle East. In the spring of 1957, the president received congressional endorsement of the so-called "Eisenhower Doctrine," a pledge to defend Middle Eastern countries "against overt armed aggression from any nation controlled by international communism." Anticolonial, nationalist movements aligned with Nasser's vision were gaining support in the region. Although designs by "international communism" hardly described the multiple causes of rising nationalism and civil unrest in many nations, anticommunist rhetoric did provide justification for maintaining governments that supported the West's need for oil. When elites in Lebanon and Jordan, fearful of revolts by forces friendly to Nasser, asked the United States and Britain to stabilize their countries, Eisenhower agreed. More than 14,000 U.S. marines surprised sunbathers on Lebanese beaches, waded ashore, and set up an anti-Nasser government in Beirut. A British incursion simultaneously restored King

Hussein to the throne in Jordan. These actions were part of Eisenhower's policy to support friendly, conservative governments in the Middle East, but Western military intervention also intensified Arab nationalism and anti-Americanism.

The Eisenhower administration tried to thwart revolutionary political movements elsewhere in the world. In 1958 the president approved a plan to support an uprising against Achmed Sukarno, the president of Indonesia, who drew support from Indonesia's large Communist Party. When civil war broke out, the CIA furnished planes, pilots, and encouragement to the rebels. But when the rebellion failed, the CIA abandoned its Indonesian allies, and Sukarno tightened his grip on power. In the next few years, CIA activities included various schemes to assassinate Fidel Castro (these efforts failed) and Patrice Lumumba, a popular black nationalist in the Congo (Lumumba was killed in 1961, although the degree of CIA involvement in his death is still debated by scholars).

Vietnam

Eisenhower's strategy of thwarting communism and neutralism in the Third World set the stage for the nation's most fateful foreign policy involvement since the Second World War: Vietnam.

In Vietnam, communist-nationalist forces led by Ho Chi Minh were fighting for independence from France. Ho Chi Minh, born in the southern part of Vietnam, had studied in France and in the Soviet Union before returning to lead his country's anticolonial insurgency. At the end of the Second World War, as Japan withdrew from its wartime occupation of Vietnam, Ho Chi Minh appealed in vain to the United States to support Vietnamese independence rather than allow the return of French colonial administration. But U.S. leaders, despite their wartime criticism of colonialism, backed France and its ally in the South, the government of Bao Dai. Ho Chi Minh went to war against the French who, after a major defeat at Dien Bien Phu in 1954, decided to withdraw. The subsequent Geneva Peace Accords of 1954 eliminated French control over all of Indochina and divided it into Laos, Cambodia, and Vietnam. Vietnam itself was split into two jurisdictions—North Vietnam and South Vietnam—until an election could be held to unify the country under one leader.

Eisenhower's advisers felt that Ho Chi Minh's powerful communist-nationalist appeal might set off a geopolitical chain reaction. Using familiar Cold War language, the Eisenhower administration took the position that "the loss of any of the countries of Southeast Asia to Communist aggression" would ultimately "endanger the stability and security of Europe" and of Japan. This formulation, known as the "domino theory," would continue to be invoked by many subsequent presidents. As Ho Chi Minh's government established itself in North Vietnam, Eisenhower supported a noncommunist government in the South, turning to economic strategies and covert operations to prevent Ho Chi Minh from becoming the elected leader of a unified Vietnam.

Colonel Edward Lansdale, who had directed CIA efforts against a leftist insurgency in the Philippines from 1950 to 1953, arrived in Saigon, capital of the South, in 1954. Lansdale was to mastermind the building of a pro-U.S. government in South Vietnam under Ngo Dinh Diem, an anticommunist Catholic who had been educated at a seminary in New Jersey. At first, Lansdale seemed to be succeeding. Diem's government, with U.S. concurrence, denounced the Geneva Peace Accords and refused to take part in elections to create a unified government for Vietnam. It extended its control over the South, redistributed land formerly owned by the French, built up its army, and launched a program of industrialization. But Diem alienated much of South Vietnam's predominantly Buddhist population, and his narrowing circle of political allies was notoriously corrupt. As time passed, Diem grew more and more isolated from his own people and almost totally dependent on the United States. As early as 1955 the French prime minister had warned the United States that Diem was "not only incapable but mad." But the Eisenhower administration could see no alternative. By 1960 the United States had sent billions of American dollars and 900 advisers to prop up Diem's government.

The domestic opposition to Diem coalesced in the National Liberation Front (NLF). The NLF, formed in December 1960, was an amalgam of nationalists who resented Diem's dependence on the United States, communists who demanded more extensive land reform, and politicians who decried Diem's corruption and cronyism. It was a South Vietnamese movement, allied with the Viet Minh communists of the North, from which it gradually received more and more supplies.

Although Eisenhower warned that military intervention in Indochina would be a "tragedy" (and he himself had refused direct military intervention to help the French in 1954), he committed more and more aid and national prestige to South Vietnam and tied America's honor to Diem's diminishing political fortunes. The decision of whether to turn these commitments into a large-scale military intervention would fall to Eisenhower's successors in the White House.

In his farewell address of 1961, Eisenhower warned that the greatest danger to the United States was not communism but the nation's own "military-industrial complex." Despite his desire to limit militarism and lower the pitch of Cold War rivalries, however, Eisenhower and Secretary of State Dulles had nevertheless directed a resolutely anticommunist foreign policy that helped fuel the nuclear arms race and accelerate superpower contests in the Third World.

Affluence—A "People of Plenty"

In 1940 the United States had still teetered on the brink of economic depression. Only a decade and a half later, the nation's GNP had soared. It was more than 5 times greater than that of Great Britain and more than 10 times greater than that of Japan. The output of corporations such as General Motors surpassed the GNP of many nations. Writing in 1954, the historian David Potter called Americans a "people of plenty."

The 1950s marked the midpoint of a period of generally steady economic growth that began during the Second World War and continued until the early 1970s. Corporations turned out vast quantities of consumer goods and enjoyed rising rates of profit. Investments and business ventures overseas boosted corporate profits at home. The domestic economy intersected with an international marketplace that was dominated by firms based in the United States. The label "made in America" symbolized both the quality of particular products and the economic

The Age of Affluence • Wheaties, the "Breakfast of Champions," ran a promotional campaign that featured the new array of consumer products that were becoming associated with a life of affluence and leisure.

Steady Growth of Gross National Product, 1940–1970

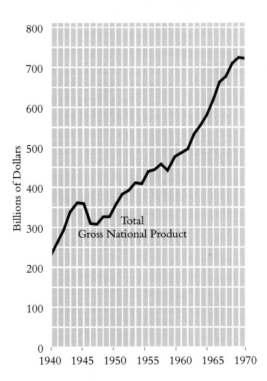

power of the nation at large. National security policies helped to keep the economy growing by facilitating access to raw materials and energy from the Third World. Abundant supplies of inexpensive oil and natural gas lowered production costs and allowed industries to replace domestic coal with less costly, and less polluting, energy sources from abroad.

Newer industries, such as chemicals and electronics, became particularly dominant in the world market. Using new chemical technologies, the Corning Glass Company reported that most of its sales in the mid-1950s came from products that had not even existed in 1940. General Electric, whose corporate spokesperson was the actor Ronald Reagan, proclaimed that "progress is our most important product."

Government spending on national security pumped money into the general economy and stimulated specific industries. In 1955 military expenditures accounted for about 10 percent of the GNP. The fact that the business of national

Barbie • The Mattel Toy Company introduced the first Barbie doll at the New York Toy Fair in 1959. An 11-inch doll with a voluptuous figure, Barbie proved to be an instant hit with young girls and went on to become the best-selling toy in the world. Barbie's extensive wardrobe and collection of accessories meant that purchasing her likeness was just the beginning of the consuming cycle.

security had become big business was dramatized by President Eisenhower's selection of Charles Wilson of General Motors in 1953 and Neil McElroy of Procter and Gamble in 1957 to head the Department of Defense.

Highways and Waterways

Although some experts argued that greater government expenditures for nonmilitary programs would generate even greater economic growth, Eisenhower remained cautious. Fearing that such spending would fuel an inflationary spiral of rising prices and destabilize the economy, his administration kept nonmilitary spending under tight control. After 1955 even the Pentagon's budget was reduced; and for several years, the federal government itself ran a balanced budget.

Eisenhower did, however, eventually endorse several costly new domestic programs. He supported the Highway Act of 1956, though even here national security considerations shaped his thinking. (In a national emergency, military supplies and personnel, it was thought, could speed along the new superhighways.) Financed by a national tax on gasoline and other highway-related products, the Highway Act provided 90 percent of the funds for the construction of a national system of limited-access, high-speed expressways. Touted as the largest public works project in the history of the world, this program delighted the auto, oil, concrete, and tire industries; provided steady work for construction firms; and boosted the interstate trucking business. It was the first centrally planned transportation system in the nation's history.

By the mid-1950s, U.S. highways were crowded with chrome-encrusted, gas-hungry automobiles that rivaled suburban homes as symbols of abundance. With autos built overseas considered either luxuries or curiosities, shoppers needed no reminders to "buy American." Automakers touted their annual model changes and their increasingly larger engines—and their 1955 sales reached almost 8 million cars. That was about one-third of all the automobiles owned by Americans on the eve of the Second World War. Speed and power, rather than safety and reliability, were the key selling points at auto showrooms. Detroit's auto industry helped to support other domestic industries such as steel. In 1956 the steel industry could boast of being three and a half times more efficient than its fledgling Japanese rival.

The Eisenhower administration and members of Congress also invoked national security to justify high-cost river-diversion projects in the Far West. Lyndon Johnson, leader of the Senate Democrats, hailed water management as "a decisive tool in our mighty struggle for national security and world peace." The Army Corps of Engineers and the Bureau of Reclamation, agencies with many supporters in business and in Congress, spent billions of dollars on dams, irrigation canals, and reservoirs. Irrigation turned desert into crop land, and elaborate pumping systems even allowed rivers to flow uphill. No society in world history had ever devoted a similar portion of its national treasury to water projects. By 1960, the western states had access to trillions of gallons of water per year, and the basis for new economic growth in Texas, California, and Arizona was established.

These water projects came at a high price. Technologically complicated and costly, they generated similarly complex and expensive bureaucracies to sustain them. As a consequence of this dynamic, ordinary people lost power to the government agencies and private entrepreneurs who worked, in concert, to dominate the water-dependent

Auto Sales, 1940–1970

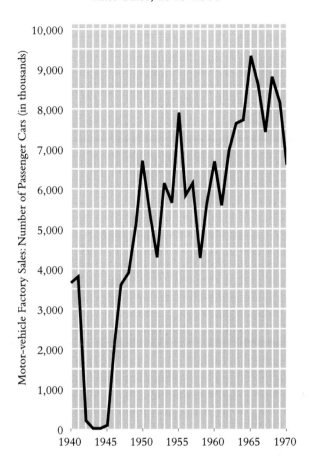

economy of the postwar West. Increasingly, large corporate-style operations pushed out smaller farmers and ranchers. In addition, American Indians found portions of their tribal lands being flooded, to serve as large water reservoirs, or being purchased by agribusinesses or by large ranching interests. Finally, the vast water projects laid the basis for ecological problems. Plans to divert surface waters, to tap into groundwater tables, and to dot the West with dams and reservoirs began to take their toll upon the land. Worse, the buildup of salt byproducts in the water and the soil, the inevitable consequence of massive efforts to harness water resources, was accompanied in the postwar West by the disastrous overuse of pesticides such as DDT.

Labor-Management Accord

Most corporate leaders, having accepted the kind of government involvement in the "free" enterprise economy required to build interstate highways and water projects, were learning to live with labor unions as well. The auto industry, where management and labor leaders had negotiated a mutually acceptable work contract in 1950, led the way.

Closer cooperation with corporate management, labor leaders reasoned, could guarantee employment stability and political influence for their unions. Taking their cue from the United Auto Workers, which had been one of the most militant CIO unions during the 1930s and had pioneered the sit-down strike, labor dropped the demand for greater union involvement in corporate decision making and agreed to bargain in a "responsible, businesslike" manner. In exchange for recognizing "management prerogatives" over crucial issues—such as the organization of the daily work routine, the introduction of new technologies, and investment priorities—union leaders could still bargain aggressively for wages and fringe benefits.

Moreover, union leaders guaranteed management that rank-and-file workers would abide by the terms of their union contracts and disavow the wildcat tactics used in the 1930s and 1940s. To police this new labor-management détente, both sides looked to the federal government's National Labor Relations Board (NLRB) as an impartial umpire. Meanwhile, in 1955, the AFL and the CIO, which had long differed on labor-organizing strategy, merged—another sign of declining militancy within the labor movement. The 1950s thus ended the fierce labor-capital conflicts that had marked the 1930s and had continued through the 1940s.

Business leaders regarded this labor-management accord as a substantial victory. *Fortune* magazine noted that General Motors had paid a price in terms of more costly employee benefit packages and higher wages in the 1950s, but that "it got a bargain" in terms of labor peace and "regained control over . . . the crucial management function." To safeguard that control, corporations regularly expanded their supervisory staffs. That practice drove up consumer prices and deprived workers of active participation in planning the work process. This accord may also have helped to divide industrial workers from one another, as those who worked in the more prosperous sectors of the economy, such as the auto industry, were able to bargain more effectively than those who worked in peripheral areas.

Most workers, however, did make economic gains. During the 1950s and early 1960s, real wages (what workers make after their paychecks are adjusted for inflation) steadily rose; the rate of industrial accidents dropped; fringe benefits (what workers receive in terms of health insurance, paid vacation time, and pension plans) improved; and job security was generally high.

Economic growth, according to celebrants of the 1950s, had made the United States the envy of the world. Widespread ownership of kitchen appliances, television sets, and automobiles supported the claim that American consumers were enjoying a culture of abundance. Theories about class conflict and the limits of capitalism, widely expressed during the 1930s, now seemed irrelevant. Capitalism worked, and it worked spectacularly well. Indeed, it seemed so successful that only a new vocabulary of superlatives could describe its wonders. In 1955 *Fortune* hailed "The Changing American Market" and highlighted "The Rich Middle-Income Class" and "The Wonderful Ordinary Luxury Market." Harvard's celebrated economist John Kenneth Galbraith had simply entitled his 1952 study of the economy *American Capitalism;* his 1958 follow-up was *The Affluent Society,* a book that topped the best-seller lists for nearly six months.

Although Galbraith's second study was actually much more critical of economic affairs than his first, the term "affluence" conjured up images of change and fluidity and fit nicely with the vision of constant economic growth. It also directed attention away from the deeply rooted inequalities that persisted in American society. Talking about affluence, for example, meant that one could avoid using the word "wealth," which might suggest its opposite, "poverty," a term seldom used in economic analyses of the mid-1950s. And by shifting the focus from what people *actually owned*—their accumulated wealth—to their affluence—what they could, with the aid of generous credit terms, *consume*—observers found that the "American way of life" was constantly improving.

The most buoyant observers even detected a leveling out of living standards between the top and the bottom levels of this consumer society. The gulf was no longer between people with cars and people without cars, they declared, but between people with Cadillacs and Lincolns and those with Chevrolets and Fords. "Luxury has reached the masses," proclaimed *Fortune.*

Political Pluralism

Many observers also credited economic affluence with giving rise to a new political structure. Giant corporations, they argued, were no longer cause for political concern. Galbraith, for example, suggested that unions, consumer lobbies, farm organizations, and other noncorporate groups could exert effective "countervailing power" against corporations.

Only a few mavericks, such as the sociologist C. Wright Mills, disagreed. Mills saw corporate leaders as members of a small "power elite" that dominated American life. Tracing the development of an interlocking group of business executives, military chieftains, and political leaders back to the Second World War, he claimed that this elite had made all of the big decisions on foreign and domestic policy in the decade since. Its influence over politics and the economy, he believed, was destroying democracy in the United States.

In Mills's critique, the nation's Cold War policies represented an unwise, potentially disastrous, extension of government power at home and overseas. And in the vaunted affluent society, work was becoming more regimented, jobs were bringing little satisfaction, and workers were spending their leisure time on corporation-dominated amusements rather than on community-based activities that they themselves directed. Although Mills anticipated and inspired critics of the 1960s and early 1970s, most of his contemporaries dismissed his power elite thesis as a simplistic conspiracy theory.

To those who subscribed to the dominant view, called "pluralism," no power elite could ever dominate the political process. According to pluralist accounts, public policymaking proceeded from wide participation in public debate by a broad range of different interest groups. Short-term conflicts over specific issues would obviously continue to arise, but pluralism's celebrants believed that affluence had effectively moderated political passions and had fostered a set of procedures by which different interests eventually could frame a consensus. As Henry Hart, a professor at Harvard Law School, put it, constant economic growth meant that "in any conflict of interest," it was "always possible to work out a solution" because affluence guaranteed that all interests would be "better off than before."

When discussion shifted from this celebratory view of *process* to an evaluation of the *substance* of recent decision making, pluralists praised postwar leaders for finding "realistic" solutions to difficult problems. The acid test of political "realism" in the 1950s was whether or not the national government was updating policies from the 1940s: containment of international communism; maintenance of a powerful national security state; and promotion of domestic programs based on the theory of constant economic growth.

A Religious People

The celebration of political pluralism dovetailed with an exaltation of the role, in an anticommunist era, of religion in American life. Members of Congress, as part of the crusade against "atheistic communism," emphasized religious values by constructing a nondenominational prayer room on Capitol Hill; by adding the phrase "under God" to the Pledge of Allegiance; and declaring the phrase "In God We Trust," which had been emblazoned on U.S. currency for nearly a century, the official national motto.

The emphasis on a pluralistic, transdenominational religious faith was not simply a product of anticommunism. Intense religious commitments, most analysts insisted, no longer divided people as much as in the past; religious belief was now often praised for bringing people together. President Eisenhower, who had belonged to no church until he entered politics, captured this when he urged people to practice their own religious creed, whatever it might be. "Our government makes no sense," he declared "unless it is founded in a deeply felt religious faith—and I don't care what it is." Tommy Sands, a young pop singer, advised his teenage fans that "all religions are the greatest."

Religious leaders offered a more sophisticated version of the same idea. Will Herberg's *Protestant-Catholic-Jew* (1955) argued that these three faiths were really "'saying the same thing' in affirming the 'spiritual ideals' and 'moral values' of the American Way of Life." Rabbi Morris Kretzer, head of the Jewish Chaplain's Organization, reassured Protestants and Catholics that they and their Jewish neighbors shared "the same rich heritage of the Old Testament . . . the sanctity of the Ten Commandments, the wisdom of the prophets, and the brotherhood of man." A 1954 survey indicated that more than 95 per cent of the population identified with one of the three major faiths, and religious commentators increasingly talked about the "Judeo-Christian traditon."

Individual religious leaders became national celebrities. Norman Vincent Peale, a Protestant minister who emphasized the relationship between religious faith and "peace of mind," sold millions of books declaring that belief in a Higher Power could reinvigorate daily life "with health, happiness, and goodness." His *The Power of Positive Thinking* (1952) remained a best-seller throughout the 1950s. The Catholic Bishop Fulton J. Sheen hosted an Emmy-winning, prime-time, TV program called *Life Is Worth Living*. Oral Roberts and Billy Graham—two younger, more charismatic TV ministers—began to spread their fiery brand of Protestant evangelism during the 1950s. Roberts, who claimed religious faith could heal even serious physical afflictions, remained on the fringes of respectability during the Eisenhower era; Graham, in contrast, became one of the most widely admired people in the country and a confidante of presidents.

Peale, Sheen, Roberts, and Graham identified themselves with conservative, anti-communist causes, but an emphasis on religious faith was hardly limited to the political right during the age of affluence. Dorothy Day, who had been involved in grass-roots activism since the early 1930s, continued to crusade for world peace and for a program aimed at redistributing wealth at home through the pages of *The Catholic Worker.* Church leaders and laypeople from all of the three major denominations supported the antidiscrimination cause and came to play important roles in the civil rights movement. Even so, the revival of religious faith during the 1950s remained closely identified with the culture of affluence.

Discontents of Affluence

Alongside the celebrations of economic affluence, political pluralism, and religious faith, the 1950s still produced a good deal of social criticism—especially about conformity, youth, mass culture, discrimination, and inequality.

Conformity in an Affluent Society

In *The Organization Man* (1956), the sociologist William H. Whyte Jr. indicted the business corporation for contributing to one of the problems produced by affluence: conformity. Criticizing the social, cultural, psychological (though not the economic) impact of large corporations, Whyte saw middle-class corporate employees accepting the values of their employers, at the expense of their own individuality. The security of knowing what the corporate hierarchy wanted—and when it wanted it—outweighed the organization man's concerns about a loss of individuality, Whyte argued.

In *The Lonely Crowd* (1950), David Riesman, another sociologist, offered a broader analysis of conformity. Riesman wrote of the shift—among members of the middle class—from an "inner-directed" society in which people looked to themselves and to their immediate families for a sense of identity and self-worth to an "other-directed" society in which people looked to peer groups for approval and measured their worth against mass-mediated models. A nation of other-directed citizens emphasized "adjustment" to the expectations of others rather than the individual "autonomy" displayed by an inner-directed citizenry. Riesman subsequently conceded that his autonomy-to-adjustment thesis might be overly broad but still insisted that he had correctly identified a growing trend toward conformity in American life.

To illustrate the subtle manner in which conformist values were taught to children, Riesman pointed to *Tootle the Engine,* a popular children's book of the 1950s. When Tootle showed a preference for frolicking in the fields beside the tracks, people came to him, not to scold or discipline him, but to exert peer pressure on him as a means of getting him to conform. If Tootle stayed on tracks laid down by others, they assured him, he would grow up to be a powerful and fast-moving streamliner. This message of unprotesting adjustment to peer expectations in this "modern cautionary tale," Riesman argued, contrasted vividly with the conflict-filled fairy tales, such as *Little Red Riding Hood,* on which earlier generations of young people had been raised.

The critique of conformity reached a broad audience through the best-selling books of journalist Vance Packard. *The Hidden Persuaders* (1957) argued that advertising—especially through calculated, subtle appeals to the insecurities of consumers—produced conformity. The book, Packard wrote his publisher, was designed to show "how to achieve a creative life in these conforming times" when so many people "are left only with the roles of being consumers or spectators."

Critics such as Whyte, Riesman, and Packard wrote primarily about the plight of middle-class men, but other writers, such as Betty Friedan, claimed to find a similar psychological malaise among many women. Corporation managers, for example, were criticized for expecting the wives of their male executives to behave properly at social functions; to help their husbands deal with the demands of corporate life, including the need for frequent relocation; and to help other wives adjust to the corporate world. The organization man, it was said, found that his ascent up the corporate ladder depended on how well his wife performed her informal corporate duties in an equally conformist social world.

Youth Culture

Concerns about young people also intensified during the 1950s. Many criminologists linked burgeoning sales of comic books to an alleged rise in juvenile delinquency, even among young people from "good" families. The psychologist Frederick Wertham, in *The Seduction of the Innocent* (1954), blamed comics displaying sex and violence for "mass-conditioning" children and for stimulating a wave of juvenile unrest that was becoming "virtually [a] new social phenomenon." Responding to local legislation and to calls for federal regulation, the comic book industry resorted to self-censorship. Publishers who adhered to new guidelines for the portrayal of violence and deviant behavior could display a seal of approval, and the great comic book scare soon faded away.

Critics of the youth culture, however, easily found other worrisome signs. In 1954 Elvis Presley, a former truck driver from Memphis, rocked the pop music establishment with a string of hits on the local Sun record label. Presley's sensual, electric stage presence thrilled his youthful admirers and outraged critics. Presley ("The King") and other youthful rock stars—such as Buddy Holly from West Texas, Richard Valenzuela (Richie Valens) from East Los Angeles, and Frankie Lymon from Spanish Harlem—crossed cultural and ethnic barriers and shaped new musical forms from older ones, especially African American rhythm and blues (R&B) and the "hillbilly" music of southern whites.

The first rock 'n' rollers inspired millions of fans and thousands of imitators. They sang about the joys of "having a ball tonight"; the pain of the "summertime blues"; the torment of being "a teenager in love"; and the hope of deliverance, through the power of rock, from "the days of old." Songs such as "Roll over Beethoven" by Chuck Berry (a singer-songwriter who merged southern hillbilly music with the blues of his native St. Louis) became powerful teen anthems, celebrating a new, consumer-oriented youth culture.

Drag Strip Protest • Although youthful protests are usually associated with the later 1960s and the war in Vietnam, teenagers were already staging demonstrations long before the anti-war movement took hold. Here, protesters take to the streets in 1960 to demand that San Diego create a drag strip. Their protest was labeled a "riot" by local authorities.

Guardians of older, family-oriented forms of mass culture found rock 'n' roll music even more frightening than comic books. They denounced its sparse lyrics, pulsating guitars, and screeching saxophones as an assault on the very idea of music. Religious groups condemned it as the "devil's music"; red-hunters detected a communist plan to corrupt youth; and segregationists found it to be part of a sinister plot to mix the races. The dangers of rock 'n' roll were abundantly evident in *The Blackboard Jungle* (1955), a film in which a racially mixed gang of high school students terrorized teachers, smashed jazz records, and mocked adult authority. The film's soundtrack featured another popular hit, "Rock around the Clock."

Some rock 'n' roll music looked critically at daily life in the 1950s. The satirical song "Charley Brown" contrasted pieties about staying in school with the bleak educational opportunities open to many students. Chuck Berry sang of alienated teenagers riding around "with no particular place to go." This kind of implied social criticism, which most older listeners failed to decode, anticipated the more overtly rebellious rock music of the 1960s.

But rock music and the larger youth culture gradually merged into the mass-consumption economy of the 1950s. Top-40 radio stations and the producers of 45-rpm records identified middle-class teenagers, whose average weekly income/allowance reached $10 by 1958, as a market worth targeting. Chuck Berry's "Sweet Little Sixteen" portrayed an affluent teenager eagerly chasing after the latest

The Drive-In • Whether it was called the Aztec (the name of this restaurant in southern California) or Porky's or King's, the drive-in became a nighttime magnet for an automobile-centered youth culture. The Aztec was eventually transformed into the Jack-in-the-Box chain.

fashions, the next rock 'n' roll concert, and "about half-a-million famed autographs." By 1960, record companies and disk jockeys promoted songs and performers exalting the pursuit of "fun, fun, fun" with the help of clothes, cars, and rock 'n' roll records. Rock music—and the product-centered culture of youth—had come to celebrate the ethic of a people of plenty.

The Mass Culture Debate

Criticism of conformity and of youth culture merged into a wider debate over the allegedly stultifying effects of mass culture. Much of the anxiety about the decline of individualism and the rise of rock 'n' roll could be traced to fears that "hidden persuaders" were now conditioning millions of people.

Custodians of culture decried mass-marketed products. According to the cultural critic Dwight MacDonald, "bad" art—such as rock music and Mickey Spillane's best-selling Mike Hammer series—was driving "good" art from the marketplace and making it difficult for people to distinguish between them. Consumed as rapidly as they were produced, works of mass culture said nothing about the complexities of life, MacDonald claimed. He and other critics of mass culture argued that entrepreneurs, by treating millions of consumers as if they were all the same, obscured difficult social issues with a blur of pleasant, superficial imagery. Critics also charged mass culture with destroying the richness of local differences. In a classic study of a small town in upstate New York, a team of sociologists claimed that the mass media were "so overwhelming that little scope is left for the expression of local cultural forms."

Television became a prominent target. Evolving out of network radio, television was dominated by three major corporations (NBC, CBS, and ABC) and sustained by advertisers, euphemistically called sponsors. Picturing millions of seemingly passive

TV: The "Electronic Hearth" • Advertisers and family advice books of the 1950s touted the television set as more than an electronic device. Sold as a piece of fine furniture, it was supposed to replace the traditional fireplace as the centerpiece of a home devoted to "family togetherness."

viewers gathered around "the boob tube," critics decried both the quality of mass-produced programming and its impact on the public. Situation comedies, such as *Father Knows Best,* generally featured middle-class, consumption-oriented suburban families. At the same time, network television responded to pressure from advertisers and avoided programs with contemporary themes in favor of ones that, according to TV's critics, encouraged retreat into unrealities such as the mythical, heroic Old West. In 1958, there were 25 westerns on network TV during prime time.

These critics also worried about how mass culture, especially television, seemed to be transforming the fabric of everyday life. Architects were calling for the rearrangement of living space within middle-class homes so that the television set could become the new focal point for family life, serving as an electronic substitute for the traditional fireplace hearth. Entire new lines of products—such as the frozen TV dinner, the TV tray, the recliner chair, and the influential magazine *TV Guide*—became extensions of the new televisual culture. And the TV set itself, which was almost always encased in some kind of substantial wood cabinet during the 1950s, became an important symbol of postwar affluence.

The Limits of the Mass Culture Debate

Most critics of mass culture doubted that things could really be changed. They acknowledged, for example, that the mass culture they detested was closely linked to the economic system they generally celebrated. Was it really possible to cure the ills of mass culture while still enjoying the benefits of affluence? Convinced that the nation, much like "Tootle the Engine," was on the right track, critics of mass culture invariably refused to join mavericks like C. Wright Mills and question the distribution of political and economic power in the United States. Radical critiques of industrial capitalism, heard so often during the 1930s, were no longer in vogue during the 1950s.

Moreover, the most obvious cures for the disease of mass culture clashed with the critics' own commitment to an open, pluralistic society. If, on the one hand, Congress were encouraged (as it had been during the comic book scare) to legislate against "dangerous" cultural products, censorship might end up curtailing the freedom of expression to which liberals of the 1950s swore allegiance. On the other hand, if local communities were to step in (as some did in the case of comics), the results might be even worse. The prospect of southern segregationists censoring civil rights literature or of local censorship boards banning movies produced in Hollywood or books published New York City hardly appealed to the cosmopolitan critics of mass culture. The critique of mass culture, in short, reached an impasse.

Meanwhile, amid the concern about mass culture, a number of other questions about the direction of postwar life were beginning to emerge. Despite the surface tranquillity of the 1950s, Americans remained especially divided over issues related to race and to the role of government.

The Fight against Discrimination, 1954–1960

When Dwight Eisenhower took office, the Supreme Court was slated to rehear a legal challenge—spearheaded by the NAACP and its legal strategist, Thurgood Marshall—to racially segregated school systems. Following the death in 1953 of Chief Justice Fred Vinson, Eisenhower rejected more conservative candidates to replace him on the Supreme Court and chose Earl Warren, a former governor of California. Under Warren, the Court would come to play an important role in the civil rights struggle, the most significant movement for change in the postwar period.

Brown v. Board

In 1954 Warren wrote the Court's unanimous opinion in *Brown* v. *Board of Education of Topeka*. While Warren was attorney general of California during the Second World War, he had pressed for the forcible detention of Japanese Americans, but he had subsequently become embarrassed by his role in this discriminatory action. In Brown, Warren embraced egalitarian principles he had earlier abandoned and declared that segregation of public schools violated the constitutional right of African American students to equal protection of the law. Although it technically applied only to educational facilities, Brown implied that all segregated public facilities, not simply schools, were open to legal challenge.

The job of carrying out the broader implications of *Brown* tested the nation's political and social institutions. The crusade against racial discrimination had long centered on the 16 states that the Census Bureau officially called "the South," but

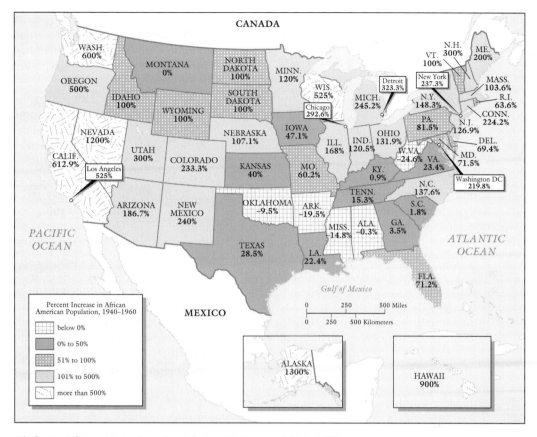

Shifts in African American Population Patterns, 1940–1960

demographic changes meant that national leaders could no longer treat the issue as simply a regional one.

The 1950s marked the beginning of a period in which the South was becoming more like the rest of the country. New cultural forces, such as network television, were linking the South more closely with a nationally based culture. Economic forces were also at work. Machines were replacing the region's predominantly black field workers, and the absence of strong labor unions and the presence of favorable tax laws were attracting national chain stores, business franchises, and northern-based industries to the South.

At the same time, the racial composition of cities in the West, Midwest, and Northeast was becoming more like that of the South. In 1940 more than three-quarters of the nation's African Americans lived in the South. Accelerating the pattern begun during the Second World War, African Americans left the rural South and settled in cities like Los Angeles, Chicago, New York, and Cleveland during the late 1940s and early 1950s. In the mid-1950s this demographic shift helped to quicken "white flight" to the suburbs and to transform political alignments. With African American voters becoming increasingly important in the North, for example, urban Democrats came to support the drive to end racial discrimination, one of the failed projects of the Fair Deal. Meanwhile, the Republicans were making small electoral gains in what had long been the Democratic Party's "solid South." Most important, African Americans themselves mounted a new attack on segregation and racial discrimination in the South.

The battle against racial discrimination was coming to dominate domestic politics. Segregationists in the South pledged "massive resistance" to the Supreme Court ruling in *Brown* v. *Board of Education*. Their lawyers resorted to traditional delaying tactics and invented new ones as well. This strategy seemed to be succeeding when in 1955 the Supreme Court ruled that school desegregation, although the law of the land, should proceed cautiously—with "all deliberate speed," as the justices put it. In the following year, 100 members of the U.S. House and Senate signed a "Southern Manifesto" in which they promised to support any state that intended "to resist forced integration by any lawful means."

Defiance went beyond the courtroom. Vigilantes unfurled the banners and donned the white robes of the Ku Klux Klan, which was joined by new racist organizations, such as the White Citizens Council. As a result, antidiscrimination activists constantly risked injury and death, while people only indirectly connected to the struggle also fell victim to racist violence. In August 1955 two white Mississippians murdered 14-year-old Emmett Till, a visitor from Chicago, for acting "disrespectful" to a white woman. Mamie Till Bradley demanded that her son's murder not remain a private incident; she insisted that his maimed corpse be displayed publicly for "the whole world to see" and that young Till's killers be punished. When their case came to trial, an all-white jury found the killers—who would subsequently confess their part in the murder—not guilty.

The Montgomery Bus Boycott and Martin Luther King Jr.

In response to the uncertainty of judicial remedies, African Americans began supplementing legal maneuvering with aggressive campaigns of direct action. In Montgomery, Alabama, Rosa Parks, a member of the local NAACP, was arrested in 1955 for refusing to obey a state segregation law that required black passengers to give up their seats to whites and sit at the back of the bus. Montgomery's black community, which had a long history of civil rights activism, responded to her arrest by boycotting public transportation and by organizing a system of private car pools as alternative transit. The resulting financial losses convinced the city's public transit system to reconsider its segregationist policy. Joining with Rosa Parks, many African American women spearheaded the bus boycott. The Montgomery boycott during 1955 and 1956 thus resulted in the desegregation of city buses and demonstrated to other black communities in the South that they could mobilize against acts of overt discrimination.

The Montgomery boycott vaulted the Reverend Martin Luther King Jr., one of its leaders, into the national spotlight. Born, raised, and educated in Atlanta, with a doctorate in theology from Boston University, King followed up the victory in Montgomery by joining with other black ministers to form the Southern Christian Leadership Conference (SCLC). In addition to pressing for the desegregation of public facilities, the SCLC launched an effort to register African American voters

Freedom Riders • Interracial groups of activists known as Freedom Riders risked racist violence in their crusade to desegregate buses in the Deep South. Here, in 1961, Freedom Riders watch a bus in which they had been traveling burn after it was firebombed in Alabama.

throughout the South. More activist than the NAACP, the SCLC served to spread King's broad vision of social change—integration forced by passive civil disobedience—throughout the nation. The purpose of civil disobedience, according to King, was to persuade people, through both words and deeds, of the moral evil of segregation and racial discrimination. The ultimate goal of the civil rights crusade was to bring "redemption and reconciliation" to American society. Aided by the national media, especially network television, King's powerful presence and religiously rooted rhetoric carried the message of the antidiscrimination movement in the South to the entire nation.

The Politics of Civil Rights

But political institutions in Washington responded very slowly. The Supreme Court expanded its definition of civil rights but generally backed away from mandating the sweeping institutional changes needed to make these rights meaningful. Congress, meanwhile, remained deeply divided on racial issues. With southern segregationists such as Harry Byrd and Howard Smith of Virginia, all of them members of the Democratic majority, holding key posts on Capitol Hill, antidiscrimination legislation faced formidable obstacles.

Even so, Congress passed its first civil rights measures in more than 80 years. The Civil Rights Act of 1957 set up a procedure for expediting lawsuits by African Americans who claimed their right to vote had been illegally abridged. It also created a permanent Commission on Civil Rights, although this was only an advisory body empowered to study alleged violations and recommend new remedies. In 1960, with the support of Lyndon Johnson of Texas, the Democratic leader in the Senate, another act promised additional federal support for blacks who were being barred from voting in the South. These civil rights initiatives, which became law against fierce opposition from southern Democrats, dramatized the difficulty of getting even relatively limited antidiscrimination measures through Congress. More sweeping civil rights laws seemed unthinkable during the 1950s.

President Eisenhower appeared largely indifferent to the issue of racial discrimination. When liberal Republicans urged him to take action—perhaps through an executive order barring racial discrimination on construction projects financed by federal funds—Ike did nothing. A gradualist on racial issues, he regarded the fight against discrimination as primarily a local matter, and he publicly doubted that any federal civil rights legislation could change the attitudes of people opposed to the integration of public facilities or job sites.

Indeed, Eisenhower's grasp of domestic issues seemed to grow more uncertain during the second term of his presidency. In the election of 1956, he achieved another landslide victory over Democrat Adlai Stevenson. Ike continued to enjoy great popularity, but his personal appeal did relatively little to help his party. In 1956 the Republicans failed to win back control of Congress from the Democrats. In fact, in this presidential election and in the off-year races of 1958, the GOP lost congressional seats as well as state legislatures and governors' mansions to the Democrats. After the 1958 elections, the Democrats outnumbered Republicans 64 to 34 in the Senate and 282 to 154 in the House. Meanwhile, Eisenhower, who had suffered a mild heart attack prior to the 1956 election, seemed progressively enfeebled, physically as well as politically. He appeared especially weak in his handling of racial issues.

In 1957, however, Eisenhower was forced to act. Orval Faubus, the segregationist governor of Arkansas, ordered his state's National Guard to block enforcement of a federal court order mandating integration of Little Rock's Central High School. Responding to this direct challenge to national authority, Eisenhower put the Arkansas National Guard under federal control and augmented it with members of the U.S. Army. Black students, escorted by armed troops, then were able to enter the high school. Despite Eisenhower's stand against Faubus during the Little Rock crisis, his overall approach to civil rights was, at best, inconsistent.

American Indian Policy

The Eisenhower administration also lacked coherent policies on issues affecting American Indians. It inherited two badly flawed programs, "termination" and "relocation," proposed during the Truman years and plunged ahead with their implementation. The termination policy, which allegedly was intended to end the status of Native Americans as "wards of the United States" and to grant them all the "rights and privileges pertaining to American citizenship," called for the national government to end its oversight of tribal affairs and to treat American Indians as individuals rather than as members of tribes. Its long-term goals, to be pursued on a tribe-by-tribe basis, were to abolish reservations, to liquidate assets of the tribes, and to end the kinds of federal services offered by the Bureau of Indian Affairs (BIA). In 1954, one year after this general policy had received congressional approval, six bills of termination were enacted. Immediately at stake was the legal status of more than 8,000 Native Americans and more than 1 million acres of tribal land. Because the Bill of Rights did not apply to Indians, those who opposed termination found it difficult to pursue legal redress: Under the Constitution, Native Americans were not entitled to civil rights protections.

Under the relocation program, which had begun in 1951 as a way of fostering "independence," Indians were encouraged to leave their rural reservations and take jobs in urban areas. In 1954 the BIA intensified its earliest relocation efforts, with Minneapolis, St. Louis, Dallas, and several other cities joining Denver, Salt Lake City, and Los Angeles as relocation sites. This program, like the termination policy, encouraged American Indians to migrate to urban areas and become assimilated into the social mainstream.

Realities mocked assimilationist theories. As several more termination bills were enacted during the Eisenhower years, almost 12,000 people lost their status as tribal members, and the bonds of communal life for many Indians grew weaker. At the same time, nearly 1.4 million acres of tribal lands were lost, often falling into the hands of real estate speculators. Indians from terminated tribes lost both their exemptions from state taxation and the social services provided by the BIA and gained almost nothing in return. Most terminated Indians sank into even deeper poverty. Relocation went no better. Promised a better life than what was available on reservations, most of the relocated Indians found only low-paying, dead-end jobs and racial discrimination. In the mid-1950s, as the issue of desegregation was still making its way through the federal court system, Indian children who had been relocated from reservations found it difficult even to enter *segregated,* let alone integrated, public schools in some cities. Despite its obvious problems, the program nevertheless continued throughout the Eisenhower years.

Total Urban and Rural Indian Population in the United States, 1940–1980

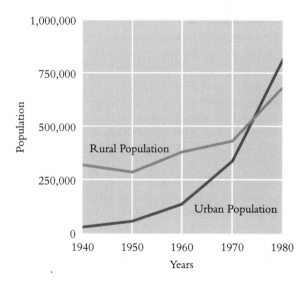

Gradually, however, both Indians and civil rights activists mobilized against the termination and relocation policies. Denounced as simply a different name for the old extermination policy of the late 19th and early 20th centuries, termination lost legitimacy rather quickly. By 1957 the BIA had scaled back its initial timetable for liquidating every tribe within five years, and in 1960 the party platforms of both the Republicans and Democrats repudiated the policy entirely. In 1962 this disastrous policy was itself terminated. Meanwhile, however, the relocation program continued, and by 1967 almost half of the nation's Indians were living in relocation cities. The policy hardly touched the deeply rooted problems that many Indians confronted, including a life expectancy only two-thirds that of whites, nor did it ever provide significantly better opportunities for employment or education.

Growth of Spanish-Speaking Populations

The millions of new Spanish-speaking people, many of whom had recently arrived in the United States, also highlighted the issue of discrimination. Taking advantage of discounted airfares between North America and the Caribbean, Puerto Ricans began moving to the mainland in large numbers. Finding only low-paying jobs and settling in older urban neighborhoods, especially in New York City, these new arrivals were U.S. citizens but often spoke only Spanish. In 1960 New York City's Puerto Rican community was nearly 100 times greater than it had been before the Second World War.

Meanwhile, large numbers of Spanish-speaking people from Mexico were moving into the Southwest, where they joined already sizable Mexican American communities. Beginning during the Second World War and continuing until 1967, the U.S. government sponsored the *bracero* (or farmhand) program, which brought nearly 5 million Mexicans northward, theoretically on short-term contracts, to serve as agricultural laborers. Many of the *braceros* remained in the United States after their contracts expired. Joining them were legal immigrants from Mexico and growing numbers of people who illegally filtered across the border. The illegal Mexican immigrants, derisively labeled "wetbacks" because they supposedly swam across the Rio Grande, became the target of an ongoing government dragnet, begun in 1950 and intensified by the Eisenhower administration, called "Operation Wetback." During a five-year period, the government claimed to have rounded up and deported to Mexico nearly 4 million people, allegedly all illegal immigrants. The well-publicized operation helped to stigmatize all people of Mexican descent and to justify discriminatory treatment by both government and private employers.

Leaders in long-established Mexican American communities mobilized to fight such discrimination. Labor organizers sought higher wages and better working conditions in the factories and fields, although the FBI labeled many of these efforts as "communist-inspired" and harassed unions—such as the United Cannery, Agricultural, Packing and Allied Workers of America (UCAPAWA)—that had large Mexican American memberships. A lengthy mining strike in New Mexico became the subject of the 1954 motion picture *Salt of the Earth*. Middle-class organizations, such as the League of United Latin American Citizens (LULAC) and the Unity League, also sought to desegregate schools, public facilities, and housing in Southern California and throughout the Southwest. In 1940 Mexican Americans had been the

"Operation Wetback" • In response to rising protests against an alleged "tidal wave" of illegal immigrants from Mexico—perjoratively called "wetbacks"—the U.S. government mounted an aggressive roundup campaign in 1954. "Operation Wetback" was a vast, military-style operation that sent more than 1 million workers back to Mexico.

most rural of all the major ethnic groups; by 1950, in contrast, more than 65 percent of Mexican Americans were living in urban areas, a figure that would climb to 85 percent by 1970. As a result of this fundamental demographic shift, Mexican Americans began to gain political clout in many southwestern cities.

Urban Issues

Ethnic issues often merged with a growing sense that the United States was bumbling toward a crisis in its cities. The growth of new, largely white, suburban areas in the 1950s was accompanied by new urban issues, many of them related to race. The restructuring of urban life, social critics charged, was another challenge to which the Eisenhower administration and Congress were devoting scant attention.

Ike's critics correctly linked the boom in suburbia with the bust in many urban areas. Throughout the 1950s, both public and private institutions were shifting money and construction projects away from the cities, especially away from neighborhoods in which Latinos and African Americans had settled. Adopting a policy called "redlining," many banks and loan institutions denied funds for home buying and business expansion in neighborhoods that were considered "decaying" or "marginal" because they contained aging buildings, dense populations, and growing numbers of nonwhites. Meanwhile, the Federal Housing Authority and other government agencies channeled most of their funds toward the new suburbs. In

1960, for example, the FHA failed to put up a single dollar for home loans in Camden or Paterson, New Jersey, cities in which nonwhite populations were growing, while it poured millions of dollars into surrounding, largely all-white suburbs.

"Urban renewal" programs, authorized by the Housing Act of 1949 (see Chapter 8), often amounted to "urban removal." Although federal housing laws called for "a feasible method for the temporary relocation" of persons displaced by urban renewal projects, developers often ignored the housing needs of the people they displaced. During the 1950s, New York City's housing czar, Robert Moses, routinely manipulated the figures in order to conceal the massive dislocations caused by his urban renewal and highway building programs. People with low-income jobs, especially African Americans and Puerto Ricans, were evicted so that their apartments and homes could be replaced by office buildings and freeways.

Public housing projects, which had been designed to provide affordable housing for low- and moderate-income families who were saving money to purchase their own homes, proved an especially grave disappointment. Although the suburbs, where land was abundant and relatively inexpensive, seemed an obvious place in which to build public housing, middle-income suburbanites blocked such construction. Consequently, public housing had to be built in the cities, where population density was high and land was expensive. At the same time, private housing interests lobbied to limit the units actually built and to ensure that public housing would offer few amenities. Originally conceived as a temporary alternative for families who would rather quickly move out to their own homes, public housing facilities became stigmatized as "the projects," housing of last resort for people with chronically low incomes and little prospect for economic advancement.

By the end of the 1950s, the urban policies of both the Fair Deal and the Eisenhower era were widely regarded as failures, especially by people in the new and growing field of urban planning. Urban renewal projects not only disrupted housing patterns but, in cities such as New York City, also helped to dislocate industries that had long provided entry-level jobs for unskilled workers. Both major presidential candidates in 1960 pledged to create a new cabinet office for urban affairs and to expand the federal government's role, a clear rejection of the stance of the Eisenhower administration.

Debates over Government's Role in the Economy

Controversy over urban issues was related to larger debates over the economic health of the country and over the role that government should play in economic life. Although Eisenhower sometimes hinted to conservative Republicans that he wanted to roll back the New Deal and the Fair Deal, he lacked both the will and the political support to do so. Actually, Eisenhower presided over a modest expansion of those earlier initiatives: an expanded Social Security system, higher minimum wages, better unemployment benefits, and a new Department of Health, Education, and Welfare (HEW). Still, as his stance on urban and racial issues showed, Eisenhower took few steps to enlarge governmental power. Dwight Eisenhower's popularity seemed to rest more on his personality rather than on the specifics of his policies, which were assailed from both right and left.

Eisenhower and the New Conservatives

As a result of his centrist position on most domestic issues, Eisenhower attracted the ire of a growing group of political conservatives. Eisenhower, of course, was the first Republican president since Herbert Hoover, but did his administration really represent basic GOP principles?

Not to Arizona's Barry Goldwater, who replaced Robert Taft as the hero of the Republican Party's right wing after Taft's death in 1953. A fervent anticommunist, who was elected to the U.S. Senate in 1952, Goldwater began to demand a more aggressive military stance than that favored by the former general. In his book *Conscience of a Conservative* (1960), Goldwater criticized postwar U.S. leaders, including Eisenhower, for failing to take stronger military measures against the Soviet Union and for not making "victory the goal of American policy." At the same time, Goldwater decried almost all domestic programs, especially civil rights legislation, as grave threats to individual liberty and came to criticize the Eisenhower administration for having aped the Democratic Party's "New Deal antics" in domestic policy-making.

At the same time that Goldwater was working to push the GOP to the right of Eisenhower's moderate Republicanism, William F. Buckley Jr. was trying to reshape a broader right-wing message for the country at large. Buckley, a devout Roman Catholic, first gained national attention while still in his twenties with a 1952 book, *God and Man at Yale,* that detected a "collectivist" and antireligious tilt in American higher education and that defended individualism and Christianity. Three years later, Buckley helped found the *National Review,* a magazine that attracted a talented group of writers.

The establishment of the *National Review* in 1955 represented an important moment for the political right. Although Buckley had earlier coauthored a defense of McCarthysim, the *National Review* moved away from extremist positions, particularly the anti-Semitism of some old-line conservatives and the hysterical anticommunism of groups such as the John Birch Society. Although this "new conservatism" began amid considerable doubts about its immediate prospects for success, Buckley's own *Up from Liberalism* (1959), Goldwater's *Conscience of a Conservative* and other books looked to a long-term strategy for building a right-of-center movement. To that end, conservatives established their own youth movement, Young Americans for Freedom (YAF), in 1960.

Advocates of a More Active Government

While the new conservatives were criticizing the Eisenhower administration for failing to break decisively with the policies of the Roosevelt and Truman years, liberals were grumbling that it was failing to address pressing public issues through the more active use of government power. They were especially critical of Eisenhower's relatively passive approach to questions involving racial discrimination. Moreover, pointing to a severe economic downturn in 1958 and 1959 when unemployment rose precipitously, critics ridiculed Eisenhower's commitment to a balanced budget as evidence of his 19th century approach and claimed that the White House was out of touch with American life. After Eisenhower suffered a second heart attack and a mild stroke during his second term, many critics talked about the need for more vigorous presidential leadership. Liberal advocates of greater governmental intervention in the economy, confident of their ability to maintain growth and prosperity, urged deficit spending by Washington as a way to stimulate continued economic expansion.

Other critics recommended dramatic increases in spending for national security. The 1957 Gaither Report, prepared by prominent people with close ties to defense industries, warned that the Soviet Union's GNP was growing even more quickly than that of the United States and that much of this expansion came in the military sector. Updating the assumptions of NSC-68 (see Chapter 8), the Gaither Report urged an immediate increase of about 25 percent in the Pentagon's budget and long-term programs for building fallout shelters, for developing intercontinental ballistic missiles (ICBMs), and for expanding conventional military forces. Another report, written by Henry Kissinger and issued by the Rockefeller Foundation, claimed that Eisenhower's New Look endangered national security because it relied too heavily on massive nuclear retaliation and downplayed nonnuclear options. It, too, called for greater spending on defense.

Eisenhower reacted cautiously to these reports. When newspapers to which the supposedly secret Gaither Report had been leaked called its findings "shocking" and judged the nation to be in grave peril, Ike calmly remarked that the report merely seemed "useful." Although he agreed to accelerate the development of ICBMs, he opposed any massive program for building fallout shelters or for fighting limited, nonnuclear wars around the globe. In fact, he reduced the size of several Army and Air Force units and kept his defense budget well below the levels his critics were proposing. Eisenhower could confidently take such steps because secret flights over the USSR by U-2 surveillance planes, which had begun in 1956, revealed that the Soviets were lagging behind, rather than outpacing, the United States in military capability.

Concerns about national security and calls for greater governmental spending also surfaced in the continuing controversy over education. Throughout the 1950s, some critics complained that schools were emphasizing "life adjustment" skills—getting along with others and accommodating to social change—instead of teaching the traditional academic subjects. Rudolf Flesch's best-selling book of 1955 wondered *Why Johnny Can't Read*. Other books suggested that Johnny and his classmates couldn't add or subtract very well either and that they lagged behind their counterparts in the Soviet Union in their mastery of science. Meanwhile, the nation's leading research universities were seeking greater government funding for higher education. In the summer of 1957, a committee of prominent scientists implored the Defense Department to expand funding for basic scientific research. "Research is a requisite for survival" in the nuclear age, they declared. Arguments for increased spending on education gained new intensity when, in October 1957, the Soviets launched the world's first artificial satellite, a 22-inch sphere called *Sputnik.*

Using the magical phrase "national security," school administrators and university researchers sought and won more federal dollars. The National Defense Education Act of 1958 funneled money to programs in science, engineering, foreign languages, and the social sciences. This act marked a milestone in the long battle to overcome congressional opposition, especially from southern segregationists who feared any intervention by Washington, to federal aid to education. A growth industry in federally supported research projects put down firm roots during the late 1950s.

Other critics urged the Eisenhower administration to seek increased federal spending for social welfare programs. Writing in 1958, in *The Affluent Society*, John Kenneth Galbraith found a dangerous tilt in the "social balance," away from "public goods." Affluent families could travel in air-conditioned, high-powered automobiles, Galbraith observed, but they must pass "through cities that are badly paved, made hideous by litter, blighted buildings," and billboards. While the researcher who develops a new carburetor or an improved household cleanser is well rewarded, the "public servant who dreams up a new public service is [labeled] a wastrel. Few public offenses are more reprehensible," Galbraith sardonically noted, than trying to advance the general welfare.

Galbraith's musings seemed mild in comparison to the jeremiads of Michael Harrington. Although his best-selling book, *The Other America* (1962), links him with the presidencies of John Kennedy and Lyndon Johnson, Harrington actually began writing about economic inequality during the 1950s. In 1959, *Commentary*, one of several influential magazines that featured social criticism during the late 1950s, published an article in which Harrington argued that the problem of economic inequality remained as urgent as it had been during the 1930s. At least one-third of the population was barely subsisting in a land of supposed affluence. Avoiding statistics and economic jargon, Harrington told dramatic stories about the ways in which poverty could ravage the bodies and spirits of people who had missed out on the affluence of the 1940s and 1950s.

During the early 1960s, when domestic policymaking became a priority of John F. Kennedy and Lyndon Baines Johnson, critics such as Galbraith and Harrington became political celebrities. But their critique should be seen as a product of the political culture of the late 1950s. The Kennedy presidency of 1961–1963 would be firmly rooted in the critique of both foreign and domestic policymaking that had emerged during the Eisenhower years.

The Kennedy Years: Foreign Policy

John Fitzgerald Kennedy, the first president to be born in the 20th century, had been groomed for the White House by his politically ambitious father. A conservative Democrat who had served as U.S. ambassador to Great Britain in the late 1930s, Joseph P. Kennedy sent his son John to Harvard. After his graduation in 1940, young John Kennedy pursued a life devoted to both private passions (especially for Hollywood movie stars) and public service. After winning military honors while serving in the U.S. Navy during the Second World War, Kennedy entered politics. In 1946 he won election from Massachusetts to the House of Representatives, and in 1952 he captured a seat in the Senate. In Washington, Kennedy was better known for his social life than for his command of legislative details, but he gradually gained a national political reputation, largely on the basis of his charm and youthful image. He was aided by his 1953 marriage to Jacqueline Bouvier. In 1956, he narrowly missed winning the Democratic vice presidential nomination.

The Election of 1960

Between 1956 and 1960, Kennedy barnstormed the country, speaking at party functions and rounding up supporters for a presidential bid. This early campaigning, along with his talented political advisers and his family's vast wealth, helped Kennedy overwhelm his primary rivals, including the more liberal Senator Hubert Humphrey of Minnesota and Lyndon Johnson. By pledging to keep his Catholic religion separate from his politics and by openly confronting those who appealed to anti-Catholic prejudice, Kennedy defused the religious issue that had doomed the candidacy of Al Smith in 1928 (see Chapter 5).

Richard Nixon, who was obliged to run on Eisenhower's record even though Ike initially seemed lukewarm about Nixon's candidacy, remained on the defensive throughout the campaign of 1960. Nixon seemed notably off balance during the first of several televised debates in which political pundits credited the cool, tanned Kennedy with a stunning victory over the pale, nervous Nixon. Despite chronic and severe health problems, which his loyal staff effectively concealed, Kennedy projected the image of a youthful, vigorous leader.

During the 1960 campaign, Kennedy stressed four issues, firmly associated with critics of the Eisenhower administration, that together made up what he called his "New Frontier" proposals. On civil rights and social programs, he espoused liberal positions that as a senator he had avoided. He pledged support for antidiscrimination efforts, which had been downplayed in the Democratic campaigns of 1952 and 1956. In an important symbolic act, he sent his aides to Georgia to assist Martin Luther King Jr., who had been sentenced to six months in jail for a minor traffic violation. Although Senator Kennedy's own civil rights record was mixed, he promised to take the kind presidential action that Eisenhower had rejected and to push for new legislation against racial discrimination. Moreover, Kennedy endorsed the sort of social programs that John Kenneth Galbraith and other liberals had been advocating. Although his proposals remained vague, he did mention greater federal spending to rebuild rural communities, to increase educational opportunities, and to improve urban conditions.

Kennedy also highlighted two other issues that had provoked debate during the 1950s: stimulating greater economic growth and conducting a more aggressive, Cold War foreign policy. Dismissing Eisenhower's cautious economic policies as ineffectual, Kennedy surrounded himself with advisers who spoke of stimulating the economy by means of tax cuts and deficit spending measures. Gradually, Kennedy embraced the promises, though not all of the specific proposals, of these progrowth economists. And on Cold War issues, he criticized Eisenhower for failing to rid the hemisphere of Castro in Cuba and for allowing a "missile gap" to develop in U.S. defenses against the Soviet Union. By spending heavily on defense, he claimed, he would create a "flexible response" against communism, especially in the Third World. Adlai Stevenson, in his 1956 campaign against Eisenhower, had said Americans could no longer "drift, we must go forward." Using similar rhetoric, Kennedy declared that his campaign rested on "the [single] assumption that the American people are tired of the drift in our national course . . . and that they are ready to move again."

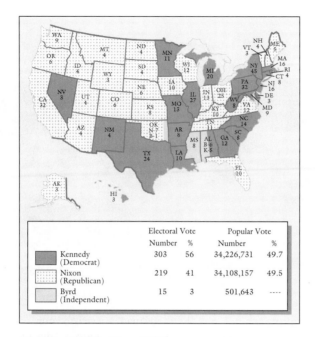

		Electoral Vote		Popular Vote	
		Number	%	Number	%
■	Kennedy (Democrat)	303	56	34,226,731	49.7
▦	Nixon (Republican)	219	41	34,108,157	49.5
▨	Byrd (Independent)	15	3	501,643	----

Presidential Election, 1960

The 1960 election defied easy analysis. Although Kennedy would claim that he had received a mandate, his margin of victory was quite narrow. Kennedy defeated Nixon by only about 100,000 popular votes and won the electoral votes of several states, including Illinois, by a razor-thin margin. Apparently hurt by the religious issue, especially in the South, Kennedy won a smaller percentage of the popular vote than most other Democrats running for lesser offices. Clearly, his victory owed a great deal to his vice presidential running mate, Lyndon Johnson, whose appeal to southern whites helped the ticket carry the Deep South and Johnson's home state of Texas.

From the outset, the president and his wife Jacqueline riveted media attention on the White House. They hobnobbed with movie stars such as Frank Sinatra and brought prominent intellectuals such as Arthur Schlesinger Jr. into the administration. The Kennedy inaugural featured designer clothing, the aged poet Robert Frost, and a stirring speech in which Kennedy challenged people to "ask not what your country can do for you; ask what you can do for your country." The "best and the brightest," the hard-driving people who joined Kennedy's New Frontier, promised to launch exciting new crusades, even to the ultimate frontier of outer space. Momentum and change, however, lay more often in rhetoric and style than in action.

Kennedy's Foreign Policy Goals

In foreign policy, Kennedy boasted of making a break with the past to wage the Cold War more vigorously. Although Secretary of Defense Robert McNamara discovered that the much-publicized "missile gap" simply did not exist, Kennedy raised

U.S. Peace Corps in the Philippines • John F. Kennedy made service to country—and to the world-wide fight against communism—the centerpiece of his administration. Under the Peace Corps program, young volunteers such as this one in the Philippines were encouraged to use their energy to assist in projects for economic development throughout the world.

the defense budget anyway. Military assistance programs, propaganda agencies, and covert action plans all received strong support from the White House. In one of his most popular initiatives, the president created the Peace Corps, a new program that sent Americans, especially young people, to nations around the world to work on development projects that were supposed to undercut the appeal of communism.

Kennedy, however, also built upon many of Eisenhower's policies. Eisenhower's last-minute efforts to reorient Latin American policies away from reliance on dictators and toward support of more progressive programs were elaborated on and repackaged as Kennedy's "Alliance for Progress." Proposed in the spring of 1961 as a way to prevent the spread of anti-Americanism and communist insurgencies, the Alliance offered $20 billion in loans over a 10-year period to Latin American countries that would undertake land reform and democratic development measures. The Alliance, based on a naive assessment of the obstacles to social and economic development, rapidly failed.

Cuba and Berlin

The worst fiasco of the Kennedy presidency, a daring but ill-conceived CIA mission against Cuba, also had its roots in the Eisenhower administration. The CIA, building on the experience of the covert actions that had overthrown leftist governments in Iran and Guatemala, was planning a secret invasion to topple Fidel Castro, Cuba's revolutionary leader. On April 17, 1961, when U.S.-backed and trained forces (mainly anticommunist Cuban exiles) landed at the Bahia de Cochinas (the Bay of Pigs) on the southern coast of Cuba, however, the expected popular uprising against Castro did not occur. The invaders were quickly surrounded and imprisoned. Kennedy refused to provide the air support that Cuban exiles had been led to expect and at first even tried to deny that the United States had been involved in the invasion. But the CIA's role quickly became public, and anti-Yankee sentiment mounted in Latin America. Castro tightened his grip over Cuba and strengthened his ties with the Soviet Union. "I have made a tragic mistake," Kennedy told Clark Clifford, an adviser. "Not only were our facts in error, but our policy was wrong." Yet, stung by the failed invasion, the Kennedy administration continued to target Castro with a covert program called Operation Mongoose, which consisted of economic destabilization activities and futile assassination plots. In one of many attempts to kill Castro, the CIA worked directly with U.S. crime figures, who also wanted revenge on Castro for shutting down their casinos.

Another dramatic Cold War confrontation loomed in Berlin. In June 1961, Nikita Khrushchev and Kennedy met in Vienna, where Khrushchev proposed ending the Western presence in Berlin and reuniting the city as part of East Germany. His proposal was motivated by the steady flow of immigrants from East Germany into West Berlin, a migration that was both embarrassing and economically draining to the German communist regime. Kennedy was forceful in his refusal to abandon West Berlin, but the East German government continued to press Khrushchev to help solve their problems. On August 13, 1961, the communist regime began to erect first a barbed-wire fence and then a concrete wall to separate East from West Berlin. East Germans attempting to escape into the West were shot. The Berlin Wall, which gradually became covered with graffiti on its westward side, became a symbol of the Cold War and of communist repression. Kennedy's assertion, *"Ich bin ein Berliner"* ("I am a Berliner"), delivered in front of the wall to a massive crowd, which cheered his pledge to defend West Berlin, became one of the most memorable lines of his presidency.

Superpower confrontation and the Kennedy administration's vendetta against Castro escalated to its most dangerous level during the Cuban Missile Crisis of 1962. The Soviet Union, responding to Castro's request, sent sophisticated weapons to Cuba. In October, after spy-plane flights confirmed the existence of missile launching sites there, the Kennedy administration publicly warned that it would not allow nuclear warheads to be installed so close to American shores. Kennedy demanded that the Soviets dismantle the missile silos they had already prepared and turn back some supply ships that were heading for Cuba. After dramatic meetings with his top advisers, Kennedy rejected an outright military strike that might have killed Soviet personnel in Cuba, setting off war between the superpowers. Instead, he ordered the U.S. Navy to "quarantine" the island. The Strategic Air Command was put on full alert for possible nuclear war. Meanwhile, both sides engaged in complicated, secret diplomatic maneuvers to prevent a nuclear confrontation.

The maneuvers succeeded. On October 28, 1962, Khrushchev ordered the missiles dismantled and the Soviet supply ships brought home; Kennedy promised not to invade Cuba and secretly assured Khrushchev that he would complete the previously ordered withdrawal of U.S. Jupiter missiles from Turkey. In the mid-1990s, with the opening of some Soviet archives, Americans learned that the crisis had

The Cuban Missile Crisis, 1962 • As the United States and the Soviet Union squared off in October 1962 over the issue of Soviet missiles in Cuba, people remained close to their TV sets in order to follow events in a confrontation that threatened to end in nuclear war. Here, a group of Cuban refugees watches an address by President John Kennedy on the state of negotiations.

been even more perilous that they had imagined. Unknown to Kennedy's circle at the time, the Soviets already had tactical nuclear weapons in Cuba that could have been launched.

After the Cuban Missile Crisis, both superpowers seemed to recognize the perils of direct conflict. Secretary of Defense McNamara later recalled leaving a presidential conference during the 13-day crisis, looking up at the sky, and wondering if the world would still be there 24 hours later. A direct phone line was established between Moscow and Washington to ensure the kind of communication that might forestall a nuclear confrontation or an accident in the future. And both nations became a bit more cautious, seeking advantage through covert action and client states rather than direct confrontation.

Southeast Asia and "Flexible Response"

In Southeast Asia, Kennedy followed Eisenhower's policy of supporting the Diem regime and trying to build South Vietnam into a viable, noncommunist state. After the Bay of Pigs disaster, in which the attempt to overthrow an already established pro-communist government had failed, Kennedy decided that the U.S. must put down communist-led "wars of national liberation" before they succeeded.

Kennedy viewed Vietnam as a test case for his new approach of "flexible response," which aimed at implementing a variety of methods to combat the growth of communist movements. Elite U.S. special forces known as Green Berets were trained in "counterinsurgency" tactics to use against communist guerrillas; cadres of social scientists charged with "nation building" were sent as advisers; Michigan State University dispatched experts to revamp South Vietnam's police forces. And when all these efforts brought nothing but greater corruption and a deeper sense of isolation to the Diem regime, the CIA gave disgruntled military officers in the South Vietnamese army the green light to orchestrate Diem's overthrow. Just weeks before Kennedy himself would be assassinated, Diem—the man whom both Eisenhower and Kennedy had tried to convert into the founding father of a democratic Vietnam—was run out of his palace and murdered. The coup against Diem brought a military leader to power, but this seemed only to breed even greater political instability in South Vietnam.

The Kennedy Years: Domestic Policy

Despite his campaign promises to increase federal spending as a way of stimulating faster economic growth, Kennedy was slow to depart from Eisenhower's cautious fiscal policies. He was fearful of angering fiscal conservatives and business leaders by running federal budget deficits greater than those of the Eisenhower years. Relations with corporate leaders still turned ugly in 1962, when Kennedy publicly clashed with the president of U.S. Steel over that company's decision to raise prices beyond the guidelines suggested by the administration.

Policymaking under Kennedy

Eventually, though, Kennedy endorsed tax breaks as a means of promoting economic growth. According to prevailing theory, lower tax rates for everyone and special deductions for corporations that invested in new plants and equipment would free up money for investment that would eventually help all Americans. Kennedy had cautiously suggested such tax breaks on business investments in 1961, and in 1962 he urged Congress to change the complex tax code. Despite opposition from those who thought the breaks would unfairly benefit corporations and the wealthy, the bill seemed headed for passage in the fall of 1963.

On matters of social welfare, the Kennedy administration, during its first two years, advanced policies that had been initiated by the Fair Deal of the 1940s—namely, a higher minimum wage and continuation of urban renewal programs. It also lent its support to the Area Redevelopment Bill, which called for directing federal grants and loans to areas (Appalachia was a favorite of Kennedy's) that had missed out on the general economic prosperity of the postwar years. Passed in 1961, the program unfortunately did little to create new jobs or promote business growth in those areas. Meanwhile, under the urban renewal programs begun during the 1940s, bulldozers were still razing large parts of urban America so that low-income housing continued to be replaced by construction projects aimed at middle- and upper-income people. Finally, the Kennedy administration made the fight against organized crime a top priority—much more so (at least initially) than the fight for racial equality.

The Civil Rights Crusade, 1960–1963

Although JFK talked about new civil rights legislation, he tried to placate segregationist Democrats—especially Virginia's Howard Smith, who controlled the Rules Committee of the House of Representatives—by doing little to press the issue for nearly the first two years of his presidency. Meanwhile, the president and his brother Robert, the attorney general, listened sympathetically to complaints from J. Edgar Hoover, director of the FBI, about the allegedly suspicious political activities of Martin Luther King Jr. and his associates. To keep tabs on King's activities and gather information that it might use against him, the FBI used surveillance and, ultimately, illegal wiretaps of his private conversations. (The Bureau also used illegal wiretaps against organized crime figures.)

Rising dissatisfaction over the slow pace of the campaign against racial discrimination, however, gradually forced the Kennedy administration to consider new initiatives. In early 1960 young African American students at North Carolina A & T College in Greensboro sat down at a dimestore lunch counter, defied state segregation laws, and asked to be served in the same manner as white patrons. It was the beginning of the "sit-in" movement, a new phase in the civil rights movement in which groups of young activists challenged legal segregation by demanding equal access to hitherto segregated public facilities. All across the South, demonstrators staged nonviolent sit-in demonstrations at restaurants, bus and train stations, and other public facilities.

The courage and commitment of the demonstrators gave the antidiscrimination movement new momentum. With songs such as "We Shall Overcome" and "Oh Freedom" inspiring solidarity, young people pledged their talents, their resources—indeed their lives—to the civil rights struggle. In 1961 interracial activists from the Congress of Racial Equality (CORE) and the Student Non-Violent Coordinating Committee (SNCC), a student group that had grown out of the sit-in movement, risked racist retaliation in "freedom rides" across the South; the freedom riders were determined that a series of federal court decisions, which had declared segregation on buses and in waiting rooms to be unconstitutional, would not be ignored by southern officials.

The new grass-roots activism, in which CORE and SNCC seized the initiative from the NAACP and the SCLC, forced the Kennedy administration to respond. In 1961 it sent federal marshals into the South in order to protect freedom riders. In 1962 and again the following year, it called on National Guard troops and federal marshals to prevent segregationists from stopping racial integration at several educational institutions in the Deep South, including the universities of Mississippi and Alabama. In November 1962, Kennedy issued a long-promised executive order that banned racial discrimination in housing financed by the national government. Several months later, in February 1963, Kennedy sent Congress a moderate civil rights bill, which focused on providing faster trial procedures in voting rights cases, in the hope of forestalling future confrontations.

But events were outpacing Kennedy's cautious policies. Racial conflict convulsed Birmingham, Alabama, in 1963. White police officers used dogs and high-power water hoses on young African Americans who were demanding an end to segregation in the city. Four children were later murdered (and 20 injured) when racists bombed Birmingham's Sixteenth Street Baptist Church, a center of the antisegregation campaign. When thousands of blacks took to the streets in protest— and two more children were killed, this time by police officers— the Kennedy administration finally took more vigorous action to prevent what it considered the possibility of "a real racial war" in Birmingham.

During the last six months of the Kennedy presidency, civil rights issues dominated domestic politics. The escalating violence in the South was becoming the subject of frequent TV specials. Kennedy himself made an emotional plea on television for a national commitment to the cause of antidiscrimination. Recent events had raised "a moral issue . . . as old as Scriptures and . . . as clear as the Constitution." The time for "patience" and "delay," he declared, had passed.

The Kennedy administration, though, still hoped to shape the direction and pace of change by passing new laws to get demonstrators "off the streets and into the courts." Thus, it supported stronger civil rights legislation, including a ban on racial discrimination in all public facilities and housing and new federal laws to guarantee the vote to millions of African Americans who were being kept from polls in the South. Later, when the administration discovered that it could not derail a grass-roots "March on Washington for Jobs and Freedom," planned for the late summer of 1963, it belatedly endorsed this demonstration.

A massive march on Washington, a dream since the 1940s of such antidiscrimination activists as union leader A. Philip Randolph, finally took place on August, 28, 1963. An integrated group of more than 200,000 people marched through the nation's capital. Leaders of the march endorsed Kennedy's new civil rights bill, but they also pressed a broader agenda. In addition to more effective civil rights legislation, the marchers' formal demands included a higher minimum wage and a federal program to guarantee new jobs. It was on behalf of a broad vision of social transformation that Martin Luther King Jr. delivered, in front of the Lincoln Memorial, his eloquent "I Have a Dream" speech. The march on Washington, which received favorable coverage from the national media, put considerable pressure on the White House and Congress to offer new legislative initiatives.

Women's Issues

The seeds of a resurgent women's movement were also being sown, although more quietly, during the Kennedy years. Kennedy's own call for young people to enter public service, in organizations such as the Peace Corps, raised young women's expectations for careers outside of marriage and child-rearing. African American activists such as Bernice Johnson Reagon (whose career with the Freedom Singers combined music and social activism) and Fannie Lou Hamer (who helped to organize an integrated Mississippi Freedom Democratic Party) fought discrimination based on both race and gender. Similarly, Chicana farm workers were key figures in the activism that led to the organization of the United Farm Workers of America, a union headed by

Cesar Chavez. Women also played an important role in protests by the Committee for a Sane Nuclear Policy (Sane) and the Women's Strike for Peace against the U.S.-Soviet arms race. All across the political spectrum, in fact, women were speaking out on contemporary issues. The new conservative movement benefited from the energy of women such as Phyllis Schlafly, whose book *A Choice, Not an Echo* (1964) became one of the leading manifestos of the Republican Party's right wing. And during Kennedy's final year in office, 1963, Betty Friedan published *The Feminine Mystique*, a very different kind of political statement. Generally credited with helping to spark a new phase of the feminist movement, Friedan's book drew on her own social criticism from the late 1950s to articulate the dissatisfactions that many middle-class women felt about the narrow confines of domestic life and the lack of public roles available to them.

To address women's issues, Kennedy appointed the Presidential Commission on the Status of Women, chaired by Eleanor Roosevelt. Negotiating differences between moderate and more militant members, the commission issued a report that documented discrimination against women in employment opportunities and wages. Kennedy responded with a presidential order designed to eliminate gender discrimination within the federal civil service system. His administration also supported the Equal Pay Act of 1963, which made it a federal crime for employers to pay lower wages to women who were doing the same work as men.

The Assassination of John F. Kennedy

By the fall of 1963 the Kennedy administration, though still worried about its ability to push legislation through a recalcitrant Congress, was preparing initiatives on civil rights and economic opportunity. Then, on November 22, 1963, John F. Kennedy was shot down as his presidential motorcade moved through Dallas, Texas. Police quickly arrested Lee Harvey Oswald as the alleged assassin. Oswald had ties to the Marcello crime family, had once lived in the Soviet Union, and had a bizarre set of political affiliations, especially with groups interested in Cuba. Oswald declared his innocence, but he was never brought to trial. Instead, Oswald himself was killed, while in the custody of the Dallas police, by Jack Ruby, a nightclub owner who also had links to powerful crime figures. A lengthy but flawed investigation by a special commission headed by Chief Justice Earl Warren concluded that both Oswald and Ruby had acted alone—but these claims came under increasing scrutiny. In 1978 a special panel of the House of Representatives claimed that Kennedy might have been the victim of an assassination plot, perhaps involving organized crime. A variety of other theories about Kennedy's assassination sprang up, including one, which pointed toward the CIA, advanced in Oliver Stone's film, *JFK* (1991).

Although most historians ridiculed Stone's scenario, his film reignited controversy over the report issued by the Warren commission. In response, Congress created the Assassinations Records Review Board as a means of preserving from destruction information about Kennedy's death. More than 35 years after Kennedy's death, competing theories about the number of shots, the trajectory of the bullets, and the nature of the president's wounds still reverberate through public discourse.

Whatever the circumstances, the brief Kennedy presidency ended in Dallas's Parkland Hospital, and Vice President Lyndon Baines Johnson of Texas inherited the burdens of framing new domestic policies and conducting a global foreign policy.

Conclusion

After 1954, the Cold War fears associated with McCarthyism began to abate. In this new atmosphere, Presidents Dwight Eisenhower and John F. Kennedy cautiously eased tensions with the Soviet Union, especially after Kennedy found himself on the brink of nuclear war over the presence of Soviet weapons in Cuba in 1962. Even so, both presidents continued to pursue similar, staunchly anticommunist, foreign policies that focused on the buildup of nuclear weapons, economic pressure, and covert activities. Developments in the Third World, particularly in Cuba and Southeast Asia, became of growing concern.

At home, the period from 1954 to 1963 was one of generally steady economic growth. A cornucopia of new consumer products encouraged talk about an age of affluence but also produced apprehension about conformity, mass culture, and the problems of youth. At the same time, the concerns of racial minorities and other people who were missing out on this period's general affluence increasingly moved to the center of public debates over the meaning of liberty and equality. The Eisenhower administration, many critics charged, seemed too reluctant to use the power of government to fight segregation or to create economic conditions that would distribute the benefits of affluence more widely. The political initiatives of the early 1960s, associated with John F. Kennedy, grew out of such criticisms.

Although Kennedy did not rush to deal with domestic issues—in large part because he believed that foreign policy needed to take precedence—the press of events gradually forced his administration to use government power to confront racial discrimination and advance the cause of equality at home. When Kennedy was killed in November 1963, a new kind of insurgent politics, growing out of the battle against racial discrimination in the Deep South, was beginning to transform political life in the United States.

In the post-Kennedy era, debates would become riveted around issues related to the government's exercise of power: Was the U.S. spreading liberty in Vietnam? Was it sufficiently active in pursuing equality for racial minorities and the poor? Lyndon Johnson's troubled presidency would grapple with these questions.

Chronology

1954 *Brown v. Board of Education of Topeka* decision • SEATO formed • Arbenz government overthrown in Guatemala • Elvis Presley releases first record on Sun label • Geneva Peace Accords in Southeast Asia

1955 Montgomery bus boycott begins • *National Review* founded

1956 Suez crisis • Anti-Soviet uprisings occur in Poland and Hungary • Federal Highway Act passed • Eisenhower reelected

1957 Eisenhower sends troops to Lebanon • Eisenhower sends troops to Little Rock • Congress passes Civil Rights Act, first civil rights legislation in 80 years • Soviets launch *Sputnik* • Gaither Report urges more defense spending

1958 National Defense Education Act passed by Congress • *The Affluent Society* published

1959 Khrushchev visits United States

1960 Civil Rights Act passed • U-2 incident ends Paris summit • Kennedy elected president • Sit-in demonstrations begin

1961   Bay of Pigs invasion fails • Berlin Wall erected • Freedom rides begin in the South • Kennedy announces Alliance for Progress

1962   Cuban missile crisis • Kennedy sends troops to University of Mississippi to enforce integration

1963   Civil rights activists undertake march on Washington • Betty Friedan's *The Feminine Mystique* published • Kennedy assassinated (November 22); Lyndon Johnson becomes president

Suggested Readings

Eisenhower's Foreign Policy

Robert Divine, *Eisenhower and the Cold War* (1981) and Blanche Wiesen Cook, *The Declassified Eisenhower* (1981) offer differing interpretations of Eisenhower's foreign policies. See also Joann P. Krieg, ed., *Dwight D. Eisenhower: Soldier, President and Statesman* (1987), and H. W. Brands, *Cold Warriors: Eisenhower's Generation and American Foreign Policy* (1988). See also the many works on Eisenhower which are cited in Chapter 8.

Specialized Studies on Foreign Policy

More specialized studies on foreign policy include Robert Divine, *Blowing In the Wind: The Nuclear Test-Ban Debate* (1978) and *The Sputnik Challenge: Eisenhower's Response to the Soviet Satellite* (1993); Allan M. Winkler, *Life Under a Cloud: American Anxiety About the Atom* (1993); Stuart W. Leslie, *The Cold War and American Science: The Military-Industrial-Academic Complex at MIT and Stanford* (1993). Regional studies include Stephen G. Rabe, *Eisenhower and Latin America: The Foreign Policy of Anticommunism* (1988); Zhang Shu Guang, *Deterrence and Strategic Culture Culture: Chinese-American Confrontations, 1949–1958* (1992); Robert J. McMahon, *The Cold War on the Periphery: The United States, India and Pakistan* (1994); Kenton J. Clymer, *Quest for Freedom: The United States and India's Independence* (1995); Isaac Alteras, *Eisenhower and Israel: U.S.-Israeli Relations, 1953–1960* (1993); Thomas G. Paterson, *Contesting Castro: The United States and the Triumph of the Cuban Revolution* (1994); Bonnie F. Saunders, *The United States and Arab Nationalism: The Syrian Case, 1953–1960* (1996); Saki Dockrill, *Eisenhower's New-Look National Security Policy, 1953–61* (1996); G. Wyn Rees, *Anglo-American Approaches to Alliance Security, 1955–60* (1996); and Cole C. Kingseed, *Eisenhower and Suez Crisis of 1956* (1995). The growing importance of intelligence agencies in foreign policy is examined in Stephen Ambrose and Richard H. Immerman, *Ike's Spies: Eisenhower and the Espionage Establishment* (1981) and *The CIA in Guatemala: The Foreign Policy of Intervention* (1982); Michael R. Beschloss, *Mayday: Eisenhower, Khrushchev, and the U-2 Affair* (1986); Rhodri Jeffreys-Jones, *The CIA and American Democracy* (1989); Loch K. Johnson, *America's Secret Power: The CIA in a Democratic Society* (1989); Thomas F. Troy, *Donovan and the CIA: A History of the Establishment of the Central Intelligence Agency* (1981); John Prados, *President's Secret Wars: CIA and Pentagon Covert Operations since World War II* (1986); Audrey R. Kahin and George McT. Kahin, *Subversion as Foreign Policy: The Secret Eisenhower and Dulles Debacle in Indonesia* (1995); and Nicholas Cullather, *Operation PSSUCCESS: The United States and Guatemala 1952–54* (1997). African Americans and foreign policy are discussed in Brenda Gayle Plummer, *Rising Wind: Black Americans and U.S. Foreign Affairs, 1935–1960* (1996) and Penny M. Von Eschen, *Race Against Empire: Black Americans and Anticolonialism, 1937–1957* (1997). On cultural diplomacy, see especially Walter L. Hixson, *Parting the Curtain: Propaganda, Culture, and the Cold War, 1945–1961* (1997), and Robert H. Haddow, *Pavilions of Plenty: Exhibiting American Culture Abroad in the 1950s* (1997).

U.S. Involvement in Vietnam

On the deepening U.S. involvement in Vietnam, see David L. Anderson, *Trapped by Success: The Eisenhower Administration and Vietnam, 1953–1961* (1991); George Herring, *America's Longest War: The United States and Vietnam, 1950–1975* (1986); Andrew J. Rotter, *The Path to Vietnam: Origins of the American Commitment to Southeast Asia* (1987); Lloyd C. Gardner, *Approaching Vietnam: From World*

War II through Dien Bien Phu (1988); James Arnold, *The First Domino: Eisenhower, the Military, and America's Intervention in Vietnam* (1991); and Melanie Billings-Yun, *Decision against War: Eisenhower and Dien Bien Phu, 1954* (1988).

Domestic Politics

Domestic politics are treated in Mark Rose, *Interstate: Express Highway Politics, 1941–1956* (1979); R. Alton Lee, *Eisenhower and Landrum Griffin: A Study in Labor-Management Politics* (1990); Richard Kluger, *Simple Justice: The History of Brown v. Board of Education and Black America's Struggle for Equality* (1975); Austin Sarat, ed., *Race, Law, and Culture: Reflections on Brown v. Board of Education* (1996); Tom Lewis, *Divided Highways: Building the Interstate Highways, Transforming American Life* (1997). Clarence G. Lasby, *Eisenhower's Heart Attack: How Ike Beat Heart Disease and Held on to the Presidency* (1996) is a interesting account.

Postwar Mass Culture

For overviews of postwar mass culture, see Andrew Ross, *No Respect: Intellectuals and Popular Culture* (1989); W. T. Lhamon Jr., *Deliberate Speed: The Origins of a Cultural Style in the American 1950s* (1990); Karal Ann Marling, *As Seen on TV: The Visual Culture of Everyday Life in the 1950s* (1994); and James L. Baughman, *The Republic of Mass Culture: Journalism, Filmmaking, and Broadcasting in America Since 1941* (2nd ed., 1996). The debates over mass culture in the 1950s can be sampled in Bernard Rosenberg and David Manning White, *Mass Culture* (1957) and *Mass Culture Revisited* (1971). James Gilbert, *A Cycle of Outrage: America's Reaction to the Juvenile Delinquent in the 1950s* (1986) critiques this debate and relates it to an emerging youth culture. On TV, see Cecelia Tichi, *The Electronic Hearth* (1991); Michael Curtin, *Redeeming the Wasteland: Television Documentary and Cold War Politics* (1995). On rock music, see Greil Marcus, *Mystery Train: Images of America in Rock n' Roll* (3rd ed., 1990); Charley Gillet, *Sound of the City: The Rise of Rock and Roll* (rev. ed., 1984); and Nelson George, *The Death of Rhythm and Blues* (1988). On the diversity of the youth culture, see William Graebner, *Coming of Age in Buffalo: Youth and Authority in the Postwar Era* (1989).

Social Issues

On social issues, see Michael Harrington's classic *The Other America: Poverty in the United States* (1962); James T. Patterson, *America's Struggle against Poverty, 1900–1980* (1981); Doug McAdam, *Political Process and the Development of Black Insurgency, 1930–1970* (1982); Harvard Sitkoff, *The Struggle for Black Equality, 1954–1992* (1993); Larry Burt, *Tribalism in Crisis: Federal Indian Policy, 1953–1961;* (1982); Donald L. Fixico, *Termination and Relocation: Federal Indian Policy, 1945–1960* (1986); Manuel Alers-Montalvo, *The Puerto Rican Migrants of New York* (1985); David Garrow, *Bearing the Cross: Martin Luther King, Jr., and the Southern Christian Leadership Conference* (1986); Joseph P. Fitzpatrick, *Puerto Rican Americans: The Meaning of Migration to the Mainland* (2nd ed., 1987); Taylor Branch, *Parting the Waters: America in the King Years, 1954–1963* (1988); Steven J. Whitfield, *A Death in the Delta: The Story of Emmett Till* (1988); Mario Garcia, *Mexican-Americans: Leadership, Ideology, Identity, 1930–1960* (1989); Ricardo Romo, *East Los Angeles: History of a Barrio* (1989); Armstead L. Robinson and Patricia Sullivan, eds., *New Directions in Civil Rights Studies* (1991); the relevant chapters of Jacqueline Jones, *The Dispossessed: America's Underclass from the Civil War to the Present* (1992); Mark V. Tushnet, *Making Civil Rights Law: Thurgood Marshall and the Supreme Court, 1936–1961* (1993); James F. Findlay, *Church People in the Struggle: The National Council of Churches and the Black Freedom Movement, 1950–1970* (1993); Maria Cristina Garcia, *Havana USA: Cuban Exiles and Cuban Americans in South Florida, 1959–1994* (1996); and David G. Gutierrez, *Walls and Mirrors: Mexican Americans, Mexican Immigrants, and the Politics of Ethnicity* (1995). Claybourne Carson, ed., *The Papers of Martin Luther King, Jr.* (Vol III., 1997) focuses on struggles during the Montgomery bus boycott; see also Richard Lischer, *The Preacher King: Martin Luther King, Jr. and the Words that Moved America* (1995); and Glenn T. Eskew, *But for Birmingham: The Local and National Movements in the Civil Rights Struggle* (1997). On civil rights issues during the Kennedy years, see Howard Zinn, *SNCC: The New Abolitionists* (1965); William Chafe, *Civilities and Civil Rights: Greensboro, North Carolina and the Black Struggle for Freedom* (1980); John Walton Cotman, *Birmingham, JFK, and the Civil Rights Act of 1963* (1989); Kenneth O'Reilly, *Racial Matters: The FBI's Secret Files on Black America,*

1960–72 (1989); Mark Stern, *Calculating Visions: Kennedy, Johnson, and Civil Rights* (1992); and many of the works listed in Chapter 10.

John F. Kennedy

Garry Wills, *Nixon Agonistes: The Crisis of the Self-Made Man* (rev. ed., 1980) and *The Kennedy Imprisonment: A Meditation on Power* (1983) offer critical viewpoints on John F. Kennedy, as does Thomas C. Reeves, *A Question of Character: A Life of John F. Kennedy* (1991). Seymour M. Hersh, *The Dark Side of Camelot* (1997) is an attempt to obliterate the Kennedy mystique. More favorable, though not uncritical, is David Burner, *John F. Kennedy and a New Generation* (1988). James N. Giglio's *The Presidency of John F. Kennedy* (1991) provides a reliable overview. For more detail, see Herbert J. Parmet's two volumes: *Jack: The Struggle of John F. Kennedy* (1980) and *JFK: The Presidency of John F. Kennedy* (1983). There are many sympathetic accounts of Kennedy's presidency by close associates; by far the best is Arthur Schlesinger Jr., *A Thousand Days* (1965). Specific policy decisions are the subject of Jim F. Heath, *John Kennedy and the Business Community* (1969); Victor Navasky, *Kennedy Justice* (1971); Carl M. Brauer, *John F. Kennedy and the Second Reconstruction* (1977); James R. Williamson, *Federal Antitrust Policy during the Kennedy-Johnson Years* (1995).

Kennedy's Foreign Policy

On Kennedy's foreign policy, see Thomas G. Paterson, ed., *Kennedy's Quest for Victory: American Foreign Policy, 1961–1963* (1989); Michael R. Beschloss, *The Crisis Years: Kennedy and Khrushchev, 1960–1963* (1991); and Noam Chomsky, *Rethinking Camelot: JFK, the Vietnam War, and U.S. Political Culture* (1993). A huge literature on the missile crisis in Cuba includes Graham T. Allison, *Essence of Decision: Explaining the Cuban Missile Crisis* (1971); Trumbell Higgins, *The Perfect Failure: Kennedy, Eisenhower, and the CIA at the Bay of Pigs* (1989); Dino A. Brugioni, *Eyeball to Eyeball: The Inside Story of the Cuban Missile Crisis* (1991); James Blight, *Cuba on the Brink: Castro, the Missile Crisis, and the Soviet Challenge* (1993); Mark J. White, *The Cuban Missile Crisis* (1996); John C. Ausland, *Kennedy, Khrushchev, and the Berlin-Cuba Crisis, 1961–1964* (1996); Timothy Naftali and Aleksandr Fursenko, *"One Hell of a Gamble": Khrushchev, Castro, and Kennedy, 1958–1964;* (1997); and Ernest R. May and Philip D. Zelikow, eds., *The Kennedy Tapes: Inside the White House during the Cuban Missile Crisis* (1997).

Kennedy's Death

Events surrounding Kennedy's death have attracted almost as much attention as his life. Michael J. Kurtz, *The Crime of the Century: The Kennedy Assassination from an Historian's Perspective* (1982) tries to offer historical grounding, while Barbie Zelizer, *Covering the Body: The Kennedy Assassination, the Media, and the Shaping of Collective Memory* (1992) is a superb cultural study. Theories of the assassination itself include Peter Dale Scott, *Deep Politics and the Death of JFK* (1993), which is critical of the Warren Commission's findings, and Gerald L. Posner, *Case Closed: Lee Harvey Oswald and the Assassination of JFK* (1993), which defends them. See also John Newman, *Oswald and the CIA* (1995).

Videos

Eisenhower (1993) is an excellent documentary in the "American Experience" series. *America's Mandarin (1954–1967)* is a one-hour video documentary of U.S. involvement in Vietnam, from Eisenhower to Johnson, in the series "Vietnam: A Television History" (1983). *The Quiz Show Scandal* (1991) and *That Rhythm, Those Blues* (1988) are solid entries in the "American Experience" series. The multipart documentary series "Eyes on the Prize" (1987) provides a dramatic, visual representation of the struggle for African American civil rights. *The Road to Brown* (1990) offers a a more limited, but still important, view. See also, *Dr. Martin Luther King Jr.: A Historical Perspective* (1993) and *Southern Justice: The Murder of Medger Evers* (1994). *The Kennedys* (1992) is a four-hour video documentary in the "American Experience" series. *Spy in the Sky* (1996) is the story of the U.S. reconnaissance program during the Eisenhower years. *Crisis: Missiles in Cuba* (1989) offers a brief, 30-minute overview.

10

America during Its Longest War, 1963–1974

L yndon Baines Johnson promised to finish what John F. Kennedy had begun. "Let *us* continue," he said in his first speech as president. That phrase, which recalled Kennedy's own "Let us begin," did characterize Johnson's first months in office. Ultimately though, Johnson's troubled presidency bore little resemblance to John Kennedy's thousand days of "Camelot."

In Southeast Asia, Johnson faced a crucial decision: Should the United States flex its vast power and introduce its own forces and weaponry in order to prop up its South Vietnamese ally? If Johnson did this, what would be the consequences?

At home, Johnson enthusiastically mobilized the federal government's power in order to promote greater equality, especially in the areas of civil rights and economic opportunity. But could federal action produce the Great Society that Johnson envisioned?

Many Americans, particularly young people, began to dissent from Johnson's foreign and domestic policies and, more broadly, from the direction of postwar life. As some dissenters took their protests to the streets, other Americans worried that liberty was degenerating into license. As a result of a war overseas and dissent at home, the late 1960s and early 1970s became a time of increasingly sharp political and cultural polarization.

Richard Nixon's presidency both suffered from—and contributed to—this polarization. By the end of America's longest war and the Watergate crisis that caused Nixon's resignation, the nation's political culture and social fabric differed significantly from what Lyndon Johnson had inherited from John Kennedy in 1963.

The Great Society

Lyndon Johnson lacked Kennedy's charisma, but he possessed political assets of his own. As a young administrator in Franklin Roosevelt's New Deal, a member of the House of Representatives during the late 1930s and early 1940s, and majority leader of the U.S. Senate in the 1950s, the gangling Texan became the consummate legislative horse trader. Unlike Kennedy, who despised paperwork, Johnson drove himself to a nearly fatal heart attack worrying over legislative details and trying to keep his Senate colleagues in line. Few issues, Johnson believed, defied consensus. Nearly everyone could be flattered, cajoled, even threatened into lending Johnson their support. During his time in Congress, LBJ's wealthy Texas benefactors gained valuable oil and gas concessions and lucrative construction contracts, while Johnson himself acquired a personal fortune. At the same time, the growth of Dallas, Houston, and other cities and the economic boom throughout the Southwest owed much to Johnson's skill in pushing measures such as federally funded irrigation and space-exploration projects through Congress.

Kennedy's death gave Johnson the opportunity to fulfill his dreams of transforming the nation, just as he had transformed Dallas and Houston. Confident that he could use the tactics he had employed in the Senate to build a national consensus for the expansion of government power, Johnson began by urging Congress to honor JFK's memory by passing legislation that Kennedy's administration had originated.

Completing Kennedy's Initiatives

More knowledgeable in the ways of Congress than Kennedy, Johnson quickly completed the major domestic goals of JFK's New Frontier. Working behind the scenes, Johnson secured passage of Kennedy's proposed $10 billion tax cut, a measure intended to stimulate the economy by making more money available for business investment. Although economic historians differ on how much the Kennedy-Johnson tax cut contributed to the economic boom of the mid-1960s, it *appeared* to work. GNP rose 7 percent in 1964 and 8 percent the following year; unemployment dropped to about 5 percent; and consumer prices rose by less than 3 percent. Claims that the Kennedy-Johnson economic program would guarantee sustained, noninflationary economic growth initially seemed credible.

Johnson also built on Kennedy-era plans for addressing the problems of people who were not yet sharing in the new economic bounty. In his January 1964 State of the Union address, Johnson announced that his administration was declaring "an unconditional war on poverty in America." With Johnson constantly prodding it, in August 1964 Congress created the Office of Economic Opportunity (OEO) to coordinate the various elements of a multifaceted antipoverty program. First headed by R. Sargent Shriver, brother-in-law of John Kennedy, the OEO was to "eliminate the paradox of poverty in the midst of plenty . . . by opening to everyone the opportunity to live in decency and in dignity." The Economic Opportunity Act of 1964, in addition to establishing OEO, mandated loans for rural and small-business development; established a program of work training called the Jobs Corps; created a domestic version of the Peace Corps program, called VISTA; provided low-wage jobs, primarily in urban areas, for young people; began a work-study plan to assist college students; and, most important, authorized the creation of additional federally funded social programs that were to be designed in concert with local community groups.

Finally, Johnson secured passage of civil rights legislation. Because he was at first distrusted by activists working to end racial discrimination, Johnson took special pride in helping to push an expanded version of Kennedy's civil rights bill through Congress in 1964. Championing the bill as a memorial to Kennedy, he nevertheless recognized that southern segregationists in the Democratic Party would try to delay and dilute the measure. Consequently, to ensure enough votes for passage, he successfully lobbied key Republicans, especially the Senate's minority leader, Everett Dirksen, for their support. Passed in July 1964 after lengthy delaying tactics by southerners, the Civil Rights Act of 1964, administered by a new Equal Employment Opportunity Commission (EEOC), strengthened federal remedies for fighting job discrimination. It also prohibited racial discrimination in public accommodations connected with interstate commerce, such as hotels and restaurants. Moreover, Title VII, a provision added to the bill during the legislative debates, barred discrimination based on sex, a provision that became extremely important to the movement for women's equality.

The Election of 1964

Civil rights legislation was also a testimony to the moral power of civil rights workers and their faith that local organizing could shape national policymaking. During the summer 1964, while Lyndon Johnson was dominating policymaking in Washington, a coalition of civil rights organizations enlisted nearly a thousand volunteers to help register voters in Mississippi—an operation they called "Freedom Summer." During that violent summer, six volunteers were murdered in Mississippi by segregationists, but their fellow civil rights workers pressed forward, only to see their political work frustrated at the Democratic national convention. Pressured by Johnson, who used the FBI to gather information on dissidents, party leaders seated Mississippi's "regular" all-white delegates rather than members of the alternative (and racially diverse) "Freedom Democratic Party."

After this rebuff, civil rights activists, such as Fannie Lou Hamer of the Freedom Democratic Party, recalled their earlier suspicions about Lyndon Johnson and the national Democratic Party. Johnson did seem more committed to change than John Kennedy had been, but would LBJ—and Hubert Humphrey, Johnson's personal choice for his vice presidential running mate—continue to press for anti-discrimination measures after the election? This question became all the more important once it became apparent that Johnson would win the 1964 presidential race.

The Republicans nominated Senator Barry Goldwater of Arizona, the hero of the GOP's conservative wing, to oppose Johnson. Goldwater's strategists, who had captured the nomination by waging a grass-roots organizing effort within the Republican Party, believed that an unabashedly conservative campaign would attract the millions of voters who were thought to be dissatisfied with both Democratic liberalism and moderate Republicanism. He denounced Johnson's foreign policies as too timid and Johnson's domestic programs as destructive of individual liberties. Goldwater, only one of eight Republican senators who had voted against the Civil Rights Act of 1964, had criticized the measure as a dangerous extension of power by the national government. (Goldwater condemned racial discrimination but insisted that the Constitution vested the power to enact remedial legislation with the states, not the federal government in Washington.)

Goldwater's penchant for blurting out ill-considered opinions allowed critics to picture him as fanatical, unpredictable, and reactionary. Goldwater suggested that people who feared nuclear war were "silly and sissified" and wondered, out loud, if Social Security could be converted to a voluntary program. U.S. weapons were so accurate, he once quipped, that the military could target the men's room in the Kremlin. Reinforcing his "radical-right" image, Goldwater declared in his acceptance speech at the 1964 Republican convention that "extremism in the pursuit of liberty is no vice" and "moderation in the pursuit of justice is no virtue."

Even many Republican voters came to view Goldwater as too extreme, and he led the GOP to a crushing defeat in November. Johnson carried 44 states and won more than 60 percent of the popular vote; in addition, Democrats gained 38 new seats in Congress. Most political pundits immediately hailed Johnson's election as a repudiation of Goldwater's brand of conservatism and a great triumph for Johnson's vision of domestic policymaking.

In retrospect, however, the 1964 election presaged significant political changes that would eventually erode support for Johnson's approach to domestic policymaking. During the Democratic primaries, for example, Alabama's segregationist governor, George Wallace, had run strongly against the president in several northern states. An opponent of civil rights legislation, Wallace attacked federal "meddling" in local affairs, injected the issue of race into politics in both South and North, and demonstrated the potential of a "white backlash" movement. The 1964 election was the last time the Democratic Party would capture the White House by hewing to the New Deal–Fair Deal tradition of urging expanded use of governmental power at home.

Goldwater's defeat seemed to invigorate, rather than discourage, his conservative supporters. His youthful campaign staff had pioneered several innovative stratagems such as direct mail fund-raising. By refining these tactics in future campaigns, conservative strategists helped to make the 1964 election the beginning, not the end, of the Republican Party's movement to the right. Moreover, Goldwater's stand against the Civil Rights Act of 1964 helped him carry five southern states, and these victories convinced Republicans that opposition to antidiscrimination measures by Washington would continue to attract white voters in the South who had once been solidly Democratic.

The Goldwater effort also propelled an attractive group of conservative leaders into national politics. Ronald Reagan, the actor and corporate spokesperson, proved such an effective campaigner in 1964 that conservative Republicans began to groom him for a political career. Other prominent conservatives such as William Rehnquist, an Arizona lawyer who had been one of Goldwater's key strategists, also entered national politics through the 1964 campaign. In the immediate aftermath of Goldwater's defeat, however, the prospect that a President Ronald Reagan would one day nominate William Rehnquist to be Chief Justice of the United States seemed beyond any conservative's wildest dream or any liberal's worst nightmare (see Chapter 12).

Lyndon Johnson's Great Society

Lyndon Johnson wanted to capitalize quickly on his electoral victory. Almost immediately after taking the oath of office in January 1965, Johnson ordered his staff to work on an ambitious new legislative agenda. Enjoying broad support in Congress, Johnson announced his plans for a "Great Society," an array of programs, funded by the national government, that he envisioned would bring economic opportunity to all the people who had missed the prosperity of the 1950s and early 1960s. Johnson called on government to help "enrich and elevate our national life" by building a society that was also wealthy "in mind and spirit."

Some of the Great Society programs fulfilled the dreams of Johnson's Democratic predecessors. Nationally funded medical coverage for the elderly (Medicare) and for low-income citizens (Medicaid) culminated efforts begun during the New Deal and revived during the Fair Deal. Similarly, an addition to the president's cabinet, the Department of Housing and Urban Development (HUD), built upon earlier plans for coordinating urban revitalization programs. Finally, the Voting Rights Act of 1965, which mandated federal oversight of elections in the South, seemed to cap federal efforts begun during the 1930s to end racial discrimination in political life.

Other programs sought to build on the prosperity of the 1960s. Roosevelt had to cope with the Great Depression, and Truman had to deal with the economic uncertainties of the postwar years. Johnson, in contrast, launched his Great Society at a time of economic boom. Even a costly war in Southeast Asia could not deter him from believing that continued economic growth would support his boldest goal: a "War on Poverty."

The array of initiatives developed under Johnson's antipoverty program heartened his supporters and appalled his conservative critics. The "Model Cities Program" was intended to demonstrate, initially through small-scale projects, how to reconstruct cities without the inequality that had marked the urban renewal efforts of the 1950s; rent supplements were designed to help low-income families maintain and eventually upgrade their living conditions; the expanded Food Stamp program was aimed at improving nutritional levels; Head Start was to help preschool youngsters from low-income families climb the educational ladder; a variety of other federally financed educational programs would upgrade classroom instruction throughout the nation, especially in low-income neighborhoods; and a legal services program would provide legal advice and access to the court system for those who could not afford private attorneys. These initiatives were intended to build services, funded by federal tax dollars, to help people fight their own way out of economic distress and into Johnson's new and greater society. Johnson insisted these government programs actually rested on the principle of individual self-help because they would be giving people a "hand-up" rather than a "hand-out."

The Great Society's Community Action Program (CAP) also promised to empower grass-roots activists. CAP, one of the most innovative parts of Johnson's agenda, encouraged citizens, working through local organizations, to design community-based projects that would be financed from Washington. Great Society programs such as Head Start and legal services grew out of the CAP process. By promoting "maximum feasible participation" by citizens themselves, CAP was supposed to end bureaucratic boondoggles and broaden civic participation through grass-roots activism. It was to use federal funds to promote the kind of community-based democracy that could transform the entire political system.

Evaluating the Great Society

Why did the Great Society become so controversial? Most obviously, Johnson's dramatic extension of Washington's power rekindled old debates about the proper role of the national government. In addition, the president's extravagant rhetoric, with its promise of an "unconditional" victory over poverty, raised expectations that could not be met in one presidency, or even in one generation. Most important, the faith that economic growth would generate the tax revenues needed to fund expanding social programs simply collapsed with the onset of economic problems during the late 1960s. Facing unexpected financial worries of their own, many people who had initially been inclined to support the Great Society came to accept the argument, first popularized by George Wallace, that bureaucrats in Washington were taking hard-earned dollars from taxpayers and redirecting them in unproductive directions. In 1964 Lyndon Johnson assumed that continued prosperity would allow him to build a consensus for the Great Society; worsening economic conditions, however, made greater federal spending for domestic programs a highly divisive policy.

Historians have evaluated Lyndon Johnson's Great Society programs in a variety of ways. Conservatives have subjected them to harsh criticism. Charles Murray's influential *Losing Ground* (1984) set the tone by charging that massive government expenditures during the Johnson years had encouraged antisocial behavior. Lured by welfare payments, he argued, many people with low incomes had abandoned the goals of marrying, settling down, and seeking jobs. According to this view, the Great Society's spending had also created huge government deficits that slowed economic growth. Had the nation's economic structure not been weakened by the Great Society, virtually everyone in America could have come to enjoy a middle-class lifestyle. This conservative argument condemned Johnson's program as the cause, not the remedy, for persistent economic inequality in America.

Historians more sympathetic to Johnson's approach have vigorously rejected the conservative argument. They find scant evidence for the claim that low-income people preferred welfare to meaningful work. Spending on the military sector far outstripped that for social programs and seemed the principal cause of burgeoning government deficits. Moreover, they note, expenditures on Great Society programs neither matched Johnson's promises nor commanded the massive amounts claimed by conservatives. Johnson proudly declared that the War on Poverty would begin with a $1 billion budget, but more than half of this figure included money already appropriated for other programs rather than new expenditures.

Observers to the left of the Great Society have persistently criticized its failure to challenge the prevailing distribution of political and economic power. The Johnson administration, they argue, remained closely wedded to large-scale bureaucratic solutions for problems that had many local variations. Generally, it worked to ensure that people loyal to the Democratic Party machinery, rather than grass-roots activists, dominated the planning and execution of new social programs. The CAP model, in other words, was quickly jettisoned. In addition, they point out, the Great Society never sought a redistribution of wealth and income. For these critics on the left, the Great Society was a noble ideal that was never seriously implemented; the War on Poverty was only a series of small skirmishes.

Although historians evaluate the impact of the Great Society in very different ways, there is broad agreement that Johnson's domestic agenda left its mark on American life. It represented the first significant new outlay of federal dollars for domestic social programs in 30 years, since the New Deal. Spending on such programs, though hardly extravagant, did increase more than 10 percent in every year of Johnson's presidency. In 1960, federal spending on social welfare comprised 28 percent of total government outlays; in 1970, such expenditures had risen to more than 40 percent. Within a decade of the beginning of the Great Society, programs such as Medicaid, legal services, and job training provided low-income individuals with some of the services more affluent Americans had long taken for granted.

The Great Society, by trying to extend the reach of the welfare state that had begun to appear in the United States during the 1930s, ignited increasingly intense public debate over how best to use the power and resources of the national government. In seeking to extend tangible assistance to the poor, how could policymakers follow the distinction, which became increasingly accepted in public discourse, between people who seemed to deserve assistance and those who seemed to be, in Lyndon Johnson's own formulation, seeking a "hand-out" rather than a "hand-up"? Partisan debates over government's social welfare policies would continue throughout the rest of the century.

Escalation in Vietnam

Johnson's crusade to build a Great Society at home had its counterpart in an ambitious extension of U.S. power abroad. The escalation of the war in Vietnam demanded increasingly more of the administration's energy and resources. Eventually, it alienated many Americans, especially the young, and divided the entire nation. The optimism and confidence of the brief Kennedy administration and the Great Society gave way to frustration and polarization.

The Tonkin Gulf Resolution

Immediately after John Kennedy's assassination in November 1963, Johnson had avoided widening the war in Vietnam. But this brash Texan, accustomed to getting his way, instinctively recoiled from appearing "soft" on communism. Insecure about his knowledge of foreign affairs and surrounded by Kennedy's Ivy League advisers, Johnson felt he had to follow up on Kennedy's commitments. Seeing no alternative to backing the government in South Vietnam, he accepted his military advisers' recommendation to forestall enemy offensives in South Vietnam by staging air strikes against the North. He prepared a congressional resolution authorizing such an escalation of hostilities.

Events in the Gulf of Tonkin, off the coast of North Vietnam, provided him with a rationale for taking the resolution to Congress and asking for support. On August 1, 1964, the U.S. destroyer *Maddox* was attacked by North Vietnamese torpedo boats while conducting an intelligence-gathering mission. Three days later, the *Maddox* returned with the destroyer *Turner Joy* and, amid severe weather conditions, reported a torpedo attack. Although the *Maddox*'s commander radioed that the "attack" might have been a false report and needed to be confirmed before a response was initiated, Johnson proclaimed that U.S. forces had been the target of "unprovoked aggression." He rushed the resolution to Congress, where he received overwhelming approval to take "all necessary measures to repel armed attack." Johnson subsequently used this Tonkin Gulf Resolution as tantamount to a congressional declaration of war and cited it as legal authorization for all subsequent military action in Vietnam. On the eve of the 1964 election, the president's tough stand dramatically increased his approval ratings in public opinion polls.

Despite his moves in the Gulf of Tonkin, the president was still able to position himself as a cautious moderate during the presidential campaign of 1964. When Barry Goldwater, his Republican opponent, urged stronger measures against North Vietnam and mentioned the possible use of tactical nuclear weapons, Johnson's supporters warned that Goldwater's approach risked expanding the conflict into a wider war with China and the Soviet Union. Johnson's campaign managers portrayed Goldwater as a threat to the survival of civilization. A TV commercial developed by the Democrats depicted a little girl picking the petals from a daisy as a nuclear bomb exploded onscreen. The implication was that a Goldwater victory would bring nuclear holocaust. Johnson promised not to commit American troops to fight a land war in Asia.

Soon after the election, however, Johnson further escalated the war. The 1963 coup against Diem (see Chapter 9) had left a political vacuum in the South, and the National Liberation Front was making rapid gains in several rural provinces. The incompetence of the South's new military-led government sparked growing discontent even in the capital city of Saigon, where strikes by workers and students brought widespread civic disorder. Soldiers deserted at an alarming rate. In January 1965, the regime fell, and factionalism prevented any stable government from emerging in its wake.

"Ten, nine, eight, seven . . .

six, five, four, three . . .

two, one . . .

These are the stakes, to make a world in which all of god's children can live . . .

or to go into the dark. We must either love each other or we must die . . .

The stakes are too high for you to stay home."

Political "Attack Ad," 1964 • This TV commercial from Lyndon Johnson's 1964 campaign portrayed Republican Barry Goldwater as a right-wing extremist who might take the country into a nuclear war. The ad's broadcast is now identified as one of the first times in which a 30-second TV spot was used to attack an opposing candidate.

Without any credible or effective government in South Vietnam, Johnson increasingly worried over his options. Should the pursuit of anticommunism turn the Vietnamese struggle into "America's war"? Were the stakes worth the potential costs? What would be the public backlash against a possible communist victory? Could the United States escalate and win the war without provoking a deadly clash with China or even the Soviet Union?

In 1965, Johnson canvassed for advice and carefully weighed his options. His advisers offered conflicting views. National Security Adviser McGeorge Bundy predicted inevitable defeat unless the United States sharply escalated its military role. Walt Rostow was optimistic about such a course. He assured Johnson that a determined effort would bring a clear-cut victory. "Historically, guerrilla wars have generally been lost or won cleanly," Rostow wrote. If all routes to victory are denied the enemy, he advised, they will give up. Undersecretary of State George Ball, by contrast, warned that greater Americanization of the war would bring defeat, not victory. "The South Vietnamese are losing the war," he wrote, and "no one has demonstrated that a white ground force of whatever size can win a guerrilla war . . . in jungle terrain in the midst of a population that refuses cooperation to the white forces." Senate Majority Leader Mike Mansfield urged the president to devise some plan that would reunite Vietnam as a neutral country. The Joint Chiefs of Staff, afflicted by interservice rivalries, provided differing military assessments and no clear advice.

Although privately doubting the long-term prospects for success, Johnson nonetheless feared the immediate political hazards of a U.S. pullout from Vietnam. Domestic criticism of a communist victory in South Vietnam, he believed, would certainly endanger his Great Society programs and, perhaps, end the effectiveness of his presidency. Moreover, to those who argued that Vietnam had little strategic importance to the United States, Johnson countered that U.S. withdrawal would set off a "domino effect": encouraging Castro-style insurgencies in Latin America, increasing pressure on West Berlin, and damaging American credibility around the world. Both Eisenhower and Kennedy, after all, had staked American prestige on preserving a noncommunist South Vietnam. Johnson now either had to retract that commitment or face—as his predecessors had not had to do—the uncertain course of ordering a massive infusion of America's own troops.

Swayed by political calculations and trapped within the Cold War mentality of the times, Johnson gambled that the weak and unpopular government in Saigon could somehow be strengthened by an escalation of the U.S. offensive. He decided on a sustained campaign of bombing in North Vietnam, code-named "Rolling Thunder." While the bombing was going on, he deployed U.S. ground forces to regain territory in the South, expanded covert operations, and stepped up economic aid to the beleaguered Saigon government. Only six months into his new term, with both civilian and military advisers divided in their recommendations, Johnson committed the United States to full-scale war against North Vietnam and risked the nation's prestige on the rescue of a tottering ally in Saigon.

The War Widens

The war grew more intense throughout 1965. Trying to break the will of the enemy, U.S. military commanders called for an all-out effort to escalate the number of casualties inflicted. Accordingly, the administration authorized the use of napalm, a chemical that charred both foliage and people, and allowed the Air Force to bomb new targets in the North. Additional combat troops arrived to secure enclaves in the South, converting the struggle into the kind of far-away ground war that most military strategists (including Dwight Eisenhower) had once said should be avoided. Each escalation seemed to make further escalation inevitable. North Vietnam's rejection of an unrealistic "peace plan," outlined by Johnson in a speech in April 1965, became a pretext for again raising the levels of U.S. military spending and action. North Vietnam's leader, Ho Chi Minh, was playing the same game of escalation and attrition, convinced that Johnson commanded meager public and congressional support for continuing the costly war.

In April 1965, Johnson brought his anticommunist crusade closer to home. Prompted by exaggerated reports of a communist threat in the Dominican Republic, Johnson sent American troops to unseat a left-leaning, elected president and to install a government favorable to U.S. economic interests. This U.S. incursion violated a long-standing, "good neighbor" pledge not to intervene militarily in the western hemisphere. Although the action was criticized throughout Latin America, the seemingly successful military ouster of a leftist regime boosted the administration's determination to hold the line against communism in Vietnam.

During the spring of 1965, as the fifth government since Diem's death took office in Saigon, U.S. strategists were still puzzling over how to prop up its South Vietnamese ally. The commander in charge of the American effort, General William Westmoreland, recommended moving U.S. forces out of their enclaves and sending them on "search and destroy" missions. In July, Johnson dispatched 50,000 additional troops to Vietnam, privately agreed to send an additional 50,000, and left

Search and Destroy Mission in Vietnam • U.S. military strategists wrongly believed that ground troops, backed by armadas of helicopters, could "pacify" the countryside in South Vietnam and thereby stabilize the government in Saigon. Costly in terms of military hardware losses and casualties to U.S. forces, this strategy seemed to guarantee long-term involvement by the United States and helped to fuel popular protests at home.

open the possibility of sending even more. He also approved saturation bombing of the countryside in the South and intensified bombing of the North.

Some of his advisers urged Johnson to admit candidly to the public that the scope of the war was being steadily enlarged. They also recommended either an outright declaration of war or some kind of emergency legislation that would formally put the United States on a wartime footing. Otherwise, the president would be unable to wield any of the economic or informational controls that past administrations had used in conflicts of this magnitude. But Johnson was unwilling to take such a step for

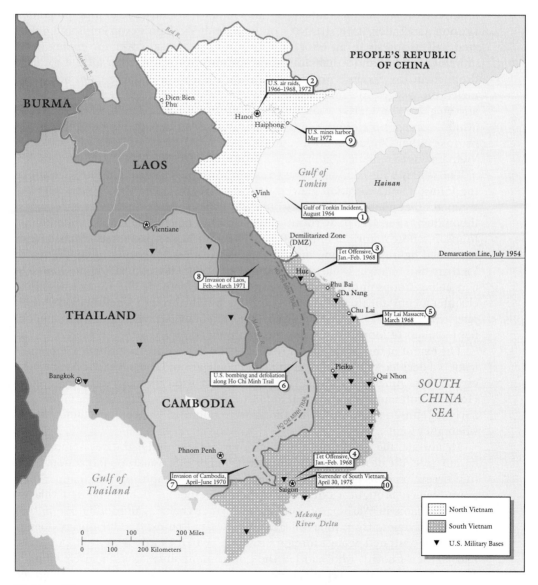

Vietnam War

fear that assuming the formal status of a belligerent would provoke the Soviet Union or China. He also worried about arousing greater protests from Congress and the public. Although Congress had approved $400 million for military expenditures in May 1965, many legislators expressed grave doubts about the war. Rather than risk open debate that might reveal his shallow political support, Johnson decided to stress the administration's efforts to negotiate and to pretend that the war was not a war. As the president talked about seeing "light at the end of the tunnel," the public was actually left in the dark as to exactly what its government was doing and why.

Over the next three years, the number of American troops increased from 50,000 to 535,000. By 1967, the United States was spending more than $2 billion a month on the war and was subjecting the Vietnamese landscape to widespread devastation. Operation RANCHHAND scorched South Vietnam's crop lands and defoliated half its forests in an effort to eliminate the natural cover for enemy troop movements. One and a half-million tons of bombs—more than all the tonnage dropped in the Second World War—leveled North Vietnamese cities and pummeled the villages and inhabitants of "free-fire zones" (designated areas in which anything was considered a fair target) in the South. Still, Johnson was careful to avoid bombing too close to the Chinese border or doing anything else that might provoke either Chinese or Soviet entry into the war. Despite the escalating violence, Vietnam was to remain a "limited" war.

The weekly body count of enemy dead, therefore, became the measure by which the Johnson administration gauged the war's progress. The strategy was attrition. Estimates that a kill ratio of 10:1 would force the North to surrender encouraged the military to inflate body count figures and to engage in indiscriminate killing. Johnson, whose notorious temper flared whenever he was presented with bad news, welcomed figures suggesting that "victory was around the corner." Actually, North Vietnam was matching each American escalation and controlling its losses by concealing troops under the jungle canopy that remained. The North was able to channel a constant flow of supplies into the South through a shifting network of jungle paths called the Ho Chi Minh Trail. The war had reached a stalemate, but few members of Johnson's administration would admit it.

The extent of the destruction wreaked by the U.S. effort gave North Vietnamese leaders a decided propaganda advantage. People around the world condemned the escalation of American attacks. The Soviet Union and China increased their aid to Ho Chi Minh and helped foment anti-Americanism elsewhere. Both at home and abroad, Johnson administration officials were hounded by protesters almost everywhere they went.

Meanwhile, the government in Saigon was reeling under the devastation of its countryside, the destabilizing effect of the flood of U.S. dollars on its economy, and the corruption of its politicians. So-called "pacification" and "strategic hamlet" programs, which brought Vietnamese farmers together in tightly guarded villages, sounded viable in Washington but caused further chaos by uprooting one in four South Vietnamese from their villages and ancestral lands. Buddhist priests persistently demonstrated against foreign influence. When Generals Nguyen Van Thieu and Nguyen Cao Ky, who had led the government since 1965, held elections in 1967 to legitimate their regime, their narrow margin of victory merely highlighted their weakness.

The Media and the War

Johnson lectured the American public about upholding national honor and standing by commitments, but criticism against the war continued to mount. In most earlier wars, Congress had imposed strict controls on what journalists could report to the public. Because the Vietnam War was undeclared, Johnson had to resort to informal, though at first effective, ways of managing information. With television coverage making Vietnam a "living room war," Johnson kept three TV sets playing in his office in order to monitor the major networks. Sometimes he would phone the news anchors after their broadcasts and castigate them for their stories. The "Johnson treatment," some called it. After one CBS report, the network's president, Frank Stanton, reportedly received this call: "Frank, are you trying to f— me? . . . This is your president, and yesterday your boys shat on the American flag." Increasingly sensitive to criticism, Johnson equated any question or doubt about his policy in Vietnam with a lack of patriotism.

Antiwar activists were equally disturbed by what they regarded as the media's uncritical reporting on the war. Most of the reporters, they claimed, relied on official handouts for their stories, spent their time in Saigon's best hotels, and took pains to avoid offending anyone at the White House. Indeed, especially in the early years, few reporters filed hard-hitting stories. Though the press corps did not invite Americans to love the war, as it had during the two world wars, neither did it encourage much criticism.

In time, however, news coverage and its impact became less ambiguous. The unrelenting images of destruction on the nightly news and in *Life* magazine's photos, whatever their intent, turned people against the war. In addition, a few journalists forthrightly expressed their opposition. Harrison Salisbury of *The New York Times* sent reports from Vietnam that dramatized the destructiveness of U.S. bombing missions. Gloria Emerson wrote grim and widely read reports, picturing the war as a class-based effort in which the United States used poor and disproportionately nonwhite fighting forces, while rich men with draft-exempt sons raked in war profits.

As the war dragged on and more Americans began to question the purpose and strategy of the United States in Vietnam, the country became polarized into "hawks" and "doves." Johnson insisted that he was merely following the policy of containment favored by Eisenhower and Kennedy. Secretary of State Dean Rusk spoke of the dangers of "appeasement." But influential senators—including J. William Fulbright of Arkansas, chair of the powerful Foreign Relations Committee, and Eugene McCarthy of Minnesota—warned of misplaced priorities and an "arrogance of power." Meanwhile, antiwar protestors began challenge the structure of American society itself.

The War at Home

Millions came to oppose the war in Southeast Asia, and backing eroded for the Great Society at home. Tensions that had been slowly building over recent years appeared to be reaching a critical point, threatening the stability of the entire nation.

The Rise of the New Left

During the early 1960s small groups of young people, many of them college students, came to reject the welfare-state policies of the postwar years. In 1962, two years after activists on the right had formed Young Americans for Freedom (YAF), insurgents on the left established a political organization called Students for a Democratic Society (SDS). While YAF was quietly working to build a "New Right," SDS captured the media's attention. Although SDS endorsed familiar causes, especially the fight against racial discrimination, its founding "Port Huron Statement" also spoke of new issues: the "loneliness, estrangement, isolation" of postwar society.

SDS became part of a new political initiative, popularly known as the "New Left," that tried to distance itself from both the welfare-state policies of the Great Society and the "old" communist-inspired Left. By confronting the dominant culture, which allegedly valued bureaucratic expertise over citizen engagement and conspicuous consumption over meaningful work, members of the New Left sought to create an alternative social vision. They called for "participatory democracy," grass-roots politics responsive to the wishes of local communities rather than the preferences of national elites. "We felt that we were different, and that we were going to do things differently," recalled one early SDS member. "It felt like the dawn of a new age."

During the early 1960s, many young, white college students found inspiration from the antidiscrimination movement in the Deep South. Risking racist violence, they went to the South where they forged bonds of community with African American activists and began to believe they could create a new interracial society. Some stayed in the South or moved on to political projects in northern neighborhoods. Others returned to their college campuses and joined protests, often associated with the New Left, against both the war in Southeast Asia and social conditions at home.

These dissenting students denounced the nation's prestigious colleges and universities as part of a vast "establishment" that resisted significant change. Giant universities, they claimed, were sustained by funds from government and corporations and seemed oblivious to the social and moral implications of their war-related research. Student dissidents charged faculty and administrators with ignoring the relevant issues of the day in favor of traditional, required courses. Moreover, restrictions on personal freedoms, such as student dress codes and mandatory dormitory hours, were labeled as relics of an authoritarian past in which colleges and universities acted *in loco parentis* (in place of parents) and in which students were passive and unprotesting. During the Berkeley "student revolt" of 1964 and 1965, students and sympathetic faculty protested the university administration's restrictions on political activity on campus and then moved on to broader issues such as Vietnam and racism. Thus the student revolt, which disrupted classes and embittered many moderate professors, ushered in nearly a decade of turmoil.

By 1966 the war in Vietnam had come to dominate the agenda of student protesters. For young men, the antiwar movement became, in part, a matter of self-interest; when they reached age 18 they were required by federal law to register for possible military service. They were to carry a draft card that signified their military obligation. Local draft boards usually granted men who were attending college a student deferment, but these expired upon graduation and could, in some instances, be revoked or denied. The draft became a prominent campus issue. The

Draft Card Burning • As a means of protesting U.S. involvement in Vietnam, young men began burning their draft cards. Because the law required every male over the age of 18 to carry a draft card, such burnings became a symbolic act of resistance against the war.

burning of draft cards, as a symbolic protest against both the war and universal military service for men, became a central feature of many antiwar protests.

Meanwhile, many campuses became embroiled in bitter strife. At "teach-ins," supporters and opponents of the war presented their positions and debated the morality of the involvement of universities in national security policies. Teach-ins soon gave way to less-structured demonstrations, on and off campus. As antiwar sentiments grew more intense, campus supporters of the war claimed that *their* right to free speech was being threatened. Conservatives, along with many moderates, pressured college administrators to crack down on "troublemakers" and return "civility" to the campus. As the debate broadened, conservatives—including Ronald Reagan, who was elected governor of California in 1966—made opposition to campus protests a prominent part of their new agenda.

The Counterculture

Accompanying the spread of New Left politics was the rise of an antiestablishment "counterculture." Even though only a relatively small percentage of young people fully embraced countercultural values, they came to symbolize, especially in the mass media, the youthful ferment of the late 1960s. Ridiculing traditional attitudes on such matters as clothing, hair styles, and sexuality, devotees of the counterculture sought an open and experimental approach to daily life. Caricatured as "hippies," they dabbled with mind-altering drugs, communal living arrangements, and new forms of folk-rock music. Bob Dylan, who had been a central figure in the revival of acoustical folk music in the early 1960s, suddenly "went electric" in 1965.

The Counterculture on Wheels • A bus named the Road Hog carries members of a New Mexico countercultural commune to a Fourth of July parade in 1968. The inspiration for this bus was the one—immortalized by Tom Wolfe in his book *The Electric Kool-Aid Acid Test*— that carried the novelist Ken Kesey and his "Merry Pranksters" on their LSD-inspired trips.

Reworking musical idioms used by African American blues artists such as Muddy Waters, Dylan's "Like a Rolling Stone" (1965) exploded onto both the Top 40 charts of AM radio and the freewheeling play lists of the new, alternative FM stations. Although Dylan never sought the role, members of the counterculture and the media cast him as the musical prophet for an entire generation.

The trappings of the counterculture soon found a ready market among middle-class consumers. Impressed by the success of hippie bands like San Francisco's Grateful Dead and the Jefferson Airplane, the mass culture industry welcomed the youth rebellion. The Rolling Stones made big money with their ode to a "Street Fighting Man" (1968) and their pledge of "Sympathy for the Devil" (1968). The Beatles made even more money and attracted critical acclaim with *Sgt. Pepper's Lonely Hearts Club Band* (1967) and *The Beatles* (The White Album) (1968). Hollywood tapped the youth culture market with *The Graduate* (1967) and *Bonnie and Clyde* (1967) and followed up with a brief cycle of films, such as *Easy Rider* (1969) and *Wild in the Streets* (1968), that portrayed adult authority figures as vampirish, even murderous, ravagers of youth.

A lively debate arose over the media's increasingly sensationalized coverage of the counterculture. Critics of the youth culture charged the media with spreading dangerous, antisocial images. According to conservative critics, the media's extensive coverage of demonstrations in which young radicals and countercultural musicians joined with older opponents of the war helped to exaggerate the strength of the antiwar movement. At the same time, ironically, veterans of earlier New Left protests claimed that the media's unrelenting attention on the counterculture actually undercut antiwar politics. The media's insatiable need for spectacular demonstrations and more exciting celebrities from the youth culture, they charged, trivialized the serious issues that the dissidents were seeking to articulate.

The media's coverage of an antiwar march on the Pentagon in 1967 crystallized this debate. Rejecting political speeches and the ritualistic burning of draft cards as too dull, some of the marchers amused themselves—and the media camera crews—by trying to levitate the Pentagon. Abbie Hoffman, self-proclaimed leader of the fictitious Youth International Party (the "Yippies"), facetiously urged "loot-ins at department stores to strike at the property fetish that underlies genocidal war" in Vietnam. Although the Pentagon march played well as a media spectacle—even winning Norman Mailer, who had participated in it, a National Book Award for *Armies of the Night,* his account of the event—its impact on political events was uncertain. At best, dramatic television clips conveyed the passion of dissenters; at worst, a colorful mélange of media-conscious demonstrators helped to fuel polarization throughout American society.

From Civil Rights to Black Power

A similar debate developed over media coverage of the increasingly militant protests against racial discrimination. Early on, leaders in the fight against discrimination, notably Dr. Martin Luther King Jr., had recognized the benefits to be derived from media coverage. During King's 1965 drive to win access to the ballot box for African Americans, TV images of the racist violence in Selma, Alabama, helped to galvanize support for federal legislation. At one point, ABC television interrupted the anti-Nazi film *Judgment at Nuremburg* in order to show white Alabama state troopers beating peaceful, mostly African American, civil rights marchers. President Johnson used television to dramatize his support for voting-rights legislation and to promise that "we shall overcome" the nation's "crippling legacy of bigotry and injustice."

Selma, Alabama, 1965 • The campaign to guarantee the right to vote for African Americans in the South came together in Selma, Alabama. The effort there, and a violent reaction by racist opponents of the civil rights movement, provided the immediate impetus for Congress to pass the Voting Rights Act of 1965.

At the same time, the media became the forum for fierce debates over what was increasingly being called a "racial crisis." Conservatives argued that subversive agitators were provoking conflict and violence and that only a good dose of law and order would ease urban racial tensions. Social activists argued that a complex mix of racism, lack of educational and employment opportunities, and inadequate government responses were producing the frustration and despair that burst forth in sporadic racial violence. This debate intensified in 1965 in the wake of a devastating racial conflict in Los Angeles. A confrontation between a white Highway Patrol officer and a black motorist escalated into six days of urban violence, centered in the largely African American community of Watts in South-Central Los Angeles. Thirty-four people died; hundreds of businesses and homes were burned; the National Guard patrolled the streets of Los Angeles; and TV cameras framed the conflagration as an ongoing media spectacle. Racial violence erupted in many other U.S. cities during the remainder of the decade.

In response to these events a radical "Black Power" movement emerged. A charismatic preacher named Malcolm X had heralded its arrival. The chief spokesperson for the Nation of Islam, headed by the Honorable Elijah Muhammad, Malcolm X preached a message fundamentally at odds with that of the leaders of the civil rights movement. He denounced King's gradualist, nonviolent approach to political change as irrelevant to the social and economic problems of most African Americans and proclaimed that integration was unworkable. Although Malcolm X never called for violent confrontation, he did endorse self-defense "by any means necessary." Malcolm X, a growing group of followers argued, was simply "telling it like it is."

Racist Violence in Birmingham, 1963 • Public officials in Birmingham, Alabama, utilized fire hoses, cattle prods, and police dogs against peaceful civil rights demonstrators. The tactics backfired, however, as public opinion in the North turned decisively in favor of Congress passing new civil rights legislation.

PUBLIC NOTICE

If any voters or members of their family who are planning to vote **Tuesday,** are wanted by Law Enforcement Officials for the following offenses, **inform- ation** has been received that a list of voters has been drawn to **be arrested** after voting for the following offenses, committed in the past five years:

1. Traffic tickets
2. Speeding or negligent collision tickets.
3. Parking Tickets
4. Child Support Payments ordered by the Courts in divorce suits or child desertion.
5. Questioning by the Police for any offense.
6. Voters who have not appeared in Court as witnesses or Defendants in criminal or civil matters.
7. Voters who have not paid fines ordered by the Court.

Please take care of these matters before voting or else contact a Bail Bondsman or Lawyer before voting in order to be sure that you won't miss work or have to spend the night in jail by being arrested.

(Harris County Negro Protective Association)

Public Notice: Vote at Your Own Risk! • A handbill posted in predominantly black voting precincts in Houston, Texas, in 1964 illustrates one of the many different tactics used by opponents of the civil rights movement. The handbill's none-too-subtle threat—that African Americans who exercised their right to vote might open themselves to pressure from a white-dominated legal establishment—was designed to depress black voter turnout.

Malcolm X offered more than angry rhetoric. He called for renewed pride in the African American heritage and for vigorous efforts at community reconstruction. In order to revitalize their contemporary institutions, he urged African Americans to "recapture our heritage and identity" and "launch a cultural revolution to unbrainwash an entire people." Seeking to forge a broader movement, Malcolm X eventually broke from the Nation of Islam, established his own Organization of Afro-American Unity, and explored alliances with other insurgent groups. Murdered in 1965 by political enemies from the Nation of Islam, Malcolm X remained a powerful symbol of both militant politics and a renewed pride in African American culture.

As demonstrations against discrimination in politics, jobs, and housing erupted in both North and South, a new generation of African Americans picked up the mantle of Malcolm X. Disdaining the older integrationist agenda, the youthful militants embraced the word "black." As "black power" replaced the old civil rights call for "freedom now," advocates soon caught the media's attention and began to gain support within African American communities. "Black Is Beautiful" became the watchword. James Brown, the "Godfather of Soul," captured this new spirit with his 1965 hit song, "Papa's Got a Brand New Bag," which announced a defiant refusal to abide by old rules and restrictions. Later, Brown's "Say It Loud, I'm Black and Proud" encapsulated the cultural message of the Black Power movement.

The Black Power crusade raised philosophical and tactical disagreements within the antidiscrimination movement. Angered by the slow pace of civil rights litigation, some younger African Americans, including Stokely Carmichael, who became head of the Student Non-Violent Coordinating Committee (SNCC) in 1966, and members of the Black Panther Party, escalated attacks on the gradualist and nonviolent methods of the established civil rights organizations such as King's Southern Christian Leadership Conference. A Black Panther manifesto, for example, called for community "self-defense" groups as protection against police harassment, the release from jail of all African American prisoners (on the assumption that none had received fair trials in racist courts), and guaranteed employment for all citizens. Although opinion surveys suggested that the vast majority of African Americans still supported the integrationist agenda, the new modes of insurgency were unraveling the established, black-white civil rights alliance on which Martin Luther King Jr. and Lyndon Johnson had once relied.

Within this social context, the Civil Rights Act of 1968 passed Congress. One provision of this omnibus law, popularly known as the Fair Housing Act, sought to eliminate racial discrimination in housing. But in response to charges that antidiscrimination legislation could illegally infringe on the rights of landlords and real estate agents, the act provided exemptions for certain categories of homes and apartments, rendering the law's enforcement provisions weak. Moreover, another section was included in the law that made it a crime to cross state lines in order to incite a "riot." This antiriot provision, pushed by conservatives, was widely understood to be aimed at using the power of the federal government against radical political activists, particularly those connected with the Black Power movement.

1968: The Violence Overseas

In 1968, several shocking and violent events worsened political polarization. The first came in Vietnam. At the end of January, during a truce in observance of Tet, the lunar new year celebration, troops of the National Liberation Front (NLF) joined North Vietnamese forces in a series of coordinated surprise attacks throughout South Vietnam. Sweeping into eight provincial capitals, they even seized the grounds of the U.S. embassy in Saigon for a few hours. In some respects, the so-called "Tet offensive" was a defeat for the NLF and the North; during two weeks of intense fighting, they suffered heavy casualties and sustained no significant military victory. But Tet turned out to be a serious psychological defeat for the United States because it suggested that military claims about an imminent South Vietnamese–United States victory were not to be trusted. When General Westmoreland asked for 206,000 additional troops, most of Johnson's closest advisers, led by his new secretary of state, Clark Clifford, criticized his request and urged that South Vietnamese troops be required to assume more of the military burden. Johnson accepted these arguments, realizing that such a large troop increase would have fanned antiwar opposition at home. In a way, Tet contributed to the beginning of a policy that would later be referred to as the "Vietnamization" of the war.

The Tet offensive destroyed much of whatever political support Johnson still commanded among antiwar Democrats and threw his strategic planners into confusion. Although some analysts blamed the media for turning the Tet "victory" into a "defeat" by exaggerating the effect of the early attacks and by ignoring the heavy losses suffered by the NLF and the North Vietnamese, others pointed out that communist strength had caught the U.S. off guard, ill-prepared to take advantage of enemy losses. Faced with revolt in his own party, led by Senator Eugene McCarthy of Minnesota, Johnson suddenly declared on March 31, 1968, that he would not run for reelection. He halted the bombing of North Vietnam and promised to devote his remaining time in office to seeking an end to the war. McCarthy, campaigning on a peace platform, continued his election bid against Johnson's vice president and party stalwart, Hubert H. Humphrey.

1968: The Violence at Home

One person who rejoiced at Johnson's withdrawal was Martin Luther King Jr. Firmly opposed to Johnson's reelection, King hoped that the Democratic Party would now turn to an antiwar candidate, preferably Senator Robert Kennedy of New York, who could advance King's new vision of economic transformation for the United States. But on an April 4, 1968, trip to Memphis, Tennessee, in support of a strike by African American sanitation workers, King was assassinated, allegedly by a lone gunman named James Earl Ray. (Ray quickly pleaded guilty to being King's assailant, but he subsequently recanted and sought a new hearing. In 1997, King's family met with Ray in prison, suggested that he seemed merely a pawn in some larger conspiracy, and endorsed his call for a retrial.)

As news of King's assassination spread, violence swept through black neighborhoods around the country. More than 100 cities and towns witnessed outbreaks; 39 people died; 75,000 regular and National Guard troops were called to duty. When Johnson proclaimed Sunday, April 7, as a day of national mourning for the slain civil rights leader, parts of Washington, D.C., were still ablaze.

Meanwhile, Robert Kennedy had entered the race for the Democratic presidential nomination. His campaign brought together veterans of John Kennedy's New Frontier, youthful activists, and media celebrities. Campaigning at a feverish pace, Kennedy battled McCarthy in a series of primary elections, hoping to gain a majority of the convention delegates that had not already been pledged to Hubert Humphrey by the party's old-line bosses such as Richard J. Daley, mayor of Chicago. Then, on June 5, only minutes after claiming victory over Eugene McCarthy in California's Democratic presidential primary, Robert Kennedy fell victim to an assassin's bullets. Kennedy's nationally televised funeral was a disturbing reminder of King's recent murder and the assassination of his own brother nearly five years earlier.

The violence of 1968 continued. During the Republican national convention in Miami, as presidential candidate Richard Nixon, his political career resurrected, was promising to restore "law and order," racial violence in that same city killed four people. Later that summer, in Chicago, New Left and counterculture celebrities, Black Power advocates, and thousands of antiwar demonstrators converged on the Democratic Party's convention to protest the expected nomination of Humphrey, who was still supporting Johnson's policy in Vietnam. Taking seriously Yippie jokes about lacing the city's water supply with the drug LSD, Mayor Daley ordered police to crush the demonstrators. Responding to acts of provocation by demonstrators who seemed to welcome confrontation, members of the Chicago police department struck back with indiscriminate violence. Although an official report later characterized the conflict in the streets outside of the Democratic convention a "police riot," it was more widely interpreted in 1968 as an ominous example of the violent drift of radical politics. Hubert Humphrey easily captured the Democratic nomination, but controversy over Johnson's Vietnam policies and over Mayor Daley's response to the antiwar demonstrations left the Democratic Party badly divided.

The Election of 1968

Both Humphrey and Nixon faced a serious challenge from the political right, spearheaded by Alabama's George Wallace. After running successfully in several northern Democratic primaries, Wallace decided to seek nationwide support as a third-party candidate. A grass-roots campaign eventually placed his American Independent Party on the presidential ballot in every state. Because Wallace's opposition to racial integration was well established, he could concentrate his fire on other controversial targets, particularly the counterculture and the antiwar movement. If any long-haired, hippie demonstrator blocked his motorcade, he bragged, "it'll be the last car he'll ever lay down in front of." Moreover, Wallace recognized that many voters were beginning to lose faith in welfare-state programs and to see themselves as victims of an aloof, tax-and-spend bureaucracy in Washington.

Wallace's candidacy exacerbated the political polarization of 1968. By threatening to prevent either major-party candidate from winning a majority of the electoral votes, it raised the possibility that the choice of the nation's president would rest with the House of Representatives and that Wallace himself could act as a power broker between Democrats and Republicans. (Selection of a president by the House had happened last in 1824.) In order to capitalize on right-wing dissent against U.S. foreign policy, Wallace chose the hawkish Air Force General Curtis LeMay, the former head of the Strategic Air Command, as his running mate. LeMay's presence on the American Independent ticket was supposed to help Wallace court voters who wanted all-out victory in Vietnam, but LeMay quickly inflamed political passions when he complained that too many Americans had a "phobia" about the use nuclear weapons. Political pundits immediately labeled Wallace and LeMay the "Bombsey Twins."

Nixon narrowly prevailed in November. Although he won 56 percent of the electoral vote, he out-polled Humphrey in the popular vote by less than 1 percent. Humphrey, although burdened by his association with Johnson and by memories of the Chicago convention, had benefited when the president ordered a pause in the bombing of North Vietnam and pledged to begin peace talks in Paris; and he helped his own cause with a belated decision to distance himself from Johnson's Vietnam policies. Still, Humphrey carried only Texas in the South, losing the grip the Democratic Party had held there since Reconstruction. George Wallace picked up 46 electoral votes, all from the Deep South, and 13.5 percent of the popular vote, a total greater than that gained by any third-party candidate since Robert La Follette in 1924 (see Chapter 2). Nixon won five key southern states and attracted, all across the country, those whom he called "the forgotten Americans, the

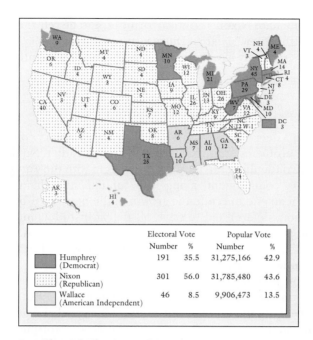

	Electoral Vote		Popular Vote	
	Number	%	Number	%
Humphrey (Democrat)	191	35.5	31,275,166	42.9
Nixon (Republican)	301	56.0	31,785,480	43.6
Wallace (American Independent)	46	8.5	9,906,473	13.5

Presidential Election, 1968

non-shouters, the non-demonstrators." Hinting that he had a plan for ending the war in Vietnam, Nixon claimed to be the candidate most likely to restore tranquillity to the domestic front. But soon after taking office, Nixon embraced policies that proved every bit as divisive as those of Lyndon Johnson.

The Nixon Years, 1969–1974

Richard Milhous Nixon was perhaps the most complex political leader of the postwar era. Raised in a modest Quaker home in southern California, Nixon graduated from Whittier College, a small Quaker school near his hometown. Three years at Duke Law School, a hitch in the Navy during the Second World War, and a job in Franklin Roosevelt's wartime bureaucracy gave Nixon a taste of new, cosmopolitan worlds. After the war, however, he returned to his small-town California law practice before beginning a meteoric political career that took him to the House of Representatives in 1946, the Senate in 1950, and the vice presidency in 1952.

Nixon's rabid anticommunism and ruthless campaign tactics initially dominated his political image. He seemed to thrive on seeking enemies, at home and abroad, and on confronting a constant series of personal challenges. He titled an early memoir of his political life *Six Crises*. Personally devastated by his narrow defeat to Kennedy in 1960, Nixon seemed crushed politically when, in 1962, he failed to win the governorship of his native California. At a postelection press conference, a bitter Nixon denounced the press for distorting his political record and announced his political retirement. But Barry Goldwater's 1964 defeat and Johnson's problems helped to revive Richard Nixon's political fortunes, and he returned to the political wars in 1968 as the "new" Nixon. During his presidency (1969–1974) this new Nixon seemed increasingly like the old Nixon in his ability to inflame, rather than to calm, political passions.

The Economy

Culminating with a deep recession in 1973, Nixon's presidency coincided with a series of economic problems unthinkable only a decade earlier. No simple cause can account for these difficulties, but most analyses begin with the war in Vietnam. This expensive military commitment, along with fundamental changes in the world economy, brought an end to economic growth of the previous two decades.

Lyndon Johnson, determined to stave off defeat in Indochina without cutting Great Society programs, had pretended that the nation could conduct its economic business as usual and had even concealed the rising costs of the war from his own advisers. Johnson bequeathed Nixon a deteriorating (though still favorable) balance of trade and a rising rate of inflation. Between 1960 and 1965, consumer prices had risen on average only about 1 percent a year; in 1967, the increase had been nearly three times this average; and in 1968, it exceeded 4 percent.

Nixon promised to check inflation, but conditions worsened. Although he pledged to cut war costs by reducing troop levels, the Vietnamization strategy still required extensive bombing and continued to drain economic resources. Moreover, although Nixon spoke of reducing domestic spending, he soon discovered that many federal programs still enjoyed support in the Democrat-controlled Congress and among voters. During his first years in office, the percentage of federal funds spent on domestic programs increased steadily.

Meanwhile, unemployment soared, topping 6 percent by 1971. According to conventional wisdom, expressed in a technical economic concept called "the Phillips curve," when unemployment rises, prices should remain constant or even decline. Yet *both* unemployment and inflation were rising, as if in tandem. Economists invented the term "stagflation" to describe this puzzling, unprecedented convergence of economic stagnation and price inflation. Along with stagflation, U.S. exports were becoming less competitive in international markets, and in 1971, for the first time in the 20th century, the United States ran a trade deficit, importing more products than it exported.

Long identified as an opponent of government regulation of the economy but fearful of the political consequences of stagflation and the trade deficit, Nixon searched for a cure for the nation's economic ills. In a reversal that one media commentator likened to a religious conversion, Nixon suddenly proclaimed himself a believer in greater government management of the economy. Gambling that inflation could be halted before the 1972 election, in August 1971 he announced a "new economic policy" that mandated a 90-day freeze on any increase in wages and prices, to be followed by government monitoring to detect "excessive" increases in either.

To try to reverse the trade deficit, Nixon also revised the U.S. relationship to the world monetary structure. Ever since the 1944 Bretton Woods agreement (see Chapter 7), the value of the dollar, the world's premier currency, had been tied to the value of gold at $35 for every ounce. This meant that the United States, to provide an anchor for world currencies, was prepared to exchange U.S. dollars for gold at that rate if any other nation's central bank requested it to do so. Other countries had fixed their own exchange rates against the dollar. But U.S. trade deficits undermined the value of the American dollar, enabling foreign banks to exchange dollars for gold at highly favorable rates. Consequently, in August 1971 the Nixon administration abandoned the fixed gold-to-dollar ratio, announcing that, after complicated negotiations had been completed (as they were in 1972), the dollar would be free to "float" against the prevailing market price of gold and against all other currencies. In 1973, the Nixon administration devalued the dollar, cheapening the price of American goods in foreign markets in order to make them more competitive. The strategy fundamentally altered the international economic order but did little to arrest the deterioration of U.S. trade balances. Over the next decade, U.S. exports more than tripled in value but imports more than quadrupled.

Social Policy

At the urging of Daniel Patrick Moynihan, a Democrat who had served in Kennedy's administration and who was now Nixon's chief adviser on domestic policy, Nixon began to consider a drastic revision of the nation's welfare programs. Moynihan insisted that Nixon, while still identifying himself as a conservative Republican, could bring about significant changes in domestic policy.

After heated debates within his inner circle, Nixon unveiled his Family Assistance Plan (FAP) during a TV address in August 1969. The centerpiece of this complex policy package was the replacement of most welfare programs, including the controversial Aid to Families with Dependent Children (AFDC), with a guaranteed annual income for all families. AFDC, a program that had become progressively more expensive since it had been reorganized under the Great Society, provided government payments to cover basic costs of care for low-income children who had lost the support of a bread-winning parent. By 1970, half of all persons in families headed by women were receiving AFDC payments.

Under Nixon's initial plan, the government would guarantee a family of four an annual income of $1,600, with the possibility of further assistance depending on how much income the family earned. In one bold stroke, FAP would replace the post–New Deal welfare system, which provided services and assistance *only* to those in particular circumstances, such as low-income mothers with small children or people who were unemployed, with a system that offered government aid to *all* low-income families. Even a family with an annual income of nearly twice Nixon's $1,600 level, according to one projection, would still benefit from FAP because of its tax refund and food stamp provisions.

FAP failed to attract significant support either in Congress or in the nation at large. Conservatives blasted the proposal, especially its provisions for supplementing the income of families that had a regularly employed, though low-paid, wage earner. In contrast, proponents of more generous government assistance programs criticized FAP's guaranteed income of $1,600 as too miserly. The House of Representatives approved a modified version of FAP in 1970, but a curious alliance of senators to the right and to the left of Nixon blocked its passage. Beset by other problems, especially the lingering war in Vietnam, Nixon let the program drop, and a general overhaul of the nation's welfare system would not come until the 1990s.

Some changes in domestic programs were enacted during the Nixon years, however. For example, Congress passed the president's much heralded revenue-sharing plan, a feature of Nixon's "new federalism." This plan provided for the return of a certain percentage of federal tax dollars to state and local governments in the form of "block grants." Instead of Washington specifying how the funds were to be used, the block grant concept left the state and local governments free, within broad limits, to spend the funds as they saw fit.

The Democratic dominated Congress itself stitched together a revised welfare program in the early 1970s. A patchwork of provisions, it included rent subsidies for people at the lowest income levels and Supplementary Security Insurance (SSI) payments for those who were elderly, blind, or disabled. The Medicare and Medicaid programs, established under Johnson's Great Society, were gradually expanded during Nixon's presidency. In 1972 Social Security benefits were "indexed," which meant they would rise with the rate of inflation. More cautious than Nixon's FAP proposals, these congressional initiatives, though they attracted relatively little attention when passed, substantially extended the nation's income-support programs, albeit only for specific groups, especially older Americans. Congress also passed in 1971, but the president vetoed, a Child Development Act, that would have set up a national system of day care centers for preschool children. Between 1970 and 1980 the federal government's spending for social welfare rose from 40.1 percent of total government outlays to slightly over 53 percent.

Social Welfare Spending, 1960–1990

As a Percentage of Total Spending

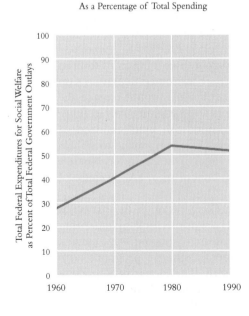

Total Expenditures

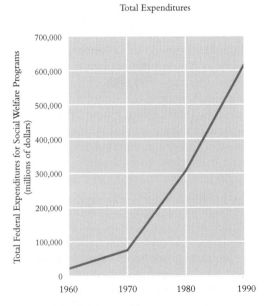

Controversies over Rights

The Nixon administration's domestic initiatives came against the backdrop of a much broader debate over how to define the federal government's responsibility to protect basic constitutional rights. In many areas of public policy, this debate raised issues of equality and became framed in terms of the constitutional guarantee of "equal protection" of the laws.

The struggle to define basic constitutional rights embroiled the U.S. Supreme Court in controversy. Under the leadership of Chief Justice Earl Warren and Associate Justice William Brennan, both appointees of Dwight Eisenhower, an "activist" majority that was devoted to recognizing a broad range of constitutionally protected rights had dominated the Court during the 1960s. Although nearly all the Warren Court's rights-related decisions, especially in the areas of school desegregation and political dissent, drew critical fire, the most emotional cases involved the rights of persons accused of violent crime. In *Miranda* v. *Arizona* (1966), the Court's activists held that the Constitution required police officers to advise people arrested for a felony offense of their constitutional rights to remain silent and to consult an attorney. While civil libertarians defended decisions such as *Miranda* as the logical extension of settled judicial precedents, the Court's numerous critics attacked the activist justices for allegedly inventing new rights that could not be found in the text of the Constitution. Amid rising public concern over crime, conservatives made *Miranda* a symbol of the judicial "coddling" of criminals. During the 1968 presidential campaign, George Wallace and Richard Nixon both attacked the Court for "making" law rather than simply "applying" it.

Richard Nixon had campaigned for president in 1968 as an opponent of the Warren Court's activist stance. Before the election, Chief Justice Warren had announced his resignation, and incoming President Nixon was therefore able to appoint a moderately conservative Republican, Warren Burger, as Chief Justice. Pledged to select only judges who would interpret rights claims narrowly, Nixon also appointed three new associate justices to the Supreme Court during his presidency—Harry Blackmun, William Rehnquist, and Lewis Powell. The Supreme Court, however, continued to face controversial new cases involving the issue of rights.

Considerable discussion focused on the constitutional status of social welfare programs. Following the logic of earlier Warren Court decisions on equal protection of the laws, activist lawyers argued that access to adequate economic assistance from the federal government should be recognized as a national right every bit as fundamental as, say, the right to vote. Many observers expected that the Court, even with the retirement of Warren, might soon take this step. In 1970, however, in *Dandridge* v. *Williams,* the Court rejected the argument that laws capping the amount a state would pay to welfare recipients violated the Constitution's requirement that the government must extend equal protection of the laws to all citizens. The Court drew a sharp distinction between the government's responsibility to respect the individual liberties of all citizens, such as the right to vote and freedom of speech, and its discretionary ability to make distinctions in the administration of spending programs such as AFDC. In short, the Court refused to hold, as a matter of constitutional law, that welfare was a national right.

Another controversial aspect of the rights debate involved issues of health and safety. A vigorous consumer rights movement, which had initially drawn inspiration from Ralph Nader's exposé about auto safety, titled *Unsafe at Any Speed* (1965), attracted immediate political support. Under Nader's leadership, consumer advocates lobbied for federal legislation to protect the right to safety in the workplace, the right to safe consumer products, and the right to a healthy environment. This effort, despite strong opposition from many business groups, found expression in such legislation as the Occupational Safety Act of 1973, stronger consumer protection laws,

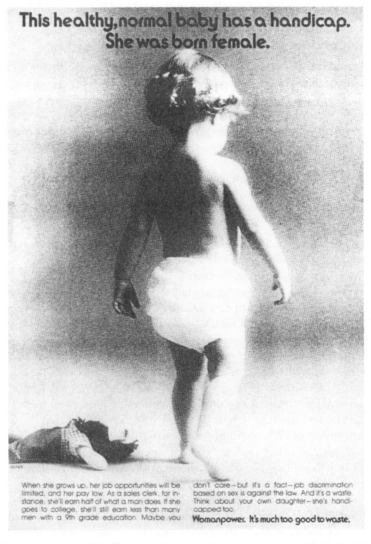

Gender Should Not Be a Handicap. • This advertisement, sponsored by the National Organization for Women (NOW), dramatized the group's efforts to make the elimination of gender inequalities a central part of the "rights revolution."

and new environmental legislation (see Chapter 11)—measures that the courts invariably sustained against constitutional challenges.

At the same time, a newly energized women's rights movement pushed its own set of issues. The National Organization for Women (NOW), founded in 1966, backed a constitutional change, an Equal Rights Amendment (ERA), that would explicitly guarantee women the same legal rights as men. After having been passed by Congress in 1972 and quickly ratified by more than half the states, the ERA suddenly emerged as one of the most divisive domestic issues of the early 1970s. Conservative women's groups, such as Phyllis Schlafly's "Stop ERA," charged that equal rights for women (including the right to equality within the military) would undermine traditional "family values." At anti-ERA rallies, children carried signs that read "Please Don't Send My Mommy to War." As a result of such opposition, the ERA, which once seemed assured of passage, failed to attain approval from the three-quarters of states needed for ratification. Ultimately, women's groups abandoned the ERA effort in favor of urging the courts to recognize women's equal rights on a case-by-case, issue-by-issue basis.

One of these specific issues, involving a woman's right to a safe and legal abortion, became even more controversial than the ERA. In *Roe* v. *Wade* (1973), the Supreme Court ruled that a state law making abortion a criminal offense violated a woman's right of privacy. The *Roe* decision outraged conservatives. Rallying under the "Right to Life" slogan and focusing on the rights of the unborn fetus, anti-abortion groups showed that the language of constitutional rights could be used by the political right as well as by liberals and the left. Antiabortion forces labeled *Roe* v. *Wade* as another threat to family values, and in 1976 they succeeded in persuading Congress to ban the use of federal funds to finance abortions for women with low incomes. Standing behind the right to privacy—and behind any woman's right to have access to a safe, medically supervised abortion—feminist groups made the issue of individual choice in reproductive decisions a principal rallying point.

Richard Nixon had promised an administration that, in contrast to Lyndon Johnson's, would "bring us together." Instead, bitter divisions over economic policies, government spending programs, and the meaning of basic constitutional guarantees made the Nixon presidency a period of increasing, rather than decreasing, polarization.

Foreign Policy under Nixon and Kissinger

While attempting to deal with divisive domestic concerns, the Nixon administration was far more preoccupied with international affairs, especially the war in Vietnam and other Cold War issues. Nixon appointed Henry Kissinger, a political scientist from Harvard, as his national security adviser. Under Kissinger, the National Security Council (NSC) emerged as the most powerful shaper of foreign policy within the government, eclipsing the State Department and its head, William Rogers. In 1973 Kissinger was himself appointed Secretary of State, a position that he continued to hold until 1977. Kissinger was the dominant personality of the Nixon and Gerald Ford administrations and one of the few top advisers who managed to remain unscathed by the scandals that ended Nixon's presidency. With Nixon,

Kissinger orchestrated a grand strategy for foreign policy: détente with the Soviet Union, normalization of relations with China, and disengagement from direct military involvement in Southeast Asia and other parts of the world.

Détente

Although Nixon had built his political career on hard-line anticommunism, the Nixon-Kissinger team mapped a foreign policy that aimed at easing tensions with the two major communist nations, the Soviet Union and China. Kissinger surmised that, as both nations began to seek favor with the United States, they might ease up on their support for North Vietnam, facilitating America's ability to withdraw from the war that was dividing the nation.

Arms control talks took top priority in U.S.-Soviet relations. In 1969 the two superpowers opened the Strategic Arms Limitation Talks (SALT), and after several years of high-level diplomacy they signed an agreement (SALT I) that limited further development of both antiballistic missiles (ABMs) and offensive intercontinental ballistic missiles (ICBMs). The impact of SALT I on the arms race was negligible because it did not limit the number of warheads that could be carried by each missile. Still, the very fact that the Soviet Union and the United States had concluded high-level discussions on arms control signaled a shift. Moreover, to promote an agreement on arms control, the Nixon administration took another step toward accommodation. It offered greater access to U.S. trade and technology to help the faltering Soviet economy.

Nixon's steps toward normalizing relations with the People's Republic of China brought an even more dramatic break with the Cold War past. Nixon had been one of the most vocal critics of the communist regime that had come to power in China in 1949. Now, tentative conversations arranged through the embassies of both countries in Poland led to a slight easing of U.S. trade restrictions against China in early 1971 and then to an invitation from China for Americans to compete in a ping-pong tournament. This celebrated exhibition became a prelude to more significant exchange. In 1972 Nixon himself visited China, posing for photos with Mao Zedong and strolling along the Great Wall. Relations between the two countries remained difficult, especially over the status of Taiwan, which the United States still recognized as the legitimate government of China. A few months after Nixon's visit, however, the United Nations admitted the People's Republic as the representative of China, and in 1973 the United States and China exchanged informal diplomatic missions.

Vietnamization

While the Nixon administration was eagerly seeking rapprochement with China and the Soviet Union, it continued to wage war in Vietnam. After a review of Vietnam policy in 1969, Nixon and Kissinger decided to start the withdrawal of U.S. ground forces (a policy called "Vietnamization") while stepping up the air war and intensifying diplomatic efforts to reach a settlement. In July of that year, the president publicly announced the "Nixon Doctrine," which pledged that the United States would provide military assistance to anticommunist governments in Asia but would leave it to them to provide their own military forces.

The goal of Vietnamization was to withdraw U.S. ground troops without accepting compromise or defeat. Like Johnson before him, Nixon hoped that U.S. technology could bring military victory. While officially adhering to Johnson's 1968 bombing halt over the North, Nixon and Kissinger accelerated both the ground war and the air war by launching new offensives in the South and, in April 1970, by approving a military incursion into Cambodia, an ostensibly neutral country. Extending the war into Cambodia revealed how powerful Kissinger had become in shaping the nation's foreign policy. Both Secretary of State William Rogers and Secretary of Defense Melvin Laird had advised against such a drastic step.

The move set off a new wave of protest at home. Campuses exploded in anger, and bomb threats led many colleges to close early for the 1970 summer recess. White police officers killed two students at the all-black Jackson State College in Mississippi, and National Guard troops at Kent State University in Ohio fired on demonstrators and killed four students. As growing numbers of protestors took to the streets, moderate business and political leaders turned against the war, alarmed by how it was dividing the country. Disillusionment with the war also grew from revelations that, a month after Tet, troops led by U.S. Lieutenant William Calley had entered a small hamlet called My Lai and shot more than 200 people, mostly women and children. This massacre of South Vietnamese civilians had become public in 1969; in 1971 a military court convicted Calley and, in a controversial decision, sentenced him to life imprisonment.

The Cambodian incursion of 1970 was part of a widening secret war in Cambodia and Laos. Although the U.S. government denied that it was waging any such war, large areas of those rich agricultural countries were disrupted by American bombing. As the number of Cambodian refugees swelled and food supplies dwindled, the communist guerrilla force in Cambodia—the Khmer Rouge—grew into a well-disciplined army. The Khmer Rouge would later seize the government and, in an attempt to stabilize its power by eliminating all potential dissent, turn Cambodia into what was later termed a "killing field." While Nixon continued to talk about U.S. troop withdrawals and while peace negotiations with North Vietnam proceeded in Paris, the Vietnam War actually broadened into a war that destabilized the entire region of Indochina.

Even greater violence was yet to come. In the spring of 1972 a North Vietnamese offensive approached within 30 miles of Saigon. U.S. generals warned of imminent defeat unless something was done. Nixon responded by resuming the bombing of North Vietnam and by mining its harbors. Just weeks before the 1972 election, Kissinger again promised peace and announced a cease-fire. After the election, however, the United States unleashed even greater firepower. In the so-called Christmas bombing of December 1972, the heaviest bombardment in history, B-52 bombers pounded North Vietnamese military and civilian targets around the clock.

By this time, however, much of the media, the Congress, and the public had become sickened by the violence and apprehensive over the extent of government secrecy and surveillance at home. At last, Nixon proceeded with full-scale Vietnamization of the war. In January 1973 North Vietnam and the United States signed peace accords in Paris that provided for the withdrawal of U.S. troops. As U.S. troops pulled out, the South Vietnamese government, headed by Nguyen Van Thieu, continued to fight, though it was growing increasingly demoralized and disorganized.

In the spring of 1975, nearly two years after the Paris accords, South Vietnam's army was unable to withstand the advance of North Vietnam's skilled general

Nguyen Giap. Thieu's government collapsed, North Vietnamese armies entered Saigon, and U.S. helicopters scrambled to airlift the last remaining officials out of the besieged U.S. embassy. America's longest war had ended in defeat.

The Aftermath of War

Between 1960 and 1973, approximately 3.5 million American men and women served in Vietnam: 58,000 died; 150,000 were wounded; 2,000 remain missing. In the aftermath of this long, costly war, many Americans struggled to find meaning. Why had their country failed to prevail over a small, barely industrialized nation? Conservatives, arguing that the war had been lost at home, blamed the uncensored and irresponsible media, the coddling of dissenters, the "failure of will" in Congress, and "neo-isolationism." The goals of the war, they believed, were laudable; politicians, setting unrealistic limits on the war due to fear of domestic dissent and concern over possible Chinese involvement, had denied the military the means to attain victory. By contrast, those who had opposed the war stressed the overextension of American power, the misguided belief that the United States was unbeatable, the deceitfulness of governmental leaders, and the incompetence of bureaucratic processes. For them, the war was in the wrong place and waged for the wrong reasons; and the human costs to Indochina outweighed any possible gain for U.S. national security.

The Vietnam War Memorial in Washington, D.C. • A kind of wailing wall that contains the names of every American who lost his or her life in the Vietnam War, the Vietnam Memorial became a powerful, and unifying, symbol of a bitterly divisive crusade. It was dedicated in November 1982.

Regardless of their positions on the war, most Americans could agree on one proposition: There should be "no more Vietnams." Within the Pentagon, especially, the lesson of Vietnam was unambiguous. The United States should not undertake future military involvements unless there were clear and compelling political objectives, demonstrable public support, and the provision of adequate means to accomplish the goal.

The Nixon Doctrine

Although the Nixon Doctrine received its fullest articulation in the Vietnamization of the war in Indochina, Nixon and Kissinger extended the basic premise of that doctrine to other areas as well. In molding foreign policy, Kissinger relied increasingly on pro-U.S. anticommunist allies to police their own regions of the world. Kissinger made it clear that the United States would not dispatch troops to oppose revolutionary insurgencies but would give generous assistance to anticommunist regimes or factions that were willing to fight the battle themselves.

During the early 1970s, America's Cold War strategy came to rely on supporting staunchly anticommunist regional powers: nations such as Iran under Shah Reza Pahlavi, South Africa with its apartheid regime, and Brazil with its repressive military dictatorship. All of these states built large military establishments trained by the United States. U.S. military assistance, together with covert CIA operations, also incubated and protected anticommunist dictatorships in South Korea, in the Philippines, and in much of Latin America. U.S. arms sales to the rest of the world skyrocketed from $1.8 billion in 1970 to $15.2 billion six years later. In one of its most controversial foreign policies, the Nixon administration employed covert action against the elected socialist government of Salvador Allende Gossens in Chile in 1970. After Allende took office, Kissinger gave top priority to encouraging destabilization of his government, and in 1973 Allende was overthrown by the Chilean military, who immediately suspended democratic rule and announced that Allende had committed suicide.

Critics charged that the United States, in the name of anticommunism, had too often wedded its diplomatic fortunes to such questionable covert actions and unpopular military governments. In 1975 Senator Frank Church conducted widely-publicized Senate hearings into possible abuses by the CIA (including the action in Chile). But supporters of the Nixon Doctrine applauded the administration's strengthening of a system of allies and its tough anticommunism. In many circles, Nixon received high marks for a pragmatic foreign policy that combined détente toward the communist giants with strong containment against the further global spread of revolutionary regimes.

The Wars of Watergate

Nixon's presidency ultimately collapsed as a result of horrendous decisions made in the president's own Oval Office. From the time Nixon entered the White House, he had been deeply suspicious of nearly every person and institution in Washington. He pressed the Internal Revenue Service to harass prominent Democrats with expensive audits and suspected the IRS of disloyalty when it seemed to be moving too slowly. Such suspicions centered on antiwar activists and old political opponents but even extended to likely allies, such as J. Edgar Hoover, the staunchly conservative director of the FBI. Isolated behind a close-knit group of advisers, Nixon ultimately set up his own secret intelligence operation, which was separate from the FBI.

During the summer of 1971 Daniel Ellsberg, a dissident member of the national security bureaucracy, leaked to the press a top-secret history of U.S. involvement in the Vietnam War, subsequently known as the "Pentagon Papers." Nixon responded by seeking, unsuccessfully, a court injunction to stop publication of the study and, more ominously, by unleashing his secret intelligence unit, dubbed "the plumbers," to stop the leaking of information to the media. Looking for materials that might discredit Ellsberg, the plumbers burglarized his psychiatrist's office. Thus began a series of "dirty tricks" and outright illegalities, often financed by funds illegally solicited for Nixon's 1972 reelection campaign, that would culminate in the political scandal and constitutional crisis known as "Watergate."

The Election of 1972

As the 1972 election approached, Nixon's political strategists worried that economic troubles and the war might deny the president reelection. Creating a campaign organization separate from that of the Republican Party, with the ironic acronym of CREEP (Committee to Re-Elect the President), they secretly raised millions of dollars, much of it from illegal contributions.

As the 1972 campaign proceeded, Nixon's chances of reelection dramatically improved. An assassination attempt crippled George Wallace, Nixon's major right-wing challenger. Meanwhile, Senator Edmund Muskie of Maine, who was trying to translate his impressive showing as Hubert Humphrey's running mate in 1968 into a Democratic presidential bid of his own, made a series of blunders (some of them precipitated by Republican "dirty tricksters") that derailed his campaign. Eventually, Senator George McGovern of South Dakota, an outspoken opponent of the Vietnam War, won the Democratic nomination.

McGovern never seriously challenged Nixon. During the campaign, McGovern called for higher taxes on the wealthy, a guaranteed minimum income for all Americans, amnesty for Vietnam War draft resisters, and the decriminalization of marijuana—positions significantly to the left of the views of many traditional Democrats. In foreign policy, McGovern called for deep cuts in defense spending and for vigorous efforts to achieve peace in Vietnam—positions that Nixon successfully portrayed as signs of "weakness."

Nixon won an easy victory in the November elections. McGovern lost traditional Democrats without attracting a significant number of new or disaffected voters. The president received the Electoral College votes of all but one state and the District of Columbia, won more than 60 percent of the popular vote, and carried virtually every traditional Democratic bloc except the African American vote. His margin of victory was one of the largest in U.S. history, only slightly below that of Johnson's 1964 landslide. Although the Twenty-sixth Amendment, ratified a year before the election, had lowered the voting age to 18, relatively few of the newly enfranchised voters cast ballots.

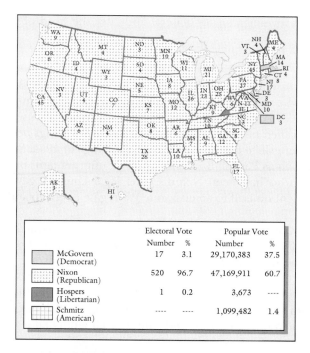

	Electoral Vote		Popular Vote	
	Number	%	Number	%
McGovern (Democrat)	17	3.1	29,170,383	37.5
Nixon (Republican)	520	96.7	47,169,911	60.7
Hospers (Libertarian)	1	0.2	3,673	----
Schmitz (American)	----	----	1,099,482	1.4

Presidential Election, 1972

Nixon Pursued

In achieving that victory, however, the president's team left a trail of corruption that cut short Nixon's second term. The campaign effort, as both federal prosecutors and investigative journalists soon discovered, had been marked by a variety of questionable and clearly illegal activities. In June 1972 a surveillance team with links to both CREEP and the White House had been arrested while adjusting some eavesdropping equipment that it had installed earlier in the Democratic Party's headquarters in Washington's Watergate office complex. In public, Nixon's spokespersons dismissed the Watergate break-in as an insignificant "third-rate burglary"; privately, Nixon and his closest aides immediately launched an illegal cover-up. They paid hush money to the Watergate burglars and had the CIA falsely warn the FBI that any investigation into the break-in would jeopardize national security.

While reporters from the *Washington Post* took the lead in pursuing the taint of scandal, members of Congress and the federal judiciary sought evidence on possible violations of the law. In January 1973 Judge John Sirica, a Republican appointee who was presiding over the trial of the Watergate burglars, refused to accept their claim that neither CREEP nor the White House had been involved in the break-in. While Sirica pushed for more information, Senate leaders convened a special Watergate Committee, headed by North Carolina's conservative Democratic Senator Sam Ervin, to look into the "dirty tricks" that had allegedly been played on the Democrats during the 1972 campaign. Meanwhile, federal prosecutors uncovered evidence that seemed to link key administration and White House figures, including John

Mitchell, Nixon's former attorney general and later the head of CREEP, to illegal activities.

Nixon's political and legal difficulties grew steadily worse during 1973. In March, under unyielding pressure from Judge Sirica, one of the Watergate burglars, a former CIA officer working for CREEP, finally broke his silence. By May, he joined other witnesses who testified before the Senate's Watergate Committee about various illegal activities committed by CREEP and the White House. Nixon's closest aides were soon called before the committee, and the hearings became the biggest political soap opera since the Army-McCarthy hearings of 1954. Some of the president's people, such as Patrick Buchanan, proved unrepentant, but others, including John Dean, who had been Nixon's chief legal counsel, gave testimony that linked the president himself to an elaborate Watergate cover-up and to other illegal activities.

Along the way, Senate investigators discovered that a voice-activated taping machine had recorded every conversation held in Nixon's Oval Office. Now it was possible to determine whether the president or John Dean, Nixon's primary accuser, was lying. Nixon claimed an "executive privilege" to keep the tapes from being released to other branches of government, but Judge Sirica, Archibald Cox (a Harvard Law School professor who had been appointed as a special, independent prosecutor in the Watergate case), and Congress all launched legal moves to gain access to them.

If Nixon's own problems were not enough, his vice president, Spiro Agnew, resigned in October 1973 after pleading "no contest" to income tax evasion. He agreed to a plea-bargain arrangement in order to avoid prosecution for having accepted illegal kickbacks while he was in Maryland politics. Acting under the Twenty-fifth Amendment (ratified in 1967), Nixon appointed—and both houses of Congress confirmed—Representative Gerald Ford of Michigan, a Republican Party stalwart, as the new vice president. Although an amiable, unpretentious person, Ford seemed so lacking in presidential qualities that pundits joked that his ascension to the nation's second-highest office provided Nixon with a valuable insurance policy against impeachment.

Nixon's Final Days

By the early summer of 1974, though, the likelihood of Nixon's impeachment—and of a Ford presidency—no longer seemed unthinkable. The nation's legal-constitutional system was closing in on Nixon, and the president's inept attempts to sidetrack his pursuers only redounded against him. During the previous autumn, shortly after Agnew's embarrassing departure, for example, Nixon had clumsily orchestrated the firing of Archibald Cox, hoping to prevent him from gaining access to the White House tapes. When this rash action was greeted by a public outcry—the affair came to be known as Nixon's "Saturday Night Massacre"—the president was obliged to appoint another independent prosecutor, Leon Jaworski, who proved as tenacious as Cox. Similarly, Nixon's own release of edited, and occasionally garbled, transcripts of a series of Watergate-related conversations, merely prompted people to demand the original tape recordings. Finally, by announcing that he would only obey a "definitive" Supreme Court decision on the tapes' legal

Impeach Nixon • As Richard Nixon's legal problems became more serious in 1973, sign-carrying opponents took to the streets of Washington, D.C. One protest technique not depicted here encouraged popular participation by urging motorists to "Honk if You Think He's Guilty."

status, Nixon was all but inviting the justices, including some he himself had appointed, to reach a unanimous decision. And on July 24, 1974, the Court did just that in the case of *U.S.* v. *Nixon*. By this time, Nixon was in desperate straits. While the Supreme Court was unanimously ruling that Nixon's claim of "executive privilege" over the tapes could not justify his refusal to release evidence needed in a criminal investigation, the Judiciary Committee of the House of Representatives was already moving toward a vote on impeachment.

By the end of July, only a few loyalists stood behind Richard Nixon. After nearly a full week of televised deliberations, a majority of the House Judiciary Committee, including some Republicans, voted three formal articles of impeachment against the president for (1) his obstruction of justice in the cover-up of Watergate; (2) his violation of constitutional liberties (as in his use of illegal wiretaps); and (3) his refusal to produce evidence requested during the impeachment process. Nixon boasted that he would fight these accusations before the Senate, the body authorized by the Constitution (Article I, Section 3) to render a verdict of guilty or innocent after the House votes impeachment.

Nixon's closest aides, however, were already making ready for his departure. One of his own attorneys, while preparing Nixon's defense, discovered that a tape Nixon had been withholding contained the long-sought "smoking gun": a 1972 conversation confirming that Nixon himself had agreed to a plan by which the CIA would advance the fraudulent claim of national security in order to stop the FBI from investigating the Watergate burglary. At this point, Nixon's secretary of defense ordered all military commanders to ignore any order from the president, their titular commander in chief, unless it was countersigned by the secretary. Checkmated by his own aides, abandoned by almost every prominent Republican, and about to confront a Senate prepared to vote him guilty on the impeachment charges, Nixon caved in. He went on television on August 8, 1974, to announce that he would resign from office, effective at noon on the following day. On August 9, Gerald Ford became the nation's 38th president.

In 1974, most people believed that Watergate was one of the gravest crises in the history of the republic and that the lawless Nixon administration had posed a serious threat to constitutional government. As time passed, though, the public's recollection and knowledge of the Watergate illegalities and Nixon's forced resignation faded. Opinion polls conducted on the 20th anniversary of Nixon's resignation suggested that most Americans retained only a dim memory of Watergate.

One reason may be that although nearly a dozen members of the Nixon administration—including its chief law enforcement officer, John Mitchell—were convicted of criminal activities, the president himself escaped punishment. Only a month after Nixon's resignation, Gerald Ford granted Nixon an unconditional presidential pardon. The nation was spared the spectacle of witnessing a former president undergoing a lengthy, perhaps divisive trial; but it was also denied an authoritative accounting, in a court of law, of the full range of Nixon's misdeeds. In time, Nixon even underwent yet another political resurrection and emerged, prior to his death in 1994, as an honored elder statesperson.

Another reason for the fading memory of Watergate may be the popular penchant for linking it to nearly every political scandal of the post-Nixon era. The suffix "–gate" became attached, especially in the mass media, to grave constitutional episodes (such as Ronald Reagan's "Iran-Contragate" affair) and to the most trivial of political events (such as the brief "Nannygate" controversy that eliminated one of President Bill Clinton's nominees for attorney general in 1993). By the end of the 20th century, much of public discourse, it seemed, framed the dramatic events of 1973 and 1974 as another example of routine political corruption rather than as a unique, serious constitutional crisis.

Finally, what the historian Stanley Kutler has called the "wars of Watergate" may have been overshadowed by the enormity of the turmoil and loss Americans experienced as a result of America's longest war. In this sense, Watergate tends to blend into a broader pattern of political, social, economic, and cultural turmoil that emerged during the lengthy, increasingly divisive war in Southeast Asia. Indeed, divisions from the Vietnam era would continue to strain American life during the rest of the 20th century.

Conclusion

The power of the national government expanded during the 1960s. Lyndon Johnson's Great Society created a blueprint for an expanding welfare state, financed from Washington. Federal programs, Johnson believed, could ignite a War on Poverty, lifting the economic and spiritual well-being of all. The Great Society, however, was quickly overshadowed by the escalation of the war in Vietnam, a struggle that consumed increasingly more of the nation's wealth in order to prevent communism from gaining a victory in southeast Asia.

This growth of governmental power—both the enlargement of domestic social programs and the waging of war abroad—prompted divisive debates that polarized the country. The economy faltered, and top leaders became discredited. Johnson left the presidency a broken man. And his Republican successor, Richard Nixon, in trying to control the divisions at home, let loose an abuse of power that ultimately drove him from office in disgrace and left the presidency itself tainted. The exalted hopes of the early 1960s—that the U.S. government would be able to enhance liberty and equality both in America and throughout the rest of the world—ended in frustration in domestic policy and defeat in Vietnam.

The era of America's longest war was a time of street demonstrations, of high political passions, of generational and racial conflict, of differing definitions of patriotism. It saw the slow convergence of an antiwar movement, along with the emergence of a youthful counterculture, of "Black Power," of "women's liberation," and of a variety of contests over what constituted basic rights for Americans. Different groups assigned different causes to explain the failures of both the Great Society and the war, and the polarization from these years, over the war and over a variety of social issues, shaped the fault lines of politics for years to come. Nearly all Americans, however, became much more reserved, many even cynical, about further enlarging the power of the federal government.

Chronology

1963 Johnson assumes presidency and pledges to continue Kennedy's initiatives

1964 Congress passes Kennedy's tax bill, the Civil Rights Act of 1964, and the Economic Opportunity Act • Gulf of Tonkin Resolution gives Johnson authority to conduct undeclared war • Johnson defeats Barry Goldwater in presidential election

1965 Johnson announces plans for the Great Society • Malcolm X assassinated • U.S. intervenes in Dominican Republic • Johnson announces significant U.S. troop deployments in Vietnam • Congress passes Voting Rights Act • Violence rocks Los Angeles and other urban areas

1966 Black Power movement emerges • *Miranda* v. *Arizona* decision guarantees rights of criminal suspects • Ronald Reagan elected governor of California • U.S. begins massive air strikes in North Vietnam

1967 Large antiwar demonstrations begin • Beatles release *Sgt. Pepper's Lonely Hearts Club Band*

1968 Tet offensive (January) • Martin Luther King Jr. assassinated (April) • Robert Kennedy assassinated (June) • Violence at Democratic national convention in Chicago • Civil Rights Act of 1968 passed • Vietnam peace talks begin in Paris • Richard Nixon elected president

1969 Nixon announces "Vietnamization" policy • Pictures of My Lai massacre become public

1970 U.S. troops enter Cambodia • Student demonstrators killed at Kent State and Jackson State

1971 "Pentagon Papers" published; White House "plumbers" formed • Military court convicts Lieutenant Calley for My Lai incident

1972 Nixon crushes McGovern in presidential election

1973 Paris peace accords signed • *Roe* v. *Wade* upholds women's right to abortion • Nixon's Watergate troubles begin to escalate

1974 House votes impeachment, and Nixon resigns • Ford assumes presidency

1975 Saigon falls to North Vietnamese forces

Suggested Readings

Lyndon Johnson

On Lyndon Johnson see Paul K. Conkin, *Big Daddy from the Pedernales: Lyndon Baines Johnson* (1986); Robert Caro, *The Path to Power* (1982) and *Means of Ascent* (1990); Robert J. Dallek, *Lone*

Star Rising: Lyndon Johnson and His Times, 1908–1960 (1991); and Irving Bernstein, *Guns or Butter: The Presidency of Lyndon Johnson* (1996). Other titles include Vaughn Davis Bornet, *The Presidency of Lyndon Baines Johnson* (1993), which is relatively sympathetic, and Doris Kearns Goodwin, *Lyndon Johnson and the American Dream* (1976). Joseph A. Califano, Jr., *The Triumph and Tragedy of Lyndon Johnson: The White House Years* (1991) is an interesting memoir, and Michael R. Beschloss, ed., *Taking Charge: The Johnson White House Tapes, 1963–1964* (1997) offers fascinating insights. On the Warren Court see Morton J. Horwitz, *The Warren Court and the Pursuit of Justice* (1998).

Civil Rights

Civil rights issues are treated in David Garrow, *Protest at Selma: Martin Luther King, Jr., and the Voting Rights Act of 1965* (1980); Clayborne Carson, *In Struggle: SNCC and the Black Awakening of the 1960s* (1981); Doug McAdam, *Freedom Summer* (1988); Emily Stoper, *The Student Non-Violent Coordinating Committee: The Growth of Radicalism in a Civil Rights Organization* (1989); Mark Stern, *Calculating Visions: Kennedy, Johnson, and Civil Rights* (1992); William L. Van Deburg, *New Day in Babylon: The Black Power Movement and American Culture, 1965–1975* (1992); Gerald Horne, *Fire This Time: The Watts Uprising and the 1960s* (1995); David J. Armor, *Forced Justice: School Desegregation and the Law* (1995); Richard Griswold del Castillo and Richard A. Garcia, *Cesar Chavez: A Triumph of Spirit* (1995); Louis A. DeCaro Jr., *On the Side of My People: A Religious Life of Malcolm X* (1996); Michael Eric Dyson, *Making Malcolm: the Myth and Meaning of Malcolm X* (1995); Charles M. Payne, *I've Got the Light of Freedom: The Organizing Tradition and the Mississippi Freedom Struggle* (1995); and Taylor Branch, *Pillar of Fire: America in the King Years, 1963–65* (1998).

The Great Society and the War on Poverty

The Great Society and the War on Poverty receive a critical assessment in Alan J. Matusow, *The Unraveling of America: A History of Liberalism in the 1960s* (1984). The most influential analysis from the right of Great Society liberalism has been Charles Murray's *Losing Ground: American Social Policy, 1950–1980* (1984), which can be compared with Christopher Jencks, *Rethinking Social Policy: Race, Poverty and the Underclass* (1992). A recent overview is Gareth Davies, *From Opportunity to Entitlement: The Transformation and Decline of Great Society Liberalism* (1996). See also Michael L. Gillette, *Launching the War on Poverty: An Oral History* (1996).

Johnson's Foreign Policies

Johnson's foreign policies are treated in Bernard Firestone and Robert C. Vogt, eds., *Lyndon Baines Johnson and the Uses of Power* (1988); Warren I. Cohen and Nancy Bernkopf Tucker, eds., *Lyndon Johnson Confronts the World: American Foreign Policy, 1963–1968* (1994); Diane Kunz, ed., *The Diplomacy of the Crucial Decade: American Foreign Relations during the 1960s* (1994). On the Dominican intervention see Bruce Palmer, Jr., *Intervention in the Caribbean: The Dominican Crisis of 1965* (1989); and Abraham F. Lowenthal, *The Dominican Intervention* (1995).

Johnson's Policies in Vietnam

Johnson's policies in Vietnam have attracted an immense literature. Representative titles include George Herring, *America's Longest War: The United States and Vietnam, 1950–1975* (1986); Marilyn Blatt Young, *The Vietnam-American Wars, 1945–1990* (1991); David L. DiLeo, *George Ball, Vietnam, and the Rethinking of Containment* (1991); Melvin Small, *Johnson, Nixon, and the Doves* (1988); Larry Berman, *Lyndon Johnson's War: The Road to Stalemate in Vietnam* (1989); Marilyn Young and Jon Livingston, *The Vietnam War: How the United States Intervened in the History of Southeast Asia* (1990); Gabriel Kolko, *Anatomy of War: Vietnam, The United States, and the Modern Historical Experience* (1994); Lloyd C. Gardner, *Approaching Vietnam: From World War II through Dien Bien Phu* (1988); George McT. Kahin, *Intervention: How America Became Involved in Vietnam* (1986); R.B. Smith, *An International History of the Vietnam War* (1983); James J. Wirtz, *The Tet Offensive: Intelligence Failure in War* (1991); Ronald Spector, *After Tet: The Bloodiest Year in Vietnam* (1993); David M. Barrett, *Uncertain Warriors: Lyndon Johnson and His Vietnam Advisors* (1993); David L. Anderson, ed., *Facing My Lai: Moving Beyond the Massacre* (1997); Michael Hunt, *Lyndon Johnson's War: America's Cold War*

Crusade in Vietnam, 1945–1968 (1996); Robert Buzzanco, *Masters of War: Military Dissent and Politics in the Vietnam Era* (1996); Richard A. Hunt, *Pacification: The American Struggle for Vietnam's Hearts and Minds* (1995); Edwin Moise, *Tonkin Gulf and the Escalation of the Vietnam War* (1996); Roger Warner, *Back Fire: The CIA's Secret War in Laos and Its Link to the Vietnam War* (1995); and Robert D. Schulzinger, *A Time for War: The United States and Vietnam, 1941–1975* (1997).

Cultural Debates Generated by the War in Vietnam

For cultural debates generated by the war in Vietnam, see Loren Baritz, *Backfire: A History of How American Culture Led Us into Vietnam and Made Us Fight the Way We Did* (1985); Kathleen Turner, *Lyndon Johnson's Dual War: Vietnam and the Press* (1985); Susan Jeffords, *The Remasculinization of America: Gender and the Vietnam War* (1989); Albert Auster and Leonard Quart, *How the War Was Remembered: Hollywood and Vietnam* (1988); John Carlos Rowe and Rick Berg, eds., *The Vietnam War and American Culture* (1991); Michael Gregg, ed., *Inventing Vietnam: The War in Film and Television* (1991); David W. Levy, *The Debate over Vietnam* (2nd ed., 1995); and Fred Turner, *Echoes of Combat: The Vietnam War in American Memory* (1996).

Political Insurgency of the 1960s

On the political insurgency of the 1960s see W. J. Rorbaugh, *Berkeley at War: The 1960s* (1989); Barbara Tischler, ed., *Sights on the Sixties* (1992); David Chalmers, *And the Crooked Place Made Straight: The Struggle for Social Change in the 1960s* (1996); Timothy Miller, *The Hippies and American Values* (1991); Peter Collier and David Horowitz, *Destructive Generation: Second Thoughts about the Sixties* (1996); Paul Berman, *A Tale of Two Utopias: The Political Journey of the Generation of 1968* (1998); David Farber, ed., *The Sixties: From Memory to History* (1994); Alexander Bloom and Wini Breines, eds., *"Takin it to the Streets": A Sixties Reader* (1995); Paul Lyons, *New Left, New Right, and the Legacy of the Sixties* (1996); Jonah Raskin, *For the Hell of It: The Life and Times of Abbie Hoffman* (1996); and David Burner, *Making Peace with the Sixties* (1996). The conservative insurgency is the subject of Mary C. Brennan, *Turning Right in the Sixties: The Conservative Capture of the GOP* (1995); Robert Alan Goldberg, *Barry Goldwater* (1995); and John A. Andrew III, *The Other Side of the Sixties: Young Americans for Freedom and the Rise of Conservative Politics* (1997).

Opposition to the War

On opposition to the war, see Charles De Benedetti, *An American Ordeal: The Anti-War Movement of the Vietnam Era* (1990); Melvin Small and William D. Hoover, eds., *Give Peace a Chance* (1992); Kenneth J. Heineman, *Campus Wars: The Peace Movement at American State Universities in the Vietnam Era* (1993); Amy Swerdlow, *Women Strike for Peace: Traditional Motherhood and Radical Politics in the 1960s* (1993); Tom Wells, *The War Within: America's Battle Over Vietnam* (1993); Adam Garfinkle, *Telltale Hearts: The Origins and Impact of the Vietnam Antiwar Movement* (1995). Todd Gitlin indicts the media for speeding the fall of opposition efforts in *The Whole World is Watching: Mass Media in the Making and Unmaking of the New Left* (1980), while Maurice Isserman's *If I Had a Hammer: The Death of the Old Left and the Birth of the New Left* (1987) looks at the general conflict among radicals. See also Wini Breines, *Community and Organization in the New Left, 1962–1968* (1982); Jim Miller, *Democracy Is in the Streets: From Port Huron to the Siege of Chicago* (1987); Todd Gitlin, *The Sixties: Years of Hope, Days of Rage* (1987); and Douglas Knight, *Streets of Dreams: The Nature and Legacy of the 1960s* (1989). On the politics of 1968 see Lewis Gould, *1968: The Election That Changed America* (1993).

Richard Nixon and His Policies

On Richard Nixon and his policies, see Garry Wills, *Nixon Agonistes* (rev. ed., 1980); Bruce Odes, ed., *From the President: Richard Nixon's Secret Files* (1989); Stephen Ambrose, *Nixon* (1989); Roger Morris, *Richard Milhous Nixon: The Rise of an American Politician* (1990); Joan Hoff, *Nixon Reconsidered* (1994); and Terry Terriff, *The Nixon Administration and the Making of U.S. Nuclear Strategy* (1995). On economic policy see Diane B. Kunz, *Butter and Guns: America's Cold War Economic Policy* (1997); and Allen J. Matusow, *Nixon's Economy: Booms, Busts, Dollars, and Votes* (1997).

Watergate

On Watergate and the broader ethos of secret government, see Peter Schrag, *Test of Loyalty: Daniel Ellsberg and the Rituals of Secret Government* (1974); Theodore White, *Breach of Faith: The Fall of Richard Nixon* (1975); Athan Theoharis, *Spying on Americans: Political Surveillance from Hoover to the Huston Plan* (1978); Frank J. Donner, *The Age of Surveillance: The Aims and Methods of America's Surveillance System* (1980); L. H. LaRue, *Political Discourse: A Case Study of the Watergate Affair* (1988); Stanley I. Kutler, *The Wars of Watergate: The Last Crisis of Richard Nixon* (1990) and *Abuse of Power: The New Nixon Tapes* (1998); and Michael Schudson, *Watergate in American Memory: How We Remember, Forget, and Reconstruct the Past* (1992).

Videos

LBJ (1991) is a four-hour video documentary in the "American Experience" series; *Chicago, 1968* (1995) is a solid, one-hour entry in the same series. There are a number of video accounts of Malcolm X, including *Malcolm X: Make It Plain* (1993) and *The Real Malcolm X: An Intimate Portrait of the Man* (1992). On civil rights, also consult the appropriate one-hour segments in the longer "Eyes on the Prize" series. On the political insurgency of the 1960s, see *Making Peace with the Sixties* (1991), a three-part series and the more limited, but more insightful, *Berkeley in the Sixties* (1990). *Watergate* (1994) is a multipart documentary produced in Great Britain.

11

America in Transition: Economics, Culture, and Social Change in the Late 20th Century

A s the end of the 20th century approached, historians tried to assess several decades of remarkable economic and cultural changes. The 1960s—fraught with political assassinations, a lengthy foreign war, and domestic dissent— had once seemed a period peculiar for its upheavals. In fact, the decades that followed brought even more far-reaching, although less violent, changes. Increasing immigration, urbanization, and movement of people southward and westward altered the demographics of American life. A transformation from manufacturing to postindustrial employment swept the economy. A digital revolution transfigured systems of information and entertainment. And social movements associated with environmentalism, women's rights, gay pride, racial and ethnic solidarity, and the New Right affected both politics and the ways that Americans defined themselves.

A Changing People

In demographic terms, the post-1970 period marked a watershed in American life. The population was becoming older, more urban, and more ethnically and racially diverse. Moreover, the nation's center of power was shifting away from the Northeast and toward the South and West.

An Aging Population

After about 1970 the birth rate slowed dramatically. During the 1950s, the height of the baby boom, the population had grown by 1.8 percent a year; during the 1970s and 1980s, even with a wave of new immigration and longer life expectancy, the growth rate was only about 1 percent a year. Birth rates sank to their lowest levels, except for the Great Depression decade of the 1930s, in U.S. history. Most young people were delaying marriage until well into their twenties, and the number of women in their mid-thirties who had never married tripled between 1970 and 1990 to 16 percent.

As a result of declining birth rates, rising life expectancy, and the aging of the baby boom generation, the median age of the population rose steadily. In 1970, at

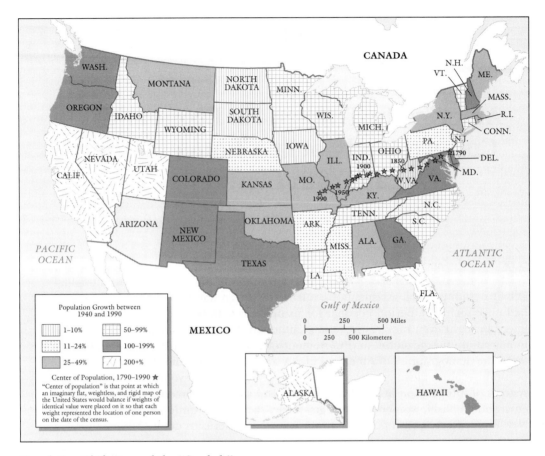

Population Shifts toward the "Sunbelt"

the height of student protests and the youth culture, the median age of Americans was 28; by the middle of the 1990s, it had risen to 34. The catch phrase of the 1960s counterculture, "Don't trust anyone over 30," had taken on a certain irony. Advertising agencies and TV serials turned to midlife appeals. As aging baby boomers pondered retirement, policymakers grew concerned that the projected payouts in Social Security and Medicare benefits would bequeath a staggering cost burden to the smaller post–baby boom generation of workers. During the 1990s, halting the rise of health care costs, revamping health payment systems, and guaranteeing Social Security benefits became major public policy issues.

Rise of the Sunbelt

Not only did population growth slow in the 1970s and 1980s, but the regional pattern of population distribution began to shift political and economic power within the country. Historically, European settlement had proceeded from east to west. The nation's political capital was in the East, and so were its financial, industrial, and cultural centers. Between 1970 and 1990, however, 90 percent of the nation's population growth came in the South and the West. The census of 1980 revealed that for the first time more Americans were living in the South and the West than were living in the North and the East. From 1940 on, Nevada, California, Florida, Arizona, and (after 1959) Alaska were the fastest-growing states, and by 1990 more than 1 in 10 Americans lived in California.

The population shift profoundly reshaped national politics. In the late 1960s, Republican political analyst Kevin Phillips looked at the region extending from Florida to California—the Sunbelt—and predicted that its voters would join together in a conservative coalition. It was just such a coalition that elected Californian Ronald Reagan president in 1980. The South, once solidly Democratic, finally developed a two-party system. And in the reapportionment of seats in the House of Representatives during the early 1990s, California gained seven seats, Florida gained four, New York lost three, and several other northeastern states lost two. The focus of electoral politics shifted from the northeastern states to Florida, Texas, and California.

There were many reasons for this demographic shift. One was the availability of affordable air-conditioning for homes and offices. Another was the rise of tourism and the proliferation of new retirement communities in Nevada, California, Arizona, and Florida. Also, lower labor costs and the absence of strong unions prompted manufacturers to build new plants and relocate old ones in the Sunbelt. Equally important was the growth of a weapons industry.

The Sunbelt was also the gunbelt. Continuous governmental spending on research and manufacture of advanced weaponry and aerospace technology since the Second World War shifted the center of industrial activity from the Mid-Atlantic states to the South and the West, especially California. A perimeter of high-tech industries emerged, with their economic fortunes tied to military-industrial spending.

Those industries attracted highly skilled engineers and scientists. Silicon Valley in Santa Clara County, near San Francisco, had been a rural area until 1940. From then on, it doubled its population every decade. This spectacular growth was triggered by the new semiconductor industry and its network of electronics-related suppliers. For a time, Silicon Valley boasted one of the highest median family incomes in the country. Clogged freeways, heavy air pollution, and rapidly rising housing costs (nearly the highest in the nation), however, slowed growth during the 1980s, and some industries moved out of Silicon Valley. Other high-tech concentrations in the Sunbelt followed a similar pattern, with population growth lively during the 1960s and 1970s, then falling off in the 1980s and early 1990s, only to rebound as the economic boom of the mid-1990s again expanded consumer-driven, high-tech industries.

Government spending on the space program also helped shift research and technology to the Sunbelt, especially to Florida and Texas. After the Soviet Union's launch of its *Sputnik* satellite in 1957, the United States stepped up its own space program under the newly formed National Aeronautics and Space Administration (NASA). In 1961 President Kennedy announced plans for the Apollo program, promising a manned mission to the moon by 1970. In July 1969 astronauts Neil Armstrong and Edwin ("Buzz") Aldrin stepped from their spacecraft onto the moon, planted the American flag, and gathered 47 pounds of lunar rocks for later study. Apollo flights continued until 1972, when NASA turned to the development of a space station, an earth-orbiting platform from which to conduct experiments and research. In the 1980s NASA began launching a series of "space shuttles," manned rockets that served as scientific laboratories and could be flown back to earth for reuse. This progression of ever more innovative, and costly, advances in space technology spurred economic development in the nation's high-tech perimeter.

New Immigration

Another reason for the sharp rise in the population of the Sunbelt was a dramatic increase in immigration. Before 1960, most immigrants had come from Europe and entered the country through the cities of the Northeast. During the 1970s and 1980s, however, 10 million immigrants from Asia and Latin America arrived in the United States, six times the number of European immigrants arriving over the same period. (If illegal immigrants were included, the count would be far higher; Los Angeles officials estimated that 1.5 million illegals arrived in that city in 1993 alone.)

The largest number of non-European immigrants came from Mexico. Many Americans of Mexican ancestry, of course, were not recent immigrants; perhaps 80,000 Mexicans were living in the Southwest at the time northern Mexico had been annexed by the United States in 1848. Immigration into the United States, however, became significant in the 20th century, spurred by the Mexican revolution after 1910 (see Chapter 5) and responding to U.S. labor shortages during the First World War, the Second World War, and the Korean War. In every decade of the postwar period, both legal and illegal immigration from Mexico rose substantially. Many migrants came as seasonal agricultural workers; many others formed permanent communities. Ninety percent of all Mexican Americans lived in the Southwest, primarily in Texas and California.

Although Mexican Americans comprised the majority of the Spanish-speaking population across the country in the late 20th century, Puerto Ricans were more numerous on the East Coast. The United States annexed Puerto Rico after the Spanish-American War of 1898 (see Chapter 3) and in 1917 granted U.S. citizenship to its inhabitants. Puerto Ricans, therefore, were not really immigrants but could come and go freely from island to mainland. Before the Second World War, the Puerto Rican population in the United States was small and centered in New York City. After the war, however, immigration rose significantly (see Chapter 9). By the 1970s, more Puerto Ricans were living in New York City than in San Juan, Puerto Rico's capital. Sizable Puerto Rican communities also developed in Chicago and in industrial cities in New England and Ohio. By 1990 the Puerto Rican population had grown to over 2 million.

Cubans comprised the third most numerous Spanish-speaking group in the U.S. population, largely as a result of Fidel Castro's revolution in Cuba. In 1962 congressional action designated Cubans who were fleeing Castro's regime as refugees eligible for admittance. Over the next 30 years, 800,000 Cubans quickly established themselves in South Florida. By 1990 Cubans comprised one-third of the population in Miami and had become an economic and political force.

President Lyndon Johnson's Immigration Act of 1965, one of the least controversial but ultimately most important pieces of Great Society legislation, sharply altered immigration policy. Since the 1920s, rates of immigration had been determined by quotas based on national origins (see Chapter 5). The 1965 act ended

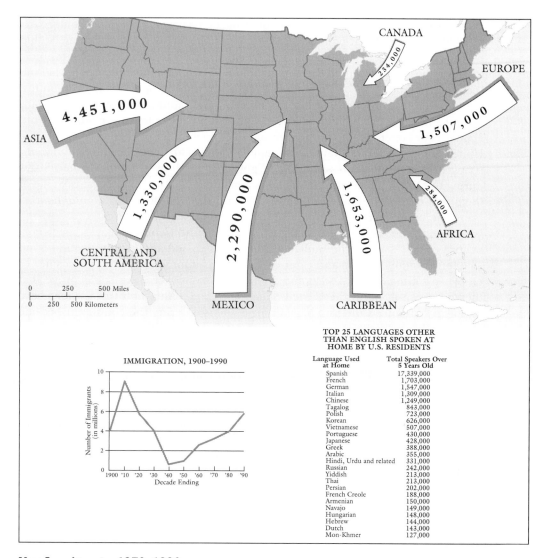

New Immigrants, 1970–1990

these quotas and, although unforeseen at the time, laid the basis not only for a resumption of high-volume immigration but also for a substantial shift in region of origin. The law placed a ceiling of 20,000 immigrants for every country, gave preference to those with close family ties in the United States, and accorded priority to those with special skills and those classified as "refugees." Under the new act, large numbers of people immigrated from Korea, China, the Philippines, the Dominican Republic, Colombia, and countries in the Middle East. In the aftermath of the Vietnam War, Presidents Ford and Carter ordered the admittance of many Vietnamese, Cambodians, Laotians, and Hmong (an ethnically distinct people who inhabited lands extending across the borders of all three countries in Indochina) who had assisted the United States during the war and whose families were consequently in peril.

In response to the surge in number of refugees, Congress passed the Refugee Act of 1980. It specified that political refugees, "those fleeing overt persecution," would be admitted but that refugees who were seeking simply to improve their economic lot would be denied entry to the United States. In practice, the terms "political" and "economic" tended to be applied in such a way that people fleeing communist regimes were usually admitted but those fleeing right-wing oppression were usually turned away or deported. For example, Cubans and Soviet Jews were admitted, but Haitians were often denied immigrant status. (The number of Haitians entering the United States illegally, however, rose rapidly.) Many Guatemalans and Salvadorans, trying to escape the repressive military governments backed by the United States during the 1980s, stood little chance of being admitted as legal immigrants. Some of them, however, were helped into the U.S. and then harbored by a church-based "sanctuary movement" that opposed U.S. policies in Central America.

As illegal immigration, especially from Mexico and Central America, became a major political issue in the mid-1980s, Congress passed another immigration law. The Immigration Reform and Control Act of 1987 imposed penalties on businesses employing illegal aliens and granted residency to workers who could prove that they had been living in the United States since 1982. Although this law may have temporarily reduced the number of illegal aliens entering the country, it became increasingly ineffective during the 1990s. Old sources of illegal immigration from Latin America and new ones, especially from China, continued to transform the American population.

Los Angeles became a microcosm of world cultures. By the mid 1990s, fewer than half of the schoolchildren in Los Angeles were proficient in English, and some 80 different languages were spoken in homes there. The slogan "A City Divided and Proud of It" described Los Angeles's ambivalence about the issue of separate versus common identities.

In 1990 a new museum opened in the old immigrant reception center on Ellis Island in New York harbor. It celebrated America's immigrant origins at the same time that the nation was once again being reshaped by newcomers. Like the immigration that had peaked shortly after 1900, the immigration of the late 20th century was accompanied not only by hopes but also by ethnic rivalries and tensions.

Urbanization and Suburbanization

Urban-suburban demographics were also in a state of flux. By 1990 nearly 80 percent of Americans were living in metropolitan areas. As those areas continued to expand, the relationship between central city and adjacent suburbs changed. The suburbs melded into "urban corridors," metropolitan strips often running between older cities, as between Los Angeles and San Diego, Washington and Baltimore, Seattle and Tacoma, or into "edge cities," former suburban areas such as the Galleria area west of Houston, the Perimeter Center south of Atlanta, and Tysons Corner near Washington, D.C., that came to rival the cities themselves as centers of business and population.

Meanwhile, central cities were transformed. As suburban shopping malls surpassed the old downtown shopping areas in retail sales, the cities became centers primarily of financial, administrative, and entertainment activity. During the 1970s

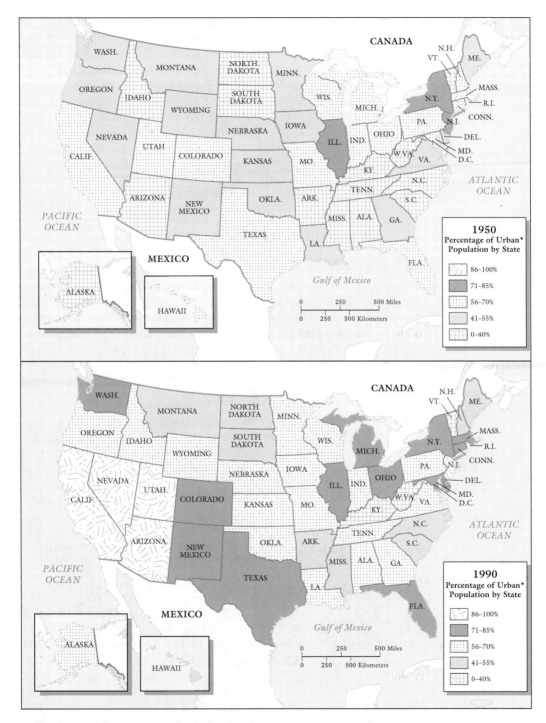

Urbanization of American Life, 1950–1990

*An urbanized area is defined as a city of 50,000 or more (or twin cities meeting this criterion) and the surrounding closely settled areas, including incorporated places and unincorporated territory.

and 1980s, the percentage of upper- and middle-income residents within city boundaries fell, and tax bases declined at the same time that an influx of low-income populations placed greater demands on public services. Higher rates of homelessness and crime, together with deteriorating schools and urban infra-structures (such as sewer and water systems), plagued most large cities. Big-city mayors complained about the decline of federal funding, which decreased from $64 per urban resident in 1980 to under $30 per resident by 1993. Although some central cities began to revive during the mid-1990s—as a result of general economic growth, lower crime rates, better policing, and the renewed desire to enjoy the amenities of an urban lifestyle—the population growth of urban corridors continued to outpace that of traditional cities.

Economic Transformations

A typical American adult of the 1990s would likely awake to a digital alarm clock, pop breakfast into a microwave oven, work at a desktop computer, and relax with a movie or TV program taped earlier on the VCR, while the children amused themselves with Nintendo or surfed the Internet. None of these products or activities had been known in the early 1960s. The pace of technological change had brought an astonishing transformation in consumer products, production processes, and the structure of the labor force.

New Technologies

The most noteworthy technological advances were made in biotechnology, high-performance computing, and communications systems. By the early 1990s the federal government was allocating approximately $4 billion a year to research in biotechnology. As scientists deepened their understanding of DNA and genetic engineering, they devised new techniques of gene transfer, embryo manipulation, tissue regeneration, and even cloning. Those techniques led the way to possible breakthroughs in cancer treatment, alteration of genetically inherited diseases, new and improved crops, waste conversion, and toxic cleanup. But biotechnology, especially genetic engineering, also raised fears about the decline in the variety of biological organisms, what scientists called "biodiversity," and prompted ethical questions about the role of science in manipulating reproduction.

The computer revolution, which began after the Second World War, entered a new phase during the 1970s, when the availability of microchips boosted the capability and reduced the size and cost of computer hardware. Sales of home computers soared, led by a fledgling company, Apple, and by its formidable rival, IBM. High-performance computers with powerful memory capabilities and "parallel processors," which allow many operations to run simultaneously, began to transform both industry and information systems. Computerized factories and robotics heightened efficiency by lowering labor costs, making production schedules more flexible, and rendering obsolete the giant warehouses that had once held goods until they were shipped. "Artificial intelligence" capabilities emerged, along with voice interaction between people and machines.

The computer revolution, enhanced by new communications technologies such as fiber-optic networks and satellite transmission, fueled an "information revolution." Libraries replaced card catalogs with computer networks, and librarians facilitated access to specialized national and international databases. Electronic mail, fax transmissions, voice mail, and the World Wide Web rapidly came to supplement posted (sometimes called "snail") mail and telephone conversations. Cellular phones became a staple among people who believed that they needed instant communication at all times and places. The variety of ways in which people could speedily communicate with other people or with information-bearing machines changed the patterns of human interaction and work. "Telecommuting" from home became common as electronic networks made it less necessary for workers to appear in person at a distant office.

Big Business

Computerized communications helped transform ways of doing business by enabling the growth of electronic banking, far-flung business franchising, and huge globalized industries.

Although buying on credit had been widespread in the United States since the 1920s, Bank of America's introduction of its Visa credit card lifted credit-buying to new levels, efficiently organized through computer systems. From the 1970s on, use of bank-issued credit cards mounted; by 1990, there were 4,000 bankcard issuers serving 75 million cardholding customers. Private debt and personal bankruptcies also soared, however, and the rate of personal savings in the United States fell to the lowest in the industrialized world. Other innovations in electronic banking quickly followed: automatic teller machines (ATMs), checking (or debit) cards, automatic depositing, and electronic bill-paying moved Americans closer to a cashless economy where electronic impulses would substitute for currency. Sweeping deregulation of financial industries in the 1980s and 1990s permitted banking institutions and brokerage houses to offer most of the same financial services, accelerating competition and innovation.

Franchising and chain stores also changed the way consumer products were bought and sold. McDonald's and Holiday Inn pioneered nationwide standardization in the fast-food and travel industries during the 1950s. Other chain restaurants, such as Arby's, Wendy's, Burger King, and Pizza Hut, soon copied the McDonald's model. Later, Chili's and Cattle Country steak houses showed that franchise food need not be inexpensive. Similarly, Starbuck's parlayed a simple dietary staple, coffee, into a pricey designer commodity. Even the blues, once the preserve of wandering musicians, became a chain operation with the establishment of the House of Blues enterprise. And Sam Walton's success in building his Wal-Mart chain symbolized the transformation that was engulfing the entire retailing industry. Books, videotapes, records, electronics equipment, shoes, groceries, travel accommodations, and just about every other consumer item were made available by nationwide or regional chains that brought a greater array of merchandise and lower prices—but often offered only minimum wage, part-time, and nonunion jobs. These chains also ruined independent retailers in thousands of midsized towns across the country.

Shop until You Drop • The largest enclosed shopping center in the United States, the Mall of America in Bloomington, Minnesota, represents a four-story celebration of consumer culture. The complex includes more than 500 retail stores and 40 restaurants, an amusement park, a miniature golf course, a wedding chapel, and its own police force. Shoppers from all over the country,—and even from around the world—take advantage of special air fares to the Minneapolis–St. Paul Airport, which is only minutes from the Mall of Amer-

American chain businesses expanded overseas as well as at home. Especially after the collapse of communist regimes in the Soviet Union and Eastern Europe, they rushed to supply consumers with long-denied, American-style goods and services. McDonald's opened to great fanfare in Moscow and Budapest, while the fast-growing Hilton chain opened new hotels in Eastern European capitals. Pepsi and Coke carried on with their "cola wars" for dominance in foreign markets. In one of the more bizarre consequences of the end of the Cold War, Coke gained new popularity in Russia because its rival, Pepsi, had previously held an exclusive marketing arrangement with the discredited communist order.

Production, as well as consumption, turned international. U.S. automakers, for example, moved many of their production and assembly plants outside of the United States; by 1990 well over 50 percent of the sticker price on most "American" models went to foreign businesses and workers. Moreover, the trend toward "privatization" (the sale of government-owned industries to private business) in many economies worldwide provided American companies with new opportunities for acquisition. Foreign interests also purchased many U.S. companies and real estate

Spreading the American Diet in Moscow • With the fall of the Soviet empire, virtually every part of the world—including Russia—became open to American products and services. U.S. mass merchandising spread quickly.

holdings. In the early 1990s foreign corporations owned RCA, Doubleday, Mack Truck, Goodyear, and Pillsbury, among many other traditionally "American" brands. Even the entertainment industry, which the United States had dominated for decades, attracted significant foreign investment. A Japanese conglomerate, for example, temporarily owned Columbia Pictures during the early 1990s, and Mexico's Televiso took over U.S.-owned Univision in 1993. So many industrial giants had become globalized by the late 20th century that it was difficult to define what constituted an American or a foreign company. Drinking the most prominent brands of "Mexican" beer, after an acquisition in 1997, actually meant drinking a product of Anheuser-Busch. Assembling a Honda may have employed more U.S. workers than assembling a Pontiac.

Postindustrial Restructuring

New technologies and economic globalization brought structural changes to American business and the workforce. Citing pressure from international competition and declining profits, many companies cut their work forces and trimmed their management staffs in efforts to "downsize." In the 1970s more than a dozen major steel plants closed, and the auto industry, staggering under Japanese competition, laid off thousands of workers. The Chrysler Corporation managed to survive only after the federal government took the unprecedented step of guaranteeing loans to the company. The steel and auto industries regained profitability in the 1980s and 1990s, but other giant corporations also began to downsize. As employment in traditional manufacturing and extractive sectors decreased, jobs in service, high-technology, and the information-entertainment sector increased. By the end of the 1990s, the unemployment rate was at its lowest point in several decades, but the kinds of jobs held by Americans had shifted. Computing and other high-tech jobs brought high salaries, but jobs in the expanding service sector—clerks, servers, cleaners—tended to remain low-paid, part-time, and nonunionized.

Union membership, always highest in the manufacturing occupations that comprised a decreasing proportion of jobs in the restructuring economy, fell to under 15 percent of the labor force by the mid-1990s. While union membership rolls and political power steadily slipped, efforts to expand the base of the union movement into new sectors of the economy initially met with little success. In the mid-1970s, an attempt by Nine to Five to organize women clerical workers in Boston attracted media attention and temporarily boosted unionization drives among office workers in several large cities. Some union locals around the country also attempted to organize restaurant and hotel workers, another sector that employed many women. But businesses adamantly fought unionization, claiming that it would raise labor costs, and the AFL-CIO initially gave little support to such organizing efforts, which they considered unlikely to succeed.

Cesar Chavez's efforts during the late 1960s and early 1970s to organize agricultural workers, who were largely of Mexican and Filipino descent, also dramatized the difficulties of expanding the base of the union movement. Chavez, a charismatic leader who emulated the nonviolent tactics of Martin Luther King Jr., vaulted the United Farm Workers (UFW) into public attention. As the union president, Chavez undertook a series of personal hunger strikes and instituted several well-publicized consumer boycotts of lettuce and grapes as means of pressuring growers to bargain with the UFW. He also established close ties with liberal Democrats in California and nationally and won a major contract victory in 1970. During the late 1970s and the 1980s, however, the UFW steadily lost ground. Strong stands by growers to keep out union organizers, opposition from the Teamsters union, and the continued influx of new immigrants eager for work undercut the UFW's efforts. By the time of Chavez's death, in April 1993, the UFW was struggling to rebuild its membership and regain bargaining power.

Union organization among new, low-paying sectors of the economy expanded only slowly. The major growth for organized labor came among government employees and workers in the health care industry. But these gains did not offset the losses in union membership in the old industrial sectors.

Some economists warned that the shift to a "postindustrial" economy was "deskilling" the labor force and worsening technological unemployment—people out of work because the jobs for which they were trained no longer exist. Might a globalized economy erode the living standards in America? Critics of the new trends expressed alarm over statistics revealing that well over half the new jobs created in the U.S. economy during the 1980s paid less than $7,000 per year. Moreover, the firms that provided temporary workers to other businesses were becoming the largest employers in the country. Some analysts warned that the widening gulf between highly paid, highly skilled positions and minimum-wage jobs might ultimately undermine the middle-class nature of American society. By the late 1990s, the labor movement was hoping to revitalize itself by making part-time work and the stagnation in real wages the centerpieces of new organizing efforts; a successful Teamsters strike against United Parcel Service in 1997 dramatized this new agenda.

More optimistic observers, however, pointed out that internationalization and corporate downsizing might temporarily mean lost jobs for some people but that gains in productivity would eventually translate into lower consumer prices and rising living standards. Moreover, they claimed, new technologies promised to create business opportunities for future generations. Celebrants of change could point to many success stories, such as Microsoft.

In 1980 this small company, headed by a young engineer named Bill Gates, licensed the software for a computer operating system called MS-DOS to IBM and then to hundreds of companies who were manufacturing clones of IBM personal computers (PCs). MS-DOS became the standard operating system for PCs and, together with a succession of other software products, transformed Microsoft into one of America's most profitable corporations, rivaling giant IBM itself. In 1995 Bill Gates, with his boyish grin and shrewd business instincts, became the richest person in the country. Business analysts marveled at the meteoric growth of a company whose product had only barely been invented in 1980; one comic suggested that MS-DOS stood for "Microsoft Seeks Dominion Over Society." Although the Microsoft story clearly was exceptional, new high-tech businesses turned many computer

Bill Gates: An American Potentate? • By the end of the 20th century, Bill Gates, founder of the Microsoft computer software empire, was by far the wealthiest person in the country, and critics worried that his company's power over the new, electronically based culture might have become too great. The U.S. government charged Microsoft with violating antitrust laws, but supporters of the software giant countered that outmoded legal concepts from the industrial age could hamper efforts by visionaries such as Gates to introduce innovative technologies.

mavens into millionaires. Product innovation paved a broad avenue of upward economic mobility for those with computer-age skills.

These revolutionary changes in technology and the economy had profound effects on the lives of Americans. Skilled workers of earlier generations had tended to stick to one profession or place of employment throughout their working life. But by the end of the 20th century, even middle-income professionals were likely to switch occupations several times before retiring. The need for training and retraining programs that served all ages of people transformed ideas about education, as well as ideas about work.

The Environment

The modern environmental movement began during the 1970s, but its roots reached back to the earlier conservation and preservation movements. During the first four decades of the 20th century, the conservation movement promoted "wise use" of water, forests, and farmlands by urging government to promote scientific resource management and to designate areas as national parks and forests (see Chapter 2). A preservation movement—led by the Sierra Club, the Audubon Society, the Wilderness Society, and others—was primarily concerned with the aesthetics of nature and wanted to protect and enjoy the natural environment in a state as pristine as possible. Landmark legislation during the 1960s—the Wilderness Act of 1964, the National Wild and Scenic Rivers Act of 1968, and the National Trails Act of 1968—set aside new areas, protecting them from development. Lady Bird Johnson, President Johnson's wife, championed formation of a Commission on Natural Beauty that both reflected and promoted the nation's growing interest in its natural habitat.

Environmental Activism and Government Policy

Increasingly, the conservation and preservation movements broadened into an "environmental movement" that focused on improving people's health and on maintaining ecological balances. In 1962 Rachel Carson had published *Silent Spring,* which warned that the pesticides used in agriculture, especially DDT, threatened bird populations. Air pollution in major cities such as Los Angeles became so bad that simply breathing urban air was equivalent to smoking several packs of cigarettes a day. Industrial processes polluted water systems, and fears of overexposure to radiation mounted as a result of the testing of atomic weapons and the proliferation of nuclear power plants. In response to these concerns, environmentalists tried to focus national attention on toxic chemicals and the adverse impact of industrial development on air, water, and soil quality. The Environmental Defense Fund, a private organization formed in 1967, took the crusade against DDT and other dangerous toxins to the courts. And in 1970 activists came together for Earth Day, organized largely by college students, to raise awareness about environmental degradation and to popularize the science of ecology, a branch of biology that studies the interrelationships between living organisms and their physical environments.

During the 1970s combating environmental hazards and maintaining ecological balances emerged as major concerns of public policy. During Richard Nixon's

Declining Air Pollutant Emissions, 1970–1991

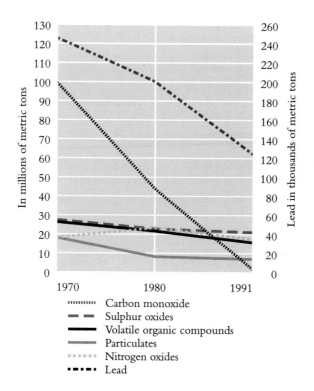

presidency, the federal government established the Environmental Protection Agency (EPA) in 1970 and enacted major pieces of environmental legislation: the Resources Recovery Act of 1970 (dealing with waste management), the Clean Air Act of 1970, the Water Pollution Control Act of 1972, the Pesticides Control Act of 1972, and the Endangered Species Act of 1973. National parks and wilderness areas were further expanded, and a new law required that "environmental impact statements" be prepared in advance of any major government project. Administering environmental policies, which substantially expanded the power of government, became a complex task requiring sophisticated research, cost-benefit balancing, and tedious negotiations among conflicting interest groups. It also prompted heated public debates. Environmentalist groups grew in size, resources, and expertise, while businesses opposed to these types of bureaucracies attacked government regulation and branded environmentalism an elitist cause that destroyed jobs and impeded economic growth.

New standards brought some significant improvements. The Clean Air Act's restrictions on auto and smokestack emissions, for example, reduced the amount of six major airborne pollutants by one-third in a single decade. The emission of lead into the atmosphere declined by 95 percent. But the remedies could also create new problems. Requiring higher smokestacks to eliminate smog helped to clear city skies but also elevated pollutants into the atmosphere, where they produced damaging "acid rain."

In the late 1970s families living at Love Canal, a housing development near Buffalo, New York, learned that the soil under their homes was contaminated by chemical wastes produced 30 years earlier. The finding explained why residents of the area suffered from high levels of cancer and had children with genetic defects. The costs of resettlement and cleanup of wastes, often the responsibility of now-defunct companies, prompted Congress to create a cleanup "Superfund" to be financed by taxes imposed on polluting industries. The most heavily contaminated areas, designated as Superfund sites, were slated for special cleanup efforts. Superfund money, however, did not begin to cover anticipated costs, and, once awareness had been aroused, additional evidence of toxic dumping rapidly multiplied the number of potential Superfund sites.

Environmental legislation prompted a backlash. President Ronald Reagan, who campaigned in 1980 on a promise to halt the growth of government power, denounced the environmental regulations of the 1970s and tried to weaken the EPA. James Watt, Reagan's first secretary of the interior, angered environmentalists by supporting the "sagebrush rebellion," in which interests in the western states demanded fewer restrictions from Washington on the use of public land within their borders. Emotional battles broke out during the 1980s over private use of resources in federal wilderness areas and over whether protection of endangered species, such as rare bird populations, should take priority over economic activities such as timber cutting.

The acrimony of environmental debates lessened during the 1990s, as all sides became more accustomed to negotiating differences rather than pressing demands. Alternative approaches to environmental management sought to promote change through incentives rather than penalties. In 1997, for example, the Conservation Reserve Program, a farm subsidy program that previously paid farmers to remove land from tillage, now stipulated payment to farmers who would restore wetlands on their properties. Wetland restoration would decrease polluted runoff into streams and preserve wildlife habitat.

The U.S. government itself, however, turned out to be one of the country's most flagrant polluters. In 1988 Secretary of Energy John Harrington admitted that the government's nuclear facilities had been lax on safety measures and estimated that cleanup would cost more than $1 billion. The revelation of hazardous conditions at sites where atomic weapons had been produced shocked nearby residents, who feared that they might have been victims of radiation poisoning. Workers at the sites had been inadequately warned about radiation, even though government officials knew of its dangers. Moreover, medical records, long suppressed by the government, revealed that people living downwind of nuclear test sites in the 1940s and 1950s had experienced an abnormally high incidence of cancer, leukemia, and thyroid disorders. In 1993 President Bill Clinton's energy secretary, Hazel O'Leary, finally released records relating to radiation testing and experimentation and promised programs to inform and compensate victims. The legacy of other kinds of military-related toxic pollutants also became evident as many of the nation's bases were closed down during the 1990s.

During the 1980s, the environmental movement increasingly focused on international, as well as national, ecological dangers. Those hazards, which threatened life on a worldwide scale, included global warming (the "greenhouse effect"); holes in the ozone layer caused by chlorofluorocarbons (CFCs), commonly used in refrigeration, aerosol sprays, and many other industrial processes; massive deforestation and desertification with accompanying climatic changes; pollution of the oceans; and the rapid decline of biological diversity among both plant and animal species. Solutions to these global problems required worldwide cooperation and restructuring toward sustainable development practices. International meetings on environmental issues became more frequent and attracted greater public interest. Conventions in Vienna in 1985, Montreal in 1987, London in 1990, and Kyoto in 1997 worked toward establishing international standards on emissions of CFCs and greenhouse gases. A so-called Earth Summit was held in Brazil in 1992, and a conference in Cairo in 1994 took up global population issues. Fear that environmental restrictions could harm economic growth and the lack of mechanisms to enforce internationally agreed-on targets, however, slowed the progress of the international environmental crusade.

Energy

The problem of global warming stemmed largely from patterns of energy use. The United States obtained 90 percent of its energy from the burning of fossil fuels, a major source of the carbon dioxide that creates the greenhouse effect. The nation's dependence on fossil fuels, especially on petroleum imported from abroad, aroused serious public concern during the 1970s. Part of the concern was simply economic. In 1973 and again in 1976 the Organization of Petroleum Exporting Countries (OPEC), a cartel dominated by the oil-rich nations of the Middle East, sharply raised the price of oil and precipitated acute shortages in the industrialized world. As Americans wearied of high prices and long lines at gas stations, President Jimmy Carter (1977–1981) promised to make the United States less dependent on imported fossil fuel. He created a new cabinet-level Department of Energy in 1977 and gave some support to conservation efforts and to the development of renewable sources such as solar and wind-generated energy.

But Carter also continued to support the use of nuclear power generated by giant reactors, a source of energy that became increasingly controversial. Boosters of the nation's atomic research program during the early days of the Cold War had promised that nuclear reactors would provide a cheap, almost limitless supply of energy. The cost of building and maintaining the reactors, however, far exceeded the original estimates, and critics charged that the reactors posed a grave safety risk. The danger was illustrated in 1979 by a malfunction at a reactor at Three Mile Island in Pennsylvania. The malfunction nearly produced a nuclear meltdown, and residents had to be evacuated from the area. In response to growing public alarm, power companies canceled orders for new nuclear reactors. During the 1980s, although existing reactors continued to operate, expansion of the nuclear power industry halted. The power company that served the state of Washington, once a leader in the use of nuclear energy, went into bankruptcy.

Meanwhile, the cost of OPEC oil was skyrocketing from $1.80 a barrel in 1971 to nearly $30 a decade later, helping to boost U.S. inflation rates during Carter's presidency. On taking office as president in 1981, Ronald Reagan promised to break OPEC's oil monopoly by encouraging the development of new sources of supply at home and in other parts of the world. Ignoring environmentalists' calls for the promotion of renewable sources, Reagan and his successor George Bush followed a "cheap oil" energy policy throughout the 1980s. The tapping of new supplies of oil, together with rivalries among OPEC members, weakened OPEC's hold over the world market and reduced energy costs. But little progress was made in breaking U.S. reliance on fossil fuels, and the United States government assumed little leadership in pushing for international standards on carbon dioxide emissions.

Media and Culture

Innovations in electronic technologies transformed America's culture as well as its economy. By 1995 virtually every residential unit in the country had at least one TV, 99 percent had a VCR, and about 80 percent had a personal computer. More than one-third of the population needed a computer in their daily work, and more than half of all schoolchildren used one in the classroom. Meanwhile, magazines and books were being produced for computer screens, and rock concerts were being carried over the Internet. The video screen seemed the preeminent symbol of the nation's mass culture.

The Video Revolution

Video monitors were everywhere. Visitors to museums and historical sites could access information about a particular display simply by pressing spots on an interactive video screen. Sports bars lined their walls with video monitors, enabling patrons to follow favorite teams or to scan several sporting events simultaneously. Meanwhile, TV screens were replacing last year's magazines in doctors' waiting rooms and auto repair shops. Air travelers, while waiting for their flights, could catch the latest news updates and weather conditions by watching a special Airport Channel.

The kind of specially targeted programming found in many airports highlighted the increasingly fragmented nature of all cultural production, especially television programming. The 1970s represented the last decade in which the three major television networks—CBS, NBC, and ABC—were able to command the daily attention of a nation of loyal viewers.

At the beginning of the 1970s, the three major TV networks still followed the practice, which had originated with network radio broadcasting in the 1930s, of offering a range of general-interest programming that was designed to attract a broadly representative, mass audience. A typical 30-minute episode of a top-rated situation comedy might draw more viewers in a single evening than a hit motion picture attracted over an entire year. The networks could promise advertisers, the companies who sponsored the programs, that a cross section of the American public would be watching their sales pitches. Various ratings devices, including the venerable Nielsen system, tracked the number of viewers who were tuning in.

The networks, in search of even greater advertising dollars, began to modify this mass-market strategy during the 1970s. Early in the decade, CBS jettisoned a number of highly rated programs, especially those popular among older and rural viewers, and replaced them with shows designed to attract younger urban and suburban viewers. (*Hee-Haw,* a country music show, and *The Beverly Hillbillies* were two of the first casualties.) This shift in strategy, CBS assured potential advertisers, would allow them concentrate on the consumers most likely to spend money on new products.

In line with this strategy of targeting specific groups, CBS began using its comedy lineup to offer more controversial programming. *All in the Family,* a sitcom that highlighted generational conflict within a blue-collar family from Queens, allowed Archie Bunker, the show's bigoted protagonist, to serve as a lightning rod for controversial issues involving race and gender. Although *The Mary Tyler Moore Show* rarely took positions that seemed overtly "feminist," this popular sitcom featured a woman who worked in a fictional TV newsroom. It portrayed the personal politics of working women of the 1970s and broke the male-dominated sitcom formula established in the 1950s. Even TV critics—who rarely seemed to like the programs they were paid to review—joined viewers in applauding new CBS shows, such as *M*A*S*H,* for integrating comedy with social commentary. NBC soon joined the trend; in 1975 *Saturday Night Live* brought the barbed humor of the 1960s counterculture to network television.

Choosing a strategy different from that of CBS or NBC, ABC cultivated the teenage audience. Aware that young people generally controlled at least one of the family's TV sets, ABC increased its ratings with sex-and-action programs *(Charley's Angels),* mildly risqué sitcoms *(Three's Company),* fast-paced police shows *(Kojak),* and a variety of upbeat programs such as the nostalgic *Happy Days* and the escapist *Fantasy Island.* ABC, which had always been the smallest of the three networks, used its soaring ratings to lure local affiliates away from its rivals.

All three networks enjoyed rising profits during the 1970s, and some media analysts likened operating a local affiliate to owning a press that printed money. At the end of the 1970s, 9 of every 10 TV sets were still tuned to a network program during prime-time viewing hours.

During the 1980s, however, the networks began to confront a slow yet steady loss of viewers. One reason was that programmers found it increasingly difficult to create successful prime-time programs. Although NBC found great success with *The Bill Cosby Show,* which featured an affluent African American family, and *Cheers,* a sitcom set in a Boston tavern where "everybody knows your name," most of its other offerings had significantly less audience appeal. NBC, like the other networks, adjusted by slashing budgets and staff, especially in the news division, and spicing its prime-time programs with sexually oriented themes.

Meanwhile, independent stations began to compete in local markets with the three network TV affiliates. At a time when the number of daily newspapers was steadily shrinking, 200 independent TV stations went on the air during the 1980s. In the middle of the decade, earnings for UHF independents (channels between 14 and 81 on the standard TV dial) more than doubled. Lacking access to new network programs, these independents targeted small but lucrative markets by strategically scheduling Hollywood films, sporting events, and reruns of canceled network programs.

Capitalizing on the rise of the independents, Rupert Murdoch's Fox television network debuted in 1988. Fox broke new ground by offering a limited, though sometimes highly rated, program schedule to previously independent stations, most of which broadcast in the UHF range. One of its first hit series, *The Simpsons,* a cartoon send-up of the venerable family sitcom, became a mass-marketing bonanza and a favorite of TV critics. Fox gradually expanded its nightly offerings and in 1993 shocked the TV industry by outbidding CBS for the rights to carry the National Football League's NFC conference games. A number of CBS affiliates followed the NFL and shifted their allegiance to Fox. In the 1990s, two other communication conglomerates, Paramount and Time-Warner, set up networks based on the Fox model and aimed much of their prime-time programming at younger, urban viewers.

New technologies were also undermining the monopoly of the major networks. At the simplest level, the remote-control device, which had been introduced during the 1960s but not widely marketed until the 1980s, gave rise to a new TV aesthetic, called "zapping" or "channel surfing," in which viewers rapidly switch from program to program, usually during commercial breaks. The mass-marketing of VCRs also gave people new control over their television viewing habits. Once the intricacies of programming a VCR's timing mechanism were mastered, they no longer had to be in front of their sets at the appointed time to see their favorite network programs.

But the greatest impact on viewing patterns came from the growth of cable television (CATV). By 1995 nearly 65 percent of the nation's homes were wired for CATV. Capable of carrying scores of different programs, most of which were aimed at very specific audiences, CATV further fragmented TV viewership. Ted Turner, one of the first to recognize the potential of CATV with his "Superstation" WTBS, later added Cable News Network (CNN), several movie channels, and even an all-cartoon network before his communications empire merged with that of Time-Warner. Cable operations—whether they featured news, cartoons, sports, public affairs, commercial-free movies, round-the-clock weather, or home shopping programs—steadily expanded. By

The End of an Era: May 14, 1998 • Patrons at a lobby bar in a Chicago hotel, part of a record national TV audience, watch the final episode of the sitcom *Seinfeld* as it ended its nine-year run on NBC. The cost of commercial time on the final *Seinfeld* episode surpassed that charged for a spot on the annual Super Bowl telecast.

1998, the percentage of television viewers watching programs on ABC, CBS, and NBC had fallen to less than 60 percent, and the media corporations that controlled the three networks were expanding into the cable market themselves.

Hollywood and the "MTV Aesthetic"

The new media environment affected nearly every aspect of mass culture. With movie ticket sales remaining about the same in 1980 as they had been in 1960, Hollywood studios raised the price of each ticket and concentrated on turning out a handful of blockbuster epics, such as *Star Wars* (1977), which earned investors a profit of nearly 2,000 percent, and an occasional surprise hit, such as Sylvester Stallone's original *Rocky* (1976). But for every *Star Wars* or *Rocky*, Hollywood moguls seemed equally able to produce expensive box-office duds like *Waterworld* (1995) or *Judge Dredd* (1995). Thus, filmmakers increasingly tended to play it safe and use the kind of story lines and special effects that had made money in the past. Classic TV series, such as *Batman* and *Leave It to Beaver*, became motion pictures. Blockbuster hits such as *Jurassic Park* (1993) spawned sequels such as *Lost World* (1996). And following ABC's TV strategy, Hollywood also made teenagers a major target for films such as *The Breakfast Club* (1985), *Ferris Bueller's Day Off* (1986), and *Clueless* (1995). CATV and VCRs did, however, provide Hollywood with new sources of revenue, even from films that had been long ago relegated to the storage vaults. Although huge multiplex movie theaters opened in suburban shopping areas throughout the 1980s and 1990s, video rental stores surpassed them in number, and VCR sales soared. During the 1990s, most of the smaller video stores faced often-fatal competition from giant

What Do You Know about History? • In a media-saturated culture, traditional methods of telling stories about the past were challenged by new forms. The popular films of director Oliver Stone—including *Platoon, JFK, Nixon,* and *Born on the 4th of July*—offered powerful images of the recent past. Even professional historians who criticized Stone's interpretations could not ignore the wide appeal of his work.

Grammy Award Winner, 1996 • As old-time rock 'n' roll began to lose its innovative edge in the 1980s, rap music, once dismissed by rock critics as another passing fad, became increasingly popular. Naughty By Nature's *Poverty's Progress* won the Grammy Award in 1996 for the best rap album. The group also operated a Web site and sold its "Naughty Gear" clothing line over the Internet.

chains like Blockbuster and from corner gas-marts and convenience stores. More and more people were using VCRs and the various all-movie CATV channels to convert their TV sets, with ever larger screens, into home movie theaters.

CATV and VCRs helped to transform the pop music industry as well. Music Television (MTV), initially offering a 24-hour supply of rock videos, was launched in 1981. Critics charged it with consistently portraying women as sex objects and with excluding artists of color. Eventually, however, MTV defused complaints—especially after Michael Jackson's 29-minute video based on his hit single "Thriller" (1983) set new standards for video production and opened the way for artists such as Prince and Los Lobos. Several years later, Madonna used MTV to create a new relationship between music and visual image—what some critics called the "MTV aesthetic"— and launched her meteoric career. A decade later, Madonna's first MTV videos migrated to VH-1, the CATV channel whose musical format catered to older, post-MTV viewers. By the late 1990s, the entertainment industry was releasing VHS and CD-ROM musical packages, as well as singles and albums on tape and compact disc (CD), and was introducing new mini-disk and DVD technologies. The 45-rpm record and the LP, which had been at the heart of the musical revolutions of the 1950s and 1960s, disappeared or became collector's items for those who claimed that the new technologies failed to match the rich sound of music recorded on vinyl.

The New Mass Culture Debate

Mass commercial culture, as it had in the 1950s (see Chapter 9), generated controversy. In 1975 the Federal Communications Commission (FCC), the agency charged with oversight of the broadcasting industry, ordered the TV networks to dedicate the first 60 minutes of prime time each evening to "family" programming free of violence or "mature" themes. Several TV production companies immediately challenged this family-hour requirement as government censorship, and a federal court ruled that it was a violation of the First Amendment's guarantee of free speech. Demands that the government regulate rock lyrics and album covers also ran afoul of complaints that this constituted illegal censorship. Although governmental efforts faltered, private organizations, many of them associated with conservative religious groups, were more successful in pressing media companies to practice self-censorship. In 1992 pressure on Time-Warner resulted in the withdrawal of a song titled "Cop Killer" by the African American rap artist Ice-T; television networks subsequently adopted a rating system designed to inform parents about the amount of violence and sexual content in prime-time programs.

Meanwhile, a new generation of writers, reviewers, and university professors were paying serious attention to mass culture. Unlike the critics of the 1950s, who dismissed mass culture as trivial and condemned its effects on American life, the critics of the 1980s and 1990s often became fans of the cultural products they were reviewing. Instead of comparing mass culture to "high" culture (the so-called classical works of Western civilization), many in the new generation of cultural critics abandoned the distinction between lowbrow and highbrow. They insisted that music of the Beatles should be studied along with that of Beethoven and argued that the lyrics of Chuck Berry and Bob Dylan merited academic analysis. Observers of contemporary culture debated the meaning of the MTV aesthetic and wrote scholarly essays and books about Madonna.

These new analysts also studied the ways in which consumers integrated the products of mass culture into their daily lives. Again rejecting the cultural criticism of the 1950s—which saw the consumers of mass culture as dupes who passively soaked up worthless products—they stressed ordinary people's creative, interactive engagement with mass culture texts. Much of this affirmative cultural criticism came from professors in the new field of "cultural studies," who focused on how people reworked images from the mass media. Scholarly studies of *Star Trek*, for example, explored the ways in which loyal fans had kept this popular TV series of the 1960s alive in syndication and had subsequently prompted a succession of Hollywood motion pictures and several new *Star Trek* television series for the syndication market. Moreover, through conventions, self-produced magazines (called fanzines"), and Web sites, fans of *Star Trek* ("Trekkies") and of shows such as *Xena* created a grass-roots subculture that used TV programs as vehicles for discussing social and political issues, especially ones that touched on race, gender, and sexuality. Those who advocated cultural studies argued that students should study such popular phenomena and also that they should be exposed to a range of works by women, people of color, and political outsiders. Moreover, they encouraged students to reinterpret traditional texts in light of their political and historical contexts rather than simply as great, timeless works.

Political and social conservatives condemned the introduction of cultural studies into the college curriculum and viewed such teaching as evidence of "the closing of the American mind" (which became the title of a best-selling 1987 book by Allan Bloom) and of the "opening" of students' minds only to what was trendy and "politically correct" (or "PC"). They charged that such fascination with mass culture represented a debasement of intellectual life that was also spreading beyond the classroom. *U.S. News & World Report,* for example, built an advertising campaign—

which, ironically, was featured on CATV—around the fact that its rivals, *Time* and *Newsweek,* carried cover stories about such "trivia" as *Superman.*

The Debate over Multicultural Education

Debates over mass culture often merged with controversies over educational policies in an increasingly pluralistic and fragmented society. Cultural studies, multiculturalism, and political correctness became fighting words. During the late 1970s, the government-funded National Endowment for the Humanities (NEH) and the National Endowment for the Arts (NEA) began to provide financial backing for projects that focused on America's cultural diversity and on politically sensitive reinterpretations of traditional works. In the 1980s conservative Republicans launched a counterattack. Ronald Reagan's secretary of education, William Bennett, used his office to crusade against multicultural education, while Lynn Cheney, head of the NEH, championed traditional programs. Seeking to placate conservatives such as North Carolina's Senator Jesse Helms, President George Bush's administration pressured the NEA to cancel grants to controversial artistic projects, especially those relating to feminism or homosexuality. Controversies over the funding, and even the continued survival, of the NEA and the NEH continued through the 1990s. On college campuses, meanwhile, faculty and students heatedly debated, amidst pressures from wealthy conservative donors, the value of multicultural curricula.

Conservative pressure groups mounted a parallel critique of educational practices in public schools. This phase of the conservative movement, which had initially

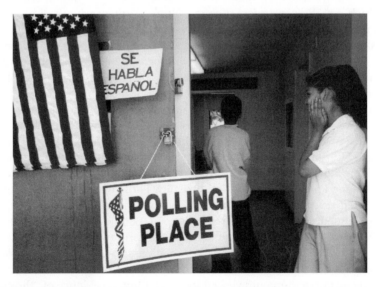

Se Habla Español • New immigrants from Asia and Latin America created controversies in the 1990s relating to multiculturalism and multilingualism. Some critics of multiculturalism insisted that public life in the United States should be conducted primarily in the English language. Campaigns were mounted to limit the use of signs in foreign languages, cut back on bilingual educational programs, and even to forbid the transaction of any public business in a language other than English.

begun in response to the Supreme Court decisions of the 1960s that barred state-sponsored prayers and Bible-reading in public schools, argued that cultural and educational innovations were manifestations of an antireligious philosophy they called "secular humanism." In the 1950s and 1960s, liberal opponents of Bible-reading and prayer in public schools had insisted that students should not be forced to participate in religious activities. In the 1980s conservatives adapted this argument for their cause and insisted that children should not be coerced into participating in secular-humanist activities that contradicted the religious teachings of their families and churches.

Originating in a complex and electronically mediated environment, the controversy over mass culture extended from the White House to the local schoolhouse. During the 1992 presidential campaign, Bill Clinton eagerly appeared on MTV, while his running mate's spouse, Tipper Gore, suddenly disassociated herself from her earlier, well-publicized effort to censor rock lyrics. The Republican Party's national platform, in contrast, strongly attacked the new cultural climate. Meanwhile, in communities across the country, militant conservatives mobilized to elect school boards that opposed multicultural curricula and other educational changes. As the United States became the home to increasingly fragmented and highly politicized cultures, people debated the complex meanings of multiculturalism and tolerance.

Social Activism

Although the 1960s and early 1970s have been frequently characterized as a unique time of heightened social activism, the post-Vietnam decades that followed probably saw an intensification, rather than a diminution, of such ferment. No document attracted the attention aroused by the Port Huron Statement of 1962; no demonstration ever rivaled the drama or symbolic importance of the 1963 civil rights march on Washington; and no cause generated the emotions sparked by the antiwar movement. Yet the legacy of activism from the 1960s had become deeply embedded in American life and rippled through the decades that followed.

The mass demonstration remained a tool of social activists representing all kinds of causes. Washington, D.C., continued to provide a favorite stage where huge rallies could attract the attention of national lawmakers and the media, but activists also mounted smaller rallies and protests that recalled the demonstrations of the 1960s. The antinuclear movement, in particular, employed nonviolent, direct-action tactics. In the early 1980s the Clamshell Alliance mounted a campaign of civil disobedience against a nuclear reactor being built in Seabrook, New Hampshire, while a broad coalition of West Coast activists waged an unsuccessful three-year struggle to shut down the University of California's Lawrence Livermore National Laboratory, which was producing nuclear weapons. Women's groups staged annual "Take Back the Night" marches in major cities to protest the rising tide of sexual assaults, and both pro-choice and anti-abortion groups sponsored demonstrations in Washington, D.C., and in local communities. In October 1995, the "Million Man March" in Washington, D.C., sought to mobilize African American men behind a campaign of social reconstruction in black communities, and two years later an evangelical men's group called the "Promise Keepers" filled

Washington's Mall with men rallying behind calls for Christian commitment and taking greater responsibility for families.

Mass demonstrations, however, had lost much of their power to attract media attention by the end of the 20th century. During a period of violence in May 1991 in Los Angeles, 30,000 Korean Americans staged a march for peace. Although it was the largest demonstration ever conducted by any Asian American group, even the local media ignored it. For most social activists, politics-in-the-streets became only one of many available political tactics.

A New Women's Movement

During the 1960s the ideology of domesticity, which had dominated the public rhetoric of the previous decade, continued to clash with the experiences and aspirations of millions of women. More and more women were working outside the home, postponing marriage, remaining single, or getting divorced. Moreover, the development of the birth-control pill gave women more control over reproduction and significantly changed the nature of sexual relationships. Younger activists began to move beyond the agenda that had been set in the mid-1960s by middle-class feminists—people such as Betty Friedan and organizations such as NOW (see Chapter 10).

As they participated in various activist causes and pursued other activities outside their homes, women came to realize the extent of gender discrimination and to ask new questions about the gender-based division of both public and private power arrangements. Even many of the men who were involved in movements for social change saw no contradiction between women's second-class status and men's positions of authority and leadership. Some male leaders of these movements expected female members to provide secretarial or sexual services and complained that raising issues of sexual equality "interfered" with the movements' primary tasks of redirecting racial and foreign policies. As a result, struggles for gender equality emerged within various older insurgency movements. African American women, such as the cultural critic bell hooks, advocated black feminism; Chicana groups coalesced within the United Farm Workers movement and within Mexican American organizations; radical feminists split off from the antiwar movement; other women challenged the ethics of capitalism by forming new, female-directed cooperatives.

Throughout the 1970s groups of women came together in "consciousness-raising" sessions to discuss issues and share perspectives. These discussions produced a growing conviction that women's larger *political* concerns about the maldistribution of power in the United States could not be separated from the very *personal* power relationships that shaped their own lives. "The personal is political" became the watchword for this new generation of feminists. Although the women's movement did not ignore traditional public issues, such as antidiscrimination efforts, it did prompt discussion of a wide range of personal questions involving housework, child-rearing, sexuality, and economic independence. By addressing these issues, which cut to the heart of everyday social relationships, the new feminism ensured that it would remain a significant force during the last three decades of the 20th century.

Economic self-sufficiency became a pressing issue for many women. Although women increasingly entered the professions and gained unionized positions (by

1990, fully 37 percent of union members were women, compared with about 18 percent in 1960), the average female worker throughout the 1970s and 1980s continued to earn about 60 cents for every dollar earned by the average male worker. During the 1960s, social welfare benefits for single mothers with children had been boosted by higher AFDC payments and by the Food Stamp program. But in the 1970s and 1980s, with inflation gripping the economy, the real monetary value of these benefits, measured in constant dollars, steadily decreased. In 1972, for example, a family of four, headed by a woman, received AFDC and Food Stamp benefits that, on average, were worth about $577 per month; by 1990, the monthly value of this same package had fallen to about $430. Homeless shelters, which once catered primarily to single men, increasingly had to address the needs of women and children. Throughout the 1970s and 1980s, this "feminization of poverty," and the growing number of children raised in low-income, female-headed families, became a fact of life.

Feminism grew into a highly diverse movement with agendas diverging along lines of class, race, ethnicity, and region. Yet diversity and division proved a strength to women's activism, not a weakness. Women from all sectors of society built new institutions to address needs that had been long ignored by male leaders. American life was greatly influenced by an explosion of female-oriented organizations: battered-women's shelters, health and birthing clinics specializing in women's medicine, rape crisis centers, economic development counseling for women-owned businesses, union-organizing efforts led by women, organizations of women in specific businesses or professions, women's studies programs in colleges and universities, and academic journals devoted to historical and contemporary research on women.

Pressure to end gender discrimination changed existing institutions as well. Previously all-male bastions, such as country clubs and service organizations, were

The New Women's Movement Protests the Miss America Pageant • Critics in the late 1960s contended that the Miss America contest trivialized women by emphasizing only their attractiveness to men. In response, the pageant changed somewhat, trying to accentuate the intellectual accomplishments of its contestants as well as their beauty.

pressured into admitting women. Most mainline Protestant churches and Reform Jewish congregations were challenged to accept women into the ministry. Educational institutions, under feminist pressure, began to adopt "gender-fair" hiring practices and curricula. The everyday lives of most American women by the end of the 20th century took place in an institutional environment very different from that of their mothers a generation earlier. New concerns related to gender equality had been elevated to a visible place in public discussions.

Sexual harassment, to take only one of the new concerns, became a significant issue among feminists, although there was no unanimity of views. Some feminists, including the charismatic Camille Paglia, argued that to focus on sexual harassment—or on the related issue of pornography—would tend to identify feminism with a kind of sexual puritanism that the women's movement had once promised to end. Most activists, however, continued to push government organizations and private employers to ban behavior, whether verbal or physical, that demeaned women and exploited their lack of power vis-à-vis male supervisors and male coworkers. In 1986 the U.S. Supreme Court ruled that sexual harassment constituted a form of discrimination covered under the 1964 Civil Rights Act.

In 1991 the issue of sexual harassment attracted national attention when Clarence Thomas, an African American nominee for the Supreme Court, was accused by Anita Hill, an African American law professor, of sexually harassing her when both had worked for the Office of Economic Opportunity. Feminists were angered when the all-male Senate Judiciary Committee, which was responsible for considering Thomas's qualifications for the Supreme Court, seemed unable to understand the issues raised by Hill's charges. When the Senate confirmed Thomas's nomination, women's groups gained new converts to their views on sexual harassment. In addition, political observers credited anger over the Thomas-Hill hearings with helping to mobilize female voters to elect four women to the U.S. Senate in 1992.

Sexual harassment became an even more controversial issue within the U.S. military, which began to recruit women more actively in the 1970s. West Point and the other service academies began accepting female cadets, and women seemed to be finding places of equality within the post-Vietnam military establishment. Sexual harassment had always been an issue in this new military order, but it became front-page news with revelations about harassment and even sexual assaults against female naval officers by their male comrades at the 1991 "Tailhook" convention. Attempts by Navy officials to cover up the incident provoked outrage in Congress and among the public. Despite this scandal, which ended the careers of several high-ranking officers, sexual harassment continued to be an issue within regular military units, at the service academies, and at military schools.

Sexual Politics

Debates over gender and sexuality became extremely divisive when it came to issues involving gays and lesbians. Some homosexuals, especially gay men affiliated with the left-leaning Mattachine Society and lesbians who organized the Daughters of Bilitis, had already begun to claim rights on the basis of their sexuality in the 1950s (see Chapter 8). A new spirit of insurgence and self-assurance emerged toward the end of the 1960s. In 1969, New York City police raided the Stonewall Inn, a gay bar in Greenwich Village. Patrons resisted arrest, and the confrontation pitted homosexuals, who claimed the right to be free from police harassment, against law-enforcement officials.

"Stonewall" marked a turning point in homosexual politics. New York City's Gay Liberation Front (GLF) provided a model for similar groups across the country, which also borrowed ideas and rhetoric from the civil rights and feminist movements. Within a decade after Stonewall, thousands of gay and lesbian advocacy groups sprang up, and many homosexuals came "out of the closet," proudly proclaiming their sexual orientation.

Soon, newspapers, theaters, nightspots, and religious groups identifying themselves with the homosexual community became part of daily life in cities and large towns. Specific forms of popular entertainment, such as the disco craze of the 1970s, became closely identified with the gay and lesbian subcultures. As a cultural movement, homosexuality benefited significantly at the end of the 20th century from a general relaxation of legal and cultural controls over the portrayal and practice of *all* forms of explicit sexuality.

Homosexuals pressured state and local governments to enact laws prohibiting discrimination in housing and jobs on the basis of sexual preference. Moreover, they demanded that the police treat attacks on homosexuals, known as "gay bashing," no less seriously than they treated other forms of violent crime. By the 1990s gays and lesbians had gained political power, especially within the national Democratic Party and in city councils and state legislatures. Activism by homosexuals, however, was also met with either indifference or determined opposition, especially by conservatives.

In addition to battling traditional forms of discrimination, broadly labeled as "homophobia," gays faced a new issue: acquired immunodeficiency syndrome (AIDS), a fatal and contagious condition that attacks a person's immune system. First identified in the early 1980s, AIDS quickly became an intensely emotional and often misunderstood medical and political issue. Epidemiologists correctly recognized AIDS as a health problem for the general public. The disease could be transmitted through the careless use of intravenous drugs, tainted blood supplies, and "unprotected" heterosexual intercourse. At first, however, its incidence in the United States was limited almost solely to gay men. As a consequence of this association, gay activists charged, the Reagan and Bush administrations responded to conservative pressure and placed a low priority on medical efforts to check the spread of AIDS or to find a cure for it. The controversy over AIDS and medical funding galvanized gay and lesbian activists to assert more forcefully their concerns and political power.

Race, Ethnicity, and Social Activism

The emphasis on group identity as the basis for activism grew especially strong among various racial and ethnic communities in the late 20th century. In movements that both built upon and transcended the activism of the 1960, groups emphasized pride in their distinctive traditions and declared that cultural differences among Americans should be affirmed rather than feared, celebrated rather than simply tolerated. Especially with the influx of new immigrants, multiculturalism became a major issue within American society and politics.

Debates within African American Culture

African Americans had developed a strong sense of cultural identity during the civil rights and black power struggles of the 1960s (see Chapters 9 and 10). Battles against discrimination and for cultural pride continued in the post-Vietnam era. Controversies over future directions, however, also emerged.

During the 1970s a movement called "Afrocentrism" began to attract a number of African American intellectuals and professionals. In contrast to the cold rationality of "Eurocentrists," it was argued, African Americans, with a cultural heritage reaching back to ancient Egypt, understood people and knowledge in broader, more empathetic ways. Afrocentrists encouraged blacks to take pride in heroic figures from the recent past, especially Malcolm X (see Chapter 10). A trend that one African American writer called "Malcolmania" accelerated with the appearance of Spike Lee's film *Malcolm X* (1991). The stress on racial pride was also prominent in rap and hip-hop music. Touting rap music as a source of information and ideas for black communities, Afrocentric rappers urged people to look "to the East blackwards." Seeking to institutionalize this philosophy, by 1990 more than 300 private schools and even some public systems were offering black students an "Afrocentric" curriculum.

Pride in racial identity and an African heritage became a complex, contested proposition. African American women who identified with feminist issues tended to view Afrocentrism and some male rap music as infected with misogyny. Queen Latifah, one of the first female rappers to incorporate feminist themes in her music, sang songs like "Ladies First," which criticized what she saw to be the gender stereotyping and the romanticizing of a mythical African past in many rap lyrics. African American women's groups organized to pressure record companies and radio stations to censor some rap music, especially "gangsta rap," which they considered misogynistic.

Similarly in academia, most programs in African American studies veered away from a strict Afrocentric approach in order to acknowledge the diversity and complexity of a heritage that stemmed from a multiplicity of African and American cultural influences. African American scholars such as Henry Lewis Gates Jr., who became head of Harvard's Afro-American studies department in 1991, made pride in the black experience one part of a larger multicultural vision. African American culture, in Gates's view, was not "a thing apart, separate from the whole, having no influence on the shape and shaping of American culture." Gates urged that African American authors, such as Toni Morrison (who won the Nobel Prize for Literature in 1993) and Alice Walker, be viewed as writers who take "the blackness of the culture for granted, as a springboard to write about those human emotions that we share with everyone else, and that we have always shared with each other." Although African American cultures could be seen as unique and different, said Gates, they should not be considered apart from their interaction with American culture generally.

This issue of whether African Americans should cultivate separateness or seek more interaction with the broader American culture surfaced at the NAACP convention in 1997. Leaders opened for debate the possibility that the NAACP should no longer adhere to its long-standing agenda favoring school integration, the issue that had effectively defined the civil rights movement of the 1950s and 1960s. Although the venerable organization did not change its stance, the very discussion of returning to separatist schools illustrated both frustration over the test scores of African American children in integrated public education and the impact of Afrocentric influences.

Other developments underscored the fact that a broad spectrum of views existed among African Americans. The controversy over the appointment of Clarence Thomas to the U.S. Supreme Court divided African Americans, just as it divided whites. Some, especially African American feminists, saw Anita Hill's testimony against Thomas as evidence of pervasive sexism within black culture, but many other African Americans remained focused on race. No white nominee, they argued, would ever have faced the kind of personal scrutiny that Thomas confronted. Opinion polls also suggested that a majority of African Americans thought protecting Thomas's position as a successful African American male was more important than attacking his conservative politics or exploring any of the gender issues raised by Hill.

The 1996 trial of sports star O. J. Simpson, which became a media spectacle for nearly a year, raised another important debate about the place of African Americans in American life. On this issue, African Americans were less divided. In the "trial of the century," Simpson was prosecuted for two brutal murders, including that of his former wife. Simpson's defense team, headed by the African American attorney Johnnie Cochran Jr., successfully refocused the trial on alleged misconduct by racist officers within the Los Angeles police department, and a largely black jury returned a verdict of not-guilty. Opinion polls indicated a significant division along racial lines: Whites were solidly convinced of Simpson's guilt, and African Americans overwhelmingly believed he was innocent. (Simpson was subsequently found liable for the murders in a civil trial for monetary damages, a judicial proceeding in which the laws of evidence and burden of proof are different from those required in criminal prosecution.) Quite apart from whatever the criminal trial proved about Simpson's guilt or innocence, it indicated an enormous gulf between whites and African Americans because of the distrust of police and the legal system in African American communities, a distrust that efforts to develop "community policing" and more racially diverse police forces had not yet overcome.

American Indians

American Indians pursued a variety of different strategies for social change during the 1970s and 1980s. In 1969 activists began a two-year sit-in, designed to dramatize a history of broken treaty promises over land claims, at the former federal prison on Alcatraz Island in San Francisco harbor. Expanding on this tactic, the American Indian Movement (AIM), which had been created in 1968 by young activists from several Northern Plains tribes, adopted a confrontational approach. Clashes, with both federal officials and more conservative Indian leaders, eventually erupted in early 1973 on the Pine Ridge Reservation in South Dakota. In response, the FBI and federal prosecutors targeted members of AIM for illegal surveillance and criminal prosecutions.

Many American Indians, like other ethnic groups, emphasized building a stronger sense of identity through the recovery, or the reinvention, of traditional cultural practices. To forestall the disappearance of their languages, Indian activists urged bilingualism and the revival of traditional rituals. AIM forged links with aboriginal peoples throughout the Americas and the South Pacific and organized trips to Central and South America to draw international attention to the problems faced by aboriginal peoples there. At home, AIM denounced the use of stereotypical Indian names in amateur and professional sports. Teams that had long called themselves "Chiefs" or "Redskins" were pressured to seek new names.

Meanwhile, important legal changes were taking place. The omnibus Civil Rights Act of 1968 contained six sections that became known as the "Indian Bill of Rights." In these, Congress finally extended most of the provisions of the constitutional Bill of Rights to reservation Indians while still upholding the legitimacy of tribal laws. Federal legislation and several Supreme Court decisions in the 1970s subsequently reinforced the broad principle of tribal self-determination.

Following the suggestion of American Indian lawyers and tapping the expertise of the Native American Rights Fund (NARF), many tribes used the courts aggressively to press legal demands that derived from old treaties with the U.S. government and the unique status of tribal nations. Some tribal representatives insisted that their traditional fishing and agricultural rights be restored, a demand that often provoked resentment among non-Indians, who complained that such special claims should not take precedence over state and local laws. At the same time, Indians also sued to protect tribal water rights and traditional religious ceremonies (some of which include the ritual use of drugs such as peyote) and to secure repatriation of Native American skeletal remains that were being displayed or simply stored in museums across the country. (At one point, the Smithsonian Institution was housing the remains of more than 18,000 Indians, supposedly for historical and scientific purposes.) Pressure from Indian rights groups led several states and finally Congress to pass laws that provided for the repatriation of both Indian remains and sacred religious artifacts.

Tribes also used the courts to press claims related to gambling. Claiming exemption from state gaming laws, Indians opened bingo halls and then full-blown gambling casinos. In 1988 the Supreme Court ruled that states could not prohibit gambling operations on tribal land, and Congress soon passed the Indian Gaming Regulatory Act, which gave a seal of approval to their casino operations. By the mid-1990s gambling had become one of the most lucrative sectors of the nation's entertainment business, and Indian-owned casinos had become a major part of this controversial phenomenon. In states such as Connecticut, Minnesota, and Wisconsin, Indian gaming establishments became a major source of employment for Indians and non-Indians alike. Vividly underscoring the contradictions within Indian culture, the glitzy postmodernism of Las Vegas–style casinos existed alongside tribal powwows and efforts to revive older tribal practices. Indeed, the Mashantucket Pequot tribe in Connecticut used the profits from its Foxwoods casino to finance one the nation's largest powwows, which offered nearly $ 1 million in prizes for entrants in its Indian dance contests.

Mystic Lake Casino, Prior Lake, Minnesota • A Las Vegas–style casino and hotel complex, owned by the Shakopee Mdewakanton Sioux (Dakota) community, the Mystic Lake Casino blends American Indian traditions into the design of its marquee. The casino's circular construction was designed to represent the Dakota's four-cycle view of life and to suggest the seven tribes that make up the Dakota nation. Searchlights atop the casino symbolize a "tepee of light."

Spanish-Speaking Americans

The media, citing the surge of immigration from South and Central America and from the Caribbean and noting the high birth rates for Spanish-speaking women in the United States, proclaimed the 1980s the "decade of the Hispanics." (Many Spanish-speaking people preferred the term "Latino.") Whether "Hispanic" or "Latino," the designation signified a population that soon would comprise America's largest minority group. Beneath this designation and a common language, however, was enormous diversity. For example, Cuban Americans, most of whom came to South Florida in the 1960s and 1970s, generally enjoyed greater access to education and higher incomes than did other Latinos. They also tended to be politically conservative, strongly supporting a hard-line stance against the communist government of

Cuba's Fidel Castro. Émigrés from Puerto Rico were already U.S. citizens and focused some of their political energies on the persistent "status" question—that is, whether Puerto Rico should hope for independence, strive for statehood, or retain a "commonwealth" connection to the mainland. Immigrants from the Dominican Republic and Central America (both legal and illegal) generally were the most recent and most impoverished newcomers.

Mexican Americans comprised the oldest and most numerous Spanish-speaking group in the United States. Among them, a spirit of *Chicanismo,* a populistic pride in a heritage that could be traced back to the ancient civilizations of Middle America, emerged in the late 1960s. Young activists made "Chicano," once a term of derision that most Mexican Americans avoided, a rallying cry. In cities in the Southwest, advocates of *Chicanismo,* though they remained a minority within Mexican American life, gained considerable cultural influence. Attempts by the police to crack down on Chicano activism during the 1970s backfired, especially in Los Angeles, and increasing numbers of young Mexican Americans came to identify with the new insurgent spirit.

Cities in the Southwest with large Mexican American populations experienced widespread ferment in the 1970s. The La Raza Unida movement, founded in 1967, began to win local elections during the early 1970s. At the same time, *Chicanismo* continued to stimulate a cultural flowering. Although Catholic priests generally avoided militancy, many of them opened their churches to groups devoted to ethnic dancing, mural painting, poetry, and literature. And Spanish-language newspapers and journals reinforced the growing sense of pride. Mexican Americans pushed for Chicano studies at colleges and universities.

Developments in San Antonio, a city with a large Mexican American population, suggested the potential fruits of grass-roots political organizing. In the 1970s Ernesto Cortes Jr. took the lead in founding COPS (Communities Organized for Public Service), a group that focused on achieving concrete, tangible changes that touched the everyday lives of ordinary citizens. In San Antonio this strategy meant that Mexican American activists worked with Anglo business leaders and with Democratic politicians like Henry Cisneros, who became the city's mayor in 1981. (In 1993 Cisneros and Federico Peña, a former mayor of Denver, both joined President Clinton's cabinet.) COPS brought many Mexican Americans, particularly women, into the public arena for the first time.

By the 1990s Mexican American politics was becoming increasingly diverse. La Raza Unida continued its activities during the 1980s but never became a national force. Instead, the Mexican American Legal Defense and Educational Fund (MALDEF), established in 1968 with funding from the Ford Foundation, emerged as the most visible national group ready to lobby or litigate on behalf of Mexican Americans. At the local level, organizations formed on the model of COPS, such as UNO (United Neighborhood Organization) in Los Angeles, continued to work on community concerns. The 1990 census reported that 40 percent of the general population and 60 percent of school-age children in Los Angeles were Latino. Meanwhile, as the U.S. economy of the 1990s offered expanding employment and educational opportunities, especially for women, many Mexican Americans were encouraged to pursue their own career advancement. For example, the National Network of Hispanic Women, founded in the 1970s, represented Chicanas who had

***Huelga!* (Strike!)** • As the United States became a more multicultural society, political expression on the streets broadened as well. Here, members of the United Farm Workers (UFW) march through San Diego in support of striking agricultural workers.

obtained positions in the professions and business corporations. Linda Chavez, who had moved from the business world to the Reagan administration and then to a prominent public-policy institute, came to symbolize the possibility of mobility for conservative Mexican American professionals and businesspeople.

Asian Americans

Diverse people with ancestral roots in Asia increasingly used the term "Asian American" as a way of signifying a new ethnic consciousness. Especially at colleges and universities on the West Coast, courses and then programs in Asian American studies were established during the 1970s. By the early 1980s political activists were gaining influence, especially within the Democratic Party, and a number of Asian American politicians were elected to office during the late 1980s and early 1990s. During the 1970s, older Japanese Americans finally began to talk about what had long been unspoken—their experiences in internment camps during the Second World World (see Chapter 7). Talk eventually turned to political agitation, and in 1988 Congress issued a formal apology and voted a reparations payment of $20,000 to every living Japanese American who had been confined in the camps.

The new Asian American vision encouraged Americans of Chinese, Japanese, Korean, Filipino, and other backgrounds to join together in a single pan-Asian movement. Organizations such as the Asian Pacific Planning Council (APPCON), founded in 1976, lobbied to obtain government funding for projects that benefited Asian American communities. The Asian Law Caucus, founded in the early 1970s by opponents of U.S. intervention in Vietnam, and the Committee Against Anti-Asian Violence, created a decade later in response to a wave of racist attacks, mobilized to fight a wide range of legal battles. And in 1997, the National Asian Pacific American Network Council, the first civil rights group to be formed by Asian Americans, began to lobby on issues related to immigration and education.

Emphasis on ethnic identity, however, raised problems of inclusion and exclusion. Activists who were Filipino American, the second largest Asian American group in the United States in 1990, often resisted the Asian American label because they felt that Chinese Americans and Japanese Americans dominated groups such as APPCON. As a result of complex pressures from different ethnic groups, the federal government finally decided to designate "Asian or Pacific Islanders" (API) as a single pan-ethnic category in the 1990 census, but it also provided nine specifically enumerated subcategories (such as Hawaiian or Filipino) and allowed other API groups (such as Hmong and Thai) to write in their respective ethnic identifications.

Socioeconomic differences also divided Asian Americans. Although in the late 1980s and early 1990s many Asian American groups showed remarkable upward mobility, demonstrating both economic and educational achievement, others such as Hmong immigrants and Chinese American garment workers, struggled to find jobs that paid more than the minimum wage. Thus, the term "Asian American"—which, by the end of the 20th century, applied to more than 10 million people and dozens of different ethnicities—both reflected and was challenged by the new emphasis on ethnic identity.

Dilemmas of Antidiscrimination Efforts

The assertion of racial and ethnic solidarity raised difficult questions about the meaning of equality. Between the end of the Second World War and about 1970, the antidiscrimination movement had demanded that the government not be permitted to categorize people according to group identities based on race or ethnicity. On matters such as education, housing, or employment—as the Supreme Court decisions and civil rights laws of the 1950s and 1960s had reaffirmed—the law must remain "color-blind," and government should strike down discriminatory laws and practices and enact measures that effectively secure equality of opportunity for all individuals.

The insurgencies of the 1960s and the upsurge in immigration gradually began to modify this agenda, as more and more ethnic groups embraced the politics of group identity. With people taking new pride in their ethnic heritage, there was a subtle, yet profound, shift of emphasis in social programs away from individual advancement and toward ethnic-group interests. By the 1970s this shift helped to produce a new vision of antidiscrimination in which government was to move beyond simply eliminating discriminatory barriers to *individual* opportunity. Social justice, according to the new antidiscrimination credo, required government to take "affirmative action" so that *groups* that had historically faced discrimination would now receive an equitable share of the nation's jobs, public spending, and educational programs. It was not enough, in short, that individual members of ethnic minorities theoretically be permitted to compete for jobs and educational opportunities; government needed to make sure that a representative number of people from different groups had a reasonable chance of acceptance. Affirmative action, supporters argued, would help compensate for historic discrimination and hidden racial attitudes that continued to disadvantage members of minority groups.

Affirmative action sparked fierce controversy. Many people who had supported previous policies against discrimination based on a color-blind commitment to guaranteeing individual opportunity found affirmative action a dangerous form of racialistic thought. Setting aside jobs or openings in educational institutions for certain racial or ethnic groups smacked of racist "quotas," these opponents of affirmative action charged. Moreover, was not affirmative action *on behalf of* some groups inevitably also "reverse discrimination" *against* others? The issue of reverse discrimination became particularly emotional when members of one ethnic group received jobs or entry to educational institutions despite lower scores on admissions exams. Even some beneficiaries of affirmative action programs began to feel that their own accomplishments would be denigrated because they were stigmatized, no matter what their individual talents, by the "affirmative action" label.

Meanwhile, courts found it difficult to square affirmative action programs with already mandated antidiscrimination policies. The pattern of judicial decision making in this new area of law satisfied neither proponents nor opponents of affirmative action. As a general rule, courts tended to strike down as unconstitutional those affirmative action plans that seemed to contain inflexible ethnic quotas but to uphold those plans that intended to remedy past patterns of discrimination and to make ethnicity only one of several criteria in hiring or educational decisions.

But the movement to eliminate, or scale back radically, affirmative action plans gained momentum during the 1990s. In 1996, after a hotly contested referendum campaign, voters in California passed Proposition 209, which aimed at ending most affirmative action measures in California by abolishing racial or gender "preference" in state hiring, contracting, and college admissions. The number of African Americans and Latinos admitted to the state's most prestigious law and medical schools immediately dropped (and most of those who were admitted chose to go elsewhere), and proponents of affirmative action immediately challenged Proposition 209 as discriminatory.

Ironically, the late 20th century debates over identity politics and affirmative action coincided with a rise in racial and ethnic intermarriage—a movement that might, in time, change the entire basis of discussion about equality. In the 1990s, growing numbers of people identified themselves as "mixed race" and either could not or would not claim a single ethnic-racial identity. In 1997, the media hailed Eldrick ("Tiger") Woods as the first African American golfer to win the prestigious Masters tournament. But Woods, whose mother was from Thailand, fiercely resisted being assigned any particular ethnic identification. In an official statement to the media, he said he was "EQUALLY PROUD" to be "both African American and Asian!" But he hoped that he could also "be just a golfer and a human being."

The New Right

The most successful social and cultural movement to emerge during the late 20th century was a newly militant conservatism, "the New Right." Beginning in the mid-1970s, a diverse coalition mobilized on behalf of the conservative reconstruction of American life. By the 1980s and 1990s this new conservative vision had captured the imagination of millions.

Several different constituencies comprised the New Right. Older activists, who had rallied around William F. Buckley's *National Review* in the 1950s and behind Barry Goldwater in the mid-1960s, contributed continuity (see Chapter 9). Espousing anticommunism and denouncing domestic spending programs, they also spoke out on an ever wider range of social issues. Phyllis Schlafly assumed a prominent role in mobilizing opposition to ratification of the Equal Rights Amendment, and Buckley's broad-ranging *Firing Line* became one of public television's most successful programs.

Neoconservatives

These established activists were joined by a group of intellectuals called the "neoconservatives." Many neoconservatives, such as Norman Podhoretz, Midge Dector, Irving Kristol, Gertrude Himmelfarb, and Jeane Kirkpatrick, had been anticommunist liberals during the 1950s and early 1960s. Unsettled by the insurgencies of the mid-1960s, they had criticized the Democratic Party for retreating from an anticommunist foreign policy and catering to social and cultural activists. In 1968 most had still supported Democrat Hubert Humphrey over Republican Richard Nixon, but the left-leaning candidacy of George McGovern in 1972 prompted a rush to the right.

Although neoconservatives remained true to their Cold War roots, many simultaneously renounced their support of domestic social programs. Their lively essays, written for established organs of conservatism such as *National Review* and *The Wall Street Journal* and for avowedly neoconservative publications such as *Commentary, The Public Interest,* and *The New Criterion,* denounced any movement associated with the 1960s, especially affirmative action. Neoconservatives offered intellectual sustenance to a new generation of conservative thinkers who worked to reinvigorate the nation's anticommunist foreign policy and celebrate its capitalist economic system.

A new militancy among conservative business leaders contributed to this movement. Arguing that the Great Society and even the Nixon administration had gone too far in areas such as health and safety regulations and environmental protection, pro-business lobbyists advocated that the United States rededicate itself to "economic freedom." Generous funding by corporations and conservative philanthropic organizations helped to staff right-leaning research institutions (such as the American Enterprise Institute and Heritage Foundation) and to finance new lobbying organizations (such as the Committee on the Present Danger). Conservatism even gained considerable ground on college campuses, the birthplace of the New Left and the counterculture during the 1960s.

The New Religious Right

The New Right of the 1970s also attracted much grass-roots support from Protestants who belonged to fundamentalist and evangelical churches. (Fundamentalists preach the necessity of fidelity to a strict moral code, of an individual commitment to Christ, and of a faith in the literal truth of the Bible. Evangelicals generally espouse the same doctrinal tenets as fundamentalists but place more emphasis on converting non-Christians and less on defending the literal truth of the Bible.) The Supreme Court's abortion decision in *Roe* v. *Wade* (1973) mobilized fundamentalist and evangelical leaders. Since the 1920s, fundamentalist and evangelical Protestants had generally stayed clear of partisan politics. Most, for instance, had dismissed abortion as a "Catholic issue." Now, fundamentalists and evangelicals who formed the core of this "New Religious Right" found themselves uniting with Catholic conservatives over opposition to abortion and other social and cultural issues. Because "liberals have been imposing morality on us for the last fifty years," declared Reverend Jerry Falwell of the Thomas Road Baptist Church and the "Old Time Gospel Hour" television ministry, *Roe* showed that it was time to fight back, even if this meant entering the political arena. Leaders of the New Religious Right also embarked on a lengthy legal battle to prevent the Internal Revenue Service from denying tax-exempt status to private Christian colleges and academies, particularly in the South, that allegedly discriminated against students of color.

Conservative Politics

Political developments of the 1970s also contributed to the emergence of the New Right. The declining political fortunes of George Wallace, who was badly wounded in the 1972 attempt on his life, left many conservatives, especially southerners, looking for new leadership. Similarly, many on the right had ultimately judged Richard Nixon more of an Eisenhower-style moderate than a Goldwater-style conservative. The end of Nixon's presidency in 1974 only intensified the desire for a "real" conservative leader. This desire became a crusade after Nixon's successor, Gerald Ford, selected the standard-bearer of Republican liberalism, Nelson Rockefeller, as his vice president. "I could hardly have been more upset if Ford had selected Teddy Kennedy," one disappointed conservative lamented (see Chapter 12).

George Wallace's campaigns had indicated that conservative politics, especially when focused on social and cultural issues, could excite millions of voters. Eventually, activists such as Richard Viguerie and Paul Weyrich organized the National Conservative Political Action Committee in 1975, the first of a number of organizations, including the Conservative Caucus, The Committee for the Survival of a Free Congress, and Jerry Falwell's Moral Majority. Although these organizations initially focused on lobbying in Washington and electing conservative Republicans, they also had broader cultural and social goals. As one architect of the New Right coalition put it, they fervently believed that "God's truth ought to be manifest politically."

Increasingly, this crusading spirit became phrased in terms of defending "family values" and of opposing what the religious right considered to be "degenerate lifestyles," particularly those espoused by feminists and homosexuals. Jerry Falwell's *Listen America!* (1980) suggested that the nation's military establishment was "under the complete control of avid supporters of the women's liberation movement." Because homosexuality was "one of the gravest sins condemned in the Scriptures," argued Paul Weyrich, the issue of gay and lesbian rights was not a matter of private lifestyles but a "question of morality which . . . affects the society as a whole." American institutions, particularly the male-headed nuclear family, needed protection. Similarly, parents needed to be able to protect their children from educational "experiments." School boards and liberal educators, religious conservatives argued, were not only challenging Biblical precepts by teaching evolution but were advancing dangerous new ideas such as multiculturalism and gender-fair educational curricula. To conservatives, it seemed that educational bureaucrats were forcing students to accept values that violated their personal religous values.

The New Right proved adept in publicizing its crusade. Right-leaning foundations funded conferences and radio and TV programs. The New Religious Right mastered the media, and preachers such as Pat Robertson capitalized on the expansion of CATV in the 1970s and early 1980s. Following in Jerry Falwell's footsteps, Robertson built a multimedia empire that included the 24-hour Christian Broadcasting Network (later renamed "The Family Channel"). During the 1980s, scandals and financial problems overtook some religious broadcasters, including Jimmy Swaggart and Jim Bakker, but Robertson's *700 Club,* a program that adapted his conservative evangelicalism to the talk-show and morning-news formats, grew steadily. At the same time, broadcasters associated with the New Right used talk-radio programs at both the local and national levels to spread the conservative message.

On its fringes, the New Right attracted support from ultralibertarian paramilitary groups who denounced gun control laws, taxes, and the federal government, particularly the Bureau of Alcohol, Tobacco, and Firearms. Violent confrontations between such groups and federal authorities, especially the government's ill-conceived and poorly managed assault on the Branch Davidian group in Texas (in which 78 people, including many children, were killed), left supporters of paramilitary politics feeling besieged. Any symbol of the federal government, one paramilitary leader claimed, could be considered a *"strategic military target."* In April 1995, on the second anniversary of the government's attack on the Branch Davidians, the Alfred P. Murrah Federal Building in Oklahoma City became such a target. A powerful bomb ripped through the building and killed 168 people, many of them children who were playing in a day care center. This bombing, for which a paramilitary loner named Timothy McVeigh was convicted and sentenced to death in 1997 (and for which accomplice Terry Nichols was convicted of conspiracy), discredited the extremist, antigovernment movement, as conservatives and liberals alike denounced the violent tendencies of paramilitary groups.

The New Right, a coalition of disparate parts, became a powerful force in both American culture and, increasingly, in American politics. After the middle of the 1970s, the many strains of the new conservatism helped to challenge New Deal–Great Society liberalism and to remap the ways in which the nation's political system dealt with questions of liberty and power.

Conclusion

Sweeping changes occurred in demographics, economics, culture, and society during the last quarter of the 20th century. The nation aged, and more of its people gravitated to the Sunbelt. Sprawling "urban corridors" and "edge cities" challenged older central cities as sites for commercial, as well as residential, development. Rapid technological change fueled the growth of globalized industries, restructuring the labor force to fit a "postindustrial" economy. Americans also developed a new environmental consciousness. Air and water quality standards improved, even though larger problems such as toxic wastes, ozone depletion, and global warming remained.

In American mass culture, the most prominent development was the proliferation of the video screen, an omnipresent conveyer of visual images. Television and motion pictures increasingly targeted specific audiences, and the fragmented nature of cultural reception was exemplified by the rise of new, particularistic media ventures such as CNN and MTV.

Meanwhile, American society itself also seemed to fragment into specialized identifications. Social activism often organized around sexual, ethnic, and racial identities: the women's movement, gay and lesbian pride, Afrocentrism, Indian rights, and movements that represented people of Latino and Asian ancestry. Multiculturalists celebrated this fragmentation while another activist movement, the New Right, argued that it was dividing the nation. The New Right's stress on conservative social values and the necessity for limiting the power of government increasingly came to set the terms for political debate during the 1980s and 1990s, reconfiguring discussions about how to respond to transformations associated with cultural diversity.

Chronology

1965 Congress passes Immigration Act of 1965

1968 Indian Bill of Rights extends most provisions of the Constitution's Bill of Rights to Native Americans

1970 First Earth Day observed • Environmental Protection Act passed • Clean Air Act passed

1973 *Roe* v. *Wade* decision upholds women's right to abortion • Endangered Species Act passed • Sudden rise in oil prices as result of OPEC

1980 Microsoft licenses its first PC software

1981 MTV debuts

1986 Supreme Court holds that sexual harassment qualifies as "discrimination"

1987 Immigration Reform and Control Act toughens laws against illegal aliens

1992 "Earth Summit" held in Brazil

1995 Million Man March takes place in Washington, D.C.

1996 O. J. Simpson tried and acquitted of murder

Suggested Readings

Social, Economic, and Demographic Developments

On social, economic, and demographic developments, see Raymond Mohl, ed., *Searching for the Sunbelt: Historical Perspectives on a Region* (1990); Mike Davis, *City of Quartz: Excavating the Future in Los Angeles* (1990); Alejandro Portes and Alex Stepick, *City on the Edge: The Transformation of Miami* (1993); Merry Ovnick, *Los Angeles: The End of the Rainbow* (1994); Nathan Glazer, ed., *Clamor at the Gates: The New American Immigration* (1985); Michael D'Innocenzo and Josef P. Sirefman, eds., *Immigration and Ethnicity* (1992); Alejandro Portes and Ruben G. Rumbaut, *Immigrant America: A Portrait* (1996); Norman L. Zucker and Naomi Flink Zucker, *Desperate Crossings: Seeking Refuge in America* (1996); Robert J. Samuelson, *The American Dream in the Age of Entitlement, 1945–1995*

(1996); Steven P. Dandaneau, *A Town Abandoned: Flint, Michigan, Confronts Deindustrialization* (1996); Ruth Milkman, *Farewell to the Factory: Auto Workers in the Late Twentieth Century* (1997); Charles Noble, *Welfare as We Knew It: A Political History of the American Welfare State* (1997); and Allen J. Scott and Edward W. Soja, *The City: Los Angeles and Urban Theory at the End of the Twentieth Century* (1996).

Changes in Technology and the Environment

On changes in technology and the environment, see Robert Reich, *The Work of Nations: Preparing Ourselves for 21st Century Capitalism* (1991); Kirkpatrick Sale, *The Green Revolution; The Environmental Movement* (1993); James W. Cortada, *The Computer in the United States: From Laboratory to Market, 1930–1960* (1993); Daniel Yergin, *The Prize: The Epic Quest for Oil, Money, and Power* (1991) and *The Commanding Heights: The Battle between Government and the Marketplace That is Remaking the Modern World* (1998); Samuel P. Hays, *Beauty, Health, and Permanence: Environmental Politics in the United States, 1955–1985* (1987); Craig E. Coltren and Peter N. Skinner, *The Road to Love Canal: Managing Industrial Waste before the EPA* (1996); Michele Stenehjem Gerber, *On the Home Front: The Cold War Legacy of the Hanford Nuclear Site* (1992); Terence Kehoe, *Cleaning Up the Great Lakes: From Cooperation to Confrontation* (1997); (1987); Ann Markusen et al., *The Rise of the Gunbelt: The Military Remapping of Industrial America* (1991); and Philip Shabecoff, *A Fierce Green Fire: The American Environmental Movement* (1993).

Changes in the Media Environment and Mass Culture

On changes in the media environment and mass culture, see Todd Gitlin, *Inside Prime Time* (1983); John Fiske, *Television Culture* (1987); Mark Crispin Miller, *Boxed-In: The Culture of TV* (1988); Robert Kolker, *Cinema of Loneliness: Penn, Kubrick, Scorcese, Spielberg, Altman* (rev. ed., 1988); Marsha Kinder, *Playing with Power in Movies, Television, and Video Games* (1991); Elizabeth G. Traube, *Dreaming Identities: Class, Gender, and Generation in the 1980s Hollywood Movies* (1992); Andrew Goodwin, *Dancing in the Distraction Factory: Music Television and Popular Culture* (1992); Henry Jenkins, *Textual Poachers: Television Fans & Participatory Culture* (1992); Anne Friedberg, *Window Shopping: Cinema and the Postmodern* (1993); Jane Feuer, *Seeing Through the Eighties: Television and Reaganism* (1995); Alan Nadel *Flatlining on the Field of Dreams: Cultural Narratives in the Films of President Reagan's America* (1997); Henry A. Giroux, *Channel Surfing: Race Talk and the Destruction of Today's Youth* (1997); Joseph Turow, *Breaking Up America: Advertisers and the New Media World* (1997).

Continuation of Political Insurgency

On the continuation of political insurgency, begin with Barbara Epstein, *Political Protest and Cultural Revolution: Non-Violent Direct Action in the 1970s* (1991). See also Paul Chaat Smith and Robert Allen Warrior, *Like a Hurricane: The Indian Movement from Alcatraz to Wounded Knee* (1996). Sara Evans, *Personal Politics: The Roots of Women's Liberation in the Civil Rights Movement and the New Left* (1979); Alice Echols, *Daring to Be Bad: Radical Feminism in America, 1967–1975* (1989); Nancy Whittier, *Feminist Generations: the Persistence of the Radical Women's Movement* (1995) seek to trace the emergence of a new feminism out of the male-dominated ethos of the New Left and the counterculture and to suggest that the 1960s did not represent a sudden end to insurgent movements. See also Jane J. Mansbridge, *Why We Lost the Era* (1986); Mary Frances Berry, *Why ERA Failed: Politics, Women's Rights, and the Amending Process of the Constitution* (1986); Johnnetta B. Cole, ed., *All American Women: Lines That Divide, Ties That Bind* (1986); Catherine MacKinnon, *Feminism Unmodified: Discourses on Life and Law* (1988); Susan Staggenborg, *The Pro-Choice Movement: Organization and Activism in the Abortion Conflict* (1991); and the relevant chapters of Leslie Reagan, *When Abortion Was a Crime: Women, Medicine, and Law in the United States, 1867–1973* (1997). On the gay and lesbian rights movement, see John D'Emilio and Estelle B. Freedman, *Intimate Matters: A History of Sexuality in America* (1988); Randy Shilts, *And the Band Played On: Politics, People, and the AIDS Epidemic* (1987); Steven Epstein, *Impure Science: AIDS, Aids Activism, and the Politics of Science* (1996).

Race and Multiculturalism

On the dilemmas of race and multiculturalism see Russell Ferguson, et al., eds., *Out There: Marginalization and Contemporary Cultures* (1990); Toni Morrison, ed., *Race-ing Justice, En-Gendering Power:*

Essays on Anita Hill, Clarence Thomas, and the Construction of Social Reality (1992); Andrew Hacker, *Two Nations: Black and White, Separate, Hostile, and Unequal* (1992); bell hooks, *Black Looks: Race and Representation* (1992); Michael Eric Dyson, *Reflecting Black: African-American Cultural Criticism* (1993); Cornel West, *Race Matters* (1993) and *Beyond Eurocentrism and Multiculturalism* (1993); Celeste Olalquiaga, *Megalopolis: Contemporary Cultural Sensibilities* (1992); James Davison Hunter, *Culture Wars: The Struggle to Define America* (1991); Henry Louis Gates, Jr., *Loose Canons: Notes on the Culture Wars* (1992); Patricia Turner, *I Heard it Through the Grapevine: Rumor in African-American Culture* (1993); Russell A. Potter, *Spectacular Vernaculars: Hip-Hop and the Politics of Postmodernism* (1995); David A. Hollinger, *Post-Ethnic America: Beyond Multiculturalism* (1995); Robert C. Smith, *Racism in the Post–Civil Rights Era; Now You See It, Now You Don't* (1995); Roger Waldinger, *Still the Promised City? African-Americans and New Immigrants in Postindustrial New York* (1996); Mattias Gardell, *In the Name of Elijah Muhammed: Louis Farrakhan and the Nation of Islam* (1996); Michael Eric Dyson, *Between God and Gangsta Rap: Bearing Witness to Black Culture* (1996); Jennifer L. Hochschild, *Facing Up to the American Dream: Race, Class, and the Soul of the Nation* (1995); Toni Morrison ed., *Birth of a Nation 'Hood: Gaze, Script, and Spectacle in the O.J. Simpson Case* (1997); Elaine Bell Kaplan, *Not Our Kind of Girl: Unravelling the Myths of Black Teenage Motherhood* (1997); Pyong Gap, Min, *Caught in the Middle: Korean Merchants in America's Multiethnic Cities* (1996); Fergus M. Bordewich, *Killing the White Man's Indian: Reinventing Native Americans at the End of the Twentieth Century* (1996); Ambrose I. Lane, Sr., *Return of the Buffalo: the Story Behind America's Indian Gaming Explosion* (1995); Raymond Tatalovich, *Nativism Reborn? The Official English Language Movement and the American States* (1995); Gary Y. Okihiro, *Margins and Mainstreams: Asians in American History and Culture* (1994); John William Sayer, *Ghost Dancing and the Law: The Wounded Knee Trials* (1997); Joane Nagel, *American Indian Ethnic Revival: Red Power and the Resurgence of Identity and Culture* (1996); Rennard Strickland, *Tonto's Revenge: Reflections on American Indian Culture and Policy* (1997); Pierrette Hondagneu-Sotelo, *Gendered Transitions: Mexican Experiences of Immigration* (1994); Alan Klein, *Baseball on the Border: A Tale of Two Laredos* (1997) offers a unique look, through the American pastime, of multiculturalism.

Conservative Politics

The growth of the "new conservatism" may be traced in David Reinhard, *The Republican Right Since 1945* (1983); Jerome Himmelstein, *To the Right: The Transformation of American Conservatism* (1990); Walter Capps, *The New Religious Right: Piety, Patriotism, and Politics* (1990); Walter Hixson, *Searching for the American Right* (1992); Michael Lienesch, *Redeeming America: Piety and Politics in the New Christian Right* (1993); Mary C. Brennan, *Turning Right in the Sixties: The Conservative Capture of the GOP* (1995); Robert Alan Goldberg, *Barry Goldwater* (1995); Dan T. Carter, *The Politics of Rage: George C. Wallace, the Origins of the New Conservatism, and the Transformation of American Politics* (1995); Catherine McNicol Stock, *Rural Radicals: Righteous Rage in the American Grain* (1996); James D. Tabor and Eugene V. Gallagher, *Why Waco? Cults and the Battle for Religious Freedom in America* (1995); Mark J. Rozell and Clyde Wilcox, *Second Coming: The New Christian Right in Virginia Politics* (1996); Raymond Wolters, *Right Turn: William Bradford Reynolds, the Reagan Administration, and Black Civil Rights* (1996); and Didi Herman, *The Antigay Agenda: Orthodox Vision and the Christian Right* (1997).

Videos

DreamWorlds II: Desire, Sex, and Power in Music Video (1996) is an award-winning critique of the images in rock videos, while Michael Eric Dyson, *Material Witness: Race, Identity and the Politics of Gangsta Rap* (1996) offers a more complex view. *The Myth of the Liberal Media* (1994) is a three-part critique, by Noam Chomsky and Edward Herman, of how the U.S. media shapes popular understandings.

12

Winds of Change: Politics and Foreign Policy from Ford to Clinton

T he power of the national government continually expanded during the three decades after the Second World War. Most people supported augmenting the government's military and intelligence capabilities so that the United States could play a dominant role in world affairs. Both Democrats and Republicans also generally endorsed the use of government power to cushion against economic downturns and to assist needy families.

The Vietnam War and the Watergate scandals (see Chapter 10), however, shook faith in government. Disillusionment with secrecy, corruption, bloated budgets, and failed crusades (especially the intervention in Vietnam and the War on Poverty) bred cynicism about the use of government power. The social and economic changes that were transforming daily life and lowering the real wages of many families bred a feeling that the national government no longer operated effectively. Political leaders from Gerald Ford to Bill Clinton had to operate within this culture of distrust.

In this environment, divisive debates punctuated political life. How might a stagnating economy and a beleaguered welfare system be reshaped? Should there be more governmental activism in addressing persistent problems of poverty and inequality, or would conditions improve if government's role were reduced?

Disagreements also focused on foreign policy. Should the United States set aside anticommunism to pursue other goals, as President Jimmy Carter initially suggested, or should it wage the Cold War even more vigorously, as his successor Ronald Reagan advocated? Then, in 1989, the Cold War came to an unexpected end, and the United States faced the task of reorienting its foreign policy in a world without a Soviet threat.

The post–Cold War environment also affected domestic politics. Americans still debated the proper relationship of government power to the preservation of liberty and equality, but as the economy strengthened during the mid-1990s, domestic issues seemed less divisive than they had been only a decade earlier.

The Ford Presidency

Gerald Ford, the first person to become vice president and then president without having been elected to either office, promised to mend the divisions that had split

476

the nation during the 1960s and early 1970s. He believed he could draw on the connections he had forged during many years in the House of Representatives to reestablish the presidency as a focus of national unity. But Ford's ability to "heal the land," as he put it, proved limited. A genial, unpretentious person—he asked that his entry to public events be accompanied by the fight song of his alma mater, the University of Michigan, rather than "Hail to the Chief"—Ford could not shake the impression, fueled by critics in the media, that he was a weak, indecisive chief executive.

Domestic Issues under Ford

Ford, who hoped to rebuild his own party around an updated version of the moderate Republicanism of the 1950s (Chapter 8), quickly ran into trouble. Needing to appoint a new vice president (subject to congressional approval), Ford picked New York's Nelson Rockefeller. The choice of Rockefeller, one of the GOP's most liberal figures, generated infighting in Ford's own administration and infuriated conservatives within the Republican Party. One prominent conservative newspaper began calling the president "Jerry the Jerk." Granting a presidential pardon to former President Nixon, in September 1974, proved even more controversial. Citing the need for healing, Ford pardoned Nixon for all federal crimes he "committed or may have committed or taken part in" while president. This decision provoked widespread controversy, and Ford's approval rating sharply plummeted.

Economic problems soon dominated the domestic side of Ford's presidency. Focusing on rising prices, rather than on increasing unemployment, Ford touted a program he called "Whip Inflation Now" (WIN). It offered a one-year income tax surcharge and cuts in federal spending as solutions to inflation. But escalating prices, contrary to what prevailing economic wisdom still predicted, were accompanied by a sharp recession. As both prices and unemployment continued to rise—the condition that had become known during Nixon's presidency as "stagflation"—Ford abandoned WIN. In 1975, the employment rate reached 8.5 per cent while the rate of inflation topped 9 percent.

Meanwhile, Ford and the Democratic-controlled Congress differed over how to deal with stagflation. Ford vetoed 39 spending bills during his brief, 865-day presidency. He eventually acquiesced, though, to an economic program that included a tax cut, an increase in unemployment benefits, an unbalanced federal budget, and a limited set of controls over oil prices. Even Republicans worried that he could neither implement coherent programs of his own nor stand up to Democrats in Congress.

Foreign Policy under Ford

While struggling with economic problems at home, Ford steered the nation through its final involvement in the war in Southeast Asia. Upon assuming office, Ford assured South Vietnam that the United States would renew its military support if the government in Saigon ever became directly menaced by North Vietnamese troops. The antiwar mood in Congress and throughout the country, however, made fulfilling this commitment impossible. North Vietnam's armies, sensing final victory, moved rapidly through the South in March 1975, and Congress, relieved that American troops had finally been withdrawn following the 1973 Paris peace accords, refused to reintroduce U.S. military power.

The spring of 1975 brought the communist victories that U.S. intervention had been designed to prevent. In early April, Khmer Rouge forces in Cambodia drove the American-backed government from the capital of Phnom Phen, and on April 30, 1975, North Vietnamese troops overran the South Vietnamese capital of Saigon, renaming it Ho Chi Minh City. The final defeat reignited the debate over U.S. policy in Indochina: Former "doves" lamented the lives lost and money wasted, while former "hawks" derided their country's "failure of will."

Within this charged atmosphere, Ford immediately sought to demonstrate that the United States could still conduct an assertive foreign policy. In May 1975, the Khmer Rouge boarded a U.S. ship, the *Mayaguez,* and seized its crew. Secretary of State Henry Kissinger, declaring that it was time to "look ferocious," convinced Ford to order a mission to rescue the *Mayaguez*'s crew and bombing strikes against Cambodia. This military response, along with pressure on the Khmer Rouge from China, secured the release of the *Mayaguez* and its crew. The president's approval ratings briefly shot up, but the incident did little to allay growing doubts about Ford's ability to handle complex foreign policy issues. The White House seemed primarily interested in looking tough, and more U.S. troops were lost than people rescued during the *Mayaguez* incident. Meanwhile, the president's other foreign policy initiatives, which included extending Nixon's policy of detente with the Soviet Union and pursuing a peace treaty for the Middle East, achieved little. Gerald Ford increasingly seemed to be a caretaker president.

The Election of 1976

In fact, conservative Republicans rallied behind Ronald Reagan, the former governor of California, and nearly denied Ford the GOP presidential nomination in 1976. Reagan's campaign, burdened by ill-focused ideas about shifting the cost of domestic programs from the federal to the state level, initially floundered, but it suddenly caught fire when his advisers urged him to forgo specific proposals and to highlight his image as a true conservative who, unlike Ford, was not beholden to Washington insiders. By this time, however, Ford had already won just enough delegates in the early primaries to eke out a narrow, first-ballot victory at the Republican Party's national convention.

The Democrats turned to an outsider, James Earl (Jimmy) Carter, the former governor of Georgia. Carter had graduated from the Naval Academy with a degree in nuclear engineering and, as a young officer, had worked on the nuclear submarine program. His military career had been cut short in the early 1950s, when he returned to Plains, Georgia, to run his family's peanut farming business following the death of his father. Later, Carter had entered state politics, gaining the reputation of being a moderate on racial issues and a fiscal conservative. When he announced his intention to run for the presidency in 1976, few people took him seriously; no governor, including people with far greater national reputations than Jimmy Carter, had captured the White House since Franklin Roosevelt in 1932.

Carter campaigned as a person of many virtues. With Watergate still a vivid memory in voters' minds, he emphasized his personal character and the fact that most

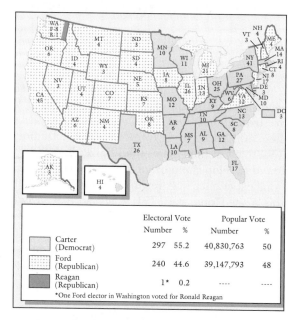

		Electoral Vote		Popular Vote	
		Number	%	Number	%
	Carter (Democrat)	297	55.2	40,830,763	50
	Ford (Republican)	240	44.6	39,147,793	48
	Reagan (Republican)	1*	0.2	----	----

*One Ford elector in Washington voted for Ronald Reagan

Presidential Election, 1976

of his life had been spent outside of politics. Highlighting his small-town roots, he pledged to "give the government of this country back to the people of this country." A devout Baptist, Carter campaigned as a born-again Christian. He also touted his record as a successful governor and asked people "to help me evolve an efficient, economical, purposeful and manageable government for our nation." And in order to counterbalance his own status as a Washington outsider, he picked a member of the Senate, Walter Mondale, as his running mate. Although economic conditions seemed to be improving—the unemployment rate for the year dropped to 7.7 percent and the rate of inflation declined to less than 6 percent in 1976—it was not enough to secure Ford's reelection. In November, Carter won a narrow victory over Ford.

Carter owed his election to a diverse, transitory coalition. Capitalizing on his regional appeal, he carried every southern state except Virginia. He ran well among southern whites who belonged to fundamentalist and evangelical churches. Still, his victory in the South rested on a strong turnout among African Americans, the beneficiaries of federal voter protection laws enacted during the 1960s. Meanwhile, across the country, Carter courted the youth vote by promising to pardon most of the young men who had resisted the draft during the Vietnam War. Mondale's appeal to traditional Democrats helped Carter narrowly capture three key states that had long been Democratic strongholds—New York, Pennsylvania, and Ohio. Even so, Carter won by less than 2 million popular votes, and by the close margin of 297 to 241 in the electoral vote. Not only was his margin of victory over Ford slight, but millions of people had not bothered to vote at all. Only about 54 percent of eligible voters went to the polls in 1976, the lowest turnout since the end of the Second World War.

The Carter Presidency: Domestic Issues

Jimmy Carter's lack of a popular mandate and his image as an outsider proved serious handicaps. Powerful constituencies, including both labor unions and multinational corporations, feared that Carter might prove to be an unpredictable leader. Moreover, many Democratic members of Congress, especially those who had first been elected in 1974 in the immediate aftermath of Watergate, stressed their independence from the White House, even though it was now occupied by a president from their own party. In 1976 most of these Democrats, after all, had rolled up higher vote totals in their states than Carter had.

Carter also failed to develop the aura of a national leader. Although he brought some people with long experience in government into his cabinet, he relied mainly on the Georgians on his White House staff. This small cadre of advisers, which the Washington press corps dubbed the "Georgia Mafia," overestimated the value of Carter's outsider image. After leaving government, Carter reflected on his difficulties: "I had a different way of governing. . . . I was a southerner, a born-again Christian, a Baptist, a newcomer. . . . As an engineer and a governor I was more inclined to move rapidly and without equivocation."

Welfare and Energy

In trying to frame his agenda, Jimmy Carter found himself caught between those who claimed that the power of the national government had already expanded too much and those who argued that Washington was doing too little to address social and economic problems. Unlike Richard Nixon, who had unveiled a bold Family Assistance Plan (FAP) in 1969 (Chapter 10), Carter temporized on what to do about social welfare policy. His advisers were divided between those who favored a more complicated version of FAP, which would have granted greater monetary assistance to low-income families, and those who thought the national government should create several million new public service jobs. Carter, while opposing any increase in the federal budget, asked Congress for a program that included both additional cash assistance and more jobs. He presented his proposal to Congress in 1977, where it quickly died in committee. Two years later, the House of Representatives turned down Carter's revised plan for job creation, although it passed a controversial bill that called for cash assistance to low-income families. The Senate rejected that measure, however, and the effort to change the welfare system stalled.

Carter pushed harder on energy issues. In response to soaring Middle East oil prices (see Chapter 11), he delegated James Schlesinger, a veteran of both the Nixon and the Ford administrations, to develop a sweeping energy plan. Schlesinger, Carter's secretary of energy, came up with a set of ambitious goals: a decrease in U.S. reliance on foreign oil and natural gas; the expansion of domestic energy production through new tax incentives and the repeal of regulations on the production of natural gas; the levying of new taxes to discourage use of gasoline; the fostering of conservation by encouraging greater reliance on insulation and other energy-saving measures; and the promotion of alternative sources of energy, especially coal and nuclear power. Neither Carter nor Schlesinger, who had drafted the plan in secret, consulted Congress or even some key members of the president's own administration. Instead,

Carter went on national television, in April 1977, to announce a complicated energy plan that included more than 100 interrelated provisions.

Congress quickly rejected the Carter-Schlesinger plan. Legislators from oil-producing states opposed the proposal for higher taxes on gasoline, and critics of the big oil companies blocked the idea of rapid deregulation of oil and natural gas production. Meanwhile, environmentalists opposed any increase in coal production because of coal's contribution to air pollution. And most Americans simply ignored Carter's claim that the nation's struggle with its energy problems amounted to "the moral equivalent of war."

Economic Policy

Carter had no greater success with economic policy. He inherited the economic problems—especially "stagflation," sluggish economic growth coupled with high rates of inflation—that had bedeviled Nixon and Ford. When Carter entered the White House in January 1977, unemployment stood at slightly under 7 percent and inflation was running a bit under 6 percent. Carter pledged to lower both unemployment and inflation, to stimulate greater economic growth, and to balance the federal budget (which had showed a deficit of about $70 billion in 1976). Instead, by 1980 the economy had almost stopped expanding, unemployment (after to dipping to a rate of under 6 percent in 1979) was beginning to rise again, and inflation topped 13 per cent. Most voters, according to opinion polls, believed that economic conditions were dramatically deteriorating during Carter's presidency.

The economic difficulties of the 1970s were not limited to individuals. New York City, beset by long-term economic and social problems and short-term fiscal mismanagement, faced bankruptcy. It could neither meet its financial obligations nor borrow money through the usual channels. Finally, private bankers and public officials collaborated on congressional legislation to provide the nation's largest city with federal loan guarantees. New York's troubles were symptomatic of a broader urban crisis. According to one estimate, New York City lost 600,000 manufacturing jobs in the 1970s; Chicago lost 200,000. During the 1970s a leading export of St. Louis, Missouri, was bricks from demolished industrial-era buildings. As a consequence of such trouble, increasing numbers of people living in central cities could find only low-paying, short-term jobs that carried no fringe benefits. Many found no jobs at all. Rising crime rates and deteriorating downtown neighborhoods afflicted most American cities, just when the impact of inflation further eroded city budgets.

What went wrong? Tax cuts and increased spending on public works projects had temporarily lowered the unemployment rate. And the Federal Reserve Board, hoping to add its own economic stimulus, had permitted a growth in the supply of money. Those very measures, which were designed to stimulate recovery, however, fueled price inflation. Meanwhile, the continued rise in international oil prices triggered a series of increases for gasoline and home heating fuel that rippled through the economy. Inflation and high interest rates choked off productivity and economic growth.

Conservative economists and business groups argued that the domestic programs favored by most congressional Democrats also contributed to the spiral of rising prices. By increasing the minimum wage and by vigorously enforcing safety and antipollution regulations, conservatives argued, the national government had driven up the cost of doing business and had forced companies to pass on this increase to consumers in the form of higher prices. During the last two years of his presidency, Carter himself seemed to agree with some of this analysis when, over the protests of members of his own party, he reduced spending for a variety of social programs, supported a law that reduced the capital gains taxes paid by wealthier citizens, and began a process of deregulating transportation industries, such as trucking and airlines.

The Carter Presidency: Foreign Policy

In foreign policy, as in domestic policy, Carter promised a significant change of direction. On his first day in office, he extended amnesty to those who had resisted the draft in the Vietnam War. He also declared that he would not be afflicted by an "inordinate fear of communism" and would put a concern for "human rights" at the center of U.S. foreign policy. After four years, however, his foreign policy initiatives were in disarray; even those who supported his goals conceded that Carter's leadership projected a lack of confidence in himself and in the nation. Ronald Reagan's "get-tough-again" presidential campaign of 1980 would make Carter a symbol of foreign policy ineptitude.

That caricature stemmed, in part, from fundamental flaws in Carter's foreign policymaking process. Carter himself, although skillful in handling small-group negotiations, had little experience working with long-term foreign policy issues. Furthermore, his top policy advisers—Cyrus Vance as secretary of state and Zbigniew Brzezinski as national security adviser—often had contradictory approaches to policymaking. Brzezinski favored a hard-line, anti-Soviet policy with an emphasis on military muscle; Vance preferred avoiding public confrontations and emphasized the virtues of quiet diplomacy. Pulled in divergent directions, Carter's policy often seemed to waffle. Still, Carter set some important new directions, emphasizing negotiation in particular trouble spots of the world and elevating a concern for human rights into a foreign policy priority.

Negotiations in Panama and the Middle East

One of the first concerns of the Carter administration involved the Panama Canal treaties. The status of the Panama Canal Zone had been under negotiation for 13 years. U. S. ownership of the canal, a legacy of turn-of-the-century imperialism, had sparked growing anti-Yankee sentiment throughout Latin America. Moreover, Carter argued, the canal was no longer the economic and strategic necessity it had once been. Despite strong opposition from those who saw ownership of the Canal Zone as a symbol of America's power in the world, Carter adroitly managed public and congressional relations to obtain ratification of treaties that granted Panama increasing jurisdiction over the canal, with full control after the year 2000.

Carter's faith in negotiations, and in his personal skill as a facilitator, again emerged in the Camp David peace accords of 1978. Relations between Egypt and

Israel had been strained ever since the Yom Kippur War of 1973, when Israel repelled an Egyptian attack and then seized the Sinai Peninsula and territory along the West Bank (of the Jordan River). Reviving Henry Kissinger's earlier efforts to mediate Arab-Israeli conflicts, Carter brought Menachem Begin and Anwar Sadat, leaders of Israel and Egypt, respectively, to the Camp David presidential retreat. After 13 days of bargaining, the three leaders announced the framework for a negotiating process and a peace treaty. Although Middle East tensions hardly vanished, the Camp David accords kept high-level discussions alive, lowered the level of acrimony between Egypt and Israel, and bound both sides to the United States through its promises of economic aid.

In Asia and Africa, the Carter administration also emphasized accommodation. Building on Nixon's initiative, Carter expanded economic and cultural relations with China and finally established formal diplomatic ties with the People's Republic on New Year's Day 1979. In Africa, Carter abandoned Kissinger's reliance on white colonial regimes and supported the transition of Zimbabwe (formerly Rhodesia) to a government run by the black majority.

Human Rights Policy

Carter's foreign policy became best known for its emphasis on human rights. Cold War alliances with anticommunist dictatorships, Carter believed, were undermining U.S. influence in the world. In his 1976 campaign he had criticized Nixon for supporting repressive regimes. In the long run, Carter's policy helped to raise consciousness around the world about human rights issues and made a regime's behavior a criterion in decisions about the extension of U.S. foreign aid. The trend toward democratization that occurred in many nations during the 1980s and 1990s was partially triggered by the rising awareness associated with Carter's stress on human rights.

The immediate impact of the human rights policy, however, was ambiguous. Because Carter applied the policy inconsistently, many of America's most repressive allies, such as Ferdinand Marcos in the Philippines, felt little pressure to change their ways. Moreover, Carter's rhetoric about human rights helped spark revolutionary movements against America's long-standing dictator-allies in Nicaragua and Iran. These revolutions, fueled by resentment against the United States, brought anti-American regimes to power and presented Carter with thorny policy dilemmas. In Nicaragua, for example, the Sandinista revolution toppled dictator Anastasio Somoza, whom the United States had long supported. The Sandinistas, initially a coalition of moderate democrats and communists, quickly drifted toward a more militant Marxism and began to expropriate property. Carter opposed Nicaragua's movement to the left but could not change the revolution's course. The president's Republican critics charged that his policies had given a green light to communism in Central America and pledged that they would work to oust the Sandinista government.

The Hostage Crisis in Iran

Events in Iran dramatically eroded Carter's standing. Shah Reza Pahlavi had regained his throne with the help of Western intelligence agencies in a 1953 coup, and the United States had subsequently showered him with military hardware. The overthrow of the Shah by an Islamic fundamentalist revolution in January 1979 thus signaled a massive rejection of U.S. influence in Iran. When the Carter administration bowed to political pressure and allowed the deposed and ailing Shah to enter the United States for medical treatment in November 1979, a group of Iranians took 66 Americans hostage at the U.S. embassy compound in Teheran; they demanded the return of the Shah in exchange for the release of the hostages.

As the hostage incident gripped the country, Carter's critics cited it as evidence of how weak and impotent the United States had become. Carter talked tough; levied economic reprisals against Iran; and, over Vance's objections, sent a military mission to rescue the hostages. (Vance subsequently resigned.) But the mission proved an embarrassing failure, and Carter never managed to resolve the situation. After his defeat in the 1980 election, diplomatic efforts finally brought the hostages home, but the United States and Iran remained at odds.

Meanwhile, criticism of Carter intensified when the Soviet Union invaded Afghanistan in December 1979, a move that may have been sparked by Soviet fear of the growing influence of Islamic fundamentalists along its borders. Many Americans interpreted the invasion as a simple sign that the Soviets now dismissed the United States as too weak to contain their expansionism. Carter, who had followed Henry Kissinger's pursuit of détente in an attempt to lessen superpower conflict, could never shake the charge that he was afflicted with "post-Vietnam syndrome," a failure to act strongly in foreign affairs. Carter halted grain exports to the Soviet Union (angering his farm constituency), organized a boycott of the 1980 Olympic Games in Moscow, withdrew a new Strategic Arms Limitation Treaty (SALT) from the Senate, and revived registration for the military draft. Still, conservatives charged Carter with presiding over a decline of American power and prestige, and Ronald Reagan made constant reference to Iran and Afghanistan as he prepared for the 1980 elections.

The Election of 1980

For a time, when Senator Edward Kennedy of Massachusetts entered the party's 1980 presidential primaries, it seemed that the Democrats might not even allow Carter to run for a second term. Carter responded to Kennedy's campaign by adopting a "Rose Garden" strategy. Insisting that events in Iran demanded his full attention, he stayed near the White House, acted "presidential," and ignored Kennedy. Kennedy's own personal and political liabilities, along with Carter's solid support among southern Democrats, eventually helped the president turn back Kennedy's challenge.

Kennedy's campaign, however, underscored Carter's vulnerability. Kennedy popularized anti-Carter themes that Republicans gleefully embraced. "It's time to say no more hostages, no more high interest rates, no more high inflation, and no more Jimmy Carter," went one of Kennedy's stump speeches. More than one-third of the people who supported Kennedy in the final eight Democratic primaries (five of which Kennedy won) were conservative Democrats who told pollsters they would likely vote Republican in the general election. As Carter entered the fall campaign against the Republicans, he seemed a likely loser.

Republican challenger Ronald Reagan exuded confidence. He stressed his opposition to federal social programs and his support for a stronger national defense. His successful primary campaign glossed over specific details, especially those related to his promise of tax cuts, and highlighted an optimistic vision of a rejuvenated America and a supply of movie-inspired quips. To remind voters of the alleged failures of the Carter presidency, he asked repeatedly, "Are you better off now than you were four years ago?" He quickly answered his own question by invoking what he called a "misery index," which added the rate of inflation to the rate of unemployment.

Reagan's optimism allowed him to seize an issue that Democrats had long regarded as their own: economic growth. In 1979 Alfred Kahn, one of Jimmy Carter's economic advisers, had gloomily suggested that the nation's economic problems were so severe that there was "no way we can avoid a decline in our standard of living. All we can do is adapt to it." In contrast, Reagan optimistically promised that tax cuts would bring back the kind of economic expansion the nation had enjoyed during the 1950s and 1960s. During a crucial television debate, when Carter tried to criticize Reagan's promises for their lack of specificity, a smiling Reagan spotlighted Carter's apparent pessimism by repeatedly quipping, "There you go again!"

Reagan won the November presidential election with only slightly more than 50 percent of the popular vote. (Moderate Republican John Anderson, who ran an independent campaign for the White House, won about 7 percent.) But Reagan's margin over Carter in the Electoral College was overwhelming: 489 to 49. In the South, Carter carried just 35 percent of the white vote and only his home state of Georgia. Moreover, Republicans took 12 Senate seats away from Democrats, gaining control of the Senate for the first time since 1954.

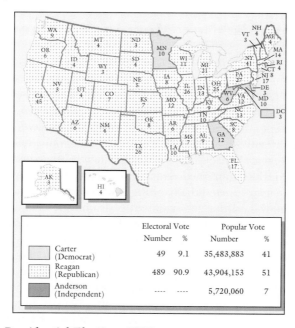

		Electoral Vote		Popular Vote	
		Number	%	Number	%
	Carter (Democrat)	49	9.1	35,483,883	41
	Reagan (Republican)	489	90.9	43,904,153	51
	Anderson (Independent)	----	----	5,720,060	7

Presidential Election, 1980

Many Democrats initially tried to dismiss the election as a fluke. Noting Reagan's slim majority in the popular vote, they portrayed 1980 as more of a defeat for Carter than a victory for the Republicans. By reducing expenditures for domestic programs and lowering taxes on capital gains, according to this analysis, Carter had alienated traditional Democratic voters. Moreover, Reagan's sophisticated media campaign was credited with temporarily misleading voters; in due course, these Democrats claimed, Reagan would be unmasked as a media-manufactured president.

Democrats, however, failed to recognize that their own domestic agenda had been steadily losing support. In 1980 voters turned seven prominent liberal Democratic senators, including former presidential candidate George McGovern, out of office. The real income of the average American family, which had risen at an annual rate of just under 3 percent per year between 1950 and 1965, rose only 1.7 percent a year between 1965 and 1980, with the worst years coming after 1973. In such a stagnant economic climate, middle-income taxpayers, who were themselves struggling to make ends meet, found Democratic social welfare programs far less palatable than they had found them in more prosperous times.

During the 1970s, then, public support for domestic spending programs had begun to fade, and the United States had entered a new, more conservative era in social policymaking. Liberals continued to talk about how to improve, and even expand, welfare-state initiatives. But conservatives advocated a radical reduction in government spending programs, decrying public housing as a waste of tax dollars and denouncing AFDC (Aid to Families with Dependent Children) and food stamps as socially debilitating for their recipients and a drag on the national economy. More and more voters came to identify with the position championed by Ronald Reagan.

Reagan's "New Morning in America"

Reagan's advisers set about crafting a bold, conservative agenda. Tapping anxieties about declining national power and eroding living standards, Reagan promised a "new morning in America," especially in the area of taxation. A taxpayer revolt, which had emerged in California in the late 1970s, provided a model for Reagan's attack on federal spending for domestic programs. (There was something ironic in this situation: California's tax revolt had emerged in response to increases that had occurred while Reagan himself had been the state's governor.) Across the country, people responded to Reagan's tax-reduction message.

In addition, Reagan courted the New Right with opposition to abortion, support for prayer in school, and the endorsement of traditional "family values." Conservative religious figures, including Jerry Falwell and Pat Robertson, onetime Democrats, joined Reagan's new Republican coalition. Even Carter's own Southern Baptists, who had rallied behind him in 1976, along with born-again Christians across the country, flocked to Reagan in 1980. Reagan also found a way to reach white (especially male) voters, who were upset over affirmative action, while avoiding being charged with making racist appeals. Reagan himself proclaimed a commitment to "color-blind" social policies and appointed conservative African American and Hispanic leaders to his administration. "Guaranteeing equality of treatment is the government's proper function," Reagan proclaimed at one of his first presidential press conferences.

Reagan's First Term: Economic Issues

To justify cutting taxes, Reagan touted a theory called "supply-side economics." This theory held that tax reductions would stimulate the economy by putting more money in the hands of investors and consumers, thereby reversing the economic stagnation of the 1970s. Reagan pushed his tax plan through Congress during the summer of 1981. The new law significantly reduced taxes for people who earned high incomes and already possessed significant wealth. Taxes on businesses were also slashed to encourage investment in new facilities and equipment. Most Democrats, who had supported tax reductions under Carter in 1978, endorsed Reagan's plan. At the same time, the Federal Reserve Board under Paul Volker, a Carter appointee, pursued a policy of keeping interest rates high in order to drive down inflation.

After a severe recession in 1981 and 1982, the worst since the Great Depression of the 1930s, the economy rebounded and entered a period of noninflationary growth. Between 1982 and 1986, more than 11 million new jobs were added to the economy. By 1986, the GNP was steadily climbing, while the rate of inflation had plunged to less than 2 percent; unemployment figures, however, stubbornly refused to drop. Still, Reagan's supporters called the turnaround an "economic miracle" and hailed the "Reagan Revolution."

The economic revival of the 1980s sparked debate over the cumulative impact of annual federal budget deficits and the consequences of the economic expansion. On the first issue—budget deficits—Reagan's critics pointed out that his tax cuts had not been matched by budget reductions. Although Reagan constantly inveighed against budget deficits and big spenders, his administration actually rolled up the most extraordinary record of deficits and spending in U.S. history. During his presidency, the annual deficits tripled to nearly $300 billion. To finance such spending, the United States borrowed abroad and piled up the largest foreign debt in the world. Reagan's "Revolution," critics charged, brought short-term recovery for some people by courting a long-term budget crisis that would harm people with low incomes, who relied on government programs, and would imperil future generations, who would have to pay for the soaring government debt.

On the second issue—the soundness of the U.S. economy—critics charged that the new economic growth was unevenly distributed. They complained that Reagan's policies were creating a "Swiss-cheese" economy, one that was full of holes. Farmers in the Midwest were especially battered during the recession of 1981–1982, as falling crop prices made it difficult for them to make payments on the high-interest loans contracted during the inflation-ridden 1970s. The value of land, a farmer's primary asset, plummeted. A series of mortgage foreclosures, reminiscent of the 1930s, hit farm states, and the ripple effect decimated many small-town businesses. At the same time, urban families, who were struggling to get by on low-paying jobs and declining welfare benefits, were also puzzled by talk about a "Reagan boom." Many of the jobs created in the 1980s were in the nonunionized service sector and offered relatively low wages and few, if any, fringe benefits. In 1981 the average weekly paycheck was $270; measured in constant dollars, the same check was worth only $254 in 1991. The minimum wage, when measured in constant dollars, fell throughout Reagan's presidency.

In communities of color, this uneven pattern was especially glaring. From the late 1960s on, people of color with educational credentials and marketable skills had made—and would continue to make—significant economic gains. The number of African American families making a solid middle-class income more than doubled between 1970 and 1990. African American college graduates could expect incomes comparable to those of white college graduates, partly as a result of the affirmative action hiring plans that the federal government was enforcing. Many persons of color, therefore, could afford to move away from inner-city neighborhoods. But the story of mobility was very different for an "underclass" of people who were persistently unemployed and trapped in declining urban centers. At the end of the 1980s, one-third of all black families lived in poverty and the number making under $15,000 per year had doubled since 1970. In inner cities, less than half of African American children were completing high school, and more than 60 percent were unemployed. Throughout America, the gap between rich and poor widened significantly.

Implementing a Conservative Agenda

Meanwhile, Reagan made changes in other areas. In 1981 he pleased his conservative, pro-business supporters—and enraged union members and their supporters—by firing the nation's air traffic controllers when their union refused to halt a nationwide strike. Overall, union membership continued to decline, as both the Reagan administration and many large businesses pursued aggressive antiunion strategies during the 1980s. The percentage of non-farmworkers who were unionized, which had been declining since the 1960s, fell to just 16 percent by the end of Reagan's presidency. Workers, who recognized that the balance of power was tilting against them, increasingly turned away from strikes as an economic weapon.

Reagan also placed a conservative stamp on the federal court system. Almost immediately, Reagan was able to nominate a Supreme Court justice, Sandra Day O'Connor, the first woman to sit on the High Court. Justice O'Connor initially seemed a staunch conservative, particularly when deciding cases having to do with social issues or criminal justice matters. During Reagan's first term, when the Republican Party controlled the Senate, Reagan also named prominent conservative jurists, such as Robert Bork and Antonin Scalia, to lower federal courts. Conservatives, who had long decried the decisions of the Court under Earl Warren and even many of those handed down under Warren Burger, welcomed the influx of judges from the political right. Civil libertarians complained that the federal courts were becoming less hospitable to legal claims made by criminal defendants, labor unions, and political dissenters. Because of the retirement of a number of older judges, by 1989 about 50 percent of the federal judiciary had been nominated and confirmed during Ronald Reagan's presidency.

In his non-judicial appointments, Reagan also looked for staunch conservatives. With presidential counselor Edwin Meese overseeing the selection process, Reagan filled the Justice Department with lawyers who were eager to end the "rights

Value of the Minimum Wage, 1955–1995
(adjusted for inflation to 1995 dollars)

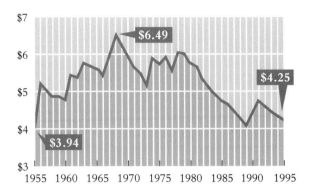

Source: Data from U.S. Department of Labor.

revolution" and affirmative action programs. He appointed James Watt, an outspoken critic of environmental legislation, as secretary of the interior, the department that guides the nation's conservation policy. Reagan's first two appointees to the Department of Energy actually proposed eliminating the department they headed—an idea that Congress successfully blocked. Reagan himself mused about abolishing the Department of Education and often criticized programs espoused by his own secretary of education. Finally, having staffed most of the administrative agencies with conservatives, Reagan sought to ease regulations on businesses by relaxing enforcement of the safety and environmental laws that conservative economists had blamed for escalating the costs of doing business. The administration also eased the enforcement of affirmative action laws, in line with Reagan's call for a "color-blind" approach on racial issues.

In addition, Reagan eliminated some social welfare programs, most notably the Comprehensive Employment and Training Act (CETA), which had been established during Richard Nixon's first term, and reduced funding for others, such as food stamps. Reagan proved to be much more conservative on domestic issues than Richard Nixon, who had allowed social expenditures to increase, had courted some labor union leaders, and had advanced his guaranteed-income program, FAP. Nevertheless, Reagan pledged that Washington would still maintain a "safety net" for those who were really in need of governmental assistance.

Critics complained, however, that—after having declined throughout the 1970s—there was a rise in the number of people whose total package of income and government benefits fell below what economists considered the "poverty" level. Conditions would have been worse if the nation's most popular welfare program, Social Security, had not been redesigned in the 1970s so that its benefits automatically increased along with the rate of inflation (an arrangement called "indexing"). Rising Social Security payments, along with Medicare benefits, enabled millions of older Americans who might otherwise have fallen below the official poverty line to hold their own economically during the Reagan years. The burden of the growing poverty,

A Dwindling Number of Strikes

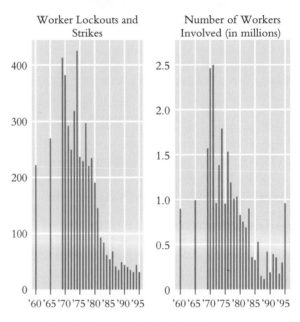

Source: Data from Bureau of Labor Statistics

then, fell disproportionately on female-headed households and especially on children. By the end of the 1980s, one of every five children was being raised in a household whose total income fell below the official poverty line.

Amid the controversies over the growing budget deficit and the inequalities in wealth, Reagan became known as the "Teflon president." No matter what problems beset his administration, nothing negative ever seemed to stick to Reagan himself. His genial optimism seemed unshakable. He even appeared to rebound quickly after being shot by a would-be assassin in March 1981.

The Election of 1984

Democrats continued to underestimate Reagan's popular appeal—a miscalculation that doomed their 1984 presidential campaign. Walter Mondale, Jimmy Carter's vice president from 1976 to 1980, ran on a platform that followed the party's postwar tradition of calling for "the eradication of discrimination in all aspects of American life" and for an expansion of domestic spending programs by the national government. Mondale even predicted higher taxes to pay for his proposals. His running mate, Representative Geraldine Ferraro of New York, was the first woman ever to run for president or vice president on a major-party ticket. Convinced that Reagan's "economic miracle" would eventually self-destruct, Mondale stuck to his basic themes, particularly on taxes. Reagan would soon have to raise taxes to cover the burgeoning federal deficit, Mondale bravely declared, and "so will I. He won't tell you; I just did."

The Republicans ran a textbook-perfect campaign. The president, while emphasizing the accomplishments of his first term, criticized Mondale for living in the past. He labeled Mondale's support by labor and civil rights groups as a vestige of the old politics of "special interests" and denounced Mondale's tax proposal as a reminder of the "wasteful tax-and-spend policies" that he claimed had precipitated the stagflation of the 1970s. Reagan's surrogates criticized Mondale's selection of Ferraro as another example of his kowtowing to special interests—in this case, feminist and pro-choice groups. Reagan himself continued to sketch, in the broadest possible strokes, the picture of a bright, conservative future for America. In his campaign films, the United States appeared as a glowing landscape of bustling small towns and lush farmland. His campaign slogan was "It's Morning Again in America," and his campaign song was "I'm Proud to Be an American." The 1984 presidential election ended with Mondale carrying only his home state of Minnesota and the District of Columbia. In 1964, the Republican Party had hit bottom with Barry Goldwater's defeat; 20 years later, Ronald Reagan's victory capped a remarkable revival for the GOP.

Reagan and his conservative supporters succeeded in giving new meanings to many traditional political terms. "Liberal" no longer meant a set of government programs that would stimulate the economy and help people to buy new homes and more consumer goods. Instead, Republicans made "liberalism" a code word for supposedly wasteful social programs devised by a bloated federal government that gouged hardworking people and gave their dollars to people who were undeserving and lazy. The term "conservative," as used by Republicans, came to mean economic growth through limited government and support for traditional social-cultural values.

Renewing the Cold War

Reagan quickly established foreign policy themes that dominated both of his terms in office. Under Carter, he claimed, the nation's power had been eroded by the "Vietnam syndrome" of passivity and "loss of will." Reagan promised to reverse that trend. In contrast to Carter's amnesty for Vietnam War resisters, Reagan declared that the war had been a "noble cause" that the government had refused to win. Although he did not repudiate Carter's human rights policy, he called it into the service of a renewed Cold War against the Soviet Union, highlighting the Soviet Union's mistreatment of its Jewish population and ethnic minorities. Reagan hoped that his renewal of the Cold War crusade, along with his conservative domestic agenda, would complete the effort, begun under Nixon, to forge a new Republican majority.

The Defense Buildup

The United States, Reagan claimed, had "unilaterally disarmed" during the 1970s, while the Soviets were staging a massive military buildup. He called for a new battle against what he called the "evil empire" of the Soviet Union. He dismissed critics of his foreign policy as the "Blame-America-First Crowd" and as "the strangest collection of misfits, loony tunes, and squalid criminals since the advent of the Third Reich."

Closing what Reagan called America's "window of vulnerability" against Soviet military power, however, would be expensive. Although his tax cuts would inevitably reduce government revenues, Reagan nonetheless asked Congress for dramatic increases in military spending. The Pentagon launched programs to enlarge the Navy and to modernize strategic nuclear forces, concentrating especially on missile systems. It also deployed new missiles throughout Western Europe, despite vigorous protests by many people who lived there. At the height of Reagan's military buildup, the Pentagon was purchasing about 20 percent of the nation's manufacturing output.

In 1984 Reagan surprised even his closest advisers by proposing the most expensive defense system in history—a space-based shield against incoming missiles. Although it was a nebulous idea when announced, the Strategic Defense Initiative (SDI) soon had its own agency in the Pentagon that projected a need for $26 billion over five years, just for start-up research. Controversy swirled around the SDI program. Critics dubbed it "Star Wars," and many members of Congress shuddered at its astronomical costs. Although most scientists considered the project impractical, Congress voted appropriations for SDI, and throughout his presidency Reagan clung to the idea of a defensive shield. SDI dominated both the strategic debate at home and arms talks with the Soviet Union. (Reagan's successors quietly reduced support for the project after the end of the Cold War.)

Greater defense spending had another strategic dimension. Secretary of Defense Caspar Weinberger suggested that, as the Soviets increased the burden on their own faltering economy in order to compete in the accelerating arms race, the Soviet Union itself might collapse under the economic strain. This had been an implicit goal of the containment policy since NSC-68.

Military Actions in Lebanon, Grenada, Nicaragua, and Libya

In waging the renewed Cold War, Reagan promised vigorous support to "democratic" revolutions around the globe, a move designed to make it harder for the Soviet Union to maintain its sphere of influence. Reagan's UN representative, Jeane Kirkpatrick, wrote that "democratic" forces included almost any movement, no matter how autocratic, that was noncommunist. Throughout the world the United States thus funded opposition movements in countries that were aligned with the Soviet Union: Ethiopia, Angola, South Yemen, Cambodia, Grenada, Cuba, Nicaragua, and Afghanistan. Reagan called the participants in such movements "freedom fighters," although few had any visible commitment to liberty or equality.

The Reagan administration also displayed a new willingness to unleash U.S. military power. The first occasion was in southern Lebanon, where Israeli troops were facing off against Lebanese Moslems supported by Syria and the Soviet Union. Alarmed by the gains the Moslems were achieving, the Reagan administration in 1982 convinced Israel to withdraw and sent 1,600 American marines as part of a "peacekeeping force" to restore stability. But Moslem fighters then turned their wrath against the Americans. After a suicide commando mission into a U.S. military compound killed 241 marines, Reagan decided that this ill-defined undertaking could never win public support. He subsequently pulled out U.S. troops and disengaged from the conflict.

Although the debacle in Lebanon raised questions about Reagan's leadership, another military intervention restored his popularity. In October 1983 Reagan sent 2,000 U.S. troops to the tiny Caribbean island of Grenada, whose socialist leader was forging ties with Castro's Cuba. U.S. troops overthrew the government and installed one friendly to American interests. Although later studies revealed that the invasion was plagued by lack of coordination, poor planning, and needless casualties, tight military control over news coverage shielded the administration from criticism at the time and allowed it to declare Grenada a complete foreign policy victory.

Buoyed by events in Grenada, the Reagan administration fixed its sights on the Central American country of Nicaragua. The socialist government, led by the Sandinista party, was trying to build ties with Cuba in hopes that Nicaragua could break its historic dependence on the United States. In a clear threat to invade Nicaragua, the United States augmented its military forces in neighboring Honduras and conducted training exercises throughout the area. But any overt military action in Nicaragua would involve far greater costs than the invasion of tiny Grenada. Reagan consequently decided to use covert means to topple the Sandinista regime. Following the pattern of previous covert operations, the United States tightened its economic stranglehold on Nicaragua and launched a psychological offensive to discredit the Sandinistas. These measures were designed to erode the regime's popularity at home and abroad and to give the United States time to train and equip an opposition military force of Nicaraguans, the *contras*. Meanwhile, the administration supported murderous dictatorships in nearby El Salvador and Guatemala to prevent other leftist insurgencies from gaining ground in Central America.

U.S. initiatives in Central America became the most controversial aspect of Reagan's foreign policy. U.S. backed regimes were clearly implicated in abuses of human rights, not only against their own people but also against American nuns, journalists, and humanitarian-aid workers. Mounting evidence of the brutality and corruption of the Nicaraguan *contras*—Reagan's so-called "freedom fighters"— brought growing public criticism. In 1984, the Democratic-controlled Congress broke with the president's policy and denied further military aid to the *contras*.

The Reagan administration quickly sought ways around the congressional ban. One solution was to encourage wealthy U.S. conservatives and other governments to donate money to the *contras*. In June 1984, at a top secret meeting of the National Security Planning Group, Reagan and his top advisers discussed the legality of pressing "third parties" to contribute to the *contra* cause. Reagan ended the meeting with a bid for secrecy: "If such a story gets out, we'll all be hanging by our thumbs in front of the White House."

Meanwhile, violence continued to escalate throughout the Middle East. Militant Islamic groups stepped up the use of terrorism against Israel and Western powers; bombings and the kidnaping of Western hostages became more frequent. Apparently, such activities were being encouraged by Libyan leader Muammar al-Qaddafi as well as by Iran. In the spring of 1986 Reagan undertook a military action in the Middle East that did not require the commitment of U.S. ground troops. As part of a broad plan to destroy Qaddafi's power, the United States launched an air strike into Libya aimed at Qaddafi's personal compound. The bombs did serious damage and killed Qaddafi's young daughter, but Qaddafi and his government survived.

Despite some public criticism of this action, which looked like a long-range assassination attempt against a foreign leader (an action outlawed by Congress), Americans generally approved of using strong measures against sponsors of terrorism and hostage-taking.

Other Initiatives

Reagan's foreign policy included initiatives other than military incursions. In a new "informational" offensive, the administration funded a variety of conservative groups around the world and established Radio Martí, a Florida radio station beamed at Cuba and designed to discredit Fidel Castro. When the United Nations agency UNESCO criticized the global dominance of the U.S. media and called for a "New World Information Order" that would reduce the overwhelming influence of U.S.-originated news and information, Reagan cut off U.S. contributions to UNESCO and demanded changes in the organization and operation of the UN. Reagan also championed free markets, urging other nations to minimize tariffs and restrictions on foreign investment. His Caribbean Basin Initiative, for example, rewarded with U.S. aid those small nations in the Caribbean region that adhered to free-market principles.

The CIA, under Director William Casey, stepped up covert activities, some of which became so obvious that they were hardly "covert." It was no secret, for example, that the United States was aiding anticommunist forces in Afghanistan and the *contras* in Nicaragua, but the extent and nature of that aid were not officially acknowledged by the U.S. government. The Reagan administration's zeal for covert action, secret and not so secret, gave rise to the administration's most dubious legacy: the Iran-*Contra* affair.

*The Iran-***Contra*** Affair*

In November 1986, a magazine in Lebanon reported that the Reagan administration was selling arms to Iran as part of a secret deal to secure the release of Americans being held hostage by Middle Eastern factions friendly to Iran's government. The story quickly became front-page news in the United States because such a deal would be in clear conflict with the Reagan administration's stated policies that it would not sell arms to Iran and that it would not reward hostage-taking by negotiating for the release of any captives.

As Congress began to investigate the arms-for-hostages story, matters turned even more bizarre. Reagan's attorney general, Edwin Meese, revealed that profits from secret arms sales to Iran had been channeled to the *contra* forces in Nicaragua as a means of circumventing the congressional ban on U.S. military aid. Oliver North, a lieutenant colonel who worked in the office of the national security adviser, had directed the effort, apparently with the approval of the head of the CIA, the national security adviser, and other officials. Responsibility for carrying out the deal, subsequent investigations showed, had been entrusted to a secret unit in the National Security Council, shadowy international arms dealers, and private go-betweens who were immune from public accountability. North had been running a covert operation that violated both the stated policy of the White House and the ban legislated by Congress.

The arms-for-hostages idea dovetailed with Reagan's foreign policy priorities. During the 1980 campaign, Reagan had made hostages a symbol of U.S. weakness under Carter; as Iranian-backed groups continued to kidnap Americans, Reagan began to worry that the hostage issue might be as disastrous for his presidency as it had been for Carter's. Meanwhile, Iran was waging a prolonged war with Iraq, led by Saddam Hussein. Although the United States allowed arms sales to Iraq, it had organized a ban on the sale of arms to Iran by Western powers because of Iran's connection with hostage-taking. The arms-for-hostages deal thus evolved out of mutual interests and fears: Despite the public enmity between the two nations, Iran needed arms to fight its war with Iraq, and the Reagan administration needed to show that it could bring hostages home. The secret deal satisfied both countries. Even better, the United States could use the profits from the sale secretly to fund other projects—such as the *contra* cause—that had to be hidden from Congress and the public.

This scheme seemed to cut at the heart of democratic processes, but everyone involved escaped accountability. Ronald Reagan, in a remarkable display of forgetfulness, maintained that he could not remember any details about either the release of the hostages or the funding of the *contras*. His management style might deserve criticism, he admitted, but no legal issues were involved. Vice President George Bush also escaped censure by claiming ignorance. Oliver North and National Security Adviser John Poindexter were convicted of felonies, including falsification of documents and lying to Congress, but their convictions were overturned on appeal. Six years later, on Christmas Eve of 1992 and just a few days before the end of his presidency, George Bush pardoned six former officials who had been involved in the Iran-*Contra* affair.

Beginning of the End of the Cold War

Although Reagan's first six years in office had revived the Cold War confrontation, his last two years saw a sudden thaw in U.S.-Soviet relations and a movement toward détente. The economic cost of superpower rivalry was burdening both nations. Moreover, changes within the Soviet Union were eliminating the reasons for confrontation. Mikhail Gorbachev, who became general secretary of the Communist Party in 1985, was a new style of Soviet leader. Familiar with the pace of technological change in Western democracies as economies and communications became globally integrated, he realized that his isolated country was facing economic stagnation and an environmental crisis brought on by decades of poorly planned industrial development. To redirect his country's course, he championed a major political transformation. He withdrew Soviet troops from the costly and unpopular war in Afghanistan, reduced commitments to Cuba and Nicaragua, proclaimed a policy of *glasnost* ("openness"), and began to implement *perestroika* ("economic liberalization") at home.

Soon Gorbachev was pursuing policies that brought him acclaim throughout the West and stirred winds of change throughout the Soviet empire. He began summit meetings with the United States on arms control. At Reykjavik, Iceland, in October 1986, Reagan shocked both Gorbachev and his own advisers by proposing a wholesale

The Great Communicator Visits the Evil Empire • Ronald Reagan's all-out crusade against the Soviet Union drew some criticism because of its expense and rhetorical bombast. But toward the end of his second term, Reagan softened his tone and even visited the Soviet Union in response to Mikhail Gorbachev's new policies of *glasnost* and *perestroika*. Within a year of this 1988 visit, the Soviet Union itself had collapsed.

ban on nuclear weapons. Although negotiations at Reykjavik stumbled over Gorbachev's insistence that the United States abandon its "Star Wars" program, the next year Gorbachev dropped that condition. In December 1987 Reagan and Gorbachev signed a major arms treaty that reduced the number of intermediate-range missiles held by each nation and allowed for on-site verification, something the Soviets had never before permitted. The next year, Gorbachev scrapped the policy, from the era of Leonid Brezhnev, that forbade any nation under Soviet influence from renouncing communism. In effect, Gorbachev, who was elected president in the first competitive election in the Soviet Union in 1989, was unilaterally declaring an end to the Cold War. And within the next few years, the Soviet sphere of influence—and then the Soviet Union itself—would cease to exist.

From Reagan to Bush

During his first term, Ronald Reagan became America's most popular president since Franklin Roosevelt. But even before the Iran-*Contra* affair, his presidential image and influence were beginning to fade. Even members of the New Right came to criticize the president for failing to support their agendas vigorously enough, while economic problems—especially the growing federal deficit and the disarray in the financial sector—sparked broader-based calls for more assured leadership from the White House.

Domestic Policy during Reagan's Second Term

During Reagan's second term, the White House and Congress began to address two long-term domestic issues: reduction of the federal budget and reform of the welfare system. First, the Gramm-Rudman-Hollings Act of 1985 mandated a balanced federal budget by 1991, but neither Congress nor the Reagan administration seemed eager to implement that goal or the larger one of reducing the soaring government deficit. Second, the Family Support Act of 1988 required states to inaugurate work training programs and to move people, even mothers receiving AFDC, off the welfare rolls. But this law, its critics noted, did little to guarantee that its work training provision would actually result in people finding—and then keeping—jobs. Without a plan to create new employment opportunities, the Family Support Act seemed to have more to do with the desire among politicians of both parties to line up in favor of cutting domestic programs and less to do with finding actual alternatives to the existing welfare system. Yet, despite their limitations, Gramm-Rudman-Hollings and the Family Support Act set policymakers in the White House and in Congress on a course of action that would eventually culminate in a comprehensive budget-reduction and welfare-reform package nearly a decade later.

Even many of Ronald Reagan's own supporters became disappointed by domestic developments during his second term. In 1986, following the resignation of Warren Burger, the Senate confirmed William Rehnquist as chief justice of the United States, and Antonin Scalia, another staunch conservative, to replace Rehnquist as associate justice of the Supreme Court. But in 1987 the Senate rebuffed Reagan's attempt to elevate Robert Bork, another conservative, to the Court. Bork's rejection sparked discord among conservatives, many of whom blamed Reagan for not working hard enough to secure his confirmation. Meanwhile, members of the Religious Right chafed at what they considered Reagan's tepid support for their antiabortion crusade. And Reagan himself rebuffed conservative ideas about modifying the Social Security system. Meanwhile, his massive spending for military programs undermined the conservative dream of decreasing the federal budget and reducing the long-term federal debt.

Reagan's second term was also marked by charges of mismanagement and corruption. The process of banking deregulation became linked to malfeasance in financial circles and to risky speculation that critics called "casino capitalism." Problems in the savings and loan industry reached crisis proportions. During a period of lax oversight by federal regulators, many savings and loan institutions (S&Ls) had extended too much money to risky ventures, particularly in the overbuilt real estate market, and had incurred financial obligations far beyond their means. As hundreds of S&Ls fell insolvent, the people and the businesses to whom they had lent money also faced financial disaster. The agency that regulated S&Ls predicted an impending crisis as early as the spring of 1985, but the Reagan administration and most members of Congress, hoping to delay any decisive response until after the 1988 election, dismissed the warning as unduly alarmist.

Finally, in 1989 Congress was forced to act. It enacted an expensive bailout plan, designed to save some institutions and to provide a means of transferring the assets of failed S&Ls to those that were still solvent. Even as taxpayers began paying for the plan, corruption plagued its execution; large, well-connected commercial banks, for instance, purchased the assets of bankrupt S&Ls at bargain prices. By the time the Treasury Department stepped in, early in 1994, most of the larger S&Ls had already been sold. As a consequence, some shareholders had been defrauded, and the banking industry had undergone a sudden, unplanned consolidation.

The Election of 1988

Despite the growing criticism of Reagan's leadership at home, Cold War détente boosted the 1988 presidential prospects of his heir-apparent, Vice President George Bush, who easily gained the Republican nomination. Part of a prominent Republican family from Connecticut, Bush had gone to Texas and entered the oil business as a young man. His lengthy political resume included a time in the House of Representatives and a stint as director of the CIA. Bush was both a less charismatic and a more establishment-style politician than Reagan: He was "Reagan plus water," quipped one analyst. Bush chose as his running mate Senator J. Danforth Quayle, a staunch conservative better known for playing golf than for drafting legislation. The selection of Quayle pleased the Republican right—and delighted political comedians, who found the bumbling Quayle a rich source for new comic material.

Governor Michael Dukakis of Massachusetts emerged from the primaries as the Democratic presidential candidate. In an effort to distance himself from the disastrous Democratic effort in 1984 and to draw attention to the stain of corruption that was finally sticking to Reagan, Dukakis avoided talk of new domestic programs and higher taxes. Instead, he pledged to bring competence and honesty to the White House and boasted of how he had mobilized private experts to help streamline the government and stimulate the economy of Massachusetts. By running a cautious campaign and avoiding controversial domestic issues, Dukakis gambled that he could defeat Bush, who was burdened by Reagan's domestic failures.

The election of 1988, the last to be conducted during the Cold War era, was dominated by negative campaigning, especially on behalf of George Bush. Pro-Bush television commercials usually presented Dukakis bathed in shadows and always showed him with a frown on his face. In the campaign's most infamous ad, Dukakis was linked to Willie Horton, an African American prison inmate who had committed a rape while on furlough from a Massachusetts prison. Clearly designed to play on racial fears, the ad also implied that Dukakis, whom Bush assailed as a "card-carrying member of the American Civil Liberties Union," was soft on crime. Rising rates of violent crime during the late 1980s, much of it stemming from the spread of crack cocaine, alarmed Americans across the country. As one pundit put it, the Bush campaign made it seem that Willie Horton was Dukakis's running mate.

Bush won a solid majority in both the popular vote and the Electoral College. Yet, he carried so many states by such small margins that relatively minor shifts in voter turnouts, especially among Black and Latino voters who failed to support Dukakis as strongly as they had supported Mondale four years earlier, could have given the victory to Dukakis. Dukakis did better in 1988 than Mondale had done in 1984, winning 111 electoral votes. Outside the South, which went heavily for Bush, Dukakis carried more than 500 counties that had supported Reagan in 1984. Overall, voter turnout was the lowest it had been in any national election since 1924, and polls suggested that a majority of voters considered neither Bush nor Dukakis worthy of being president.

A Gathering of Five Presidents, 1991 • Republican dominance of the White House between 1968 and 1992 is graphically depicted in this executive assemblage at dedication ceremonies for the Ronald Reagan Presidential Library in Simi Valley, California. Jimmy Carter (1977–1981) is the lone Democrat present among former GOP stalwarts Richard Nixon (1969–1974), Gerald Ford (1974–1977), Ronald Reagan (1981–1989), and George Bush (1989–1993).

Although conservatives hoped Bush would build on the Reagan presidency, many doubted his commitment to their cause. Might not his campaign pledge of a "kinder, gentler America" be meant as a veiled criticism of Reagan's domestic policies? Bush, after all, had once endorsed abortion rights. Some grumbled when John Tower, a zealous advocate for the military, failed to gain Senate confirmation as secretary of defense and criticized Bush for not doing enough to assist his own nominee. Bush angered many conservatives by agreeing to an increase in the minimum wage and by failing to veto the Civil Rights Act of 1991, a law they wrongly claimed set up quotas for the preferential hiring of women and people of color in business and government. Most important, in 1990 he broke his campaign promise of "no new taxes," the issue on which most conservatives came to judge his worthiness as Reagan's successor, and accepted a tax increase as a means of dealing with the rising federal deficit.

Moreover, there was a growing popular perception that the national government, divided between a Democratic-controlled Congress and a Republican-occupied White House, was suffering from "gridlock." Little seemed to be getting done on domestic issues, especially on reorganization of the health care and welfare systems.

Bush's failure to respond to urban issues was highlighted in April 1992 when South–Central Los Angeles erupted in violence. After the acquittal of four police officers charged with beating Rodney King, an African American, several days of racial conflict resulted in 53 deaths, thousands of injuries, countless fires, and more than one billion dollars in property damage. Confused over an appropriate response,

Conflagration in LA, 1992 • The acquittal by an all-white jury of four white police officers on charges that they had beaten Rodney King, an African American motorist, sparked several days of violence in Los Angeles beginning on April 29, 1992. More than 50 people were killed, a thousand buildings were destroyed, and several thousand people were injured. Five years later, only two-thirds of the buildings that were leveled during the violence had been rebuilt, and a majority of respondents to a newspaper poll indicated that race relations in Los Angeles remained tense.

Bush temporized and ended up pleasing neither law-and-order advocates nor those who were still looking for his "kinder, gentler America."

Meanwhile, the economic growth of the Reagan years was slowing, and the budget deficit was expanding. George Bush's chances for a second term, it became clear, would depend on his record in foreign, rather than domestic, policy.

Foreign Policy under Bush

During Bush's presidency Soviet communism collapsed. As communist states fell like dominoes, the international order underwent its greatest transformation since the end of the Second World War.

The End of the Cold War

Beginning in 1989, political change swept through Eastern and Central Europe. In Poland, the anticommunist labor party, Solidarity, ousted the pro-Soviet regime. The pro-Soviet government in East Germany fell in November 1989, and Germans from both West and East hacked down the Berlin Wall. Divided since the Second World War, Germany began the difficult process of reunification. In Czechoslovakia,

Hungary, Romania, and Bulgaria, public demonstrations forced out communist governments. Yugoslavia disintegrated, and warfare ensued as ethnic groups tried to recreate the separate states of Slovenia, Serbia, Bosnia, and Croatia. The Baltic countries of Latvia, Lithuania, and Estonia, which had been under Soviet control since the Second World War, declared their independence. And most dramatic, the major provinces that had comprised the Soviet Union itself assumed self-government. The president of the new state of Russia, Boris Yeltsin, put down a coup by hard-line communists in August 1991 and his popularity rapidly eclipsed that of Mikhail Gorbachev. Yeltsin urged that the Soviet Union be abolished and replaced with 11 republics, loosely joined in a Commonwealth of Independent States. In December 1991, the Russian Parliament ratified that plan.

As the map of Europe changed, the United States faced the task of establishing diplomatic relations with many new and reconfigured countries. Most of these former communist states began to experiment with elections and democracy, raising

The Symbolic End of the Cold War, 1989 • The dismantling of the Berlin Wall, which had been erected in 1962, marked the end of a divided Germany and symbolized the victory of the "free world" over communism.

difficult questions about how the United States might help democratic governments to succeed by fostering economic stability in the Soviet Union's old empire. In December 1991 Congress authorized $400 million to help the Soviet Union's successor states, especially Ukraine, dismantle their nuclear weaponry, and it allotted an equivalent amount the next year for promoting democracy in the new European republics. Critics charged that these sums for peace-building were minuscule compared to the funds that had been appropriated for military containment. But Bush, who feared being charged with slighting domestic problems, felt reluctant to press for more assistance.

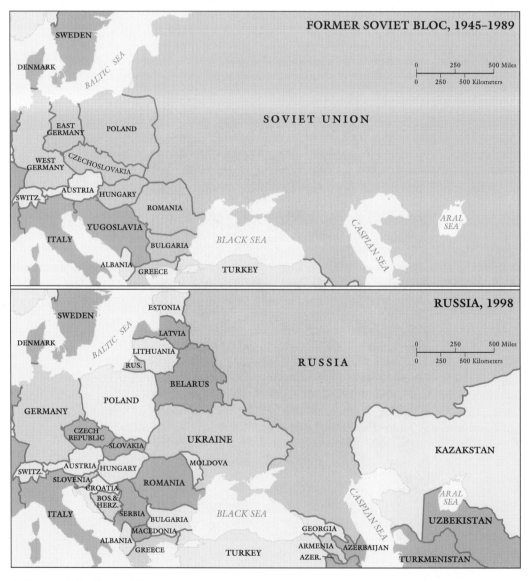

Collapse of the Soviet Bloc

Meanwhile, the international economic picture was improving. In the mid-1980s, huge debts that Third World nations owed to U.S. banks had threatened to shake the international banking system, but by the end of the decade most of these obligations had been renegotiated. Free-market economies began to emerge in the former communist states, and Western Europe moved toward economic integration. The nations of the Pacific Rim continued to prosper, and Bush pressed for a North American Free Trade Agreement (NAFTA) that would bring Canada, the United States, and Mexico together to form the largest free-market zone in the world.

As the likelihood of armed conflict with the Soviet Union faded, the Bush administration set about redefining "national security." The leftist threats in Central America, which had preoccupied the Reagan administration, suddenly ameliorated with the end of the Cold War. The Sandinistas were voted out of office in Nicaragua and became just another political party in a multiparty state. Supported by the United States, the United Nations began to assist both El Salvador and Guatemala in charting a course that would turn armed conflicts into electoral ones. The Pentagon thus began to consider new missions for its military forces. Future action, its planners predicted, would take the form of rapid, sharply targeted strikes rather than lengthy campaigns. Military troops might even be used to fight a "war against drugs," which Bush had promised during his 1988 presidential campaign. In Latin America, the Bush administration sponsored missions to destroy drug crops and interdict drug shipments. Such initiatives, however, merely annoyed the highly elusive drug dealers.

A more accessible target, the Bush administration decided, was the country of Panama, whose government, headed by General Manuel Noriega, was deeply involved in the drug trade. The Reagan administration had secured an indictment in the United States against Noriega for drug trafficking and had tried to force him from power through economic pressure. But this had only deepened Noriega's reliance on drug revenues. Deciding how to deal with Noriega was a significant problem for U.S. policymakers. First, there was the embarrassing fact that Noriega had been recruited as a CIA "asset" in the mid-1970s, when Bush himself was the agency's director. In addition, the United States needed a friendly, responsible government in Panama in order to complete the transfer of the Panama Canal to Panamanian sovereignty by the end of the century. Bush finally decided to topple Noriega. In a military incursion called "Operation Just Cause" and broadcast live on television throughout the world, U.S. marines landed in Panama in December 1989, pin-pointed Noriega's whereabouts, and put him under siege. Soon he surrendered and was extradited to stand trial in Florida. In April 1992 he was convicted of cocaine trafficking and imprisoned.

Seizing the leader of a foreign government in this manner raised questions of international law, and the resort to military force in a region long sensitive to U.S. intervention sparked controversy. Still, this military action, which involved 25,000 troops but only about two dozen U.S. casualties, boosted Bush's popularity at home. It also provided a new model for post–Cold War military action. The Pentagon firmed up plans for phasing out its older military bases, particularly in Germany and the Philippines, and for creating highly mobile, rapid-deployment forces that could respond quickly to a variety of perceived threats to U.S. national interests. A test of this new strategy came in the Persian Gulf War.

The Persian Gulf War

On August 2, 1990, President Saddam Hussein of Iraq ordered his troops to occupy the small neighboring emirate of Kuwait. Within a day, Iraq's forces had taken control of Kuwait, and Saddam Hussein quickly declared it the 19th province of Iraq. This move caught the United States off guard. Although Iraq had been massing troops on Kuwait's border and denouncing Kuwaiti oil producers, U.S. intelligence forecasters had doubted that it was about to take over the country. Now, however, they warned that Iraq might make Saudi Arabia, the largest oil exporter in the Middle East and a longtime friend of the United States, its next target.

Moving swiftly, Bush organized an international response. He convinced the Saudi government, which was at first reluctant to harbor Western troops on its soil, to accept a U.S. military presence. Four days after Iraq's invasion of Kuwait, Bush launched operation "Desert Shield" by sending 230,000 troops to protect Saudi Arabia. After consulting with European leaders, he took the matter to the United Nations. The UN denounced Iraqi aggression, ordered economic sanctions against Saddam Hussein's regime, and authorized the United States to lead an international force to restore the government of Kuwait if Saddam Hussein had not withdrawn his troops by January 15, 1991. Bush assembled a massive force, ultimately deploying nearly half a million American troops and some 200,000 from other countries, and he persuaded Congress to approve a resolution backing his use of force, although it passed by only five votes in the Senate. Although Bush claimed a moral obligation to rescue Kuwait, his policymakers spoke frankly about the economic peril Hussein's aggression posed for the United States and other oil-dependant economies. Secretary of State James Baker summed up the national interest of the United States in one word: "Jobs."

Just after the January 15 deadline passed, the United States launched an air war on Iraq. "Pools" of journalists, whose movements were carefully controlled by the military, focused mainly on new military technology, especially the antimissile missile called the "Patriot." TV networks showed Patriots, in video game fashion, intercepting and downing Iraqi "Scud" missiles. (Later, careful studies significantly reduced claims about the success rate of the Patriot missiles.) The media also highlighted the new role that women played in America's modernized military. After six weeks of devastating aerial bombardment and economic sanctions against Iraq, General Colin Powell ordered a ground offensive on February 24. Over the next four days Saddam Hussein's armies were shattered. The United States, with its control of the skies, kept its casualties relatively light (148 deaths in battle). Estimates of Iraq's casualties ranged from 25,000 to 100,000 deaths. Although the conflict had lasted scarcely six weeks, the destruction of highways, bridges, communications, and other infrastructure in both Iraq and Kuwait was enormous.

In a controversial decision, Bush decided not to force Saddam Hussein's ouster, an ambitious goal that the UN had never approved and that military advisers had considered costly to achieve. Instead, the United States, backed by the UN, maintained its economic pressure, worked to dismantle Iraq's nuclear and bacteriological capabilities, and enforced a "no-fly" zone over northern Iraq to protect the Kurdish population, which was being persecuted by Saddam Hussein. The government of Iraq survived, still headed by Saddam Hussein, an implacable foe of the

The Destruction of Iraqi Forces, 1991 • The brief Persian Gulf War of 1991 demonstrated the degree of firepower that the technologically sophisticated U.S. military could bring to bear on global conflicts in the post–Cold War era.

United States. Even so, the Persian Gulf War boosted George Bush's popularity and seemed to assure his reelection.

Bush, however, proved less adept in articulating long-term diplomatic goals for a post–Cold War world than in conducting a brief military confrontation. The end of the Cold War had eliminated some foreign policy issues, but new ones emerged. Turmoil broke out in some of the former Soviet provinces, and Russia struggled to develop a private-property, free-market economy. Full-scale warfare erupted among the states of the former Yugoslavia, with Serbians launching a brutal campaign of aggrandizement and "ethnic cleansing" against Bosnian Muslims. In the Far East, Japan's economic strength prompted Americans to grumble about adverse trade balances and unfair competition. In Africa, when severe famine struck the country of Somalia, Bush ordered in American troops to establish humanitarian supply lines, but the American public remained wary of this military mission.

In confronting such diverse global issues, Bush met with mixed success. He could claim significant foreign policy accomplishments: He had assembled and held together an international coalition against Iraq, had constructively assisted the transition in Russia and Eastern Europe at the end of the Cold War, and had begun a process of trade liberalization that his successor would implement. But when Bush spoke about creating a "new world order," neither he nor his advisers could explain just what that meant. The old reference points that had defined national security, especially containment of the Soviet enemy, had disappeared, and Bush never effectively articulated a new vision that could firmly establish his reputation as a foreign policy leader.

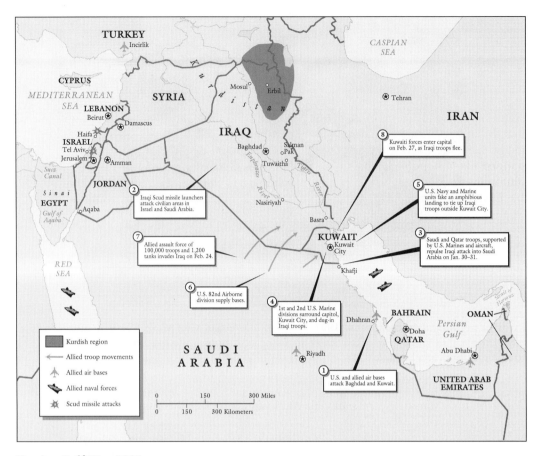

Persian Gulf War, 1991

Toward the 21st Century

Flux and uncertainty marked politics during the 1990s. The unraveling of George Bush's presidency and the mercurial rise of Democrat Bill Clinton in 1992 was followed, in congressional elections two years later, by a surprising Republican triumph. These abrupt swings suggested, among other things, a suspicion of national political leaders and a declining loyalty to political parties, particularly among people who had come to oppose many of the domestic policies that had been championed by the Democratic Party since the 1930s.

The Election of 1992

The inability to portray a coherent vision of either foreign or domestic policy threatened Bush's reelection and forced him to make concessions to the New Right. Dan Quayle returned as his running mate, and the president allowed conservative activists to dominate the 1992 Republican national convention. They talked about "a religious war" for "the soul of America" and pictured Democrats as the enemies of "family values." But conservative Democrats and independents, who had supported Ronald Reagan and George Bush in the previous three presidential elections, found this rhetoric no substitute for policies that addressed domestic problems, particularly the sluggish economy.

Not surprisingly, Bush's Democratic challenger, Governor Bill Clinton of Arkansas, did concentrate on economic issues, pledging to increase government spending for job creation and long-term economic growth. Addressing a concern that apparently cut across partisan lines, Clinton promised a comprehensive revision of the nation's health care system. On other domestic issues, Clinton almost sounded like a Republican. "It's time to end this [welfare] system as we know it," Clinton insisted. "People who can work ought to go to work, and no one should be able to stay on welfare forever." He claimed to be a "new Democrat" who would reduce taxes for middle-class Americans, cut the federal deficit, and shrink the size of government. Clinton, in short, highlighted economic issues while making it difficult for Bush to label him as a "big government" liberal.

This focus on economics also helped to deflect attention from social-cultural issues on which Clinton appeared vulnerable. As a college student in the 1960s, he had not only avoided service in Vietnam but also had participated in antiwar demonstrations while in England as a Rhodes Scholar. When Bush, a decorated veteran of the Second World War, challenged Clinton's patriotism, Clinton countered by emphasizing, rather than repudiating, his roots in the rock 'n' roll and Vietnam War generation. He became the first presidential candidate to campaign on MTV. In addition, he chose Senator Albert Gore, who had served in Vietnam, as his running mate. And when Clinton's personal life and financial dealings in Arkansas drew Republican fire, Bill and Hillary Rodham Clinton acknowledged past problems but defended their marriage as an effective, ongoing partnership. Hillary Rodham Clinton's career as a lawyer and advocate for children's issues, the couple insisted, would be an asset to a Clinton presidency.

The 1992 presidential campaign was enlivened by the third-party candidacy of Ross Perot, a billionaire from Texas who spent $60 million of his own money on a quixotic run for the White House. A blunt, folksy speaker, Perot entered politics by appearing on TV and radio talk shows to expound a quasi-conspiratorial view of recent U.S. history: Political insiders in Washington, both Republicans and Democrats, had created a "mess" that insulted the common sense of the American people and satisfied only special interests. "The last time we all sacrificed together," Perot argued, was during the Second World War. If people would only come together in the 1990s as they had done in the 1940s, he claimed, they could "take back our country." After suddenly dropping out of the presidential race in July, the unpredictable Perot returned in October with a $37 million media blitz that apparently hurt Bush more than Clinton.

Clinton won by a comfortable margin. He garnered 43 percent of the popular vote and won 370 electoral votes by carrying 32 states and the District of Columbia. Perot gained no electoral votes but did attract 19 million popular votes. Meanwhile, the 1992 election was a crushing defeat for George Bush. He won a majority only among white Protestants in the South. In contrast, Clinton carried the Jewish, African American, and Latino vote by large margins, and he even gained a plurality among people who had served in the Vietnam War. He also ran very well among independents, voters whom Reagan and Bush had carried during the 1980s and on whom Perot had counted in 1992. Perhaps most surprising, about 55 percent of eligible voters went to the polls, a turnout that reversed 32 years of steady decline in voter participation.

Clinton's Domestic Policies

Bill Clinton, the first Democratic president in 12 years and the first from the generation that had come of age during the Vietnam era, brought an emphasis on youth, vitality, and cultural diversity to Washington. The African American author Maya Angelou delivered a poem especially commissioned for his inauguration, and there were different inaugural balls for different musical tastes, including one (broadcast live on MTV) that featured rock 'n' roll. Clinton's initial appointments underscored diversity. His first cabinet included three African Americans and two Latinos; three cabinet posts went to women. As his first nomination to the Supreme Court, he chose Ruth Bader Ginsburg, only the second woman to sit on the Court. And as representative to the United Nations, Clinton named Madeleine Albright, a woman who would become the country's first female secretary of state during his second term.

On social issues, Clinton claimed several victories during his first term. He ended the Reagan era's ban on abortion counseling in family planning clinics; pushed a family leave program for working parents through Congress; established a program, Americorps, that allowed students to repay their college loans through community service; and secured passage of the Brady Bill, which instituted a five-day waiting period for the purchase of handguns. Limited college loan and youth training programs also received funding.

But health care reform, a central feature of Clinton's 1992 campaign, collapsed. Hillary Rodham Clinton led a task force that produced a plan so complex that few understood it; worse, it pleased virtually no one. Republicans used the health care fiasco to paint Clinton, more successfully than during the 1992 campaign, as an advocate of "big government" spending and bureaucratic feather-bedding. The administration's health care proposal quickly died in Congress.

Meanwhile, Clinton faced problems of his own. Hillary Rodham Clinton's prominent role in the failed health care effort fueled criticism of her public activities, and the Clintons' joint involvement in financial dealings in Arkansas—particularly those connected to a bankrupt S&L and to a failed land development called "Whitewater"—drew renewed criticism. In August 1994 Kenneth Starr, a Republican, was appointed as an independent prosecutor charged with investigating the allegations. Starr soon negotiated guilty pleas from several people in Arkansas who were connected to Whitewater and pressed forward with an investigation that seemed aimed at securing an indictment against one of the Clintons. Led by the outspoken Rush Limbaugh, conservative talk show hosts leveled a nonstop barrage of criticism against the president. The elections of 1994 showcased the conservative movement, which had been gaining strength for several decades, and highlighted Clinton's vulnerabilities.

The 1994 elections brought a dramatic GOP victory. Republicans secured control of both houses of Congress for the first time in 40 years; they won several new governorships; gained ground in most state legislatures; and made significant headway in many city and county elections, particularly across the South. Led by Representative Newt Gingrich of Georgia, conservative Republicans hailed these gains as a mandate for their new agenda called the "Contract with America," which aimed at rolling back federal spending and a variety of governmental programs and regulations.

Congressional Republicans, however, overplayed their hand. Opinion polls suggested that people found Gingrich, the GOP's primary spokesperson, less trustworthy and competent than the president, whose character and policies the Republicans planned to assail during the two years leading up to the 1996 elections. Moreover, surveys also showed little support for the kind of thoroughgoing "revolution" against federal programs that was being proposed by the conservatives in Congress. When conflict between the Democratic president and GOP Congress over budget issues led to two brief shutdowns of many government agencies (November 14–20, 1995, and December 16, 1995–January 4, 1996), most people blamed the Republicans in Congress, rather than the White House, for the impasse.

Most important, while Washington seemed to have problems moving in any direction, a revived U.S. economy worked to Clinton's advantage. As low rates of inflation accompanied steady economic growth, new jobs were created at a rate that surpassed even the president's most optimistic predictions. Although the specific benefits of this general expansion were distributed almost as unequally as those that had accompanied the "economic miracle" of the 1980s, many people, especially those most likely to vote, saw their economic fortunes improving dramatically during Clinton's first term. The stock exchanges, in the midst of the longest bull market in the nation's history, created hundreds of thousands of new millionaires.

A backlash against the budget gridlock of 1995, together with the signs of continued economic growth, inclined both the White House and Congress to cooperate on overhauling the welfare system. In his 1996 State of the Union address, the president declared that "the era of big government is over." Repudiating the legacy of the New Deal and Great Society, Clinton and the Republican Congress began to redesign the nation's welfare policies.

The Personal Responsibility and Work Opportunity Reconciliation Act of 1996 represented a series of compromises that pleased conservatives more than liberals. Relatively noncontroversial sections of the law tightened collection of child support payments and reorganized nutrition and child care programs. Clinton, while voicing concern about provisions that cut the Food Stamp program and benefits for recent immigrants, embraced the law's central feature: the replacement of the AFDC program, which had promised a minimum level of funds and social services to poor families headed by single unemployed women, by a flexible system of block grants to individual states. Under the new program, entitled Temporary Assistance to Needy Families (TANF), states were to design their own welfare-to-work programs under broad federal guidelines.

TANF, which effectively ended the welfare system that had been in place since the New Deal, provoked bitter controversy. Its proponents claimed it would encourage states to experiment with new programs, many of which were to be developed by private corporations, that would reduce their welfare costs. Critics worried that its provisions, including those that limited a person to five years of government assistance during his or her lifetime and authorized states to cut off support if recipients did not find employment within two years, ignored the difficulty that people without job skills faced. They also feared the impact that TANF might have on daily lives of children, especially if states provided inadequate child care, nutritional, and medical care programs. Studies showed that one of every four children, including many from families in which at least one parent was working, already lived in poverty. By pushing further debate over such issues into the future, however, the new welfare law helped to remove a number of potential domestic issues from the political campaign of 1996, a turn that especially helped Bill Clinton.

Clinton's Foreign Policy

Clinton, like Bush, faced the task of reorienting U.S. foreign policy. For nearly half a century, anticommunism and rivalry with the Soviet Union had shaped policy-making. The United States now had to redefine national security to fit a multipolar world. Clinton often articulated an expansive, internationalist vision: improving relations with the UN, expanding NATO, advancing human rights and democracy abroad, reducing nuclear threats, working on global environmental concerns, and promoting free-market policies. During both of his presidential campaigns, however, Clinton focused primarily on domestic issues, and the public seemed suspicious of new international commitments.

One of the most perplexing issues involved revamping the U.S. military for the post–Cold War world. Under what conditions should U.S. troops participate in "peacekeeping" missions? Some people saw any reluctance to use military power as a "new isolationism." Others cautioned against drifting into long-term, ill-defined commitments.

Several trouble spots sparked debate. In the African country of Somalia, U.S. troops, under the umbrella of a UN mission, had been assisting a humanitarian effort to provide food and relief supplies since May 1992. Caught in factional fighting, however, U.S. troops suffered well-publicized casualties, and Clinton ordered a pullout during the spring of 1994. In Haiti, closer to home, U.S. interests seemed clearer, and Clinton vowed to help reestablish Haiti's elected president, Jean-Bertrand Aristide. In September 1994, the first 3,000 of a projected force of 15,000 troops landed in Haiti, in cooperation with the UN, and last-minute negotiations by former president Jimmy Carter persuaded the Haitian military peacefully to step aside. After six months, with Aristide in power and political institutions functioning again, U.S. soldiers handed over the responsibility for keeping civil order to UN forces, and most returned home. In the former Yugoslavia, the United States also committed troops, under the umbrella of NATO, to halt the massacre of Bosnian Muslims by Bosnian Serbs and to oversee a cease-fire and peace-building process that all parties to the conflict had accepted in the U.S.-brokered Dayton (Ohio) accords of 1995.

To clarify U.S. policy related to peacekeeping efforts, in January 1994 Clinton announced that Washington would act only in urgent situations, only if other countries shared the cost, and only if American troops remained primarily under U.S. command.

Meanwhile, other post–Cold War concerns drew Clinton's attention. In February 1994, the CIA was rocked by the biggest scandal of its history when a high ranking official, Aldrich Ames, and his wife were arrested on charges of selling information to the Soviet Union and Russia over the preceding decade, contributing to the deaths of several CIA agents. Ames subsequently pled guilty to espionage and was sentenced to life in prison; his wife received a lesser sentence. A year later, it was revealed that the CIA had maintained connections to unsavory death squads in Guatemala, which had been responsible for murdering American citizens in that country. Mindful of calls for reform of the agency, the CIA tried to chart new, post–Cold War missions. International drug traffickers and other criminal syndicates, some specializing in nuclear materials, posed potential threats. And the CIA also targeted international terrorism. In early 1993, a bomb rocked the World Trade Center in New York City, killing 6 people and injuring nearly 1,000. Investigators arrested four Muslims, who had links to previous terrorist acts, and cited the incident as proof that the United States needed a global intelligence network.

Clinton also shaped new policies on weapons of mass destruction. He dismantled some of the U.S. nuclear arsenal and tried to curtail the potential danger from other nuclear powers. When the Soviet Union collapsed and its nuclear weapons became dispersed among several independent states, the Clinton administration feared these might be sold on the black market to terrorists. In early 1994 Clinton increased economic aid for the newly independent state of Ukraine, then the third greatest nuclear power in the world, in return for promises to disarm its 1,600 warheads. In the same year, a highly secret "Project Sapphire" transferred enriched uranium stocks from Kazakstan, another former Soviet state, to storage facilities in the United States. Also, Jimmy Carter, responding to Clinton's request, helped negotiate a complicated agreement with North Korea over nuclear weapons, signed in 1994. North Korea agreed to begin dismantling its nuclear program and permit international inspections as soon as the United States helped it construct safer, lightwater nuclear reactors for its energy needs. Throughout the rest of the world, the United States successfully pressed many nations to sign a new Nuclear Nonproliferation Treaty in the spring of 1995. In early 1998, Clinton went to the brink of war with Iraq to maintain international inspections of Saddam Hussein's weapons programs, which experts feared were developing dangerous chemical and biological capabilities.

A principal goal of Clinton's foreign policy was to lower trade barriers and expand global markets. Building on the Reagan-Bush legacy, Clinton argued that such policies would boost prosperity and, in turn, foster democracy around the world. Consequently, his administration consummated several historic trade agreements. Despite opposition from labor unions and other groups that usually supported his Democratic Party, Clinton strongly backed the North American Free Trade Agreement (NAFTA), which projected cutting tariffs and eliminating other trade barriers between the United States, Canada, and Mexico over a 15-year period. After adding new provisions on labor and environmental issues, in December 1993 he muscled the bill through Congress in a close vote that depended on Republican support. NAFTA took effect on January 1, 1994. Then, in early 1995, Mexico's severe debt crisis and a dramatic devaluation of its peso prompted Clinton to extend a $20 billion loan from America's Exchange Stabilization Fund, a unprecedented act that stabilized the economy of this important trading partner. Clinton's trade negotiators completed the so-called "Uruguay Round" of the General Agreement on Trade and Tariffs (GATT) in late 1993, and in early 1995 GATT was replaced by a new World Trade Organization (WTO), a more powerful multilateral group created to enlarge world trade by implementing new agreements and mediating disputes. Clinton also reversed his election-year position and granted China, despite its dismal record on human rights, equal trading status with other nations. To justify this turnaround, Clinton argued that increased trade with China would contribute to long-term pressures for democratization there. Similarly, in February 1994, the United States ended its 19-year-old trade embargo against Vietnam, and American traders began doing business with a regime that had once been cast as a major threat to U.S. global interests.

Clinton claimed that all of these measures on behalf of market expansion, along with the emergence of free-market economies in Eastern Europe and Latin America, provided the framework for a new era of global prosperity. When Asian economies faltered during 1998, the president strongly supported acting with the International Monetary Fund to provide huge emergency credits to reform and restore financial systems from Korea to Indonesia.

Election of 1996 and Aftermath

The election of 1996 brought few political changes. The special Whitewater prosecutor had failed, despite GOP hopes, to secure any new indictments, and "corruption"

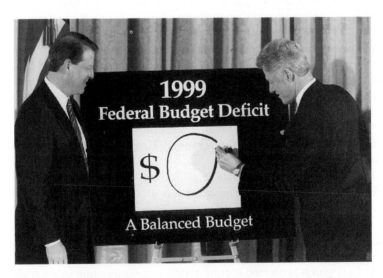

End of the Federal Budget Deficit? • After more than two decades of controversy about annual federal deficits—yearly governmental outlays that exceeded tax revenues—President Bill Clinton and Vice President Al Gore unveil a budget for Fiscal Year 1999 that projected no deficit, the first such balanced budget since 1976. The situation came about through cooperation in budget reductions between the White House and the Republican-controlled Congress and, more importantly, from a surging economy that swelled the federal treasury with greater tax revenues.

in the White House never became a major issue during the campaign. The Clinton-Gore team, benefiting from the generally burgeoning economy, defeated the Republican ticket of Bob Dole and Jack Kemp by about the same margin that it had beaten Bush and Quayle in 1992. (In contrast to 1992, the independent candidacy of Ross Perot made almost no impact in 1996.) Exit polls revealed that Clinton and most other Democrats ran particularly well among African Americans, women, and Hispanic voters. Republicans retained control of Congress and gained several new governorships, but Democrats still held a majority of the seats in state legislatures, a sign that many voters found ticket-splitting (voting for both Democrats and Republicans) a sensible course. After the election, Clinton and congressional Republicans responded by cooperating to pass legislation that promised broadly distributed tax cuts and phased reductions in the federal deficit. In his 1998 State of the Union address, Clinton proudly proclaimed that the budget deficit would soon move to zero, and both parties even began debating what might be done with potential surpluses.

After the election of 1996, however, national politics increasingly came to revolve around Starr's investigations of the president and his administration. The White House had hoped to focus Clinton's second term on a new "national conversation" about racial issues and on programs to improve education, but the media highlighted a seemingly endless array of legal allegations leveled against the president and his

The Clinton Presidency at High Tide • A January 26, 1998, magazine cover reflects the stature that Bill Clinton, a "new Democrat," had achieved after six years in office.

associates. While Starr continued to press forward on matters related to the involvement of the Clintons in the Whitewater land deal, he broadened his inquiry to include claims that the president had carried on a sexual relationship with a White House intern, Monica Lewinsky, and that he had tried to obstruct justice by either committing perjury himself or by pressuring others to offer false accounts of his behavior.

Clinton's presidency, though still judged to be an overwhelming success by a majority of people in public opinion surveys, came under constant scrutiny from Republicans and a broad cross-section of the media. Republicans charged the White House with impeding Starr's investigation and the president of lying, and some began to talk about impeaching the president for obstruction of justice. The president's defenders charged Starr's office with engaging in a partisan vendetta against Clinton, leaking secret testimony to the media, and working in concert with the conservative political action committees that were financing a private lawsuit against the president by Paula Corbin Jones for an incident of sexual harassment that had allegedly occurred when Clinton had been governor of Arkansas. Media outlets, particularly those on cable

Will the Clinton Presidency Sink? • Only one week after celebrating Bill Clinton's accomplishments as chief executive, *U.S. News & World Report* joined the rest of the media in speculating about the end of his presidency because of allegations that he had lied in a legal deposition about sexual involvement with a White House employee. Clinton spent much of his second term in office trying to respond to an aggressive investigation, headed by independent prosecutor Kenneth Starr, into his business and personal life.

television, framed the president's problems with sensationalized themes such as "The White House Under Siege." But with economic statistics remaining positive, Clinton's approval rating went up, while that of Starr plummeted.

In mid-August 1998, Starr obtained secret grand jury testimony from Lewinsky and, later, Clinton. Afterward, Clinton went on national television to concede an "inappropriate" personal relationship with Lewinsky, deny any legal wrongdoing, and condemn Starr's investigation into his "private" life. Required to report to Congress, the independent prosecutor submitted a report in September that outlined 11 possible grounds for impeachment (including perjury and obstruction of justice) and, within weeks, the House of Representatives voted to begin impeachment hearings against Clinton.

Conclusion

Winds of change swept over American life during the final 25 years of the 20th century. In foreign policy, people had to adjust to the trauma of Vietnam, to the sudden end of the Cold War, and to a global environment in which U.S. economic and strategic interests seemed in a state of constant flux. How and where should U.S. military and economic power—which remained considerable—be exercised?

At home, the Watergate scandal and the economic problems of the 1970s helped to breed cynicism about government. Support for extending the power of the national government in order to address domestic problems slowly eroded. Meanwhile, the "Reagan Revolution" of the 1980s marked the emergence of a new conservative movement that had been born in the shadow of Lyndon Johnson's Great Society. The strength of the Republican Party, which by 1996 could claim nearly as many supporters as the once-dominant Democratic Party, and the presidency of Bill Clinton, a "new Democrat" who declared that the era of "big government" had ended, suggested that many people now rejected the idea that increasing the power of the government in Washington meant progress. But how, without mobilizing the power of the national government, could a diverse nation confront economic and social problems? As the 21st century drew near, Americans continued to debate how to deal with the diverse forces that were transforming the country.

Chronology

1974 Nixon resigns and Ford becomes president; Ford soon pardons Nixon

1975 South Vietnam falls to North Vietnam • Ford asserts U.S. power in *Mayaquez* incident

1976 Jimmy Carter elected president

1978 Carter helps negotiate Camp David peace accords on Middle East

1979 Soviet Union invades Afghanistan • Sandinista Party comes to power in Nicaragua • U.S. hostages seized in Iran

1980 Reagan elected president • U.S. hostages in Iran released

1981 Reagan tax cut passed • Economic downturn, the most severe since 1930s, begins

1983 U.S. troops removed from Lebanon • U.S. troops invade Grenada • Reagan announces SDI ("Star Wars") program

1984 Reagan defeats Walter Mondale

1986 Reagan administration rocked by revelation of Iran-*Contra* affair

1988 George Bush defeats Michael Dukakis in presidential election

1989 Communist regimes in Eastern Europe collapse; Berlin Wall falls • Cold War, in effect, ends

1990 Bush angers conservative Republicans by agreeing to a tax increase

1991 Bush orchestrates Persian Gulf War against Iraq

1992 Bill Clinton defeats Bush and third-party candidate Ross Perot in presidential race

1993 Congress approves North American Free Trade Agreement (NAFTA) and the General Agreement on Trade and Tariffs (GATT)

1994 Republicans gain control of both houses of Congress and pledge to enact their "Contract with America"

1995 Special prosecutor Kenneth Starr takes over the investigation of "Whitewater" allegations

1996 Personal Responsibility and Work Opportunity Reconciliation Act becomes first major overhaul of the national welfare system since the 1930s • Clinton defeats Robert Dole in the presidential race

1997 Congress and the White House agree on legislation aimed at reducing taxes and rolling back the federal deficit

Suggested Readings

General Surveys of Recent Political Trends

General surveys of recent political trends include Martin T. Wattenberg, *The Decline of American Political Parties, 1952–1980* (1984); Ryan Barilleaux, *The Post-Modern Presidency: The Office After Ronald Reagan* (1988); Kathleen Hall Jamieson, *Packaging the Presidency: A History and Criticism of Presidential Campaign Advertising* (3rd ed., 1996); William Greider, *Who Will Tell the People: The Betrayal of American Democracy* (1992); Thomas Byrne and Mary D. Edsall, *Chain Reaction: The Impact of Race, Rights, and Taxes on American Politics* (1992); Kevin Phillips, *Boiling Point: Republicans, Democrats, and the Decline of Middle Class Prosperity* (1993); William C. Berman *America's Right Turn: From Nixon to Bush* (1994); Ronald Radosh, *Divided They Fell: The Demise of the Democratic Party, 1964–1996 (1996)*; and Philip John Davies, *An American Quarter Century: U.S. Politics from Vietnam to Clinton* (1995).

Foreign Policy

On general trends and specific episodes in foreign policy, see Paul Kennedy, *The Rise and Fall of the Great Powers: Economic Change and Military Conflict from 1500 to 2000* (1987); Walter LaFeber, *Inevitable Revolutions: The United States in Central America* (1983); Raymond Garthoff, *Detente and Confrontation: American-Soviet Relations from Nixon to Reagan* (1985); Gaddis Smith, *Morality Reason, and Power: American Diplomacy in the Carter Years* (1986) and *The Last Years of the Monroe Doctrine, 1945–1993*; Herbert D. Rosenbaum and Alexej Ugrinsky, eds. *Jimmy Carter: Foreign Policy and Post-Presidential Years* (1994); Richard C. Thornton, *The Carter Years: Toward a New Global Order* (1991); David Skidmore, *Reversing Course: Carter's Foreign Policy, Domestic Politics, and the Failure of Reform* (1996); Timothy P. Maga, *The World of Jimmy Carter: U.S. Foreign Policy, 1977–1981* (1994); Joanna Spear, *Carter and Arms: Implementing the Carter Administration's Arms Transfer Restraint Policy* (1995); John Dumbrell, *American Foreign Policy: Carter to Clinton* (1996); Robert A. Pastor, *Whirlpool: U.S. Foreign Policy Toward Latin America and the Caribbean* (1992); Raymond Garthoff, *The Great Transition: America-Soviet Relations and the End of the Cold War* (1994); Keith L. Nelson, *The Making of Detente: Soviet-American Relations in the Shadow of Vietnam* (1995); Michael R. Beschloss and Strobe Talbott, *At the Highest Levels: The Inside Story of the End of the Cold War* (1993); Theodore Draper, *A Very Thin Line: The Iran-Contra Affairs* (1991); Gary Sick, *October Surprise: America's Hostages in Iran and the Election of Ronald Reagan* (1991); Morris H. Morley, ed. *Crisis and Confrontation: Ronald Reagan's Foreign Policy* (1988); H. Bruce Franklin, *War Stars: The Superweapon and the American Imagination* (1988); John Lewis Gaddis, *The United States and the End of the Cold War: Implications, Reconsiderations, Provocations* (1991) and *We Now Know* (1997); Michael Hogan, ed., *The End of the Cold War: Its Meaning and Implications* (1992).

The Gulf War

For the Gulf War, specifically, see Lawrence Freedman and Efraim Karsh, *The Gulf Conflict, 1990–1991: Diplomacy and War in the New World Order* (1993); Dilip Hiro, *Desert Shield to Desert Storm: The Second Gulf War* (1992); Douglas Kellner, *The Persian Gulf TV War* (1992); Richard Hallion, *Storm Over Iraq: Air Power and the Gulf War* (1992); Susan Jeffords and Lauren Rabinovitz, eds. *Seeing Through the Media: The Persian Gulf War* (1994); Frank N. Schubert and Theresa L. Kraus, *The Whirlwind War: The United States Army in Operations Desert Shield and Desert Storm* (1995).

The Brief Ford Presidency

On the brief Ford presidency, see Edward L. and Frederick H. Schapsmeier, *Gerald R. Ford's Date with Destiny: A Political Biography* (1989); James Cannon, *Time and Chance: Gerald Ford's Appointment with History* (1994); John R. Greene, *The Presidency of Gerald R. Ford* (1995); and John F. Guilmartin Jr., *A Very Short War: The Mayaguez and the Battle of Koh Tang* (1995).

The Carter Years

On the Carter years, see Burton I. Kaufman, *The Presidency of James Earl Carter Jr.* (1993); Betty Glad, *Jimmy Carter: In Search of the Great White House* (1980); Erwin C. Hargrove, *Jimmy Carter as President* (1988); Garland Haas, *Jimmy Carter and the Politics of Frustration* (1992); Kenneth Morris, *Jimmy Carter: American Moralist* (1996); Anthony S. Campagna, *Economic Policy in the Carter Administration* (1995); and Gary M. Fink and Hugh Davis Graham, *The Carter Presidency: Policy Choices in the Post–New Deal Era* (1998).

The Reagan Era

On the Reagan era, see Sidney Blumenthal and Thomas Byrne Edsall, eds., *The Reagan Legacy* (1988); Robert Dallek, *Ronald Reagan: The Politics of Symbolism* (1984); Garry Wills, *Reagan's America: Innocents at Home* (1987); Robert E. Denton Jr., *The Primetime Presidency of Ronald Reagan* (1988); Michael Schaller, *Reckoning With Reagan* (1992); James E. Combs, *The Reagan Range: The Nostalgic Myth in American Politics* (1993); William Pemberton, *Exit with Honor: The Life and Presidency of Ronald Reagan* (1997); John Lofand, *Polite Protesters: The American Peace Movement of the 1980s* (1993); Raymond Wolters, *Right Turn: William Bradford Reynolds, the Reagan Administration, and Black Civil Rights* (1996); Diane Vaughan, *The Challenger Launch Decision: Risky Technology, Culture and Deviance at NASA* (1997); and Beth A. Fischer, *The Reagan Reversal: Foreign Policy at the End of the Cold War* (1998).

The Bush Presidency

On the Bush presidency see Michael Duffy and Dan Goodgame, *Marching in Place: The Status Quo Presidency of George Bush* (1992); David Mervin, *George Bush and the Guardian Presidency* (1996); John Podhoretz, *Hell of a Ride: Backstage at the White House Follies 1989–1993* (1993); Charles Kolb, *White House Daze: The Unmaking of Domestic Policy in the Bush Years* (1994); and Herbert S. Parmet, *George Bush: The Life of a Lone Star Yankee* (1997).

Politics of the 1990s

On the politics of the 1990s, see Jack W. Germond and Jules Witcover, *Mad as Hell: Revolt at the Ballot Box 1992* (1993); David Maraniss, *First in His Class: A Biography of Bill Clinton* (1995); Bob Woodward, *The Agenda: Inside the Clinton White House* (1994); Michael Lienesch, *Redeeming America; Piety and Politics in the New Christian Right* (1993); James Gibson, *Warrior Dreams: Paramilitary Culture in*

Post Vietnam America (1994); Sara Diamond, *Roads to Dominion: Right-Wing Power and Political Power in the United States* (1995); Catherine McNicol Stock, *Rural Radicals: Righteous Rage in the American Grain* (1996); Kathryn S. Olmsted, *Challenging the Secret Government: The Post-Watergate Investigations of the CIA and the FBI* (1996); Theda Skocpol, *Boomerang: Clinton's Health Security Effort and the Turn against Government in U.S. Politics* (1996); Jacob S. Hacker, *The Road to Nowhere: The Genesis of President Clinton's Plan for Health Security* (1997); John Hohenberg, *Reelecting Bill Clinton: Why America Chose a "New" Democrat* (1997); and Robert Reich, *Locked in the Cabinet* (1997).

Videos

The "A & E Biography Series" contains a number of videos appropriate for these years, including *Jimmy Carter: To the White House and Beyond* (1995). The Gulf War is covered in *A Line in the Sand* (1990), *Desert Triumph* (1991), a three-part series, and *The Gulf War* (1997), also a three-part series. *Rush to Judgment: The Anita Hill Story* (1997) offers interviews with both advocates and critics of Justice Clarence Thomas's chief accuser. *The War Room* (1994) provides a candid, behind-the-scenes look at the 1992 Clinton campaign. *An American Journey: The Great Society to the Reagan Revolution* (1998) is a five-part overview of the period.

Appendix

**The Constitution of the
United States of America**

Population of the United States, 1890–1998

Presidential Elections, 1892–1996

**Presidents, Vice Presidents, and Cabinet
Members (since 1893)**

The Constitution of the United States of America

We the People of the United States, in Order to form a more perfect Union, establish Justice, insure domestic Tranquility, provide for the common defence, promote the general Welfare, and secure the Blessings of Liberty to ourselves and our Posterity, do ordain and establish this Constitution for the United States of America.

Article I.

SECTION 1. All legislative Powers herein granted shall be vested in a Congress of the United States, which shall consist of a Senate and House of Representatives.

SECTION 2. The House of Representatives shall be composed of Members chosen every second Year by the People of the several States, and the Electors in each State shall have the Qualifications requisite for Electors of the most numerous Branch of the State Legislature.

No Person shall be a Representative who shall not have attained to the Age of twenty five Years, and been seven Years a Citizen of the United States, and who shall not, when elected, be an Inhabitant of that State in which he shall be chosen.

Representatives and direct Taxes[1] shall be apportioned among the several States which may be included within this Union, according to their respective Numbers, which shall be determined by adding to the whole Number of free Persons, including those bound to Service for a Term of Years, and excluding Indians not taxed, three fifths of all other Persons.[2] The actual Enumeration shall be made within three Years after the first Meeting of the Congress of the United States, and within every subsequent Term of ten Years, in such Manner as they shall by Law direct. The Number of Representatives shall not exceed one for every thirty Thousand, but each State shall have at Least one Representative; and until such enumeration shall be made, the State of New Hampshire shall be entitled to chuse three; Massachusetts eight; Rhode Island and Providence Plantations one; Connecticut five; New York six; New Jersey four; Pennsylvania eight; Delaware one; Maryland six; Virginia ten; North Carolina five; South Carolina five; and Georgia three.

When vacancies happen in the Representation from any State, the Executive Authority thereof shall issue Writs of Election to fill such Vacancies.

The House of Representatives shall chuse their Speaker and other Officers; and shall have the sole Power of Impeachment.

SECTION 3. The Senate of the United States shall be composed of two Senators from each State, chosen by the Legislature thereof, for six Years; and each Senator shall have one Vote.[3]

Immediately after they shall be assembled in Consequence of the first Election, they shall be divided as equally as may be into three Classes. The Seats of the Senators of the first Class shall be vacated at the Expiration of the second Year, of the

---

Text is from the engrossed copy in the National Archives. Original spelling, capitalization, and punctuation have been retained.

[1]Modified by the Sixteenth Amendment.

[2]Replaced by the Fourteenth Amendment.

[3]Superseded by the Seventeenth Amendment.

second Class at the Expiration of the fourth Year, and of the third Class at the Expiration of the sixth Year, so that one third may be chosen every second Year; and if Vacancies happen by Resignation, or otherwise, during the Recess of the Legislature of any State, the Executive thereof may make temporary Appointments until the next Meeting of the Legislature, which shall then fill such Vacancies.[4]

No Person shall be a Senator who shall not have attained to the Age of thirty Years, and been nine Years a Citizen of the United States, and who shall not, when elected, be an Inhabitant of that State for which he shall be chosen.

The Vice President of the United States shall be President of the Senate, but shall have no Vote, unless they be equally divided.

The Senate shall chuse their other Officers, and also a President pro tempore, in the Absence of the Vice President, or when he shall exercise the Office of President of the United States.

The Senate shall have the sole Power to try all Impeachments. When sitting for that Purpose, they shall be on Oath or Affirmation. When the President of the United States is tried, the Chief Justice shall preside: And no Person shall be convicted without the Concurrence of two thirds of the Members present.

Judgment in Cases of Impeachment shall not extend further than to removal from Office, and disqualification to hold and enjoy any Office of honor, Trust or Profit under the United States: but the Party convicted shall nevertheless be liable and subject to Indictment, Trial, Judgment and Punishment, according to Law.

SECTION 4. The Times, Places and Manner of holding Elections for Senators and Representatives, shall be prescribed in each State by the Legislature thereof, but the Congress may at any time by Law make or alter such Regulation, except as to the Places of chusing Senators.

The Congress shall assemble at least once in every Year, and such Meeting shall be on the first Monday in December, unless they shall by Law appoint a different Day.[5]

SECTION 5. Each House shall be the Judge of the Elections, Returns and Qualifications of its own Members, and a Majority of each shall constitute a Quorum to do Business; but a smaller Number may adjourn from day to day, and may be authorized to compel the Attendance of absent Members, in such Manner, and under such Penalties as each House may provide.

Each House may determine the Rules of its Proceedings, punish its Members for disorderly Behaviour, and, with the Concurrence of two thirds, expel a Member.

Each House shall keep a Journal of its Proceedings, and from time to time publish the same, excepting such Parts as may in their Judgment require Secrecy; and the Yeas and Nays of the Members of either House on any question shall, at the Desire of one fifth of those Present, be entered on the Journal.

Neither House, during the Session of Congress, shall, without the Consent of the other, adjourn for more than three days, nor to any other Place than that in which the two Houses shall be sitting.

SECTION 6. The Senators and Representatives shall receive a Compensation for their Services, to be ascertained by Law, and paid out of the Treasury of the United

---

[4]Modified by the Seventeenth Amendment.

[5]Superseded by the Twentieth Amendment.

States. They shall in all Cases, except Treason, Felony and Breach of the Peace, be privileged from Arrest during their Attendance at the Session of their respective Houses, and in going to and returning from the same; and for any Speech or Debate in either House, they shall not be questioned in any other Place.

No Senator or Representative shall, during the Time for which he was elected, be appointed to any civil Office under the Authority of the United States, which shall have been created, or the Emoluments whereof shall have been encreased during such time; and no Person holding any Office under the United States, shall be a Member of either House during his Continuance in Office.

SECTION 7. All Bills for raising Revenue shall originate in the House of Representatives; but the Senate may propose or concur with Amendments as on other Bills.

Every Bill which shall have passed the House of Representatives and the Senate shall, before it become a Law, be presented to the President of the United States; If he approve he shall sign it, but if not he shall return it, with his Objections to that House in which it shall have originated, who shall enter the Objections at large on their Journal, and proceed to reconsider it. If after such Reconsideration two thirds of that House shall agree to pass the Bill, it shall be sent, together with the Objections, to the other House, by which it shall likewise be reconsidered, and if approved by two thirds of that House, it shall become a Law. But in all such Cases the Votes of both Houses shall be determined by yeas and Nays, and the Names of the Persons voting for and against the Bill shall be entered on the Journal of each House respectively. If any Bill shall not be returned by the President within ten Days (Sundays excepted) after it shall have been presented to him, the Same shall be a Law, in like Manner as if he had signed it, unless the Congress by their Adjournment prevent its Return, in which Case it shall not be a Law.

Every Order, Resolution, or Vote to which the Concurrence of the Senate and House of Representatives may be necessary (except on a question of Adjournment) shall be presented to the President of the United States; and before the Same shall take Effect, shall be approved by him, or being disapproved by him shall be repassed by two thirds of the Senate and House of Representatives, according to the Rules and Limitations prescribed in the Case of a Bill.

SECTION 8. The Congress shall have power To lay and collect Taxes, Duties, Imposts and Excises, to pay the Debts and provide for the common Defence and general Welfare of the United States; but all Duties, Imposts and Excises shall be uniform throughout the United States;

To borrow Money on the credit of the United States;

To regulate Commerce with foreign Nations, and among the several States, and with the Indian Tribes;

To establish an uniform Rule of Naturalization, and uniform Laws on the subject of Bankruptcies throughout the United States;

To coin Money, regulate the Value thereof, and of foreign Coin, and fix the Standard of Weights and Measures;

To provide for the Punishment of counterfeiting the Securities and current Coin of the United States;

To establish Post Offices and post Roads;

To promote the Progress of Science and useful Arts, by securing for limited Times to Authors and Inventors the exclusive Right to their respective Writings and Discoveries;

To constitute Tribunals inferior to the supreme Court;

To define and punish Piracies and Felonies committed on the high Seas, and Offences against the Law of Nations;

To declare War, grant Letters of Marque and Reprisal, and make Rules concerning Captures on Land and Water;

To raise and support Armies, but no Appropriation of Money to that Use shall be for a longer Term than two Years;

To provide and maintain a Navy;

To make Rules for the Government and Regulation of the land and naval Forces;

To provide for calling forth the Militia to execute the Laws of the Union, suppress Insurrections and repel Invasions;

To provide for organizing, arming, and disciplining, the Militia, and for governing such Part of them as may be employed in the Service of the United States, reserving to the States respectively, the Appointment of the Officers, and the Authority of training the Militia according to the discipline prescribed by Congress;

To exercise exclusive Legislation in all Cases whatsoever, over such District (not exceeding ten Miles square) as may, by Cession of particular States, and the Acceptance of Congress, become the Seat of the Government of the United States, and to exercise like Authority over all Places purchased by the Consent of the Legislature of the State in which the Same shall be, for the Erection of Forts, Magazines, Arsenals, dock-Yards, and other needful Buildings;—And

To make all Laws which shall be necessary and proper for carrying into Execution the foregoing Powers, and all other Powers vested by this Constitution in the Government of the United States, or in any Department or Officer thereof.

SECTION 9. The Migration or Importation of such Persons as any of the States now existing shall think proper to admit, shall not be prohibited by the Congress prior to the Year one thousand eight hundred and eight, but a Tax or duty may be imposed on such Importation, not exceeding ten dollars for each Person.

The Privilege of the Writ of Habeas Corpus shall not be suspended, unless when in Cases of Rebellion or Invasion the public Safety may require it.

No Bill of Attainder or ex post facto Law shall be passed.

No Capitation, or other direct, Tax shall be laid, unless in Proportion to the Census or Enumeration herein before directed to be taken.

No Tax or Duty shall be laid on Articles exported from any State.

No Preference shall be given by any Regulation of Commerce or Revenue to the Ports of one State over those of another: nor shall Vessels bound to, or from, one State, be obliged to enter, clear, or pay Duties in another.

No Money shall be drawn from the Treasury, but in Consequence of Appropriations made by Law, and a regular Statement and Account of the Receipts and Expenditures of all public Money shall be published from time to time.

No Title of Nobility shall be granted by the United States: And no Person holding any Office of Profit or Trust under them, shall, without the Consent of the Congress, accept of any present, Emolument, Office, or Title, of any kind whatever, from any King, Prince, or foreign State.

SECTION 10. No State shall enter into any Treaty, Alliance, or Confederation; grant Letters of Marque and Reprisal; coin Money; emit Bills of Credit; make any Thing but gold and silver Coin a Tender in Payment of Debts; pass any Bill of Attainder, ex post facto Law, or Law impairing the Obligation of Contracts, or grant any Title of Nobility.

No State shall, without the Consent of the Congress, lay any Imposts or Duties on Imports or Exports, except what may be absolutely necessary for executing its inspection Laws: and the net Produce of all Duties and Imposts, laid by any State on Imports or Exports, shall be for the Use of the Treasury of the United States; and all such Laws shall be subject to the Revision and Controul of the Congress.

No State shall, without the Consent of Congress, lay any Duty of Tonnage, keep Troops, or Ships of War in time of Peace, enter into any Agreement or Compact with another State, or with a foreign Power, or engage in War, unless actually invaded, or in such imminent Danger as will not admit of delay.

Article II.

SECTION 1. The executive Power shall be vested in a President of the United States of America. He shall hold his Office during the Term of four Years, and, together with the Vice President, chosen for the same Term, be elected, as follows:

Each State shall appoint, in such Manner as the Legislature thereof may direct, a Number of Electors, equal to the whole Number of Senators and Representatives to which the State may be entitled in the Congress: but no Senator or Representative, or Person holding an Office of Trust or Profit under the United States, shall be appointed an Elector.

The Electors shall meet in their respective States, and vote by Ballot for two Persons, of whom one at least shall not be an Inhabitant of the same State with themselves. And they shall make a List of all the Persons voted for, and of the Number of Votes for each; which List they shall sign and certify, and transmit sealed to the Seat of the Government of the United States, directed to the President of the Senate. The President of the Senate shall, in the Presence of the Senate and House of Representatives, open all the Certificates, and the Votes shall then be counted. The Person having the greatest Number of Votes shall be the President, if such Number be a Majority of the whole Number of Electors appointed; and if there be more than one who have such Majority, and have an equal Number of Votes, then the House of Representatives shall immediately chuse by Ballot one of them for President; and if no Person have a Majority, then from the five highest on the List the said House shall in like Manner chuse the President. But in chusing the President, the Votes shall be taken by States, the Representation from each State having one Vote; A quorum for this Purpose shall consist of a Member or Members from two thirds of the States, and a Majority of all the States shall be necessary to a Choice. In every Case, after the Choice of the President, the Person having the greatest Number of Votes of the Electors shall be the Vice President. But if there should remain two or more who have equal Votes, the Senate shall chuse from them by Ballot the Vice President.[6]

The Congress may determine the Time of chusing the Electors, and the Day on which they shall give their Votes; which Day shall be the same throughout the United States.

No Person except a natural born Citizen, or a Citizen of the United States, at the time of the Adoption of this Constitution, shall be eligible to the Office of Presi-

---

[6]Superseded by the Twelfth Amendment.

dent, neither shall any Person be eligible to that Office who shall not have attained to the Age of thirty five Years, and been fourteen Years a Resident within the United States.

In Case of the Removal of the President from Office, or of his Death, Resignation, or Inability to discharge the Powers and Duties of the said Office, the Same shall devolve on the Vice President, and the Congress may by Law provide for the Case of Removal, Death, Resignation or Inability, both of the President and Vice President, declaring what Officer shall then act as President, and such Officer shall act accordingly, until the Disability be removed, or a President shall be elected.[7]

The President shall, at stated Times, receive for his Services, a Compensation, which shall neither be encreased nor diminished during the Period for which he shall have been elected, and he shall not receive within that Period any other Emolument from the United States, or any of them.

Before he enter on the Execution of his Office, he shall take the following Oath or Affirmation:—"I do solemnly swear (or affirm) that I will faithfully execute the Office of President of the United States, and will to the best of my Ability, preserve, protect and defend the Constitution of the United States."

SECTION 2. The President shall be Commander in Chief of the Army and Navy of the United States, and of the Militia of the several States, when called into the actual Service of the United States; he may require the Opinion, in writing, of the principal Officer in each of the executive Departments, upon any Subject relating to the Duties of their respective Offices, and he shall have Power to grant Reprieves and Pardons for Offences against the United States, except in Cases of Impeachment.

He shall have Power, by and with the Advice and Consent of the Senate, to make Treaties, provided two thirds of the Senators present concur; and he shall nominate, and by and with the Advice and Consent of the Senate, shall appoint Ambassadors, other public Ministers and Consuls, Judges of the supreme Court, and all other Officers of the United States, whose Appointments are not herein otherwise provided for, and which shall be established by Law; but the Congress may by Law vest the Appointment of such inferior Officers, as they think proper, in the President alone, in the Courts of Law, or in the Heads of Departments.

The President shall have Power to fill up all Vacancies that may happen during the Recess of the Senate, by granting Commissions which shall expire at the End of their next Session.

SECTION 3. He shall from time to time give the Congress Information of the State of the Union, and recommend to their Consideration such Measures as he shall judge necessary and expedient; he may, on extraordinary Occasions, convene both Houses, or either of them, and in Case of Disagreement between them, with Respect to the Time of Adjournment, he may adjourn them to such Time as he shall think proper; he shall receive Ambassadors and other public Ministers; he shall take Care that the Laws be faithfully executed, and shall Commission all the Officers of the United States.

SECTION 4. The President, Vice President and all civil Officers of the United States, shall be removed from Office on Impeachment for, and Conviction of, Treason, Bribery, or other high Crimes and Misdemeanors.

---

[7]Modified by the Twenty-fifth Amendment.

Article III.

SECTION 1. The judicial Power of the United States, shall be vested in one supreme Court, and in such inferior Courts as the Congress may from time to time ordain and establish. The Judges, both of the supreme and inferior Courts, shall hold their Offices during good Behaviour, and shall, at stated Times, receive for their Services, a Compensation, which shall not be diminished during their Continuance in Office.

SECTION 2. The judicial Power shall extend to all Cases, in Law and Equity, arising under this Constitution, the Laws of the United States, and Treaties made, or which shall be made, under their Authority;—to all Cases affecting Ambassadors, other public Ministers and Consuls;—to all Cases of admiralty and maritime Jurisdiction;—to Controversies to which the United States shall be a Party;—to Controversies between two or more States;—between a State and Citizens of another State;[8]—between Citizens of different States,—between Citizens of the same State claiming Lands under Grants of different States, and between a State, or the Citizens thereof, and foreign States, Citizens or Subjects.

In all Cases affecting Ambassadors, other public Ministers and Consuls, and those in which a State shall be Party, the supreme Court shall have original Jurisdiction. In all the other Cases before mentioned, the supreme Court shall have appellate Jurisdiction, both as to Law and Fact, with such Exceptions, and under such Regulations as the Congress shall make.

The Trial of all Crimes, except in Cases of Impeachment, shall be by Jury; and such Trial shall be held in the State where the said Crimes shall have been committed; but when not committed within any State, the Trial shall be at such Place or Places as the Congress may by Law have directed.

SECTION 3. Treason against the United States, shall consist only in levying War against them, or in adhering to their Enemies, giving them Aid and Comfort. No Person shall be convicted of Treason unless on the Testimony of two Witnesses to the same overt Act, or on Confession in open Court.

The Congress shall have Power to declare the Punishment of Treason, but no Attainder of Treason shall work Corruption of Blood, or Forfeiture except during the Life of the Person attainted.

Article IV.

SECTION 1. Full Faith and Credit shall be given in each State to the public Acts, Records, and judicial Proceedings of every other State. And the Congress may by general Laws prescribe the Manner in which such Acts, Records and Proceedings shall be proved, and the Effect thereof.

SECTION 2. The Citizens of each State shall be entitled to all Privileges and Immunities of Citizens in the several States.

A Person charged in any State with Treason, Felony, or other Crime, who shall flee from Justice, and be found in another State, shall on Demand of the executive Authority of the State from which he fled, be delivered up, to be removed to the State having Jurisdiction of the Crime.

---

[8]Modified by the Eleventh Amendment.

No Person held to Service or Labour in one State, under the Laws thereof, escaping into another, shall, in Consequence of any Law or Regulation therein, be discharged from such Service or Labour, but shall be delivered up on Claim of the Party to whom such Service or Labour may be due.

SECTION 3. New States may be admitted by the Congress into this Union; but no new State shall be formed or erected within the Jurisdiction of any other State, nor any State be formed by the Junction of two or more States, or Parts of States, without the Consent of the Legislatures of the States concerned as well as of the Congress.

The Congress shall have Power to dispose of and make all needful Rules and Regulations respecting the Territory or other Property belonging to the United States; and nothing in this Constitution shall be so construed as to Prejudice any Claims of the United States, or of any particular State.

SECTION 4. The United States shall guarantee to every State in this Union a Republican Form of Government, and shall protect each of them against Invasion; and on Application of the Legislature, or of the Executive (when the Legislature cannot be convened) against domestic Violence.

Article V.

The Congress, whenever two thirds of both Houses shall deem it necessary, shall propose Amendments to this Constitution, or, on the Application of the Legislatures of two thirds of the several States, shall call a Convention for proposing Amendments, which, in either Case, shall be valid to all Intents and Purposes, as Part of this Constitution, when ratified by the Legislatures of three fourths of the several States, or by Conventions in three fourths thereof, as the one or the other Mode of Ratification may be proposed by the Congress; Provided that no Amendment which may be made prior to the Year One thousand eight hundred and eight shall in any Manner affect the first and fourth Clauses in the Ninth Section of the first Article; and that no State, without its Consent, shall be deprived of its equal Suffrage in the Senate.

Article VI.

All Debts contracted and Engagements entered into, before the Adoption of this Constitution, shall be as valid against the United States under this Constitution, as under the Confederation.

This Constitution, and the Laws of the United States which shall be made in Pursuance thereof; and all Treaties made, or which shall be made, under the Authority of the United States, shall be the supreme Law of the Land; and the Judges in every State shall be bound thereby, any Thing in the Constitution or Laws of any State to the Contrary notwithstanding.

The Senators and Representatives before mentioned, and the Members of the several State Legislatures, and all executive and judicial Officers, both of the United States and of the several States, shall be bound by Oath or Affirmation, to support this Constitution; but no religious Test shall ever be required as a Qualification to any Office or public Trust under the United States.

Article VII.

The Ratification of the Conventions of nine States, shall be sufficient for the Establishment of this Constitution between the States so ratifying the Same.

Done in Convention by the Unanimous Consent of the States present the Seventeenth Day of September in the Year of our Lord one thousand seven hundred and Eighty seven and of the Independence of the United States of America the Twelfth. In witness whereof We have hereunto subscribed our Names,

Articles in Addition to, and Amendment of, the Constitution of the United States of America, Proposed by Congress, and Ratified by the Legislatures of the Several States, Pursuant to the Fifth Article of the Original Constitution.

Amendment I[9]

Congress shall make no law respecting an establishment of religion, or prohibiting the free exercise thereof; or abridging the freedom of speech, or of the press; or the right of the people peaceably to assemble, and to petition the Government for a redress of grievances.

Amendment II

A well regulated Militia, being necessary to the security of a free State, the right of the people to keep and bear Arms shall not be infringed.

Amendment III

No Soldier shall, in time of peace, be quartered in any house, without the consent of the Owner, nor in time of war, but in a manner to be prescribed by law.

Amendment IV

The right of the people to be secure in their persons, houses, papers, and effects, against unreasonable searches and seizures, shall not be violated, and no Warrants shall issue, but upon probable cause, supported by Oath or affirmation, and particularly describing the place to be searched, and the persons or things to be seized.

Amendment V

No person shall be held to answer for a capital or otherwise infamous crime, unless on a presentment or indictment of a Grand Jury, except in cases arising in the land or naval forces, or in the Militia, when in actual service in time of War or public danger; nor shall any person be subject for the same offence to be twice put in jeopardy of life or limb; nor shall be compelled in any criminal case to be a witness against himself, nor be deprived of life, liberty, or property, without due process of law; nor shall private property be taken for public use, without just compensation.

---

[9]The first 10 amendments were passed by Congress September 25, 1789. They were ratified by three-fourths of the states December 15, 1791.

Amendment VI

In all criminal prosecutions, the accused shall enjoy the right to a speedy and public trial, by an impartial jury of the State and district wherein the crime shall have been committed, which district shall have been previously ascertained by law, and to be informed of the nature and cause of the accusation; to be confronted with the witnesses against him; to have compulsory process for obtaining witnesses in his favor, and to have the Assistance of Counsel for his defence.

Amendment VII

In suits at common law, where the value in controversy shall exceed twenty dollars, the right of trial by jury shall be preserved, and no fact tried by a jury, shall be otherwise reexamined in any Court of the United States, than according to the rules of the common law.

Amendment VIII

Excessive bail shall not be required, nor excessive fines imposed, nor cruel and unusual punishments inflicted.

Amendment IX

The enumeration in the Constitution, of certain rights, shall not be construed to deny or disparage others retained by the people.

Amendment X

The powers not delegated to the United States by the Constitution; nor prohibited by it to the States, are reserved to the States respectively, or to the people.

Amendment XI[10]

The Judicial power of the United States shall not be construed to extend to any suit in law or equity, commenced or prosecuted against one of the United States by Citizens of another State, or by Citizens or Subjects of any Foreign State.

Amendment XII[11]

The Electors shall meet in their respective States and vote by ballot for President and Vice-President, one of whom, at least, shall not be an inhabitant of the same State with themselves; they shall name in their ballots the person voted for as President, and in distinct ballots the person voted for as Vice-President, and they shall make distinct lists of all persons voted for as President, and of all persons voted for as Vice-President, and of the number of votes for each, which lists they shall sign and certify, and transmit sealed to the seat of the government of the United States, directed to the President of the Senate;—The President of the Senate shall, in the

---

[10]Passed March 4, 1794. Ratified January 23, 1795.

[11]Passed December 9, 1803. Ratified June 15, 1804.

presence of the Senate and House of Representatives, open all the certificates and the votes shall then be counted;—The person having the greatest number of votes for President, shall be the President, if such number be a majority of the whole number of Electors appointed; and if no person have such majority, then from the persons having the highest numbers not exceeding three on the list of those voted for as President, the House of Representatives shall choose immediately, by ballot, the President. But in choosing the President, the votes shall be taken by states, the representation from each state having one vote; a quorum for this purpose shall consist of a member or members from two-thirds of the states, and a majority of all the states shall be necessary to a choice. And if the House of Representatives shall not choose a President whenever the right of choice shall devolve upon them, before the fourth day of March next following, then the Vice-President shall act as President, as in the case of the death or other constitutional disability of the President.—The person having the greatest number of votes as Vice-President, shall be the Vice-President, if such number be a majority of the whole number of Electors appointed, and if no person have a majority, then from the two highest numbers on the list, the Senate shall choose the Vice-President; a quorum for the purpose shall consist of two-thirds of the whole number of Senators, and a majority of the whole number shall be necessary to a choice. But no person constitutionally ineligible to the office of President shall be eligible to that of Vice-President of the United States.

Amendment XIII[12]

SECTION 1. Neither slavery nor involuntary servitude, except as a punishment for crime whereof the party shall have been duly convicted, shall exist within the United States, or any place subject to their jurisdiction.

SECTION 2. Congress shall have power to enforce this article by appropriate legislation.

Amendment XIV[13]

SECTION 1. All persons born or naturalized in the United States, and subject to the jurisdiction thereof, are citizens of the United States and of the State wherein they reside. No State shall make or enforce any law which shall abridge the privileges or immunities of citizens of the United States; nor shall any State deprive any person of life, liberty, or property, without due process of law; nor deny to any person within its jurisdiction the equal protection of the laws.

SECTION 2. Representatives shall be apportioned among the several States according to their respective numbers, counting the whole number of persons in each State, excluding Indians not taxed. But when the right to vote at any election for the choice of electors for President and Vice-President of the United States, Representatives in Congress, the Executive and Judicial officers of a State, or the members of the Legislature thereof, is denied to any of the male inhabitants of such State, being twenty-

---

[12]Passed January 31, 1865. Ratified December 6, 1865.

[13]Passed June 13, 1866. Ratified July 9, 1868.

one years of age, and citizens of the United States, or in any way abridged, except for participation in rebellion, or other crime, the basis of representation therein shall be reduced in the proportion which the number of such male citizens shall bear to the whole number of male citizens twenty-one years of age in such State.

SECTION 3. No person shall be a Senator or Representative in Congress, or elector of President and Vice-President, or hold any office, civil or military, under the United States, or under any State, who, having previously taken an oath, as a member of Congress, or as an officer of the United States, or as a member of any State legislature, or as an executive or judicial officer of any State, to support the Constitution of the United States, shall have engaged in insurrection or rebellion against the same, or given aid or comfort to the enemies thereof. But Congress may by a vote of two-thirds of each House, remove such disability.

SECTION 4. The validity of the public debt of the United States, authorized by law, including debts incurred for payment of pensions and bounties for services in suppressing insurrection or rebellion, shall not be questioned. But neither the United States nor any State shall assume or pay any debt or obligation incurred in aid of insurrection or rebellion against the United States, or any claim for the loss or emancipation of any slave; but all such debts, obligations, and claims shall be held illegal and void.

SECTION 5. The Congress shall have the power to enforce, by appropriate legislation, the provisions of this article.

Amendment XV[14]

SECTION 1. The right of citizens of the United States to vote shall not be denied or abridged by the United States or by any State on account of race, color, or previous conditions of servitude—

SECTION 2. The Congress shall have power to enforce this article by appropriate legislation.

Amendment XVI

The Congress shall have power to lay and collect taxes on incomes, from whatever source derived, without apportionment among the several States, and without regard to any census or enumeration.

Amendment XVII[15]

The Senate of the United States shall be composed of two Senators from each State, elected by the people thereof, for six years; and each Senator shall have one vote. The electors in each State shall have the qualifications requisite for electors of the most numerous branch of the State legislatures.

When vacancies happen in the representation of any State in the Senate, the executive authority of such State shall issue writs of election to fill such vacancies: *Provided,* That the legislature of any State may empower the executive thereof to

---

[14]Passed February 26, 1869. Ratified February 2, 1870.

[15]Passed May 13, 1912. Ratified April 8, 1913.

make temporary appointments until the people fill the vacancies by election as the legislature may direct.

This amendment shall not be so construed as to affect the election or term of any Senator chosen before it becomes valid as part of the Constitution.

Amendment XVIII[16]

SECTION 1. After one year from the ratification of this article the manufacture, sale, or transportation of intoxicating liquors within, the importation thereof into, or the exportation thereof from the United States and all territory subject to the jurisdiction thereof for beverage purposes is hereby prohibited.

SECTION 2. The Congress and the several States shall have concurrent power to enforce this article by appropriate legislation.

SECTION 3. This article shall be inoperative unless it shall have been ratified as an amendment to the Constitution by the legislatures of the several States, as provided in the Constitution, within seven years from the date of the submission hereof to the States by the Congress.

Amendment XIX[17]

The right of citizens of the United States to vote shall not be denied or abridged by the United States or by any State on account of sex.

Congress shall have power to enforce this article by appropriate legislation.

Amendment XX[18]

SECTION 1. The terms of the President and Vice-President shall end at noon on the 20th day of January, and the terms of Senators and Representatives at noon on the 3d day of January, of the years in which such terms would have ended if this article had not been ratified; and the terms of their successors shall then begin.

SECTION 2. The Congress shall assemble at least once in every year, and such meeting shall begin at noon on the 3d day of January, unless they shall by law appoint a different day.

SECTION 3. If, at the time fixed for the beginning of the term of the President, the President elect shall have died, the Vice-President elect shall become President. If a President shall not have been chosen before the time fixed for the beginning of his term, or if the President elect shall have failed to qualify, then the Vice-President elect shall act as President until a President shall have qualified; and the Congress may by law provide for the case wherein neither a President elect nor a Vice-President elect shall have qualified, declaring who shall then act as President, or the manner in which one who is to act shall be selected, and such person shall act accordingly until a President or Vice-President shall have qualified.

SECTION 4. The Congress may by law provide for the case of the death of any of the persons from whom the House of Representatives may choose a President

---

[16]Passed December 18, 1917. Ratified January 16, 1919.

[17]Passed June 4, 1919. Ratified August 18, 1920.

[18]Passed March 2, 1932. Ratified January 23, 1933.

whenever the right of choice shall have devolved upon them, and for the case of the death of any of the persons from whom the Senate may choose a Vice-President whenever the right of choice shall have devolved upon them.

SECTION 5. Sections 1 and 2 shall take effect on the 15th day of October following the ratification of this article.

SECTION 6. This article shall be inoperative unless it shall have been ratified as an amendment to the Constitution by the legislatures of three-fourths of the several States within seven years from the date of its submission.

Amendment XXI[19]

SECTION 1. The eighteenth article of amendment to the Constitution of the United States is hereby repealed.

SECTION 2. The transportation or importation into any State, Territory, or possession of the United States for delivery or use therein of intoxicating liquors, in violation of the laws thereof, is hereby prohibited.

SECTION 3. This article shall be inoperative unless it shall have been ratified as an amendment to the Constitution by conventions in the several States, as provided in the Constitution, within seven years from the date of the submission hereof to the States by the Congress.

Amendment XXII[20]

No person shall be elected to the office of the President more than twice, and no person who has held the office of President, or acted as President, for more than two years of a term to which some other person was elected President shall be elected to the office of the President more than once.

But this Article shall not apply to any person holding the office of President when this Article was proposed by the Congress, and shall not prevent any person who may be holding the office of President, or acting as President, during the term within which this Article becomes operative from holding the office of President or acting as President during the remainder of such term.

Amendment XXIII[21]

SECTION 1. The District constituting the seat of Government of the United States shall appoint in such manner as the Congress may direct:

A number of electors of President and Vice President equal to the whole number of Senators and Representatives in Congress to which the District would be entitled if it were a State, but in no event more than the least populous State; they shall be in addition to those appointed by the States, but they shall be considered, for the purposes of the election of President and Vice President, to be electors appointed by the State; and they shall meet in the District and perform such duties as provided by the twelfth article of amendment.

---

[19]Passed February 20, 1933. Ratified December 5, 1933.

[20]Passed March 12, 1947. Ratified March 1, 1951.

[21]Passed June 16, 1960. Ratified April 3, 1961.

SECTION 2. The Congress shall have power to enforce this article by appropriate legislation.

Amendment XXIV[22]

SECTION 1. The right of citizens of the United States to vote in any primary or other election for President or Vice President, or for Senator or Representative in Congress, shall not be denied or abridged by the United States or any State by reason of failure to pay any poll tax or other tax.

SECTION 2. The Congress shall have power to enforce this article by appropriate legislation.

Amendment XXV[23]

SECTION 1. In case of the removal of the President from office or of his death or resignation, the Vice President shall become President.

SECTION 2. Whenever there is a vacancy in the office of the Vice President, the President shall nominate a Vice President who shall take office upon confirmation by a majority vote of both Houses of Congress.

SECTION 3. Whenever the President transmits to the President pro tempore of the Senate and the Speaker of the House of Representatives his written declaration that he is unable to discharge the powers and duties of his office, and until he transmits them a written declaration to the contrary, such powers and duties shall be discharged by the Vice President as Acting President.

SECTION 4. Whenever the Vice President and a majority of either the principal officers of the executive department or of such other body as Congress may by law provide, transmit to the President pro tempore of the Senate and the Speaker of the House of Representatives their written declaration that the President is unable to discharge the powers and duties of his office, the Vice President shall immediately assume the powers and duties of the office of Acting President.

Thereafter, when the President transmits to the President pro tempore of the Senate and the Speaker of the House of Representatives his written declaration that no inability exists, he shall resume the powers and duties of his office unless the Vice President and a majority of either the principal officers of the executive department or of such other body as Congress may by law provide, transmit within four days to the President pro tempore of the Senate and the Speaker of the House of Representatives their written declaration that the President is unable to discharge the powers and duties of his office. Thereupon Congress shall decide the issue, assembling within forty-eight hours for that purpose if not in session. If the Congress, within twenty-one days after receipt of the latter written declaration, or, if Congress is not in session, within twenty-one days after Congress is required to assemble, determines by two-thirds vote of both Houses that the President is unable to discharge the powers and duties of his office, the Vice President shall continue to discharge the same as Acting President; otherwise, the President shall resume the powers and duties of his office.

---

[22]Passed August 27, 1962. Ratified January 23, 1964.

[23]Passed July 6, 1965. Ratified February 11, 1967.

Amendment XXVI[24]

SECTION 1. The right of citizens of the United States, who are eighteen years of age or older, to vote shall not be denied or abridged by the United States or by any State on account of age.

SECTION 2. The Congress shall have power to enforce this article by appropriate legislation.

Amendment XXVII[25]

No law, varying the compensation for the service of the Senators and Representatives, shall take effect, until an election of Representatives shall have intervened.

---

[24]Passed March 23, 1971. Ratified July 5, 1971.

[25]Passed September 25, 1789. Ratified May 7, 1992.

Population of the United States (1890–1998)

Year	Total Population	Number per Square Mile	Year	Total Population[1]	Number per Square Mile	Year	Total Population[1]	Number per Square Mile
1890	63,056	21.2	1927	119,038		1963	189,197	
1891	64,361		1928	120,501		1964	191,833	
1892	65,666		1929	121,700		1965	194,237	
1893	66,970		1930	122,775	41.2	1966	196,485	
1894	68,275		1931	124,040		1967	198,629	
1895	69,580		1932	124,840		1968	200,619	
1896	70,885		1933	125,579		1969	202,599	
1897	72,189		1934	126,374		1970	203,875	57.5[2]
1898	73,494		1935	127,250		1971	207,045	
1899	74,799		1936	128,053		1972	208,842	
1900	76,094	25.6	1937	128,825		1973	210,396	
1901	77,585		1938	129,825		1974	211,894	
1902	79,160		1939	130,880		1975	213,631	
1903	80,632		1940	131,669	44.2	1976	215,152	
1904	82,165		1941	133,894		1977	216,880	
1905	83,820		1942	135,361		1978	218,717	
1906	85,437		1943	137,250		1979	220,584	
1907	87,000		1944	138,916		1980	226,546	64.0
1908	88,709		1945	140,468		1981	230,138	
1909	90,492		1946	141,936		1982	232,520	
1910	92,407	31.0	1947	144,698		1983	234,799	
1911	93,868		1948	147,208		1984	237,001	
1912	95,331		1949	149,767		1985	239,283	
1913	97,227		1950	150,697	50.7	1986	241,596	
1914	99,118		1951	154,878		1987	234,773	
1915	100,549		1952	157,553		1988	245,051	
1916	101,966		1953	160,184		1989	247,350	
1917	103,414		1954	163,026		1990	250,122	
1918	104,550		1955	165,931		1991	254,521	
1919	105,063		1956	168,903		1992	245,908	
1920	106,466	35.6	1957	171,984		1993	257,908	
1921	108,541		1958	174,882		1994	261,875	
1922	110,055		1959	177,830		1995	263,434	
1923	111,950		1960	178,464	60.1	1996	266,096	
1924	114,113		1961	183,672		1997	267,901	
1925	115,832		1962	186,504		1998	269,501	
1926	117,399							

Figures are from *Historical Statistics of the United States, Colonial Times to 1957* (1961), pp. 7, 8; *Statistical Abstract of the United States: 1974*, p. 5, Census Bureau for 1974 and 1975; and *Statistical Abstract of the United States: 1988*, p. 7.

Note: Population figures are in thousands. Density figures are for land area of continental United States.

[1]Figures after 1940 represent total population including armed forces abroad, except in official census years.

[2]Figure includes Alaska and Hawaii.

Presidential Elections (1892–1996)

Year	Number of States	Candidates	Parties	Popular Vote	Electoral Vote	Percentage of Popular Vote[1]
1892	44	**Grover Cleveland**	Democratic	5,555,426	277	46.1
		Benjamin Harrison	Republican	5,182,690	145	43.0
		James B. Weaver	People's	1,029,846	22	8.5
		John Bidwell	Prohibition	264,133		2.2
1896	45	**William McKinley**	Republican	7,102,246	271	51.1
		William J. Bryan	Democratic	6,492,559	176	47.7
1900	45	**William McKinley**	Republican	7,218,491	292	51.7
		William J. Bryan	Democratic; Populist	6,356,734	155	45.5
		John C. Wooley	Prohibition	208,914		1.5
1904	45	**Theodore Roosevelt**	Republican	7,628,461	336	57.4
		Alton B. Parker	Democratic	5,084,223	140	37.6
		Eugene V. Debs	Socialist	402,283		3.0
		Silas C. Swallow	Prohibition	258,536		1.9
1908	46	**William H. Taft**	Republican	7,675,320	321	51.6
		William J. Bryan	Democratic	6,412,294	162	43.1
		Eugene V. Debs	Socialist	420,793		2.8
		Eugene W. Chafin	Prohibition	253,840		1.7
1912	48	**Woodrow Wilson**	Democratic	6,296,547	435	41.9
		Theodore Roosevelt	Progressive	4,118,571	88	27.4
		William H. Taft	Republican	3,486,720	8	23.2
		Eugene V. Debs	Socialist	900,672		6.0
		Eugene W. Chafin	Prohibition	206,275		1.4
1916	48	**Woodrow Wilson**	Democratic	9,127,695	277	49.4
		Charles E. Hughes	Republican	8,533,507	254	46.2
		A. L. Benson	Socialist	585,113		3.2
		J. Frank Hanly	Prohibition	220,506		1.2
1920	48	**Warren G. Harding**	Republican	16,143,407	404	60.4
		James N. Cox	Democratic	9,130,328	127	34.2
		Eugene V. Debs	Socialist	919,799		3.4
		P. P. Christensen	Farmer-Labor	265,411		1.0
1924	48	**Calvin Coolidge**	Republican	15,718,211	382	54.0
		John W. Davis	Democratic	8,385,283	136	28.8
		Robert M. La Follette	Progressive	4,831,289	13	16.6
1928	48	**Herbert C. Hoover**	Republican	21,391,993	444	58.2
		Alfred E. Smith	Democratic	15,016,169	87	40.9
1932	48	**Franklin D. Roosevelt**	Democratic	22,809,638	472	57.4
		Herbert C. Hoover	Republican	15,758,901	59	39.7
		Norman Thomas	Socialist	881,951		2.2
1936	48	**Franklin D. Roosevelt**	Democratic	27,752,869	523	60.8
		Alfred M. Landon	Republican	16,674,665	8	36.5
		William Lemke	Union	882,479		1.9

[1]Candidates receiving less than 1 percent of the popular vote have been omitted. For that reason the percentage of popular vote given for any election year may not total 100 percent.

Year	Number of States	Candidates	Parties	Popular Vote	Electoral Vote	Percentage of Popular Vote[1]
1940	48	**Franklin D. Roosevelt**	Democratic	27,307,819	449	54.8
		Wendell L. Willkie	Republican	22,321,018	82	44.8
1944	48	**Franklin D. Roosevelt**	Democratic	25,606,585	432	53.5
		Thomas E. Dewey	Republican	22,014,745	99	46.0
1948	48	**Harry S Truman**	Democratic	24,105,812	303	49.5
		Thomas E. Dewey	Republican	21,970,065	189	45.1
		J. Strom Thurmond	States' Rights	1,169,063	39	2.4
		Henry A. Wallace	Progressive	1,157,172		2.4
1952	48	**Dwight D. Eisenhower**	Republican	33,936,234	442	55.1
		Adlai E. Stevenson	Democratic	27,314,992	89	44.4
1956	48	**Dwight D. Eisenhower**	Republican	35,590,472	457	57.6
		Adlai E. Stevenson	Democratic	26,022,752	73	42.1
1960	50	**John F. Kennedy**	Democratic	34,227,096	303	49.9
		Richard M. Nixon	Republican	34,108,546	219	49.6
1964	50	**Lyndon B. Johnson**	Democratic	43,126,506	486	61.1
		Barry M. Goldwater	Republican	27,176,799	52	38.5
1968	50	**Richard M. Nixon**	Republican	31,785,480	301	43.4
		Hubert H. Humphrey	Democratic	31,275,165	191	42.7
		George C. Wallace	American Independent	9,906,473	46	13.5
1972	50	**Richard M. Nixon**	Republican	47,169,911	520	60.7
		George S. McGovern	Democratic	29,170,383	17	37.5
1976	50	**Jimmy Carter**	Democratic	40,827,394	297	50.0
		Gerald R. Ford	Republican	39,145,977	240	47.9
1980	50	**Ronald W. Reagan**	Republican	43,899,248	489	50.8
		Jimmy Carter	Democratic	35,481,435	49	41.0
		John B. Anderson	Independent	5,719,437		6.6
		Ed Clark	Libertarian	920,859		1.0
1984	50	**Ronald W. Reagan**	Republican	54,281,858	525	59.2
		Walter F. Mondale	Democratic	37,457,215	13	40.8
1988	50	**George H. Bush**	Republican	47,917,341	426	54
		Michael Dukakis	Democratic	41,013,030	112	46
1992	50	**William Clinton**	Democratic	44,908,254	370	43.0
		George H. Bush	Republican	39,102,343	168	37.4
		Ross Perot	Independent	19,741,065		18.9
1996	50	**William Clinton**	Democratic	45,628,667	379	49.2
		Robert Dole	Republican	37,869,435	159	40.8
		Ross Perot	Reform	7,874,283	0	8.5

[1]Candidates receiving less than 1 percent of the popular vote have been omitted. For that reason the percentage of popular vote given for any election year may not total 100 percent.

Presidential Administrations (since 1893)

President	Vice President	Secretary of State	Secretary of Treasury	Secretary of War	Secretary of Navy
Grover Cleveland 1893–1897	Adlai E. Stevenson 1893–1897	Walter Q. Gresham 1893–1895 Richard Olney 1895–1897	John G. Carlisle 1893–1897	Daniel S. Lamont 1893–1897	Hilary A. Herbert 1893–1897
William McKinley 1897–1901	Garret A. Hobart 1897–1899 Thedore Roosevelt 1901	John Sherman 1897–1898 William R. Day 1898 John Hay 1898–1901	Lyman J. Gage 1897–1901	Russell A. Alger 1897–1899 Elihu Root 1899–1901	John D. Long 1897–1901
Theodore Roosevelt 1901–1909	Charles Fairbanks 1905–1909	John Hay 1901–1905 Elihu Root 1905–1909 Robert Bacon 1909	Lyman J. Gage 1901–1902 Leslie M. Shaw 1902–1907 George B. Cortelyou 1907–1909	Elihu Root 1901–1904 William H. Taft 1904–1908 Luke E. Wright 1908–1909	John D. Long 1901–1902 William H. Moody 1902–1904 Paul Morton 1904–1905 Charles J. Bonaparte 1905–1906 Victor H. Metcalf 1906–1908 T. H. Newberry 1908–1909
William H. Taft 1909–1913	James S. Sherman 1909–1913	Philander C. Knox 1909–1913	Franklin MacVeagh 1909–1913	Jacob M. Dickinson 1909–1911 Henry L. Stimson 1911–1913	George von L. Meyer 1909–1913
Woodrow Wilson 1913–1921	Thomas R. Marshall 1913–1921	William J. Bryan 1913–1915 Robert Lansing 1915–1920 Bainbridge Colby 1920–1921	William G. McAdoo 1913–1918 Carter Glass 1918–1920 David F. Houston 1920–1921	Lindley M. Garrison 1913–1916 Newton D. Baker 1916–1921	Josephus Daniels 1913–1921
Warren G. Harding 1921–1923	Calvin Coolidge 1921–1923	Charles E. Hughes 1921–1923	Andrew W. Mellon 1921–1923	John W. Weeks 1921–1923	Edwin Denby 1921–1923
Calvin Coolidge 1923–1929	Charles G. Dawes 1925–1929	Charles E. Hughes 1923–1925 Frank B. Kellogg 1925–1929	Andrew W. Mellon 1923–1929	John W. Weeks 1923–1925 Dwight F. Davis 1925–1929	Edwin Denby 1923–1924 Curtis D. Wilbur 1924–1929

Postmaster General	Attorney General	Secretary of Interior	Secretary of Agriculture	Secretary of Commerce and Labor
Wilson S. Bissel 1893–1895 William L. Wilson 1895–1897	Richard Olney 1893–1895 Judson Harmon 1895–1897	Hoke Smith 1893–1896 David R. Francis 1896–1897	J. Sterling Morton 1893–1897	
James A. Gary 1897–1898 Charles E. Smith 1898–1901	Joseph McKenna 1897–1898 John W. Griggs 1898–1901 Philander C. Knox 1901	Cornelius N. Bliss 1897–1898 E. A. Hitchcock 1898–1901	James Wilson 1897–1901	
Charles E. Smith 1901–1902 Henry C. Payne 1902–1904 Robert J. Wynne 1904–1905 George B. Cortelyou 1905–1907 George von L. Meyer 1907–1909	Philander C. Knox 1901–1904 William H. Moody 1904–1906 Charles J. Bonaparte 1906–1909	E. A. Hitchcock 1901–1907 James R. Garfield 1907–1909	James Wilson 1901–1909	George B. Cortelyou 1903–1904 Victor H. Metcalf 1904–1906 Oscar S. Straus 1906–1909
Frank H. Hitchcock 1909–1913	G. W. Wickersham 1909–1913	R. A. Ballinger 1909–1911 Walter L. Fisher 1911–1913	James Wilson 1909–1913	Charles Nagel 1909–1913

				Secretary of Commerce	Secretary of Labor
Albert S. Burleson 1913–1921	J. C. McReynolds 1913–1914 T. W. Gregory 1914–1919 A. Mitchell Palmer 1919–1921	Franklin K. Lane 1913–1920 John B. Payne 1920–1921	David F. Houston 1913–1920 E. T. Meredith 1920–1921	W. C. Redfield 1913–1919 J. W. Alexander 1919–1921	William B. Wilson 1913–1921
Will H. Hays 1921–1922 Hubert Work 1922–1923 Harry S. New 1923	H. M. Daugherty 1921–1923	Albert B. Fall 1921–1923 Hubert Work 1923	Henry C. Wallace 1921–1923	Herbert C. Hoover 1921–1923	James J. Davis 1921–1923
Harry S. New 1923–1929	H. M. Daugherty 1923–1924 Harlan F. Stone 1924–1925 John G. Sargent 1925–1929	Hubert Work 1923–1928 Roy O. West 1928–1929	Henry C. Wallace 1923–1924 Howard M. Gore 1924–1925 W. J. Jardine 1925–1929	Herbert C. Hoover 1923–1928 William F. Whiting 1928–1929	James J. Davis 1923–1929

(continued)

President	Vice President	Secretary of State	Secretary of Treasury	Secretary of War	Secretary of Navy	Postmaster General	Attorney General
Herbert C. Hoover 1929–1933	Charles Curtis 1929–1933	Henry L. Stimson 1929–1933	Andrew W. Mellon 1929–1932 Ogden L. Mills 1932–1933	James W. Good 1929 Patrick J. Hurley 1929–1933	Charles F. Adams 1929–1933	Walter F. Brown 1929–1933	J. D. Mitchell 1929–1933
Franklin Delano Roosevelt 1933–1945	John Nance Garner 1933–1941 Henry A. Wallace 1941–1945 Harry S Truman 1945	Cordell Hull 1933–1944 E. R. Stettinius, Jr. 1944–1945	William H. Woodin 1933–1934 Henry Morgenthau, Jr. 1934–1945	George H. Dern 1933–1936 Harry H. Woodring 1936–1934 Henry L. Stimson 1940–1945	Claude A. Swanson 1933–1940 Charles Edison 1940 Frank Knox 1940–1944 James V. Forrestal 1944–1945	James A. Farley 1933–1940 Frank C. Walker 1940–1945	H. S. Cummings 1933–1939 Frank Murphy 1939–1940 Robert Jackson 1940–1941 Francis Biddel 1941–1945
Harry S. Truman 1945–1953	Alben W. Barkley 1949–1953	James F. Byrnes 1945–1947 George C. Marshall 1947–1949 Dean G. Acheson 1949–1953	Fred M. Vinson 1945–1946 John W. Snyder 1946–1953	Robert P. Patterson 1945–1947 Kenneth C. Royall 1947	James V. Forrestal 1945–1947	R. E. Hannegan 1945–1947 Jesse M. Donaldson 1947–1953	Tom C. Clark 1945–1949 J. H. McGrath 1949–1952 James P. McGranery 1952–1953

Secretary of Defense

James V. Forrestal
1947–1949
Louis A. Johnson
1949–1950
George C. Marshall
1950–1951
Robert A. Lovett
1951–1953

President	Vice President	Secretary of State	Secretary of Treasury	Secretary of War	Secretary of Navy	Postmaster General	Attorney General
Dwight D. Eisenhower 1953–1961	Richard M. Nixon 1953–1961	John Foster Dulles 1953–1959 Christian A. Herter 1957–1961	George M. Humphrey 1953–1957 Robert B. Anderson 1957–1961	Charles E. Wilson 1953–1957 Neil H. McElroy 1957–1961 Thomas S. Gates 1959–1961	A. E. Summerfield 1953–1961	H. Brownell, Jr. 1953–1957 William P. Rogers 1957–1961
John F. Kennedy 1961–1963	Lyndon B. Johnson 1961–1963	Dean Rusk 1961–1963	C. Douglas Dillon 1961–1963	Robert S. McNamara 1961–1963	J. Edward Day 1961–1963 John A. Gronouski 1961–1963	Robert F. Kennedy 1961–1963
Lyndon B. Johnson 1963–1969	Hubert H. Humphrey 1965–1969	Dean Rusk 1963–1969	C. Douglas Dillon 1963–1965 Henry H. Fowler 1965–1968 Joseph W. Barr 1968–1969	Robert S. McNamara 1963–1968 Clark M. Clifford 1968–1969	John A. Gronouski 1963–1965 Lawrence F. O'Brien 1965–1968 W. Marvin Watson 1968–1969	Robert F. Kennedy 1963–1965 N. deB. Katzenbach 1965–1967 Ramsey Clark 1967–1969

Secretary of Interior	Secretary of Agriculture	Secretary of Commerce	Secretary of Labor	Secretary of Health, Education, and Welfare	Secretary of Housing and Urban Development	Secretary of Transportation
Ray L. Wilbur 1929–1933	Arthur M. Hyde 1929–1933 Roy D. Chapin 1932–1933	Robert P. Lamont 1929–1932 William N. Doak 1930–1933	James J. Davis 1929–1930			
Harold L. Ickes 1933–1945	Henry A. Wallace 1933–1940 Claude R. Wickard 1940–1945	Daniel C. Roper 1933–1939 Harry L. Hopkins 1939–1940 Jesse Jones 1940–1945 Henry A. Wallace 1945	Frances Perkins 1933–1945			
Harold L. Ickes 1945–1946 Julius A. Krug 1946–1949 Oscar L. Chapman 1949–1953	C. P. Anderson 1945–1948 C. F. Brannan 1948–1953	W. A. Harriman 1946–1948 Charles Sawyer 1948–1953	L. B. Schwellenbach 1945–1948 Maurice J. Tobin 1948–1953			
Douglas McKay 1953–1956 Fred Seaton 1956–1961	Ezra T. Benson 1953–1961	Sinclair Weeks 1953–1958 Lewis L. Strauss 1958–1961	Martin P. Durkin 1953 James P. Mitchell 1953–1961	Oveta Culp Hobby 1953–1955 Marion B. Folsom 1955–1958 Arthur S. Flemming 1958–1961		
Stewart L. Udall 1961–1963	Orville L. Freeman 1961–1963	Luther H. Hodges 1961–1963	Arthur J. Goldberg 1961–1963 W. Willard Wirtz 1962–1963	A. H. Ribicoff 1961–1963 Anthony J. Celebrezze 1962–1963		
Stewart L. Udall 1963–1969	Orville L. Freeman 1963–1969	Luther H. Hodges 1963–1965 John T. Connor 1965–1967 Alexander B. Trowbridge 1967–1968 C. R. Smith 1968–1969	W. Willard Wirtz 1963–1969	Anthony J. Celebrezze 1963–1965 John W. Gardner 1965–1968 Wilbur J. Cohen 1968–1969	Robert C. Weaver 1966–1968 Robert C. Wood 1968–1969	Alan S. Boyd 1966–1969

(continued)

President	Vice President	Secretary of State	Secretary of Treasury	Secretary of Defense	Postmaster General[1]	Attorney General	Secretary of Interior	Secretary of Agriculture
Richard M. Nixon 1969–1974	Spiro T. Agnew 1969–1973 Gerald R. Ford 1973–1974	William P. Rogers 1969–1973 Henry A. Kissinger 1973–1974	David M. Kennedy 1969–1970 John B. Connally 1970–1972 George P. Schultz 1972–1974 William E. Simon 1974	Melvin R. Laird 1969–1973 Elliot L. Richardson 1973 James R. Schlesinger 1973–1974	William M. Blount 1969–1971	John M. Mitchell 1969–1972 Richard G. Kleindienst 1972–1973 Elliot L. Richardson 1973 William B. Saxbe 1974	Walter J. Hickel 1969–1971 Rogers C. B. Morton 1971–1974	Clifford M. Hardin 1969–1971 Earl L. Butz 1971–1974
Gerald R. Ford 1974–1977	Nelson A. Rockefeller 1974–1977	Henry A. Kissinger 1974–1977	William E. Simon 1974–1977	James R. Schlesinger 1974–1975 Donald H. Rumsfeld 1975–1977		William B. Saxbe 1974–1975 Edward H. Levi 1975–1977	Rogers C. B. Morton 1974–1975 Stanley K. Hathaway 1975 Thomas D. Kleppe 1975–1977	Earl L. Butz 1974–1976
Jimmy Carter 1977–1981	Walter F. Mondale 1977–1981	Cyrus R. Vance 1977–1980 Edmund S. Muskie 1980–1981	W. Michael Blumenthal 1977–1979 G. William Miller 1979–1981	Harold Brown 1977–1981		Griffin Bell 1977–1979 Benjamin R. Civiletti 1979–1981	Cecil D. Andrus 1977–1981	Robert Bergland 1977–1981
Ronald W. Reagan 1981–1989	George H. Bush 1981–1989	Alexander M. Haig, Jr. 1981–1982 George P. Shultz 1982–1989	Donald T. Regan 1981–1985 James A. Baker 1985–1988 Nicholas F. Brady 1988–1989	Caspar W. Weinberger 1981–1987 Frank C. Carlucci 1987–1989		William French Smith 1981–1985 Edwin Meese 1985–1988 Richard Thornburgh 1988–1989	James G. Watt 1981–1983 William P. Clark 1983–1985 Donald P. Hodel 1985–1989	John R. Block 1981–1986 Richard E. Lyng 1986–1989
George H. Bush 1989–1992	J. Danforth Quayle 1989–1992	James A. Baker 1989–1992 Lawrence S. Eagleburger 1992	Nicholas F. Brady 1989–1992	Richard Cheney 1989–1992		Richard Thornburgh 1989–1990 William Barr 1990–1992	Manuel Lujan 1989–1992	Clayton Yeutter 1989–1990 Edward Madigan 1990–1992
William Clinton 1993–	Albert Gore 1993–	Warren M. Christopher 1993–1996 Madeleine K. Albright 1997–	Lloyd Bentsen 1993–1994 Robert E. Rubin 1994–	Les Aspin 1993–1994 William J. Perry 1994–1996 William S. Cohen 1997–		Janet Reno 1993–	Bruce Babbitt 1993–	Mike Espy 1993–1994 Dan Glickman 1995–

[1]On July 1, 1971, the Post Office became an independent agency. After that date, the Postmaster General was no longer a member of the Cabinet.

Secretary of Commerce	Secretary of Labor	Secretary of Health, Education, and Welfare	Secretary of Housing and Urban Development	Secretary of Transportation	Secretary of Energy	Secretary of Veterans' Affairs
Maurice H. Stans 1969–1972 Peter G. Peterson 1972 Frederick B. Dent 1972–1974	George P. Shultz 1969–1970 James D. Hodgson 1970–1973 Peter J. Brennan 1973–1974	Robert H. Finch 1969–1970 Elliot L. Richardson 1970–1973 Caspar W. Weinberger 1973–1974	George W. Romney 1969–1973 James T. Lynn 1973–1974	John A. Volpe 1969–1973 Claude S. Brinegar 1973–1974		
Frederick B. Dent 1974–1975 Rogers C. B. Morton 1975 Elliot L. Richardson 1975–1977	Peter J. Brennan 1974–1975 John T. Dunlop 1975–1976 W. J. Usery 1976–1977	Caspar W. Weinberger 1974–1975 Forrest D. Matthews 1975–1977	James T. Lynn 1974–1975 Carla A. Hills 1975–1977	Claude S. Brinegar 1974–1975 William T. Coleman 1975–1977		
Juanita Kreps 1977–1981	F. Ray Marshall 1977–1981	Joseph Califano 1977–1979 Patricia Roberts Harris 1979–1980 **Secretary of Health and Human Services** Patricia Roberts Harris 1980–1981 — **Secretary of Education** Shirley M. Hufstedler 1980–1981	Patricia Roberts Harris 1977–1979 Moon Landrieu 1979–1981	Brock Adams 1977–1979 Neil E. Goldschmidt 1979–1981	James R. Schlesinger 1977–1979 Charles W. Duncan, Jr. 1979–1981	
Malcolm Baldridge 1981–1987 C. William Verity, Jr. 1987–1989	Raymond J. Donovan 1981–1985 William E. Brock 1985–1987 Ann Dore McLaughlin 1987–1989	Richard S. Schweiker 1981–1983 Margaret M. Heckler 1983–1985 Otis R. Bowen 1985–1989 — Terrell H. Bell 1981–1985 William J. Bennett 1985–1988 Lauro Fred Cavazos 1988–1989	Samuel R. Pierce, Jr. 1981–1989	Drew Lewis 1981–1983 Elizabeth H. Dole 1983–1987 James H. Burnley 1987–1989	James B. Edwards 1981–1982 Donald P. Hodel 1982–1985 John S. Harrington 1985–1989	
Robert Mosbacher 1989–1991 Barbara Franklin 1991–1992	Elizabeth Dole 1989–1992 Lynn Martin 1992	Louis Sullivan 1989–1992 — Lamar Alexander 1990–1992	Jack Kemp 1989–1992	Samuel Skinner 1989–1990 Andrew Card 1990–1992	James Watkins 1989–1992	Edward J. Derwinski 1989–1992
Ronald H. Brown 1993–1996 William M. Daley 1997–	Robert B. Reich 1993–1996 Alexis M. Herman 1997–	Donna E. Shalala 1993– — Richard W. Riley 1993–	Henry G. Cisneros 1993–1996 Andrew M. Cuomo 1997–	Federico F. Peña 1993–1996 Rodney E. Slater 1997–	Hazel O'Leary 1993–1996 Federico F. Peña 1997–	Jesse Brown 1993–1997 Togo D. West, Jr.[2] 1998–

[2]Acting Secretary

Photo Credits

Prologue

Page 2 © 1899 By L. Frank Baum and W. W. Denslow; p. 5 Corbis-Bettmann; p. 8 Reproduced for the collections of the Library of Congress.

Chapter 1

Page 14 Courtesy Sears, Roebuck & Co.; p. 18 from the Collections of the Library of Congress; p. 26 Photograph by Byron, the Byron Collection, Museum of the City of New York; p. 30 © Collection of the New York Historical Society; p. 33 Reproduced from the collections of the Library of Congress; p. 38 the Granger Collection, New York; p. 39 Photograph by Byron, the Byron Collection, Museum of the City of New York; p. 41 Corbis-Bettmann; p. 43 San Diego Historical Society, Photograph Collection.

Chapter 2

Page 52 UPI/Corbis-Bettmann; p. 53 Photograph by Jessie Tarbox Beals, the Jacob A. Riis Collection, #502, Museum of the City of New York; p. 55 Courtesy Chicago Historical Society; p. 59 New York University, Tamiment Library; p. 69 State Historical Society of Wisconsin, WHi (X3) 49413; p. 72 Culver Pictures, Inc.; p. 77 Chicago Historical Society; p. 78 Corbis-Bettmann; p. 86 Underwood Photo Archives, S.F.

Chapter 3

Page 98 the Granger Collection, New York; p. 101 © Collection of the New York Historical Society; p. 102 Reproduced from the Collections of the Library of Congress; p. 104 National Archives #111-RB-2839; p. 109 UPI/Corbis-Bettmann; p. 111 Keyston-Mast Collection, California Museum of Photography, University of California, Riverside; p. 115 the Granger Collection; p. 117 UPI/Corbis-Bettmann; p. 119 Corbis-Bettmann; p. 122 Washington Evening Star, Library of Congress.

Chapter 4

Page 130 U.S. Signal Corps Photo No. 111-SC-94980 in the National Archives; p. 133 National Archives #165-WW-165-1; p. 141 Courtesy of the Schomburg Center For Research in Black Culture, the New York Public Library, New York; p. 142 Photo by J. E. Stimson, Wyoming Division of Cultural Resources, Wyoming State Museum; p. 144 the Granger Collection, New York; p. 147 Ellis Island Immigration Museum, Statue of Liberty National Monument; p. 148 National Archives; p. 152 *The New York Times*, 1919; p. 159 U.S. War Dept. General Staff photo no. 165-WW-464E-1 in the National Archives; p. 163 Moorland-Springarn Research Center, Howard University.

Chapter 5

Page 168 the Granger Collection, New York; p. 172 UPI/Corbis-Bettmann; p. 174 Courtesy of the Rhode Island Historical Society, neg # RHi(x3) 8860; p. 178 Corbis-Bettmann; p. 180 Corbis-Bettmann; p. 185 Courtesy Sears, Roebuck and Co.; p. 187 UPI/Corbis-Bettmann; p. 193 UPI/Corbis-Bettmann; p. 197 Frank Driggs/Corbis-Bettmann; p. 199 UPI/Corbis-Bettmann; p. 203 UPI/Corbis-Bettmann.

Chapter 6

Page 216 National Archives; p. 219 Corbis-Bettmann; p. 227 Corbis-Bettmann; p. 231 UPI/Corbis-Bettmann; p. 235 UPI/

Corbis-Bettmann; p. 237 Fine Arts Program, Public Buildings Service, U.S. General Services Administration; p. 239 UPI/Corbis-Bettmann; p. 241 UPI/Corbis-Bettmann; p. 244 UPI/Corbis-Bettmann; p. 246 UPI/Corbis-Bettmann.

Chapter 7

Page 267 Navy Department Photo No. 80-G-421289 in the National Archives; p. 269 Franklin D. Roosevelt Library; p. 275 U.S. Army Photograph #299/129; p. 276 San Diego Historical Society, Photograph Collection; p. 280 San Diego Historical Society, Union-Tribune Collection; p. 284 Office of War Information, OWI Poster #20; p. 285 Wamsutta Mills, New Bedford, Massachusetts (Chisolm Gallery); p. 287 Photographs and Prints Division, Schomburg Center for Research in Black Culture, the New York Public Library. Astor, Lenox and Tilden Foundations. Office of War Information; p. 288 UPI/Corbis-Bettmann; p. 290 Dust Storm at Manzanar, photo by Dorothea Lange from the National Archives.

Chapter 8

Page 305 Michael Barson Collection; p. 308 Stock Montage, Inc.; p. 313 AP/Wide World Photos; p. 317 San Diego Historical Society, Union-Tribune Collection; p. 325 © 1950 Time Inc., Reprinted by Permission; p. 326 Look Magazine, 1950s; p. 328 UPI/Corbis-Bettmann; p. 330 © Elliott Erwitt/Magnum Photos, Inc.; p. 332 UPI/Corbis-Bettmann; p. 337 Michael Barson; p. 340 San Diego Historical Society, Photograph Collection.

Chapter 9

Page 355 AP/Wide World Photos; p. 363 San Diego Historical Society, Union-Tribune Collection; p. 364 San Diego Historical Society, Photograph Collection; p. 365 Archive Photos/Lambert; p. 369 UPI/Corbis-Bettmann; p. 373 UPI/Corbis-Bettmann; p. 380 AP/Wide World Photos; p. 382 Corbis-UPI/Bettmann.

Chapter 10

Page 400 AP/Wide World Photos; p. 405 AP/Wide World Photos; p. 406 © Lisa Law/The Image Works; p. 407 © 1965 Bruce Davidson/Magnum Photos, Inc.; p. 408 UPI/Corbis-Bettmann; p. 409 AP/Wide World Photos; p. 418 National Organization for Women; p. 422 © Steve Weber/Stock, Boston; p. 427 UPI/Corbis-Bettmann.

Chapter 11

Page 442 © 1994 Martin Parr/Magnum Photos, Inc.; p. 443 © 1995 Chris Steele-Perkins/Magnum Photos, Inc.; p. 445 MIKE SMITH reprinted by permission of United Feature Syndicate, Inc.; p. 452 AP/Wide World Photos; p. 453 Oliver Stone cartoon, 1995 Dayton Daily News, Distributed by Tribune Media Services, reprinted with permission; p. 454 Corbis-Bettmann; p. 456 AP/Wide World Photos; p. 459 UPI/Corbis-Bettmann; p. 465 © Bill Pugliano/Gamma Liaison; p. 467 San Diego Historical Society, Union-Tribune Collection.

Chapter 12

Page 496 Reuters/Corbis-Bettmann; p. 499 Photograph by David Hume Kennerly; p. 500 AP/Wide World Photos; p. 501 Jacques Witt/SIPA; p. 505 AP/Wide World; p. 512 Agence France Presse/Corbis-Bettmann; p. 513 © 1/26/98, U.S. News & World Report; p. 514 © 2/2/98, U.S. News & World Report.

Index

Abbott, Edith, 56
Abortion rights, 419, 457, 471, 508
Abraham Lincoln battalion, 256
Accommodationism, 3, 5, 71
Acheson, Dean, 311, 322
Acid rain, 447
ACLU. *See* American Civil Liberties Union
Activism, 457–461. *See also* New Deal
  African American, 462–463
  Asian American, 467–468
  environmental, 446–449
  governmental, 375–377
  Hispanic, 465–467
  homosexual, 460–461
  Native American, 463–465
  race, ethnicity, and, 4–7, 461–463
  sexual politics and, 460–461
  social, 457–461
  of women, 54–58, 458–459
  women's movement and, 458–460
Adams, Henry, 22
Adams, Sherman, 341
Adamson Act, 89
Addams, Jane, 50–51, 54–55, 56–57, 65, 72–73, 133–134
Administrations (presidential), A22–A27
Advertising, 171–172, 283, 354
AEF. *See* American Expeditionary Force
AFDC. *See* Aid to Families with Dependent Children (AFDC)
Affirmative action, 469, 488, 489
Affluence
  discontents of, 347, 361–366
  mass culture and, 364–366
  in 1950s, 353–361
Affluent Society, The (Galbraith), 358, 377
AFL. *See* American Federation of Labor (AFL)
AFL-CIO, 358, 444
Africa. *See also* Third World
  North Africa (Second World War), 264–265, 266 (map)
  Somalia, 505, 510
  South Africa and, 316
African Americans. *See also* Affirmative action; Civil rights struggle

in armed forces, 103, 104
in baseball, 331–332
black nationalism and, 162–163
civil rights and, 71–72, 329–331
communities of, 195–196
culture of, 196
in Democratic Party, 232–233
disfranchisement of, 65
after First World War, 161–163
in First World War military, 143–144
Harlem Renaissance and, 197–198
Ku Klux Klan and, 187–188
labor and, 33–35, 37
migration to North, 141–142
in New Deal, 235, 240–241
poverty and, 488
race riots and, 288–289
resistance by, 4–6
in Second World War, 280, 286–291
social activism and, 462–463
in Twenties, 195–196
in U.S. population, 367–368, 367 (map)
Wilson and, 88
women and, 338, 385, 462
Afrocentrism, 462
Aggression, before Second World War, 254–263
Aging. *See* Elderly
Agnew, Spiro, 426
"Agrarians, the" (writers), 202
Agricultural Adjustment Act, 218, 219, 220
Agricultural Adjustment Administration, 241
Agricultural workers, 444
Agriculture. *See also* Farms and farming
  depression in Twenties, 183–184
  in 1890s, 1–3
  immigrant labor in, 26–27
  Japanese immigrants and, 30
  in New Deal, 218–219
  subsidies to, 22
  tariffs and, 210
Agriculture Department, 78
Aguinaldo, Emilio, 106

AIDS (acquired immunodeficiency syndrome), 461
Aid to Families with Dependent Children (AFDC), 415, 486, 497, 509
AIM. *See* American Indian Movement
Aircraft Production Board, 140
Airplanes, 129
Air pollution, 446, 447
Air power, 273
Alabama, school integration in, 370
Alcatraz, sit-in at, 463
Alcohol and alcoholism, 57
  ethnicity and, 57
  Prohibition and, 149, 185–186
Aldrich, Nelson, 74
Aldrin, Edwin ("Buzz"), 435
All-American Canal, 224
Allende Gossens, Salvador, 423
Alliance for Progress, 351, 380
Alliances. *See also* Military alliances
  in First World War, 127, 129
  in Second World War, 257
Allies (Allied Powers)
  in First World War, 127
  in Second World War, 257, 258, 268 (map)
All in the Family (television show), 451
All Quiet on the Western Front (movie), 255
Altgeld, John P., 55
Amalgamated Clothing Workers, 175, 238
Amendments, A10–A17. *See also* specific amendments
America First Committee, 259
American Civil Liberties Union, 191–192, 498
American Communist Party. *See* Communist Party, American
American Dilemma, An (Myrdal), 290
American Economic Association, 69
American Enterprise Institute, 470
American Expeditionary Force, 137–139, 144–145
American Federation of Labor (AFL), 35–37, 143, 238, 358
American-Filipino War, 107–108

American Hospital Association (AHA), 328
American Indian Movement, 462–463
American Indians. *See* Native Americans
American Medical Association (AMA), 328
American Protective League, 150, 160
American Railway Union, 4
American Smelting and Refining Company, 20
American Telephone and Telegraph, 15
American Tobacco Company, 15, 96
American Union Against Militarism, 134
Ames, Aldrich, 511
Amlie, Tom, 228
Amsterdam News (newspaper), 286
Amusement parks, 11, 39
Anacostia Flats, Bonus Army at, 212
Anarchists, 20, 160
Anderson, John, 485
Anderson, Marian, 240
Anderson, Sherwood, 201–202
Anglo Saxons
   Ku Klux Klan and, 187
   racial superiority and, 21
Annexation
   of Hawaii, 99
   of Puerto Rico, 109
Anthony, Susan B., 67
Anticommunism, 316. *See also* Subversives
   courts and, 321–322
   gays and, 320
   labor movement and, 317–318
Antidiscrimination movement. *See* Civil rights struggle; Discrimination; Segregation
Anti-German crusade, in First World War, 148–149
Anti-Imperialist League, 106–107
Anti-Japanese sentiment, 117
Anti-Saloon League, 57
Anti-Semitism, 24, 260. *See also* Jews and Judaism
   of Coughlin, 225
   Holocaust and, 268–270
Antitrust movement, 15
Antiwar movement, 403, 404–405, 407, 411–412, 421
ANZUS collective security pact, 315

Apartheid, 316
API. *See* "Asian or Pacific Islander" (API)
Appalachia, 291, 383
Appliances, 169, 335, 358
Arab world. *See also* Camp David accords
   Nasser and, 351–352
   oil resources in, 449–450
Arbenz Guzmán, Jacobo, 349
Arbitration, UMW and, 76
Architecture, realism in, 54
Area Redevelopment Bill, 383
Argonne forest, battle in, 139
Aristide, Jean-Bertrand, 510
Armed forces. *See also* Casualties; Military; Navy; specific wars
   African Americans in, 103, 104
   discrimination in, 286–287, 288
   First World War and, 127, 132, 143–145
   Japanese Americans in, 291
   propaganda in Second World War and, 283
   segregation in, 143–144, 330
   Soviet, 349
   in Spanish-American War, 100, 101
   women in, 284, 285
Armenia, immigrants from, 24
Armies of the Night (Mailer), 407
Armistice, for First World War, 139
Armour meatpacking company, 15
Arms and armaments. *See* Weapons
Arms control
   under Eisenhower, 348
   under Nixon, 420
   SALT and, 420
Armstrong, Louis, 196
Armstrong, Neil, 435
Army-McCarthy hearings, 341
Arnold, Henry Harley ("Hap"), 273
Arrowsmith (Lewis), 201
Arsenal of democracy, U.S. as, 260–261
Art(s). *See also* Mass culture; National Endowment for the Arts (NEA); specific arts
   African American culture and, 462
   Harlem Renaissance and, 197–198
   "Lost Generation" and, 201–203
   masculinity in, 237
   mass culture and, 455

music and, 196, 362–364
New Deal and, 231
realism in, 53–54
WPA and, 232
Articles of Constitution. *See* Constitution of the United States
Artificial intelligence, 440
ARU. *See* American Railway Union
"Aryan" Race, 255
Ashcan school, 53–54
Asia. *See also* East Asia; Immigrants and immigration; Pacific region; Southeast Asia; specific countries
   anti-immigrant attitudes toward, 118
   China and Open Door policy in, 110–112
   economic failure in, 512
   Five-Power Treaty and, 181
   immigration from, 149, 436
   imperialism and, 96
   Japanese aggression in, 262–263
   Pacific Rim region and, 503
   racism toward immigrants from, 6
   refugees from, 437
   Roosevelt, Theodore, and, 116–119
   after Second World War, 295
   Second World War and, 255
Asian Americans, 6, 467–468. *See also* specific groups
Asian Law Caucus, 467–468
"Asian or Pacific Islander" (API), 468
Asian Pacific Planning Council (APPCON), 467
Asiatic Barred Zone, 149
Assembly line, 17–18
"Associationalism," of Hoover, 179–180, 181
Astronauts. *See* Space program
Aswan Dam, 351
Atheism, 360
Athletics. *See* Sports; specific sports
Atlantic Charter, 261
Atlantic Monthly, 52
Atlantic region, in Second World War, 263, 264–270
ATMs. *See* Automatic teller machines
Atomic Energy Commission (AEC), 315
Atomic weapons. *See also* Nuclear weapons

Japan and, 274–277
radioactivity from tests, 348–349
Soviets and, 311
Truman and, 302
Attorney General's list, 304
Australia, 315
Australian ballot, 64
Austria, 348
Hitler and, 257
Austria-Hungary, First World War
and, 127, 131
Automatic teller machines (ATMs),
441
Automation, in workplace, 326
Automobiles, 11, 169. *See also* Ford,
Henry; Ford Motor Com-
pany; General Motors
emissions from, 447
in 1950s, 356–357
sales of (1940–1970), 357
Axis powers, 257, 295–296

Babbitt (Lewis), 201
Baby and Child Care (Spock),
335–337
Baby boom, 333, 433
Baer, George F., 76
Baker, James, 504
Baker, Josephine, 168
Bakker, Jim, 472
Baldwin, Hanson, 277
Balkan region, First World War
and, 128–129
Ballinger-Pinchot controversy,
81–82
Baltic region, 152, 257, 293, 501
"Bank holiday," 216
Banking Act (1935), 232
Bank of America, 30, 234
Banks and banking
electronic, 441
Federal Reserve and, 87–88
Glass-Steagall Act and, 211
Hoover and, 212
investment bankers and, 15
in New Deal, 216
Roosevelt, Theodore, and, 80
Bara, Theda, 41
Barbie dolls, 355
Barrios, 289
Barton, Bruce, 171, 173
Baruch, Bernard, 302
Baseball, 193
integration of, 331–332
Basie, "Count," 196

Batista, Fulgencio, 350
Battles. *See* specific battles
Baum, L. Frank, 1, 2
Bay of Pigs disaster, 381, 382
Beard, Charles, 53
Beatles, 406
Beer-Wine Revenue Act (1933),
218
Begin, Menachem, 483
Behrman, Martin, 31
Beijing, 256
Belgium, First World War and, 129
Bellows, George, 53
Benefits (for workers), 174, 358,
374, 416
Bennett, William, 456
Berger, Victor, 60
Berkeley, student unrest at, 404
Berkman, Alexander, 20
Berle, Adolph, 215
Berlin
division of, 294
Kennedy and, 381
Berlin blockade, 307
Berlin Wall, 381
destruction of, 500, 501
Bernays, Edward, 171
Berry, Chuck, 362, 363
Bethune, Mary McLeod, 235
Beveridge, Albert J., 79, 97
BIA. *See* Bureau of Indian Affairs
(BIA)
Bible, Scopes trial and evolutionary
theory, 191–192
Bicycles, 21
Big Four (First World War), 152
Big Parade, The (movie), 255
Big stick policy, of Roosevelt,
Theodore, 119
Big Three (First World War), 152
Bilingual education, 456
Bill Cosby Show (television show), 451
Bill of Rights. *See* "Indian Bill of
Rights"; Second Bill of
Rights
Biotechnology, 440
Birmingham, Alabama, racial
struggles in, 385, 408
Birth control, 42
Birth of a Nation (film), 187
Birth rate, 433
Blackboard Jungle, The (movie), 363
Black Cabinet, 241
Blacklist, in Hollywood, 319
Blackmun, Harry, 417

Black Muslims. *See* Nation of Islam
Black nationalism, 162–163, 196
Black Panther Party, 410
Black Power movement, 408–410
Blacks. *See* African Americans
Black Star Line, 162
"Black Tuesday," 208
Blease, Coleman, 228
Blitzkrieg, 257
Blockades, in First World War, 131
Bloom, Allan, 455
Blue Cross and Blue Shield, 328
Bohemian immigrants, 24
Bolshevik Party (Russia), 137, 160
Bombs and bombings, 273. *See also*
Atomic weapons
atomic bomb and, 274–277
Blitzkrieg, 257
hydrogen bomb, 311
at Murrah Federal Building, 472
of Vietnam, 399, 421
at World Trade Center, 511
Bonneville Dam, 222
Bonus Army, 212–213
Boom-and-bust economic cycles,
325
Bootlegging, 32
Borah, William, 155
Border Patrol, 199
Bork, Robert, 488, 497
Bosnia, 128, 501, 505
Bosses, political, 31–32, 63
Boston
elite in, 22
strikes in, 158–159
Boulder Dam, 222, 224
Boxer Rebellion, 111–112
Boycott, of Montgomery buses, 368
Bracero program, 279
Brady Bill, 508
Branch Davidian group, 472
Brandeis, Louis D., 54, 70, 81, 89
Brannan, Charles, 327
Brazil, 423
Breckinridge, Sophonisba, 56
Brennan, William, 417
Brest-Litovsk, Treaty of, 137
Bretton Woods agreement, 293,
414–415
Briand, Aristide, 182
Britain. *See* England (Britain)
Brotherhood of Sleeping Car
Porters, 196
Brown, Andy, 197
Brown, Henry Billings, 4

Brown, Herman and George, 234
Brown, James, 410
Brown v. *Board of Education of Topeka,* 366, 368
Bryan, William Jennings, 1, 51, 81, 106, 131, 132, 134, 214
  "Cross of Gold" speech of, 7
  election of 1896 and, 7–9
  Scopes trial and, 191–192
Bryce, James, 116
Brzezinski, Zbigniew, 482
Buchanan, Patrick, 426
Buckley, William F., Jr., 375, 470
Budget (federal). *See also* Carter, James Earl (Jimmy); Great Society
  Clinton and, 509, 512
  Reagan and, 497
Bulgaria, 24, 294, 501
Bulge, Battle of, 267
Bull Moose party. *See* Progressive Party, in 1912
Bunau-Varilla, Philippe, 115–116
Bundy, McGeorge, 399
Bureau of Immigration and Naturalization, 64
Bureau of Indian Affairs (BIA), 243, 370, 372
Bureau of Reclamation, 223–224
Burger, Warren, 417, 488, 497
Burleson, Albert, 88, 151
Bush, George, 499
  election of 1988 and, 498–500
  election of 1992 and, 506–508
  foreign policy of, 500–505
  Iran-*Contra* and, 495
  NEA and, 456
  Persian Gulf War and, 504–505
Bush, Vannevar, 278
Business, 441–443. *See also* Corporations
  Coolidge and, 177–179
  corporate consolidation and, 15–16
  Duke and, 14
  economic change and, 1
  FDR and, 233–234
  imperialism and, 96–97
  industrialization and, 10
  internationalization of, 442–443, 445
  labor conflict and, 158–160
  management revolution and, 16
  neoconservatives and, 470
  overseas expansion of, 442

  politics of, 176–183
  Reagan and, 488
  robber barons in, 19–20
  in Second World War, 278–279
  in Twenties, 173

Cable television (CATV), 452–453, 454
California. *See also* Los Angeles
  anti-Japanese sentiment in, 117
  immigrants in, 436
  Japanese in, 30
  Mexicans in, 199–200
  Proposition 209 in, 469
  Silicon Valley and, 435
  water projects and, 224
Californios, 199
Calley, William, 421
Cambodia, 352, 421, 437, 478
Camp David accords (1978), 482–483
Canada. *See also* North American Free Trade Agreement (NAFTA)
  immigrants from, 23, 24
Canals, 356
Canal Zone. *See* Panama Canal
Cannon, Joseph G., 74, 81
Capitalism
  affluence and, 358
  after First World War, 170
  welfare capitalism and, 173, 174
Capone, Al, 32, 186
Capra, Frank, 238–239, 283
Caribbean Basin Initiative, 494
Caribbean region
  dollar diplomacy in, 120
  U.S. dominance in, 110
  Wilson's policy in, 121
Carmichael, Stokely, 410
Carnegie, Andrew, 3, 15, 20, 106, 159
Carnegie foundations, 20
Caroline Islands, 295
Carranza, Venustiano, 122–123
Cars. *See* Automobile industry
Carson, Rachel, 446
Cartels, 15
Carter, James Earl (Jimmy), 309, 400, 476, 511
  economic policy of, 481–482
  election of 1976 and, 478–479, 479 (map)
  election of 1980 and, 484–486, 485 (map)

  energy and, 449, 480–481
  foreign policy of, 482–484
  hostage crisis and, 483–484
  human rights policy of, 483
  Panama Canal and, 116
  presidency of, 480–484
Casablanca meeting, 264
Casey, William, 494
"Cash-and-carry" policy, 256, 259
Castro, Fidel, 350–351, 378, 380–381, 494
Casualties
  in American-Filipino War, 107–108
  in First World War, 130
  in Second World War, 254
  in Vietnam War, 422
Catalog sales, of houses, 185
Catholics
  FDR's advisers and, 234–235
  Kennedy as, 378
  Klan and, 187, 188
  Smith as presidential candidate and, 194
Catholic schools, 193
Catholic Worker, The, 361
Catt, Carrie Chapman, 68, 133
CATV. *See* Cable television (CATV)
Caute, David, 320
CD-ROM, 454
CDs. *See* Compact discs (CDs)
Censorship, 362
CENTO. *See* Central Treaty Organization
Central America. *See also* specific countries
  Bush and, 503
  immigration from, 438
  Reagan and, 493
  United Fruit Company in, 120–121
Central Intelligence Agency (CIA), 306, 307
  Ames scandal and, 511
  Bay of Pigs invasion and, 381
  covert activities of, 349–350, 423, 494
  Diem coup and, 383
Central Powers, 131
Central Treaty Organization, 348
Central Valley Project, 224
CETA. *See* Comprehensive Employment and Training Act (CETA)
CFCs. *See* Chlorofluorocarbons (CFCs)

Chain stores, 441–442
Charity. *See* Philanthropy
Chavez, Cesar, 386, 444
Cheers (television show), 451
Cheney, Lynn, 456
Chiang Kai-shek. *See* Jiang Jieshi
Chicago
  black workers in, 34
  Capone in, 32
  Democratic Convention in
    (1968), 411–412
  Hull House in, 54–56
  Pullman strike and, 4
  race riot in, 162
  reform in, 61
Chicana and Chicano farm work-
    ers, 385
Chicanos, 242–243, 466
Child Development Act, 416
Child labor, outlawing of, 89
Children, 361–362
Chile, 423
China
  Boxer Rebellion in, 111–112
  Cold War and, 311
  immigration from, 23, 24, 438
  Japanese invasion of, 256–257
  Korean War and, 313–315
  Mao Zedong in, 271, 311
  Nixon and, 420
  Open Door policy and, 110–112,
    117, 120
  Second World War and, 271
  trade with, 512
China lobby, 271
Chinese Americans, 467, 468
Chinese Exclusion Act (1882), 6,
    118
Chlorofluorocarbons (CFCs), 449
Choice, Not an Echo, A (Schlafly),
    386
Christian Broadcasting Network,
    472
Christianity. *See also* Protestantism;
    Religion
Chrysler Corporation, 443
Church, Frank, 423
Churchill, Winston, 264, 293–294
  Atlantic Charter and, 261
CIA. *See* Central Intelligence
    Agency (CIA)
Cigarettes
  American Tobacco Company
    and, 15
  Duke and, 14

CIO. *See* Congress of Industrial Or-
    ganizations (CIO)
Cisneros, Henry, 466
Cities and towns, 39–40. *See also*
    Urban areas; Urbanization
  costs of reform in, 62
  municipal reform and, 61–62
  population and economic
    changes in, 438–440
  racial composition of, 367–368
  transportation in, 11
Citizenship
  education in, 193
  for Hawaiians, 105
  naturalization and, 194
  for Puerto Ricans, 110, 436
City commission plan, 61–62
City manager plan, 62
Civil defense work, 280
Civilian Conservation Corps, 216,
    217, 278
Civil Rights Act
  of 1960, 460
  of 1964, 393
  of 1968, 410, 464
Civil rights and liberties, 4–7,
    71–73. *See also* Civil rights
    struggle; House Committee
    on Un-American Activities
    (HUAC); NAACP; Women
  accommodationism and, 71
  African Americans and, 287–288
  of communists, 321–322
  gender equality and, 418–419
  Johnson and, 392–393
  Kennedy and, 378, 384–385
  NAACP and, 72–73
  New Deal and, 233
  Nixon and, 417–419
  politics of, 369–370
  Reagan and, 488
  Roosevelt, Eleanor, and, 286
  Truman and, 329–331
Civil rights bill, of Kennedy, 385
Civil rights struggle, 407. *See also*
    Civil rights and liberties
  Black Power movement and,
    408–410
  King, Martin Luther, Jr., and,
    368–369
  Montgomery bus boycott and,
    368–369
  New Left and, 404
Civil war, in Spain, 256
Civil Works Administration, 217–218

Clamshell Alliance, 457
Clark, Champ, 84
Clark, Tom, 319, 336
Class(es). *See also* Elites; Middle
    class
  class warfare and, 44
  divisions among, 146
Clayton Act, 88
Clean Air Act (1970), 447
"Clear and present danger" doc-
    trine, 321–322
Clemenceau, Georges, 152, 153
Cleveland, Grover, 3, 106
  election of 1896 and, 7
  Hawaii and, 98–99
  Pullman strike and, 4
Cleveland, Ohio, reform in, 61
Clinton, Bill
  domestic policy of, 508–510
  election of 1992 and, 506–508
  election of 1996 and, 512–513
  environment and, 448
  foreign policy of, 510–512
  "Nannygate" and, 428
  sex scandals and, 514
  Whitewater and, 508
Clinton, Hillary Rodham, 507, 508
Closed shops, 318
Clubwomen, 57–58
Coal industry, 81
Coca-Cola, 279, 325
Cochran, Johnnie, Jr., 463
Codes
  Japanese, 263, 270
  Navajo language and, 272
Coeur d'Alene, Idaho, strike in, 3
Cohen, Ben, 234
Cold War, 301–303. *See also* Com-
    munism
  containment at home and,
    316–323
  détente policy and, 420
  end of, 476, 495–496, 500–502,
    502 (map)
  Kennedy and, 378
  Nixon Doctrine and, 423
  Reagan and, 491–492
Collective bargaining, 36
  Railway Labor Act and, 180
Collective security, 292, 315
Collier, John, 243, 244
Colombia, Panama Canal and,
    114–116
Colonialism, 99, 105–112. *See also*
    Imperialism

First World War and, 129
freedom from, 151
after Second World War, 295
Coloreds. *See* African Americans
Color line, Robinson, Jackie, and, 331–332
Comic book industry, 362
Commentary, 470
Commission on Civil Rights, 369
Commission on Protecting and Reducing Government Secrecy, 321
Committee Against Anti-Asian Violence, 468
Committee for Public Information, 146–147, 221
Committee for the Survival of a Free Congress, 471
Committee on the Present Danger, 470
Committee to Defend America by Aiding the Allies, 260
Commons, John R., 51, 69
Communications, 10
Communism. *See also* Containment policy; Covert activities; House Committee on Un-American Activities (HUAC); Subversives
in China, 311
containment of, 304
détente policy and, 420
Eisenhower and, 341–342
end of Cold War and, 500–502
FBI and, 319–320
NSC-68 and, 311–312
Rosenberg case and, 320–322
in Russia, 137
in Vietnam, 352–353
Communist Control Act (1950), 341
Communist Party
American, 229, 318, 321–322
McCarthy and, 322–323
Communities. *See also* Cities and towns; Suburbs; Urbanization
African-American, 34–35
Community Action Program (CAP), 395
Compact discs (CDs), 454
Competition
athletic, 21
corporate consolidation and, 15
Comprehensive Employment and Training Act (CETA), 489

Computer revolution, 440–441, 445–446
Coney Island, 39
Conformity, social, 361–362
Congress
elections of 1994 and, 508–509
New Deal legislation and, 278
radicals in, 228
Taft and, 81
Congressional Government (Wilson), 83
Congress of Industrial Organizations (CIO), 227, 238, 318, 358
Congress on Racial Equality, 289–290, 384
Conscience of a Conservative (Goldwater), 375
Conscription, 143
Conservationist movement, 77–79
Conservation Reserve Program (1997), 448
Conservatism, 471–472. *See also* New Right
campus unrest and, 404
cultural, 56–57
Eisenhower and, 375
neoconservatives and, 470
in Protestantism, 190–191
Reagan and, 486, 488–490
Conservative Caucus, 471
Consolidation, corporate, 15–16
Constitution of the United States, A2–A10 *See also* specific amendments
amendments to, A10–A17
civil rights issues and, 417
Indians and, 371
national security and, 323
Consumer society
advertising and mass marketing in, 171–172
credit in, 170
after First World War, 169–170
franchising and, 441
in 1950s, 353–361
rural dwellers and, 184–185
safety and, 417
after Second World War, 325
Second World War propaganda and, 283
Containment policy, 301. *See also* Society
Cold War and, 301–303

Korean War and, 315–316
Truman Doctrine and, 303–304
in United States, 317–331
Contras, 493, 494–495. *See also* Iran-*Contra* affair
Coolidge, Calvin, 158–169, 173, 177–179, 182, 194
Cooper, Harry, 197
Cooperative Marketing Act (1926), 180
COPS (Communities Organized for Public Service), 466
Corcoran, Thomas "Tommy the Cork," 234
CORE. *See* Congress on Racial Equality
Corporations, 1, 10. *See also* Business
consolidation among, 15–16
FDR and, 233–234
growth of, 12–13
labor accords with, 358–359
management revolution and, 16
progressivism and, 79–80
in Second World War, 279
Corridos, 200
Corruption, in government, 176–177
Cortes, Ernest, Jr., 466
Costa Rica, 121, 350
Cotton Club, 197
Cotton industry, 26
Coughlin, Charles, 225
Council of Economic Advisers, 324
Counterculture, 405–407
Counterintelligence, 304
Coups. *See* Central Intelligence Agency (CIA); Diem, Ngo Dinh
Courts. *See* Supreme Court
Cousins, Norman, 236
Covert activities, 307, 347, 349–350, 380–381, 423, 494
Cox, Archibald, 426
Cox, James M., 176
Coxey, Jacob, 3
Coxey's army, 3
CP. *See* Communist Party, American
CPI. *See* Committee for Public Information
Craft unions, 36–37
Cramer, Charles, 177
Credit, consumer, 170
Creel, George, 146
CREEP (Committee to Re-Elect the President), 424, 425, 426

Crime and criminals. *See also* Gun control
  cities and, 481
  Kennedy and, 384
  Miranda rights and, 417
  organized crime and, 32
Crisis, The, 73, 161, 287
"Crisis of the 1890s," 7
Croatia and Croatians, 24, 128–129, 501
Croker, "King Richard," 31
"Cross of Gold" speech (Bryan), 7
Cuba, 245, 350–351
  control of, 108–109
  immigrants from, 436, 438, 465–466
  Kennedy and, 380–381
  Spanish-American War and, 99–100, 101–102
  troops in, 114
Cuban Missile Crisis (1962), 381
Cullen, Countee, 197
Cultural pluralism, 244
Cultural studies, 455–456
Culture. *See also* Harlem Renaissance; specific groups
  of African Americans, 196, 197–198
  in Great Depression, 208
  mass, 364–366, 454–456
  media and, 450–457
  of Mexican Americans, 198–200, 242–243
  military, 286
  of Native Americans, 6
  youth, 362–364
cummings, e. e., 201
Curley, James Michael, 31
Currency. *See* Gold standard
CWA. *See* Civil Works Administration
Czechoslovakia, 152, 257, 500

Daley, Richard J., 411
Dams, 222, 356. *See also* Water projects
Dandridge v. *Williams,* 417
Danish West Indies. *See* Virgin Islands
DAR. *See* Daughters of the American Revolution
Darlan, Jean, 265
Darrow, Clarence, 55, 60, 191
Darwin, Charles, 22–23, 191–192
Daugherty, Harry, 176

Daughters of Bilitis, 460
Daughters of the American Revolution, 240
Davis, John W., 194
Dawes Act (1887), 6, 243
Dawes Plan, 182
Day, Dorothy, 361
Day care, 285–286, 416
Dayton, Ohio
  accords in (1995), 510
  municipal reform in, 62
D-Day, 265–267
DDT, 357, 446
Dean, John, 426
Death(s). *See* Casualties
Death camps (Germany), 260, 269
Debs, Eugene V., 4, 58, 59, 60, 85, 134, 150, 160, 176
Debt. *See* Budget (federal)
Decolonization
  after First World War, 152–153
  after Second World War, 295
Dector, Midge, 470
Deep South. *See* Civil rights struggle; South
Defense Department, 306, 316, 376
Defense strategy. *See also* Foreign policy; National defense; Weapons
  of Eisenhower, 348–349
  Gaither Report, 376
  of Reagan, 491–492
Deficit (federal), 230. *See also* Budget (federal)
Deflation, 2, 9
Delano family, 213
De Lôme, Enrique Dupuy, 100
Demilitarization, of Rhine, 153
Democracy. *See also* Roosevelt, Franklin D.
  in former Soviet bloc, 501–502
  intellectuals on, 201–202
Democratic Party, 203. *See also* Dixiecrats; Roosevelt, Franklin D.; specific presidents and issues
  constituents of, 233–234
  election of 1896 and, 7–9
  election of 1912 and, 84–86, 85 (map)
  ethnics and, 194
  1968 convention of, 411–412
  in Twenties, 214–215
  Wilson and, 83–86
Demographics. *See also* Population

  race and population shift, 367–368
  Sunbelt and, 434–436
Demonstrations. *See* Antiwar movement; Civil rights struggle; Women's rights movement
Denmark, 153
Dennis v. *U.S.,* 322
Denslow, William, 2
Depression. *See also* Great Depression
  agricultural, 183–184
Deregulation, of financial industries, 441
Desegregation
  civil rights movement and, 384–385
  in military, 330
  official efforts toward, 368
"Deskilling," of labor force, 444
Détente policy, 420
Detroit, race riot in, 288, 289
Dewey, George, 100
Dewey, John, 53, 55, 60, 65, 73, 202, 203
Dewey, Thomas E., 307–309
Diaz, Adolfo, 121
Diaz, Porfirio, 121
Dickerson, R. Q., 197
Dictatorships. *See also* Hitler, Adolf; Mussolini, Benito; Stalin, Joseph
  in Latin America, 113, 350–351
Diem, Ngo Dinh, 352–353, 383, 398
Diplomacy. *See also* Foreign policy; Open Door policy; specific presidents
  China, Open Door policy, and, 110–112, 117, 120
  Nixon-Kissinger policies and, 420
  of Taft, William Howard, 119–121
Direct election of senators, 63
Direct primary, 63
Disarmament, 182. *See also* Arms control
Discrimination. *See also* China; Japan; Japanese Americans; Segregation
  against African Americans, 34, 37, 196
  antidiscrimination efforts and, 468–469
  against ethnic groups, 192–193
  fight against (1954–1960), 366–374

against gays, 460
gender, 393, 459–460
labor unions and, 281
in military, 286–287, 288
NAACP and, 73
against Native Americans, 370–372
against Spanish-speaking Americans, 372–373
Disease. *See also* Health and health care
in urban slums, 28
Disfranchisement, 64–65, 67–68
Distribution. *See* Mass production and distribution
Distribution of wealth, Great Depression and, 210
Dixiecrats, 307, 329–330
Dixon, Frank, 286
Doby, Larry, 331
Doheny, Edward L., 177
Dole, Bob, 513
Dollar, gold standard and, 415
Dollar diplomacy, of Taft, 119–121
Domestic policy. *See* specific presidents
Domestic service, 42
Dominican Republic, 113
intervention in, 182, 400
Wilson and, 121
Domino effect, 352, 399
Dos Passos, John, 201, 202
Doughboys, 137
Douglas, Aaron, 197
Doves (political), 403
Dower, John, 270
Dow Jones Industrial Average, 209
Downsizing, 443–444
Doyle, James, 313
Draft. *See* Conscription; Military draft
Draft card burning, 405
Draft resisters, 424
Dreiser, Theodore, 53
Drift and Mastery (Lippmann), 66
Drinking. *See* Alcohol and alcoholism
Drive-in theaters, 364
Drug trade, 503
Du Bois, W. E. B., 65, 71, 72, 73, 161, 320
black nationalism and, 163
Dukakis, Michael, 498
Duke, James B., 14, 15, 96
Dulles, John Foster, 341, 349

Dumbarton Oaks Conference, 292
Dunkirk evacuation, 257–258
DuPont, 13, 15
Dust Bowl, 219
Dylan, Bob, 405–406

Earth Summit (1992), 449
East Asia, peacekeeping in, 116–119
East Asia Co-Prosperity Sphere, 256
Eastern Europe
anti-Soviet activities in, 349
end of Cold War in, 500–502, 502 (map)
ethnic groups from, 193–195, 240
immigrants from, 24, 188
Soviet control of, 302–303
Eastern front. *See* Fronts
Easter Rebellion (Ireland), 134
East Germany, 294
Eastman, Crystal, 43
Eastman, Max, 44
EBA. *See* Emergency Banking Act
Economic and Social Council (UN), 293
Economics
immigration and, 24–25
Social Darwinism and, 22–23
Economy. *See also* Great Depression; Great Society; Immigrants and immigration; Labor; Markets; New Deal; Silver movement; Welfare programs
affluence and, 353–361
agricultural assistance and, 218–219
business and, 441–443
Carter and, 481–482, 484, 485
consumer society and, 169–170
Coolidge and, 178–179
corporate growth and, 12–13
crisis in, 1–4
election of 1896 and, 9
in First World War, 139–141
Ford and, 477
government and, 277–278, 324–327, 374–377
growth of, 10, 11–19
Hoover and, 211–212
international, 503
Kennedy-Johnson economic program and, 392–393

labor-management accords and, 357–359
Nixon and, 414–415
"people's capitalism" and, 170
prosperity in Twenties, 167–175
Reagan and, 486–487
recession of 1937–1938 and, 248–249
restructuring of, 443–446
Roosevelt, Theodore, and, 76
after Second World War, 293, 324–327
in Second World War, 277–282
technology and, 11, 440–441
underconsumptionists and, 230
Economy Act (1933), 218
Edison, Thomas, 11, 16
Education
bilingual, 456
conservatism and, 471
discrimination in, 366–368
of ethnic minorities, 193–194
federal aid to, 376–377
GI Bill and, 327
integration and, 384
multicultural, 456–457
science teaching and, 376
segregation in, 330–331
EEOC. *See* Equal Employment Opportunity Commission (EEOC)
Egypt
Camp David accords and, 482–483
Nasserism in, 351–352
Eighteenth Amendment, 57, 149, 185–186
Eighteen-year-olds, vote for, 424
Eight-hour day, 89
Einstein, Albert, 275
Eisenhower, Dwight D., 265, 269, 347
domestic policy, 341
economic role of government and, 374–377
election of 1952 and, 338–340
election of 1956 and, 370
farewell address of, 353
foreign policy under, 347–350
highways, waterways, and, 356–357
Indian policy of, 370–371
presidency of, 340–342
racial discrimination and, 370
religion and, 360

Elderly, 433–434
Elections, A20–A21
of 1892, 3
of 1896, 7–9
of 1900, 74
of 1904, 76
of 1908, 80
of 1912, 82–83, 84–86, 85 (map), 139
of 1916, 134
of 1920, 167
of 1924, 178, 194
of 1928, 194–195, 195 (map), 203
of 1932, 212, 213, 214, 215
of 1936, 232–233, 233 (map)
of 1940, 260
of 1944, 292
of 1948, 307–309, 309 (map), 329
of 1952, 338–340
of 1956, 370
of 1960, 378–379, 379 (map)
of 1964, 393–394, 398
of 1968, 411, 412–413, 413 (map)
of 1972, 421, 424, 425 (map)
of 1976, 478–479, 479 (map)
of 1980, 484–486, 485 (map)
of 1984, 490–491
of 1988, 498–500
of 1992, 506–508
of 1994, 508–509
of 1996, 512–513
direct election of senators, 63
direct primary and, 63
process of, 65–66
voter participation in presidential, 66
Electric Kool-Aid Acid Test, The (Wolfe), 406
Electric power, 11
Electronic revolution, 441–442. *See also* Video revolution
Eliot, T. S., 201, 202
Elites. *See also* Class(es)
power elite, 359
racial superiority and, 21–22
wealth of, 213
Ellington, "Duke," 196, 198
Ellsberg, Daniel, 424
Elmer Gantry (Lewis), 201
El Salvador, 438, 493, 503
Ely, Richard, 60, 69
Emergency Banking Act, 216, 218

Emergency Farm Mortgage Act (1933), 218
Emergency Fleet Corporation, 140
Emergency Relief Appropriation Act (1935), 232
Emerson, Gloria, 403
Emigration. *See* Immigrants and immigration
Empires, 129. *See also* Imperialism
Employers, welfare capitalism and, 173, 174
Employment, 443–444. *See also* Unemployment; Workforce
corporate growth and, 12–13
in 1890s, 3–4
in federal government (1891–1917), 89
postwar economic growth and, 324–327
of women, 41–42, 236, 338
women's movement and, 458–459
Employment Act (1946), 324, 326
Endangered Species Act (1973), 447
End Poverty in California (EPIC), 229
Energy, 449–450
England (Britain). *See also* First World War; Second World War
blockades in First World War, 131
Easter Rebellion and, 134
Egypt and, 351
First World War and, 127
imperialism and, 110, 111, 112
Nazi bombing of, 259
Wilson and, 131
Entente. *See* Triple Entente
Entertainment. *See also* Leisure
amusement parks, 11
in cities, 39–40
of "masses," 22
movies, 11
Entrepreneurs, ethnicity and, 29
Environment
activism and, 446–449, 481
CCC and, 216
energy issues and, 449–450
legislation and, 419
Roosevelt, Theodore, and, 77–79
water pollution and, 357
Watt and, 448, 489
Environmental Defense Fund, 446
Environmental movement, 446

Environmental Protection Agency (EPA), 447
Equal Employment Opportunity Commission (EEOC), 393
Equality. *See also* Civil rights and liberties; Civil rights struggle; specific groups
gender, 43, 284–286, 459–460
racial, 73, 286–288
Equal Pay Act (1963), 386
Equal Rights Amendment (ERA), 284, 419, 470
Ervin, Sam, 425
Espionage, Sabotage, and Sedition Acts (1917, 1918), 150
Estonia, 152, 293, 294, 501
"Ethnic" cleansing, 504
Ethnic groups. *See also* African Americans; Native Americans; Race and racism
alcohol and, 57
communities and, 28–32
in Democratic Party, 214
European Americans, 192–195
First World War prejudices and, 147
Hispanic Americans, 465–467
immigration and, 188–190
Mexican Americans, 198–200
middle class and, 29–31
New Deal and, 240
of new immigrants, 24
in Second World War, 291
Eurocentrists, 462
Europe and Europeans
ethnic immigrant communities and, 193–195
First World War and, 128–130, 154 (map)
immigration from, 23–24, 188–189
intellectual flight to, 201
Second World War and, 257–258, 258 (map), 263–270, 293–295
Evangelicals, 470–471
Evans, Hiram, 187
Evolution theory, 191–192
Excess profits tax, 145
Exchange Stabilization Fund, 512
Executive Order 9066, 290
Executive Order 9835, 304
Expansion and expansionism. *See also* First World War; Imperialism; Second World War

by Hitler, 256, 257–258, 258 (map)
Soviet, 301–302
U.S. as world power and, 95–99
Expatriates, intellectuals as, 201
Export-Import Bank, 246
Exports. *See* Trade
Extermination policy, of Hitler, 260, 269

Factories, 10
scientific management in, 16–19
in Second World War, 279–281
wages in, 27
Factory law, in Illinois, 55
Fair Deal, 327–329, 383
Fair Employment Practices Commission, 280, 287, 330
Fall, Albert, 176
Falwell, Jerry, 471, 472, 486
Family Assistance Plan (FAP), 415–416, 480
Family life
AFDC and, 415
gender and, 335–337
of immigrant laborers, 27–28
juvenile delinquency and, 336
suburban, 333–335
television and, 365
Family Support Act (1988), 497
"Family values," 471, 507
FAP. *See* Family Assistance Plan (FAP)
Far East, Second World War in, 255
Farewell to Arms, A (Hemingway), 201
Farley, Jim, 234
Farm Credit Act (1933), 218
Farmer-labor parties, 169, 183, 203
Farmers Alliance, 3
Farms and farming, 233
agricultural depression and, 183–184
cultural dislocation and, 184–185
in 1890s, 1
after First World War, 169
in Great Plains, 220
Japanese immigrants and, 30
Mexican laborers and, 198
Native Americans and, 6
in postwar period, 327
Reagan and, 487
Farm Security Administration (FSA), 278
Fascism, 255, 256

Fast-food industry, 441
"Fat Man" bomb, 276
Faubus, Orval, 370
Faulkner, William, 202
FBI. *See* Federal Bureau of Investigation (FBI)
FDIC. *See* Federal Deposit Insurance Corporation
FDR. *See* Roosevelt, Franklin D.
Federal Bureau of Investigation (FBI), 319–320, 463–464. *See also* Hoover, J. Edgar
Federal Communications Commission, 454
Federal Deposit Insurance Corporation, 217
Federal Emergency Relief Act (1933), 218
Federal Emergency Relief Administration (FERA), 217
Federal Housing Administration (FHA), 328, 333, 374
Federal Republic of Germany. *See* West Germany
Federal Reserve Act (1913), 87–88
Federal Reserve System (Fed), 209–210, 232, 249, 481, 487
Federal Trade Commission (FTC), 178–179
Federal Trade Commission Act (1914), 88
Feminine Mystique, The, 386
Femininity, in Second World War, 286
Feminism, 42–44, 458–460. *See also* Women; Women's movement
in arts, 237–238
and Kennedy administration, 385–386
women's movement and, 419
"Feminization of poverty," 459
FEPC. *See* Fair Employment Practices Commission
Ferraro, Geraldine, 490, 491
FHA. *See* Federal Housing Administration
Fifteenth Amendment, 65, 73
Filipino Americans, 467, 468. *See also* Philippines
Films. *See* Movies
Finance
in First World War, 145
in Second World War, 278–279
Financial industries, 441

Financial system, 3. *See also* Depression; Great Depression
Finland, 152
"Fireside chats," 216
First Amendment
Communist Party and, 321–322
Scopes trial and, 191
television and, 455
First New Deal (1933–1935), 215–224
First World War, 127–164, 128 (map). *See also* League of Nations; Versailles, Treaty of
armistice for, 139
escalation of, 135–136
European beginnings of, 128–130
Europe and Near East after, 154 (map)
financing, 145
labor during, 141–143
patriotism during, 146–147
peace movement in, 133–134
postwar world and, 158–163
repression during, 148–151
submarine warfare in, 131–133
United States in, 136, 138 (map)
U.S. neutrality in, 130–136
women's movement and, 68
Fitness movement. *See* Physical fitness
Fitzgerald, F. Scott, 167, 201
Fitzgerald, John Francis ("Honey Fitz"), 32
Five-Power Treaty, 181
"Flappers," in Twenties, 173
Fleischmann, Doris, 171
Flesch, Rudolf, 376
Flexible response policy, 378, 382–383
Float (economic), 415
Florida, 436
Flynn, Elizabeth Gurley, 44
"Foggy Bottom," 264
Food Administration, 140
Foods, transporting of, 169
Food Stamp program, 395, 509
Football, 21
Foraker Act (1900), 109
Forbes, Charles, 177
Ford, Gerald, 419, 426, 427, 428, 471, 476–479, 499
Ford, Henry, 11, 12, 171
black employees of, 196
scientific management and, 17

Ford, John, 239
Ford Motor Company, 13, 17–19
Foreign Affairs (journal), 304
Foreign aid, 306–307, 350
Foreign policy. *See also* Diplomacy;
    Imperialism; specific presi-
    dents and wars
  of Bush, 500–505
  of Carter, 482–484
  of Clinton, 510–512
  of Eisenhower, 341, 347–350
  First World War and, 131
  of Ford, 477–478
  of Hoover, 180–183
  isolationism and, 254–255
  of Kennedy, 379–383
  Latin America and, 182–183
  New Deal and, 245–247
  of Nixon and Kissinger, 419–423
  of Roosevelt, Theodore, 98,
    116–119
  of Taft, 119–121
  Third World and, 350–353
  of Truman, 303–304
  of Wilson, 121–123
Formosa (Taiwan), 311
442nd Regimental Combat Team,
    291
Four freedoms, 135
"Four Minute Men," 146
Fourteen Points, 137, 139, 151,
    153, 157
Fourteenth Amendment, 331
Fox television network, 451–452
France. *See also* First World War;
    Second World War
  First World War and, 127, 129,
    137, 153
  imperialism and, 110, 111, 112
  Panama Canal and, 114
  Ruhr occupation by, 181
  in Second World War, 266 (map)
  Vichy government in, 258, 264,
    265, 266 (map)
  Vietnam and, 352
Franchise. *See* Voting and voting
    rights; Woman suffrage
Franchises (business), 441
Franck, Jerome, 275
Franco, Francisco, 256
Frank, Jerome, 220
Frankfurter, Felix, 143, 202
Franz Ferdinand (Archduke), 129
Freedom Democratic Party, 393
Freedom rides, 369, 384

Freedoms. *See* Rights; specific free-
    doms
Freedom Summer, 393
"Free" enterprise economy, 357
"Free love," 42
Free-market economies, in former
    communist states, 503
Free silver, 3, 7
French Canada, immigrants from,
    23, 24
French Indochina, 315. *See also*
    Vietnam
Frick, Henry Clay, 20
Friedan, Betty, 362, 386, 458
Frontier(s), closing of western,
    96–97
Frontier thesis (Turner), 96–97
Fronts, in First World War, 129
Frost, Robert, 379
Fuel Administration, 140
Fulbright, J. William, 403
Full Employment Bill, 324
Fundamentalism, 167, 190–192,
    470–471
Fusion issue, 7, 9

Gaither Report, 376
Galbraith, John Kenneth, 358, 377,
    378
Galveston plan. *See* City commis-
    sion plan
Gambling, on Indian lands, 464,
    465
"Gangsta rap," 462
Gangsters, Prohibition and, 186
Garment workers, 26, 27, 70, 158
Garner, John Nance, 214, 215
Garrison, William Lloyd, 72
Garvey, Marcus, 162–163, 196
Gasoline-powered engine, 11
Gates, Bill, 445
Gates, Henry Lewis, Jr., 462
GATT. *See* General Agreement on
    Tariffs and Trade (GATT)
Gay Liberation Front (GLF), 461
Gays. *See* Homosexuals and homo-
    sexuality
Gehrig, Lou, 194
Gender. *See also* Women
  discrimination and, 393,
    459–460
  equality of, 43
  family life and, 335–337
  of immigrants, 25
  in New Deal, 234–238

Second World War and, 284–286
General Agreement on Tariffs and
    Trade (GATT), 293, 512
General Assembly (UN), 292
General Electric, 15
General Motors, 171, 238, 239, 353,
    358
Geneva, summit meeting in, 348
Geneva Peace Accords (1954), 352,
    353
Genocide. *See* Holocaust
Gentlemen's agreement, with
    Japan, 118
Geopolitics, of Roosevelt,
    Theodore, 112–119
German American Bund, 260
German Americans
  anti-German hysteria and,
    148–149
  First World War and, 134
German language, in First World
    War, 148–149
Germany, 247. *See also* First World
    War; Nazism; Second World
    War
  Central Powers and, 131
  containment and, 307
  Dawes Plan and, 182
  end of Cold War and, 500, 501
  after First World War, 153
  First World War and, 127,
    135–136
  imperialism and, 110, 111, 112
  Kennedy and, 381
  Mexico and, 135
  military bases in, 503
  postwar governing of, 294
  reparations and, 181
  as republic, 153
  in Second World War, 263–264,
    267–268, 268 (map)
  Soviet nonaggression pact with,
    257
  Wilson and, 131
  zones in, 294, 310 (map)
Ghetto, Harlem as, 196
Giannini, Amadeo P., 30
Giap, Nguyen, 422
GI Bill (1944), 327, 328
GI Bill of Rights (1952), 327
Gilman, Charlotte Perkins, 42
Gingrich, Newt, 509
Ginsburg, Ruth Bader, 508
Glasnost, 495, 496
Glass-Steagall Act, 211, 217, 218

Global power, of U.S., 316
Global warming, 448–449
GNP. *See* Gross national product (GNP)
God and Man at Yale (Buckley), 375
Godkin, E. L., 99
Gold, 3, 9, 211
"Gold-bug," 7
Goldman, Emma, 42
Goldman Sachs, 234
Gold Repeal Joint Resolution (1933), 218
Gold standard, 9, 414–415
Goldwater, Barry, 375, 393–394, 470
Gompers, Samuel, 36, 88, 106, 143, 160
Gomulka, Wladyslaw, 349
Gonzalez, Xavier, 237
Good Neighbor Policy, 245–246
G.O.P. *See* Grand Old Party
Gorbachev, Mikhail, 495, 496, 501
Gore, Al, 512
Gospel of wealth, 20
Gould, Jay, 20
Government. *See also* Great Society; Legislation; New Deal; Regulation; specific programs
    economic role of, 277–278, 324–327, 374–377
    Eisenhower and, 374–377
    expansion of, 234, 476
    federal employees (1891–1917), 89
    housing and, 333
    labor strikes and, 3–4, 175
    Roosevelt, Theodore, and, 75–79
    socialists and role of, 60
    spending by, 230
Graham, Billy, 360
Gramm-Rudman-Hollings Act (1985), 497
Grammy Awards, 454
Grand Coulee Dam, 222, 224
Grandfather clauses, 73
Grand Old Party, 74
Grant, Madison, 22
Grapes of Wrath, The (Steinbeck), 239
Great Britain. *See* England (Britain)
Great Depression, 208–209. *See also* New Deal
    agriculture in, 218–219
    banking in, 216
    causes of, 209–210

Hoover and, 210–212
Great Gatsby, The (Fitzgerald), 201
Great Migration, by African Americans, 141–142, 195
Great Plains
    Dust Bowl and, 220
    farming in, 1–2, 3
Great Railroad Strike (1877), 39
Great Society, 391–397, 416
Great White Fleet, 118, 119
Greece, 24, 189, 293, 303, 316
Greenhouse effect, 448–449
Greenwich Village, 42–43
Gregory, Thomas, 150, 151
Grenada, intervention in, 492
Griffith, D. W., 187
Gromyko, Andrei A., 302
Gross national product (GNP), 326, 354, 392
Guadalcanal, 270
Guam, acquisition of, 105
Guatemala, 349, 438, 493, 503, 511
Guerrilla warfare, in Vietnam, 399
Guggenheim, Daniel and Simon, 20
Guggenheim, David, 81
Gulf of Tonkin. *See* Tonkin Gulf Resolution
Gulf War. *See* Persian Gulf War
Gunbelt, 435
Gun control, 508
Gypsies, Hitler and, 260, 269

Hague, The, women's peace conference in, 134
Haiti, 121, 183, 439, 510
Hamer, Fannie Lou, 385, 393
Hamilton, Alice, 55, 56
Handguns. *See* Gun control
Hanna, Marcus, 8
Harassment. *See* Sexual harassment
Harding, Warren G., 167, 176–177, 339
Harlan, John Marshall, 4
Harlem, 195–196
Harlem Renaissance, 197–198
Harper's, 52
Harrington, John, 448
Harrington, Michael, 377
Harrison, Benjamin, 3
Harrison, Carter, Jr., 61
Hart, Henry, 359
Harvey, George, 83
Hawaii, 98–99, 105. *See also* Pearl Harbor

Hawks (political), 403
Hawley-Smoot Tariff (1930), 210
Hay, John, 100, 110, 112, 114
Hay-Bunau-Varilla Treaty, 116
Hay-Herran Treaty, 114
Hay-Pauncefote Treaty, 114
Haywood, William "Big Bill," 37, 38, 150
Head Start, 395
Health, Education, and Welfare Department, 374
Health and health care, 21, 417
    AIDS and, 461
    government programs and, 328
    nuclear tests and, 348–349
    reform of, 508
Hearst, William Randolph, 99, 100
Hefner, Hugh, 337
Heller, Walter, 326
Helms, Jesse, 456
Hemingway, Ernest, 201, 202
Henry Street Settlement, 70
Hepburn Act (1906), 76
Herberg, Will, 360
Heritage Foundation, 470
Herran, Tomas, 114
Heterodoxy, 43
HEW. *See* Health, Education, and Welfare Department
Hidden Persuaders, The (Packard), 362
Higher education, 376
Highland Park plant (Ford), 13, 17–18
High-tech jobs, 444
Highway Act (1956), 356
Hill, Anita, 460, 463
Hill, James J., 96
Hill-Burton Act, 328
Hillman, Sidney, 175, 202, 238
Himmelfarb, Gertrude, 470
Hine, Lewis, 54
Hippies, 405–406
Hiroshima, Japan, 275
Hispanic Americans, 198–200, 289, 373
Hiss, Alger, 319, 322
Hiss-Chambers-Nixon affair, 319
History and historians, 301–302, 453
Hitler, Adolf, 247, 255
    expansionism of, 256, 257–258, 258 (map)
    Holocaust and, 268–270
Hmong people, 437, 468

Ho Chi Minh, 352
Ho Chi Minh City, 478
Ho Chi Minh Trail, 402
Hoey, Jane, 235
Hoffman, Abbie, 407
Holding Company Act (1935), 231
Hollywood. *See also* Movies
  blacklist in, 319
  movie industry and, 40
  television programming and,
    453–454
Hollywood Ten, 319
Holmes, Oliver Wendell, 54
Holocaust, 268–270
Home front
  in First World War, 139–151
  in Second World War, 277–291
  in Vietnam War, 403–412
Homelessness, 459
Home Loan Bank Board, 211
Home Owners Loan Act (1933),
  218
Homestead strike, 3, 159
Homophobia, 461
Homosexuals and homosexuality
  antisubversive campaigns against,
    320
  conservatism and, 471
  Hitler and, 260, 269
  sexual politics and, 460–461
Honduras, 120
Hoover, Herbert, 176, 179–183, 194
  domestic policy of, 210–212
  Food Administration and, 140
  foreign affairs and, 180–183
Hoover, J. Edgar, 319–320, 322,
    336, 384, 424
Hoover Dam. *See* Boulder Dam
Hoover-Stimson Doctrine, 255
Hopkins, Harry, 214, 217, 219, 232
Horton, Willie, 498
Hostage crisis. *See* Iran
House, Edward M., 131, 132
House Committee on Un-American
  Activities (HUAC), 318
House-Grey memorandum (1916),
  132
Housing. *See also* Public housing
    projects
  catalog sales of, 185
  mass culture and, 365
  in postwar period, 328–329
  in postwar suburbs, 332–335
  redlining and, 373
  segregation in, 34

Housing Act (1949), 329, 374
Howells, William Dean, 73, 107
HUAC. *See* House Committee on
  Un-American Activities
  (HUAC)
Huerta, Victoriano, 122–123
Hughes, Charles Evans, 70, 134,
  176, 181
Hughes, Langston, 197, 198
Hull House, 54–56
Human rights policy, 483, 491
Humphrey, George, 341
Humphrey, Hubert H., 378, 393,
  411, 412, 413 (map), 424
"Hundred Days," 215–216, 218
Hungary, 24, 349, 501
Hunter, Robert, 28
Hurston, Zora Neale, 197, 198
Hussein, Saddam, 495, 504–505,
  511
Hydrogen bomb, 311

ICBMs. *See* Intercontinental ballis-
  tic missiles
ICC. *See* Interstate Commerce Com-
  mission
Ickes, Harold L., 240, 282
Idealism, of Wilson, 127
"I Have a Dream" speech (King),
  385
ILGWU. *See* International Ladies
  Garment Workers Union
Illegal aliens, 438
IMF. *See* International Monetary
  Fund
Immigrants and immigration,
  23–28. *See also* Ethnic
    groups; specific groups
  alcoholism and, 57
  anti-immigrant crusade and, 149
  causes of immigration, 23–24
  cultural divisions among, 147
  disfranchisement and, 64–65
  European-American ethnic com-
    munities and, 193–195
  family life and, 27–28
  First World War and, 141
  labor and, 26–28
  lifestyle of, 21–22
  limitations on Jews, 260
  living conditions and, 28
  national security and, 320
  new immigration, 4, 24,
    436–438, 437 (map)
  organized crime and, 32

patterns of immigration, 25–26
political machines and, 31–32
quotas and restrictions on,
  188–190
racism and, 22
rate of return of, 25
reformers' attitudes toward,
  56–57
sources of, 23–24
Immigration Act (1965), 436–437
Immigration and Naturalization,
  Bureau of, 64
Immigration Reform and Control
  Act (1987), 438
Immigration Restriction Act
  (1917), 149, 151
Impeachment, Nixon and, 427
Imperialism, 97–99. *See also* Colo-
  nialism
  business and, 96–97
  China and Open Door policy,
    110–112
  McKinley and, 105–107
  in Pacific region (1900), 106
    (map)
  Panama Canal and, 114–115
  Protestant missionaries and, 96
  Roosevelt, Theodore, and,
    113–119
  Social Darwinism and, 23
  Spanish-American War and,
    99–105
  Wilson and, 95
Imperial Valley, water for, 224
Imports, tariffs and, 81
Income, of laborers, 27
Income tax, 145
  progressive, 86–87
Indemnity, to Japanese Americans,
  291
Independence, Philippines and,
  108
Indexing, of benefits, 416, 489
"Indian Bill of Rights," 464
Indian Gaming Regulatory Act
  (1988), 464
Indian policy, 370–371
Indian Reorganization Act (1934),
  244
Indians. *See* Native Americans
Indochina, 352
Indonesia, 352
Industrial democracy, 143
Industrialization, 10
  economic growth and, 11–19

electric power and, 11
immigration and, 23
from 1900–1920, 12 (map)
physical fitness and, 21–23
"robber barons" and, 19–20
Industrial Relations Commission, 70
Industrial unions, 36
Industrial workers, 174–175
Industrial Workers of the World,
        37–39, 59, 90, 150
Industry
    automobile and, 11
    consumer society and, 169–170
    electric power and, 11
    emissions from, 447
    First World War and, 139–141,
        168–169
    in Great Depression, 221
    imperialism and, 95, 96–97
    in 1950s, 355–356
Inflation, 414
    Carter and, 481–482
    economy and, 487
Influence of Sea Power upon History,
    1660–1783 (Mahan), 97
Inheritance tax, 145
Inherit the Wind (movie), 192
Initiative, 63
Installment buying, 170
Institutions, in African-American
        communities, 34–35
Insular Cases, 110
Insurance, health, 328
Integration
    of baseball, 331–332
    educational, 370, 384
    Garvey and, 163
Intellectual thought. See also Settle-
        ment houses
    "Lost Generation" and, 201–203
    realism in, 53–54
    Social Darwinism and, 22
Intercontinental ballistic missiles
        (ICBMs), 376
Interior Department, 78
Intermarriage, 469
Internal combustion engine, 11
International Bank for Reconstruc-
        tion and Development. See
        World Bank
International Brotherhood of
        Teamsters, 281
International Harvester, 12–13, 15
International Ladies Garment
        Workers Union, 36, 37, 238

International Monetary Fund, 293,
        512
International organizations. See also
        League of Nations; United
        Nations
    economic, 292–293
    United Nations as, 292–293
Internment, of Japanese Americans,
        290–291, 467
Interstate Commerce Commission,
        76
Intervention and interventionism
    in Cuba, 108–109
    in Dominican Republic, 400
    in Grenada, 492
    in Haiti, 121, 183, 510
    in Latin America, 114, 182–183
    in Lebanon, 351, 492
    in Mexico, 122
    in Nicaragua, 121
    before Second World War, 256,
        260
Inventions and inventors, 11. See
        also specific inventions
Investment banking, 15, 234
Investments (international), 120
IQ testing, 144–145
Iran, 316, 423
    CIA and, 349
    hostage crisis in, 483–484
    Iraq war with, 495
    revolution in, 484
Iran-Contra affair, 428, 494–495
Iraq
    Iran war with, 495
    Persian Gulf War and, 504–505
Ireland, Easter Rebellion in, 134
Irreconcilables, 154
Irrigation, 224, 356
Islamic fundamentalists (Iran), 484
Isolationism
    League ratification and,
        154–156
    before Second World War,
        254–255, 260
Israel, 296
    Camp David accords and,
        482–483
Issei, 290
Italian Americans, 30. See also Im-
        migrants and immigration
    middle class among, 30
    Sacco-Venzetti case and, 161
Italy, 247. See also First World War
    First World War and, 129

immigration and, 24, 25, 189, 190
imperialism and, 111
Mussolini in, 255
in Second World War, 265, 266
        (map)
IWW. See Industrial Workers of the
        World

Jackson State College, 421
James, William, 53, 107
Japan, 505
    anticommunism in, 316
    anti-Japanese sentiment and, 117
    atomic bomb and, 274–277
    business competition from, 443
    China and, 256–257, 271
    immigrants from, 23, 24
    imperialism and, 110, 111, 112
    Pacific battles and, 270–274, 272
        (map)
    peace treaty with, 315
    Pearl Harbor attack by, 262–263
    Russo-Japanese War and, 117
    Second World War and, 255, 270,
        274–277
    Taft-Katsura Agreement with,
        117
Japanese Americans, 467
    internment of, 290–291
    middle class among, 30
Jaworski, Leon, 426
Jazz, 196, 197
Jazz Age, 167, 168
Jews and Judaism
    anti-Semitism and, 225, 260
    Brandeis and, 89
    FDR's advisers and, 234–235
    growth of middle class and,
        29–30
    Hitler and, 255
    Holocaust and, 268–270
    immigration and, 24, 189, 190
    Klan and, 187, 188
    Middle East homeland for, 296
    Soviet immigrants and, 438
    Zionism and, 151
Jiang Jieshi, 271, 292–293, 311
Jim Crow laws, 4, 5, 34
    Populist Party and, 7
    union membership and, 36
    Washington, Booker T., on, 5–6
Jingoism, 99
Jobs. See Employment
Jobs Corps, 392
Johnson, Charles P., 196

Johnson, Hiram W., 82, 155
Johnson, Hugh, 221, 226
Johnson, James Weldon, 195
Johnson, Lyndon B., 234, 356, 386, 391–392. *See also* Vietnam War
   civil rights and, 369
   domestic policy of, 377
   economy and, 414
   election of 1964 and, 393–394
   Great Society and, 394–397
   Kennedy's initiatives and, 392–393
   Tet offensive and, 410–411
   vice presidency and, 378, 379
Johnson, Tom, 61
Johnson-O'Malley Act (1934), 243
Johnson-Reed Act (1924), 188, 189–190, 198
Johnston, Olin T., 228
Jones, David, 197
Jones, Paula Corbin, 514–515
Jordan, 351–352
Judeo-Christian tradition, 360
Jungle, The (Sinclair), 58, 76
Justice Department, 330
Juvenile delinquency, 336

Kahn, Alfred, 485
Kaiser, Henry J., 233–234
Kaiser corporation, 279
Keating-Owen Act, 89
Keller, Helen, 60
Kelley, Florence, 55, 60
Kellogg, Frank, 182
Kellogg-Briand pact, 182
Kemp, Jack, 513
Kennan, George, 304
Kennedy, John F., 347, 377–378. *See also* Johnson, Lyndon B.; Kennedy family
   Alliance for Progress of, 351
   assassination of, 386–387
   civil rights and, 384–385
   Cuba and, 380–381
   domestic policy of, 377, 383–386
   election of 1960 and, 378–379, 379 (map)
   foreign policy of, 379–383
   women's issues and, 385–386
Kennedy, Joseph P., 377
Kennedy, Robert F., 384, 411
Kennedy family, 32. *See also* Kennedy, John F.; Kennedy, Robert F.

Edward, 484
Jacqueline Bouvier, 377
Joseph P., 32
Patrick Joseph, 32
political machines and, 32
Kent State University, 421
Kerensky, Alexander, 135, 137
Kettle Hill, battle at, 103, 104
Keynes, John Maynard, 230, 325
Key West, Florida, 222
Khmer Rouge, 421, 478
Khrushchev, Nikita, 348–349, 381–382
Kim Il-sung, 312
King, Martin Luther, Jr., 368–369, 407, 410
   assassination of, 411
   "I Have a Dream" speech of, 385
   Kennedy and, 378
King, Rodney, 499–500
Kinsey, Alfred, 320
Kinsey Report, 320
Kirkpatrick, Jeane, 470, 492
Kissinger, Henry, 376, 419–423, 478, 483
Klan. *See* Ku Klux Klan
Knights of Columbus, 188
Knox, Frank, 259
Knox, Philander C., 119, 120
Korea, 117, 118, 294, 295
Korean Americans, 458, 467
Korean War, 312–315, 314 (map)
   containment policy and, 315–316
   desegregation of forces in, 330
   Eisenhower and, 340–341
   GI Bill of Rights and, 327
Korematsu v. *U.S.,* 291
Kretzer, Morris, 360
Kristol, Irving, 470
Ku Klux Klan, 163, 167, 187–188, 368
Kurdish peoples, 504
Kutler, Stanley, 428
Kuwait, 504–505
Ky, Nguyen Cao, 402

Labor. *See also* Employment; Strikes; Women; Workforce
   African Americans and, 33–35, 196
   banning of immigrant, 149
   child, 89
   civilian, and First World War, 141–143

conditions of, 27
conflict after First World War, 158–160
ethnic groups and, 29–30
Ford and, 18
immigrants and, 27–28, 436
industrial workers and, 174–175
management accords with, 357–359
Mexicans as, 198
military, and First World War, 143–145
in New Deal, 226–228, 238–239
in New York, 70
Roosevelt, Theodore, and, 75–76
Wilson and, 88
in Wisconsin, 69
women and, 41–42
Labor-Management Relations Act. *See* Taft-Hartley Act
Labor movement, 203, 317–318
Labor's Non-Partisan League (LNPL), 238
Labor strikes. *See* Strikes
Labor unions, 27
   AFL, 35–37
   African Americans and, 196
   American Railway Union as, 4
   during First World War, 142
   membership in, 444
   in 1930s, 226–228
   political machines and, 32
   Reagan and, 488
   in Second World War, 281–282
   in textile industry, 175
Ladies Home Journal, 52
La Follette, Philip, 228
La Follette, Robert, 65, 74, 79, 134, 145, 155
   Farmer-Labor Party and, 169
   state reform and, 68–70
Laird, Melvin, 421
Laissez-faire policies, 177–179
Lakota Indians, 6
Land
   tribal, 370–371
   values of, 487
Landon, Alf, 232
Lange, Dorothea, 290
Language, voting and, 64–65
Lansdale Edward, 352, 353
Lansing, Robert, 131, 132
Laos, 352, 421, 437
La Raza Unida movement, 466
Lathrop, Julia, 55–56

Latin America
  Alliance for Progress and, 380
  Bush and, 503
  CIA covert actions in, 349
  Cuba and, 380–381
  dollar diplomacy in, 120–121
  Eisenhower's policy toward, 350–351
  FDR and, 245–246
  government policy in Twenties and, 182–183
  immigration from, 24, 436, 437, 438
  intervention in, 400
  military aid to, 315
  Panama Canal and, 114–115
  Roosevelt corollary and, 112–113
  after Second World War, 295–296
  U.S. investments in, 120
Latinos. See Hispanic Americans
Latvia, 152, 293, 294, 501
Lawrence Livermore National Laboratory, 457
League of Nations, 133, 134, 151–152, 153–158
League of United Latin American Citizens, 372
Lebanon, 24, 351, 492
Lee, Spike, 462
Left wing, 160, 316
Legal Redress Committee, of NAACP, 73
Legislation. See also specific acts
  civil rights, 392–393
  environmental, 419, 446–447
  of "Hundred Days" (1933), 218
  of Second New Deal, 230–232
Lehman Brothers, 234
Leisure
  automobile, appliances, and, 169–170
  ethnic groups and, 194
  mass marketing and, 171
LeMay, Curtis, 273, 412
Lend-lease program, 260–261
Lenin, Vladimir, 137, 160
Lesbians. See also Homosexuals and homosexuality
Levitt, William, 335
Levittown, New York, 333
Lewinsky, Monica, 514, 515
Lewis, John L., 226, 227, 238
Lewis, Sinclair, 201, 202
Liberalism. See also Progressivism
  FDR and, 214–215

Liberty Bonds, 145
Libya, 493–494
Lifestyle, of immigrant laborers, 27–28
Liliuokalani (Hawaii), 99
Lindbergh, Charles, 259
Lippmann, Walter, 60, 66, 202
Liquor. See Alcohol and alcoholism; Prohibition
Listen America! (Falwell), 471
Literacy tests, 5, 65
Literature
  African Americans and, 462
  Harlem Renaissance and, 196
  realism in, 53
  in Twenties, 201–202
Lithuania, 24, 152, 293, 294, 501
"Little Boy" bomb, 276
Little John (Chief), 244
Little Rock, 370
Lloyd, Henry Demarest, 55
Lloyd George, David, 152, 153
Lobbying, 79, 470
Lochner v. New York, 36
Locke, Alain, 197–198
Lodge, Henry Cabot, 22, 98, 155–156
Logan, Eli, 197
Lonely Crowd, The (Riesman), 361
Long, Huey, 225
Longshoremen, strike by, 227
Longworth, Alice Roosevelt, 176
Los Alamos, 274
Los Angeles
  immigrants in, 438
  King, Rodney, and rioting in, 499–500
  Mexicans in, 199–200, 242
  Watts riot in, 408
  "zoot suit" riots in, 289
Losing Ground (Murray), 396
"Lost Generation," 201–203
Love Canal, 448
Low-income housing, 374
Loyalty program, 304–305, 318–320
Luce, Clare Boothe, 286
Ludlow massacre, 38–39, 90
Luftwaffe, 259
Lunch counter sit-ins, 384
Lundeen, Ernest, 228
Lusitania (ship), 131–132
Lynchings, 71, 240
  of African Americans, 5, 161–162
  of German immigrant, 149
Lynd, Robert and Helen, 170, 202

MacArthur, Arthur, 108
MacArthur, Douglas, 212, 271–272, 313–315
MacDonald, Dwight, 364
Macedonians, 24
Machines (political). See Political machines
Machines and machinery, 13–14
MacLeish, Archibald, 259, 283
Maddox (ship), 397
Madero, Francisco, 121–122
Mafia, 32
Magazines, 52–53, 337
MAGIC code, 263
Magsaysay, Ramón, 349
Mahan, Alfred Thayer, 97–98
Mailer, Norman, 407
Maine (ship), 100, 101
Main Street (Lewis), 201
Major League Baseball. See Baseball
Malcolm X, 408–410, 462
Malcolm X (movie), 462
Management
  labor accords with, 357–359
  scientific, 16–19
Manchukuo, 255
Manchuria, 117, 118, 120, 255
Manhattan Project, 278
Manhattan Transfer (Dos Passos), 202
Manila, 100, 105
Mann Act (1910), 43
Mansfield, Mike, 399
Man That Nobody Knows, The (Barton), 173
Manufacturing, 29
Manzanar War Relocation Center, 290
Mao Zedong, 271, 311, 420
Marcantonio, Vito, 228
March, Peyton, 143
March on Washington for Jobs and Freedom (1963), 385, 457
Margin buying, 217
Mariana Islands, 272, 295
Marines. See also Armed forces; Intervention
  in Dominican Republic, 182
  in Nicaragua, 182–183
Maritime Commission, 277
Marketing
  advertising and, 171–172
  Sears, Roebuck and Co. and, 14
Markets. See also Mass production and distribution

growth of, 13
imperialism and, 97
industrial growth and, 13
Marne River, battle at, 137
Marriage
in Twenties, 173
women workers and, 279–280
Marshall, George C., 264, 276, 306, 322
Marshall Islands, 272, 295
Marshall Plan, 306–307, 326
Mary Tyler Moore Show, The (television show), 451
Masculinity, 237, 286
Mashantucket Pequot tribe, 464
Mason, Charlotte, 198
Masons, 188
Mass culture, 364–366, 454–456, 455
Masses, The (journal), 44
Massive retaliation doctrine, 348
Mass marketing, 171–172
Mass media. *See* Media
Mass merchandising, 442–443
Mass production and distribution, 12, 13–14, 17–19
Mattachine Society, 320, 460
Maverick, Maury, 228
Maxey, Leroy, 197
Mayaguez incident, 478
McAdoo, William G., 88, 140, 145, 194, 214
McCarran Internal Security Act (1950), 322
McCarran-Walter Act (1952), 320
McCarthy, Eugene, 403, 411
McCarthy, Joseph, 322–323, 339
McCarthyism, 322–323, 341
McClure's Magazine, 52
McGovern, George, 309, 424, 486
McGrath, Howard, 320
McKay, Claude, 197
McKinley, William, 8, 74, 95, 99, 105–107
McNamara, Robert, 379–380, 382
McNary-Haugen Bill, 178, 183–184
McVeigh, Timothy, 472
Meat Inspection Act (1906), 76
Meatpacking industry, 58, 76, 77
Media. *See also* Voice of America
civil rights movement and, 408
counterculture coverage and, 406–407
culture and, 450–457

Hollywood, "MTV aesthetic," and, 453–454
Persian Gulf War coverage by, 504
Reagan and, 486, 494
Truman and, 307
video revolution and, 450–453
Vietnam War coverage and, 403
Medicaid program, 416
Medical research, 440
Medicare program, 416, 489
Medicine, 328
Meese, Edwin, 488, 494
Mellon, Andrew, 176, 182
Mencken, H. L., 191, 192, 201, 202
Merger movement, 15
Metropolitan areas, 438–440
Mexican American Legal Defense and Educational Fund (MALDEF), 466
Mexican Americans, 6, 372–373, 466
farm workers and, 233
immigration restrictions on, 189–190
migration of, 142
U.S. population of, 200 (map)
women's issues and, 385–386
in workforce, 279
"zoot suit" riots and, 289
Mexican Revolution (1910), 24, 121–122
Mexico, 245–246. *See also* North American Free Trade Agreement (NAFTA)
debt crisis in, 511–512
Germany and, 135
immigrants from, 23, 436, 438
intervention in, 122
Wilson and, 121–123
Microsoft, 445
Middle class, 54. *See also* Class(es); Elites
black, 35
ethnic, 29–31
Middletown study and, 170
Middle East. *See also* specific countries
Camp David accords in, 482–483
Carter and, 480–481
after First World War, 154 (map)
Ford and, 478
immigrants from, 24
Jewish homeland in, 296
Nasserism in, 351–352

Reagan and, 493–494
Middletown (Lynd, Robert and Helen), 170, 202
Midway Island, 270
Migration
of African Americans, 33–34, 286
during First World War, 141–142
of Native Americans, 289
Militancy. *See* specific groups
Military. *See also* Armed forces
buildup of, 315–316
Eisenhower and, 347, 376
in First World War, 143–145
Reagan and, 492–494, 497
in Second World War, 264, 284, 285
segregation in, 143–144, 330
sexual harassment in, 460
spending limits, 348
Military aid, 315, 380
Military alliances, 309–311
Military Assistance Program, 350
Military bases, 503
Military draft, 143, 259
Military-industrial complex, 353
Military Training Camps Association, 260
Million Man March, 457
Mills, C. Wright, 359
Minimum wage, 374, 489
Mining industry
immigrants in, 26, 27
Ludlow massacre and, 38–39, 90
strikes in, 3, 75
Minnesota, radicalism in, 228
Minnesota Farmer-Labor (MFL) Party, 228–229
Minorities, 192–200, 239–245. *See also* specific groups
in labor unions, 281
women in workforce and, 280
Miranda v. *Arizona,* 417
Miss America Pageant, 459
Missile gap, 378, 379–380
Missiles, 376
Cuban Missile Crisis and, 381–382
in Persian Gulf War, 504
Reagan and, 492
Missionaries, 96, 244
Mississippi Freedom Democratic Party, 385, 393
Mitchell, John, 76, 425–426, 428
Mobilization
for First World War, 129
for total war, 139–151

Mobsters, Prohibition and, 186
Model A Ford, 171
Model Cities Program, 395
Model T Ford, 11, 17–18, 19, 171
Moley, Raymond, 215
Mondale, Walter, 479, 490
Money supply, 230
Monroe Doctrine, 110
  Roosevelt corollary to, 113–114
Montenegrins, 24
Moonlanding, 435
Moral Majority, 471
Morgan, J. P., 3, 15, 75, 81, 182
Morgenthau, Henry, 294
Morocco, 315
Morrison, Toni, 462
Moses, Robert, 374
Mossadegh, Mohammad, 349
Mothers. See Family life
Motion pictures. See Movies
Movies, 11, 40, 453
  counterculture and, 406
  HUAC and, 318–319
  juvenile delinquency and family
    life in, 336–337
  in 1930s, 238–239
  in Second World War, 283
Moynihan, Daniel Patrick, 415
MTV (Music Television), 454
Muckrakers, 51–54, 58
Muhammad, Elijah, 408
Muir, John, 77, 78
Multicultural education, 456–457
Multinational corporations, 96,
  442–443
Muncie, Indiana, 188
Munich Conference (1938), 257
Municipal reform, 61–62
Murdoch, Rupert, 451
Murphy, Frank, 238
Murrah Federal Building bombing,
  472
Murray, Charles, 396
Murrow, Edward R., 259
Music. See also MTV (Music Televi-
  sion)
  academic analysis of, 455
  of African Americans, 196
  at Cotton Club, 197
  counterculture and, 405–406
  Grammy Awards and, 454
  of Mexican Americans, 200
  pop industry, 454
  rock 'n roll, 362–364
Muskie, Edmund, 424

Muslims, in Bosnia, 505, 510
Mussolini, Benito, 225, 247, 255,
  256
Mutual defense pacts, 348
Mutual Security Program, 350
My Lai massacre, 421
Myrdal, Gunnar, 290

NAACP, 65, 196, 384
  founding of, 72–73
  in Second World War, 289
  separateness and, 463
Nader, Ralph, 418
NAFTA. See North American Free
  Trade Agreement (NAFTA)
Nagy, Imre, 349
Nanjing, 256, 257
"Nannygate," 428
NASA. See National Aeronautics
  and Space Administration
  (NASA)
Nasser, Gamal Abdel, 351–352
Nation, The, 99
National Aeronautics and Space
  Administration (NASA),
  435–436
National Americanization commit-
  tee, 150
National American Woman Suffrage
  Association, 67, 68, 133
National Association for the
  Advancement of Colored
  People. See NAACP
National Association of Manufac-
  turers, 324
National Civic Federation, 79
National Conservative Political
  Action Committee, 471
National defense, 315, 491–492
National Defense Education Act
  (1958), 376–377
National Endowment for the Arts
  (NEA), 456
National Endowment for the
  Humanities (NEH), 456
National Forest Service, 81
National Guard, 132
  labor strikes and, 159, 227, 238
  school integration and, 370
National Industrial Recovery Act
  (1933), 218, 221–222, 226
Nationalism. See also Colonialism; Im-
  perialism; New Nationalism
  black, 162–163
  in Egypt, 351

  Second World War and, 295
  Wilson and, 88–90
Nationalist Chinese, 271
Nationalist Party (South Africa),
  316
National Labor Relations Act
  (1935), 231, 233, 247, 248
National Labor Relations Board,
  231, 358
National Liberation Front (NLF),
  353, 398
National Network of Hispanic
  Women, 466–467
National Organization for Women
  (NOW), 419, 458
National origins, immigration
  quotas and, 436–437
National parks, 447
National Park Service, 77
National Recovery Administration,
  221, 226, 244
National Recovery Planning Board,
  278
National Review, 375, 470
National security
  Cold War and, 301–303
  containment at home and,
    316–317
  Eisenhower and, 341
  elections and, 309
  Truman Doctrine and, 303–304
  water projects and, 356
National Security Act (1947), 306,
  323
National Security Council (NSC),
  349, 419
  NSC-68 and, 311–312
National Socialist Party. See Nazism
National Union of Social Justice, 225
National Urban League. See Urban
  League
National War Labor Board, 140,
  143, 158
National Women's Party, 42, 68
National Youth Administration,
  233, 278
Nation building policy, 382
Nation of Islam, 408–409
Native American Rights Fund
  (NARF), 464
Native Americans, 243–245,
  463–465
  frontier and, 97
  government policy toward,
    370–371

migration to urban areas, 289
rights of, 6
Native Son (Wright), 320
Nativism, 4, 194
NATO. *See* North Atlantic Treaty
Organization (NATO)
Naturalized citizens, 194
Natural resources, 77–78
Navajo Indians, 272
Navy. *See also* Armed forces; Pearl
Harbor; Second World War;
Ships and shipping
Great White Fleet and, 118, 119
growth of, 97–98
Pacific ports and, 98
Panama Canal and, 114
Philippines and, 100
Nazism, 255, 294. *See also* Second
World War
Near East, 154 (map). *See also*
Middle East
Negro Cavalries, 103, 104
Negro leagues, 331
Negro World, The (Garvey), 162
Neoconservatives, 470
Network television, 450–451
Neutrality Acts (1935, 1936, 1937),
255–256, 261
Neutrality policy
in First World War, 130–136
before Second World War,
255–256, 259
New Criterion, The, 470
New Deal. *See also* Roosevelt,
Franklin D.
banking in, 216
First (1933–1935), 215–224
foreign relations and, 245–247
minorities and, 239–245
populist critics of, 224–226
Second (1935–1937), 229–239
workers for, 234–238
New Diplomacy, of Wilson, 133,
137
New Freedom, 85, 87–88, 139
New Frontier, 378, 379, 392
New immigration. *See* Immigrants
and immigration
New Left, 404–405. *See also* Counterculture
New Look, Eisenhower and,
347–349, 376
New Nationalism, 75, 82, 88–90,
139, 140
New Negro, The (Locke), 198

New Religious Right, 470–471, 472
New Right, 404, 469–472. *See also*
New Religious Right
Newspapers
foreign language, 29
muckrakers and, 52–53
Spanish-American War and, 99
New woman, 56–57
New York (city)
fiscal problems in, 481
immigrants in, 436
slums in, 28
urban renewal in, 374
New York (state), progressive re-
form in, 70
New York Journal, 99, 100
New York Stock Exchange, 170,
209, 217
New York World, 99
New Zealand, 315
Niagara movement, 71–72
Nicaragua, 246, 503
intervention in, 121, 182–183
Panama Canal and, 114
Reagan and, 493
Nicholas II (Russia), 135
Nichols, Terry, 472
Nickelodeons, 40
Nightclubs, in Harlem, 197, 198
Nimitz, Chester W., 270, 272
Nine to Five, 444
NIRA. *See* National Industrial
Recovery Act (1933)
Nisei, 290, 291
Nixon, Richard M., 339, 413–414,
499
civil rights and liberties under,
417–419
domestic policy of, 414–419
economy and, 414–415
election of 1960 and, 378–379,
379 (map), 413
election of 1968 and, 411,
412–413, 413 (map)
environment and, 446–447
foreign policy of, 419–423
HUAC hearings and, 319
Latin America and, 350
pardon of, 428, 477
presidency of, 413–428
resignation of, 427–428
vice presidency of, 350
Vietnam War and, 420–423
Watergate and, 423–428

Nixon Doctrine, 420, 423
NLF. *See* National Liberation Front
(NLF)
NLRA. *See* National Labor Rela-
tions Act (1935)
NLRB. *See* National Labor Rela-
tions Board
Nobel Prize, 117, 202
Nonaggression pact, Germany-
Soviet Union, 257
Nonpartisan League of North
Dakota, 183
Nonrecognition policy, 25
Noriega, Manuel, 503
Normandy invasion, 265–267
Norris, Frank, 53
Norris, George, 134
North, the
African Americans in, 34–35,
141–142, 194–195, 286
Ku Klux Klan in, 187
racial composition in, 367–368,
367 (map)
voting rights in, 65
North, Oliver, 495
North Africa, in Second World War,
264–265, 266 (map)
North American Free Trade Agree-
ment (NAFTA), 503, 511
North Atlantic Treaty Organization
(NATO), 309–311, 310
(map), 348, 510
Northern Securities Company, 75
North Korea, 511. *See also* Korea;
Korean War
North Vietnam, 352, 399. *See also*
Vietnam War
NOW. *See* National Organization
for Women (NOW)
NSC-68, 311–312
Nuclear fusion, 311
Nuclear power, 446, 449. *See also*
Atomic weapons; Weapons
protests against, 457
waste pollution and, 448
Nuclear weapons. *See also* Atomic
weapons
activism against, 457
ban on, 495–496
Clinton and, 511
Cuban Missile Crisis and,
381–382
hydrogen bomb, 311
testing of, 446
Nuremberg trials, 269–270

NWLB. *See* National War Labor Board

NYA. *See* National Youth Administration

Nye, Gerald, 255

Occupation, of Germany, 294

Occupational Safety Act (1973), 418

O'Connor, Sandra Day, 488

Odets, Clifford, 238

Office of Economic Opportunity (OEO), 392

Office of Facts and Figures (OFF), 283

Office of Inter-American Affairs, 295

Office of Price Administration, 277

Office of Scientific Research and Development, 278

Office of War Information, 273, 283, 284

"Ohio Gang," 176

OIAA. *See* Office of Inter-American Affairs

Oil
    Carter and, 480–481
    energy uses and, 449–450

Okies, 219, 220, 291

Okinawa, 272–273, 315

Oklahoma City bombing, 472

Old Guard
    Bull Moose Party and, 82–83
    progressivism and, 80
    in Republican Party, 74
    Roosevelt, Theodore, and, 79–80

Old immigrants, 24

O'Leary, Hazel, 448

Omaha Beach landing, 266, 267

O'Neill, Eugene, 201, 202

OPEC. *See* Organization of Petroleum Exporting Countries (OPEC)

Open Door policy, 110–112, 117, 120, 181

"Open skies" proposal, 348

"Operation Just Cause," 503

Operation OVERLORD, 265–270

Operation TORCH, 265

Operation Wetback, 372, 373

Organization Man, The (Whyte), 361

Organization of Petroleum Exporting Countries (OPEC), 449–450

Organized crime, 32, 384. *See also* Mobsters

Orlando, Vittorio, 152

Oswald, Lee Harvey, 386

Other America, The (Harrington), 377

Ottoman Empire, 127, 129, 152–153

Ovington, Mary White, 72

OWI. *See* Office of War Information

Pacific region, 503
    American empire in (1900), 106 (map)
    imperialism in, 105–108
    naval ports in, 98
    Pearl Harbor in, 98, 105, 262–263
    Second World War in, 270–277, 272 (map), 274 (map)
    trust territories in, 295

Pacifism. *See* Peace movement

Packard, Vance, 362

Paglia, Camille, 460

Pago Pago, 98

Pahlavi. *See* Shah of Iran

Painting, Ashcan school of, 53–54

Palestine, 296

Palmer, A. Mitchell, 160–161

Palmer Raids, 160–161

Panama, Bush and, 503

Panama Canal, 114–115
    Carter and, 482

Pan American Conference, 295

Pan-Asian movement, 467

Panay incident, 256

Panics (financial). *See also* Depression; Great Depression
    of 1893, 3
    of 1907, 26, 87

Paper money, 3

Paraguay, 350

Paramilitary groups, 472

Paris
    in First World War, 137
    Jazz Age in, 168
    Treaty of (1898), 105, 107

Paris peace accords (1973), 421, 478

Paris Peace Conference (1919), 151–153

Parker, Alton B., 76

Parks, Rosa, 368

Parochial schools, ethnic groups and, 193

Passing of the Great Race, The (Grant), 22

Patriotism, in First World War, 146–147, 148–151

Patton, George, 212

Paul, Alice, 42, 68

Payne-Aldrich Tariff (1909), 81

Payroll taxes, 249

Peace Corps, 380, 385

Peace efforts
    after First World War, 151–158
    after Second World War, 291–296

Peace movement, 133–134. *See also* Antiwar movement

Peace without victory, 127, 134–135

Peale, Norman Vincent, 360

Pearl Harbor, 98, 105, 262–263

Peasants, immigration of, 24–25

Peña, Federico, 466

Pendergast, Thomas J., 31, 292

Pendergast, Tom, 302

Pentagon, 376

Pentagon Papers, 424

People of color, 338, 488. *See also* African Americans; Hispanic Americans

People's Party. *See* Populist (People's) Party

People's Republic of China. *See* China

Perestroika, 495, 496

Perkins, Frances, 214, 226, 235, 236

Perot, Ross, 507–508, 513

Pershing, John J. ("Black Jack"), 122, 137, 143

Persian Gulf War, 503, 504–505, 506 (map)

Personal Responsibility and Work Opportunity Reconciliation Act (1996), 509

Peru, 350

Pesticides, 357

Pesticides Control Act (1972), 447

Petroleum. *See* Oil

Philanthropy, 20

Philippines, 271–272
    acquisition of, 105
    American-Filipino War and, 107–108
    anticolonial movement in, 105–106
    immigrants from, 23
    imperialism and, 105–108
    independence of, 295
    military and, 315, 503
    Spanish-American War and, 100

Phillips, David Graham, 51–52

Phillips, Kevin, 435
Phillips curve, 414
Philosophy, realism in, 53
Phnom Penh, 478
Photography, 54
Physical fitness, 21–22
Picketing, 36
Pinchot, Gifford, 78–79, 81–82
Pine Ridge Reservation, 463
Pingree, Hazen S., 61
Pins and Needles (musical play), 238
Pittsburgh, living conditions in, 28
Platt, Thomas C., 74
Platt Amendment, 108
Playboy magazine, 337
Pledge of Allegiance, 360
Plessy v. Ferguson, 4, 5, 330–331
Pluralism, 359–360
Podhoretz, Norman, 470
Poetry, Harlem Renaissance and, 196
Poindexter, John, 495
Poland
    anticommunist movement in, 500
    after First World War, 152, 153
    immigrants from, 24, 189, 190
    postwar period and, 294
    rebellion in (1956), 349
    Second World War and, 257, 294
    Soviets and, 294
"Politically correct" (PC), 455
Political machines, 31–32, 63, 292
Political parties. *See also* specific parties
    racial alignments in, 367–368
Political reform. *See* Reform and reformers
Politics. *See also* Conservatism; specific political parties and issues
    of business, 176–183
    conservative, 471–472
    Hoover and, 179–180
    League ratification and, 155
    in New Deal, 224–229
    New Left and, 404–405
    New Right and, 404, 469–472
    pluralism in, 359–360
    sexual, 460–461
    of socialists, 59–60
    women's movement and, 458–459
Poll taxes, 5, 65
Pollution, environment and, 357, 446–449
Pools, 15

Popular front, 229
Population. *See also* Immigrants and immigration
    African American patterns of (1940–1960), 367 (map)
    aging of, 433–434
    immigrants and, 23
    of Mexicans in U.S., 200 (map)
    movement, in Second World War, 291
    Sunbelt and, 434–436
    of urban and rural Indians (1940–1980), 371
    urbanization of, 438–440
    of urban slums, 28
    of U.S. (1890–1998), A19
Populism, 3, 224–226, 233–234
Populist (People's) Party, 1, 3, 7–9
Port Arthur, 117
Port Huron Statement, 404, 457
Portsmouth conference, 117
Portugal, immigrants from, 24
Postindustrial economy, 443–446
Postwar world
    after First World War, 158–163
    after Second World War, 291–296
Potsdam Conference, 302
Potter, David, 353
Poverty. *See also* Wealth
    feminization of, 459
    of Mexican Americans, 199
    in 1980s, 488
    Reagan and, 489–490
    relief during Depression, 217–218
    settlement house movement and, 54–56
    among workers, 175
Poverty (Hunter), 28
Powell, Colin, 504
Powell, Lewis, 417
Power elite, 359
Power of Positive Thinking (Peale), 360
Power politics, Taft and, 120
POWs. *See* Prisoners of war
Powwow, 464
Prague, 257
Preer, Andy, 197
Prejudice. *See* Discrimination; Race and racism; specific groups
Presidential Commission on the Status of Women, 386
Presidential elections. *See* Elections
Presidents of the United States, A22–A27

Presley, Elvis, 362
Price and wage freeze, 414
Principles of Scientific Management, The (Taylor), 17
Prisoners of war, 273, 340–341
Privatization, 442
Production, 168, 277, 442. *See also* Mass production and distribution
Professions, women in, 338
Progressive income tax, 86–87
Progressive Party
    in 1912, 50, 82–83
    in 1948, 307, 309
    in Wisconsin, 228
Progressivism, 50. *See also* La Follette, Robert
    civil rights and, 71–73
    cultural conservatism and, 56–57
    economic and social reform in states, 68–70
    electorate and, 63–66
    muckrakers and, 51–52
    municipal reform and, 61–62
    national reform and, 74–80
    in New York, 70
    political reform in states, 62–68
    and Protestant spirit, 50–51
    settlement houses and, 54–56
    socialism and, 58–60
    special interests and, 79–80
    Taft and, 80–82
    Wilson and, 83–90
    in Wisconsin, 68–70
    women's clubs and, 57–58
Prohibition, 32, 57, 149, 185–186, 193–194
"Project Sapphire," 511
"Promise Keepers," 457–458
Propaganda
    CPI and, 146–147
    under Eisenhower, 348
    in Second World War, 283
Property qualifications, for voting, 65
Proposition 209 (California), 469
Prosperity, after First World War, 167–175
Protective legislation, 236
Protest. *See* Antiwar movement; Counterculture; Strikes; Violence
Protestant-Catholic-Jew (Herberg), 360
Protestantism

fundamentalism and, 190–191
missionaries and, 96
progressivism and, 50–51, 84
Prohibition and, 186
among rural dwellers, 184
socialism and, 60
Public health, women in, 56
Public housing projects, 288–289, 374
Public Interest, The, 470
Public Lands Commission, 78
Public Works Administration, 221–222, 232
Pueblo Relief Act (1933), 243
Puerto Ricans, 372, 466
Puerto Rico, 109–110
acquisition of, 105
immigrants from, 436
Pulitzer, Joseph, 99
Pullman strike, 3–4
Pure Food and Drug Act (1906), 76
PWA. *See* Public Works Administration

al-Qadaffi, Muammar, 493–494
Quarantine policy, 256
Quayle, J. Danforth, 498
Quotas, 469
on immigration, 188–190, 436–437

Race and racism, 161–163. *See also* Civil rights struggle; Jim Crow laws; Population
activism, tensions, and, 4–7
affirmative action and, 469
African Americans and, 196
Asians and, 6, 468
black nationalism and, 162–163
Dixiecrats and, 329–330
after First World War, 158
immigration restrictions and, 188–190
against Japanese, 118, 290–291
Ku Klux Klan and, 187–188
Mexicans and, 6
Native Americans and, 6
New Deal and, 240–241
racial superiority and, 21–22
Second World War and, 286–291
social activism and, 461–463
in unions, 281
white flight and, 334
Race riots, 162
anti-Asian, 118

after King's death, 411
in Los Angeles, 408, 499–500
in Second World War, 288–289
in Springfield, Illinois, 71
Radford, Arthur, 348
Radicals and radicalism
after First World War, 158
in New Deal, 228
Red Scare and, 160–161
socialism and, 60
third parties and, 228–229
Radio
Coughlin and, 225
Roosevelt's "fireside chats" and, 216
Radioactivity, nuclear testing and, 348–349
Radio Asia, 348
Radio Free Europe, 348, 349
Radio Liberation, 348
Radio Martí, 494
RAF. *See* Royal Air Force
Railroad Administration, 140
Railroad Coordination Act (1933), 218
Railroads, 4, 10, 15
Railway Labor Act (1926), 180
Randolph, A. Philip, 196, 286–287, 330, 385
Rankin, Jeannette, 263
Ratification, of Versailles Treaty, 154–156
Rauschenbusch, Walter, 51
Ray, James Earl, 411
R&D. *See* Research and development
Reading Railroad, 76
Reagan, Ronald, 355, 435, 476, 499
assassination attempt on, 490
Cold War and, 491–492
domestic policy of, 486–490, 496–497
election of 1976 and, 478
election of 1980 and, 484–486, 485 (map)
election of 1984 and, 490–491
energy and, 449–450
environment and, 448
HUAC hearings and, 319
Iran-*Contra* affair and, 494–495
Iran-Contragate and, 428
multicultural education and, 456
"Reagan Revolution," 487
Reagon, Bernice Johnson, 385
Realism, 53–54, 360
Rearmament, of West Germany, 315

Recession
of 1937–1938, 248–249
in 1981–1982, 487
Reciprocal Trade Agreement, 246
Reconstruction Finance Corporation, 211, 232
Recycling, 280
Red China. *See* China
Red Cross, 280, 287
Redlining, 373
Red Scare, 160–161. *See also* Communism; McCarthyism; Subversives
Referendum, 63
Reform and reformers. *See also* Progressivism; Roosevelt, Theodore
conservatism of progressives, 56–57
costs of municipal reform, 62
economic and social, in states, 68–70
municipal reform and, 61–62
national, 74–80
in New York State, 70
political, in states, 62–68
Riis as, 22
Roosevelt, T., and, 82–83
settlement house movement and, 54–56
socialists as, 58–60
Wilson as, 84
in Wisconsin, 68–70
Refugee Act (1980), 438
Refugees, 437–438
Regulation. *See also* Securities and Exchange Commission
of capitalism, 60
Democrats and, 214
of mass culture, 454–456
muckrakers and, 58
of S&Ls, 497
of trusts, 75
of voting, 63
Wilson and, 88
in Wisconsin, 69
Rehnquist, William, 417, 497
Relief programs, 216–217, 236
Religion. *See also* specific religions
bigotry, immigration, and, 188–190
among ethnic groups, 192–194
fundamentalism in, 167, 190–191
of new immigrants, 24
in 1950s, 360–361

progressivism and, 51
Scopes trial and, 191–192
Religious Right, 497
Relocation policy, for Indians, 370, 371
Remington, Frederick, 102
Reparations, from Germany, 153, 181
Repression, 148–151, 160–161
Republican Party, 203. *See also* specific presidents
Bull Moose campaign (1912) and, 82–83
divisions in, 80
election of 1896 and, 8–9
election of 1952 and, 338–340
elections of 1994 and, 508–509
League of Nations and, 155–156
McCarthyism and, 323
national reform and, 74
Research, 277–278
scientific, 376
and technology, in Sunbelt, 435–436
Reservations, 6, 289, 370, 371, 464
Resources, energy, 449–450
Resources Recovery Act (1970), 447
Restrictive covenants, 330
Retailing, 441–442
Reuben James (ship), 261
Revenue Act
of 1926, 178
of 1932, 212
Reverse discrimination, 469
Revolts, 352. *See also* Revolution(s)
Revolution(s). *See also* specific revolutions
in Cuba, 350–351
in Iran, 484
in Mexico, 24, 121–122
in Russia, 135, 137
Reykjavik summit, 495
Rhee, Syngman, 312
Rhineland, 256
Rhine River region, 153, 267
Rhodesia. *See* Zimbabwe
Rhythm and blues (R&B) music, 362
Riesman, David, 361
Rights. *See* Civil rights and liberties
"Right to Life" groups, 419
Right wing, 393–394. *See also* Conservatism
Riis, Jacob, 22, 53, 54

Rio de Janeiro conference, 295
Riots. *See* Race riots
Rivera, Diego, 231
River Rouge plant (Ford), 13
Rivers. *See* Water projects
Roads and highways, in 1950s, 356–357
Robber barons, 19–20
Roberts, Oral, 360
Roberts, Owen J., 248
Robertson, Pat, 472, 486
Robeson, Paul, 320
Robinson, Jackie, 331–332
Rockefeller family
John D., 20, 51
John D., Jr., 39
Nelson, 471, 477
Rockefeller Foundation, 20, 376
Rockefeller University, 20
Rock 'n roll music, 362–364
Rockwell, Norman, 283
Rocky (movie), 453
Roe v. *Wade*, 419, 471
Rogers, William, 419, 421
Rolling Stones, 406
Rolling Thunder, 399
Roman Catholics. *See* Catholics
Romania, 294, 501
Roosevelt, Eleanor, 235, 240, 286, 386
Roosevelt, Franklin D., 203, 208, 213–215, 246, 269. *See also* Foreign policy; New Deal; Second World War
Atlantic Charter and, 261
death of, 291–292
elections of, 214, 215, 232–233, 233 (map), 260, 292
Nazi aggression and, 259–261
polio of, 214, 217
Soviet postwar influence and, 294
Roosevelt, Theodore
Bull Moose campaign of 1912 and, 82–83
economy and, 76
environment and, 77–79
First World War and, 130, 132
geopolitics of, 112–119
imperialism and, 95
League of Nations and, 155
muckrakers and, 51
Panama Canal and, 114–116
peace-keeping in East Asia by, 116–119

physical fitness and, 21
progressivism and, 50, 74–80
Rough Riders and, 103
Spanish-American War and, 102
Square Deal and, 75–76
trusts and, 75
on wealth, 213
Roosevelt corollary, 113–114
Root, Elihu, 155
Root-Takahira Agreement, 118
Rosenberg case, 320–322
Rosenman, Samuel, 215, 235
Rosenwald, Julius, 20
Rostow, Walt, 399
Rothstein, Arnold, 32
Rough Riders, 103, 104
Royal Air Force, 259
Ruby, Jack, 386
Ruef, Abe, 31
Ruhr valley, 181
Rural Electrification Administration, 232, 278
Rural life, urbanization and, 184–185
Rusk, Dean, 403
Russell Sage Foundation, 203
Russia. *See also* First World War; Soviet Union
after Cold War, 501
First World War and, 127, 129, 135, 137
immigrants from, 24
imperialism and, 110, 111, 112
Russian Revolutions, 135, 137
Russo-Japanese War, 117
Ruth, Babe, 193

Saar basin, 153
SACB. *See* Subversive Activities Control Board
Sacco, Nicola, 161, 193
Sadat, Anwar, 483
Safety rights, 417
"Sagebrush rebellion," 448
Saigon. *See* Ho Chi Minh City
Sakhalin Island, 117
Salisbury, Harrison, 403
Saloons, social role of, 57
SALT. *See* Strategic Arms Limitation Talks (SALT)
Salt of the Earth (movie), 372
Samoa, 98
San Antonio, 466
Sanctuary movement, 438
Sandinistas, 493, 503

Sane Nuclear Policy, 386
San Francisco, 118, 227
Sanger, Margaret, 42
Sanitation, in urban slums, 28
San Juan Hill, battle at, 102, 104
Santiago, Cuba, 104–105
Sarajevo, Bosnia, First World War
  and, 128
Saturday Night Live (television
  show), 451
"Saturday Night Massacre," Nixon
  and, 426
Saudi Arabia, 315, 504
Savings and loan institutions
  (S&Ls), 497–498
Scalia, Antonin, 488, 497
Schlafly, Phyllis, 386, 419, 470
Schlesinger, Arthur, Jr., 378
Schlesinger, James, 480–481
Schools. *See also* Education
  ethnic minorities in, 193
  integration of, 370, 384
  segregation of, 330–331
Science
  Social Darwinism and, 22
  teaching of, 376
Scientific management, 16–19
SCLC. *See* Southern Christian Lead-
  ership Conference (SCLC)
Scopes trial, 191–192
SDI. *See* Strategic Defense Initiative
  (SDI, "Star Wars")
SDS. *See* Students for a Democratic
  Society
Seabrook nuclear reactor, 457
Seagram, 186
Sears, Roebuck and Co., 14, 20, 185
Seattle, general strike in (1919),
  158–159
Second Bill of Rights, 323–324,
  324, 329
Second New Deal (1935–1937),
  229–239
Second World War, 254
  economy during, 277–282
  events leading to, 254
  peace after, 291–296
  racial tensions during, 288–291
  social issues in, 283–291
  U.S. response to, 259–260
Secretariat (UN), 293
Secret ballot, 64
Securities Act (1933), 217, 218
Securities and Exchange Commis-
  sion, 217

Securities Exchange Act (1934),
  217
Security Council (UN), 292–293
Sedition laws, after First World War,
  160
Seduction of the Innocent, The
  (Wertham), 362
Segregation. *See also* Discrimina-
  tion; specific groups
  in armed forces, 143–144, 330
  of Asian schoolchildren, 118
  of blood, 287
  Indians and, 371
  NAACP and, 73
  of public facilities, 330
  of schools, 330–331
  sit-ins and, 384
Seinfeld (television show), 452
Selective Service Act (1917), 143
Selective Training and Service Act
  (1940), 259
Self-determination, 146, 151,
  152–153
Selma, Alabama, violence in, 407
Senate
  direct election to, 63
  Treaty of Versailles and, 154–156
Seneca Falls convention, 67
Separate-but-equal principle, 4
Separateness, Afrocentrism and,
  462–463
Serbia, 129, 501
Serbia and Serbians, 24, 505
Serviceman's Readjustment Act
  (1944). *See* GI Bill
Settlement houses, 54–57, 70
700 Club, 472
Seventeenth Amendment, 63
Sewall, Arthur, 8
Sex and sexuality
  cultural conservatism and, 57
  Kinsey and, 320
  in Twenties, 173
  women and, 40–42
  youth culture and, 362
Sexual harassment, 460, 514–515
Sexual politics, 460–461
Shah of Iran (Mohammad Reza
  Pahlavi), 349, 423, 483–484
Shandong, 256
Sharecroppers, 33, 220–221, 241
Share the Wealth clubs, 225
Sheen, Fulton J., 360
Sherman Antitrust Act (1890), 15,
  35, 88

Sherry, Michael, 316
Ships and shipping. *See also* Subma-
  rine warfare
  in First World War, 136
  Panama Canal and, 114
  Second World War and, 261
  Washington Conference and, 181
Siberia, 117
Sicilian immigrants, 32
Sicily campaign, 265
Sierra Club, 77
"Significance of the Frontier in
  American History, The"
  (Turner), 96–97
Silent Spring (Carson), 446
Silicon Valley, 435
Silver movement, 3, 7
Simpson, O. J., 463
Simpsons, The (television show),
  451–452
Sinai Peninsula, 483
Sinclair, Harry F., 177
Sinclair, Upton, 53, 58, 76, 229
Sirica, John, 425, 426
"Sit-down" strike, 238
Sit-in movement, 384
Situation comedies, 365
Sitzkrieg, 257
Six Crises (Nixon), 413
Sixteenth Amendment, 87
Slavic immigrants, 24, 25, 189
Sloan, John, 53
Slovaks, 24
Slovenia and Slovenians, 24, 501
Smith, Alfred E., 70, 179, 194, 203,
  214, 215, 240, 378
Smith, Howard, 384
Smith, Jesse, 177
Smith, Jimmy, 197
Smith, Willie, 196
SNCC. *See* Student Non-Violent
  Coordinating Committee
  (SNCC)
Social classes. *See* Class(es)
Social Darwinism, 22–23, 97, 107
Social Gospel, 51
Social institutions, ethnic, 28–29
Socialism, 62
  characteristics of followers,
    58–59
  progressivism and, 58–60
  radicalism and, 160
Socialist Party, 59
  election of 1912 and, 85
  repression of, 150

Social sciences, 22, 53
Social Security Act
    of 1935, 230–231, 233, 247, 248
    of 1950, 327
Social Security system, 327–328,
    374, 489, 497
Social welfare. *See* Welfare programs
Social work, 56
Society. *See also* Economy; Ethnic
    groups; Family life; Gender;
    Immigrants and immigra-
    tion; Religion; Women
    affluence and inequality in,
        358–359
    change and containment in,
        331–338
    class warfare and, 44
    conformity in, 361–362
    consumerism and, 169–170
    cultural dislocation of farmers
        in, 184–185
    discontents of affluence in,
        361–366
    economic crisis and, 1–4
    in First World War, 127
    industrialization and, 10
    intellectual ridicule of, 201
    realistic portrayals of, 53–54
    in Second World War, 282–291
Soil Conservation and Domestic Al-
    lotment Act (1936), 220
Soil Conservation Service (1935),
    220
Soil erosion, 220
Soldiers. *See also* Armed forces;
    Conscription; Military;
    Military draft
    Americans in Vietnam, 402
    Japanese American, 291
    recruiting of, 144
Solidarity party (Poland), 500
Solomon Islands, 270
Somalia, 505, 510
Somme River, battle at, 129
Somoza, Anastasio, 246
Sonar, 136
Sound and the Fury, The (Faulkner),
    202
South. *See also* Civil rights struggle;
    Desegregation; Sunbelt
    African American workers in, 34
    civil rights and, 329–330
    farming in, 1–2, 3
    income of laborers in, 27
    Jim Crow in, 5

Ku Klux Klan and, 187
    racial composition in, 367
    voting rights in, 65
South Africa, 316, 423
Southeast Asia, 352–353, 382–383,
    477–478. *See also* Vietnam
    War
Southeast Asia Treaty Organiza-
    tion, 348
Southern Christian Leadership
    Conference (SCLC),
    368–369, 384
Southern Europe, 24, 193–195, 240
South Korea. *See* Korean War
South Manchurian Railroad, 117,
    120
South Vietnam, 352, 398–399,
    400–401. *See also* Vietnam
    War
Southwest
    immigrants in, 24
    Mexican Americans in, 6, 466
Soviet Union. *See also* Cold War;
    Russia
    American Communist Party and,
        229
    atomic weapons of, 302
    Clinton and, 510
    Eastern Europe and, 270,
        302–303
    East Germany and, 294
    Eisenhower and, 347–349
    end of Cold War and, 495–496,
        500–502, 502 (map)
    German nonaggression pact
        with, 257
    Kennedy and, 381–382
    postwar settlement with, 293–295
    Reagan and, 491–492
    Second World War and, 264, 265,
        293
Space program, 376, 435–436
Spain, 110, 256. *See also* Spanish-
    American War
Spanish-American War, 99–105,
    103 (map)
Spanish civil war, 256
Spanish-speaking Americans,
    372–373, 465–467. *See also*
    Hispanic Americans; spe-
    cific groups
Special interests, 63, 79–80
Speculation, on stock market, 209,
    217
Speech, freedom of, 191, 455

Spheres of influence, 110,
    293–296, 316
Spies and spying, 304. *See also* Hiss,
    Alger
    Ames and, 511
    Rosenberg case and, 320–322
    U-2 incident and, 348
Spillane, Mickey, 364
Spock, Benjamin, 335–337
Sports, 21. *See also* specific sports
    integration of, 331–332
    on television, 452
    women in, 279
Springfield, Illinois, race riot in, 71
Sputnik, 376, 435
Square Deal, 75–76
Stagflation, 414, 477
Stalin, Joseph, 265, 293–294, 349
Stalingrad, battle at, 265
Stamps, Charlie, 197
Standard Oil Company, 15, 20, 51
Stanford, Leland, 20
Stanton, Elizabeth Cady, 67
Stanton, Frank, 403
Starr, Ellen Gates, 54
Starr, Kenneth, 508, 513
Star Trek (television show), 455
Star Wars (movies), 453
"Star Wars" program. *See* Strategic
    Defense Initiative (SDI,
    "Star Wars")
States
    economic and social reform in,
        68–70
    political reform in, 62–68
    racial composition of, 367–368,
        367 (map)
States' Rights Party. *See* Dixiecrats
Steam power, 11
Stearns, Harold, 201
Steel industry, 26, 27, 159–160
Steffens, Lincoln, 51, 61
Stein, Gertrude, 201
Steinbeck, John, 239
Stereotypes, racial, 22
Stevenson, Adlai, 336, 339, 370,
    378
Stilwell, Joseph W. ("Vinegar Joe"),
    271
Stimson, Henry, 259, 262, 263, 264,
    265, 275, 276, 302
Stock market, 208, 209
Stock ownership, 170
Stonewall raid, 460–461
Storey, Moorfield, 73

Strategic Arms Limitation Talks (SALT), 420
Strategic Defense Initiative (SDI, "Star Wars"), 492, 496
Strikes, 90, 317–318, 490. *See also* Labor; Labor unions
    at Coeur d'Alene, Idaho, 3
    after First World War, 158–160
    during First World War, 142
    at General Motors, 238
    Great Railroad Strike (1877), 39
    at Homestead plant, 3
    labor unions and, 35–36
    Ludlow massacre and, 38–39
    by miners, 75
    in New Deal, 227–228
    at Pullman Palace Car Company, 4
    Second World War and, 282
    "sit-down," 238
    in textile industry, 175
    by United Farm Workers, 467
Stroessner, Alfredo, 350
Strong, Josiah, 7
Student Non-Violent Coordinating Committee (SNCC), 384, 410
Students for a Democratic Society (SDS), 404
Submarine warfare, 131–133, 136
Subsidies, 220, 279
Suburbs, 438–440
    family and gender issues in, 335–337
    postwar growth of, 332–335
    urban issues and, 373
    white flight to, 334
Subversive Activities Control Board, 322
Subversives
    FBI and, 319
    after First World War, 160
    homosexuals and, 320
    labor and, 318
    loyalty program and, 304
    McCarthy and, 322–323
Subways, 11
Sudetenland, 257
Suez crisis (1956), 351–352
Suffrage. *See* Voting and voting rights
Sukarno, Achmed, 352
Sullivan, Louis, 54
Summit meetings, Geneva talks and, 348
Sunbelt, 434–436, 434 (map)

Superfund (environmental), 448
Superpowers, 348–349, 381
Supply-side economics, 487
Supreme Court
    Clinton and, 508
    communists and, 321–322
    Coolidge and, 179
    desegregation and, 368
    FDR and, 247–248
    Jim Crow and, 4, 5
    on New Deal legislation, 220
    Nixon and, 417
    Reagan and, 488
    Watergate and, 426
Survey Graphic (magazine), 197
Survival of the fittest, 22
Sussex pledge, 132
Swaggart, Jimmy, 472
Sweatshops, 29
Swift meat packing, 15
Switzerland, Holocaust and, 270
Syria, immigrants from, 24

Taft, Robert, 310, 323, 375
Taft, William Howard, 80–82, 143, 155
    dollar diplomacy of, 119–121
    Mexico and, 122
    as Philippine governor-general, 108
Taft-Hartley Act (1947), 318, 327
Taft-Katsura Agreement (1905), 117, 119
"Tailhook" convention, 460
Taiwan. *See* Formosa (Taiwan)
"Take Back the Night" marches, 457
Talk shows, New Right and, 472
Tammany Hall, 52
TANF. *See* Temporary Assistance to Needy Families (TANF)
Tanks, 129
Tarbell, Ida, 20, 51
Tariff Act (1930). *See* Hawley-Smoot Tariff (1930)
Tariffs, 184, 246
    Great Depression and, 210
    progressives and, 81
    reform of, 86–87
Taxation, 249
    on corporations, 231–232
    First World War and, 145
    Kennedy and, 383
    Reagan and, 487
Taylor, Frederick Winslow, 16–17

Teach-ins, 405
Teamsters Union, 444
Teapot Dome scandal, 176
Technology, 440–441
    economic growth and, 11
    Sunbelt and, 435–436
    television and, 452
    workplace automation and, 326
Teheran Conference, 294, 295
Telecommuting, 41
Telegraph, 10
Television, 364–365. *See also* Video revolution
    cable, 452–453
    family programming on, 455
    mass culture debate and, 454–456
    MTV and, 454
    network, 450–451
    Persian Gulf War coverage by, 504
    religion programs on, 360
    situation comedies on, 451
    video revolution and, 450–453
    Vietnam War and, 403
Temperance movement, 57
Temporary Assistance to Needy Families (TANF), 509–510
Tenant farmers, 33, 220
Tenements, 53
Tennessee Valley Authority (TVA), 222
Tennessee Valley Authority Act (1933), 218
Termination policy, for Indians, 370–371
Terrorism
    Oklahoma bombing and, 572
    World Trade Center bombing and, 511
Tesla, Nikola, 11
Tet offensive, 410–411
Texas, Mexicans in, 198
Textile industry. *See also* Cotton industry
    immigrants and, 26
    strikes in, 90, 158, 228, 282
    workers in, 175
Thieu, Nguyen Van, 402, 421
Third parties. *See also* Perot, Ross
    after First World War, 169
    radical, 228–229
    Wallace and, 412
Third Reich (Germany), 255, 268–270

Third World, 347, 349–350, 350–353, 355, 378, 503
Thomas, Clarence, 460, 463
369th Regiment, in First World War, 145
Three Mile Island, 449
Thurmond, Strom, 307, 329–330
Tibbets, Paul, 276
Till, Emmett, 368
Time-and-motion studies, 16–17
Title VII, of Civil Rights Act (1964), 393
Tobacco industry, 14, 15. *See also* Cigarettes
Tojo, Hideki, 263
Tokyo, bombing of, 273
Tonkin Gulf Resolution, 397–399
Toomer, Jean, 197
Total war, mobilization for, 139–151
Townsend, Francis E., 226
Townsend Plan, 226
Toxic wastes, 448
Trade
    Clinton and, 511–512
    tariffs and, 210
Trade deficit, 414
Trade unions. *See* Labor unions
Transportation, 10
    industrial growth and, 13
    in 1950s, 356–357
    separate but equal facilities and, 4
    urban, 11
"Treason of the Senate, The" (Phillips), 51–52
Treaties. *See also* specific treaties
    First World War and, 129, 152–153
Trench warfare, 129, 136–137
Tresca, Carlo, 44
Triangle Shirtwaist fire, 27
Tribes. *See* Native Americans
Triborough Bridge (New York), 222
Triple Alliance, 127, 129
Triple Entente, 127, 129
Troops. *See* Soldiers
Trotter, Monroe, 71, 73
Truman, Harry S., 292
    anticommunism at home and, 316–317
    atomic bomb and, 275, 276
    civil rights and, 329–331
    Cold War, containment, and, 301–307
    domestic policy of, 323–331

election of 1948 and, 307–309, 329–330
    Fair Deal of, 327–329
    loyalty program of, 304–305
    MacArthur and, 314–315
    social change under, 331–338
Truman Doctrine, 303–304
Trusteeships, after First World War, 153
Trusts (business), 15, 74
Trusts (financial), 60
Trust Territories (Pacific region), 295
Tugwell, Rexford, 202, 215, 220
Turkey, 24, 303, 316
Turner, Frederick Jackson, 96–97
Turner, George Kibbe, 51
Turnevereins, 29
Tuskegee Institute, 5
TVA. *See* Tennessee Valley Authority (TVA)
Twain, Mark, 107
Tweed, "Boss," 52
Twenties
    ethnic/racial communities in, 192–200
    farmers, small-town Protestants, moral traditionalists, and, 183–192
    "Lost Generation" and, 201–203
    politics of business in, 176–183
    Prohibition and, 185–186
    prosperity in, 167–175
    women in, 172, 173
Twenty-fifth Amendment, 426
Twenty-second Amendment, 323
Twenty-sixth Amendment, 424
Twenty-third Amendment, 323
Tydings, Millard, 323

UAW. *See* United Auto Workers
U-boats. *See* Submarine warfare
UFW. *See* United Farm Workers (UFW)
UHF television, 451
Ukraine, 24, 502
UMW. *See* United Mine Workers
UN. *See* United Nations
Unconditional surrender policy, toward Japan, 273–274
Underclass, 488
Underconsumptionists, 230
Underwood-Simmons Tariff (1913), 87
Underworld. *See* Organized crime

Unemployment, 414, 488
    Carter and, 481
    in male and female occupations, 236
    in 1929–1945, 248
Unemployment Relief Act (1933), 218
UNIA. *See* Universal Negro Improvement Association (UNIA)
Union of Soviet Socialist Republics (USSR). *See* Soviet Union
Unions. *See* Labor unions
United Auto Workers, 238, 239, 358
United Cannery, Agricultural, Packing and Allied Workers of America (UCAPAWA), 372
United Farm Workers (UFW), 385–386, 444, 467
United Fruit Company, 120–121, 349
United Mine Workers, 36, 37, 75–76, 226, 227, 238, 282
United Nations, 292–293, 351
United Parcel Service, 444
United States, as world power, 95–99, 105–119
U.S. Steel Corporation, 15–16, 26, 158, 238
United States Information Agency, 348
U.S. v. Nixon, 427
United Textile Workers, 36
Unity League, 372
Universal Negro Improvement Association (UNIA), 162, 163
Universities and colleges, 404
    antiwar protests at, 421
    cultural studies in, 455–456
    football at, 21
    New Left and, 404
    state government and, 69
University of Chicago, 20
UNO (United Neighborhood Organization), 466
Unsafe at Any Speed (Nader), 417
Up from Liberalism (Buckley), 375
Urbanization, 39–40, 438–440, 439 (map). *See also* Cities and towns
    in 1920, 186 (map)
    ethnic communities and, 28–32
    rural dwellers and, 184
    slums in, 28

social issues and, 373–374
transportation in, 11
Urban League, 73, 196
Urban renewal programs, 329, 374, 383
Uruguay Round, 512
USSR. *See* Soviet Union
Utilities, municipal reform and, 61
U-2 spy planes, 348, 376

Vance, Cyrus, 482, 484
Vandenberg, Arthur, 303
Vanderbilt, Cornelius, 209
Van Kleeck, Mary, 203, 235
Vanzetti, Bartolomeo, 161
VCRs, 453–454
Veblen, Thorstein, 53, 60
Venezuela, 113, 350
Venona files, 304–305
Veracruz, intervention in, 122
Verdun, battle at, 129
Versailles, Treaty of (1919), 152–153, 154–158
Veterans
  Bonus Army and, 212–213
  GI bills for, 327, 329
Veterans' Readjustment Assistance Act (1952). *See* GI Bill of Rights (1952)
VH-1, 454
Vichy France, 258, 264, 265
Victorianism, women and, 40–41, 57
Video revolution, 450–453
Vietnam, 437
  Diem coup and, 383
  Eisenhower's strategy in, 352–353
  Ford and, 477–478
  trade with, 512
Vietnam War, 401 (map)
  aftermath of, 422–423
  antiwar movement and, 404–405
  escalation of, 399–403
  home front during, 403–412
  media and, 403
  Tet offensive and, 410–411
  Tonkin Gulf Resolution and, 397–399
  Vietnamization policy and, 420–422
Vietnam War Memorial, 422
Vigilantes, 368
Viguerie, Richard, 471
Villa, Pancho, 122

Villard, Oswald Garrison, 72
Violence, 4. *See also* Bombs and bombings; Strikes
  antiblack, 161–162
  in civil rights struggles, 385
  in labor strikes, 228
  in 1968, 411–412
Virgin Islands, purchase of, 121
VISTA program, 392
VJ Day, 276, 277
Voice of America, 348
Volker, Paul, 487
Volstead Act, 151
Voting and voting rights, 369, 370. *See also* Referendum
  for African Americans, 5, 71–72, 73, 409
  Australian ballot and, 64
  disfranchisement and, 64–65
  for 18-year-olds, 424
  ethnic groups and, 194
  personal registration laws and, 64
  in presidential elections (1876–1920), 66
  regulation of, 63, 64
  women and, 6–7, 66–67
Voting Rights Act (1965), 407

WACs (Women's Army Corps), 285
Wages. *See also* Minimum wage
  at Ford Motor Company, 18
  immigrant labor and, 27
  Reagan and, 487–488, 489
Wagner, Robert F., 70, 214, 231, 240
Wagner Act. *See* National Labor Relations Act (1935)
Wagner-Rogers Bill, 260
Waiting for Lefty (Odets), 238
Wald, Lillian, 70
Walker, Alice, 462
Wallace, George, 396, 412, 417, 424, 471
Wallace, Henry A., 303, 307, 309
Waller, Fats, 196
Walling, William English, 72
Wall Street Journal, The, 470
Walsh, Frank, 143
War guilt, of Germany, 153
War Industries Board, 140, 158
War Labor Board, 277, 282
War Manpower Commission, 277
Warren, Earl, 386, 417, 488
Warren commission, 386

Wars and warfare. *See* Weapons; specific wars
Washington, Booker T., 3, 5, 71, 73, 76
Washington Conference on the Limitation of Armaments, 181
Washington Post, Watergate and, 425
WASPs (Women's Airforce Service Pilots), 284
Waste Land, The (Eliot), 201
Waste pollution, 447, 448
Watergate scandal, 423–428
Water pollution, 357, 446
Water Pollution Control Act (1972), 447
Water projects, in New Deal, 222–224, 223 (map)
Waterways, in 1950s, 356–357
Watson, Tom, 8, 9
Watt, James, 448, 489
Watts riot, 408
Wayland, Julius, 58
Wealth
  affluence in 1950s and, 353–361
  of elite class, 213
  maldistribution of, 210
  robber barons and, 20
  taxation of, 145
Wealth Tax Act (1935), 231–232, 233
Weapons. *See also* Gun control; Missiles
  arms race and, 302, 386
  atomic, 274–277, 302
  in First World War, 129
  intercontinental ballistic missiles, 376
  lend-lease program and, 260–261
  long-range, 315–316
  in Persian Gulf War, 504
  RAND think tank and, 315
  sonar and, 136
  submarine as, 131–133
  tanks, 129
  Washington Conference and, 181
Weaver, James B., 3
Weinberger, Caspar, 492
Welfare capitalism, 173, 174
Welfare programs
  Carter and, 480
  FDR and, 217–218
  Great Society and, 397
  Nixon and, 415–416
  Reagan and, 486, 489

Supreme Court on, 417
women's movement and, 459
Welfare state, 324, 327–329
Wells, Ida B., 5, 71, 73
Wertham, Frederick, 362
West. *See also* Sunbelt
    African American workers in, 34
    environmental preservation in,
        77–79
    water projects in, 222, 223–224,
        356
    women's voting rights in, 67, 68
West Bank, 483
Western Federation of Miners, 38
Western front, in First World War,
    129, 130, 138 (map)
Western Hemisphere, as U.S.
    sphere of influence, 110
West Germany, 294, 309, 310, 315
Westinghouse, 15
Westinghouse, George, 11
Wetbacks, 372, 373
Wetland restoration, 448
Weyler, Valeriano ("Butcher"), 99,
    100
Weyrich, Paul, 471
Wheeler, Burton K., 259, 261
Wheeler, Depriest, 197
Wheeler-Howard Act. *See* Indian
    Reorganization Act
Wherry, Kenneth, 323
Whip Inflation Now (WIN)
    program, 477
White, William Allen, 260
White Citizens Council, 368
White flight, 334
Whites. *See also* NAACP
    and civil rights alliance, 410
    Harlem Renaissance and, 198
    migration to North, 142
    separate facilities for, 4
    urban issues and, 373–374
White slave trade, 43
Whitewater, 508, 514
Why Johnny Can't Read (Flesch), 376
Whyte, William H., Jr., 361
Wilhelm II (Germany), 53, 129
Willkie, Wendell, 260
Wilson, Edith Bolling, 156
Wilson, Henry Lane, 122
Wilson, Woodrow, 83–84. *See also*
    First World War; League of
    Nations
    election of 1912 and, 84–86, 85
        (map)

First World War and, 136–139
foreign policy of, 121–123
idealism of, 127
labor and, 143
Mexico and, 121–123
New Nationalism and, 88–90
Paris Peace Conference (1919)
    and, 151–152
peace movement and, 133–134
peace vision of, 134–135
presidency of, 86–90
progressivism and, 50, 51
repression and, 149–150
stroke and death of, 156
WIN. *See* Whip Inflation Now
    (WIN) program
Winesburg, Ohio (Anderson), 201–202
Wisconsin, 68–70, 228
Wisconsin idea, 70
Wisconsin Industrial Commission,
    69–70
*Wizard of Oz, The. See Wonderful
    Wizard of Oz, The*
Wobblies. *See* Industrial Workers of
    the World
Wolfe, Tom, 406
Woman of the Year (film), 237
Woman suffrage, 66–67, 67 (map)
Women
    advertising and, 172
    African American, 462
    changing roles of, 337–338
    Chicana farm workers and, 385
    clubwomen and, 57–58
    discontents among, 362
    family life and, 335–337
    feminism and, 42–44
    in higher education
        (1870–1930), 56
    Kennedy administration and,
        385–386
    in labor unions, 281
    in military, 284, 285
    in New Deal, 235–238
    new sexuality and, 40–42
    new woman and, 56–57
    peace movement and, 133–134
    physical fitness and, 21
    settlement house movement and,
        54–56
    social status of, 6–7
    in Twenties, 172
    voting rights of, 6–7
    in workforce, 142, 279–280,
        285–286, 287

Women's Christian Temperance
    Union, 57
Women's movement, 419, 458–460
Women's Peace Party, 134
Women's rights movement, 67, 386,
    393, 419
Wonderful Wizard of Oz, The (Baum),
    1, 2, 9
Wood, Leonard, 103
Wood, Robert E., 259
Woods, Eldrick ("Tiger"), 469
Workday, 27, 76, 89
Workers. *See also* Labor; Relief
    programs; Workforce
    affluence and, 358
    black, 34
    in First World War, 141
    industrial, 174–175
    unions and, 35–39
    voting by, 228
Workforce. *See also* Women
    distribution of (1870–1920), 13
    at Ford Motor Company, 18
    immigrants in, 27–28
    in Second World War, 279–281,
        285–286, 287
Works Progress Administration,
    232, 278
Workweek, 27, 142
World Bank, 293
World Economic Conference, 245
World Trade Center bombing, 511
World Trade Organization (WTO),
    512
World War I. *See* First World War
World War II. *See* Second World
    War
Wounded Knee, battle at, 6
WPA. *See* Works Progress Adminis-
    tration
Wright, Frank Lloyd, 54, 55
Wright, Richard, 290, 320
Wrigley, 279
WTO. *See* World Trade Organiza-
    tion (WTO)
Wyoming, women's voting in, 67

Xena (television show), 455

YAF. *See* Young Americans for
    Freedom
Yalta Conference, 294, 295
"Yellow dog" contracts, 175
Yellow journalism, 99, 100
Yeltsin, Boris, 501

Yerkes, Charles T., 61
Yippies (Youth International Party), 407
York, Alvin C., 145
Young Americans for Freedom, 375, 404
Youth culture, 362–364

Youth movement. *See* Counterculture
Yugoslavia, 152, 501, 504

Zanuck, Darryl, 283
Zelaya, José Santos, 121
Zimbabwe, 483

Zimmermann telegram, 135
Zionism, 151
Zones
    in Germany, 294, 310 (map)
    in Korea, 295, 312
"Zoot suit" riots, 289